SPURGEON'S
SERMON
NOTES

OVER 250 SERMONS
INCLUDING NOTES,
COMMENTARY AND
ILLUSTRATIONS

CHARLES H. SPURGEON

HENDRICKSON
PUBLISHERS

Spurgeon's Sermon Notes
Copyright © 1997 by Hendrickson Publishers, Inc.

Published by Hendrickson Publishers, Inc.
P.O. Box 3473
Peabody, MA 01961-3473

First published in 1884
First reprinted in four volumes 1981 by Baker Books, a division of Baker Book
    House Company
First reprinted in one volume 1997 by Hendrickson Publishers, Inc.

Printed in the United States of America

ISBN 978-1-56563-829-7

Sixth printing—December 2006

All scripture quotations are taken from the King James Version.

Interior design by Pinpoint Marketing Communications, Kirkland, Wash.

TABLE OF CONTENTS

Genesis	19:15	1	Hastening Lot	1
	32:28	2	Power with God	3
	32:29	3	"He Blessed Him There"	7
	33:9, 11	4	"I Have Enough"	9
	33:13	5	Gently! Gently!	11
	41:56	6	Joseph Opening the Storehouses	14
	49:8	7	Judah	17
Exodus	12:3–4	8	Too Little for the Lamb	20
	14:15	9	Unseasonable Prayer	22
	32:26	10	Who Is on the Lord's Side?	25
Leviticus	4:29	11	Laying the Hand on the Sacrifice	28
Numbers	11:1	12	Against Murmuring	31
Deuteronomy	32:36	13	Man's Extremity, God's Opportunity	34
Joshua	24:19	14	Moral Inability	37
Judges	9:9	15	The Faithful Olive Tree	40
Ruth	1:16	16	Ruth Deciding for God	42
1 Samuel	17:47	17	The Battle Is the Lord's	45
	18:3	18	Love Plighting Troth	48
	30:20	19	David's Spoil	52
2 Samuel	7:27	20	Prayer Found in the Heart	54
1 Kings	2:28, 30	21	Clinging to the Altar	57
	10:1	22	Consulting with Jesus	60
	10:2	23	Heart-Communing	63
	19:4	24	Elijah Fainting	66
	20:40	25	A Frivolous Exercise	70
2 Kings	2:14	26	Where Is the God of Elijah?	73
	6:17	27	Eyes Opened	76
	17:25, 33	28	Half-Breeds	79
1 Chronicles	13:8, 12	29	The Lesson of Uzza	81
2 Chronicles	2:11	30	A King Sent in Love	84
	12:14	31	Rehoboam the Unready	86
	20:4	32	Help Asked and Praise Rendered	89
	28:23	33	Ruins	91
Nehemiah	1:11	34	Those Who Desire	94
	8:10, 12:43	35	The Joy of the Lord	96
Job	1:6	36	Satan Among the Saints	99
	3:23	37	The Sorrowful Man's Question	102

Job	7:20	38	The Sinner's Surrender to His Preserver . . 105
	14:4	39	Out of Nothing Comes Nothing 108
	19:25	40	Job's Sure Knowledge 110
	24:13	41	Rebelling Against the Light 114
	27:10	42	The Hypocrite Discovered 116
	34:33	43	Conceit Rebuked. 119
	34:33	44	Pride Catechized 122
	38:25–27	45	Rain and Grace: A Comparison. 124
Psalms	9:18	46	Good Cheer for the Needy. 127
	19:7	47	Revelation and Conversion 130
	37:39	48	*Salus Jehovæ*. 133
	84:3	49	Sparrows and Swallows. 136
	91:11	50	Angelic Protection in Appointed Ways . . . 139
	115:17–18	51	Living Praise 142
	119:50	52	What Is Your Comfort?. 145
	138:1–3	53	Open Praise and Public Confession 148
	143:9	54	Flight to God 151
Proverbs	15:19	55	The Thorn Hedge 154
	16:2	56	"Things Are Not What They Seem" 156
	21:2	57	Pondering Hearts 159
	23:23	58	To Heavenly Merchantmen 162
	23:26	59	Wisdom's Request to Her Son 165
	25:2	60	God's Glory in Hiding Sin 168
	25:25	61	Good News 171
	27:10	62	The Best Friend. 173
	27:18	63	The Honored Servant. 176
	29:25	64	Fear of Man Destroyed by Trust in God . . 178
Ecclesiastes	8:4	65	The Word of a King. 181
Song of Sol.	2:1	66	The Rose and the Lily. 184
	3:4	67	Constraining the Beloved. 186
	6:5	68	The Conquest of a Holy Eye. 189
Isaiah	1:18	69	Invitation to a Conference 192
	2:5	70	Walking in the Light. 195
	5:6	71	No Rain 198
	14:32	72	Enquirers Answered 200
	32:2	73	Our Hiding Place 203
	32:2	74	Rivers in the Desert. 206
	38:17	75	The Bitter and the Sweet. 209
	45:22	76	The Life-look. 211
	46:4	77	A Sermon for the Aged. 214
	49:20–21	78	Church Increase 217
	50:2–6	79	The Redeemer Described by Himself 220

Isaiah	50:7	80	The Redeemer's Face Set like a Flint	222
	53:5	81	Christopathy	225
	54:7–9	82	The Little Wrath and the Great Wrath	229
	55:7	83	Repentance	232
	55:7	84	Abundant Pardon	235
	60:8	85	The Cloud of Doves	238
Jeremiah	3:12,14, 22	86	Return! Return!	241
	3:19	87	Interrogation and Exclamation	244
	5:3	88	Decided Ungodliness	246
	6:16	89	Rest as a Test	248
	13:23	90	The Ethiopian	251
	18:11	91	Individual Repentance	254
	33:3	92	Prayer Encouraged	257
	51:50	93	Sacred Memories	260
Ezekiel	36:11	94	Better than at Your Beginnings	263
	36:30–31	95	Mistaken Notions about Repentance	266
	47:11	96	Marshes	269
Daniel	5:6	97	A Man Troubled by His Thoughts	272
	9:17	98	Prayer for the Church	275
Hosea	2:6–7	99	Ways Hedged Up	278
	2:14	100	Strange Ways of Love	280
	2:23	101	A People Who Were No People	283
	8:7	102	What Will the Harvest Be?	286
	10:2	103	Heart Disease	289
	10:12	104	The Stroke of the Clock	292
	13:10	105	Theocracy	295
Joel	2:13	106	Inward More than Outward	298
Amos	7:7	107	The Plumbline	301
Obadiah	1:3	108	Self-Deceived	304
Jonah	3:4	109	The Ninevites' Repentance	306
Micah	1:12	110	Maroth; or, the Disappointed	309
	2:8	111	The Worst of Enemies	312
	6:3	112	The Lord's Appeal to His Own People	315
Nahum	1:7	113	The Stronghold	317
Habukkuk	2:1–4	114	Watching, Waiting, Writing	320
	2:4	115	Pride the Destroyer	323
	2:4 et al.	116	Faith: Life	326
Zephaniah	2:3	117	May Be	329
	3:2	118	Fourfold Fault	331
Haggai	2:13–14	119	Defiled and Defiling	333
Zechariah	4:10	120	Small Things Not to Be Despised	336
	7:5–6	121	Self or God	339

v

Zechariah	9:11–12	122	Prisoners of Hope 342
	10:6	123	Perfect Restoration 345
	10:12	124	Spiritual Convalescence 347
	12:10	125	Mourning at the Cross 350
	12:10	126	The Bitterness of the Cross 353
	12:12–14	127	Apart 355
Malachi	1:2	128	Love Questioned and Vindicated 357
	4:2	129	Sunshine 360
Matthew	4:3	130	Sonship Questioned 363
	4:19	131	The Making of Men-catchers 366
	7:21–23	132	The Disowned 369
	8:7	133	Thy Word Suffices Me 372
	9:9	134	"A Man Named Matthew" 374
	9:36	135	A Portrait of Jesus 377
	10:27	136	Learn in Private What to Teach in Public . 380
	10:30	137	The Numbered Hairs 383
	10:38	138	Cross-bearing 386
	11:28–30	139	Rest for the Restless 388
	11:28	140	Jesus Calling 391
	14:31	141	The Why and the Wherefore of Doubt . . . 393
	20:3–4	142	From Twenty-five to Thirty-five 396
	22:8–10	143	Guests for the Wedding Feast 399
	25:10	144	Entrance and Exclusion 402
	27:29	145	Mocked of the Soldiers 405
	28:9–10	146	"All Hail!" 407
Mark	4:24	147	Hearing with Heed 410
	5:6	148	He Ran, and HE Ran 413
	5:7	149	Resistance to Salvation 415
	8:22–25	150	The Free-agency of Christ 418
	9:24	151	Feeble Faith Appealing to a Strong Savior 421
	10:49–50	152	The Blind Beggar of Jericho 424
	12:34	153	So Near 426
	14:32	154	Gethsemane 429
	14:72	155	Fountains of Repentant Tears 432
	16:10	156	A Sad Interior and a Cheery Messenger . . 435
Luke	5:26	157	Strange Things 437
	7:38	158	"At His Feet" 439
	7:42	159	Love's Foremost 442
	8:40	160	A Welcome for Jesus 444
	10:39	161	Love at Home 446

Luke	15:4–6	162	The Good Shepherd in Three Positions . . 449
	19:5	163	Must He? 452
	22:19–20	164	The Ordained Memorial 454
	22:27	165	*Servus Servorum* 457
	23:34	166	"Father, Forgive Them" 459
	24:36	167	A Divine Visitation 462
	24:50	168	Our Lord's Attitude in Ascension 465
John	1:29	169	The Baptist's Message 468
	1:47	170	The Israelite Indeed 471
	4:6	171	Jesus Sitting on the Well 473
	4:11	172	The Source 476
	5:9	173	Sabbath-work 479
	7:11	174	"Where Is He?" 482
	7:43	175	Christ the Cause of Division 484
	8:37	176	Place for the Word 487
	9:31	177	True and Not True 490
	10:9	178	The Door 493
	10:22–23	179	The Lord in Our Assemblies 496
	14:28	180	Love's Importance 498
	14:31	181	A Watchword 501
	19:14	182	"Behold Your King!" 504
	20:15	183	A Handkerchief 506
	20:17	184	*Noli Me Tangere* 509
	20:27	185	Signs and Evidences 512
	20:29	186	Faith without Sight 515
Acts	2:24	187	Bonds Which Could Not Hold 517
	2:37	188	Life-wounds 519
	4:14	189	The Golden Muzzle 522
	7:13	190	"The Second Time" 525
	7:58	191	Stephen and Saul 528
	13:26	192	"To You" 531
	19:18–20	193	Growing and Prevailing 533
	26:14	194	The Ox and the Goad 536
	28:2	195	Kindling a Fire 539
Romans	2:4	196	Concerning the Forbearance of God 542
	4:24	197	"Jesus Our Lord" 544
	6:11–12	198	Dead but Alive 547
	8:17	199	Heirs of God 550
	10:16	200	Disobedience to the Gospel 553
	12:15	201	Fellowship in Joy 555
	15:4	202	Patience, Comfort and Hope from the Scriptures 558

1 Corinthians	6:19–20	203	Bought with a Price.	561
	11:24	204	In Remembrance.	564
	11:28	205	Examination before Communion	567
	15:6	206	Fallen Asleep	569
2 Corinthians	1:3–4	207	Comforted and Comforting.	571
	1:10	208	The Tenses	574
	1:20	209	All the Promises	577
	7:1	210	Cleansing which Comes of Godliness.	580
	7:10	211	Sorrow and Sorrow.	582
Galatians	1:16	212	A Conference to Be Avoided	585
	3:23	213	Under Arrest	588
	5:7	214	Various Hindrances	591
	5:11	215	The Offence of the Cross	594
	6:2,5	216	Burden-bearing.	596
	6:7	217	Sowing and Reaping.	599
	6:14	218	Three Crucifixions	602
Ephesians	1:13–14	219	The Earnest	605
	3:15	220	The Royal Family	607
	3:16–19	221	Measuring the Immeasurable	610
	4:15–16	222	The Head and the Body	613
	4:20–21	223	True Learning	616
	5:11	224	Child of Light and Works of Darkness	618
	5:25	225	The Pattern of Love.	620
	6:15	226	Heavenly Shoes	622
Philippians	4:4	227	Joy a Duty	625
Colossians	1:16	228	Christ the Creator	628
	2:6	229	AS and SO.	630
	3:11	230	Christ Is All	633
1 Thessalonians	2:13–14	231	A Happy Minister's Meeting.	636
2 Thessalonians	3:13	232	Weariness in Well-doing	639
1 Timothy	1:15	233	The Faithful Saving	642
	1:16	234	Paul's Conversion a Pattern	644
2 Timothy	1:12	235	Our Gospel	647
	1:18	236	Mercy in the Day of Judgment.	650
	2:9	237	The Word of God Unbound.	653
Titus	2:10	238	Gospel Jewelry.	655
Hebrews	4:12	239	The Sword of the Lord	658
	4:16	240	Boldness at the Throne.	661
	5:2	241	Compassion on the Ignorant	664
	5:8	242	The Education of Sons of God.	666
	10:9	242	The First and the Second	669
	12:13	243	Lame Sheep	672

Hebrews	12:25	245	Hear! Hear!	675
	13:5	246	Never, No Never, No Never	678
James	1:12	247	The Tried Man the Blessed Man	680
	4:6	248	More and More	683
1 Peter	1:9	249	Salvation as It Is Now Received	686
	4:18	250	If So—What Then?	688
	5:1	251	A Witness and a Partaker	691
2 Peter	2:9	252	The Lord's Knowledge our Safeguard	693
1 John	3:2	253	By and By	694
	3:3	254	Purification by Hope	697
	3:14	255	Life Proved by Love	700
	3:20–21	256	The Lower Courts	703
	5:4	257	Victorious Faith	705
3 John	2	258	Soul-health	708
Jude	24–25	259	Jude's Doxology	711
Revelation	1:7	260	The Coming with the Clouds	713
	11:19	261	The Ark of His Covenant	715
	16:8–9	262	The Repentance which Glorifies God	718
	19:9	263	The Marriage Supper of the Lamb	721
	19:9	264	The Scriptures Divinely True	724

1

When the morning arose, then the angels hastened Lot.
—*Genesis 19:15*

ERE these personages angels, or divine appearances? It matters not: they were messengers sent from God to save. In any case they teach us how to deal with men if we are to arouse and bless them. We must go to their homes ("They turned in unto Lot," verse 3); they stated the case ("The Lord will destroy this city," verse 14); they urged and persuaded ("Up, get you out of this place"); and they resorted to a loving violence ("The men laid hold upon his hand," verse 16). Picture the two angels with all their four hands occupied in leading out Lot and his wife and his two daughters.

I. THE RIGHTEOUS NEED TO BE HASTENED.

1. *In what?* In matters of obedience to their Lord. Few can say, "I made haste and delayed not to keep thy commandments."
   - In coming out from the world. "He lingered." "His wife looked back" (verse 26). The urgency of the command which says, "Come ye out from among them; be ye separate," shows how loath we are to "rise up and come away."
   - In seeking the good of their families. "Hast thou here any besides?" (verse 12).
   - In general quickness of movement in spiritual things. "Escape for thy life" (verse 17). "Haste thee" (verse 22).
2. *Why?* The flesh is weak. Lot was an old man, too much tinctured with worldliness, and he was away from Abraham, the nobler spirit, who had helped to keep him right.
   - Perseverance is difficult. "I cannot escape to the mountain."
   - Sodom has a sluggish influence. We often traverse the "Enchanted ground," where sleep seizes on the traveler.
   - When our worldly occupation is incessant, and takes up most of our thoughts, we are hindered from decision.
   - Idle leisure is still worse. Men with nothing to do in the world seldom do anything in religion.
3. *By what means?* By reminding them of their obligations, their opportunities, and the days already wasted.
   - By leading them to consider the flight of time and brevity of life.
   - By warning them of the sure ruin of their impenitent friends.
   - By setting before them the fact that delay in duty is sin, and leads to other sins.

1

II. THE SINNERS NEED TO BE HASTENED.

1. *Sinners are very slow and apt to linger.*
   - They have settled down in the Sodom of sin. Like the sluggard, they desire "a little more folding of the arms to sleep."
   - They are bound by many ties to the City of Destruction.
   - They do not believe our warning. "He seemed as one that mocked unto his sons-in-law" (verse 14).
   - They trifle with our message when they dare not contradict it.
   - Delay is Satan's grand device for their ruin.
   - Procrastination baffles our persuasions. Delays act like bales of wool dropped over the wall of a besieged city to deaden the blows of a battering ram. Felix quieted his conscience by the idea of "a more convenient season."

2. *Our business is to hasten them.*
   - We must be in earnest ourselves, as these angels were.
   - We must also be patient, and repeat our pleadings.
   - We must be resolute, and lay hold on their hands.

3. *We have many arguments with which to hasten them.*
   May the Holy Spirit make them see:
   - Their imminent danger while lingering.
   - The sin of loitering when God commands them to escape for their lives.
   - The fitness of the present above any possible future.
   - The uncertainty that any available future will come"
   - The supreme necessity of immediate decision with some; for it may be "now or never" with them: they will "die in their sins" if they do not hear the voice of God today.

Illustrative Odds and Ends

A Christian tradesman bethought him that he had never spoken to a certain regular customer about his soul, though the man had called at his shop for years. He determined to plead earnestly with him the next time he came in his way. *There was no next time:* his customer died suddenly, so that he saw him no more.

When a young man made an open profession of the gospel, his father greatly offended, gave him this advice: "James, you should *first* get yourself established in a good trade, and then think of the matter of religion." "Father," said the son, "Jesus Christ advises me differently; he says, 'Seek ye *first* the kingdom of God.'"

Earnestly may we urge men to seek a present salvation since even the voluptuary pleads against delay in such words as these:

> O, gather roses while they blow,
> To-morrow's not to-day;
> Let not one moment vainly flow,
> Time fleeth fast away.

Much of the beauty of obedience lies in its being rendered at once, and without question. God's will is done in heaven immediately, because love is perfect there. That child is disobedient who is slow in obeying.

"Brother," said a dying man, "why have you not been more pressing with me about my soul?" "Dear James," replied the brother, "I have spoken to you several times." "Yes," was the answer, "you are not to blame; but you were always so quiet over it; I wish you had gone on your knees to me, or had taken me by the neck and shaken me, for I have been careless, and have nearly slept myself into hell."

The poor needle-woman with her inch of candle has work to finish. See how her fingers fly, for she fears lest she should be left in darkness, and her work undone.

Some Christians are slow to obey a command *because it has not been laid home to their hearts with power.* Fancy a child saying this to a father, or a soldier to his officer! Something else would soon be laid home with power.

Do not some professors cause sinners to loiter by their own loitering? A man taking a seat at the Tabernacle came to the minister and said, "Sir, do I understand that if I become a seat-holder I shall be expected to be converted?" "Yes," was the reply, "I hope you will, and I pray that it may be so. Do you object?" The answer was, "O Sir, I desire it above everything." Was not the man hastened by the general feeling of hopefulness which pervaded the Church? Assuredly there is much in the atmosphere which surrounds a man. Among warm-hearted Christians it is hard for the careless to remain indifferent.

2

As a prince hast thou power with God.
—*Genesis 32:28*

POWER with God is a sublime attainment: it leads to the possession of every form of power. No wonder that it is added, "and with men." When Jacob had prevailed with God he had no reason to fear Esau. Observe that it is the power of a single individual, exhibited in a time of deep distress: how much more power will be found where two or three agree in prayer! Let us note:

I. WHAT THIS POWER CANNOT BE.

- Cannot be physical force. "Hast thou an arm like God?" (Job 40:9).
- Cannot be mental energy. "Declare if thou hast understanding" (Job 38:4).
- Cannot be magical. Some seem to fancy that prayers are charms, but this is idle. "He maketh diviners mad"(Isa. 44:15). "Use not vain repetitions, as the heathen do" (Matt. 6:7).
- Cannot be meritorious. "Is it gain to him that thou makest thy ways perfect?" (Job 22:3). "If thou be righteous, what givest thou him?" (Job 35:7).
- Cannot be independent. It must be given by the Lord. "Will he plead against me with his great power? No; but he would put strength in me" (Job 23:6).

II. WHENCE THIS POWER PROCEEDS.

1. It arises from the Lord's nature: his goodness and tenderness are excited by the sight of our sorrow and weakness. A soldier about to kill a child put aside his weapon when the little one cried out, "Don't kill me, I am so little."
2. It comes out of God's promise. In his covenant, in the gospel, and in the Word, the Lord puts himself under bonds to those who know how to plead his truth and faithfulness." Put me in remembrance; let us plead together" (Isa. 43:26).
3. It springs out of the relationships of grace. A father will surely hear his own children. A friend will be true to his friend. Story of the power of a child in Athens who ruled his mother and through her his father who was the chief magistrate, and so controlled the whole city; love thus made a babe to have power over a prince and his people. The love of God to us is our power with him.
4. It grows out of the Lord's previous acts. His election of his people is a power with him since he is unchanging in his purposes. Redemption, regeneration, calling, communion, are all arguments for our final preservation, for mercy will not forsake that which wisdom has commenced. Each blessing draws on another like links of a chain. Past mercies are the best of pleas for present and future aid.

III. HOW CAN IT BE EXERCISED.

1. There must be a deep sense of weakness, "When I am weak then am I strong" (2 Cor. 12:10).
2. There must be simple faith in the goodness of the Lord. "He that believeth on me, the works that I do shall he do also" (John 14:12). Faith is the prevailing grace:

It treads on the world, and on hell;
It vanquishes death and despair:
And, what is still stranger to tell,
It overcomes heaven by prayer.

3. There must be earnest obedience to his will. "If any man doeth his will, him he heareth" (John 9:31).
4. There must be fixed resolve. "I will not let thee go, except thou bless me" (verse 26).
5. With this must be blended importunity. "There wrestled a man with him until the breaking of the day" (verse 24).
6. The whole heart must be poured out. "Yea he wept and made supplication" (Hos. 12:4).
7. Increased weakness must not make us cease. Jacob was lame yet he prevailed. "The lame take the prey" (Isa. 33:23).

IV. TO WHAT USE THIS POWER MAY BE TURNED.
1. For ourselves.
   • For our own deliverance from special trial.
   • Our honorable preferment. "Thy name shall be called Israel."
   • Our future comfort, strength, and growth, when, like Jacob, we are called to successive trials.
2. For others.
   • Jacob's wives and children were preserved, and Esau's heart was softened. If we had more power with God we should have a happier influence among our relatives.
   • In other instances, Abraham, Job, Moses, Samuel, Paul, etc., exercised power with God for the good of others.
   • We shall win souls for Jesus by this power. He that has power with God for men will have power with men for God.

O for a holy ambition to possess power with God!

If we have it, let us not lose it, but exercise it continually.

How terrible to have no power with God, but to be fighting against him with our puny arm!

Notes for Brightening
Jacob, though a man, a single man, a traveling man, a tired man, yea, though a worm, that is easily crushed and trodden under foot, and no man (Isa. 41:14), yet in private prayer he is so potent, that he overcomes the Omnipotent God; he is so mighty, that he overcomes the Almighty. —*Thomas Brooks*

A stern father has been conquered by a tear in the eye of his daughter. An unwilling heart has relented and bestowed an alms at the sight of the disappointment caused by a refusal. Sorrow constrains to pity. When importunity takes the hand of grief, and the two go together to the gate of mercy, it opens of its own accord. Sincerity, earnestness, perseverance, confidence, and expectancy are all potent instruments of power with God.

How often have I seen a little child throw its arms around its father's neck, and win, by kisses and importunities and tears, what had else been refused. Who has not yielded to importunity, even when a dumb animal looked up in our face with suppliant eyes for food? Is God less pitiful than we? —*Dr. Guthrie*

It were easy here to expatiate into a large history of the great exploits which prayer is renowned for in Holy Writ. This is the key that has opened and again shut heaven. It hath vanquished mighty armies, and unlocked such secrets as passed the skill of the very Devil himself to find out. It hath strangled desperate plots in the very womb wherein they were conceived; and made those engines of cruelty prepared against the saints recoil upon the inventors of them; so that they have inherited the gallows which they did set up for others. At the knock of prayer prison-doors have opened, the grave hath delivered up its dead; and the sea's leviathan, not able to digest his prey, hath been made to vomit it up again. It hath stopped the sun's chariot in the heavens, yea, made it to go back. And that which surpasseth all, it hath taken hold of the Almighty, when on his full march against persons and people, and hath put him to a merciful retreat. —*W. Gurnall*

In a certain town, says the Rev. Mr. Finney, there had been no revival for many years; the church was nearly run out, the youth were all unconverted, and desolation reigned unbroken. There lived in a retired part of the town an aged man, a blacksmith by trade, and of so stammering a tongue that it was painful to hear him speak. On one Friday, as he was at work in his shop alone, his mind became greatly exercised about the state of the church, and of the impenitent. His agony became so great, that he was induced to lay aside his work, lock the shop door, and spend the afternoon in prayer. He prevailed, and on the Sabbath called in the minister and desired him to appoint a conference meeting. After some hesitation, the minister consented, observing, however, that he feared but few would attend. He appointed it the same evening, at a large private house. When evening came, more assembled than could be accommodated in the house. All were silent for a time, until one sinner broke out in tears, and said, if anyone could pray, he begged him to pray for *him*. Another followed, and another, and still another, until it was found that persons from every quarter of the town were under deep convictions. And what was remarkable, was that they all dated their conviction at the hour when the old man was praying in his shop. A powerful revival followed. Then this old stammering man prevailed, and as a prince, had power with God.

3

He blessed him there.
—*Genesis 32:29*

HE main thing is to get a blessing. The angel did not gratify Jacob's curiosity when he asked his name; but he did bless him. May the same be the case with us at this time; even as it was with the disciples when they asked, "Wilt thou at this time restore the kingdom to Israel?" and the Lord replied, "It is not for you to know the times and the seasons, but ye shall receive power after that the Holy Ghost has come upon you." We need not know the future, but we do need power for the present.

I. WHAT WAS JACOB'S BLESSING IN THAT PLACE? "He blessed him."

1. He was saved from a great peril. Esau's attack. "For I fear him, lest he will come and smite me, and the mother with the children" (verse 11).
2. He was forgiven a great wrong. His supplanting of Esau was condoned by his brother.
3. He was able to feel that a great breach was healed. "Esau ran to meet him, and embraced him, and fell on his neck, and kissed him; and they wept" (Gen. 33:4).
4. He had won a new name and rank (verse 28). He was knighted on the spot, made a prince on the field.
5. He was now under a fresh anointing: he was a superior man ever after. "The angel redeemed him from all evil" (Gen. 48:16).

II. WHAT WAS THE PLACE? "He blessed him there."

1. A place of great trial (verses 6 and 7).
2. A place of humble confession. "I am not worthy of the least of all the mercies, and of all the truth, which thou hast showed to thy servant" (verse 10).
3. A place of pleading(verses 1 and 12). "There wrestled a man with him until the breaking of the day" (verse 24).
4. A place of communion. "I have seen God face to face" (verse 30).
5. A place of conscious weakness. "As he passed over Penuel, the sun rose upon him, and he halted upon his thigh."

All this is full of instruction to us, for we read in Hosea 12:4, "Yea, he had power over the angel, and prevailed: he wept, and made supplication unto him: he found him in Beth-el, *and there he spake with us.*"

III. ARE THERE OTHER SUCH PLACES?

1. Before the earth was created the Lord blessed his chosen people in Christ Jesus (Eph. 1:3–4).
   See also Matt. 25:34. "Come, ye blessed of my Father," etc.
2. At the cross, the tomb, and the throne of Jesus. "In thy seed shall all the nations of the earth be blessed" (Gen. 22:18).
3. In the heavenly places. "And made us sit together heavenly places in Christ Jesus" (Eph. 2:6).
4. At conversion. "From this day will I bless you." "Blessed is the man whose transgression is forgiven," etc. (Ps. 32:1–2).
5. In times of stripping, humbling, chastening, pleading, etc. "Blessed is the man that endureth temptation," etc. (James. 1:12).
6. In times of prompt obedience. "Blessed is the man whose delight is in the law of the Lord," etc., (Ps. 1). "In keeping of them there is great reward."
7. At the ordinances (Acts 8:39; Luke 24:30–31).

✓IV. IS THIS SUCH A PLACE?

Yes, if you are:
- Willing to give up sin.
- Willing to have Jesus for your all in all.
- Willing to resign yourself to the Father's will.
- Willing to serve God in his own way.

Go not away without a saving blessing. Believe for it. Wrestle for it. Only the Lord can give it, look to him alone for the blessing. What are means of grace unless the Lord blesses them, and blesses you in the use of them?

Remarks and Incidents

This blessing wherewith Christ here blessed Jacob was a divine blessing containing all other blessings within its bowels. It was that blessing of the *throne* which comprehended in it the blessings of the *foot-stool*. Jacob had got already a great store of foot-stool mercies—much wealth, wives, and children, etc. These worldly blessings would not (and indeed could not) content him: he tugs hard still, and must have some better mercy than these, even the *throne* mercy, to wit, peace with God; well knowing that this would bring peace with his brother, and all other good things; as Job saith, "Acquaint now thyself with him, and be at peace: thereby good shall come unto thee" (Job 22:21). He knew that his power to prevail with Emmanuel himself would fill him with power to prevail with Esau. —*Christopher Ness*

It was with a young man a day of seeking, and he entered a little sanctuary and heard a sermon from "Look unto me and be ye saved." He obeyed the Lord's command, and *he blessed him there*. Soon after he made a profession of his faith before many witnesses, declaring his consecration to the Lord, and *he blessed him there.* Anon he began to labor for the Lord in little rooms, among a few people, and *he blessed him there.* His opportunities enlarged, and by faith he ventured upon daring things for the Lord's sake, and *he blessed him there.* A household grew about him, and together with his loving wife he tried to train his children in the fear of the Lord, and *he blessed him there.* Then came sharp and frequent trial, and he was in pain and anguish, but *the Lord blessed him there.* This is that man's experience all along, from the day of his conversion to this hour: up hill and down dale his path has been a varied one, but for every part of his pilgrimage he can praise the Lord, for "*he blessed him there.*"

I have here, said Mr. Fuller, two religious characters, who were intimately acquainted in early life. Providence favored one of them with a tide of prosperity. The other, fearing for his friend, lest his heart should be overcharged with the cares of this life and the deceitfulness of riches, one day asked him whether he did not find prosperity a snare to him. He paused and answered, "I am not conscious that I do, for I enjoy God in all things." Some years afterwards his affairs took another turn; he lost, if not the whole, yet the far greater part of what he had once gained, and by this disaster was greatly reduced. His old friend being one day in his company, renewed his question, whether he did not find what had lately befallen him to be too much for him. Again he paused and answered, "I am not conscious that I do, for now I enjoy all things in God." This was truly a life of faith. To him it was as true as to Jacob. "*He blessed him there.*"—*Arvine's Anecdotes*

4

Esau said, I have enough. Jacob said, I have enough.
—*Genesis 33:9, 11*

 T is as rare as it is pleasing to meet with a man who has enough; the great majority are craving for more. Here we see two persons who were content. It is true they were both wealthy men, but these are often more greedy than the poor. To increase the wonder, we have here not only two men, but two brothers, and two brothers of dissimilar disposition, each saying "I have enough." Where shall we find two brothers like them? Surely their father's blessing was upon these contented twins. They were great wonders.

I. HERE IS AN UNGODLY MAN WHO HAS ENOUGH.

Because Esau has other faults, there is no necessity that he should be discontented and grasping: contentment is a moral excellence as much as a spiritual grace. Unconverted men are sometimes contented with their lot in this life.

1. It is not always or often so: they are mostly a dissatisfied company,
2. It is sometimes so; as in the case of Esau.
   - This may arise from a want of energy.
   - Or from a naturally easy disposition, readily pleased.
   - Or from utter recklessness which only considers present pleasure.
3 It has some good points about it
   - As preventing greed and the oppression which comes of it.
   - As often promoting a good-natured liberality, and the disposition to "live and let live."
4. Yet it has its evil side.
   - It leads men to boast of their wealth or acquirements who would not do so if they were craving for more.
   - It tends to breed a contempt for spiritual riches.
   - It may thus be a sign of having one's portion in this life.

II. HERE IS A GODLY MAN WHO HAS ENOUGH.

1. It is a pity that this is not true of every Christian man. Some appear to be eager after the world though they profess to be separated from it This creates care, fretfulness, envy of heart and leanness of soul.
2. It is delightful to have enough. Contentment surpasses riches
3. It is pleasant to have somewhat to spare for the poor; and this should be the aim of our labor: the apostle says, "Let him labor, working with his hands the thing which is good, that he may have to give to him that needeth" (Eph. 4:28).
4. It is blessed to have all this through our God. Jacob said, "God hath dealt graciously with me, and I have enough."
5. It is best of all to have all things. In the margin we read that Jacob said, "I have all things." "All things are yours" (1 Cor. 3:22).
   - All that the believer needs is promised in the Covenant.
   - All things in providence work together for his good.
   - In having God for his portion he has more than all.

Thus he has enough of strength and grace. Enough in Christ, in the Word, and in the Spirit Enough in God's love, power and faithfulness, and an immeasurable supply in God himself, whose name is "God All-sufficient."

The child of God should be ashamed of discontent, since even a common sinner may be free from it.

He should be heartily satisfied; for he has all things, and what more can he desire? "O rest in the Lord" (Ps. 37:7).

Illustrations

A poor Christian woman, who was breaking her fast upon a crust and a cup of water, exclaimed, "What! All this and Christ too!"

A Puritan preacher asking a blessing on a herring and potatoes, said, "Lord, we thank thee that thou hast ransacked sea and land to find food for thy children."

"The great cry with everybody is, 'Get on! get on!' just as if the world were traveling post. How astonished these people will be, if they arrive in heaven, to find the angels, who are much wiser than they, laying no schemes to be made archangels!" —*Maxims for Meditation*.

"Is not the bee as well contented with feeding on the dew, or sucking from a flower, as the ox that grazeth on the mountains? Contentment lies within a man, *in the heart*; and the way to be comfortable is not by having our barrels filled, but our minds quieted. The contented man (saith Seneca) is the happy man . . . discontent robs a man of the power to enjoy what he possesses. A drop or two of vinegar will sour a whole glass of wine. —*T. Watson*.

As a typical instance of the contentment of some unregenerate persons, note the following: "A captain of a whale-ship told one of the wretched natives of Greenland that he sincerely pitied the miserable life to which he was condemned. 'Miserable!' exclaimed the savage. 'I have always had a fish-bone through my nose, and plenty of train-oil to drink: what more could I desire?'"

And he said unto him, my Lord knoweth that the children are tender, and the flocks and herds with young are with me: and if men should overdrive them one day, all the flock will die.

—*Genesis 33:13*

 ACOB could have kept pace with Esau had he been alone, but not with so many children and flocks He did not expect Esau to travel at the slow rate which he was obliged to maintain, and therefore he desired to separate. Jacob, however, stated his reason plainly, and his brother felt the weight of it: if we must go different ways, let us cause our motive to be known, so that we may not be thought unkind. Matthew Henry says, "If friends cannot fall *in* with each other, they should see to it that they do not fall *out*." Jacob parted from his reconciled brother for the sake of his little ones, who were very dear to him.

I. LET US VIEW JACOB AS AN EXAMPLE TO US.

He displayed a tender consideration for the young and feeble; let us do the same. Let us consider:

1. *How we may overdrive?*
   - Puzzling them with deep and controversial points of doctrine, and condemning them because they are not quite correct in their opinions. "Them that are weak in the faith receive ye, but not to doubtful disputations" (Rom. 14:1).
   - Setting up a standard of experience, and frowning at them because they have not felt all the sorrows or ecstasies which we have known.
   - Requiring a high degree of faith, courage, patience, and other graces which in their case can only be tender buds.
   - Preaching nothing but the severer truths, or constantly urging to duty by terrible threatenings while withholding the promises and the consolatory parts of the word.
   - Manifesting austerity of manner, suspicion, harshness, censoriousness of spirit, and contempt for weaker brethren.
   - Fault-finding and never commending. "Fathers, provoke not your children to anger, lest they be discouraged" (Col. 3:21).
   - Dwelling always upon the trials, temptations, and woes of believers, and saying little about their joys and privileges.
   - In these and many other ways professed teachers show that they have need to go to school to Jacob to learn the shepherd's trade, and imitate his tender thoughtfulness.

2. *Why we should not overdrive the lambs.*
   - Common humanity forbids.
   - Our own experience when we were young should teach us better.
   - We may again become weak, and need great forbearance.
   - We love them too well to be hard with them.
   - Jesus thinks so much of them that we cannot worry them.
   - The Holy Spirit dwells in them, and we must be gentle towards the faintest beginning of his work.
   - We should be doing Satan's work if we did overburden them.
   - We should thus prove ourselves to have little wisdom and less grace. If we kill the lambs now, where shall we get our sheep from next year?
   - We dare not bear the responsibility of offending these little ones, for terrible woes are pronounced on those who do them wrong.

We remember how tender Jesus is: and this brings us to our second point.

II. LET US VIEW JACOB AS A PICTURE OF OUR LORD JESUS.

See his portrait in Isaiah 40:11: "He shall feed his flock like a shepherd: he shall gather the lambs with his arm, and carry them in his bosom, and shall gently lead those that are with young."

1. The weak have a special place in his love.
2. He will not have it that any of them should die
3. Therefore he never overdrives one of them.
4. But he suits his pace to their feebleness, "I will lead on softly" (Gen. 33:14). "I have many things to say unto you, but ye cannot bear them now."

   - Has he not thus been very tender to us? "Thy gentleness hath made me great" (Ps. 18:35).
   - Let us not fret and worry as though he were an exactor. We are not driven by Jehu, but led by Jesus. Let us rest in his love. At the same time let us not be slower than need be.
   - Towards others let us be tenderness itself, for we are to love our neighbor as ourselves.

Helpful Paragraphs

The Lord chooses under-shepherds for his flock among men subject to weakness and infirmity, that they may have a fellow-feeling for the feeble. *Lelah Merill*, in his "East of the Jordan," describes the movement of an Arab tribe, and says, "The flocks of sheep and goats were mostly driven by small children. Sometimes there were flocks of lambs and kids driven by children not much older relatively than the lambs and kids themselves. Some of the men had in their arms two, three, four, or a whole armful of kids and lambs that were too young to walk; and among some cooking utensils there was a large saucepan, and in it was a pair of small kids that were too young for the journey."

When a candle is newly lighted and needs to be moved, it must be carried at a slow pace or it will be extinguished. A fire which is almost expiring may be revived by a gentle breath, but it will be blown out if the bellows are plied at their full force. You can drown a little plant by watering it too much, and destroy a lovely flower by exposing it to too much sun.

Nothing is so strong as gentleness: nothing so gentle as real strength.
—*Frances de Sales*

Dr. Johnson declared that want of tenderness is want of parts, and that it is a proof of stupidity as well as of depravity.

At the Stockwell Orphanage the usual rule of walking is *little boys first*. In this way the younger children cannot be overdriven or left behind, and moreover all the boys can see before them, whereas by the usual practice of putting the tall fellows first the view in front is shut out from all but the few who lead the way. Let the church have great care for the weaker brethren, and shape her action with a constant reference to them. A strong Christian might do a thousand things lawfully if he only thought of himself, but he will not do one of them because he wishes to act expediently, and would not grieve his brother, or cause him to stumble.

Even in our manner there should be tenderness. A truly kind act may be so performed as to cause as much grief as joy. We have heard of one who would throw a penny at a beggar and thus hurt him while relieving him. A heart full of love has a mode of its own by which its gifts are enhanced in value. There is enough misery in the world without our carelessly adding to it. Some persons are morbidly sensitive, and this is wrong on their part; but when we are aware of their failing we must be the more careful lest we cause them needless pain. A gouty man will cry out if we walk with heavy footstep across the room. Do we censure him for this? No, we pity him, and tread softly. Let us do the same for the sensitive.

6

Joseph opened all the Storehouses.
—*Genesis 41:56*

HE story of Joseph is full of interest; but it is chiefly useful to us as being marvelously typical of the life of our Lord Jesus.

Remark the bounty of providence in raising up Joseph to save the house of Israel, yea, and the whole world, from famishing. Then note the greatness of sovereign grace in raising up Jesus to save his people, and to be God's salvation to the ends of the earth.

Joseph had beforehand filled the vast storehouses, and our text shows us how he used the store: "Joseph opened all the storehouses." How much more has been done by Jesus! O to be partakers of his grace!

I. JOSEPH OPENED THE STOREHOUSES BY ROYAL AUTHORITY.

1. The king was only to be approached through Joseph: "Go unto Joseph" (verse 55). So with Jesus. "No man cometh unto the Father but by me" (John 14:6).
2. The king Commanded that Joseph should be obeyed: "What he saith to you, do" (verse 55). "All men should honor the Son even as they honor the Father" (John 5:23).
3. In all the land no other could open a storehouse save Joseph. "The Father loveth the Son, and hath given all things into his hand" (John 3:35).

II. JOSEPH WAS A FIT PERSON TO BE THUS AUTHORIZED TO OPEN THE STOREHOUSES.

1. He planned the storehouses, and was justly appointed to control them. See verses 33 to 36. "Can we find such a one as this is?" (verse 38).
2. He carried out the storage, and so proved himself practical as well as inventive. "Joseph gathered corn as the sand" (verse 49).
3. He did it on a noble scale. He gathered corn "until he left numbering; for it was without number" (verse 49).
4. He had wisdom to distribute well.

> The parallel is easily drawn, for our Lord Jesus is that Housekeeper, one of a thousand, who has provided for our soul's famine; "For it pleased the Father that in him should all fullness dwell, and of his fullness have all we received" (Col. 1:19; John 1:16).

III. JOSEPH ACTUALLY OPENED THE STOREHOUSES.

1. For this purpose he filled them. Grace is meant to be used.
2. To have kept them closed would have been no gain to him
3. He opened them at a fit time: "All the land of Egypt was famished"; "the famine was over all the face of the earth" (verses 55–56).
4. He kept them open while the famine lasted. They were never closed while a hungering applicant drew near.
   - The corn held out through all the famine years.
   - The places of storage were convenient (verse 48).
   - There were appointed hours for distribution.
   - And proper arrangements to control and regulate the crowds.

All this is far exceeded in Jesus the Antitype, in whom a fullness abides; who is ever near us; to whom we may come daily; and in whom every seeker finds a ready supply.

IV. JOSEPH OPENED THE STOREHOUSES TO ALL COMERS.

1. There was a special eye to Israel, "God sent me before you to preserve you"; but Joseph was also "a father unto Pharaoh" and the preserver of many nations.
2. It was a privilege to dwell near the granaries; but it would have been a dreadful thing if any had died within sight of them. Beware of being "hearers only." Read 2 Kings 7:19.
3. Yet many people came from far for food: "All countries came into Egypt to Joseph for to buy corn" (verse 57).
4. We read of none being sent empty away.

> Yet Joseph did but sell while Jesus gives without money. Will you not come to him for heavenly bread?

V. JOSEPH ACQUIRED POSSESSION OF ALL EGYPT FOR THE KING.

The Egyptians gladly yielded their money, their lands, and their persons to Pharaoh, that their lives might be preserved. Even thus we surrender ourselves, our substance, our abilities, our time, our all to the Lord. Joseph's policy seems hard, but the design of Jesus is love itself. Our full submission and consecration are the grand result of infinite love.

Windows for Light

"This is the only hope of Egypt and all lands:-Joseph is exalted. Joseph is in authority. The residue of whatever supply may be available is with him. He has in his hands the keys. 'All countries came into Egypt to Joseph, for to buy corn' (verse 57). A perishing world hangs on this great fact, that Joseph reigns."
—*Dr. Candlish*

Dr. Conyers was for some years a preacher before he had felt the power of the gospel. As he was reading Ephesians 3:8 in his Greek Testament, he came to: "Unto me, who am less than the least of all saints, is this grace given, that I should preach among the Gentiles the unsearchable riches of Christ." "Riches of Christ!" said he to himself, "'Unsearchable riches of Christ'! What have I preached of these? What do I know of these?" Under the blessing of the Spirit of God he was thus awakened to a new life and a new ministry. Are there not some yet living who might put to their own consciences similar questions?

William Bridge says, "There is enough in Jesus Christ to serve us all. If two, or six, or twenty men be athirst, and they go to drink out of a bottle, while one is drinking, the other envies, because he thinks there will not be enough for him too; but if a hundred be athirst, and go to the river, while one is drinking, the other envies not, because there is enough to serve them all."

All the spiritual blessings wherewith the Church is enriched are in and by Christ. The apostle instances some of the choicest (Eph. 1:3). Our election is by him (verse 4). Our adoption is by him (verse 5). Our redemption and remission of sins are both through him. All the gracious transactions between God and his people are through Christ. God loves us through Christ; he hears our prayers through Christ; he forgives us all our sins through Christ. Through Christ he justifies us; through Christ he sanctifies us; through Christ he upholds us; through Christ he perfects us. All his relations to us are through Christ; all we have is from Christ; all we expect to have hangs upon him. He is the golden hinge upon which all our salvation turns. —*Ralph Robinson*

If any of the people of Egypt had refused to go to Joseph, they would have despised not Joseph only, but the king; and would have deserved to be denied that sustenance which he only could give them. Are not the despisers of our great Redeemer in like manner despisers of his Father who has set him as his King upon the holy hill of Zion? . . . If Joseph had thrown open his storehouses before the Egyptians felt the pressure of hunger, they might soon have wasted the fruits of his prudent care.... Hunger, though very unpleasant, is often more useful than fullness of bread. They were very willing to give the price demanded for their food as long as their money lasted. What is the reason why so many are unwilling to come and receive wine and milk without money and without price? They feel no appetite for it. They are not sensible of their need of it. —*George Lawson*

Judah, thou art he whom thy brethren shall praise: thy hand shall be in the neck of thine enemies; thy father's children shall bow down before thee.

—*Genesis 49:8*

 E shall use Judah as a type of our Lord Jesus, who sprang out of Judah, who is the heir of the royal house of David, and the Shiloh to whom the gathering of the people shall be (verse 10). We use both the man Judah and the tribe of Judah in the parallel.

I. JUDAH'S PRAISE. "Thou art he whom thy brethren shall praise."

They who know him best, to whom he is nearest in relationship, for whom he is most concerned, praise him most.

1. *He is first in intercession.*
   - This is his covenant blessing. "Hear, Lord, the voice of Judah" (Deut. 32:7).
   - This he proved in intercession with his father, Jacob (Gen. 43:3).
   - And in pleading with Joseph when he would have detained Benjamin. How touchingly he spake! how earnestly he offered himself as a substitute! (Gen. 44:14).

2. *He is first in wisdom.*
   - To Judah belonged the man who was filled with the spirit of God, by whom the tabernacle in the wilderness was erected. "See, I have called by name Bezaleel the son of Uri, the son of Hur, of the tribe of Judah: and I have filled him with the spirit of God, in wisdom, and in understanding, and in knowledge, and in all manner of workmanship" (Exod. 31:2–3).
   - To Judah came the legislative power. "Judah is my lawgiver" (Ps. 60) "The scepter shall not depart from Judah" (verse 10).

3. *He takes precedence in offering.*
   He that offered his offering the first day was of the tribe of Judah. See Numbers 7:12.

4. *He takes precedence in march.*
    In descent or ascent, in battle or in progress, in the first place went the standard of Judah. Read Numbers 10:14, Judges 1:2.
5. *In all things he has the pre-eminince.*
    David was chosen of the Lord to be king. "He refused the tabernacle of Joseph, and chose not the tribe of Ephraim, but he chose the tribe of Judah" (Ps. 78:67–68).

II. JUDAH'S TRIUMPHS ABROAD.

"Thy hand shall be in the neck of thine enemies." Illustrate by life of David:

- He passed through severe conflicts. Read 1 Samuel 17:34-36.
- He gained great victories (2 Chron. 13:14).
- He founded a peaceful empire.
- He utterly crushed the forces of his foes, and broke the neck of all opposition.
- So has our Lord done by his life, death, resurrection, reigning power, and second coming.

III. JUDAH'S HONORS AT HOME.

"Thy father's children shall bow down before thee."

1. *He became the Head of the family.*
2. *He was clothed with lion-like power.* "He couched as a lion, and as an old lion." See verse 9. "The lion of the tribe of Judah hath prevailed" (Rev. 5:5).
3. *He is the center of our assembling.* "To him shall the gathering of the people be" (verse 10).
4. *His glory is his meekness.* "Binding his foal," etc. (verse 11). "Thy King cometh, meek and sitting upon a colt the foal of an ass" (Matt. 21:5).
5. *The wine bath at his first and second advent, makes him lovely in our eyes.* Note verses 11 and 12; also "I have trodden the wine-press alone" (Isa. 63:1–3).
6. *He is King to us for ever. Hallelujah.* See Hosea 11:12. "Ephraim compasseth me about with lies, and the house of Israel with deceit: but Judah yet ruleth with God."
    - Are we among the foes against whom he fights as a lion ? Let us beware how we rouse him up (verse 9).
    - Are we among his friends for whom he fights? Let us praise him with all our hearts, and now bow down before him. Are we not his Father's children?
    - Do we hunger and thirst after heavenly food? See in the 12th verse how abundant are wine and milk with him.

Suggestions

There is abundance of suggestiveness in the text for three sermons from the one verse which we have selected as a text, and the following verses are peculiarly rich. Judah's name signifies praise; Judah in the person of David became the leader of praise. "God is praised *for* him, *in* him, and *by* him; and therefore his brethren shall praise him." See both the lion *rampant* and the lion *couchant* in our Lord Jesus, who, having spoiled principalities and powers, has gone up as a Conqueror and has couched down at the right hand of the divine majesty. "The lion of the tribe of Judah hath prevailed."

Rutherford often cried, "O for a well-tuned harp!"

The following extract from *Thomas Brooks* may help the preacher to a measure of variety in setting forth our Lord's claim to our praise. "Christians, remember this, *all the causes of prizing persons and things are eminently and only in Christ;* therefore, set a very, very high price upon the Lord Jesus. You prize some for their beauty; why, the Lord Jesus Christ is the fairest among the children of men, (Ps. 45:1–2; Song of Sol. 5:10), 'My beloved is white and ruddy, the chiefest;' or, the standard-bearer, 'among ten thousand.' You prize others for their strength (Isa. 26:4), 'Trust ye in the Lord for ever: for in the Lord Jehovah is everlasting strength.' You prize others for bearing their father's image; why, the Lord Jesus is the brightness of his Father's glory, and the express image of his person (Heb. 1:3). You prize others for their wisdom and knowledge; such a one is a very wise man, you say, and therefore you prize him; and such a one is a very knowing man, and therefore you prize him; why, all the treasures of wisdom and knowledge are in Christ (Col. 2:3). The truth is, all those perfections and excellencies that are in all angels and men, are all epitomized in Christ. All the angels in heaven have but some of those perfections that be in Christ. All wisdom, and all power, and all goodness, and all mercy, and all love, etc., is in no glorified creature; no, not in all glorified creatures put together. But now in Christ all these perfections and excellencies meet, as all water meets in the sea, and as all light meets in the sun. Others you prize for their usefulness; the more useful persons and things are, the more you prize and value them. The Lord Jesus Christ is of universal use to his people; why, he is the right eye of his people, without which they cannot see; and the right hand of his people, without which they cannot do, etc. He is of singular use to all his people. He is of use to weak saints, to strengthen them; and he is of use to doubting saints, to confirm them; and he is of use to dull saints, to quicken them; and he is of use to falling saints, to support them; and he is of use to wandering saints, to recover them. In prosperity he is of use to keep his saints humble and watchful, spotless, and fruitful; and in adversity he is of use to keep them contented and cheerful. All which should very much engage our hearts to prize this Christ."

They shall take to them every man a lamb, according to the house of their fathers, a lamb for an house: And if the household be too little for the lamb, let him and his neighbor next unto his house take it according to the number of the souls; every man according to his eating shall make your count for the lamb.

—*Exodus 12:3-4*

 HE lamb was to be eaten, all eaten, eaten by all, and eaten at once. The Lord Jesus is to be received into the soul as its food, and this is to be done with a whole Christ, by each one of his people, and done just now. The whole subject of the Passover is rich in instruction; we will confine ourselves to the particulars within this verse.

I. THE TEXT REMINDS US OF A PRIMARY PRIVILEGE.

1. That each man of Israel ate the passover *for himself;* "every man according to his eating." So do we feed upon Jesus, each one as his appetite, capacity, and strength enable him to do.
2. But this same delicious fare should be enjoyed by *all the family:* "a lamb for an house." Oh, that each of the parents, and all the children and servants may be partakers of Christ! By teaching, training, prayer, and holy example, this favor may be secured, for the Holy Spirit will add his blessing.

   Let not these two favors be despised. Let no man be content without personal salvation, nor without the salvation of his whole house. We have both promised in that famous text, "Believe on the Lord Jesus Christ, and *thou* shalt be saved, *and thy house.*"

II. THE TEXT IS SILENT AS TO A CERTAIN CONTINGENCY.

1. The lamb was never too little for the family; and assuredly the Lord Jesus is never too little even for the largest families, nor for the most sinful persons.
2. There is no reason to stint our prayers for fear we ask too much.
3. Nor to stay our labors because the Lord Jesus cannot give us strength enough, or grace enough.
4. Nor to restrain our hopes of salvation for the whole family because of some supposed narrowness in the purpose, provision, or willingness of the Lord to bless.

"Every man according to his eating" may feast to the full upon Christ. Every believing sinner may take Christ to himself, and there is no fear that one will be refused, for "it pleased the Father that in him should all fullness dwell."

III. THE TEXT MENTIONS A POSSIBILITY, AND PROVIDES FOR IT.

There may be a want of persons to feed upon the Lamb, though there can be no lack of food for them to feed upon. The last thing that was supplied to the great marriage feast was guests. The oxen and the fatlings were killed, and all things were ready, long before "the wedding was furnished with guests."

1. One family is certainly too small a reward for Jesus, too little for the Lamb.
2. One family is too little to render him all the praise, worship, service, and love which he deserves.
3. One family is too little to do all the work of proclaiming the Lamb of God, maintaining the truth, visiting the church, winning the world. Therefore let us call in the neighbor next unto our house.
   - Our next neighbor has the first claim upon us.
   - He is the most easy to reach, and by each calling his next neighbor all will be reached.
   - He is the most likely person to be influenced by us.
   - At any rate there is the rule, and we are to obey it. "Beginning at Jerusalem" (Luke 24:47). We read of Andrew, "he first findeth his own brother Simon" (John 1:41). Those who repaired Jerusalem built every man over against his own house (Neh. 3:28).
   - If our neighbor does not come when invited, we are not responsible; but if he perished because we did not invite him, bloodguiltiness would be upon us. "If thou dost not speak . . . his blood will I require at thine hand" (Ezek. 33:8).

IV. THE WHOLE SUBJECT SUGGESTS THOUGHTS UPON NEIGH-BORLY FELLOWSHIP IN THE GOSPEL.

1. It is good for individuals and families to grow out of selfishness, and to seek the good of a wide circle.
2. It is a blessed thing when the center of our society is "the Lamb."
3. Innumerable blessings already flow to us from the friendships which have sprung out of our union in Jesus. Church fellowship has been fruitful in this direction.
4. Our care for one another in Christ helps to realize the unity of the one body, even as the common eating of the Passover proclaimed and assisted the solidarity of the people of Israel as one nation. This spiritual union is a high privilege.
5. Thoroughly carried out, heaven will thus be foreshadowed upon earth, for there love to Jesus and love to one another is found in every heart.
   - Let us be personal in our piety, and never be put off with a mere national religion or family profession.
   - Let us be generous in our religion, and never neglect our families, our friends, or the neighborhood in which we dwell.

Things of Interest

A little boy asked his mother which of the characters in *The Pilgrim's Progress* she liked best. She replied, "Christian, of course; he is the hero of the whole story." Her son said, "I don't, mother, I like Christiana best; for when Christian went on his pilgrimage he started alone, but when Christiana went she took the children with her."

"The Lord said unto Noah, come *thou and all thy house* into the ark." True religion thinks of the house. I once knew a man who walked a long distance to hear what he called "the truth." Neither his wife nor any of his children went to any place of worship, and when he was asked about them by me, he told me that "the Lord would save his own"; to which I could not help replying that the Lord would not own *him*. For this he demanded a warrant, and I gave him this: "He that provideth not for those of his own house, he hath denied the faith, and is worse than an infidel." Does God acknowledge such persons as his elect?

A man was going to his work one morning, when he was told that the river had burst its banks, and was sweeping down the valley, carrying death and destruction wherever it went. His informant did not seem much concerned about the matter, but the brave workman immediately rushed off down to the lower part of the valley, shouting, "If that's so, somebody has got to let the people know." By his timely warning he saved the lives of many people.

Eating together is one of the most effectual symbols of fellowship; hence the Passover and the Lord's Supper remind us of our oneness in Christ. Never let us eat our morsel alone. When we eat the fat and drink the sweet, let us joyfully send portions to those for whom nothing is prepared.

9

Wherefore criest thou unto me?
—*Exodus 14:15*

HERE may come a time when this question needs to be asked even of a Moses. There is a period when crying should give place to action: when prayer is heard and the Red Sea is dividing, it would be shameful disobedience to remain trembling and praying. Therefore Moses must lift his rod and speak to the children of Israel that they go forward. Every fruit of the Spirit comes in its season, and is then most precious: out of season even prayer comes not to perfection. Ask, by all means; but prepare yourself to receive. Seek earnestly; but do not hold back when the hour arrives for you to find. Knock, and knock again; but hasten to enter as soon as the door is open.

When we ought to believe that we have the mercy, why do we continue to cry for it as though we had not obtained it? When increased faith is all that is wanted, why are we seeking the blessing which God places within reach of our faith? When duty is quite clear, why hesitate to perform it and make prayer an excuse for our delay?

The question should be asked of all who pray, "Wherefore criest thou unto me?"

I. SOMETIMES THE ANSWER WILL BE VERY UNSATISFACTORY.

1. Because I was brought up to do so. Some have perpetrated gross hypocrisy through repeating forms of prayer which they learned in childhood. We have heard of one who prayed for his father and mother in his old age (John 9:24).
2. It is a part of my religion. These pray as a Dervish dances or a Fakir holds his arm aloft; but they know nothing of the spiritual reality of prayer (Matt. 6:7).
3. It is a right thing to do. So indeed it is if we pray aright; but the mere repetition of pious words is vanity (Isa. 29:13).
4. I feel easier in my mind after it. Ought you to feel easier? May not your formal prayers be a mockery of God and so an increase of sin (Isa. 1:12–15; Ezek. 20:31)?
5. I think it meritorious and saving. This is sheer falsehood, and a high offence against the merit and sacrifice of the Lord Jesus.

II. SOMETIMES THE ANSWER WILL BETRAY IGNORANCE.

1. When it hinders immediate repentance. Instead of quitting sin and mourning over it, some men talk of praying. "To obey is better than sacrifice" and better than supplication.
2. When it keeps from faith in Jesus. The gospel is not "pray and be saved"; but "believe on the Lord Jesus Christ and thou shalt be saved" (Matt. 7:21; John 6:47).
3. When we suppose that it fits us for Jesus. We must come to him as sinners, and not set up our prayers as a sort of righteousness (Luke 18:11, 12).
4. When we think that prayer alone will bring a blessing.

III. SOMETIMES THE ANSWER WILL BE QUITE CORRECT.

1. Because I must. I am in trouble, and must pray or perish. Sighs and cries are not made to order, they are the irresistible outbursts of the heart (Ps. 42:1; Rom. 8:26).
2. Because I know I shall be heard, and therefore I feel a strong desire to deal with God in supplication. "Because he hath inclined his ear unto me, therefore will I call upon him" (Ps. 116:2).

3. Because I delight in it: it brings rest to my mind, and hope to my heart. It is a sweet means of communion with my God. "It is good for me to draw near to God" (Ps. 73:28).
4. Because I feel that I can best express the little faith and repentance I have by crying to the Lord for more.
5. Because these grow as I pray. No doubt we may pray ourselves into a good frame if God the Holy Ghost blesses us.
6. Because I look for all from God, and therefore I cry to him (Ps. 62:5). He will be enquired of by us (Ezek. 36: 37).
   • Where must those be who depend upon their own prayers ?
   • What are those who live without prayer ?
   • What are those who can give no reason for praying, but superstitiously repeat words without heart?

Cases in Point, etc.

An anxious enquirer to whom I had plainly put the great gospel command, "Believe in the Lord Jesus," constantly baffled my attempts to lead her out of self to Christ. At last she cried out, "Pray for me! pray for me!" She seemed greatly shocked when I replied, "I will do nothing of the kind. I have prayed for you before; but if you refuse to believe the word of the Lord, I do not see what I can pray for. The Lord bids you believe his Son, and if you will not do so, but persist in making God a liar, you will perish, and you richly deserve it." This brought her to her bearings. She begged me again to tell her the way of salvation, she quietly received it as a little child, her frame quivered, her face brightened, and she cried! "Sir! I can believe, I do believe, and I am saved. Thank you for refusing to comfort me in my unbelief. "Then she said very softly, "Will you not pray for me now?" Assuredly I did, and we rejoiced together that we could offer the prayer of faith.

A good illustration of the need of following up prayer by effort may be found in the following anecdote:

A scholar was remarkable for repeating her lessons well. Her schoolfellow, rather idly inclined, said to her one day, "How is it that you always say your lessons so perfectly?" She replied, "I always pray that I may say my lessons well." "Do you?" said the other; "well then, I will pray, too": but alas I the next morning she could not even repeat a word of her usual task. Very much confounded, she ran to her friend, and reproached her as deceitful: "I prayed," said she, "but I could not say a single word of my lesson." "Perhaps," rejoined the other, "you took no pains to learn it." "Learn it! Learn it! I did not learn it at all," answered the first, "I thought I had no occasion to learn it, when I prayed that I might say it." The mistake is a very common one.

In a great thaw on one of the American rivers, there was a man on one of the cakes of ice, which was not actually separated from the unbroken mass. In his terror, however, he did not see this, but knelt down and began to pray aloud for God to deliver him. The spectators on the shore cried loudly to him, "Man, man, stop praying, and run for the shore." So I would say to some of you, "Rest not in praying, but believe in Jesus." —*Quoted in "The Christian," 1874*

On one occasion, when Bunyan was endeavoring to pray, the tempter suggested "that neither the mercy of God, nor yet the blood of Christ, at all concerned him, nor could they help him by reason of his sin; therefore it was vain to pray." Yet he thought with himself, "I will pray." "But," said the tempter, "your sin is unpardonable." "Well," said he, "I will pray." "It is to no boot," said the adversary. And still he answered, "I will pray." And so he began his prayer, "Lord, Satan tells me that neither thy mercy nor Christ's blood is sufficient to save my soul. Lord, shall I honor thee most by believing thou wilt and canst? or him, by believing thou neither wilt nor canst? Lord, I would fain honor thee by believing that thou canst and wilt." And while he was thus speaking, "as if someone had clapped him on the back," that scripture fastened on his mind, "O man, great is thy faith."

> Seek thou thy God alone by prayer,
> And thou shalt doubt—perchance despair;
> But seek him also by endeavor,
> And thou shalt find him gracious ever.

10

Then Moses stood in the gate of the camp, and said, Who is on the Lord's side? let him come unto me. And all the sons of Levi gathered themselves together unto him.

—Exodus 32:26

 SRAEL had rebelled against Jehovah, and had set up the golden calf. Moses appeared among them, and in great wrath threw down their idol and rebuked Aaron. The people were awe-struck by the presence of the servant of the Lord, and sought their tents, save only a number of the more hardened who brazened it out. Moses, feeling that this great rebellion must be crushed and punished, summoned the faithful to his standard, and those who came were of the tribe of Levi. These, with stern fidelity, fulfilled their mission, and hence were made teachers of Israel for ever. Decision is that which the Lord looks for in his ministers, and when he sees it he will reward it. Remember the blessing of Levi, in Deuteronomy 33. "And of Levi he said, Let thy Thummin and thy Urim be with thy holy one, whom thou didst prove at Massah, and with whom thou didst strive at the waters of Meribah; Who said unto his father and to his mother, I have not seen him; neither did he acknowledge his brethren, nor knew his own children: for they have observed thy word, and kept thy covenant. They shall teach Jacob thy judgments, and Israel thy law: they shall put incense before thee, and whole burnt sacrifice upon thine altar."

All true men ought to be decided, for a dreadful conflict is going on at this present day, and a curse will fall on neutrals.

I. THE CONFLICT, AND WHICH IS THE LORD'S SIDE.

- Belief in God against Atheism and other forms of unbelief.
- Scripture in opposition to false philosophy and "modern thought."
- The gospel *versus* superstition.
- Christ *versus* self-righteousness.
- The commands of God *versus* self-pleasing.
- Holiness and right, against sin and oppression.

II. THE LORD'S FRIENDS AND WHAT THEY MUST DO.

- They must own their allegiance openly. "Consecrate yourselves today to the Lord" (verse 29).
- They should come out and rally to the standard: "Who is on the Lord's side? Iet him come unto me." We do this by open union with the church, by boldly rebuking sin, by testifying for truth, by not conforming to the world, and by conforming to Christ our Lord (2 Cor. 8:5).
- They must be willing to be in a minority: one tribe against eleven, if need be.
- They must become aggressive. "Put every man his sword by his side" (verse 27).
- Their zeal must overmaster nature's ties. "Neither did he acknowledge his brethren," etc., (Deut. 33:9).
- They must do what they are bidden. "And the children of Levi did according to the word of Moses" (Exod. 32:28).

III. THE LORD'S HOST AND ITS ENCOURAGEMENTS.

- Their cause is that of right and truth. A good cause is a firm foundation and a powerful stimulus of velour.
- It is the cause of the Almighty God. "They have observed thy word, and kept thy covenant" (Deut. 30:9).
- Christ himself is our Captain. Who can hesitate with such a Chieftain? "A leader and commander for the people" (Isa. 55:4).
- The Angels are with us. Horses of fire and chariots of fire are round about the Lord's servants (2 Kings 6:17).
- Thousands of the best of men have been on this side (Heb. 12:1).
- It is the side of conscience, and of a clean heart.
- It is that side of the warfare which ends in heaven and victory, world without end (Rev. 19:14).

IV. THE QUESTION OF THE TEXT, AND PROPOSALS FOR ENLISTMENT.

- Take the shilling: by faith receive the promise.
- Put on the colors: by confessing Christ openly in baptism.
- Submit to drill: be willing to learn, and yield to discipline.
- Put on the regimentals: wear the garments of holiness, the livery of love, the whole armor of God (Eph. 6:13-18).
- Gird on your sword: "The sword of the Spirit, which is the word of God."
- Enter on civil war first. Wage war within your own soul. Slay sin, conquer self, cast down high looks, etc.
- March to the field. Fight with falsehood, superstition, cruelty, oppression, drunkenness, uncleanness, and sin of every sort, anywhere and everywhere.

Illustrative Extracts

"We trust the Lord is on our side, Mr. Lincoln," said the speaker of a delegation of Christian people to that good man, during one of the darkest days of the American Civil War. "I do not regard that as so essential as something else," replied Mr. Lincoln. The worthy visitors looked horror-struck, until the President added: "I am most concerned to know that we are on the Lord's side."

Mr. Lincoln was right. The right side is not my side or your side. The Lord's side is the place to which every one of us should rally. His banner has right, truth, love, and holiness written on it. Be sure you stand up for God's banner, even if you stand alone.

Guizot, in his life of St. Louis of France, says that the latter had many vassals who were also vassals of the King of England, and that many subtle and difficult questions arose as to the extent of the service which they owed to these kings. At length the French king commanded all those nobles who held lands in English territory to appear before him, and then he said to them, "As it is impossible for any man living in my kingdom and having possessions in England rightly to serve two masters, you must either attach yourselves altogether to me, or inseparably to the King of England." After saying this, he gave them a certain day by which to make their choice.

> The Son of God goes forth to war,
>   A kingly crown to gain;
> His blood-red banner streams afar:
>   Who follows in his train?

"Set down my name, Sir." According to Bunyan, these were the words of the man who fought his way into the palace, and who was welcomed with the song:

> Come in, come in,
> Eternal glory thou shalt win.

A dear friend of mine, the head of a family of grown-up sons and daughters, lately passed away very suddenly. The day before he died, all the members of the household were with him, including one who had recently, like the rest, experienced the power of saving grace. The father's joy was great, as he put his hand upon one after another of his offspring, saying with an overflowing heart, "And *this one* on the Lord's side!—and *this one* on the Lord's side!" How would it be with our hearer should he have to stand at the death-bed of a godly parent? Would that parent rejoice over him because he is on the Lord's side?

He shall lay his hand upon the head of the sin offering.
—*Leviticus 4:29*

 ERE we have an emblem of the way in which a sacrifice becomes available for the offerer. The same ceremony is commanded in verses 4, 15, 24, and 33, and in other places: it is therefore important and instructive.

The question with many souls is how to obtain an interest in Christ so as to be saved by him. Never could a weightier question be asked.

It is certain that this is absolutely needful; but alas, it has been fearfully neglected by many. In vain did Christ die if he is not believed in.

It ought to be attended to at once.

The text gives us a pictorial answer to the question, How can Christ's sacrifice become available for me?

Let us learn:

I. THE INTENT OF THE SYMBOL.

1. *It was a confession of sin:* else no need of a sin offering.
   - To this was added a confession of the desert of punishment, or why should the victim be slain?
   - There was also an abandonment of all other methods of removing sin. The hands were empty, and laid alone upon the sin offering.
   - Do this at the cross; for there alone is sin put away.
2. *It was a consent to the plan of substitution.*
   - Some raise questions as to the justice and certainty of this method of salvation; but he who is to be saved does not so, for he sees that God himself is the best judge of its rightness, and if he is content we may assuredly be so.

- Substitution exceedingly honors the law, and vindicates justice.
- There is no other plan which meets the case, or even fairly looks at it. Man's sense of guilt is not met by other proposals.
- But this brings rest to the most tender conscience:

> What if we trace the globe around,
> And search from Britain to Japan,
> There shall be no religion found
> So just to God, so safe to man.

3. *It was an acceptance of the victim.*
   - Jesus is the most natural substitute, for he is the second Adam, the second head of the race; the true ideal man.
   - He is the only person able to offer satisfaction, having a perfect humanity united with his Godhead.
   - He alone is acceptable to God; he may well be acceptable to us.
4. *It was a believing transference of sin.*
   - By laying on of hands sin was typically laid on the victim.
   - It was laid there so as to be no longer on the offerer.
5. *It was a dependence-leaning on the victim.*
   - Is there not a most sure stay in Jesus for the leaning heart?
   - Consider the nature of the suffering and death by which the atonement was made, and you will rest in it.
   - Consider the dignity and worth of the sacrifice by whom the death was endured. The glory of Christ's person enhances the value of his atonement (Heb. 10:5-10).
   - Remember that none of the saints now in heaven have had any other atoning sacrifice. "Jesus only" has been the motto of all justified ones. "He offered one sacrifice for sins for ever" (Heb. 10:12).
   - Those of us who are saved are resting there alone; why should; not *you*, and every anxious one?

II. SIMPLICITY OF THE SYMBOL.

1. There were no antecedent rites. The victim was there, and hands were laid on it: nothing more. We add neither preface nor appendix to Christ: he is Alpha and Omega.
2. The offerer came in all his sin. "Just as I am." It was to have his sin removed that the offerer brought the sacrifice: not because he had himself removed it.
3. There was nothing in his hand of merit, or price.
4. There was nothing on his hand. No gold ring to indicate wealth; no signet of power; no jewel of rank. The offerer came as a man, and not as learned, rich, or honorable.

5. He performed no cunning legerdemain with his hand. By leaning upon it he took the victim to be his representative; but he placed no reliance upon ceremonial performances.

6. Nothing was done to his hand. His ground of trust was the sacrifice, not his hands. He desired his hand to be clean, but upon that fact he did not rest for pardon.

Come then, dear hearer, whether saint or sinner, and lean hard upon Jesus. He taketh away the sin of the world. Trust him with your sin, and it is for ever put away. Put forth now your hand, and adopt the expiation of the redeeming Lord as your expiation.

Anecdotes and Illustrations

A poor blind woman in Liverpool, after her conversion, committed many hymns to memory. She was an occasional attendant upon the old Earl of Derby, the grandfather of the present Earl. She repeated one of her hymns to him. The old Earl liked it, and encouraged her to repeat more. But one day, when repeating the hymn of Charles Wesley "All ye that pass by," she came to the words:

> "The Lord in the day of his anger did lay
> Your sins on the Lamb, and he bore them away."

He said, "Stop, Mrs. Brass, don't you think it should be, 'The Lord in the day of his *mercy* did lay'?" She did not think his criticism valid; but it proved that she was not repeating her verses to inattentive ears, and other indications showed that the blind woman was made a blessing to the dying nobleman. —*Paxton Hood's Life of Isaac Watts*

"When Christmas Evans was about to die, several ministers were standing round his bed. He said to them, 'Preach Christ to the people, brethren. Look at me: in myself I am nothing but ruin. But look at me in Christ; I am heaven and salvation.'"

It is not the quantity of thy faith that shall save thee. A drop of water is as true water as the whole ocean. So a little faith is as true faith as the greatest. A child eight days old is as really a man as one of sixty years; a spark of fire is as true fire as a great flame; a sickly man is as truly living as a healthy man. So it is not the measure of thy faith that saves thee—*it is the blood that it grips to that saves thee.* As the weak hand of a child, that leads the spoon to the mouth, will feed it as well as the strong arm of a man; for it is not the hand that feeds thee—albeit, it puts the meat into thy mouth, but it is the meat carried into thy stomach that feeds thee. So if thou canst grip Christ ever so weakly, he will not let thee perish. . . . The weakest hands take a gift as well as the strongest. Now, Christ is this gift, and weak faith may grip him as well as strong faith, and Christ is as truly thine when thou hast weak faith, as when thou hast come to those triumphant joys through the strength of faith. —*Welsh*

The Puritans speak of faith as a recumbency, a leaning. It needs no power to lean; it is a cessation from our own strength, and allowing our weakness to depend upon another's power. Let no man say, "I cannot lean"; it is not a question of what you can do, but a confession of what you cannot do, and a leaving of the whole matter with Jesus. No woman could say, "I cannot swoon"; it is not a matter of power. Die into the life of Christ; let him be all in all while you are nothing at all.

12

And when the people complained, it displeased the Lord: and the Lord heard it; and his anger was kindled; and the fire of the Lord burnt among them, and consumed them that were in the uttermost parts of the camp.

—Numbers 11:1

 EHEARSE the historical fact. Observe how the mischief began in the outskirts among the mixed multitude, and how the fire of the Lord burned in the uttermost parts of the camp. The great danger of the church lies in her camp-followers or hangers-on: they infect the true Israel. Hence the need of guarding the entrance of the church, and keeping up discipline within it. Grumbling, discontent, ungrateful complaining—these are grievous offences against our gracious God.

We shall consider the subject in a series of observations.

I. A DISSATISFIED SPIRIT CAUSES DISPLEASURE TO THE LORD.

1. This we might infer from our own feelings, when dependents, children, servants, or receivers of alms are always grumbling. We grow weary of them, and angry with them.
2. In the case of men towards God it is much worse for them to murmur, since they deserve no good at his hands, but the very reverse. "Wherefore doth a living man complain, a man for the punishment of his sins" (Lam. 3:39; Ps. 103:10)?
3. In that case also it is a reflection upon the Lord's goodness, wisdom, truth, and power. See the complaint in verses 4–6.
4. The evil lusting which attends the complaining proves its injurious character. We are ready for anything when we quarrel with God (1 Cor. 10:5–12).
5. God thinks so ill of it that his wrath burns, and chastisement is not long withheld. See verse 33 of this chapter, and other parts of Scripture.

II. A DISSATISFIED SPIRIT FANCIES IT WOULD FIND PLEASURE IN THINGS DENIED IT.

Israel had manna, but sighed for fish, cucumbers, melons, onions, etc. But to set an imaginary value upon that which we have not:

1. Is foolish, childish, pettish.
2. Is injurious to ourselves, for it prevents our enjoying what we already have. It leads men to slander angels' food and call it "this light bread." It led Haman to think nothing of his prosperity because a single person refused him reverence (Esther 5:13).
3. Is slanderous towards God, and ungrateful to him.
4. Leads to rebellion, falsehood, envy, and all manner of sins.

III. A DISSATISFIED SPIRIT FINDS NO PLEASURE FOR ITSELF EVEN WHEN ITS WISH IS FULFILLED.

The Israelites had flesh in superabundance in answer to their foolish prayers, but:

1. It was attended with leanness of soul (Ps. 106:15).
2. It brought satiety;-"until it come out at your nostrils, and it be loathsome unto you" (verse 20).
3. It caused death. He "slew the fattest of them" (Ps. 78:31).
4. It thus led to mourning on all sides. Kibroth Hattaavah, or, "the graves of lust," was the name of this station (verse 34).

IV. A DISSATISFIED SPIRIT SHOWS THAT THE MIND NEEDS REGULATING.

Grace would put our desires in order, and keep our thoughts and affections in their proper places, thus:

1. Content with such things as we have (Heb. 13:5).
2. Towards other things moderate in desire. "Give me neither poverty nor riches" (Prov. 30:8).
3. Concerning earthly things which may be lacking, fully resigned. "Not as I will, but as thou wilt" (Matt. 26:39).
4. First, and most eagerly, desiring God. "My soul thirsteth for God," etc., (Ps. 42:2).
5. Next, coveting earnestly the best gifts (1 Cor. 12:31).
6. Following ever in love the more excellent way (1 Cor. 12:31).

Helpful Notes

I have read of Caesar, that, having prepared a great feast for his nobles and friends, it fell out that the day appointed was so extremely foul that nothing could be done to the honor of their meeting; whereupon he was so displeased and enraged, that he commanded all them that had bows to shoot up their

arrows at Jupiter, their chief god, as in defiance of him for that rainy weather; which, when they did, their arrows fell short of heaven, and fell upon their own heads, so that many of them were very sorely wounded. So all our mutterings and murmurings, which are so many arrows shot at God himself, will return upon our own pates, or hearts; they reach not him, but they will hit us; they hurt not him, but they will wound us therefore, it is better to be mute than to murmur; it is dangerous to contend with one who is a consuming fire (Heb. 12:29).
—*Thomas Brooks*

God hath much ado with us. Either we lack health, or quietness, or children, or wealth, or company, or ourselves in all these. It is a wonder the Israelites found not fault with the want of sauce to their quails, or with their old clothes, or their solitary way. Nature is moderate in her desires; but conceit is insatiable. —*Bp. Hall*

Murmuring is a quarreling with God, and inveighing against him. "They spake against God" (Num. 21:5). The murmurer saith interpretatively that God hath not dealt well with him, and that he hath deserved better from him. The murmurer chargeth God with folly. This is the language, or rather blasphemy, of a murmuring spirit—God might have been a wiser and a better God. The murmurer is a mutineer. The Israelites are called in the same text "murmurers" and "rebels" (Num. 17:10); and is not rebellion as the sin of witchcraft? (1 Sam. 15:23). Thou that art a murmurer art in the account of God as a witch, a sorcerer, as one that deals with the devil. This is a sin of the first magnitude. Murmuring often ends in cursing: Micah's mother fell to cursing when the talents of silver were taken away (Judg. 17:2). So doth the murmurer when a part of his estate is taken away. Our murmuring is the devil's music; this is that sin which God cannot bear: "How long shall I bear with this evil congregation, which murmur against me?" (Num. 14:27). It is a sin which whets the sword against a people; it is a land-destroying sin: "Neither murmur ye, as some of them also murmured, and were destroyed of the destroyer" (1 Cor. 10:10). —*T. Watson*

Losing our temper with God is a more common thing in the spiritual life than many suppose. —*F. W. Faber*

Life is a field of nettles to some men. Their fretful, worrying tempers are always pricking out through the tender skin of their uneasiness. Why, if they were set down in Paradise, carrying their bad mind with them, they would fret at the good angels, and the climate, and the colors even of the roses. —*Dr. Bushnell*

I dare no more fret than curse or swear. —*John Wesley*

A child was crying in passion, and I heard its mother say, "If you cry for nothing, I will soon give you something to cry for." From the sound of her hand, I gathered the moral that those who cry about nothing are making a rod for their own backs, and will probably be made to smart under it.

13

For the Lord shall judge his people, and repent himself for his servants, when he seeth that their power is gone, and there is none shut up or left.

—*Deuteronomy 32:36*

o ungodly men the time of their fall is fatal; there is no rising again for them. They mount higher and higher upon the ladder of riches; but at last they can climb no higher, their feet slide, and all is over. This calamity hasteneth on. "To me belongeth vengeance, and recompense; their foot shall slide in due time: for the day of their calamity is at hand, and the things that shall come upon them make haste" (verse 35).

But it is not so with three characters of whom we will now speak: they are judged in this world that they may not be condemned hereafter (1 Cor. 11:32). Of each of them it may be said, "Though he fall, he shall not be utterly cast down" (Ps. 37:24).

I. THE LORD'S OWN CHURCH.

1. A church may be sorely tried, "power gone, none left."
   - By persecution the faithful may be cut off (Ps. 107:39).
   - By removals, death, poverty, a church may be depleted to a painful extent (Isa. 1:8–9).
   - Through the lack of a faithful ministry, there may be no increase; and those who remain may grow feeble and dispirited.
   - By general falling off of hearers, members, etc., a church may besorely distressed. Various circumstances may scatter a people, such as internal dissension, pestilent heresy, and lack of spiritual life. Where there is no spiritual food hungry souls find no home (Job 15:23).
2. But it may then cry to God.
   - If indeed *his people*, the covenant stands, and he will judge them.
   - If still *his servants*, the bond holds on his side, and he will repent himself for them.
   - His eye is ever upon *them*, and their eye should be up to *him*.
3. He will return and revive his own church. He who killed will make alive (verse 39). He pities his children when he sees them broken down under their sorrows.
4. Meanwhile the trial is permitted:
   - To find out his servants and drive out hypocrites (Isa. 33:14).
   - To test the faith of sincere saints, and to strengthen it.

- To manifest his own grace by supporting them under the trying times, and by visiting them with future blessing.
- To secure to himself the glory when the happier days are granted.

II. THE TRIED BELIEVER.

1. His power may be gone. Personally he becomes helpless. Bodily health fails, prudence is baffled, skill is taken away, courage sinks, even spiritual force departs (Lam. 3:17–18).
2. His earthly help may fail. "There is none shut up or left." A man without a friend moves the compassion of God.
3. He may be assailed by doubts and fears, and hardly know what to do with himself (Job 3:23–26). In all this there may be chastisement for sin. It is so described in the context.
4. His hope lies in the compassion of God: he has no pleasure in putting his people to grief. "He will turn again, he will have compassion" (Mic. 7:19). Such sharp trials may be sent because:
   - Nothing less would cure the evil hidden within (Isa. 27:9).
   - Nothing less might suffice to bring the whole heart to God alone.
   - Nothing less might affect the believer's future life (Isa. 38:16).
   - Nothing less might complete his experience, enlarge his acquaintance with the Word, and perfect his testimony for God.

III. THE CONVINCED SINNER.

He is cleaned out of all that wherein he prided himself.

1. His self-righteousness is gone. He has no boasting of the past, or self-trust for the future (Job 9:30–31).
2. His ability to perform acceptable works is gone. "Their power is gone." "Dead in trespasses and sins" (Eph. 2:1).
3. His secret hopes which were shut up are now all dead and buried.
4. His proud romantic dreams are gone (Isa. 29:8).
5. His worldly delights, his bold defiance, his unbelief, his big talk, his carelessness, his vain confidence, are all gone.
6. Nothing is left but the pity of God (Ps. 103:13).
   - When the tide has ebbed out to the very uttermost, it turns.
   - The Prodigal had spent all before he returned.
   - Empty-handed sinners are welcome to the fullness of Christ.
   - Since the Lord repents of the sorrows of the desponding, they may well take heed and repent of their sins.

Notes in Aid

The Church in New Park Street was sadly reduced in numbers, and from the position of its meeting-house there seemed no prospect before it, but ultimate dissolution; but there were a few in its midst who never ceased to pray for a gracious revival. The congregation became smaller and smaller, but they hoped on, hoped ever. Let it never be forgotten that when they were at their worst the Lord remembered them, and gave to them such a tide of prosperity that they have had no mourning, or doubting, but more than thirty years of continued rejoicing:

> Man's extremity is God's opportunity.
> Extremities are a warrant for importunities.
> A man at his wit s end is not at his faith's end.
> —*Matthew Henry*

Grandly did the old Scottish believer, of whom Dr. Brown tells us in his *Horæ Subsecivæ*, respond to the challenge of her pastor, regarding the ground of her faith. "Janet," said the minister, "what would you say if after all he has done for you, God should let you drop into hell?" "E'en's [even as] he likes," answered Janet. "If he does, he'll lose mair than I'll do," meaning that he would lose his honor for truth and goodness. Therefore, the Lord cannot leave his people in the hour of their need.

"Every praying Christian will find that there is no Gethsemane without its angel."

He brings his people into a wilderness, but it is that he may speak comfortably to them; he casts them into a fiery furnace, but it is that they may have more of his company. —*T. Brooks*

A person who could not swim had fallen into the water. A man who could swim sprang in to save him. Instead, however, of at once taking hold of the struggling man, he kept at some distance from him until he had ceased struggling; he then laid hold of him, and pulled him ashore. Upon the people on the pier asking him why he did not at once take hold of the drowning person, he replied, "I could not attempt to save a man so long as he could try to save himself." The Lord acts thus towards sinners: they must cease from themselves, and then he will display the power of his grace upon them.

So long as a sinner has a mouldy crust of his own he will not feed upon heavenly manna. They say that half a loaf is better than no bread; but this is not true, for on half a loaf men lead a starvation existence, but when they have no bread they fly to Jesus for the food which came down from heaven. As long as a soul has a farthing to bless itself with, it will foolishly refuse the free forgiveness of its debts, but absolute penury drives it to the true riches:

> 'Tis perfect poverty alone
> That sets the soul at large;
> While we can call one mite our own
> We get no full discharge.

14

And Joshua said unto the people, Ye cannot serve the Lord.
—*Joshua 24:19*

N answer to Joshua's challenge, the people had said, "We will serve the Lord, for he is our God." But Joshua knew them too well to trust them, and reminded them that they were undertaking, what they could not perform. They did not believe him, but cried, "Nay, but we will serve the Lord"; but their after history proved the truth of Joshua's warning. God's word knows us better than we know ourselves. God's omniscience sees each part of our being as an anatomist sees the various portions of the body, and he therefore knows our moral and spiritual nature most thoroughly. A watchmaker is the best judge of a watch; and he who made man has the best knowledge of his condition and capacity. Let us dwell upon his verdict as to human ability.

I. THE CERTAINTY OF THE TRUTH THAT UNRENEWED MEN CANNOT SERVE GOD.

It is not a physical but a moral inability, and this is not in their nature, but in their fallen nature, not of God, but of sin. It may be said that they could serve God if they liked; but in that "if" lies the hinge of the whole question. Man's inability lies in the want of moral power so to wish and will as actually to perform. This leaves him with undiminished responsibility; for he ought to be able to serve God, and his inability is his fault (Jer. 13:23).

1. The nature of God renders perfect service impossible to depraved men. "Ye cannot serve the Lord, for he is a holy God, he is a jealous God." See context.

2. The best they could render as unrenewed men would lack heart and intent, and therefore must be unacceptable. Without love and faith men cannot please God. What are the prayers, alms, and worshippings of a Christless soul (Isa. 1:15)?

3. The law of God is perfect, comprehensive, spiritual, far-reaching: who can hope to fulfill it? If a look may commit adultery, who shall in all points keep the law (Matt. 5:28)?

4. The carnal mind is inclined to self-will, self-seeking, lust, enmity, pride, and all other evils. "It is not subject to the law of God, neither indeed can be" (Rom. 8:7).

5. Let men try to be perfectly obedient. They will not try it. They argue for their ability, but they are loth enough to exert it.

II. THE DISCOURAGEMENT WHICH ARISES FROM THIS TRUTH.

It is alleged that this will drive men to despair, and our reply is that the kind of despair to which it drives men is most desirable and salutary.

1. It discourages men from an impossible task.

   They might as well hope to invent perpetual motion as to present a perfect obedience of their own, having already sinned. If a man should try to hold up a ladder with his own hand, and at the same time climb to the top of it, he would have less difficulty than in causing his evil nature to attain to holiness.

2. It discourages from a ruinous course.

   Self-righteousness is a deadly thing; it is a proud refusal of mercy, and a rebellion against grace. Self-confidence of any sort is the enemy of the Savior.

3. It discourages reliance upon ceremonies or any other outward religiousness, by assuring men that these cannot suffice.

4. It discourages from every other way of self-salvation, and thus shuts men up to faith in the Lord Jesus. Nothing better can befall them (Gal. 2:22–23).

III. THE NECESSITIES OF WHICH WE ARE REMINDED BY THIS TRUTH.

Unregenerate men, before you can serve God you need:

- A new nature, which only the Spirit of God can create in you: the old man cannot serve the Lord. An impure fountain must pour out foul streams. The tree must be made good, or the fruit will not be good.
- Reconciliation. How shall an enemy serve his king? There must be forgiveness, friendship, mutual delight. God and you must be made friends through the Mediator, or else you cannot be the servant of God.
- Acceptance. Till you are accepted, your service cannot please God. Only a perfect righteousness can make you accepted of a holy and jealous God; and none but Jesus can give you a complete justification.
- Continued aid. This you must have to keep you in the way when once you are in it (1 Sam. 2:9; Jude 24:25).
- If you cannot serve God as you are, yet trust him as he manifests himself in Christ Jesus; and do this just as you are.
- This will enable you to serve him on better principles.
- This change of your nature will be effected by the Holy Spirit, who will come and dwell in you.
- This will fit you for heaven, where "his servants shall serve him."

Striking Pieces

No wasp will make honey; before it will do that it must be transformed into a bee. A sow will not sit up to wash its face like the cat before the fire;

neither will a debauched person take delight in holiness. No devil could praise the Lord as angels do, and no unregenerate man can offer acceptable service as the saints do.

Their inability was wholly of the moral kind. They could not do it because they were not disposed to do it, just as it is said of Joseph's brethren (Gen. 37:4) that they "could not speak peaceably unto him," so strong was their personal dislike to him. . . . But an inability arising from this source was obviously inexcusable, on the same grounds that a drunkard's inability to master his propensity for strong drink is inexcusable. In like manner, the "cannot" of the impenitent sinner, in regard to the performance of his duty, is equally inexcusable. —*George Bush, in Notes on Joshua*

The existence of sin within us entails on us certain consequences which we have no more power to evade than the idiot has power to change his look of idiocy; or the palsied hand has power to free itself from its torpor. —*B. W. Newton*

"A little girl when reproved by her mother for some fault, and told that she should teach her little brothers to do right, replied, 'How can I do right when there is no right in me?' Did not Paul make the same confession" (Rom. 7:18)?

"Man cannot be saved by perfect obedience, for he cannot render it; he cannot be saved by imperfect obedience, for God will not accept it."

A man deeply exercised about his soul was conversing with a friend on the subject, when the friend said, "Come at once to Jesus, for he will take away all your sins from your back." "Yes, I am aware of that," said the other, "but what about my back?" I find I have not only sins to take away, but there is myself; what is to be done with that? And there is not only my back, but hands and feet, and head and heart are such a mass of iniquity that it's myself I want to get rid of before I can get peace. —*British Evangelist*

It is possible I may do an occasional service for one whose servant I am not, but it were mean that a great person should be served only by the servants of another lord. —*John Howe*

> Run, run, and work, the law commands,
> But gives me neither feet nor hands;
> But sweeter sounds the gospel brings,
> It bids me fly, and gives me wings.

15

But the olive tree said unto them, Should I leave my fatness, wherewith by me they honor God and man, and go to be promoted over
the trees?

—*Judges 9:9*

HE fable teaches that temptations will come to us all, however sweet,
or useful, or fruitful, even as they came to the fig, the olive, and the
vine. These temptations may take the shape of proffered honors; if
not a crown, yet some form of preferment or power may be the bribe.

The trees were under God's government and wanted no king; but in this
fable they "went forth," and so quitted their true place. Then they sought to be
like men, forgetting that God had not made them to be conformed to a fallen
race. Revolting themselves, they strove to win over those better trees which had
remained faithful.

No wonder they chose the olive, so rich and honored; for it would give their
kingdom respectability to have such a monarch; but the olive wisely declined,
and gave its reason.

I. APPARENT PROMOTIONS ARE NOT TO BE SNATCHED AT.

The question is to be asked, *Should* I? Let us never do what would be unbe-
coming, unsuitable, unwise (Gen. 39:9).

Emphasis is to be laid on the *I*. Should *I*? If God has given me peculiar gifts
or special grace, does it become me to trifle with these endowments? Should I
give them up to gain honor for myself (Neh. 6:11)?

- A higher position may seem desirable, but would it be right to gain it by
  such cost (Jer. 45:5)?
- It will involve duties and cares. "Go up and down among the trees"
  implies that there would be care, oversight, traveling, etc.
- These duties will be quite new to me; for, like an olive, I have been hitherto planted in one place. Should I run into new temptations, new difficulties, etc., of my own wanton will?
- Can I expect God's blessing upon such strange work? Put the question in
  the case of wealth, honor, power, which are set before us. Should we grasp
  at them at the risk of being less at peace, less holy, less prayerful, less useful?

II. ACTUAL ADVANTAGES ARE NOT TO BE TRIFLED WITH.

- "Should I leave my fatness?" I have this great boon, should I lightly lose it?
- It is the greatest advantage in life to be useful both to God and man."By me
  they honor God and man." We ought heartily to prize this high privilege.

- To leave this for anything which the world can offer would be great loss. "Will a man leave the snow of Lebanon?" etc., (Jer. 18:14; 2:13).
- Our possession of fatness meets the temptation to become a king. We are happy enough in Christ, in his service, with his people, and in the prospect of the reward. We cannot better ourselves by the move; let us stay as we are.
- We may also meet it by the reflection.
- That the prospect is startling—"Shall I leave my fatness?" For an olive to do this would be unnatural: for a believer to leave holy living would be worse (John 6:68).
- That the retrospect would be terrible—"leave my fatness." What must it be to have left grace, and truth, and holiness, and Christ? Remember Judas.
- That even an hour of such leaving would be a loss. What would an olive do even for a day if it left its fatness?
- That it would all end in disappointment; for nothing could compensate for leaving the Lord. All else is death (Jer. 17:13).
- That to abide firmly and reject all baits is like the saints, the martyrs, and their Lord; but to prefer honor to grace is a mere bramble folly.

III. TEMPTATION SHOULD BE TURNED TO ACCOUNT.

- Let us take deeper root. The mere proposal to leave our fatness should make us hold the faster to it.
- Let us be on the watch that we lose not our joy, which is our fatness. If we would not leave *it*, neither can we bear that it should leave *us*.
- Let us yield more fatness, and bear more fruit: he who gains largely is all the further removed from loss. The more we increase in grace the less are we likely to leave it.
- Let us feel the more content, and speak the more lovingly of our gracious state, that none may dare to entice us. When Satan sees us happily established he will have the less hope of overthrowing us.

Memoranda

Many to obtain a higher wage have left holy companionships, and sacred opportunities for hearing the word and growing in grace. They have lost their Sabbaths, quitted a soul-feeding ministry, and fallen among worldlings, to their own sorrowful loss. Such persons are as foolish as the poor Indians who gave the Spaniards gold in exchange for paltry beads. Riches procured by impoverishing the soul are always a curse. To increase your business so that you cannot attend week-night services is to become really poorer; to give up heavenly pleasure, and receive earthly cares in exchange is a sorry sort of barter.

Sir Edward Coke, Chief Justice of England in the time of James I., was a man of noble spirit, and often incurred the displeasure of the king by his patriotism. On one occasion, when an unworthy attempt was made to influence his conduct, he replied, "When the case happens I shall do that which shall be fit for a judge to do." Oh, that all Christians in trying moments would act as shall be fit for followers of Christ to do!

In Tennyson's story of the village maiden, who became the wife of the Lord of Burleigh, we see how burdensome worldly honors may prove, even when though unsought they have been honorably gained:

> But a trouble weighed upon her,
>   And perplexed her, night and morn,
> With the burthen of an honor
>   Unto which she was not born.
>
> "Were it not better to bestow
>   Some place and power on me?
> Then should thy praises with me grow,
>   And share in my degree.
>
> How know I, if thou shouldst me raise,
>   That I should then raise thee?
> Perhaps great places and thy praise
>   Do not so well agree."
>
> —*George Herbert*

Say not this calling and vocation to which God has appointed me is too small and insignificant for me. God's will is the best calling, and to be faithful to it is the worthiest. God often places great blessings in little things. Should thy proud heart learn humility and resignation by this humble work, wouldest thou not have high wages for thy low service? —*From the German*

16

And Ruth said, Entreat me not to leave thee, or to return from following after thee: for whither thou goest, I will go; and where thou lodgest, I will lodge: thy people shall be my people, and thy God my God.

—*Ruth 1:16*

 HIS is a brave, outspoken confession of faith, and it is made by a woman, a young woman, a poor woman, a widow woman, a foreigner. Her mother-in-law ought to have been cheered, notwithstanding her sharp afflictions, because her great temporal loss was accompanied by a greater spiritual gain. She lost her home in Moab, but found the soul of her daughter. Naomi's return to her true place brought Ruth to a decision: when Christians become consistent, their children and friends frequently become converted.

I. AFFECTION FOR THE GODLY SHOULD INFLUENCE US TO GODLINESS.

Many forces combine to effect this:

1. There is the influence of companionship. We ought to be affected by godly people more than we are by the wicked, since we should lend ourselves to their influence.
2. The influence of admiration. Imitation is the most sincere praise: what we favor we follow. Let us therefore copy the saints.
3. The influence of instruction. When we learn from a teacher we are affected by him in many ways. Instruction is a kind of formation.
4. The influence of reverence. Those who are older, wiser, and better than we are create in us a profound respect, and lead us to follow their example.
5. The influence of desire to cheer them. This should lead many of us to be attentive to the word, willing to go with Christian friends to worship, and happy to hearken to their conversation; for we know that this will greatly please them.
6. The influence of fear of separation. It will be an awful thing to be eternally divided from the dear ones who seek our salvation; it is even painful to have to leave them at the Lord's Table, when they partake and we do not.

II. RESOLVES TO GODLINESS WILL BE TESTED.

1. By the poverty of the godly and their other trials. Naomi was penniless, but Ruth said, "Entreat me not to leave thee." Poor saints are often despised saints, and young people are apt to decline the religion of the poor.
2. By counting the cost. You yourself will have to come out from your friends, as Ruth did. You will have to share the lot of God's people, as Ruth shared with Naomi (Heb. 11:24-26).
3. By the drawing back of others. Orpah turned back with a kiss, as many do who promised well for a time. The return of Pliable must not discourage Christian.
4. By the duties involved in religion. Ruth must work in the fields. Some proud people will not submit to the rules of Christ's house, nor to the regulations which govern the daily lives of believers.
5. By the apparent coldness of believers. Naomi does not persuade her to keep with her, but the reverse. She was a prudent woman, and did not wish Ruth to come with her by persuasion, but by conviction.

6. By the silent sorrow of some Christians. Naomi said, "Call me not Naomi, but call me Bitterness." Persons of a sorrowful spirit there always will be; but this must not hinder us from following the lord.

III. SUCH GODLINESS MUST MAINLY LIE IN THE CHOICE OF GOD.
1. This is the believer's distinguishing possession. "Thy God shall be my God."
2. His great article of belief. "I believe in God"
3. His ruler and lawgiver. "Make me to go in the path of thy commandment" (Ps. 119:38).
4. His instructor. "Teach me thy way, O Lord" (Ps. 28:2).
5. His trust and stay. See Ruth 2:12. "This God is our God for ever and ever, he will be our guide even unto death" (Ps. 48:14).

IV. BUT IT SHOULD INVOLVE THE CHOICE OF HIS PEOPLE. "Thy people shall be my people."
- They are ill spoken of by the other kingdom.
- Not all we could wish them to be.
- Not a people out of whom much is to be gained.
- But Jehovah is their God, and they are his people.
- Our eternal inheritance is part and parcel of theirs.
- A near kinsman is among them. The true Boaz is willing to take us to himself, and to redeem our inheritance.
- Let us make deliberate, humble, firm, joyful, immediate choice for God and his saints; accepting their lodging in this world, and going with them whither they are going.
- What say our hearers to this? Will you cling to your godly relatives? Or do you now take another road, and so choose an end far removed from theirs?

Lights
Often have I met with cases where love to mother has created in the young bosom a desire to know mother's God. The idea of never seeing again a departed father has full often led children to seek the Lord. Is not human love a highly suitable means for heavenly love to use? Babes are induced to walk by their desire to be in their mother's arms; many have made their first essays at faith because they would fain give a dear parent delight.

The converted freedman gave happy expression to his decided adhesion to Christ when he said, "I have got safe past de *go-back corner*. I'm goin' all de journey home. And if you don't see me at de first of them twelve gates up dere, just look on to de next one, for I'm bound to be dere." Alas! for thousands in all our congregations; they never get by the "go-back corner." —*Dr. Cuyler*

The power of Christian character shining forth from the face, form, and through the speech of a Christian man, is finely illustrated in the following incident: An Afghan once spent an hour in the company of Dr. William Marsh, of England. When he heard that Dr. Marsh was dead, he said: "His religion shall now be my religion; his God shall be my God; for I must go where he is, and see his face again."

I know his sackcloth and ashes are better than the fool's laughter. —*Rutherford*

In a memoir of the Rev. G. G. Letters, it is stated that he was converted at a prayer-meeting one Sabbath evening. That same evening as his mother sat with her children by the fire, she talked of the delight it would give her if they, as one family, were traveling together on the King's highway. Suddenly, George sprang up, and looking around him, said, with calm resolute voice, "I, for one, have decided for Christ." —*Wesleyan Methodist Magazine*

Open union with the people of God is most desirable. It would argue disloyalty in a soldier if he would not wear his regimentals, and refused to take his place in the ranks. True, he might fight alone, but it would probably turn out to be a sorry business. If God's people will not be ashamed of us we need not be ashamed of them. I should not like to go into a public assembly disguised in the dress of a thief; I prefer my own clothes, and I cannot understand how Christians can bear themselves in the array of worldlings.

17

And all this assembly shall know that the Lord saveth not with sword and spear: for the battle is the Lord's and he will give you into our hands.

—*1 Samuel 17:47*

 HERE are always two ways of handling the same doctrine. The truth in the text may be used as a narcotic or as a stimulant. Some are so wicked as to say that if it be the Lord's battle, we are excused from fighting: as if, seeing the harvest is the Lord's, we might justly refuse to sow or reap, We see how David used this truth: it fired his soul and nerved his arm. We are all battling on one side or the other, and the worst of all are those who boast their neutrality. To the Christian man these words are so true that he may emblazon them on his banner, and write them as the headline of "the book of the wars of the Lord."

I. THE GREAT FACT: "The battle is the Lord's."

1. Inasmuch as it is for truth, right, holiness, love, and all those things which the Lord loves, the battle is the Lord's (Ps. 45:4).
2. His name and glory are the object of it. It is his honor to see righteousness established in the earth. The gospel greatly glorifies God: men strike at the divine honor when they oppose it, and the Lord will vindicate his own name; thus our conflict becomes God's battle (Isa. 40:5).
3. We fight only by his power. The Holy Ghost is our strength; we can do nothing without the Lord: hence the battle is his in the highest degree (2 Chron. 13:12; 20:12).
4. He has bidden us fight. At our monarch's bidding we go upon this warfare. We are not free-lances on our own account, but warriors under his command (1 Tim. 6:12).
5. He has bound himself to fight this battle. The reward promised to his Son, the covenant of grace, and the distinct pledges of his word, make it his battle. His fidelity is engaged to cause the Lord Jesus to divide the spoil with the strong. He must bruise Satan under our feet shortly (Rom. 16:20).
6. When the battle is fully won, the glory will be unto the Lord alone (Ps. 98:1). "He hath triumphed gloriously" (Exod. 15:1).

II. ITS INFLUENCE ON OUR MINDS.

1. We make light of opposition. Who can stand against the Lord?
2. We are not cowed by our weakness. "When I am weak then am I strong." The Lord will make us mighty in his own fight.
3. We throw ourselves into the work heartily. We owe so much to the Lord Jesus that we must fight for him (1 Cor. 16:13).
4. We choose the best weapons. We dare not fire the Lord's cannons with the devil's powder. Love, truth, zeal, prayer, and patience should be at their best in God's battle (2 Cor. 10:4).
5. We are confident of victory. Can the Lord be defeated? He vanquished Pharaoh, and he will do the same with Satan in due season (1 Cor. 15:25).

III. LESSONS IN CONNECTION WITH IT.

Make it God's cause. Never let it sink into a selfish matter.
- By your motive. Aim at his glory only. Keep clear of all sinister designs.
- By your method. Contend for the faith as Jesus would have contended, and not in a way which the Lord would disapprove.
- By your faith. Can you not trust God to fight his own battles?

Do not forget that it is the Lord's cause.
- Or you will bring self into it.
- You will begin to judge the conflict; and as it is on too huge a scale for human comprehension, you will fall into many errors, expecting

defeat where victory is sure, or hoping for success in ways which lead to disaster.

- You will be enervated by fear, for the battle must end in your destruction if the Lord's hand be not with you.

Since it is his battle:

- Be happy if personally defeated; for Jesus is still highly exalted.
- Be calm and confident always; for there cannot be the smallest cause for fear as to the ultimate issue. "In quietness and in confidence shall be your strength" (Isa. 30:15).

This assembly does know that the battle is the Lord's. Does it not? Are all in this assembly on the conquering side? Why not look to him who is himself our salvation? He needs not our sword or spear; but will himself deliver those who trust in him.

Aids to Attention

Mr. Oncken told me that he was summoned before the burgomaster of Hamburg, who bade him cease from holding religious meetings. "Do you see that little finger?" cried he. "As long as I can move that finger I will put down the Baptists." "Yes," said Oncken, "I see your little finger, and I also see a great arm which you cannot see. As long as the great arm of God is lifted on our behalf, your little finger will have no terror for us "

We are like William of Orange, with a few followers and an empty purse, making war against the master of half the world, with the mines of Peru for a treasury. But like William, too, when questioned concerning our resources, we can reply, "Before we took up this cause we entered into a close alliance with the King of kings." —*David Gracey, in "The Sword and the Trowel"*

When Tarik the Saracen went to vanquish Spain, he informed his followers that he had been favored by Heaven with a dream which had given him the fullest assurance of success. He had seen the prophet Mohammed surrounded by those holy saints and faithful companions who had adhered to his cause while he was an exile in Medina. They stood close by his couch with their swords unsheathed and their bows bent, and he heard the prophet say, "Take courage, O Tarik, and accomplish what thou art destined to perform." He then saw the prophet and his companions entering Spain as if to herald the way for the faithful followers of Islam. With a truer vision and more confident assurance may we enter the lists, go on to the struggle, and engage in the warfare of those who are fighting beneath the leadership of the cross. For, as surely as day conquers night, the cause of Heaven shall prevail, and he shall reign whose right it is to reign. —*G. McMichael, in "The Baptist Magazine"*

It is not the will of God that his people should be a timorous people. —*Matthew Henry*

It has been said of the persecuted Quakers, that, looking steadfastly at the strength of their Almighty leader, they

> Said not, who am I? but rather,
> Whose am I, that I should fear?
> —*Annals of the Early Friends*

Luther's strength lay in the way in which he laid the burden of the Reformation upon the Lord. Continually in prayer he pleaded, "Lord, this is thy cause, not mine. Therefore, do thine own work; for if this gospel do not prosper, it will not be Luther alone who will be a loser, but thine own name will be dishonored."

Our Lord does not expect us to go a warfare at our own charges. No soldier finds himself in rations or ammunition. Our King is never ungenerous: if he sends us to battle he will go with us, both to cover our head and nerve our arm. If we will but care for his cause, he will care for us. Queen Elizabeth requested a merchant to go abroad on her service, and when he mentioned that his own business would be ruined, she replied, "You mind my business and I will mind yours." If it be but the Lord's battle, we may be sure that he will see us through with it.

18

Then Jonathan and David made a covenant, because he loved him as his own soul.

—*1 Samuel 18:3*

And Jonathan caused David to swear again, because he loved him; for he loved him as he loved his own soul.

—*1 Samuel 20:17*

 HY so many sermons on Jonah, and so few on Jonathan? Are the cross-grained more worthy of study than the gentle and generous? This noble prince counted it his joy to further the interests of the man who was to be preferred before him. There was something very beautiful in Jonathan, and this came out in his unselfish, magnanimous love of David. How much more beauty is there in the unparalleled love of Jesus to us poor sinners!

I. GREAT LOVE DESIRES TO BIND ITSELF TO THE BELOVED ONE.

- "Jonathan and David made a covenant, because he loved him."

- The covenant was made, not so much because of their mutual love, but because Jonathan loved David. "Thy love to me was wonderful, passing the love of women" (2 Sam. 1:26).

1. *Jesus bound himself to us by covenant bonds.* He undertook the charge of us as our Surety in the covenant of grace.
   - He entered into our nature to represent us, thus becoming the second Adam (1 Cor. 15:47).
   - He pledged himself to redeem us with the sacrifice of himself. "He loved me, and gave himself for me" (Gal. 2:20).
   - He took us into union with himself. "For we are members of his body, of his flesh, and of his bones" (Eph. 5:30).
   - He has bound up our future lives with his own. "Your life is hid with Christ in God" (Col. 3:3). "Because I live, ye shall live also" (John 14:19) "Father, I will that they also whom thou hast given me be with me where I am" (John 17:24) "Ye in me and I in you." Seven golden words.
   - He has made us share in all that he has, changing garments with us, as in this narrative (1 Sam. 18:4).
   - He could not come nearer to us, or he would.
   - In all these covenant deeds he proves his perfect love.
2. *Jesus would have us bound to him on our part:* therefore he would, have us,
   - Submit ourselves to the saving power of his love.
   - Love him for his great love; even as David loved Jonathan.
   - Own that we are his by choice, purchase, and power; and do this deliberately and solemnly, as men make a covenant.
   - Join ourselves to his people; for he reckons them to be himself.
   - Show kindness to all who are his, for his sake; even as David was good to Mephibosheth (2 Sam. 9).
   - More and more merge our interests in his, and find our gain in advancing his honor (2 Cor. 5:14–15). "Bound in the bundle of life with the Lord thy God" (1 Sam. 25:29). What an expression! Yet how true!
3. *If this be our Lord's desire, shall we not fulfill it?*
   - Let the bonds be mutual and indissoluble (Song of Sol. 2:16).
   - Let us accept the priceless gifts of the Prince, and then give ourselves to him without reserve.
   - Let us love him as we love ourselves, for he loved us better than himself (Matt. 27:42).
   - Let this be a time of love, a season for renewing our vows, a time of fuller self-merging into Jesus (Gal. 2:20).

II. GREAT LOVE DESIRES RENEWED PLEDGES FROM ITS OBJECT.

"Jonathan caused David to swear again."

- Not out of selfishness, but from a sacred jealousy. "The Lord thy God is a jealous God." See also Song of Solomon 8:6.
- It is the only return love can receive. We can love Jesus, we can do no more. "O love the Lord, all ye his saints" (Ps. 31:23).
- It is for our highest benefit. Bound to the horns of the altar we are free. Wedded to Christ we are blessed.
- We are so chill already that we have need to renew the flame of affection with fresh coals of loving communion.
- We are so tempted and assailed that the more solemnly and the more often we renew our vows, the better for us.
- We are most unhappy if drawn aside: every backsliding is misery, Therefore, let us be bound firmly to our Lord.
- Hence he invites us to new pledges (Song of Sol. 9:8).
- Our first surrender was attended with a solemn dedication.
- Our baptism was his own appointed token of our being one with him in his death, burial, and resurrection (Rom. 6:4).
- Our communions should be hallowed renewals of our covenant:

> Let every act of worship be,
> Like our espousals, Lord, to thee;
> Like the dear hour when from above,
> We first received thy pledge of love.

- Our restorations from sickness ought to be remembered with special praise, and we should pay our vows in the presence of the Lord's people (Ps. 116:8, 14).
- Our fresh conditions should be attended with extraordinary devotion. Removal, promotion, marriage, birth of children, death of relatives, etc., are notable seasons for rededication.
- Our times of spiritual revival, when we are full of hearty fellowship with the Lord and his saints, should be new departures.
- Come and let us renew our loves at this good hour.
- Let us get alone, and express our pure desires before our well-beloved, when only he can hear.
- Let us think of some special act of devotion by which to express our affection, and let us carry it out at once. Have we no alabaster box Can we not wash the Beloved's feet, and kiss them with reverent affection

Windows of Agate

A little girl was playing with her doll in a room where her mother was busily engaged in some literary work. When she had finished her writing, she said,

"You can come now, Alice, I have done all I want to do this morning." The child ran to her mother, exclaiming, "I am so glad, for I wanted to love you so much." "But I thought you were very happy with dolly." "Yes, mother, I was, but I soon get tired of loving her, for she cannot love me back." "And is that why you love me—because I can love you back?" "That is one why, but not the first or best why." "What is the first and best why?" "Because you loved me when I was too little to love you back." Mother's eyes filled with tears as she whispered, "*We love* HIM *because* HE *first loved us.*"

Lord Brooke was so delighted with the friendship of Sir Philip Sydney that he ordered to be engraved upon his tomb nothing but this, "Here lies the friend of Sir Philip Sydney."

Christ and the believer that loves him live as if they had but one soul betwixt them. It is not the distance between earth and heaven that can separate them: true love will find out Christ wherever he is. When he was upon the earth, they that loved him kept his company; and now that he is gone to heaven, and out of sight, those that love him are frequently sending up their hearts unto him. And, indeed, they never think themselves intelligent in any thing that is worth the knowing, until they have made their souls much acquainted and familiar with their crucified Savior (1 Cor. 2:2). —*The Morning Exercises*

"Lovest thou me" "Feed my sheep." It was a tender act on our Lord's part to allow Peter three times to speak his love, and then all the rest of his life to exercise that love by giving him work to do. Jesus, the Friend, asks thrice, and then appoints a token: Peter, out of sincere love, answers thrice, and renders the life-long token. Love is conspicuous on either side.

Saints are to look upon themselves as wholly the Lord's, in opposition to all competitors. The Lord will not divide with rivals; if ye take him these must go. The soul till it comes within the covenant is in a restless case, like a bee going from flower to flower, or a bird from bush to bush; but when it is married to Christ it is settled with him, and breaks its league with all others.

Remember, the covenant ye have entered into is an offensive and defensive league. You are to have common friends and common foes with the Lord. His people must be your people, and his enemies your enemies.

Remember that your ears are bored to the Lord's doorposts, you have opened your mouth to the Lord, and you cannot go back. You must be his without end, and without interruption. It is a laudable practice of saints to go over the bargain again, hold by it, seal it afresh, and evermore look at themselves as the Lord's. There is a backsliding disposition in the best; but a renewal of our covenant is an antidote for this poison. Moreover, he that hath truly made such a covenant has given himself to Christ without reserve, and hath put a blank into the Lord's hand, saying, with Paul, "Lord, what wilt thou have me to do?" This is well-pleasing unto our God. —*Thomas Boston*

19

This is David's spoil.
—*1 Samuel 30:20*

E see in David a type of the Lord Jesus, in his conflicts and victories, and as in a thousand things beside, so also in the spoil. To him as a warrior against evil the spoils of war belong. Jehovah saith, "I will divide him a portion with the great; and he shall divide the spoil with the strong" (Isa. 53:12). We may say of him, "Thou art more glorious and excellent than the mountains of prey" (Ps. 76:4).

I. ALL THE GOOD THAT WE ENJOY COMES TO US THROUGH JESUS.

All that we held under the law the spoiler has taken.

By our own efforts we can never gain what we have lost.

Our great Leader has made us share the spoil.

1. It was for David's sake that God gave success to the hosts of Israel.

2. It was under David's leadership that they won the battle.

- Even thus is Jesus the Captain of our salvation (Heb. 2:10).
- Within us he has wrought a great deliverance. He has overcome the strong man, taken from him all his armor, and divided his spoils (Luke 11:22). He can say with Job, "I plucked the spoil out of his teeth" (Job 29:17).
- We had lost all by sin, but Jesus has restored it: "Then I restored that which I took not away" (Ps. 69:4). "David recovered all that the Amalekites had carried away" (verse 18).
- Our very selves were captive; he has set us free. "David rescued his two wives. And there was nothing lacking to them, neither small nor great, neither sons nor daughters, neither spoil, nor anything that they had taken to them" (verses 18–19).
- Our eternal heritage was forfeited; he has redeemed it (Eph. 1:14). The prey is taken from the mighty. "David recovered all."
- Our enemies have been made to enrich us, and to glorify his name. "Having spoiled principalities and powers, he made a show of them openly, triumphing over them in it" (Col. 2:15). Now is fulfilled the promise, "They that spoil thee shall be a spoil" (Jer. 30:16).

II. THAT WHICH IS OVER AND ABOVE WHAT WE LOST BY SIN COMES BY JESUS. "And David took all the flocks and the herds, which they drave before those other cattle, and said, This is David's spoil" (verse 20).

As Jesus has made us more safe than we were before the fall, so has he also made us more rich.

1. The exaltation of humanity to kinship with God. This was not ours at the first, but it is acquired for us by the Lord Jesus.

    Election, sonship, heirship, spiritual life, union to Christ, espousal to Jesus, fellowship with God, and the glory of the future wedding-feast— all these are choice spoils.

2. The fact that we are redeemed creatures, for whom the Creator suffered, is an honor belonging to none but men, and not to men except through Jesus Christ (Heb. 2:16).

    As ransomed persons we are bound to our Redeemer by special ties. "Ye are not your own, for ye are bought with a price" (1 Cor. 6:19–20).

3. Our singular condition as creatures who have known sin, and have been delivered from it, comes by our Lord Jesus Christ. Our perfection will be that of voluntary agents, who will for ever abhor the evil from which they have been saved, and love the good unto which they have been wedded by the grace of God. This belongs not to the angels.

> Never did angels taste above
> Redeeming grace and dying love.

4. Our resurrection, which is a gem not found in the crown of seraphs, comes by our risen Lord (2 Cor. 4:14).

5. Our relation to God, and yet to materialism, is another rare gift of Jesus. We are kings and priests unto God on behalf of the universe; the sanctification of mind and matter is consummated in our favored persons.

6. Our manifestation of the full glory of the Lord. Our experience will declare to all intelligent beings the choicest wisdom, love, power, and faithfulness of God (Eph. 3:10).

    Truly all these things make us cry, "I rejoice at thy word, as one that findeth great spoil" (Ps. 119:162).

III. THAT WHICH WE WILLINGLY GIVE TO JESUS MAY BE CALLED HIS SPOIL.

1. Our hearts are his alone for ever. Hence, all that we have and are belongs to him. "This is David's spoil"—the love and gratitude of our lives (1 John 9:19).

2. Our special gifts. Our tithes and dedicated things are for him. Let us give plentifully (Mal. 3:10). Abraham gave Melchizedek the tenth of the spoil (Gen. 14:20).

3. Our homage as a Church is to him. He is Head over all things to his Church. It is his reward to reign in Zion.

4. Our race must yet bow before him; all thrones and powers acknowledge his supremacy. This also is our David's spoil.

- Yield to Jesus now, and find in him your safety, your heaven.
- What say you? Are you David's spoil?
- If not, sin and Satan are spoiling you every day.

Notabilia

(1) Sin contracts no guilt that grace does not more than remove, (2) sin deforms no beauty that grace does not more than renew, (3) sin loses no blessedness that grace does not more than restore. —*Outline of Sermon on Romans 5:20, by the late Charles Vince*

In 1741, at the Northampton Assizes, a poor Irishman was sentenced to death for murder. Dr. Doddridge believed him innocent, and so exerted himself in his behalf that a respite was obtained. Nothing could be more touching than the poor fellow's expressions of gratitude. He said, "Every drop of my blood thanks you, for you have had compassion on every drop of it. You are my deliverer, and you have a right to me. If I live I am your property, and I will be a faithful servant."

We all remember the poem of "The man of Ross." Every good thing in the place came from him. Ask who did this or that, "The man of Ross," each lisping babe replies.

Even so, as we survey each blessing of our happy estate, and ask whence it came, the only answer is, "This is Jesus' spoil The crucified hand has won this for us."

A Pastor in Cumberland has formed in his church a Good Intent Society, composed of poor persons who have no money to give, but yet desire to do something for the Lord Jesus. These give one hour in the week to some charitable work, or to some labor by which they earn a few pence which is given to the service of the Lord. Each one, according to her several ability, does something distinctly for Jesus. These people find a blessing in so doing. Should we not each one regularly and systematically set aside a portion for our Lord and Savior, and say, "This is David's spoil"?

20

For thou, O Lord of Hosts, God of Israel, hast revealed to thy servant, saying, I will build thee an house: therefore hath thy servant found in his heart to pray this prayer unto thee.

—*2 Samuel 7:27*

 ow often God does for his servants what they desire to do for him! David desired to build the Lord a house, and the Lord built him a house. When God's servants are not accepted one way, they are another. Neither do they take it ill that the Lord puts them off from the work upon which they had set their desires; but they learn his will, bow before it, and praise him for it. David went in and sat before the Lord, and offered prayer, for he felt moved in heart, so that he could not do otherwise. When the Lord promises, we should supplicate: his giving times should create for us special asking times.

I. HOW DID HE COME BY HIS PRAYER? He "found in his heart to pray this prayer."

- He found it, which is a sign he looked for it. Those who pray at random will never be accepted: we must carefully seek out our prayers (Job 13:4).
- In his heart-not in a book, nor in his memory, nor in his head, nor in his imagination, nor only on his tongue (Ps. 84:2).
- It is proof that he had a heart, knew where it was, could look into it, and did often search it (Ps. 77:6).
- It must have been a living heart, or a living prayer would not have been within it.
- It must have been a believing heart, or he would not have found "this prayer" in it.
- It must have been a serious heart, not flippant, forgetful, cold, indifferent, or he would have found a thousand vanities in it, but no prayer. Question: Would prayer be found in your heart at this time (Hosea 7:11)?
- It must have been a humble heart, for such was the prayer.
- Is this the way you pray? Do you answer, "I never pray"? God grant you may yet find it in your heart to do so.
- Is this the way you pray? Do you answer, "I say my prayers"? How can prayers which do not come from *your* heart ever reach God's heart?

II. HOW DID HIS PRAYER COME TO BE IN HIS HEART?

Through the Lord's being there, and putting it there.

1. The Lord's own Spirit instructed him how to pray.
   - By giving him a sense of need. Great blessings teach us our necessity, as in David's case.
   - By giving him faith in God. When sure that God will keep his promise we are moved to plead it.
   - By bringing before his mind the appropriate promise. "Thou hast revealed; therefore hath thy servant found in his heart to pray this prayer unto thee."
2. The Lord inclined him to pray.
   - It has been said that an absolute promise would render prayer needless; whereas the first influence of such a promise is to suggest prayer. The Lord inclined David's heart:
   - By warming his heart. Prayer does not grow in an ice-well.

- By gladdening him with bright prospects. Prayer comes flying in by the open window of hope.
- By communing with him. When God speaks to us we are moved to speak to him.

3. The Lord encouraged him to pray, by means of:
   - A promise spoken. "I will build thee an house."
   - A promise sealed home to the heart. "Thou hast revealed to thy servant."
   - His covenant is ordained on purpose to excite prayer. "I will yet for this be enquired of" (Ezek. 36:37).
   - His former great mercy, his previous answers to our petitions, his immutable goodness, his undiminished power, and his unquestioned faithfulness, all lead us to pray.
   - His Son Jesus is an Intercessor who is always pleading with success, and this puts it into our heart to pray.
   - His Holy Spirit has undertaken to help our infirmity in prayer, and this again suggests prayer.

III. HOW MAY YOU FIND PRAYER IN YOUR HEARTS?

- Look into your heart, and make diligent search.
- Think of your own need, and this will suggest petitions.
- Think of your ill-desert, and you will humbly cry to the Lord.
- Think of the promises, the precepts, and the doctrines of truth, and each one of these will summon you to your knees.
- Have Christ in your heart, and prayer will follow (Acts 9:11).
- Live near to God, and then you will often speak to him.
- Do you find prayers and other holy things in your heart? Or is it full of vanity, worldliness, ambition, and ungodliness?
- Remember that you are what your heart is (Prov. 23:7).

Things to the Point

In prayer the lips ne'er act the winning part,
Without the sweet concurrence of the heart.
—*R. Herrick*

On the cover of his "Kyrie Eleison," the great musician Beethoven wrote, "From the heart it has come to the heart it shall penetrate."

The Asiatic Russians say that it is only upon the Baikal—an exceedingly dangerous lake in Siberia—in autumn, that a man learns to pray from his heart.

"A great part of my time," said M'Cheyne, "is spent in getting my heart in tune for prayer."

It is not the gilded paper and good writing of a petition that prevails with a king, but the moving sense of it. And to that King who discerns the heart,

heart-sense is the sense of all, and that which he only regards; he listens to hear what that speaks, and takes all as nothing where that is silent. All other excellence in prayer is but the outside and fashion of it; this is the life of it. —*Leighton*

I asked a young friend, "Did you pray before conversion?" She answered that she did after a sort. I then enquired, "What is the difference between your present prayers and those before you knew the Lord?" Her answer was, "Then I said my prayers, but now I *mean* them. Then I said the prayers which other people taught me, but now I find them in my heart."

There is good reason to cry "Eureka!" when we find prayer in our heart. Holy Bradford would never cease praying or praising till he found his heart thoroughly engaged in the holy exercise. If it be not in my heart to pray, I must pray till it is. But oh, the delight of pleading with God when the heart casts forth mighty jets of supplication, like a geyser in full action! How mighty is supplication when the whole soul becomes one living, hungering, expecting desire!

Remember, God respecteth not the arithmetic of our prayers, how many they are; nor the rhetoric of our prayers, how long they are; nor the music of our prayers, how methodical they are; but the divinity of our prayers, how heart-sprung they are. Not gifts, but graces, prevail in prayer. —*Trapp*

21

Joab fled unto the tabernacle of the Lord, and caught hold on the horns of the altar. . . . And Benaiah came to the tabernacle of the Lord, and said unto him, Thus saith the king, Come forth. And he said, Nay; but I will die here.

—*1 Kings 2:28, 30*

 OAB's conscience pricks him when he hears that Solomon is dealing with other offenders.

Joab was a remorseless warrior, yet when his own turn comes he flies from death.

Joab had little enough of religion, yet he flies to the altar when the sword pursues him.

Joab refuses to quit his shelter, and falls slain at the altar.

Many are for running to the use of external religion when death threatens them. Then they go to greater lengths than Scripture prescribes; they not only go to the tabernacle of the Lord, but they must needs cling to the altar.

I. AN OUTWARD RESORT TO ORDINANCES AVAILS NOT FOR SALVATION.

- If a man will rest in external rites he will die there.
- Sacraments, in health or in sickness, are unavailing as means of salvation. They are intended only for those saved already, and will be injurious to others (1 Cor. 11:29).
- Religious observances: such as frequenting sermons, attending prayer-meetings, joining in Bible-readings, practicing family-prayer: all these put together cannot save a man from the punishment due to his sins. They are good things, but the merely formal practice of them cannot save.
- Ministers. These are looked upon by some dying persons with foolish reverence. In the hour of death resort is made to their prayers at the bedside. Importance is attached to funeral sermons, and ceremonials. What superstition!
- Professions. These may be correct, long, reputable, and eminent; but yet they may not be proofs of safety. Connection with the most pure of churches would be a poor ground of trust.
- Orthodoxy in doctrine, ordinances, and religious practices is much thought of by some; but it is terribly insufficient.
- Feelings. Dread, delight, dreaminess, despondency: these have, each in its turn, been relied upon as grounds of hope; but they are all futile.

What an awful thing to perish with your hand on the altar of God! Yet you must, unless your heart is renewed by divine grace.

The outward altar was never intended to be a sanctuary for the guilty. Read Exodus 21:14, where it is said of the criminal, "Thou shalt take him from mine altar, that he may die."

II. A SPIRITUAL RESORT TO THE TRUE ALTAR AVAILS FOR SALVATION. We will use Joab's case as an illustration.

1. His act: he "caught hold on the horns of the altar."
   - We do this spiritually by flying from the sword of Justice to the person of Jesus.
   - And by taking hold upon his great atoning work, and thus through faith uniting ourselves to his propitiation.
2. The fierce demand of his adversary: "Thus saith the king, Come forth!" This is the demand of:
   - Unbelieving Pharisees who teach salvation by works.
   - Accusing Conscience within the man.
   - Satan, quoting Holy Scripture falsely.
3. The desperate resolve of Joab, "Nay, but I will die here." This is a wise resolution, for we:

- Must perish elsewhere.
- Cannot make our case worse by clinging to Christ.
- Have nowhere else to cling. No other righteousness or sacrifice.
- Cannot be dragged away if we cling to Jesus.
- Receive hope from the fact that none have perished here.

4. The assured security. "He that believeth on the Son hath ever lasting life" (John 3:36).
   - If you perished trusting in Jesus your ruin would
   - Defeat God.
   - Dishonor Christ.
   - Dishearten Sinners from coming to Jesus
   - Discourage Saints, making them doubt all the promises.
   - Distress the Glorified, who have rejoiced over penitents, and would now see that they were mistaken.
   - Come, then, at once to the Lord Jesus, and lay hold on eternal life.
   - You may come; he invites you.
   - You should come; he commands you.
   - You should come now; for now is the accepted time.

Cases in Point, etc.

During an epidemic of cholera, I remember being called up, at dead of night, to pray with a dying person. He had spent the Sabbath in going out upon an excursion, and at three on Monday morning I was standing by his bed. There was no Bible in the house, and he had often ridiculed the preacher; but before his senses left him he begged his servant to send for me. What could I do? He was unconscious; and there I stood, musing sadly upon the wretched condition of a man who had wickedly refused Christ, and yet superstitiously fled to his minister.

"Will you put it down in black and white what I am to believe?" wrote a lady to the Rev. Robert Howie. "I have been told of many different texts; and they are so many that I am bewildered. Please tell me one text, and I will try to believe it." The answer came, "It is not any one text, nor any number of texts that saves, any more than the man who fled to the City of Refuge was saved by reading the directions on the finger-posts. It is by believing on the person and work of the Lord Jesus that we are brought into life; and, once born again, are kept in that life."

When a man goes thirsty to the well, his thirst is not allayed merely by going there. On the contrary, it is increased by every step he goes. It is by what he draws out of the well that his thirst is satisfied. Just so it is not by the mere bodily exercise of waiting upon ordinances that you will ever come to peace, but by tasting of Jesus in the ordinances, whose flesh is meat indeed, and his blood drink indeed. —M'Cheyne

The Lord Jesus is well pleased that poor sinners should fly to him, and lay hold upon him; for this is to give him due glory as a gracious Savior, and this is to fulfill the purpose for which he has set himself apart. He claims to be a Deliverer; let us use him as what he professes to be, and so do him that honor which he most esteems. A Pilot loves to get the helm in his hand, a Physician delights to be trusted with hard cases, an Advocate is glad to get his brief; even so is Jesus happy to be used. Jesus longs to bless, and therefore he says to every sinner, as he did to the woman at the well, "Give me to drink." Oh to think that you can refresh your Redeemer! Poor sinner, haste to do it.

22

And when the Queen of Sheba heard of the fame of Solomon, concerning the name of the Lord, she came to prove him with hard questions.

—1 Kings 10:1

 E may profitably consider the Queen of Sheba in her visit to Solomon, for she is given as a sign to us (Matt. 12:42). Surely she came from Arabia the Happy; but it is to be feared that many around us are dwellers in Arabia the Stony, for their hearts are hard as rocks. Jesus is greater than Solomon in wisdom, for he knows the Father himself, and all the riches of wisdom and knowledge are treasured up in him. It will be to our advantage to go to Jesus with all our doubts and troubles, and prove his love and wisdom.

I. LET US ADMIRE THE QUEEN'S MODE OF PROCEDURE.

1. She would prove the king's wisdom by learning from him. The best way of knowing Christ is by becoming his disciple.
2. She would prove him with many questions. Many are the knots in the line of life. "If any man lack wisdom let him ask of God."
3. Those she asked were hard questions.
   - Beyond herself.
   - Beyond her wise men.
   - But not beyond the capacious mind of Solomon.
   - To ask such questions was to use the rare opportunity before her.
   - Great wisdom deserves hard questions.
   - Use Jesus as he is. "An Interpreter, one among a thousand."
   - To be asked such questions would please Solomon.

- Would show her belief in the report of his glory and learning.
- Would also ease her own mind; for many a perplexity would be removed for ever. The same is true of Jesus.

II. LET US IMITATE HER EXAMPLE, AND PROVE OUR GREATER SOLOMON WITH HARD QUESTIONS.

Here are a few of them to begin with:

1. How can a man be just with God?
2. How can God be just and the Justifier of him that believeth?
3. How can a man be saved by faith alone without works, while yet it is true that a saved man must have good works?
4. How can a man be born when he is old?
5. How is it that God sees all things and yet no more sees the sins of believers?
6. How can a man see the Father, who is invisible?
7. How can it be true that that which is born of God sinneth not, and yet men born of God daily confess sin?
8. How can a man be a new man, and yet have to sigh because of the old man?
9. How can a man be sorrowful yet always rejoicing?
10. How can a man's life be in heaven while yet he lives on the earth?
    We read that Solomon told her all her questions, and we may rest assured that Jesus will teach us all that we need to know, for "in him are hid all the treasures of wisdom and knowledge" (Col. 2:3).

III. LET US ATTEND TO CERTAIN QUESTIONS OF A TRULY PRACTICAL CHARACTER.

- How can we come to Christ?
- How can we ask hard questions of Christ?
- How can he reply to us? By his Word, his Spirit, his Providence.
- How is it that none can come but those whom Jesus draws, and yet him that cometh to him he will in no wise cast out? Try both truths in your own experience, and they will prove themselves.
- How is it that there is a set time and a limited day, and yet the Lord bids us come to Jesus at once? Come and see.
- How is it that we have not come long ago?
- Why should we not come at this very moment?

Apples of Gold for Baskets of Silver

Philosophy was born a Pagan; but she may become a Christian, and should be christened "Mary." She may be proud to sit at Jesus' feet. Hellas coming to Judea's Messiah is a rarely beautiful sight.—*Dr. Duncan*

Questioners must be teachable. When Haydn was in London, a nobleman came to him for lessons in music, but found fault with all that Haydn said. At last, out of patience, the musician exclaimed, "I see, my lord, that it is you who are so good as to give lessons to me, and I am obliged to confess that I do not merit the honor of having such a master. "

Do not suppose that Wisdom is so much flattered at having you for a pupil that she will set you easy lessons and yet give you the gold medal — *T. T. Lynch*

An example of the strange riddles of Christian experience is given in one of Ralph Erskine's "Gospel Sonnets":

> I'm sinful, yet I have no sin;
> All spotted o'er, yet wholly clean;
> Blackness and beauty both I share,
> A hellish black, a heavenly fair.

The pilgrims when staying in the house of Gaius spent their time in asking and answering such riddles.

Those who lose their way because they will not ask are rather to be blamed than pitied. Men pay a great deal to obtain the opinion of a great physician; what shall we say of sick persons who will not consult the infallible Healer, though his cures are without fee? Jesus waits to be enquired of; but the most of men had rather follow their own crude thoughts than accept his infallible teachings. Let us not be among these; but having the golden opportunity of intercourse with such a Teacher, let us bring before him every difficulty, and, like Mary, sit at Jesus' feet, and learn of him.

The hard questions of life prove us, and make us see our own ignorance and folly. Yet we would not be without them, for they also prove Jesus, and display to us his knowledge and wisdom. We can remember hard questions in Providence which we could not answer, but he has made them clear as noonday; hard questions of inward conflict, which he has fully resolved; hard questions as to apparently unfulfilled promises, which we now comprehend; and hard questions of gospel doctrine, which we now see to be the truth in himself. Let us go on proving our Lord, but yet never tempting him. Every fair test, though it be far more stringent than those which Sheba's Queen imposed upon Solomon, Jesus is more than able to endure.

23

And she came to Jerusalem with a very great train, with camels that bare spices, and very much gold, and precious stones: and when she was come to Solomon, she communed with him of all that was in her heart.

—1 Kings 10:2

 T is not generally a wise thing to tell out all your heart. Samson reached the climax of folly when he did this to Delilah. Yet if we could meet with a Solomon who could solve all our difficulties, we might wisely do so.

We have a greater than Solomon in Jesus, who is incarnate Wisdom. The mischief is, that with him we are too silent, and with worldly friends, too communicative. This evil should be rectified.

I. WE OUGHT TO COMMUNE WITH HIM OF ALL THAT IS IN OUR HEART.

1. Neglect of intercourse with Jesus is very unkind; for he invites us to talk with him, saying, "Let me see thy countenance, let me hear thy voice; for sweet is thy voice, and thy countenance is comely" (Song of Sol. 2:14). Shall our heavenly Bridegroom be deprived of the fellowship of our souls?

2. To conceal anything from so true a Friend betrays the sad fact that there is something wrong to be concealed.

3. It shows a want of confidence in his love, or his sympathy, or his wisdom, if we cannot tell Jesus all that is in or upon our hearts. Between bride and Bridegroom there should be no secrets, or love will be wounded.

4. It will be the cause of uneasiness to ourselves if we withhold anything from him. The responsibility will all rest with us, and this will weigh heavily.

5. It will involve the loss of his counsel and help; for when we unbosom ourselves to him, he meets our case. If we hide our trouble, he may leave us to fret until we confide more fully in him.

6. Reticence towards Jesus is greatly aggravated by our usual eagerness to tell our troubles to others. Will we make a confidant of man, and hide the matter from our God?

II. WE NEED NOT CEASE COMMUNING FOR WANT OF TOPICS.

1. Our sorrows. He knows what they are, will comfort us under them, help us to profit by them, and in due time remove them.

2. Our joys. He will sober and salt them. Joy without Jesus is the sun without light, the essence of it is gone. Joy without Jesus would be as evil as the golden calf which provoked the Lord to jealousy.
3. Our service. He was a Servant, and therefore he knows our heart, and will sympathize with our difficulties. Let us speak freely.
4. Our plans. He had zeal and ardor, and was quick of understanding in the fear of the Lord: he will gladly commune with us concerning all that is in our hearts to do for the Father.
5. Our successes and failures should be reported at head-quarters. The disciples of the martyred John took up the body, and went and told Jesus (Matt. 14:12). Our Lord's own evangelists returned and told what had been done (Luke 9:10).
6. Our desires. Holiness, usefulness, heaven: all these awaken the sympathy of Jesus: he prays for us about these things.
7. Our fears: fears of falling, needing, failing, fainting, dying. To mention these to Jesus is to end them.
8. Our loves. Of earth and of heaven, towards others and to himself. That love which we dare not tell to Jesus is an evil lusting.
9. Our mysteries: incomprehensible feelings, undefinable uneasinesses, and complex emotions, will be all the better for being ventilated in Jesus's presence.

III. NOR SHALL WE CEASE COMMUNING FOR WANT OF REASONS.
1. How ennobling and elevating is intercourse with the Son of God!
2. How consoling and encouraging is fellowship with him who has overcome the world!
3. How sanctifying and refining is union with the perfect One, who is the Lord our righteousness!
4. How safe and healthy is a daily walk with the ever-blessed Son of man!
5. How proper and natural for disciples to talk with their Teacher, and saints with their Savior!
6. How delightful and heavenly is rapturous converse with the Beloved of our souls!
   • Warning to those who never speak with Jesus. Will he not say at the last, "I never knew you"?
   • Complaint of those who seldom commune with him. "Is this thy kindness to thy friend?"
   • Hint to those who usually live in communion with him. Be sure: to keep up the holy intercourse; and to this end be very thorough, unlock every room in your house, and let Jesus enter.
   • Congratulation of those who have long enjoyed his fellowship.

Things to Strike and Stick

A workman in time of need would part with everything before his tools for to lose them would be to lose all. Reading the Word of God and prayer are the tools of the Christian's craft: without them he is helpless. How is it, then, that when time presses, he so often foregoes these, or shortens them? What is this but to sell his tools?

If there be anything I do, if there be anything I leave undone, let me be perfect in prayer. —*Henry Martyn*

Blessed be God that I may pray. —*David Brainerd*

> He oft finds help who doth his grief impart,
> And to tell sorrow halfens sorrow's smart.
> —*Spenser*

What would be said of a member of a family who refused to speak with his father or his brother? What a source of unhappiness to have such a person in the house! What, then, must be thought of a professed spouse of Jesus who has had no personal intercourse with him by the month together? Lack of holy communion is a very grievous thing. True love is communicative; it cannot bear to keep its secrets from its Beloved, nor to be restrained in its converse with him. Let the believer see to it that he is not like one of whom we asked, "How long is it since you had fellowship with Jesus?" and he answered, "It is so long ago that I have almost forgotten it." Was not this an evil sign?

> Let us be simple with him then,
> Not backward, stiff, or cold;
> As though our Bethlehem could be
> What Sinai was of old.

The believer should be familiar in the house over which Christ is set, and draw near with full assurance of faith. Come and tell him all your wants and desires freely, without concealing anything from him, for that would argue distance and distrust. The stronger faith is, the more wants it tells, and the more fully it tells them. Do you want anything of which you cannot tell your Lord? It argues either no real need, or else little faith. Strong faith hath free communion with heaven, and conceals nothing, but tells all (Eph. 3:12). "In whom we have boldness." The word translated boldness is *"telling all."* —*Thomas Boston*

> Sing a hymn to Jesus, when the heart is faint;
> Tell it all to Jesus, comfort or complaint:
> If the work is sorrow, if the way is long,
> If thou dread's" the morrow, tell it him in song;
> Though thy heart be aching for the crown and palm,
> Keep thy spirit waking with a faithful psalm.
> —*E. Paxton Hood*

24

But he himself went a day's journey into the wilderness, and came and sat down under a juniper tree: and he requested for himself that he might die; and said, It is enough; now, O Lord, take away my life; for I am not better than my fathers.

—1 Kings 19:4

 E may learn much from the lives of others Elijah himself is not only a prophet but a prophecy. His experience is our instruction. Sometimes we enter into a strange and mysterious state of depression, and it is well to learn from Scripture that another has been in that Valley of Deathshade. Weary, and sick at heart, sorely tried ones are apt to faint. At such a time they imagine that some strange thing has happened unto them; but, indeed, it is not so. Looking down upon the sands of time they may see the print of a man's foot, and it ought to comfort them when they learn that he was no mean man, but a mighty servant of the Lord. Let us study:

I. ELIJAH'S WEAKNESS. "He requested for himself that he might die."

1. He was a man of like passions with us (James 5:17).
   - He failed in the point wherein he was strongest; as many other saints have done. Abraham, Job, Moses, Peter, etc.
   - This proved that he was strong not by nature, but in divine strength. He was no unfeeling man of iron, with nerves of steel. The wonder is not that he fainted, but that he ever stood up in the fierce heat which beat upon him.
2. He suffered from a terrible reaction. Those who go up go down. The depth of depression is equal to the height of rapture.
3. He suffered grievous disappointment, for Ahab was still under Jezebel's sway, and Israel was not won to Jehovah.
4. He was sadly weary with the excitement of Carmel, and the unwonted run by the side of Ahab's chariot.
5. His wish was folly. "O Lord, take away my life."
   - He fled from death. If he wished to die, Jezebel would have obliged him, and he needed not to have fled.
   - He was more needed than ever to maintain the good cause.
   - That cause was also more than ordinarily hopeful, and he ought to have wished to live to see better times.
   - He was never to die. Strange that he who was to escape death should cry, "Take away my life!" How unwise are our prayers when our spirits sink!

6. His reason was untrue. It was not enough: and the Lord had made him, in some respects, better than his fathers.

- He had more to do than they, and he was stronger, more bold, more lonely in witness, and more terrible in majesty.
- He had more to enjoy than most of the other prophets, for he had greater power with God, and had wrought miracles surpassed by none.
- He had been more favored by special providence and peculiar grace, and was yet to rise above all others in the manner of his departure: the chariots of God were to wait upon him.

II. GOD'S TENDERNESS TO HIM.

1. He allowed him to sleep: this was better than medicine, or inward rebuke, or spiritual instruction.
2. He fed him with food convenient and miraculously nourishing.
3. He made him perceive angelic care. "An angel touched him."
4. He allowed him to tell his grief (verse 10): this is often the readiest relief. He stated his case, and in so doing eased his mind.
5. He revealed himself and his ways. The wind, earthquake, fire, and still small voice were voices from God. When we know what God is we are less troubled about other matters.
6. He told him good news: "Yet I have left me seven thousand in Israel" (verse 18). His sense of loneliness was thus removed.
7. He gave him more to do-to anoint others by whom the Lord's purposes of chastisement and instruction should be carried on.

Let us learn some useful lessons.

- It is seldom right to pray to die; that matter is best left with God; we may not destroy our own lives, nor ask the Lord to do so.
- To the sinner it is never right to seek to die; for death to him is hell. The willful suicide seals his own sure condemnation.
- To the saint such a wish is allowable, only within bounds. He may long for heaven, but not for the mere sake of getting away from service or suffering, disappointment or dishonor.
- To desire death may be proper under some aspects; but not to pray for it with eagerness.
- When we do wish to die, the reason must not be impatient, passionate, petulant, proud, or indolent.
- We have no idea of what is in store for us in this life. We may yet see the cause prosper and ourselves successful.
- In any case let us trust in the Lord and do good, and we need never be afraid.

Selections

What is this we hear? Elijah fainting and giving up! that heroical spirit dejected and prostrate! He that durst say to Ahab's face, "It is thou and thy father's house that trouble Israel"; he that could raise the dead, open and shut the heavens, fetch down both fire and water with his prayers; he that durst chide and contest with all Israel; that durst kill the four hundred and fifty Baalites with the sword—doth he shrink at the frowns and threats of a woman? Doth he wish to be rid of his life, because he feared to lose it? Who can expect an undaunted constancy from flesh and blood when Elijah fails? The strongest and holiest saint upon earth is subject to some qualms of fear and infirmity: to be always and unchangeably good is proper only to the glorious spirits in heaven. Thus the wise and holy God will have his power perfected in our weakness. It is in vain for us, while we carry this flesh about us, to hope for so exact health as not to be cast down sometimes with fits of spiritual distemper. It is no new thing for holy men to wish for death: who can either marvel at or blame the desire of advantage? For the weary traveler to long for rest, the prisoner for liberty, the banished for home, it is so natural, that the contrary disposition were monstrous. The benefit of the change is a just motive to our appetition; but to call for death out of a satiety of life, out of an impatience of suffering, is a weakness unbeseeming a saint. It is not enough, O Elijah! God hath more work yet for thee: thy God hath more honored thee than thy fathers, and thou shalt live to honor him.

Toil and sorrow have lulled the prophet asleep under this junipertree; that wholesome shade was well chosen for his repose. While death was called for, the cozen of death comes unbidden; the angel of God waits on him in that hard lodging. No wilderness is too solitary for the attendance of those blessed spirits. As he is guarded, so is he awaked by that messenger of God, and stirred up from his rest to his repast; while he slept, his breakfast is made ready for him by those spiritual hands: "There was a cake baked on the coals, and a cruse of water at his head." Oh, the never-ceasing care and providence of the Almighty, not to be barred by any place, by any condition! When means are wanting to us, when we are wanting to ourselves, when to God, even then cloth he follow us with his mercy, and cast favor upon us, beyond, against expectation! What variety of purveyance cloth he make for his servant! One while the ravens, then the Sareptan, now the angel, shall be his caterer; none of them without a miracle: those other provided for him waking, this sleeping. O God! the eye of thy providence is not dimmer, the hand of thy power is not shorter: only teach thou us to serve thee, to trust thee. —Bp. Hall

Elijah "arose and went for his life." But better he had stood to his task as a prophet, and answered as Chrysostom did when Eudoxia the empress threatened him. "Go tell her," said he, "I fear nothing but sin"; or as Basil did, when Valens, the Arian emperor, sent him word that he would be the death of him: "I would he would," said he, "I shall but go to heaven the sooner." Luther had his fits of fear, though ordinarily he could say, "I care neither for the Pope's favor nor fury." Gregory doubted not to say, that because Elijah began to be tickled with high conceits of himself for the great acts which he had done, he was suffered thus to fear, and to fall beneath himself, for his humiliation. The like we see in Peter, scared by a silly wench: to show us how weak, even as water, we are, when left a little to ourselves. —*John Trapp*

Who told Elijah it was "enough"? God did not; he knew what was enough for Elijah to do and to suffer. It was not enough. God had more to teach him, and had more work for him to do. If the Lord had taken him at his word, and had also said "it is enough," Elijah's history would have wanted its crowning glory. —*Kitto*

It cannot be denied, that in the expression "it is enough!" we behold the anguish of a soul which, disappointed in its fairest expectations, seems to despair of God and of the world, and is impatient and weary of the cross; a soul which, like Jonah, is dissatisfied with the dealings of the Almighty, and by desiring death, seeks, as it were, to give him to understand, that it is come to such an extremity, that nothing is left but the melancholy wish to escape by death from its sufferings. Nevertheless, a Divine and believing longing accompanied even this carnal excitement in the soul of Elijah, which, thirsting after God, struck its pinions upwards to the eternal light; yes, the key-note of this mournful lamentation was the filial thought that the heart of his Father in heaven would be moved towards him, that his merciful God would again shine forth upon his darkness, and comfort the soul of his servant. Thus we see, in the prayer of our prophet, the elements of the natural and of the spiritual life fermenting together in strange intermixture. The sparks of nature and of grace, mutually opposing each other, blaze up together in one flame. The metal is in the furnace, the heat of which brings impurity to light; but who does not forget the scum and the dross at the sight of the fine gold? —*F. W. Krummacher*

I. *The cause of Elijah's despondency.* (1) Relaxation of physical strength. (2) Second cause—Want of sympathy. "I, even I only, am left." Lay the stress on *only*. The loneliness of his position was shocking to Elijah. (3) Want of occupation. As long as Elijah had a prophet's work to do, severe as that work was, all went on healthily: but his occupation was gone. Tomorrow and the day after, what has he left on earth to do? The misery of having nothing to do proceeds from causes voluntary or involuntary in their nature. (4) Fourth cause— Disappointment in his expectations of success. On Carmel the great object for which Elijah had lived seemed on the point of being realized. Baal's prophets were slain—Jehovah acknowledged with one voice: false worship put down. Elijah's life-aim—the transformation of Israel into a kingdom of God—was all but accomplished. In a single day all this bright picture was annihilated. II. *God's treatment of it.* (1) First, he recruited his servant's exhausted strength.

Read the history. Miraculous meals are given—then Elijah sleeps, wakes, and eats: on the strength of that, he goes forty days' journey. (2) Next, Jehovah calmed his stormy mind by the healing influences of nature. He commanded the hurricane to sweep the sky, and the earthquake to shake the ground. He lighted up the heavens till they were one mass of fire. All this expressed and reflected Elijah's feelings. The mode in which nature soothes us is by finding meeter and nobler utterances for our feelings than we can find in words—by expressing and exalting them. In expression there is relief. (3) Besides, God made him feel the earnestness of life. What *doest* thou here, Elijah? Life is for doing. A prophet's life for nobler doing—and the prophet was not doing, but moaning. Such a voice repeats itself to all of us, rousing us from our lethargy, or our despondency, or our protracted leisure, "What doest thou here?" here in this short life. (4) He completed the cure by the assurance of victory. "Yet have I left me seven thousand in Israel who have not bowed the knee to Baal." So, then, Elijah's life had no failure after all. —*F. W. Robertson*

25

And as thy servant was busy here and there, he was gone. And the king of Israel said unto him, So shall thy judgment be; thyself hast decided it.

—*1 Kings 20:40*

 MAN must be hard run indeed when he cannot forge an excuse. This is a very common one for the loss of the soul: "I was very busy, and had no time to attend to religion." They say, "a bad excuse is better than none:" this is very questionable. Here is an excuse which condemned the man who made it. The man in the prophet's story was ordered to keep a prisoner, and it became his first duty to do so; but he preferred to follow out his own wishes, and attend to his private concerns, and so the prisoner "was gone." It is clear that he had power to have attended to the king's business, for he attended to his own. His excuse was a confession that he was willfully disobedient.

I. IT IS AN EXCUSE WHICH SOME CANNOT USE.

1. They have but little to occupy them. They are noblemen, or ladies with no occupation, or persons of large leisure, or invalids who can do nothing for a livelihood, and therefore have ample time for reflection and reading.

2. They have done all their hard work, and are retired upon their savings, and find it hard to pass their time.

3. They are never busy, for they are idlers whom nothing could provoke to industry. They kill time.

II. IT IS AN EXCUSE WHICH IS NOT VALID.

1. There was no absolute need to be so busy. Many people make slaves of themselves with a view to gain, when they could earn enough for their needs, and yet have abundant leisure to care for their souls.
2. To have believed in the Lord would have lessened the needful care of life, and so the pressure of business would have been lightened. The fact is that no man can afford to neglect his soul, for thus he hinders his own life-work.
3. You find time for other necessaries,-to eat, drink, dress, converse, and sleep. And have you no time to feed your soul, to drink the living water, to put on the robe of righteousness, to talk with God, and to find rest in Christ?
4. You have time for diversion. Think of the many hours wasted in idle chat, unprofitable reading, or worse. If offered a holiday, or an evening's entertainment, you make time if you cannot find it. You have, then, time for weightier matters.
5. You find time for judging others, questioning great truths, spying out difficulties, and quibbling over trifles. Have you no time for self-examination, study of the word, and seeking, the Lord! Of course you have; where is it?

III. IT IS AN EXCUSE WHICH ACCUSES THE PERSON WHO MAKES IT.

1. You have enjoyed many mercies in your daily work, for you have been able to attend to your business; should not these have won your gratitude?
2. You have seen many trials while busy here and there; why did they not lead you to God?
3. You have abilities for business; and these should have been used for God. Did he not give them to you? Why expend them on your own selfish money-getting?

IV. IT IS AN EXCUSE WHICH WILL WOUND THE MEMORY OF SOME.

- To have worked hard for nothing: to live hard, and lie hard, and yet to fail, and die poor at last, will be sad.
- To have to leave all when you have succeeded in accumulating wealth will be wretched work. Yet so it must be.

V. IT IS AN EXCUSE WHICH CANNOT RESTORE THE LOSS.

- If you have lost the time, you certainly had it entrusted to you, and you will be called to account for it: but you cannot regain it, nor make up for its loss.

- How wretched to have spent a life in idly traveling, collecting shells, reading novels, etc., and to have therefore left no space for serving God, and knowing the Redeemer!
- Men do worse than this: they sin, they lead others to sin, they invent ways of killing time, and then say they have no time.
- They give their minds to skeptical thought, to propagating atheism, undermining Scripture, or arguing against the gospel, and yet have no time to believe and live!
- Call to the young to use time while time is theirs.
- Call to the aged to spend the remnant of their days well.
- Call to Christians to look well to their children's souls, lest they slip from under their influence while they are busy here and there.
- Call to experienced believers to see to their own joy in the Lord, lest they lose it in the throng.

In London, such is the hum of business, that the great clock of St. Paul's may strike many times and not be heard. God speaks often, and men hear him not because other voices deafen them. A great earthquake happened when two armies were in the heat of battle, and none of the combatants knew of it. Preoccupation of mind will prevent the most solemn things from having due weight with us.

Nero, when Rome was famishing, sent ships to Alexandria, not to bring corn for the starving people, but to fetch sand for the arena. He fiddled while Rome was burning Are not many thus cruel to themselves? Are they not spending, on fleeting merriments, precious hours, which should be used in seeking after pleasures for evermore?

Whatever negligence may creep into your studies, or into your pursuits of pleasure or of business, let there be one point, at least, on which you are always watchful, always alive: I mean, in the performance of your religious duties. Let nothing induce you, even for a day, to neglect the perusal of Scripture. You know the value of prayer; it is precious beyond all price. Never, never neglect it. —*Buxton to his Son*

King Henry the Fourth asked the Duke of Alva if he had observed the great eclipse of the sun which had lately happened. "No," said the Duke, "I have so much to do on earth, that I have no leisure to look up to heaven." Ah, that this were not true of professors in these days! It is sad to think how their hearts and time are so taken up with earthly things, that they have no leisure to look after Christ and the things that belong to their everlasting peace. —*Thomas Brooks*

A treatise on the excellence and dignity of the soul, by Claude, Bishop of Toul, ends thus: "I have but one soul, and I will value it."

Moments seize;
Heaven's on their wing: a moment we may wish,
When worlds want wealth to buy.

—*Young*

Grotius, the historian, cried in death, "Ah, I have consumed my life in a laborious doing of nothing. I would give all my learning and honor for the plain integrity of John Urick" (a poor man of eminent piety).

A dying nobleman exclaimed, "Good God, how have I employed myself! In what delirium has my life been passed! What have I been doing while the sun in its race, and the stars in their courses, have lent their beams, perhaps only to light me to perdition! I have pursued shadows, and entertained myself with dreams. I have been treasuring up dust, and sporting myself with the wind. I might have grazed with the beasts of the field, or sung with the birds of the woods, to much better purpose than any for which I have lived."

26

And he took the mantle of Elijah that fell from him, and smote the waters, and said, Where is the Lord God of Elijah?

—*2 Kings 2:14*

HE great object to be desired is God, Jehovah, Elijah's God. With him all things flourish. His absence is our decline and death.

Those entering on any holy work should seek for the God who was with their predecessors. What a mercy that the God of Elijah is also the God of Elisha! He will also be with us, for "this God is our God, for ever and ever, he will be our guide even unto death" (Ps. 48:14).

In great difficulties no name will help but that of God. How else can Jordan be divided but by Jehovah, God of Elijah?

Elisha sought first for the Lord, and inquired, "Where is he?" Elijah was gone, and he did not seek *him*, but his God.

He used Elijah's old mantle, and did not invent novelties; desiring to have the aid of the same God, he was content to wear the mantle of his predecessor. The true is not new.

Still we do not need antiquities from the past, nor novelties of the present, nor marvels for the future; we only want the Triune God, Father, Son, and Holy Spirit, and we shall then see among us wonders equal to those of Elijah's age. "Where is the Lord God of Elijah?" The old mantle, used with faith in the same God, parted the waters hither and thither. The power is where it used to be.

I. THE QUESTION TURNED INTO PRAYER.

I. THE QUESTION TURNED INTO PRAYER. It is as though he cried, "O thou, who wast with Elijah, be thou also with me!" At this day our one need is Elijah's God.

1. The God who kept him faithful must make us stand firm should we be left alone in the truth (1 Cor. 1:8).
2. The God who heard *his* prayer must give us also the effectual in-wrought prayer of the righteous man (James 5:16).
3. The God who provided for him at Cherith and Zarephath, and in the wilderness, must also supply all our needs (Ps. 23:1).
4. The God who raised the dead by him must cause us to bring men up from their death in sin (1 Kings 17:22).
5. The God who answered by fire must put life, energy, and enthusiasm into our hearts (1 Kings 18:38).
6. The God who gave him food for a long journey must fit us for the pilgrimage of life, and preserve us to the end (1 Kings 19:8).
7. The God who gave him courage to face kings must also make us very bold, so as to be free from the fear of man (1 Kings 21:20).
8. The God who divided Jordan for the prophet will not fail us when we are crossing into our Canaan (2 Kings 2:8).
9. The God who took him away in a chariot of fire will send a convoy of angels, and we shall enter into glory.

II. THE QUESTION ANSWERED. The Lord God of Elijah is not dead, nor sleeping, nor on a journey.

1. He is still in heaven regarding his own reserved ones. They may be hidden in caves, but the Lord knoweth them that are his.
2. He is still to be moved by prayer to bless a thirsty land.
3. He is still able to keep us faithful in the midst of a faithless generation, so that we shall not bow the knee to Baal.
4. He is still in the still small voice. Quietly he speaks to reverent minds: by calm and brave spirits he is achieving his purposes.
5. He is still reigning in providence to overturn oppressors (1 Kings 21:18–19), to preserve his own servants (2 Kings 1:10), and to secure a succession of faithful men (1 Kings 19:16).
6. He is coming in vengeance. Hear ye not his chariot-wheels? He will bear away his people, but, sorely, O ye unbelievers! shall ye rue the day wherein ye cried in scorn, "Where is the Lord God of Elijah?"
   - Oh, to be so engaged that we can court the presence of God!
   - Oh, to be so consecrated that we may expect his benediction!
   - Oh, to have that presence, so as to be girded with his strength!
   - Oh, to live so as never more to ask this question!

Auxiliary Extracts

"God of Queen Clotilda," cried out the infidel Clovis I of France, when in trouble on the field of battle, "God of Queen Clotilda! grant me the victory!" Why did he not call upon his own god? Saunderson, who was a great admirer of Sir Isaac Newton's talents, and who made light of his religion in health, was, nevertheless, heard to say in dismal accents on a dying-bed, "God of Sir Isaac Newton, have mercy on me!" Why this changing of gods in a dying hour? — *"Addresses to Young Men," by Rev. Daniel Baker*

1. *The God of Elijah gave him the sweet experience of keeping warm and lively in a very cold and dead generation;* so that he was best when others were worst. . . . But where is the Lord God of Elijah in these dregs of time, wherein professors generally are carried away, with the stream of impiety, from all their liveliness and tenderness that aforetime have been among them, when the more wickedness set. up its head, the more piety is made to hide its head? It is a sad evidence that God is gone from us, when the standard of wickedness makes advances, and that of shining holiness is retreating, and can hardly get hands to hold it up.

2. *The God of Elijah gave him the sweet experience of the power of prayer* (James 5:17). But where is the God of Elijah, while the trade with heaven by prayer is so very low? Alas, for the dead, cold, and flat prayers that come from the lips of professors at this day, so weak and languishing that they cannot reach heaven!

3. *The God of Elijah gave him the experience of the sweet fruits of dependence on the Lord,* and of a little going far, with his blessing (1 Kings 17:16). But where is the God of Elijah at this day, when what we have seems to be blown upon, that it goes in effect for nothing? Our table is plentifully covered, yet our souls are starved; our goodness sometimes looks as a morning cloud, it blackens the face of the heavens, and promises a heavy shower, but quickly proves as a little cloud, like unto a man's hand, which is ready to go for nothing; yea, this generation is blinded by the means that have a natural tendency to give light. Ah! "Where is the Lord God of Elijah?"

4. *The God of Elijah gave him the experience of a gracious boldness to face the most daring wickedness* of the generation he lived in, though it was one of the worst. This eminently appeared in his encounter with Ahab (1 Kings 18:1). But where is the God of Elijah now, while the iniquities of our day meet with such faint resistance, while a brave brow for the cause of God, a tongue to speak for him, and a heart to act, are so much wanting? The wicked of the world, though they have an ill cause in hand, yet they pursue it boldly; but, alas! the people of God shame their honest cause by their cowardice and faint appearing in it. If God give us not another spirit, more fitted for such a day, we shall betray our trust, and bring the curse of the succeeding generation on us.

5. *The God of Elijah gave him the experience of a glorious and powerful manifestation of himself, in a solemn ordinance,* even at the sacrifice on Mount Carmel, which was ushered in with the spirit of prayer in Elijah (1 Kings 18:37–39). But where

is the God of Elijah, when so little of the Spirit's influences is found in ordinances, even solemn ordinances? Here is the mantle, but where is the God of Elijah? Here are the grave-clothes, in which sometimes the Lord was wrapt up, but where is he himself? Communion-days have sometimes been glorious days in, Scotland, and sometimes the gospel hath done much good, so that ministers have had almost as much to do to heal broken hearts as now to get hard hearts broken; but where now is the God of Elijah?

6. *The God of Elijah gave him the experience of being enabled to go far upon a meal* (1 Kings 19:8). But where now are such experiences, while there is so little strength in the spiritual meals to which we now sit down? This is a time wherein there is much need of such an experience; the Lord seems to be saying to his people, "Rise and eat, for the journey is long"; and what a hard journey some may have, ere they get another meal, who knows? Oh, for more feeding power in the doctrine preached among us!

7. *The God of Elijah gave him the experience of the Lord's removing difficulties out of his way, when he himself could do nothing at them*: Jordan divided. So Peter had the iron gate opened to him of its own accord: for when the Lord takes the work in hand, were it never so desperate as to us, it will succeed well with him. Sure we have need of this experience this day. How is the case of many souls so embarrassed at this day that they cannot extricate themselves, by reason of long and continued departures from God, so that all they can do is that they are fleeing and going backward! Ah! where is the God of Elijah, to dry up those devouring deeps? Enemies have surrounded the church, and brought her to the brow of the hill, ready to cast her over; where is the God of Elijah, to make a way for her escape? —*Thomas Boston*

27

And Elisha prayed, and said, Lord, I pray thee, open his eyes, that he may see. And the Lord opened the eyes of the young man; and he saw: and, behold, the mountain was full of horses and chariots of fire round about Elisha.

—2 Kings 6:17

 AITH serves the believer for eyes, and makes him see what others cannot. This keeps the man himself quiet and calm, and enables him to check the fears of those who cry, "Alas, my master! how shall we do" (verse 15)?

From this narrative we learn how much may be about us, and yet it may be invisible to the natural eye. We shall use it to teach:

I. THAT THE NATURAL EYE IS BLIND TO HEAVENLY THINGS.

- God is everywhere; yet sin-blinded eyes see him not.
- His law touches the thoughts and intents of the heart; yet its wonderful spiritual meaning is not perceived.
- Men themselves are evil, guilty, fallen; yet they see not their own wounds, and bruises, and putrefying sores.
- Their danger is imminent; yet they sport on, blindly dancing at hell's mouth. There is a man at Brighton who wears a placard about his neck, on which are these words, "I am *quite* blind." This might suit such foolish ones.
- Jesus is near, and ready to help; but their eyes are holden so that they know not that it is Jesus. He is altogether lovely, and desirable, the sun of the soul, yet is he altogether unknown.
- This want of spiritual discernment makes man ignoble. Samson blinded is a sorry spectacle: from a judge in Israel he sinks to a slave in Philistia.
- This keeps a man content with the world: he does not see how poor a thing it is, for which he sweats, and smarts, and sins, and sacrifices heaven.
- This causes many men to pursue the monotonous task of avarice; never more aspiring after better things, but pursuing the dreary round of incessant moil and toil, as blind horses go round and round the mill.
- This makes men proud. They think they know all things because they see so little of what can be known.
- This places men in danger. "If the blind lead the blind, both shall fall into the ditch" (Matt. 15:14).

II. THAT GOD ALONE CAN OPEN MAN'S EYES.

- We can lead the blind, but we cannot make them see; we can put truth before them, but we cannot open their eyes; that work remains with God alone.
- Some use artificial eyes, others try spectacles, telescopes, colored glasses, etc., but all in vain, while the eyes are blind. The cure is of the Lord alone.
1. To give sight is the same wonder as creation. Who can make an eye? In the sinner the faculty of spiritual vision is gone.
2. The man is born blind. His darkness is part of himself. "Since the world began was it not heard that any man opened the eyes of one that was born blind" (John 9:32).
3. The man is willfully blind. None so blind as those who will not see. "The blind people that have eyes" (Isa. 43:8).
4. Opening of the eyes is set down as a covenant blessing. The Lord has given his Son "for a covenant of the people, to open the blind eyes" (Isa. 42:6–7).

    Satan counterfeited this in the garden when he said, "Your eyes shall be opened, and ye shall be as gods" (Gen. 3:5).

III. THAT WE MAY PRAY HIM TO OPEN MEN'S EYES. We ought to cry, "Lord, I pray thee, open his eyes, that he may see."

1. When we see sinners in trouble it is a hopeful sign, and we should pray for them with double importunity (Isa. 26:2).
2. When we hear them inquiring, we should inquire of the Lord for them. Their prayer should call up ours.
3. When we ourselves see much, we should see for them.
4. When their blindness astonishes us, it should drive us to our knees.
5 The prayers of others availed for us, and therefore we ought to repay the blessing to the prayer-treasury of the church.
6. It will glorify God to open their eyes; let us pray with great expectancy, believing that he will honor his Son.

IV. THAT GOD DOES OPEN MEN'S EYES.

1. He has done it in a moment. Notice the many miracles performed by our Lord on blind men.
2. He specially opens the eyes of the young. "The Lord opened the eyes of the young man." See the text.
3. He can open *your* eyes. Many are the forms of blindness, but they are all comprehended in that grand statement, "The Lord openeth the eyes of the blind" (Ps. 146:8).
4. He can in an instant cause you to see his grace in its all-sufficiency and nearness. Hagar and the well (Gen. 21:19).

V. THAT EVEN THOSE WHO SEE NEED MORE SIGHT. Elisha's young man could see; yet he had his eyes more fully opened.

1. In the Scriptures more is to be seen. "Open thou mine eyes, that I may behold wondrous things out of thy law" (Ps. 119:18).
2. In the great doctrines of the gospel there is much latent light.
3. In Providence there are great marvels. To see God's hand in everything is a great attainment, specially glorifying to his name (Ps. 107:24).
4. In self, sin, Satan, etc., there are depths which it were well for us to see. May we be men with our eyes opened.
5. In Christ Jesus himself there are hidden glories. "Sir, we would see Jesus" (John 12:21; Heb. 2:9).

> Have you spiritual sight? Then behold angels and spiritual things. Better still—behold your Lord!

Gleanings

One of the saddest conditions of a human creature is to read God's word with a veil upon the heart, to pass blindfolded through all the wondrous testimonies of redeeming love and grace which the Scriptures contain. And it is sad, also, if not actually censurable, to pass blindfolded through the works of God, to live in a world of flowers, and stars, and sunsets, and a thousand glorious objects of nature, and never to have a passing interest awakened by any of them. —*Dean Goulbourn*

A lady once said to Turner, when he was painting: "Why do you put such extravagant colors into your pictures? I never see anything like them in nature." "Don't you wish you did, madam?" said he. It was a sufficient answer. *He* saw them, if *she* did not. So believers, like the prophet, see many divine wonders which worldlings cannot perceive.

> If his word once teach us, shoot a ray
> Through all the heart's dark chambers, and reveal
> Truths undiscerned but by that holy light,
> Then all is plain.
>
> —*Cowper*

The dying prayer of William Tyndale, the martyr, uttered "with a fervent zeal and a loud voice," was this: "Lord open the king of England's eyes!"

28

And so it was at the beginning of their dwelling there, that they feared not the Lord: therefore the Lord sent lions among them, which slew some of them.... They feared the Lord, and served their own gods, after the manner of the nations whom they carried away from thence. Unto this day they do after the former manners: they fear not the Lord, neither do they after their statutes, or after their ordinances, or after the law and commandment which the Lord commanded the children of Jacob, whom he named Israel.

—*2 Kings 17:25, 33–34*

 т is as needful to warn you against the false as to urge you to the true. Conversion, which is a divine change, is imitated, and the spurious palmed off as genuine. This answers the devil's purpose in several ways; it eases the conscience of the double-minded, adulterates the church, injures its testimony, and dishonors true religion.

I. THEIR FIRST ESTATE. "They feared not the Lord."

1. They had little or no religion of any sort.
2. They were not troubled about serving the true God.
3. Probably they even ridiculed Jehovah and his people.

4. But they were near a God-fearing people, and near to king Hezekiah, under whom there had been a great revival. Such influence creates a great deal of religiousness.

II. THEIR SHAM CONVERSION. "They feared the Lord."

1. They were wrought upon by fear only: the "lions" were their evangelists, and their teeth were cutting arguments.
2. They remained in ignorance of the character of Jehovah, and only wished to know "the manner of the god of the land." Outside religion is enough for many; they care not for God himself.
3. They were instructed by an unfaithful priest; one of those who had practiced calf-worship, and now failed to rebuke their love of false gods. Such persons have much to answer for.
4. They showed their conversion by outward observances, multiplying priests, and setting up altars on high places.
5. But their conversion was radically defective, for:
   • There was no repentance.
   • No expiatory sacrifice was offered on God's one altar.
   • The false gods were not put away. "Every nation made gods of their own" (verse 29). While sin reigns grace is absent.
   • They showed no love to God. They *feared*, but did not trust or love.
   • They rendered no obedience to him. Even their worship was will-worship. "They feared the Lord, and *served* their own gods": a very significant distinction.
   • They did not abandon false trusts: they looked not to the Lord.
   Case examples:
   • The religious drunkard. See him weep! Hear him talk! He has a dread of God, but he serves Bacchus.
   • The unchaste hypocrite, whose real worship goes to the vilest lusts, and yet he dreads to be found out.
   • The pious Sabbath-breaker. Very devout, but serves out poison on Sundays, or prefers recreation to regeneration.
   • The saintly skinflint. He has "a saving faith" in the worst sense.
   • The slandering professor. Under pretense of greater holiness he abuses the righteous.

III. THEIR REAL STATE. "They fear not the Lord."

1. They own him not as God alone. The admission of other gods is apostasy from the true God. He will be all or nothing.
2. They do not really obey him; for else they would quit their idols, sins, and false trusts.
3. He has no covenant with them. They ignore it altogether.

4. He has not wrought salvation for them.

5. They act so as to prove that they are not his. See the future history of these Samaritans in the book of Nehemiah, of which these are the items:
   - They desire to unite with Israel for the sake of advantage;
   - They become enemies when refused;
   - They grow proud and judge the true Israel. They say they are better than "those who profess so much." They measure the corn of the sincere with the bushel of their own deceit.

In real conversion there must be
   - Idol-breaking. Sin and self must be abandoned.
   - Concentration. Our only God must be adored and served.
   - Christ-trusting. His one sacrifice must be presented and relied upon.
   - Full surrender. Our heart must yield to God and delight in his ways.

29

And David and all Israel played before God with all their might, and with singing, and with harps, and with psalteries, and with timbrels, and with cymbals, and with trumpets.". . . And David was afraid of God that day, saying, how shall I bring the ark of God home to me?
—1 Chronicles 13:8, 12

So David, and the elders of Israel, and the captains over thousands, went to bring up the ark of the covenant of the Lord out of the house of Obed-edom with joy.
—1 Chronicles 15:25

AVID loved his God and venerated the symbol of his presence. He desired to restore the Lord's appointed worship, and to place the ark where it should be, as the most sacred center of worship. But right things must be done in a right manner, or they will fail. In this case the failure was sad and signal, for Uzza died, and the ark turned aside to the house of Obed-edom.

I. THE FAILURE. First Text: 1 Chron. 13:8.
   - Here were multitudes, "David and all Israel," and yet the business came to naught. Crowds do not ensure blessing.
   - Here was pomp—singing, harps, trumpets, etc.—yet it ended in mourning. Gorgeous ceremonial is no guarantee of grace.

- Here was energy: "they played before God with all their might." This was no dull and sleepy worship, but a bright, lively service, and yet the matter fell through.
- But there was no thought as to God's mind. David confessed, "we sought him not after the due order" (1 Chron. 15:13).
- There was very little spiritual feeling. More music than grace.
- The priests were not in their places, nor the Levites to carry the ark: oxen took the place of willing men. The worship was not sufficiently spiritual and humble.
- There was no sacrifice. This was a fatal flaw; for how can we serve the Lord apart from sacrifice?
- There was little reverence. We hear little of prayer, but we hear much of oxen, a cart, and the too familiar hand of Uzza.
- Now, even a David must keep his place, and the Lord's command must not be supplanted by will-worship. Therefore the Lord made a breach upon Uzza, and David was greatly afraid.
- May we not expect similar failures unless we are careful to act obediently, and serve the Lord with holy awe? Are all the observances and practices of our churches scriptural? Are not some of them purely will-worship?

II. THE FEAR. Second Text: 1 Chron. 13:12.

- The terrible death of Uzza caused great fear. Thus the Lord slew Nadab and Abihu for offering strange fire; and the men of Beth-shemesh for looking into the ark. The Lord has said, "I will be sanctified in them that come nigh me, and before all the people I will be glorified" (Lev. 10:3).
- His own sense of wrong feeling caused this fear in David, for we read, "and David was displeased" (verse 11). We are too apt to be displeased with God because he is displeased with us.
- His own sense of unworthiness for such holy work made him cry, "How shall I bring the ark of God home to me?"
- His feeling that he failed in that which God expected of his servants created a holy fear. "Sanctify yourselves, that ye may bring up the ark of the Lord God" (1 Chron. 15:12).
- He meant well, but he had erred, and so he came to a pause; yet not for long. The ark of God remained with Obed-edom three months, but not more (verse 14).
- Some make the holiness of God and the strictness of his rule an excuse for wicked neglect.
- Others are overwhelmed with holy fear; and therefore pause a while, till they are better prepared for the holy service.

III. THE JOY. Third Text: 1 Chron. 15:25.

1. God blessed Obed-edom. Thus, may humble souls dwell with God and die not. Those houses which entertain the ark of the Lord shall be well rewarded.
2. Preparation was made and thought exercised by David and his people when a second time they set about moving the ark of the covenant. Read the whole of the chapter.
3. The mind of the Lord was considered: "And the children of the Levites bare the ark of God upon their shoulders, with the staves thereof, as Moses commanded, according to the word of the Lord" (verse 15).
4. The priests were in their places: "So the priests and the Levites sanctified themselves." Men and methods must both be ruled by God (verse 14).
5. Sacrifices were offered: "And it came to pass, when God helped, the Levites that bare the ark of the covenant of the Lord, that they offered seven bullocks and seven rams" (verse 26). The great and perfect sacrifice must ever be to the front.
6. Now came the exceeding joy (verse 28).
   • Do we draw near to God in all holy exercises after this careful, spiritual, reverent fashion?
   • If so, we may safely exhibit our delight, and our hearts may dance before the Lord as king David did (verse 29).

For Emphasis

When after long disuse ordinances come to be revived, it is too common for even wise and good men to make some mistakes. Who would have thought that David should have made such a blunder as this, to carry the ark upon a cart (verse 7)? Because the Philistines so carried it, and a special providence drove the cart (1 Sam. 6:12), he thought they might do so too. But we must walk by rule, not by example, when it varies from the rule; no, not those examples that providence has owned. —*Matthew Henry*

1. *The matter and right manner of performing duties are, in the command of God, linked together.* He will have his service well done as well as really done. We must serve God with a perfect heart and a willing mind, for the Lord searcheth all hearts, and understandeth all the imaginations of the thoughts. Masters on earth challenge to themselves a power to oblige their servants, not only to do their work, but to do it so-and-so; and though they do the thing itself, yet if not in the manner required, it cannot be accepted.

2. *The doing of a duty in a wrong manner alters the nature of it, and makes it sin.* Hence "the ploughing of the wicked is sin" (Prov. 21:4). Hence prayer is accounted a howling upon their beds (Hos. 7:14). Unworthy communicating is not counted as eating the Lord's supper (1 Cor. 11:20). If a house

be built of never so strong timber and good stones, yet if it be not well founded, and rightly built, the inhabitant may curse the day he came under the roof of it.

3. *Duties not performed according to the right order are but the half of the service we owe to God, and the worst half too. —Thomas Boston*

30

Then Huram the king of Tyre answered in writing, which he sent to Solomon, Because the Lord hath loved his people, he hath made thee king over them.

—2 Chronicles 2:11

UCH was the character of Solomon, that even Huram could see that he was a blessing to the people over whom he ruled. Be it ours to bless others, whatever our station may be. May it be observed concerning us that, because the Lord loved the family he made us heads of it, friends to it, or servants in it; and so forth.

Even a heathen could trace great blessings to God's love; what heathens those are who do not speak of the Lord's goodness, but talk of "chance" and "good luck"!

It is a great blessing when communications between rulers savor of a pious courtesy, as these between Solomon and Huram.

This verse may well be applied to our Lord Jesus. May the Holy Spirit bless our meditation thereon.

I. THE LOVE OF GOD HAS MADE JESUS OUR KING.

1. It is not, then, a burden to be under law to Christ: his commandments are not grievous (1 John 5:3).
2. Jesus did not need us for subjects, but we needed to be under the rule and headship of Jesus. It is for our guidance, comfort, honor, growth, success, peace, and safety.
3. It brings us great happiness to obey our Prince. His laws are simply indications of where our felicity lies.
4. The personal character of our King is such that it is a great blessing to his subjects to have him as their Monarch.
   • So wise: therefore able to judge and to direct.
   • So powerful: therefore able to enrich and to defend.
   • So gracious: therefore laying himself out to benefit us all.

- So holy: therefore elevating and purifying his people. In this Solomon failed, but Jesus succeeded.

5. His relationship to us makes it a great blessing to have him for our King. We are not under the tyranny of a stranger; but to us is fulfilled the word of the prophet: "Their nobles shall be of themselves, and their governor shall proceed from the midst of them" (Jer. 30:21).

The Lord Jesus is, to all of us who are believers:

- Our Brother. Therefore it is no bondage to follow him.
- Our Redeemer. Therefore it is joy to own his property in us.
- Our Husband. Who would not do the bidding of one so loving?

It is a delight to obey him in all things who has blessed us in all things.

II. THE LOVE OF GOD HAS MADE US THE SUBJECTS OF JESUS.

1. We see this in the choice which the Lord has made of us.
We were like Israel:
- Insignificant in rank, power, or wisdom.
- Erring, and continually apt to revolt from our King.
- Poor, and therefore unable to pay him any great revenue.
- Feeble, and therefore no help to him in his grand designs.
- Fickle, and consequently a wretched people to rule and lead.

2. We see this in his subduing us.
We began with rebellion, but our Prince conquered us, and brought us under happy subjection because of his great love.

3. We see this in the healthy order he maintains. It is good for us to be under so wise a rule. Love gives rebels a powerful, gracious, and forbearing ruler. A firm hand and a loving heart will tame the unruly, and be a boon to them.

4. We see this in the peace which he creates: the quiet within and without: in the heart and in the church (1 Kings 4:24).

5. We see this in the plenty which he scatters. "And the king made silver and gold at Jerusalem as plenteous as stones, and cedar trees made he as the sycamore trees that are in the vale for abundance" (2 Chron. 1:15). Far greater are the riches of grace which the reign of Jesus brings to us.

6. We see this in the honor he puts upon us, making us all to be kings and priests with him (Rev. 1:5–6).

III. OUR LOVE TO GOD MAKES THE REIGN OF JESUS BLESSED TO US.

1. It makes his courts our delight.
2. It makes his service our recreation.
3. It makes his revenue our riches.
4. It makes his glory our honor.

5. It makes his cross our crown.
6. It makes himself our heaven.
   - Lord, bless thy people, by keeping them loyal and obedient.
   - Lord, bless rebellious ones, by bringing them to bow before so gracious and wise a Prince.
   - Lord, we now bless thee for exalting Jesus, to be a Prince and a Savior to us. May his Spirit rest upon us!

And he did evil, because he prepared not his heart to seek the Lord.
—2 Chronicles 12:14

THIS is the summing up of Rehoboam's life: he was not so bad as some, but he did evil in various ways, not so much from design as from neglect.

The evil effects of the father's sin and the mother's idolatry were seen in their son, yet there was another cause, namely, a want of heart-preparation. The son of Solomon very naturally desired many wives (2 Chron. 11:23); and it was no marvel that the child of Naamah the Ammonitess allowed images and groves to defile the land; yet there was a deeper cause of his life's evil, and that lay in himself. His heart was not thorough with the Lord, and he, himself, was not carefully consecrated to the worship of Jehovah. He might have done well had he not been Rehoboam the Unready.

I. HE DID NOT BEGIN LIFE WITH SEEKING THE LORD.

1. He was young, and should have sought wisdom of God; but he went to Shechem to meet the people without prayer or sacrifice (2 Chron. 10:1). That which commences without God will end in failure.
2. He leaned on counselors, saying, "What advice give ye?" Of those counselors he chose the worst, namely, the younger and prouder nobles (2 Chron. 10:8). Those who reject divine wisdom generally refuse all other wisdom.
3. He committed great folly by threatening the people, and refusing their just demands; and that while as yet he had not been accepted as their king (2 Chron. 10:13–14). He had none of his father's wisdom. How can they act prudently and prosperously who are not guided of the Lord?

II. HE SHOWED NO HEART IN SEEKING THE LORD AFTERWARDS.

1. He obeyed the prophet's voice when the man of God forbade him to fight with Israel; yet afterwards he forsook the law of the Lord (2 Chron. 12:1). He is said to have been "young and tender-hearted," which means *soft* (2 Chron. 13:7).
2. He winked at the most horrible crimes among the people whom he ought to have judged (1 Kings 14:24).
3. He fell into his father's sins.
4. He busied himself more for the world than for God. We hear nothing of his worship but much of his building, nothing of his faith but much of his fickleness (2 Chron. 11:5-12).

III. HE WAS NOT FIXED AND PERSEVERING IN HIS SEEKING THE LORD.

1. For three years his loyalty to his God made him prosper, by bringing into Judah all the better sort of people who fled from Jeroboam's calf-worship (2 Chron. 11:13-17), yet he forsook the Lord who had prospered him.
2. He grew proud, and God handed him over to Shishak (verse 5).
3. He humbled himself and was pardoned, yet he stripped the Lord's house to buy off the king of Egypt.
4. He wrought no great reforms and celebrated no great passover, yet he owned, "the Lord is righteous" (verse 6).

IV. HE HAD NO CARE TO SEEK THE LORD THOROUGHLY.

Yet no man is good by accident: no one goes right who has not intended to do so. Without heart, religion must die.

1. Human nature departs from the right way, especially in kings, who are tolerated in more sin than others.
2. Courtiers usually run the wrong way, especially the young, proud, and frivolous. Rehoboam loved the gay and proud, and gave himself up to their lead.
3. Underlings are apt to follow us and applaud us if we go in an evil path, even as Judah followed Rehoboam. Thus, those who should lead are themselves led.
   - The kind of preparation required by me, in order to the diligent and acceptable seeking of the Lord, my God, is somewhat after this fashion:
     - To feel and confess my need of God in the whole of my life.
     - To cry unto him for help and wisdom.
     - To yield to his guidance, and not to follow the counsel of vain persons, nor to bluster at those around me.
     - To be anxious to be right in everything, searching the Scriptures, and seeking by prayer, to know what I should do.

- To serve the Lord carefully and earnestly, leaving nothing to chance, passion, fashion, or whim.
- Are there any professors among us of the same sort as Rehoboam?
- Are there any hopeful young men who lack whole-hearted devotion to the Lord?
- Are there any older men who have suffered already from vacillation, hesitation, or double-mindedness?
- Are there any just escaped from such trouble who nevertheless are not firm, and ready even now?

Oh, for a clear sense of the evil and folly of such a condition!
Oh, for the confirming power of the Holy Ghost!
Oh, for vital union with the Lord Jesus!

Examples

Before the University Boat race comes off, the men undergo a long and severe training. They would not think of contending for the mastery without preparation; and do we imagine that we can win the race of life at a venture, without bringing under the body and cultivating the mind? The preacher studies his discourse carefully, though it will only occupy part of an hour; and is our life-sermon worthy of no care and consideration? A saintly life is a work of far higher art than the most valuable painting or precious statue, yet neither of these can be produced without thought. A man must be at his best to produce an immortal poem, yet a few hundred lines will sum it all up. Let us not dream that the far greater poem of a holy life can be made to flow forth like impromptu verse.

Well known to me was a kindly, well-disposed gentleman, who, like Rehoboam, was tender-hearted or persuasible. He was a worldling of pleasing manners, who delighted in the esteem of the circle which surrounded him. He had a great respect for religious persons, and especially for ministers; but he could not afford to be a godly man himself, for then he might have become unpopular with a large circle of worldly fashionables. He once quitted an assembly which I addressed, because he said, "I felt almost on the go, and should soon have been converted if I had not rushed out." "There," said he, "Spurgeon, I am like an india-rubber doll when you are preaching; you can make me into any shape you like; but then I get back into my old form when you have done." He was an accurate reproduction of the soft-soured son of Solomon: a very Pliable, easily persuaded to set out on pilgrimage, but equally ready to return at the world's call.

The parable of the two sons will come in here. Rehoboam said, "I go, Sir"; but he went not. The modern Rehoboam is a perfect gentleman: if he did but know his own mind, he would also be a man. He is inclined to obey God, but others incline him to keep in the fashion. He is like the pear which the French call *Bon Chrétien*, very promising, but apt to become sleepy, and to rot at the core. This sort of people is not of much use either to the good cause or to its opposite.

32

And Judah gathered themselves together, to ask help of the Lord: even out of all the cities of Judah they came to seek the Lord.

—2 Chronicles 20:4

HE sudden news of a great invasion came to Jehoshaphat, and, like a true man of God, he set himself to seek the Lord, and proclaimed a fast. The people came together with all speed, and the whole nation earnestly cried to the Lord for his aid.

Let us notice carefully:

I. HOW THEY ASKED HELP.
- They expressed their confidence; Jehoshaphat cried, "Art not thou God in heaven? In thine hand Is there not power and might" (verse 6)?
- They pleaded his past acts. "Art not thou our God, who didst drive out the inhabitants of this land?" (verse 7).
- They urged the promise given at the dedication of the temple. Read verse 9. "Thou wilt hear and help."
- They confessed their condition: humbly did they acknowledge their danger and their impotence. They had:
  - No power. "We have no might against this great company."
  - No plan. "Neither know we what to do" (verse 12).
  - No allies. Their wives and their little ones only increased their care (verse 13).
- They then lifted their souls to God. "Our eyes are upon thee." Where could they look with more certainty?

II. HOW THEY RECEIVED IT.
- By renewed assurance. "The Lord will be with you" (verse 17).
- By the calming of their fears. "Be not afraid!" "Fear not, nor be dismayed." Courage keeps the field, but fear flies.
- By urging them to greater faith. "Believe in the Lord your God, so shall ye be established" (verse 20).
- By distinct direction. "Tomorrow go ye down against them; ye shall find them at the end of the brook" (verse 16).

- By actual deliverance. The Moabites and Ammonites slew the Edomites, and Israel triumphed without striking a blow.
- It shall be greatly to our joy to see the right hand of the Lord getting us the victory.

III. HOW THEY ACTED BY THIS HELP.

- They worshipped. With every sign of reverence, the king and; his people bowed before Jehovah (verse 18). Worship girds us for warfare.
- They praised. Before they received the mercy, "He appointed singers unto the Lord." Read verse 21.
- They went forth, preceded by the singers, till they reached "the watch-tower in the wilderness" (verse 24).
- They saw the promise fulfilled. "They looked unto the multitude, and, behold, they were dead bodies" (verse 24).
- They gathered the spoil. "They were three days in gathering of the spoil, it was so much" (verse 25).
- They blessed the Lord (verse 26). The valley of Berachah heard their joyful notes, and then they returned to the house of the Lord with harps and psalteries and trumpets.
- They had rest. "So the realm of Jehoshaphat was quiet: for his God gave him rest round about" (verse 30). God's victories end the war. The fear of God fell on all the kingdoms, and they dared not invade Judah.
- Let us when in difficulties have immediate resort to the Lord.
- Let us do this in the spirit of confidence and praise.
- Is there not a cause for our assembling even now to plead against the Moabites, Ammonites, and Edomites of superstition, worldliness, and infidelity?

Observations

This chapter, which begins with danger, fear, and trouble all round, ends with joy, peace, quiet, and rest. Two words seem to stand out in this chapter— PRAISE and PRAYER—twin sisters which should always go together. One word links them here—FAITH.

"Jehoshaphat set himself to seek the Lord." His good example was soon followed. "Judah gathered themselves together, to ask help of the Lord: even out of all the cities of Judah they came to seek the Lord." What a prayer-meeting—a real one, a united one, with a definite object, and the king presiding! Notice the prayer (verse 5). It is a pattern one. Jehoshaphat felt his weakness and need; but he recognized that God is all, and over all, and has all power and might. He brings forward every plea and argument. He appeals to God's power and promises, to his justice and love, and winds up with simple yet prevailing faith in God himself. "We have no might, neither know we what to

do; but our eyes are upon thee" (verse 12). Placing all the responsibility on God, and they just looking to him, waiting for him: God answered at once.
—*Captain Dawson, in "Thoughts in the Valleys"*

33

But they were the ruin of him, and of all Israel.
—*2 Chronicles 28:23*

ARRATE the actual circumstances. Ahaz turned away from Jehovah to serve the gods of Damascus, because Syria enjoyed prosperity. "For he sacrificed unto the gods of Damascus, which smote him: and he said, Because the gods of the kings of Syria help them, therefore will I sacrifice to them, that they may help me. But they were the ruin of, him, and of all Israel."

The consequent introduction of false deities and defilement of the worship of God became the ruin of Ahaz and his kingdom.

We fear lest this should be the ruin of England; for the idols of the Papists and the doctrines of Rome are again being set up in our land. Though no country prospers in which these prevail, yet besotted minds are laboring to restore the gods of the Vatican. This subject deserves many faithful sermons.

At this time we shall turn the text to more general use.

I. THE MAN RUINING HIMSELF. Ahaz is the type of many selfdestroyers. "O Israel, thou hast destroyed thyself" (Hos. 13:9).

- He would be his own master. This ruined the prodigal, and will ruin millions more.
- He was high-handed in sin. "He walked in the way of the kings of Israel" (2 Kings 16:3–4). This is a race to ruin.
- He lavished treasure upon it. He spent much but gained little. Profligacy and many other wrong ways are expensive and ruinous.
- He defied chastisement. "In the time of his distress did he trespass yet more against the Lord" (2 Chron. 28:22). This defiance of correction leads to sure ruin.
- He was exceedingly clever, and curried favor with the great. He made a copy of a classic altar, and sent it home. More men perish through being too clever than by being simple.
- He was a man of taste. He admired the antique, and the esthetic in religion.

- He had officials to back him. "Urijah, the priest, built an altar according to all that king Ahaz had sent from Damascus" (2 Kings 16:11). Bad ministers are terrible destroyers.
- He imitated prosperous sinners. The king of Assyria became his type. This is ruinous conduct.
- He abandoned all worship of God. "He shut up the doors of the house of the Lord" (verse 24). This is the climax of rebellion, and the seal of ruin.

But he did not prosper; the false gods were the ruin of him.

II. THE MAN IN RUINS. We leave Ahaz to think of some around us.

- The man becomes eaten up with secret vice. A rotting ruin haunted by bats and owls, and foul creatures of the night.
- The man of drinking habits, not fit for society, a brute, a fiend.
- The man of evil company and foul speech: likely to be soon in prison, or an outcast.
- The man of unbelieving notions and blasphemous conversation, lost to God, to goodness, and moral sense.
- All around us we see such spiritual ruins.
- Turned from holy uses to be moldering wastes.

The man is ruined in:

- Peace, character, usefulness, prospects. Worst of all, he is himself a ruin, and will be so for ever.
- A ruin suggests many reflections.
- What it was! What it might have been!
- What it is! What it will be!
- Meditations among ruins may be useful to those who are inclined to repeat the experiment of Ahaz.

III. OTHERS RUINED WITH HIM. "They were the ruin of him, *and of all Israel.*"

- Designedly. Some men by example create drunkards, by teaching make infidels, by seduction ruin virtue, by their very presence destroy all that is good in their associates.
- Incidentally; even without intent they spread the contagion of sin. Their irreligion ruins the young, their conduct influences the unsettled, their language inflames the wicked.
- Sin will ruin you, if persisted in.
- Your downfall will drag down others.
- Will you not endeavor to escape from ruin?
- Jesus is the Restorer of the wastes.

Relics

There is an Australian missile called the boomerang, which is thrown so as to describe singular curves, and to return at last to the hand of the thrower. Sin is a kind of boomerang, which goes off into space curiously, but turns again upon its author, and with tenfold force strikes the guilty soul that launched it.

We might illustrate the evil of sin by the following comparison: "Suppose I were going along a street, and were to dash my hand through a large pane of glass, what harm would I receive?" "You would be punished for breaking the glass." "Would that be all the harm I should receive?" "Your hand would be cut by the glass." "Yes; and so it is with sin. If you break God's laws, you shall be punished for breaking them; and your soul is hurt by the very act of breaking them." —*J. Inglis*

I have heard that a shepherd once stood and watched an eagle soar out from a cliff. The bird flew far up into the air, and presently became unsteady, and reeled in its flight. First one wing dropped, and then the other; presently, with accelerated speed, the poor bird fell rapidly to the ground. The shepherd was curious to know the secret of its fall. He went and picked it up. He saw that when the eagle lighted last on a cliff, a little serpent had fastened itself upon him; and as the serpent gnawed in farther and farther, the eagle in its agony reeled in the air. When the serpent touched its heart, the eagle fell. Have you never seen a man or woman in the church, or in society, rising and rising; the man becoming more and more influential, apparently strong, widely known, asserting power far and near; but, by and by, growing unsteady, uncertain, reeling, as it were, in uncertainty and inconsistency, and at last falling to the earth, and lying there in hopeless disgrace, a spectacle for angels to weep over, and scoffers and devils to jeer at? You do not know the secret of the fall, but the omniscient eye of God saw it. That neglect of prayer, that secret dishonesty in business, that stealthy indulgence in the intoxicating cup, that licentiousness and profligacy unseen of men, that secret tampering with unbelief and error, was the serpent at the heart that brought the eagle down. —*T. Cuyler.*

Sages of old contended that no sin was ever committed whose consequences rested on the head of the sinner alone; that no man could do ill and his fellows not suffer. They illustrated it thus: "A vessel, sailing from Joppa, carried a passenger, who, beneath his berth, cut a hole through the ship's side. When the men of the watch expostulated with him, saying, 'What doest thou, O miserable man?' the offender calmly replied, 'What matters it to you? The hole I have made lies under my own berth.'" This ancient parable is worthy of the utmost consideration. No man perishes alone in his iniquity; no man can guess the full consequences of his transgression.

34

O Lord, I beseech thee, let now thine ear be attentive to the prayer of thy servant, and to the prayer of thy servants, who desire to fear thy name.

—Nehemiah 1:11

EHEMIAH believed that there were others praying besides himself. He was not so gloomy, so self-opinionated, so uncharitable as to think that he alone loved the house of the Lord, and prayed for it. He believed that the Lord had many praying servants besides himself. In this he was more hopeful than Elijah (1 Kings 19:10, 18).

Nehemiah valued the prayers of his fellow-servants, and felt supported in his own supplications by the fact that he was one of a crowd of pleaders.

Even those of the feebler sort, who could get no further than desiring to fear God, were prized by this holy man when they lifted up their prayers. The littles of supplication, when multiplied by the number of those who present them, help to turn the scale.

Who are the persons that make up this class: "Who desire to fear thy name"? We will try to find them out.

I. THIS INCLUDES ALL WHO HAVE ANY TRUE RELIGION.

1. True godliness is always a matter of desire.
   - Not of custom, fashion, habit, excitement, passion, or chance.
   - Nor of unwilling dread, or compulsion, or bribery.
   - Nor of boasted full attainment and conceited self-satisfaction.
2. Every part of it is a matter of desire.
   - Repentance, faith, love, etc. None of these can be found in a man unless he desires to have them.
   - Prayer, praise, service, alms, and all good deeds, are matters of the heart's desire. Oh, to abound in them!
   - Progress and maturity of grace are never so far attained as to content us. They are still matters of desire.
   - So, too, usefulness among our fellows, the prevalence of truth, the prosperity of the church, and the spread of Christ's kingdom ever remain things of desire.
   - The same may be said of heaven, of resurrection, and of the future glories of Christ's reign on earth.
   - Good men are like Daniel, men of desires (Dan. 9:23, margin). Desire is the life-blood of piety, the egg of holiness, the dawn of grace, the promise of perfection.

3. The desire is accepted where there can be no more.

In giving, in working, in self-dedication, the Lord takes the will for the deed where the power to perform is absent. To him the essence of even the most self-sacrificing action is found, not in the suffering involved, but in a desire for God's glory.

4. But without even the desire, man is in a condition of spiritual death, and all that he does is as dead as himself.

II. THIS INCLUDES MANY GRADES OF GRACE.

Not the merely temporary wishers and resolvers, for these are only blossoms, and the bulk of blossoms never turn to fruit; of such we may say with Solomon, "The soul of the sluggard desireth, and hath nothing" (Prov. 13:4). But

1. Those who earnestly and heartily long to be right with God, though afraid to think themselves saved. These are always desiring.

2. Those who do believe, but fear lest there should be presumption in their calling themselves God's people. Their faith shows itself far more in desire than in a sense of having obtained the object of their search.

3. Those who know that they fear God, but desire to fear him more. Some of the best of men are of this order.

4. Those who wish to serve the Lord with greater freedom, constancy, delight, and power. What would they not do if they could but obtain their heart's desire?

5. Those who delight in the ways of God, and long to abide in them all their days. No man perseveres in holiness unless he desires to do so. Tender desires breed watchful walking, and, by God's Spirit, lead to consistent living.

- Now all these people can pray acceptably: indeed, they are always praying, for desires are true prayers.
- We need the prayers of all these people, as well as of advanced saints. The rank and file are the main part of the army. If none but eminent believers prayed, our treasury of supplication would be scantily furnished.
- We should gratefully associate such beginners with us in our cries for prosperity to the cause of God: their struggling petitions will excite us all to pray better, and the exercise will increase their own prayer-power.
- Lastly, LET US PRAY NOW—all of us, great and small. In the Holy Ghost let us pray, and thereby support our ministers, missionaries, and other workers, who, like Nehemiah, lead the way in holy service.

Spices

This description of God's servants—"who desire to fear thy name"—reminds us how largely their religion in this world consists of "desire." They have real piety, but are dissatisfied with their attainments, and aspire to better things. Their desire is, however, to be carefully distinguished from that of many who substitute occasional good wishes for actual piety. The real Christian's desire impels him to the diligent use of all those means by which a higher life is reached. He "exercises himself unto godliness"; and what he attains he employs in spiritual and moral living. But the word used rather signifies "delight," expressing the pleasure which God's servants feel in their religion.—*Pulpit Commentary*

That which we desire when we have it not we delight in when we obtain it. At least, this is the case in matters which are really worth desiring. Those who never pine for grace will never prize grace.

When Napoleon returned from Elba, a man at work in a garden recognized the emperor, and at once followed him. Napoleon welcomed him cheerfully, saying, "Here we have our first recruit." When even one person begins to pray for us, however feeble his prayers, we ought to welcome him. He who prays for me enriches me.

The gospel ministry is so dependent upon the power of prayer that it should be a pastor's main object to educate the praying faculty among his people. There should be numerous prayer meetings, and these of a varied order, that women, youths, children, and illiterate persons may unite in the holy exercise. Every little helps. Grains of sand and drops of rain combine for the greatest of purposes, and achieve them. There may be more real prayer in a little gathering of obscure desirers than in the great assembly where everything is done with ability rather than with agony of desire.

Never let your pastor lose his prayer book. It should be written in the hearts of his people. If you cannot preach, or give largely, or become a church officer, you can, at least, pray without ceasing.

35

Then he said unto them, Go your way, eat the fat, and drink the sweet, and send portions unto them for whom nothing is prepared: for this day is holy unto our Lord: neither be ye sorry; for the joy of the Lord is your strength.

—Nehemiah 8:10

Also that day they offered great sacrifices, and rejoiced; for God had made them rejoice with great joy: the wives also and the children rejoiced; so that the joy of Jerusalem was heard even afar off.

—Nehemiah 12:43

HE people who had wept before, under a sense of sin, were now called upon to rejoice. Holy mourning prepares the way for spiritual mirth. Clear shining follows rain.

It was well that they kept themselves under such control that they could weep or rejoice as they were bidden.

Their joy was remarkable for its spirituality and universality, and in these and other ways it was an example for us.

I. THERE IS A JOY OF DIVINE ORIGIN. "The joy of the Lord."

1. It rejoices in God himself, his character, his doings, his commands, and all that makes up his glory. It rejoices especially that he himself is ours. "Finally, my brethren, rejoice in the Lord (Phil. 3:1).
2. It possesses a deep sense of reconciliation, acceptance, adoption, and union with Christ Jesus. Joy must necessarily flow from all these founts of blessing (Isa. 12:3).
3. It enjoys assurance of future perseverance, victory, and perfection, by reason of the finished work of Christ, and the immutability and omnipotence of divine grace (Heb. 6: 17–18).
4. It is exalted by the present personal fellowship with God out of which it springs. "We also joy in God" (Rom. 5:11).
5. It is happy in the honor of service (1 Tim. 1:12).
6. It is acquiescent in the divine will, in providence, affliction, disappointment, etc. (Rom. 5: 3).
7. It is full of hope for the future-a well of delight.

II. THAT JOY IS A SOURCE OF STRENGTH. "The joy of the Lord is your strength."

1. It arises from considerations which strengthen. The same truths which make us glad also make us strong.
2. It is sustained by a life which is strong, even the life of Christ within us, maintained by the Holy Ghost.
3. It fortifies against temptation, or persecution, or affliction, and so it proves a present strength in time of need.
4. It fits for abounding service. He who is joyous of heart himself will seek the good of others.
5. It forbids all fear by giving a sense of ability to face every enemy. It is calm, constant, humble, real, deep-seated strength.

III. THAT STRENGTH WHICH COMES OF HOLY JOY LEADS TO PRACTICAL RESULTS.

1. Praise: "Ezra blessed the Lord, the great God; and all the people answered, Amen, Amen" (verse 6).

2. Sacrifices of joy: "They offered great sacrifices, and rejoiced."
3. Expressions of joy: "God had made them rejoice with great joy."
4. Family happiness: "The wives also and the children rejoiced."
5. This joy ensured the notice of the neighbors, "so that the joy of Jerusalem was heard even afar off."

IV. THAT JOY IS WITHIN REACH.
It was God's gift, but it came by:
- Hearing attentively. "The ears of all the people were attentive unto the book of the law" (verse 3).
- Worshipping devoutly. "They bowed their heads, and worshipped the Lord" (verse 6).
- Mourning penitently. "All the people wept, when they heard the words of the law" (verse 9).
- Understanding clearly. "Great mirth, because they had understood the words that were declared unto them" (verse 12).
- Obeying earnestly. "They made booths, and sat under the booths," etc. (verse 17).
- Let us seek after joy in God, through our Lord Jesus Christ, by whom we have received the atonement; for this is a true, safe, sanctifying joy. It is such an ornament as well becomes the thoroughly devoted believer while on earth, and prepares him to unite in the hallelujahs of heaven.
- There is such a thing as a joyless heart. God help us to have no personal experience of it!
- There are also deadly joys. From these let us flee to the living joys of grace.

Sparkles
It is a bad fireplace where all the heat goes up the chimney: true religion spreads joy over all around. Yet the fire warms first the chimney in which it burns, and grace comforts the heart in which it dwells. Nobody will be warmed by a cold hearth.

Faith is the key of happiness; use it at the gates of the Lord's house, and chambers of bliss shall open to you. If your religion only admits you into vaults and dungeons it must be very incomplete. Christ comes from ivory palaces, and leads his chosen into banqueting houses.

That the Christian religion is favorable to human happiness, is, I believe, the secret conviction even of many who may not openly confess it; hence it is no uncommon thing to hear even the openly wicked say, "I believe that the real Christian is the happiest man in the world." I recollect the remark of a certain skeptic, made to myself, in the hour of affliction: "Oh, sir, you Christians have the advantage of us." —*Addresses to Young Men by Rev. Daniel Baker*

Mr. Moody says, "I never knew a case where God used a discouraged man or woman to accomplish any great thing for him. Let a minister go into the pulpit in a discouraged state of mind, and it becomes contagious: it will soon reach the pews, and the whole church will be discouraged. So with a Sabbath-school teacher: I never knew a worker of any kind who was full of discouragement, and who met with great success in the Lord's work. It seems as if God cannot make large use of such men."

When we are weakened by sadness we do not speak attractively. Our statements lack certainty, and energy. We are apt to quarrel over trifles, to be turned aside by discouragements, and in general to do our work badly. Soldiers march best to music, and sailors work most happily when they can join in a cheery note; and I am sure we do the same.

Joyful Christians set the sinner's mouth a watering for the dainties of true religion. When the prodigal returned, he was shod, and clothed, and adorned, but we do not read that the servants were to put meat into his mouth. Yet they were to feed him, and they did so by themselves feasting: "Let *us* eat and be merry." This would be the surest way to induce the poor hungry son to make a meal. If saints were happier, sinners would be far more ready to believe.

36

Now there was a day when the sons of God came to present themselves before the Lord, and Satan came also among them.

—Job 1:6

T is idle to enquire what day this was. Perhaps it was a special Sabbath kept both in earth and heaven, a day of solemn convocation. In the earliest ages the godly gathered together for worship, with the Lord as their center. Both in heaven and earth they so gather: the communion of saints is one. Alas, how soon the evil entered among the righteous! There is no need that the devil should have been in heaven as a place; but looking down from his throne the Lord saw Satan mingling with those who worshipped him; and he had a word for him. In a rightly-ordered congregation even the wicked have their portion.

From Satan's presence among the sons of God we learn:

I. THAT THE MERE ASSEMBLING OF OURSELVES WITH GOD'S PEOPLE IS OF NO VALUE.

1. Very clearly, it is not acceptable worship to God: for nothing that Satan does can be accepted. His presence among the sons of God is presumption, and not reverence.

2. It is not beneficial to the person's own self; for the fallen spirit remained a devil, and acted like one, even in the presence of God. We must come to the Lord by faith, or our worship is dead and unprofitable.

3. It may be the occasion of more sin; for in the assembly Satan belied Job, and plotted his destruction.

From this we learn:

II. THAT THE BEST ASSEMBLIES ARE NOT FREE FROM EVIL ONES.

1. This should make us continue to meet with the saints even though we know of some in the assembly who are false to their profession. Should the sons of God cease to meet because Satan may come among them?

2. This should cause great heart-searching and the prompt inquiry, "Lord, is it I?" Out of twelve apostles one was a devil, and he was with the Lord at his farewell passover.

3. This should make us watchful even while we are praying.

4. This should make ministers faithful, so that the devil may not be at home in the congregation, but may be annoyed by the truth which he hates.

5. This should make us long for the perfect assembly above where there will be no mixture, but a sinless congregation.

III. THAT SATAN MAY ASSEMBLE WITH THE SONS OF GOD.

1. To do mischief to saints:
   - By accusing them before the Lord, even in their holy things.
   - By calling off their thoughts from heavenly concerns, and making them heavy of heart and distracted with care.
   - By setting them to criticize instead of hearing to profit.
   - By sowing dissensions even in their holy service.
   - By exciting pride in preachers, in singers, in those who publicly pray, and in those who give. This is shown in different persons in their style, their tone, their dress, etc.
   - By cooling down their ardor, abating their love, chilling their praise, freezing their prayer, and, in general, killing their zeal and joy.

2. To do mischief to unconverted hearers:
   - By distracting attention from saving truth.
   - By raising doubts; by suggesting skeptical ideas, raising dark questions, and putting the man before the Master.
   - By suggesting delay to those who may be impressed.
   - By quenching prayer, hindering enjoyment, preventing profit, deadening feeling, and robbing God of glory.
   - By taking away the word which had been sown; as birds peck up the seed scattered on the highway.

IV. THAT IT IS POSSIBLE TO BE ALL THE MORE SATANIC FOR ASSEMBLING WITH THE SONS OF GOD.

Satan showed the cloven foot in that sacred gathering more than ever.

1. He was brazenly impudent with his Maker.
2. He railed at God's people, even at one of the best of them, whom the Lord himself called "perfect."
3. He resolved to tempt him, to torture him, and to lead him into rebellion against God, if he could.
   - The devil is here at this moment.
   - Let us not yield to his suggestions.
   - Let us cry to the Lord at once, and trust in the Lord Jesus, who can preserve us from the evil one, even when he is present.

Addenda

As soon as the sower goes forth to sow his seed, the fowls of the air go forth also. The more good is being done in any place, the more surely will Satan oppose it. Unusual provocations will be given to lukewarm professors by those whose zeal is aroused; and so there will be bickerings. Ready offense will be taken by cross-grained brethren during a revival; for things are apt to be a little out of the regular order; and here is another root of bitterness. Unusually large numbers of hypocrites will come forward, just as snails and slugs come creeping forth on a rainy day. Unusual bitterness will be felt by worldlings, and, as a consequence, unusual slanders will be current against the more active assailants of the enemy's kingdom. You cannot destroy a wasp's nest without being attacked in return. Yet this is better than stagnation. In a slumbering church it is the adversary's chief business to rock the cradle, hush all noise, and drive away even a fly which might light upon the sleeper's face; Satan's great dread is lest the church should be aroused from her dreamy slumbers.

Since Satan will enter our assemblies, it behoves us to see (1) that no one of us brings him in our company; (2) that no one gives place to him when he enters the congregation; (3) that, like Abram with the ravenous birds, we drive him away; or (4) that we pray with all the more earnestness, "Deliver us from the evil one."

George Marsh, who was martyred in the reign of Queen Mary, in a letter to some friends at Manchester, wrote: "The servants of God cannot at any time come and stand before God, that is, lead a godly life, and walk innocently before God, but Satan cometh also among them, that is, he daily accuseth, findeth fault, vexeth, persecuteth, and troubleth the godly; for it is the nature and property of the devil always to hurt, and do mischief, unless he be forbidden of God; but unless God doth permit him, he can do nothing at all, not so much as enter into a filthy hog." —*Fox's Book of Martyrs*

Did Satan review himself at the end of that Sabbath? Did he feel any compunction at having defied his Maker, at having intruded among the saints, and at having done them wrong in their own Father's Palace? We suppose not. But hearers, who are not Satan's, would do well to lay to heart the character of any one of their Lord's-days as God sees it. Sabbath sins well weighed and studied furnish plentiful material for repentance. Perhaps if this theme were well applied to the conscience it might arouse the heart to penitence, and lead it to faith.

Luther was in great danger of being stabbed by a Jew; but a friend sent him a portrait of the assassin, and so he was put upon his guard. We ought to be forearmed by being forewarned. The great enemy cannot now pounce upon us at unawares while we are at our devotions; for we are not ignorant of his devices We are bidden to watch as well as pray, to watch before we pray, and to watch when we pray.

37

Why is light given to a man whose way is hid, and whom God hath hedged in?

—Job 3:23

 OB'S case was such that life itself became irksome He wondered why he should be kept alive to suffer. Could not mercy have permitted him to die out of hand? Light is most precious, yet we may come to ask why it is given. See the small value of temporal things, for we may have them and loathe them; we may have the light of life and prefer the darkness of death under the sorrowful conditions which surround us. Hence Job asks, "Wherefore is light given to him that is in misery, and life unto the bitter in soul; which long for death, but it cometh not; and dig for it more than for hid treasures?"

We hope that our hearers are not in Job's condition; but if they are, we desire to comfort them.

I. THE CASE WHICH RAISES THE QUESTION: "A man whose way is hid, and whom God hath hedged in." He has the light of life, but not the light of comfort.

   1. He walks in deep trouble, so deep that he cannot see the bottom of it. Nothing prospers, either in temporals or in spirituals. He is greatly depressed in spirit. He can see no help for his burden, or alleviation of his misery. He cannot see any ground for comfort either in God or in man. "His way is hid."

2. He can see no cause for it. No special sin has been committed. No possible good appears to be coming out of it. When we can see no cause we must not infer that there is none. Judging by the sight of the eyes is dangerous.

3. He cannot tell what to do in it. Patience is hard, wisdom is difficult, confidence scarce, and joy out of reach, while the mind is in deep gloom. Mystery brings misery.

4. He cannot see the way out of it. He seems to hear the enemy say, "They are entangled in the land, the wilderness hath shut them in" (Exod. 14:3). He cannot escape through the hedge of thorn, nor see an end to it: his way is straitened as well as darkened. Men in such a case feel their griefs intensely, and speak too bitterly.

If we were in such misery, we, too, might raise the question; therefore let us consider:

II. THE QUESTION ITSELF: "Why is light given?" etc.

This inquiry, unless prosecuted with great humility and child-like confidence, is to be condemned:

1. It is an unsafe one. It is an undue exaltation of human judgment. Ignorance should shun arrogance. What can we know?

2. It reflects upon God It insinuates that his ways need explanation, and are either unreasonable, unjust, unwise, or unkind.

3. There must be an answer to the question; but it may not be one intelligible to us. The Lord has a "therefore" in answer to every "wherefore"; but he does not often reveal it; for "he giveth not account of any of his matters" (Job 33:13).

4. It is not the most profitable question. Why we are allowed to live in sorrow is a question which we need not answer. We might gain far more by inquiring how to use our prolonged life.

III. ANSWERS WHICH MAY BE GIVEN TO THE QUESTION.

1. Suppose the answer should be, "God wills it." Is not that enough? "I opened not my mouth; because thou didst it" (Ps. 39:9).

2. To an ungodly man sufficient answers are at hand.
   • It is mercy which, by prolonging the light of life, keeps you from worse suffering. For you to desire death is to be eager for hell. Be not so foolish.
   • It is wisdom which restrains you from sin, by hedging up your way, and darkening your spirit. It is better for you to be downcast than dissolute.
   • It is love which calls you to repent. Every sorrow is intended to whip you Godward.

3. To the godly man there are yet more apparent reasons. Your trials are sent:
   • To let you see all that is in you. In deep soul-trouble we discover what we are made of.

- To bring you nearer to God. The hedges shut you up to God; the darkness makes you cling close to him. Life is continued that grace may be increased
- To make you an example to others. Some are chosen to be monuments of the Lord's special dealings; a sort of lighthouse to other mariners.
- To magnify the grace of God. If our way were always bright we could not so well exhibit the sustaining, consoling, and delivering power of the Lord.
- To prepare you for greater prosperity. Without your life being preserved, you could not reach that halcyon period which is reserved for you; nor would you be fitted for it if you were not disciplined by previous trials.
- To make you like your Lord Jesus, who lived in affliction. For him death was no escape from his burdens: he said, "It is finished," before he gave up the ghost.

Be not too ready to ask unbelieving questions.

Be sure that life is never too long.

Be prepared of the Holy Spirit to keep to the way even when it is hid, and to walk on between the hedges when they are not hedges of roses, but fences of briar.

Suggestions

When it is asked why a man is kept in misery on earth, when he would be glad to be released by death, perhaps the following among others may be the reasons: (1) those sufferings may be the very means which are needful to develop the true state of his soul. Such was the case with Job; (2) they may be the proper punishment of sin in the heart, of which the individual was not fully aware, but which may be distinctly seen by God. There may be pride, and the love of ease, and self-confidence, and ambition, and a desire of reputation. Such appear to have been some of the besetting sins of Job; (3) they are needful to teach true submission, and to show whether a man is willing to resign himself to God; (4) they may be the very things which are necessary to prepare the individual to die. At the same time that men often desire death, and feel that it would be a relief, it might be to them the greatest possible calamity. They may be wholly unprepared for it. For a sinner, the grave contains no rest; the eternal world furnishes no repose. One design of God in such sorrows may be to show to the wicked how intolerable will be future pain, and how important it is for them to be ready to die. If they cannot bear the pains and sorrows of a few hours in this short life, how can they endure eternal sufferings? If it is so desirable to be released from the sorrows of the body here, if it is felt that the grave, with all that is repulsive in it, would be a place of repose, how important is it to find some way to be secured from everlasting pains! The true place of release from suffering, for a sinner, is not the grave; it is in the pardoning mercy of God, and in that pure heaven to which he is invited through the blood of the cross. In that holy heaven is the only real repose from suffering and from sin; and heaven will be all the sweeter in proportion to the extremity of pain which is endured on earth. —*Barnes*

38

I have sinned; what shall I do unto thee, O thou preserver of men?
—Job 7:20

 ob could defend himself before men, but he used another tone when bowing before the Lord: there he cried, "I have sinned." The words would suit any afflicted saint; for, indeed, they were uttered by such an one; but they may also be used by the penitent sinner, and we will on this occasion direct them to that use.

1. A CONFESSION. "I have sinned."

In words this is no more than a hypocrite, nay, a Judas, might say. Do not many call themselves "miserable sinners" who are indeed despicable mockers? Yet seeing Job's heart was right his confession was accepted.

1. It was very brief, but yet very full. It was more full in its generality than if he had descended to particulars. We may use it as a summary of our life: "I have sinned." What else is certain in my whole career? This is most sure and undeniable.

2. It was personal. *I* have sinned, whatever others may have done.

3. It was to the Lord. He addresses the confession not to his fellowman but to the Preserver of men.

4. It was a confession wrought by the Spirit. See verse 18, where he ascribes his grief to the visitation of God.

5. It was sincere. No complimentary talk, or matter of ritualistic form, or passing acknowledgment. His heart cried, "I have sinned," and he meant it.

6. It was feeling. He was cut to the quick by it. Read the whole chapter. This one fact, "I have sinned," is enough to brand the soul with the mark of Cain, and burn it with the flames of hell.

7. It was a believing confession. Mingled with much unbelief Job still had faith in God's power to pardon. An unbelieving confession may increase sin.

II. AN INQUIRY. "What shall I do unto thee?"

In this question we see:

1. His willingness to do anything, whatever the Lord might demand, thus proving his earnestness.
2. His bewilderment: he could not tell what to offer, or where to turn; yet something must be done.
3. His surrender at discretion. He makes no conditions, he only begs to know the Lord's terms.
4. The inquiry may be answered negatively.
   - What can I do to escape thee? Thou art all around me.
   - Can past obedience atone? Alas! As I look back I am unable to find anything in my life but sin.
   - Can I bring a sacrifice? Would grief, fasting, long prayers, ceremonies, or self-denial avail? I know they would not.
5. It may be answered evangelically:
   - Confess the sin. "If we confess our sins," etc.
   - Renounce it. By his grace we can "cease to do evil and learn to do well."
   - Obey the message of peace: believe in the Lord Jesus and live.

III. A TITLE. "O thou preserver of men!"

Observer of men, therefore aware of my case, my misery, my confession, my desire for pardon, my utter helplessness.

Preserver of men.

- By his infinite long-suffering refraining from punishment.
- By daily bounties of supply, keeping the ungrateful alive.
- By the plan of salvation, delivering men from going down into the pit, snatching the brands from the burning.
- By daily grace, preventing the backsliding and apostasy of believers.

We must view the way and character of God in Christ if we would find comfort; and from his gracious habit of preserving men we infer that he will preserve us, guilty though we be.

Address upon the point in hand:

- The impenitent, urging them to confession.
- The unconcerned, moving them to enquire, "What must we do to be saved?"
- The ungrateful, exhibiting the preserving goodness of God as a motive for love to him.

Cross Lights

No sooner had Job confessed his sin, but he is desirous to know a remedy. Reprobates can cry, "Peccavi," I have sinned; but then they proceed not to say as here, "What shall I do?" They open their wound, but lay not on a plaster, and so the wounds made by sin are more putrefied, and grow more dangerous. Job would be directed what to do for remedy: he would have pardoning grace and prevailing grace, upon any terms. —*Trapp*

Job was one of those whom Scripture describes as "perfect," yet he cried, "I have sinned." Noah was perfect in his generation, but no drunkard will allow us to forget that he had his fault. Abraham received the command, "Walk before me and be thou perfect," but he was not absolutely sinless. Zecharias and Elizabeth were blameless, and yet there was enough unbelief in Zecharias to make him dumb for nine months. The doctrine of sinless perfection in the flesh is not of God, and he who makes his boast of possessing such perfection has at once declared his own ignorance of himself and of the law of the Lord. Nothing discovers an evil heart more surely than a glorying in its own goodness. He that proclaimeth his own praise publisheth his own shame.

Man is in himself so feeble a creature, that it is a great wonder that he has not long ago been crushed by the elements, exterminated by wild beasts, or extirpated by disease. Omnipotence has bowed itself to his preservation, and compelled all visible things to form the Bodyguard of Man. We believe that the same Preserver of men who has thus guarded the race, watches with equal assiduity over every individual. Our own life contains instances of deliverance so remarkable, that the doctrine of a special providence needs to us no further proof. Kept alive, with death so near, we have been compelled to cry, "This is the finger of God!" Now, this preserving grace is a fair ground for hope as to forgiving love. He who has been thus careful to keep us in being must have designs for our well-being. Marvelously has he protected us, sinners though we be; and, therefore, we need not question his willingness to save us from all iniquity.

The unconditional surrender implied in the question, "What shall I do unto thee?" is absolutely essential from every man who hopes to be saved. God will never raise the siege until we hand out the keys of the city, open every gate, and bid the Conqueror ride through every street, and take possession of the citadel. The traitor must deliver up himself and trust the prince's clemency. Till this is done the battle will continue; for the first requisite for peace with God is complete submission.

39

Who can bring a clean thing out of an unclean? Not one.
—Job 14:4

OB had a deep sense of the need of being clean before God, and indeed he was clean in heart and hand beyond his fellows. But he saw that he could not of himself produce holiness in his own nature, and therefore, he asked this question, and answered it in the negative without a moment's hesitation. The best of men are as incapable as the worst of men of bringing out from human nature that which is not there.

I. MATTERS OF IMPOSSIBILITY IN NATURE.

1. Innocent children from fallen parents.
2. A holy nature from the depraved nature of any one individual.
3. Pure acts from an impure heart.
4. Perfect acts from imperfect men.
5. Heavenly life from nature's moral death.

II. SUBJECTS FOR PRACTICAL CONSIDERATION FOR EVERYONE.

1. That we must be clean to be accepted.
2. That our fallen nature is essentially unclean.
3. That this does not deliver us from our responsibility: we are none the less bound to be clean because our nature inclines us to be unclean; a man who is a rogue to the core of his heart is not thereby delivered from the obligation to be honest.
4. That we cannot do the needful work of cleansing by our own strength.
   - Depravity cannot make itself desirous to be right with God.
   - Corruption cannot make itself fit to speak with God.
   - Unholiness cannot make itself meet to dwell with God.
5. That it will be well for us to look to the Strong for strength, to the Righteous One for righteousness, to the Creating Spirit for new creation. Jehovah brought all things out of nothing, light out of darkness, and order out of confusion; and it is to such a Worker as He that we must look for salvation from our fallen state.

III. PROVISIONS TO MEET THE CASE.

1. The fitness of the gospel for sinners. "When we were yet without strength, in due time Christ died for the ungodly." The gospel contemplates doing that for us which we cannot attempt for ourselves.

2. The cleansing power of the blood. Jesus would not have died if sin could have been removed by other means
3. The renewing work of the Spirit. The Holy Ghost would not regenerate us if we could regenerate ourselves.
4. The omnipotence of God in spiritual creation, resurrection, quickening, preservation, and perfecting. This meets our inability and death.
   - Despair of drawing any good out of the dry well of the creature.
   - Have hope for the utmost cleansing, since God has become the worker of it.

Observations

The word which we render "clean" signifies shining, beautiful: a substance so pure and transparent that we may see through it, so pure that it is free from all spot or defilement, from all blackness and darkness. Who can bring such a clean thing out of an unclean? The Hebrew word (*tama*) comes near the word (*contaminatum*), which is used by the Latins for "unclean," and it speaks the greatest pollution, the sordidness and filthiness of habit, the gore of blood, the muddiness of water, whatever is loathsome or unlovely, noisome or unsightly. All these meet in and make up the meaning of this word, "Who can bring a clean thing out of this uncleanness?" —*Caryl*

The depravity of man is universally hereditary. Adam is said to have begotten "a son in his own likeness," sinful as he was as well as mortal and miserable. Yea, the holiest saint upon earth communicates a corrupt and sinful nature to his child: as the circumcised Jew begat an uncircumcised child; and as the wheat, cleansed and fanned, being sown comes up with a husk (John 3:6). —*Gurnall*

It would be labor in vain to endeavor to cleanse the stream of a polluted fountain. No, the source must be changed, or the flow will be unaltered. Prune the crab as you please, it will not bring forth apples: nor will a thorn under the best cultivation produce figs. Regeneration is a change of nature, but it is by no means a natural change; it is supernatural in its origin, execution, and consequences. It must be wrought by a power from above, since there is neither will nor power to work it from below.

40

For I know that my Redeemer liveth.
—*Job 19:25*

IFFICULTIES of translation very great. We prefer a candid reading to one which might be obtained by pious fraud. It would seem that Job, driven to desperation, fell back upon the truth and justice of God. He declared that he should be vindicated somehow or other, and even if he died there would certainly come a rectification after death. He could not believe that he would be left to remain under the slanderous accusations which had been heaped upon him He was driven by his solemn assurance of the justice and faithfulness of God to believe in a future state, and in a Vindicator who would one day or other set crooked things straight. We may use the words in the most complete evangelical sense, and not be guilty of straining them; indeed, no other sense will fairly set forth the patriarch's meaning. From what other hope could he obtain consolation but from that of future life and glory?

I. JOB HAD A TRUE FRIEND AMID CRUEL FRIENDS. He calls him his
Redeemer, and looks to him in his trouble.

The Hebrew word will bear three renderings, as follows:

1. His Kinsman.
   - Nearest akin of all. No kinsman is so near as Jesus. None so kinned, and none so kind.
   - Voluntarily so. Not forced to be a brother, but so in heart, and by his own choice of our nature: therefore more than brother.
   - Not ashamed to own it. "He is not ashamed to call them brethren" (Heb. 2:11). Even when they had forsaken him he called them "my brethren" (Matt. 28:10).
   - Eternally so. Who shall separate us (Rom. 8:35)?

2. His Vindicator.
   - From every false charge: by pleading the causes of our soul.
   - From every jibe and jest: for he that believeth in him shall not be ashamed or confounded.
   - From true charges, too; by bearing our sin himself and becoming our righteousness, thus justifying us.
   - From accusations of Satan. "The Lord rebuke thee, O Satan!" (Zech. 3:2). "The accuser of our brethren is cast down" (Rev. 12:10).

3. His Redeemer.
   - Of his person from bondage.

- Of his lost estates, privileges, and joys, from the hand of the enemy.
- Redeeming both by price and by power.

II. JOB HAD REAL PROPERTY AMID ABSOLUTE POVERTY. He speaks of "my Redeemer," as much as to say, "Everything else is gone, but my Redeemer is still my own, and lives for me."

He means:

1. I accept him as such, leaving myself in his hands.
2. I have felt somewhat of his power already, and I am confident that all is well with me even now, since he is my Protector.
3. I will cling to him for ever. He shall be my only hope in life and death. I may lose all else, but never the Redemption of my God, the Kinship of my Savior.

III. JOB HAD A LIVING KINSMAN AMID A DYING FAMILY. "My Redeemer liveth."

He owned the great Lord as ever living:

- As "the Everlasting Father," to sustain and solace him.
- As Head of his house, to represent him.
- As Intercessor, to plead in heaven for him.
- As Defender, to preserve his rights on earth.
- As his Righteousness, to clear him at last.

What have we to do with the dead Christ of the church of Rome? *Our* Redeemer lives.

What with the departed Christ of Unitarians? Our divine Vindicator abides in the power of an endless life.

IV. JOB HAD ABSOLUTE CERTAINTY AMID UNCERTAIN AFFAIRS. "I know." He had no sort of doubt upon that matter. Everything else was questionable, but this was certain.

- His faith made him certain. Faith brings sure evidence; it substantiates what it receives, and makes us know.
- His trials could not make him doubt. Why should they? They touched not the relationship of his God, or the heart of his Redeemer, or the life of his Vindicator.
- His difficulties could not make him fear failure on this point, for *the life* of his Redeemer was a source of deliverance which lay out of himself, and was never doubtful
- His caviling friends could not move him from the assured conviction that the Lord would vindicate his righteous cause.

While Jesus lives our characters are safe. Happy he who can say, "I know that my Redeemer liveth."

- Have you this great knowledge?
- Do you act in accordance with such an assurance?
- Will you not at this hour devoutly adore your loving Kinsman?

Rough Thoughts

"*My Redeemer.*" The word has the general meaning "ransomer," "deliverer," and specially denotes one who takes up a man's cause and vindicates his rights, either by avenging him on his foes, or by restoring him or his heirs to possessions of which he has been defrauded. Job has already expressed a wish that there might be an *umpire* between him and God: then he goes further, and desires an *advocate*: then declares that he has a witness, one who exactly knows his rights, in heaven: then calls upon God himself to be his advocate. He now takes a stronger position, and declares his certainty that there is One who adds to all these conditions that which gives them solidity, and assures his final triumph: there lives One who will vindicate his righteousness, and clear his cause completely. —*Speaker's Commentary*

In times of sharp trials believers are: (1) driven out of themselves to look to their God, their Redeemer; (2) driven to look within themselves for a knowledge sure and unquestioning—"I know"; (3) driven to hold by personal faith to that which is set forth in the covenant of grace—"my Redeemer"; (4) driven to live much upon the unseen—the living Redeemer, and his advent in the latter day.

Tried saints, when greatly in the dark, have been led to great discoveries of comfortable truth. "Necessity is the mother of invention." Here Job found an argument from the justice of God for his own comfort. God could not leave his sincere servant under slander: therefore if he died undefended, and years passed away so that the worms consumed his body, yet a Vindicator would arise, and the maligned and injured Job would be cleared. Thus the Spirit revealed to the afflicted patriarch a future state, a living Next-of-Kin, a future judgment, a resurrection, and an eternal justification of saints. Great light came in through a narrow window, and Job was an infinite gainer by his temporary losses.

A weak faith is glad to look off from all difficulties, for it shrinks back at them: as Martha, considering Lazarus was four days dead, and began to putrefy, her faith began to fail her; it was too late now to remove the gravestone. But Faith in its strength considers all these, urges these impossibilities, and yet overcomes them: as Elijah, in his dispute with Baal's priests, took all the disadvantages to himself. "Pour on water," said he; and again, "Pour on more water"; faith shall fetch fire from heaven to enflame the sacrifice. "So," saith Job, "let me die, and rot, and putrefy in the grave, nay, let the fire burn my body, or the sea swallow it, or wild beasts devour it, yet it shall be restored to me; death shall be *prœdœ suœ custos*, like the lion that killed the prophet, and then stood by his body, and did not consume it." Job's faith laughs at impossibilities, is ashamed to talk of difficulties; with Abraham, considers not his own dead body, but believes above and against hope; knew God would restore it. —*R. Brownrig*

These words are ushered in with a solemn preface, containing in them some notable truth: "Oh, that my words were now written! Oh, that they were printed in a book! That they were graven with an iron pen and lead in the rock for ever! For I know," etc. Surely such a passionate preface will become no other matter so well as the great mystical truths of the Christian faith.

Faith is, or should be, strongly persuaded of what it believeth. It is an evidence, not a conjecture; not a surmise, but a firm assurance. We should certainly know what we believe: "We know that thou art a Teacher come from God" (John 3:2). "We believe, and are sure, that thou art that Christ, the Son of the living God" (John 6:69). "We know that we have a building of God" (1 Cor. 5:1). "We know that we shall see him as he is!" (1 John 3:2). "Be ye steadfast, unmoveable, always abounding in the work of the Lord, forasmuch as ye know that your labor is not in vain in the Lord" (1 Cor. 15:58). Invisible things revealed by God should be certainly known, because God hath told us that such clear, firm apprehensions become us. Faith is not a bare conjecture, but a certain knowledge; not "we think," "we hope well," but "we know" is the language of faith. It is not a bare possibility we go upon, nor a probable opinion, but a certain, infallible truth I put you upon this, partly because we have a great argument in the text. If Job could see it so long before it came to pass, should not we see it now? Believers of old shame us, who live in the clear sunshine of the gospel Job lived long before the gospel was revealed; the redemption of souls was at that time a great mystery, being sparingly revealed to a few; only one of a thousand could bring this message to a condemned sinner, that God had found a ransom (Job 33:23). —*Manton*

If we are sure about anything, let it be concerning the Redeemer. If we have an indefeasible claim to anything, let it be to our Redeemer. If we cling with tenacity to any truth, let it be our Redeemer's resurrection and life. Everything hangs here; this is the keystone of the gospel, the foundation of our faith, and the pinnacle of our hope: "Because I live ye shall live also." Oh for more of Job's certainty, even if the cost were Job's afflictions!

41

They are of those that rebel against the light.
—*Job 24:13*

HESE evidently had the light, and this should be esteemed as no small privilege, since to wander on the dark mountains is a terrible curse. Yet this privilege may turn into an occasion of evil.

Most of us have received light in several forms, such as instruction, conscience, reason, revelation, experience, the Holy Spirit. The degree of light differs, but we have each received some measure thereof.

Light has a sovereignty in it, so that to resist it is to rebel against it. God has given it to be a display of himself, for God is light; and he has clothed it with a measure of his majesty and power of judgment.

Rebellion against light has in it a high degree of sin. It might be virtue to rebel against darkness, but what shall be said of those who withstand the light, resisting truth, holiness, and knowledge?

I. DETECT THE REBELS.

- Well-instructed persons, who have been accustomed to teach others, and yet turn aside to evil: these are grievous traitors.
- Children of Christian parents who sin against their early training; upon whom prayer and entreaty, precept and example are thrown away.
- Hearers of the word, who quench convictions deliberately, frequently, and with violence.
- Men with keen moral sense, who rush on, despite the reins of conscience which should restrain them.
- Lewd professors who, nevertheless, talk orthodoxy and condemn others, thereby assuredly pronouncing their own doom.

II. DESCRIBE THE FORMS OF THIS REBELLION.

- Some refuse light, being unwilling to know more than would be convenient; therefore they deny themselves time for thought, absent themselves from sermons, neglect godly reading, shun pious company, avoid reproof, etc.
- Others scoff and fight against it, calling light darkness, and darkness light. Infidelity, ribaldry, persecution, and such like, become their resort and shelter.
- Persons run contrary to it in their lives; of set purpose, or through willful carelessness. Walking away from the light is rebelling against it. Setting up your own wishes in opposition to the laws of morality and holiness, is open revolt against the light. Many presume upon their

possession of light, imagining that knowledge and orthodox belief will save them.

- Many darken it for others, hindering its operations among men, hiding their own light under a bushel, ridiculing the efforts of others, etc.
- All darkness is a rebellion against light. Let us "have no fellowship with the unfruitful works of darkness."

III. DENOUNCE THE PUNISHMENT OF THIS REBELLION.
- To have the light removed.
- To lose eyes to see it even when present.
- To remain unforgiven, as culprits blindfolded for death, as those do who resist the light of the Holy Spirit.
- To sin with tenfold guilt, with awful willfulness of heart.
- To descend for ever into that darkness which increases in blackness throughout eternity.

IV. DECLARE THE FOLLY OF THIS REBELLION.
- Light is our best friend, and it is wisdom to obey it: to resist it is to rebel against our own interest.
- Light triumphs still. Owls hoot, but the moon shines. Opposition to truth and righteousness is useless, it may even promote that which it aims to prevent.
- Light would lead to more light. Consent to it, for it will be beneficial to your own soul.
- Light would lead to heaven, which is the center of light.
- Light even here would give peace, comfort, rest, holiness, and communion with God.
- Let us not rebel against light, but yield to its lead; yea, leap forward to follow its blessed track.
- Let us become the allies of light, and spread it. It is a noble thing to live as light-bearers of "the Lord and Giver of Light."
- Let us walk in the light, as God is in the light; and so our personal enjoyment will support our Life-work. Light must be our life if our life is to be light.

Lights

Off the coast of New Zealand, a captain lost his vessel by steering in the face of the warning light, till he dashed upon the rock immediately beneath the lighthouse. He said that he was asleep; but this did not restore the wreck, nor save him from condemnation. It is a terrible thing for rays of gospel light to guide a man to his doom.

The sins of the godly have this aggravation in them, that they sin against clearer illumination than the wicked. "They are of those that rebel against the light" (Job 24:13). Light is there taken figuratively for knowledge. It cannot be denied that the wicked sin knowingly; but the godly have a light beyond other men, such a divine, penetrating light as no hypocrite can attain to. They have better eyes to see sin than others; and for them to meddle with sin, and embrace this dunghill, must needs provoke God, and make the fury rise up in his face. Oh, therefore, you that are the people of God, flee from sin; your sins are more enhanced, and have worse aggravations in them, than the sins of the unregenerate. —*Thomas Watson*

Sins of ignorance are truly sins, for every lawgiver takes it for granted that his subjects seek to know his laws. But the deliberate commission of known trespass, and the willful neglect of known duty, have in them elements of great disloyalty. He who knew his Lord's will and did it not was beaten with many stripes. If a man puts his hand into the fire knowing that it burns, no one will pity him; if he wantonly enters a pesthouse, no one can wonder that he is smitten with disease. When the ice is marked "DANGEROUS," the warning should be sufficient for any reasonable man; and when the notice is repeated at every corner, and set up in great capital letters, he who ventures on the rotten ice will be not only a fool but a suicide, should he perish in his rashness.

42

Will he always call upon God?
—*Job 27:10*

 HYPOCRITE may be a very neat imitation of a Christian. He professes to know God, to converse with him, to be dedicated to his service, and to invoke his protection: he even practices prayer, or at least feigns it. Yet the cleverest counterfeit fails somewhere, and may be discovered by certain signs. The test is here: "Will he always call upon God?"

I. WILL HE PRAY AT ALL SEASONS OF PRAYER?
- Will he pray in private? Or is he dependent upon the human eye, and the applause of men?
- Will he pray if forbidden? Daniel did so. Will he?
- Will he pray in business? Will he practice ejaculatory prayer? Will he look for hourly guidance?
- Will he pray in pleasure? Will he have a holy fear of offending with his tongue? Or will company make him forget his God?
- Will he pray in darkness of soul? Or will he sulk in silence?

II. WILL HE PRAY CONSTANTLY?

If he exercises the occasional *act* of prayer, will he possess the spirit of prayer which never ceases to plead with the Lord? We ought to be continually in prayer, because we are:

- Always dependent for life, both temporal and spiritual, upon God.

> Long as they live should Christians pray,
> For only while they pray they live.

- Always needing something, nay, a thousand things.
- Always receiving, and therefore always needing fresh grace wherewith to use the blessing worthily.
- Always in danger. Seen or unseen danger is always near, and none but God can cover our head.
- Always weak, inclined to evil, apt to catch every infection of soul-sickness, "ready to perish" (Isa. 27:13).
- Always needing strength, for suffering, learning, song, or service.
- Always sinning. Even in our holy things sin defiles us, and we need constant washing.
- Always weighted with other men's needs. Especially if rulers, pastors, teachers, parents.
- Always having the cause of God near our heart if we are right, and in its interests finding crowds of reasons for prayer.

III. WILL HE PRAY IMPORTUNATELY?

- If no answer comes, will he persevere? Is he like the brave horse who will pull at a post at his master's bidding?
- If a rough answer comes, will he plead on? Does he know how to wrestle with the angel, and give tug for tug?
- If no one else prays, will he be singular, and plead on against wind and tide?
- If God answer him by disappointment and defeat, will he feel that delays are not denials, and still pray?

IV. WILL HE CONTINUE TO PRAY THROUGHOUT THE WHOLE OF LIFE?

- The hypocrite soon gives up prayer under certain circumstances.
- If he is in trouble, he will not pray, but will run to human helpers.
- If he gets out of trouble, he will not pray, but quite forget his vows.
- If men laugh at him, he will not dare to pray.
- If men smile on him, he will not care to pray.
1. He grows formal. He is half asleep, not watchful for the answer. He falls into a dead routine of forms and words.

2. He grows weary. He can make a spurt, but he cannot keep it up. Short prayers are sweet to him.
3. He grows secure. Things go well and he sees no need of prayer; or he is too holy to pray.
4. He grows infidel, and fancies it is all useless, dreams that prayer is not philosophical.

Illustrations

We have heard of a child who said her prayers, and then added, "Good bye, God; we are all going to Saratoga, and pa and ma won't go to meeting, or pray any more till we come back again." We fear that many who go to the seaside, or other holiday resorts, give God the go-by in much the same manner.

There was a celebrated poet who was an atheist, or at least professed to be so. According to him there was no God—the belief in a God was a delusion, prayer a base superstition, and religion but the iron fetters of a rapacious priest-hood So he held when sailing over the unruffled surface of the Ægean Sea. But the scene changed; and with the scene his creed. The heavens began to scowl on him; and the deep uttered an angry voice, and, as if in astonishment at this God-denying man, *"lifted up his hands on high."* The storm increased until the ship became unmanageable. She drifted before the tempest. The terrible cry, "Breakers ahead!" was soon heard; and how they trembled to see death seated on the horrid reef, waiting for his prey! A few moments more, and the crash comes. They are overwhelmed in the devouring sea? No. They were saved by a singular Providence. Like apprehended evils, which in a Christian's experience prove to be blessings, the wave, which flung them forward on the horrid reef, came on in such mountain volume as to bear and float them over into the safety of deep and ample sea room. But ere that happened, a companion of the atheist—who, seated on the prow, had been taking his last regretful look of heaven and earth, sea and sky—turned his eyes down upon the deck, and there, among Papists, who told their beads and cried to the Virgin, he saw the atheist prostrated with fear. The tempest had blown away his fine-spun speculations like so many cobwebs, and he was on his knees, imploring God for mercy. —*Guthrie*

The hypocrite is not for prayer always. He will pray when he seeth his own time. He will stint God in time as well as in measure. He will be master, not only of his own time, but of God's too. "When will the Sabbath be gone?" (Amos 8:5). Sometimes he will delight himself in the Almighty: but will he always call upon God? Everyone that knows him can make the answer for him, "No, he will not": especially in secret, where none but God's eye can behold him. Upon some extraordinary occasions, in extraordinary cases, he may seem very devout; but he is modest, he will not trouble God too far, nor too often. Ahaz will not ask a sign, even when God bids him, lest he should tempt the Lord (Isa. 7:10-12): a great piece of modesty in show; but a sure symptom of infidelity. He would not ask a sign because he could not believe the thing; not to avoid troubling of God, but himself. He seems very mannerly, but shows himself very malapert.

Thus, this hypocrite will serve God only by fits and starts, when he himself lists. He never troubles God but when God troubles him. In health, wealth, peace, he can comfort himself. He never prays but in trouble: in his affliction he will seek God early (Hos. 5:15). God is fain to go away, and return to his place, else this man would never look after him. When God hath touched him, he acquaints God with his misery, but when times grow better with him, he excludes God from his mirth. —*Samuel Crook*

43
Should it be according to thy mind?
—Job 34:33

 HE verse is written in language of the most ancient kind, which is but little understood. Moreover, it is extremely pithy and sententious, and hence it is obscure. The sense given in our version is, however, that which sums up the other translations, and we prefer to adhere to it.

I. DO MEN REALLY THINK THAT THINGS SHOULD BE ACCORDING TO THEIR MIND?

1. Concerning God. Their ideas of him are according to what they think he should be; but could he be God at all if he were such as the human mind would have him to be?
2. Concerning providence on a large scale, would men re-write history? Do they imagine that their arrangements would be an improvement upon infinite wisdom? In their own case they would arrange all matters selfishly. Should it be so?
3. Concerning the Gospel, its doctrines, its precepts, its results, should men have their own way? Should the atonement be left out, or the statement of it be modified to suit them?
4. Concerning the Church. Should they be head and lord?
   - Should their liberal ideas erase inspiration?
   - Should Baptism and the Lord's Supper be distorted to gratify them? Should gaudy ceremonies drive the Lord's homely ordinances out of doors? Should priestcraft crush out spiritual life? Should taste override divine commands?

- Should the Ministry exist only for their special consolation, and be molded at their bidding?

II. WHAT LEADS THEM TO THINK SO?
1. Self-importance, and selfishness.
2. Self-conceit, and pride.
3. A murmuring spirit which must needs grumble at everything.
4. Want of faith in Christ leading to a doubt of the power of his gospel.
5. Want of love to God, souring the mind and leading it to kick at a thing simply because the Lord prescribes it.

III. WHAT A MERCY THAT THINGS ARE NOT ACCORDING TO THEIR MIND!
1. God's glory would be obscured.
2. Many would suffer to enable one man to play the Dictator.
3. We should, any one of us, have an awful responsibility resting upon us if our own mind had the regulation of affairs.
4. Our temptations would be increased. We should be proud if we succeeded, and despairing if we met with failure.
5. Our desires would become more greedy.
6. Our sins would be uncorrected; for we should never allow a rod or a rebuke to come at us.
7. There would be universal strife; for every man would want to rule and command (James 4:5). If it ought to be according to your mind, why not according to mine?

IV. LET US CHECK THE SPIRIT WHICH SUGGESTS SUCH CONCEIT.
1. It is impracticable; for things can never be as so many different minds would have them.
2. It is unreasonable; for things ought not so to be.
3. It is unchristian; for even Christ Jesus pleased not himself, but cried, "Not as I will" (Matt. 26:39).
4. It is atheistic; for it dethrones God to set up puny man.
   - Pray God to bring your mind to his will.
   - Cultivate admiration for the arrangements of the Divine mind.
   - Above all, accept the gospel as it is, and accept it now.

Helps
Should it be according to thy mind? Many appear to think so. If we may judge by their conduct, they think that the Most High should have consulted their ease, their fancy, and their aggrandizement. The gospel is not just what they would like it to be. Providence does not work as they desire. Few things are exactly as they should be.

Complaining mortal! Should it be according to thy mind? Is not thy mind carnal? Is it not selfish? Is it not prejudiced? If it were according to thy mind, would not God's glory be obscured? Would not others suffer? Would not thy lusts be fed? Would not thy temptations be stronger? Would not thy danger be greater?

Is not thy God wiser, kinder, and holier than thou art? Does he not love justice? Are not his mercies over all his works? True, you may be afflicted, you may be poor, you may be sickly; what then? You are wishing for health, for a competency, for freedom from trials; but, "should it be according to thy mind?"

Beloved, let us guard against such a spirit. It is common, but it is unreasonable, it is criminal, it is dangerous. The thing is impracticable. Your God must govern, he is wonderful in counsel, and excellent in working. His ways are just, his plans are wise, his designs are merciful, and when the work is complete, every part will reflect his glory. —*James Smith*

We are all very apt to believe in Providence when we get our own way; but when things go awry, we think, if there is a God, He is in Heaven and not upon the earth. The cricket, in the spring, builds his house in the meadow, and chirps for joy because all is going so well with him. But when he hears the sound of the plow a few furrows off, and the thunder of the oxen's tread, then his sky begins to darken, and his young heart fails him. By-and-by the plow comes crunching along, turns his dwelling bottom-side up, and as he goes rolling over and over, without a house and without a home, "Oh," he says, "the foundations of the world are breaking up, and everything is hastening to destruction." But the husbandman, as he walks behind the plow, does he think the foundations of the world are breaking up? No. He is thinking only of the harvest that is to follow in the wake of the plow; and the cricket, if it will but wait, will see the husbandman's purpose. My hearers, we are all like crickets. When we get our own way, we are happy and contented. When we are subjected to disappointment, we become the victims of despair. —*Dr. A. B. Jack, in "The Preacher and Homiletic Monthly"*

Man would have God go according to his mind in chastening and afflicting him. He would have God correct him only in such a kind, in such a manner and measure as he would choose. He saith in his heart, If God would correct me in this or that, I could bear it; but I do not like to be corrected in the present way. One saith, If God would smite me in my estate I could bear it, but not in my body; another saith, If God should smite me with sickness, I could bear it, but not in my children; or, If God would afflict me only in such a degree, I could submit; but my heart can hardly yield to so great a measure of affliction. Thus we would have it according to our minds as to the measure or the continuance of our afflictions. We would be corrected for so many days; but to have months of vanity and years of trouble, is not according to our mind.

Man would have God govern (not only himself, but) the whole world according to his mind. Man hath much of this in him. Luther wrote to Melancthon, when he was so exceedingly troubled at the providence of God in the world: "Our brother Philip is to be admonished that he would forbear governing the world." We can hardly let God alone to rule that world which Himself alone hath made. —*Caryl*

44

Should it be according to thy mind? He will recompense it, whether thou refuse, or whether thou choose; and not I: therefore speak what thou knowest.

—Job 34:33

 T is never wise to dispute with God. Especially upon the matter of salvation. No sinner seeking pardon should be so foolish as to dispute with his Sovereign Savior.

I. A QUESTION. "Should it be according to thy mind?"

Should salvation be planned to suit you? Should beggars be choosers? Should these who profess penitence become dictators?

1. What is it to which you object?
   - Is there something objectionable in the plan of salvation? Is it too much of grace? Is it too simple? Is it too general? Is it too humbling? Do you dislike the method of substitution? Do you rebel against the Deity of the Savior?
   - Is there a cause of stumbling in the working out of salvation? Does the cross scandalize you? Do you dislike the work of the Holy Spirit? Are his operations too radical? Is regeneration too spiritual? Is holiness irksome?
   - Are its requirements too exact? Too Puritanical?
   - Are its statements too humiliating? Too denunciatory?
   - Is its term of service too protracted? Would you prefer a temporary faith? A transient obedience?
2. Should not God have his way? He is the Donor of salvation; shall he not do as he wills with his own?
3. Is not God's way best? Is not the Infinitely Good the best Controller, the best Ruler of the feast?
4. Should it be according to a mind that is ignorant? Fickle? Feeble? Selfish? Short-sighted? Is not yours such?
5. Why is your mind to be supreme? Why not another man's mind? You see the absurdity in that case; why not in your own?

II. A WARNING. "He will recompense it, whether thou refuse, or whether thou choose."

Whether sinners accept or refuse salvation:

1. God will perform his pleasure.
2. God will punish sin.
3. God will glorify Christ by conversions.
4. God will magnify his own name before an assembled universe.
5. God will carry on his work of mercy in the one way which he has chosen, and he will not alter one jot or tittle to please vainglorious man.

III. A PROTEST. "And not I."

1. I am not the person to be disputed with: you are not dealing with man but with God. "He will recompense it . . . and not I." Therefore there is no use in deceit or in defiance: thus you may overcome a mortal, but not the Eternal.
2. I will not be responsible for you. You yourself are sinning, and must answer for it, and no friend or minister can stand for you when God recompenses your sin upon you.
3. I will not share in your rebellion. "Not I." We must keep clear of complicity with the obstinate man who dictates to his God. It is a grand thing to be able to say distinctly, "Not I."

IV. AN INVITATION. "Therefore speak what thou knowest."

1. Exercise your freedom. Choose or reject; it is at your own peril.
2. Exercise your reason. Be sure that you know by personal observation and experience, and let your decision be based upon unquestionable knowledge.
3. Exercise your influence and speak as you think; but mind what you do; for an account must be given of your words.
4. Better exercise your truthfulness and bear witness to facts, rather than criticize the methods of the Lord.
   - Do not cavil at God's methods of grace, for certainly you cannot alter them, and if you could alter them you would not improve them.
   - Join not with others in their cavilings. It may be fashionable to criticize and doubt, but it is mischievous, presumptuous, and rebellious. Doubters may be in great repute among their own class, but they are poor creatures after all. Those who are wiser than God are fools in capitals.
   - Decide for yourself, but let it be with knowledge and thought; and when you have decided do not think that everybody else is to bow to your judgment. Bow before the Lord, and let your judgment be more eager to obey the truth for itself, than to rule over others.

45

Who hath divided a watercourse for the overflowing of waters, or a way for the lightning of thunder; To cause it to rain on the earth, where no man is; on the wilderness, wherein there is no man; To satisfy the desolate and waste ground; and to cause the bud of the tender herb to spring forth?

—Job 38:25–27

 OD challengeth man to compare with his Maker even in the one matter of the rain. Can he create it? Can he send a shower upon the desert, to water the lone herbs which else would perish in the burning heat? No, he would not even think of doing such a thing. That generous act cometh of the Lord alone. We shall work out a parallel between grace and rain.

I. GOD ALONE GIVETH RAIN, AND THE SAME IS TRUE OF GRACE.

- We say of rain and of grace, God is the sole Author of it.
- He devised and prepared the channel by which it comes to earth. He hath "divided a watercourse for the overflowing of waters." The Lord makes a way for grace to reach his people.
- He directs each drop, and gives each blade of grass its own drop of dew, to every believer his portion of grace.
- He moderates the force, so that it does not beat down or drown the tender herb. Grace comes in its own gentle way. Conviction, enlightenment, etc., are sent in due measure.
- He holds it in his power. Absolutely at his own will does God bestow either rain for the earth, or grace for the soul.

II. RAIN FALLS IRRESPECTIVE OF MEN, AND SO DOES GRACE.

- Grace waits not man's observation. As the rain falls where no man is, so grace courts not publicity.
- Nor his cooperation. It "tarrieth not for man, nor waiteth for the sons of men" (Mic. 5:7).
- Nor his prayers. Grass calls not for rain, yet it comes. "I am found of them that sought me not" (Isa. 65:1).
- Nor his merits. Rain falls on the waste ground.

> Ah, grace, into unlikeliest hearts,
> It is thy wont to come;
> The glory of thy light to find
> In darkest spots a home.

III. RAIN FALLS WHERE WE MIGHT LEAST HAVE EXPECTED IT.

- It falls where there is no trace of former showers, even upon the desolate wilderness: so does grace enter hearts which had hitherto been unblessed, where great need was the only plea which rose to heaven (Isa. 35:7).
- It falls where there seems nothing to repay the boon. Many hearts are naturally as barren as the desert (Isa. 35:6).
- It falls where the need seems insatiable, "to satisfy the desolate." Some cases seem to demand an ocean of grace, but the Lord meets the need; and his grace falls where the joy and glory are all directed to God by grateful hearts. Twice we are told that the rain falls "where no man is." When conversion is wrought of the Lord, no man is seen. The Lord alone is exalted.

IV. THIS RAIN IS MOST VALUED BY LIFE.

- The rain gives joy to seeds and plants in which there is life. Budding life knows of it; the tenderest herb rejoices in it. So is it with those who begin to repent, who feebly believe, and thus are just alive.
- The rain causes development. Grace also perfects grace. Buds of hope grow into strong faith. Buds of feeling expand into love. Buds of desire rise to resolve. Buds of confession come to open avowal. Buds of usefulness swell into fruit.
- The rain causes health and vigor of life. Is it not so with grace?
- The rain creates the flower with its color and perfume, and God is pleased. The full outgrowth of renewed nature cometh of grace, and the Lord is well pleased therewith.
- Let us acknowledge the sovereignty of God as to grace.
- Let us cry to him for grace.
- Let us expect him to send it, though we may feel sadly barren, and quite out of the way of the usual means of grace.

To Interest the Hearer

A lady traveling in Palestine writes: "Rain began to fall in torrents; Mohammed, our groom, threw a large Arab cloak over me, saying, 'May Allah preserve you, O lady! while he is blessing the fields.'"

Oh, how pleasant are the effects of rain to languishing plants, to make them green and beautiful, lively and strong, fragrant and delightful! So the effects of Christ's influences are most desirable to drooping souls, for enlightening and enlivening them, for confirming and strengthening them, for comforting and enlarging them, for appetizing and satisfying them, transforming and beautifying them. —*John Willison*

Be not to me as a cloud without rain, lest I be to thee like a tree without fruit. —*Spurstowe*

My stock lies dead, and no increase
Doth my dull husbandry improve:
O let thy graces without cease
           Drop from above!

The dew cloth every morning fall;
And shall the dew outstrip thy Dove?
The dew, for which grass cannot call,
           Drop from above!
              —George Herbert

The grass springs up, the bud opens, the leaf expands, the flowers breathe forth their fragrance as if they were under the most careful cultivation. All this must be the work of God, since it cannot even be pretended that man is there to produce these effects. Perhaps one would be more deeply impressed with a sense of the presence of God in the pathless desert, or on the boundless prairie, where no man is, than in the most splendid park, or the most tastefully cultivated garden which man could make. In the one case, the hand of God alone is seen; in the other, we are constantly admiring the skill of man. *—Barnes*

The careful providence of God extends itself to all places, even to places uninhabited. This consideration may strengthen our dependence on God, though we are brought into a wilderness condition, where there is no man to pity us, or give us a morsel of bread. Surely the Lord that feeds the wild beasts where there is no man, can and will provide for his own people, when the hearts of all men are shut up against them; he can make the fowls of the air and the beasts of the earth to bring them food, as the ravens did to Elijah. *—Caryl*

This should tend to humble human pride: humanity is not the only creature that God careth for. Man is not the center and pivot of the world. God cares for oxen, birds, insects, and everything that lives. He works the mystic machinery of heaven to water meadows untrodden of the foot of man. No flower is born to blush unseen and waste its sweetness; for God sees it, and that is enough. The earth is the Lord's and the fullness thereof, and man is but one servitor out of the many which are created for God's pleasure. Let him take his place as one among many servants, and no longer dream that all things are made for him, and that they are wasted if he does not derive some benefit from them.

46

For the needy shall not always be forgotten; the expectation of the poor shall not perish for ever.

—Psalm 9:18

HE practical value of a text very much depends upon the man to whom it comes The song of the troubadour was charming to Richard Coeur-de-Lion because he knew the responsive verses. The trail is full of meaning to the Indian, for his quick eye knows how to follow it; it would not mean a tithe as much to a white man. The sight of the lighthouse is cheering to the mariner, for from it he gathers his whereabouts. So will those who are spiritually poor and needy eagerly lay hold on this promise, prize it, and live upon it with content.

It is literally true that the needy are remembered of God, and though they may be overlooked by man's laws, the Lord will rectify that error at the last. In better times also he will so order governments that they shall look with peculiar interest upon the poor. Using the text spiritually we see:

I. TWO BITTER EXPERIENCES ENDED.

1. "The needy shall not always be forgotten." You have been forgotten-
   - By former friends and admirers.
   - In arrangements made, and plans projected.
   - In judgments formed, and in praises distributed.
   - In help estimated, and reliance expressed.

In fact, you have not been a factor in the calculation; you have been forgotten as a dead man out of mind. This has wounded you deeply, for there was a time when you were consulted among the first.

This will not be so always.

2. "The expectation of the poor shall not perish for ever." You have been disappointed:
   - In your natural expectation from justice, gratitude, relationship, age, sympathy, charity, etc.
   - In your confidence in man.
   - In your judgment of yourself.
   - In your expectations of providence.

This disappointment shall only be temporary. Your expectation shall not perish for ever: you shall yet receive more than you expected.

II. TWO SAD FEARS REMOVED, FEARS WHICH ARE NORMALLY SUGGESTED BY WHAT YOU HAVE ALREADY EXPERIENCED.

1. Not for ever shall you be forgotten:
   - You shall not meet with final forgetfulness
   - In the day of severe trouble.
   - In the night of grief and alarm for sin.
   - In the hour of death.
2. Nor shall your expectation perish:
   - Your weakness shall not frustrate the power of God.
   - Your sin shall not dry up the grace of God.
   - Your constitutional infirmities shall not cause your overthrow.
   - Your future trials shall not be too much for you.

III. TWO SWEET PROMISES GIVEN.

1. "Not always be forgotten;" you shall not be overlooked:
   - In the arrangements of providence.
   - At the mercy-seat, when you are pleading.
   - From the pulpit, and in the Word, when your soul is hungering.
   - At the Breaking of Bread, when you long for communion with your Lord.
   - In your sufferings and service, when to be thought of by the Lord will be your main consolation.
   - By the angels, or by any other spiritual agencies.
   - By the Father, Son, or Holy Ghost.
2. "Expectation shall not perish for ever." You shall not be disappointed:
   - Peace shall visit your heart.
   - Sin shall be vanquished without and within.
   - Mercy shall deliver in trial and out of trial.
   - Assurance shall be gained, and all its strong confidence.
   - Eminent joys shall be obtained, and an abundant entrance into glory.
   - Let the poor man hope in God.
   - Let him feast on the future if he find the present to be scant.
   - Above all, let him rest in the promise of a faithful God.

Illuminators

The pain of being forgotten is forcibly expressed in the words ascribed by Cowper to Alexander Selkirk in his solitude:

> My friends, do they now and then send
> A wish or a thought after me?
> O tell me I yet have a friend
> Though a friend I am never to see.

An aged Christian, lying, on his death-bed in a state of such extreme weakness that he was often entirely unconscious of all around him, was asked the cause of his perfect peace. He replied, "When I am able to think, I think of Jesus; and when I am unable to think of him, I know he is thinking of me."

Thirty years ago, before the Lord caused me to wander from my father's house and from my native place, I put my mark upon this passage in Isaiah: "Thou shalt know that I am the Lord" (Isa. 49:23.) Of the many books I now possess, the Bible that bears this mark is the only one that belonged to me at that time. It now lies before me, and I find that, although the hair which then was dark as night has meanwhile become as sable silvered, the ink which marked this text has grown into intensity of blackness as the time advanced, corresponding with, and in fact recording, the growing intensity of the conviction that "they shall not be ashamed" who wait for Thee. I believed it then, but I know it now, and I can write "Probatum est" with my whole heart over against the symbol which that mark is to me of my ancient faith. . . . Under many perilous circumstances, in many most trying scenes, amid faintings within and fears without, and under tortures that rend the heart, and troubles that crush it down, I have waited for Thee, and lo I stand this day as One not ashamed —*Dr. John Kitto*

In choosing a minister, and in all other church acts, let us be sure to remember the poor of the flock; they should, in fact, have double consideration, for the Lord would not have them to be overlooked. Do not let them suppose that they are forgotten.

Let us beware of disappointing a needy person. He sets great store by a promise when he greatly needs the help, and if it does not come in due time it causes him sharp distress. Let us never disappoint one of the Lord's poor, for the Lord will never do so himself.

What recompenses there will be in the eternal state, and what changes of position! Reputations will have a resurrection as well as bodies. Dishonor and neglect shall be rewarded with glory and honor. Disappointment through unjust withholding shall be doubly repaid by surprises of unlooked-for happiness. The wheel will turn, and that part of it which touched the dust shall mount aloft. Those words, "not always," are a wonderful abatement to present ingratitude, and those, "not for ever," are an equal *solatium* under this life's trials.

47

The law of the Lord is perfect, converting the soul; the testimony of the Lord is sure, making wise the simple.

—Psalm 19:7

REES are known by their fruit, and books by their effect upon the mind. It is not the elegance of its diction but the excellence of its influence by which a book is to be estimated.

By "the law of the Lord" David means the whole revelation of God, as far as it had been given in his day; but his remark is equally true of all that God has since been pleased to speak by his Spirit.

This holy law may be judged of by its effect upon our own selves; It touches man's very soul, with the best conceivable result; and hence the Psalmist speaks of it in the most eulogistic manner as both perfect and sure. Its effects prove it to be complete and certain.

I. THE WORK OF THE WORD OF GOD IN CONVERSION.

Not apart from the Spirit, but as it is used by the Spirit for diverse ends, all needful to salvation.

1. To convince men of sin: they see what perfection is, that God demands it, and that they are far from it.
2. To drive men from false methods of seeking salvation, to bring them to self-despair, and to shut them up to God's method of saving them.
3. To reveal the way of salvation, by grace, through Christ, by faith.
4. To enable the soul to embrace Christ as its all in all. By setting forth promises and invitations, which are opened up to the understanding and sealed to the heart, etc.
5. To bring the heart nearer and nearer to God. Emotions of love, desires for holiness, devotion, self-searching, love to men, humility, etc.—these are all excited, sustained, and perfected in the heart by the Word of God.
6. To restore the soul when it has wandered. Renewing tenderness, hope, love, joy, etc., by its gentle reminders.
7. To perfect the nature. The highest flights of holy enjoyment are not above or beyond the Word. Nothing is purer or more elevated than Holy Scripture. The Word also slays all sin, promotes ffery virtue, prepares for every duty, etc.

II. THE EXCELLENCE OF THIS WORK DONE BY THE WORD.

The operations of grace by the Word are altogether good and not evil; and they are timed and balanced with infinite discretion. The Word of the Lord works marvelously, perfectly, and surely.

1. It removes despair without quenching repentance.
2. Gives pardon, but does not create presumption.
3. Gives rest, but excites the soul to progress.
4. Breathes security, but engenders watchfulness.
5. Bestows strength and holiness, but begets no boasting.
6. Gives harmony to duties, emotions, hopes, and enjoyments.
7. Brings the man to live for God, before God. and with God; and yet makes him none the less fitted for the daily duties of life.

III. THE CONSEQUENT EXCELLENCE OF THE WORD.

1. We need not add to it if we would secure conversion in any special case, or on the largest scale.
2. We need not keep back any doctrine for fear of damping the flame of a true revival.
3. We need not extraordinary gifts with which to preach it: the Word will do its own work.
4. We have but to follow the Word to be converted. It would be useless to run after new doctrine in the hope of being more powerfully affected. The old is better, and nothing better than the old Gospel can be imagined. It fits a man's needs as a key fits a lock.
5 We have but to keep to it to become truly wise: wise as the aged, wise as necessity requires, wise as the age, wise as eternity demands, wise with the wisdom of Christ.
   • Cling to the Scripture.
   • Study the whole revelation of God.
   • Use it as your chief instrument in all holy service.

Modern Instances

A remarkable proof that the Bible is its own witness is given by a writer from Oporto, who records the following reply of a man he met crouching in a ditch, to an inquiry as to what book he was reading:-"Well, if you won't betray me, I acknowledge that this is a New Testament. I bought it of a man who was selling such books, and determined to know something of its contents. I dare not tell anybody that I have it, not even my wife. So I have no one to teach me. Yet it is not difficult to understand, for as I read *it makes itself plain to me.*"

"The process of enlightenment in many Romanist minds," says an observer, "is shadowed forth by the experience of one whom I saw but last week. He sat down to read the Bible an hour each evening with his wife. In a few evenings he stopped in the midst of his reading, and said *'Wife, if this book is true, we are wrong.'* He read on, and in a few days longer, said, *'Wife, if this book is true, we are lost.'* Riveted to the book, and deeply anxious, he still read, and in a week more joyfully exclaimed, *'Wife, if this book is true, we may be saved.'* A few weeks more reading, and taught by the Spirit of God through the exhortations and instructions of a City Missionary, they both placed their faith in Christ, and are now rejoicing in hope." —*Christian Treasury*

I have many books that I cannot sit down to read; they are, indeed, good and sound, but, like halfpence, there goes a great quantity to a small amount; there are silver books, and a very few golden books; but I have one book worth them all, called the Bible. —*John Newton*

> It is the Book of God. What if I should
> Say, God of Books?
> Let him that looks
> Angry at that expression, as too bold,
> His thoughts in silence smother
> Till he find such another.
> —*Christopher Harvey*

The longer I live the higher is my estimate of an expository ministry, embracing the whole Word of God. I have on purpose tried certain truths to see if they will produce conversion, and I have not failed in any case. Outlying doctrines meet with certain outlying minds which could not be reached by the usual range of teaching. What would seem to be the eccentricities of truth are all needed for impressing eccentric conditions of thought and heart. I prayerfully preached the Resurrection and many were raised to spiritual life; I preached divine sovereignty when a revival was in full swing and it deepened and continued the work. The omission of certain truths from certain ministries may account for their barrenness. O that ministers would believe that the Word needs no improving, but is already perfect, "converting the soul"; and that it requires no suiting to the times, for it still makes wise the simple.

If there is any knowledge fully in our possession, it is certainly that which comes to us by experience. That a certain material will float in the water may be proved by a knowledge of its specific gravity; but we will feel more fully assured of the fact if we have seen it tried, and we will regard our answer to an objector, "I have seen it floating in water frequently," as simply sufficient to silence all objections. Ay, we will regard such a statement as fully more conclusive than, "It must float, for its specific gravity is lighter than water." On this same principle-and it is the principle of common sense-how fully we can prove that the Bible is the Word of God! Yes, every Christian carries the proof with him in his own experience. A poor Italian woman, a fruit-seller, had received the Word of God in her heart, and became persuaded of the truth of it. Seated at her modest stall at the head of a bridge she made use of every moment in which she was unoccupied in her small traffic, in order to study the sacred volume. "What are you reading there, my good woman?" said a gentleman one day, as he came up to the stall to purchase some fruit. "It is the Word of God," replied the fruit-vendor. "The Word of God! Who told you that?" "He told me so Himself." "Have you ever spoken with Him, then?" The poor woman felt a little embarrassed, more especially as the gentleman insisted on her giving him some proof of what she believed. Unused to discussion, and feeling greatly at a loss for arguments, she at length exclaimed, looking upward, "Can you prove to me, sir, that there is a sun up in the sky?" "Prove it!" he replied. "Why, the best proof is that it warms me, and that I can see its light." "So it is with me," she replied joyously; "the proof of this Book's being the Word of God is that it warms and lights my soul" —*Bertram's Homiletic Encyclopedia*

McCheyne somewhere says "Depend upon it; it is God's word, not man's comment on God's word, which converts souls." I have frequently observed that this is the case. A discourse has been the means of conviction or of decision; but usually upon close inquiry I have found that the real instrument was a scripture quoted by the preacher. A large fruit may contain and nourish a tiny seed; when the fruit falls into the ground and the shoot springs up, the real life was in the central pip, and not in the juicy fruit which encompassed it. So the divine truth is the living and incorruptible seed: the sermon is as needful as the apple to its pip; but still the vitality, the energy, the saving power, was in the pip of the Word, and only in a minor sense in the surrounding apple of human exposition and exhortation.

48

But the salvation of the righteous is of the Lord.
—*Psalm 37:39*

ALVATION is a very large term, and describes the whole life of true believers-their whole experience, from their first consciousness of the ruin of the fall to their entrance into glory. They feel their need of being perpetually saved from self, sin, Satan, and the world. They trust in God for preservation, and their end is peace (verse 37).

The prosperous sinner is on another tack, and comes to another conclusion: he disowns all need of salvation, and considers his success to be of his own winning. Alas, there comes to him a turning of the tables before long; according to the preceding verse: "The transgressors shall be destroyed together; the end of the wicked shall be cut off." God is not with the unrighteous; they have neither safety, nor strength, nor salvation in their time of trouble.

Our text contains a broad statement, of which we may say:

I. THIS IS THE ESSENCE OF SOUND DOCTRINE.

The salvation of the righteous is of the Lord, even of the Triune Jehovah, Father, Son and Holy Ghost in:

1. The planning.
2. The providing.
3. The beginning.
4 The carrying on.
5. The completion.

II. THIS IS A NECESSARY FACT. The saints recognize it; for

1. Their inward conflicts make them know that God alone must work salvation. They are too fickle and feeble to save themselves.
2. Their outward temptations drive them to the same conclusion. They are well kept whom God keeps, but none else.
3. The world's hate drives them away from all hope in that quarter. God is greater than a world in arms.
4 Their daily trials and afflictions would crush them if Omnipotence did not sustain them. Only God's grace can be all-sufficient.
5. The perishing of hypocrites is a sad proof of how little man can do. Temporary believers perish like blossoms which never knit to fruit, and therefore fall from the tree.

III. THIS IS A SWEET CONSOLATION. This truth, that unto God the Lord belongeth the salvation of his saints, acts graciously,:

1. Leading them to solid trust.
2. Exciting them to believing prayer.
3. Urging them to look out of self.
4. Inspiring them with great thoughts of God, and
5. Leading them to offer adoring praise unto their Redeemer.

IV. THIS IS A REASON FOR HUMILITY.

1. It strips the righteous of all pride in the fact of their being saved.
2. Of all exultation in self because they continue in their integrity.
3. Of all undue censure of the fallen; for they themselves would have failed, had not the Lord upheld them.
4. Of all self-confidence as to the future, since their weakness is inherent and abiding.
5. Of all self-glorying, even in heaven, since in all things they are debtors to sovereign grace.

V. THIS IS A FRUITFUL GROUND OF HOPE.

1. In reference to our own difficulties: God can give us deliverance.

2. In reference to our tried brethren: the Lord can sustain, sanctify, and deliver them.

3. In reference to seeking souls: we may leave their cases in the Savior's hands. He is able to save to the uttermost.

4. In reference to sinners: they cannot be too degraded, obstinate, ignorant, or false; God can work salvation even in the worst.

Golden Bells

"Salvation is of the Lord." This is the sum of Jonah's discourse; one word for all; the very moral of his history. The mariners might have written upon their ship, instead of Castor and Pollux, or the like device, "*Salvation is the Lord's*," the Ninevites in the next chapter might have written upon their gates, "*Salvation is the Lord's*," and all mankind, whose cause is pitted and pleaded by God against the hardness of Jonah's heart, might have written in the palms of their hands, "*Salvation is the Lord's*." It is the argument of both the Testaments, the staff and support of heaven and earth They would both sink, and all their joints be severed, if the salvation of the Lord were not. The birds in the air sing no other note, the beasts in the field give no other voice than Salus Jehovæ, *Salvation is the Lord's*. . . . And "what shall I more say?" as the Apostle asked (Heb. 11) when he had spoken much, and there was much more behind, but time failed him. Rather, what should I not say? for the world is my theater at this time, and I neither think nor can feign to myself anything that hath not dependence upon this acclamation, *Salvation is the Lord's. —King on Jonah*

Thus the saints hold heaven. Not by conquest, but by heritage. Won by another arm than their own, it presents the strongest imaginable contrast to the spectacle in England's palace that day when the King demanded to know of his assembled nobles by what title they held their lands? What title! At the rash question a hundred swords leapt from their scabbards. Advancing on the alarmed monarch, "By these," they said, "we won, and by these will keep them." How different the scene which heaven presents! All eyes are turned on Jesus with looks of love; gratitude glows in every bosom, and swells every song; now with golden harps they sound his praise; and now, descending from their thrones to do him homage, they cast their crowns in one glittering heap at the feet which were nailed on Calvary. From this scene, learn in whose name to seek salvation, and through whose merits to hope for it; and with a faith in harmony with the worship of the skies, be this your language: "Not unto us, O Lord, not unto us, but unto thy name give glory." —*Dr. Guthrie*

"This brook will soon run dry," said one. "Nay," quoth his fellow, "it flows from a living spring, which was never known to fail in summer or in winter." A man was reputed to be very rich by those who saw his expensive houses, and horses, and charges; but there were others who judged that his name would soon be in the Gazette, for he had no capital. "There is nothing at the back of it," said one, and the saying meant much. Now, the believer has the eternal deep for his spring of supply, and the all-sufficiency of God as the substance of his wealth. What cause has he to fear?

If salvation were partly of God and partly of man it would be as sorry an affair as that image of Nebuchadnezzar's dream, which was part of iron and part of clay. It would end in a break-down. If our dependence were upon Jesus in a measure, and our own works in some degree, our foundation would be partly on the rock and partly on the sand, and the whole structure would fall. O to know the full meaning of the words, *"Salvation is of the Lord"*!

Experience alone can beat this truth into men's minds. A man will lie broken at the foot of the precipice, every bone dislocated by the fall, and yet hope to save himself. Piles of sin will fall upon him and bury him, and yet his self-trust will live. Mountains of actual transgression will overwhelm him, and yet he will stir himself to self-confident effort, working like the Cyclops with Etna heaped upon them. Crushed to atoms, every particle of our nature reeks with conceit. Ground to powder, our very dust is pungent with pride. Only the Holy Ghost can make a man receive that humbling sentence — *"Salvation is of the Lord."*

49

Yea, the sparrow hath found a house, and the swallow a nest for herself, where she may lay her young, even thine altars, O Lord of hosts, my King, and my God.

—Psalm 84:3

AVID, as an exile, envied the birds which dwelt around the house of the Lord. So the Christian, when debarred the assembly of the saints, under spiritual desertion, will pine to be once more at home with God.

These birds found in the sanctuary what we would find in God.

I. HOUSES FOR THEMSELVES.

That they should find houses in and around the Lord's house is remarkable, and David dwelt on it with pleasure.

1. Consider what they were. Sparrows.
   - Worthless creatures. Five for two farthings.
   - Needy creatures, requiring both nests, food, and everything else.
   - Uninvited guests. The temple did not need them; it might have been all the better without them
   - Numerous creatures; but none were driven away.

2. Consider what they did: "Found a house," a comfortable, suitable, permanent abode.
   - They looked for it, or they could not have been described as having found it.
   - It was there already, or they could not have found it.
   - They appropriated it. Their right lay in discovery; they found a house and occupied it without question. O for an appropriating faith!

3 Consider what they enjoyed?
   - Safety. Rest. Abode. Delight. Society. Nearness.
   - All this in the house of God, hard by his altars.
   - Thus do believers find all in Christ Jesus.

And so, secondarily, they find the same things *in the assembly of the saints,* in the place where God's honor dwelleth.
   - We come to the house of the Lord with joy.
   - We remain in it with delight.
   - We sit and sing in it with pleasure.
   - We commune with our fellow-songsters with much content.

It is not every bird that does this. The eagle is too ambitious. The vulture too foul. The cormorant too greedy. The hawk too warlike. The ostrich too wild. The barn-door fowl too dependent upon man. The owl too fond of darkness. These sparrows were little and loving.

II. NESTS FOR THEIR YOUNG.

Some persons are not so much in need of a house for themselves, for, like swallows, they live on the wing, and are active and energetic; but they need a nest for their young, for whom they are greatly anxious. They long to see the young people settled, happy, and safe in God.

Children should be housed in the house of God. The sanctuary of God should be the nursery of the young.

1. They will be safe there, and free there. The swallow, the "bird of liberty," is satisfied to find a nest for herself near the altars of God. She is not afraid of bondage there either for herself or her young.
2. They will be joyful there. We should try to make our little ones happy in God, and in his holy worship. Dull Sabbaths and dreary services should not be mentioned among us.
3. They are near the blessing, when we bring them near the house of the Lord.
4. They are in choice society; their companions will be the companions of Jesus.
5. They are likely to return to the nest as the swallows do; even as the young salmon return to the rivulet where they were hatched. Young folks remember their first impressions.

6. Children truly brought to Christ have every blessing in that fact.
- They are rich: they dwell in God's palace.
- They are educated: they abide in the Lord's temple.
- They are safe for time and eternity.

The second blessing of a nest for our young often follows on the first, or getting a house for ourselves.
- But it needs prayer, example, and precept. Children do not take to religion as ducks to water; they must be led and trained with earnest care.
- Are you sighing after Christ for yourself and your children?
- Are you content without Christ? Then you are not likely to care about your children.
- Do you already possess a home in Jesus? Rest not till all yours are housed in the same place.

Fragments

Sir Thomas More used to attend the parish church at Chelsea, and there, putting on a surplice, he would sing with the choristers at matins and high mass. It happened, one day, that the Duke of Norfolk, coming to Chelsea to dine with him, found him at church thus engaged As they walked home together arm-in-arm after service, the duke exclaimed, "My Lord Chancellor a parish clerk! A parish clerk! You dishonor the King and his office!" "Nay," he replied, smiling, "your Grace cannot suppose that the King, our master, will be offended with me for serving his Master, or thereby account his office dishonored."

> I'm only a little sparrow,
> A bird of low degree;
> My life is of little value,
> But the dear Lord cares for me.

Tennyson plaintively refers to the song of the linnets:

> I do but sing because I must,
> And pipe but as the linnets sing,
> And one is glad—her note is gay—
> For now her little ones have ranged;
> And one is sad—her note is changed—
> Because her brood is stolen away.

The feeling of the linnets may serve as an analog. Christian parents have a gay note when their little ones have ranged at their sweet will in the paths of duty; but their note must be one of sadness when the brood is stolen away from truth and righteousness. —*W. Norris.*

"God fails not," as one has beautifully said, "to find a house for the most *worthless*, and the nest for the most *restless* of birds." What confidence this should give us! How we should rest! What repose the soul finds that casts itself on the watchful, tender care of Him who provides so fully for the need of all His creatures! We know what the expression of "nest" conveys, just as well as that of "a house." Is it not a place of security, a shelter from storm. a covert to hide one's self in, from every evil, a protection from all that can harm, "a place to rest in, to nestle in, to joy in?" — *Things New and Old*

A custom, existing among several nations of antiquity, is deemed capable of illustrating the present passage. For birds whose nests chanced to be built on the temples, or within the limits of them, were not allowed to be driven away, much less to be killed, but found there a secure and undisturbed abode. — *W. K. Clay*

As a rule, the children of godly parents are godly. In cases where this is not the case there is a reason. I have carefully observed and detected the absence of family prayer, gross inconsistency, harshness, indulgence, or neglect of admonition. If trained in God's ways, they do not depart from them.

50

For he shall give his angels charge over thee, to keep thee in all thy ways.

—*Psalm 91:11*

 HE Lord gave his people shelter in the time of pestilence, for he had promised, "There shall no evil befall thee; neither shall any plague come nigh thy dwelling." The former verses celebrate the Passover of those who dwell in God.

After the Passover came a journey to Canaan; and the promise of the covenant angel and his keeping them in all their ways, fitly follow upon the rescue from the plague.

We, too, are pilgrims on our way to Canaan. He who set us free by the Passover deliverance also provides for our journey to the land which floweth with milk and honey. All the way to the promised land is covered by this divine safe conduct.

I. THERE ARE WAYS WHICH ARE NOT IN THE PROMISE.

"All thy ways" are mentioned; but some tracks are not to be followed by children of God, and are not their ways.

    1. Ways of presumption. In these men court danger, and, as it were, defy God. "Cast thyself down," said Satan to our Lord, and then urged this promise (Matt. 4:6).

2. Ways of sin, dishonesty, lying, vice, worldly conformity, etc. We have no permit to bow in the house of Rimmon (Eph. 5:12).

3. Ways of worldliness, selfishness, greed, ambition. The ways by which men seek personal aggrandizement are usually dark, and crooked, and are not of God (Prov. 28:22; 1 Tim. 6:9).

4. Ways of pride, self-conceit, boastful promisings, pretended perfection, etc. "Pride goeth before destruction."

5. Ways of will worship, willfulness, obstinacy, fancy, day-dreaming, absurd impulse, etc. (Jer. 2:18).

6. Ways of erroneous doctrine, novel practice, fashionable ceremonial, flattering delusion, etc. (2 Tim. 3:5).

II. THERE ARE WAYS IN WHICH SAFETY IS GUARANTEED.

1. The way of humble faith in the Lord Jesus.
2. The way of obedience to divine precepts.
3. The way of childlike trust in providential guidance.
4 The way of strict principle, and stern integrity.
5. The way of consecrated service, and seeking God's glory.
6. The way of holy separation, and walking with God.

III. THESE WAYS LEAD US INTO VARIED CONDITIONS.

1. They are changeful and varied: "all thy ways."
2. They are sometimes stony with difficulty: "foot against a stone."
3. They may be terrible with temptation.
4 They may be mysteriously trying. Devils may throng the path, only to be met by holy angels.
5. They are essentially safe, while the smooth and easy roads are perilous.

IV. BUT WHILE WALKING IN THEM ALL BELIEVERS ARE SECURE.

1. The Lord Himself concerns Himself about them: "*He* shall give his angels charge over thee." He will personally command those holy beings to have an eye to His children. David charged his troops to spare Absalom, but his bidding was disregarded. It is not so with God.

2. Mysterious agencies protect them: angels bear them up in their hands, as nurses carry little children. Wonderful tenderness and power! Angels acting as servants to men!

3. All things are on their side, both visible and invisible. Command is laid on all to protect the saints. "Thou hast given commandment to save me" (Ps. 71:3).

4. Each one is personally watched over. "Charge over *thee* to keep *thee* (Isa. 13:6; Gen. 28:15).

5. That watchfulness is perpetual "All thy ways" (Ps. 121:3–4).

6. This guard also confers honor. How noble a thing to have the courtiers of heaven for a *corps de garde!*

7. All this comes to them by Jesus, whose the angels are, and whom they serve (Isa. 43:4).

- See how the lowest employment is consistent with the highest enjoyment. Keeping guard over the Lord's stumbling children is no discredit to angels.
- How cheerfully we should watch over others! How vigorously should we hold them up whenever it is in our power! To cast off a stumbling brother is not angelic, but the reverse.
- How safe we ought to feel, how fully trustful we ought to be! Alexander slept soundly, "for," said he, "Parmenio wakes."
- How holy we should be with such holy ones for watchers! Great privileges involve heavy responsibilities.

Garnishing

Whilst King William, at a battle in Flanders,was giving orders in the thickest of the fight, he saw to his surprise among his staff one Michael Godfrey, a merchant of London, and Deputy Governor of the Bank of England, who had thus exposed himself in order to gratify his curiosity. The king, riding up to him, said, "Sir, you ought not to run these hazards; you are not a soldier, you can be of no use here." "Sire," answered Godfrey, "I run no more hazard than your majesty." "Not so," said William, "I am here where it is my duty to be, and I may, without presumption, commit my life to God's keeping; but you—" The sentence needed no completion, for at that very moment a cannon ball laid Godfrey lifeless at the king's feet. He had been wise had he restricted himself to the ways of his calling and duty.

Old Humphrey has a good paper against wandering from the path of duty, suggested by a notice at the entrance of a park: "Take notice. In walking through these grounds, you are requested to keep the footpath." Bunyan has supplied the same theme for solemn warning, in the pilgrim straying into *Bye-path meadow. —Bowes*

> Angels our servants are,
>   And keep in all our ways;
> And in their watchful hands they bear
>   The sacred sons of grace:
> Unto that heavenly bliss
>   They all our steps attend;
> And God himself our Father is,
>   And Jesus is our Friend.
>
> *—Wesley*

A dying saint asked that his name should be put upon his tombstone with the dates of his birth and death, and the one word, "*Kept.*"

Our protection is in other hands than our own. In the way of duty we are as safe as in heaven. Not alone in great dangers, but in little ones we are secure if we are in the right way, for we are kept from stumbling-stones as well as from fiery darts. Our guards are such as no enemy can resist, for they are strong; such as no evil can escape, for they are swift; such as no weariness can tire, for they are never weary. We have a body-guard of Immortals, each one of them invincible, unflagging, loyal, loving, and full of fire. Each angel may truly say, "A charge to keep I have."

Keep it he will till the Lord Himself shall receive our spirit. No angel will give in his account with sorrow, saying, "I could not keep him; the stones were too many, his feet too feeble, the way too long." No, we shall be kept to the end; for in addition to angels, we have the safeguard of their Lord: He keepeth the feet of His saints (1 Sam. 2:9).

51

The dead praise not the Lord, neither any that go down into silence. But we will bless the Lord from this time forth and for evermore. Praise the Lord.

—Psalm 115:17–18

 HE living God should be adored by a living people. A blessing God should be blessed by a blessing people. Whatever others do, we ought to bless Jehovah. When we bless him we should not rest till others do the same: we should cry to them, "Praise the Lord." Our example and our persuasion should rouse them to praise.

I. A MOURNFUL MEMORY. "The dead praise not the Lord, neither any that go down into silence." This reminds us:

1. Of silenced voices in the choirs of Zion. Good men and true who neither sing nor speak among us any longer.
2. Of our own speedy silence: so far as this world is concerned, we shall soon be among the dead and silent ones.
3. Of the ungodly around us, who are already spiritually dead, and can no more praise the Lord than if they were dumb.
4. Of lost souls in hell. Never will these bless the Lord.

II. A HAPPY RESOLUTION. "But we will bless the Lord."

In heart, song, testimony, action, we are resolved to give the Lord our loving praise, because:

1. We live. Shall we not bless him who keeps us in being?
2. We live spiritually, and this demands perpetual thanksgiving.
3. We are blessed of the Lord: shall we not bless him?
4. He will bless us. More and more will he reveal his love to us: let us praise him more and more. Be this our steadfast vow, that we will bless the Lord, come what may.

III. AN APPROPRIATE COMMENCEMENT. "We will bless the Lord from this time forth."

1. When the heathen ask, "Where is now their God?" (verse 2), let us reply courageously to all atheistic questions, and meet infidelity with joyous adoration.
2. When under a sense of mercy, we are led to sing "The Lord hath been mindful of us" (verse 12), let us then bless him.
3 When spiritually renewed and comforted. When the four times repeated words, "He will bless," have come true in our experience, and the Lord has increased us with every personal and family blessing (verses 12-14), then let all that is within us bless the holy name of the Lord.
4. When led to confess Christ. Then should we begin the never-ending life-psalm. Service and song should go together.
5. When years end and begin New Years' days, birthdays, etc., let us bless God for:
   - Sin of the year forgiven.
   - Need of the year supplied.
   - Mercy of the year enjoyed.
   - Fears of the year removed.
   - Hopes of the year fulfilled.

Let us from this very moment magnify the name of the Lord. Let our hearts turn each beat into music as we inwardly bless him. We have robbed him of his glory long enough.

IV. AN EVERLASTING CONTINUANCE. "From this time forth and for evermore."

1. Weariness shall not suspend it. We will renew our strength as we bless the Lord.
2. Final falling shall not end it: the Lord will keep our soul in his way, and make us praise him all our days.
3. Nor shall death so much as interrupt our songs, but raise them to a purer and fuller strain.

4. Nor shall any supposable calamity deprive the Lord of our gratitude. "The Lord gave, and the Lord hath taken away; blessed be the name of the Lord" (Job 1:21).
   - One by one the singers in the consecrated choir steal away from us, and we miss their music: let us feel as if baptized for the dead.
   - Will no one here engage in the choir, and rehearse on earth the sonnets of heaven?

Joy-Notes

Praise is the highest function that any creature can discharge. The Rabbis have a beautiful bit of teaching buried among their rubbish about angels. They say that there are two kinds of angels, the angels of service and the angels of praise, of which two orders the latter is the higher, and that no angel in it praises God twice; but having lifted up his voice in the psalm of heaven, then ceases to be. He has perfected his being, he has reached the height of his greatness, he has done what he was made for; let him fade away. The garb of legend is mean enough, but the thought it embodies is that ever true and solemn one, without which life is naught: "Man's chief end is to glorify God." —*Dr. Maclaren*

There is no heaven, either in this world, or in the world to come, for people who do not praise God. If you do not enter into the spirit and worship of heaven, how should the spirit and joy of heaven enter into you? Selfishness makes long prayers, but love makes short prayers, that it may continue longer in praise. —*Pulsford*

> King of glory, King of peace,
>   I will love thee:
> And that love may never cease,
>   I will move thee.
>
> Seven whole days, not one in seven,
>   I will praise thee.
> In my heart, though not in heaven,
>   I can raise thee.
>
> Small it is, in this poor sort
>   To enroll thee:
> Even eternity is too short
>   To extol thee.
>   —*George Herbert*

On Thursday evening, March 29th, 1883, for above an hour all who had occasion to use the telephone in Chicago found it vibrating to musical tones. Private and public telephones, and even the police and fire-alarm instruments, were alike affected. The source of the music was a mystery until the following day, when it was learned that a telegraph wire, which passes near most of the telephone wires, was connected with the harmonic system, that tunes were being played over it, and that the telephone wires took up the sounds by induction. If one wire carrying sweet sounds from place to place could so affect another wire by simply being near to it, how ought Christians, in communication with their Father in heaven, to affect all with whom they come in contact in the world! The divine music of love and gentleness in their lives should be a blessing to society. —*The Pulpit Treasury, New York*

When we bless God for mercies we prolong them, and when we bless him for miseries we usually end them. When we reach to praise we have compassed the design of a dispensation, and have reaped the harvest of it. Praise is a soul in flower, and a secret, hearty blessing of the Lord is the soul fruit-bearing. Praise is the honey of life, which a devout heart sucks from every bloom of providence and grace. As well be dead as be without praise: it is the crown of life.

52

This is my comfort in my affliction: for thy word hath quickened me.
—*Psalm 119:50*

 N some respects the same event happens to us all: to good men, to great men, to well-instructed men, as well as to the wicked, the obscure, and the ignorant. Each of these can speak of "my affliction." "The heart knoweth his own bitterness" (Prov. 14:10).

It is a grand matter when "my affliction" is in each case balanced by "my comfort." It was so in David's case, and he is a fair representative of all believers. How is it with each one of our hearers?

I. BELIEVERS HAVE THEIR PECULIAR COMFORT. Each tried child of God can say, "This is my comfort."

1. *This*, as different from others. Worldly men get their drops of comfort from such sources as they prefer; but the godly man looks to his experience of the Word, and says, "This is my comfort" (Ps. 4:6).
2. *This*, as understanding what it is. He knew his consolation as well as he knew his tribulation. He was not like Hagar, who could not see the well which was so near her (Gen. 21: 19).
3. *This*, as having it near at hand. He does not say that, as if he pointed it out in the distance; but this, as grasping it.
4. *This*, as pleading in prayer that which he had enjoyed; urging upon the Lord the mercy already received.

II. THAT COMFORT COMES FROM A PECULIAR SOURCE. "Thy word hath quickened me."

1. In part it is outward.
   - The word of God, full of promises, is our comfort (Rom. 15:4).
   - The word of God, full of records of his goodness, is the confirmation of our confidence (Ps. 77:5–10).
   - The word of God, full of power, is our strength (Eccles. 8:4).
2. In part it is inward: "Thy word hath quickened me."
   - In past experience he had felt the power of the word in raising him:
   - Into life from death (Ps. 116:8).
   - Into energy from lethargy (Song of Sol. 6:12).
   - Into higher life from lower (Ps. 119:67).
   - In all things it had been a source of quickening to him.
   - In present experience he was then feeling its power in making
   - His mind less worldly.
   - His heart more prayerful.
   - His spirit more tender.
   - His faith more simple.
   - If the word has done and is doing all this, we may expect it to do more, and to magnify its power in our complete rescue.

III. THAT COMFORT IS VALUABLE UNDER PECULIAR TRIALS.

1. Hope deferred. Study the context. "Remember the word unto thy servant, upon which thou hast caused me to hope" (verse 49). Quickening enables us to hope on.
2. Trial endured (verse 50). Comfort is most needed in trouble, and there is no comfort like quickening.
3. Scorn suffered. "The proud have had me greatly in derision" (verse 51). We care nothing for mockers when we are lively in spiritual things.
4. Sin of others. "Horror hath taken hold upon me because of the wicked" (verse 53). More grace will enable us to bear up under abounding sin.
5. Changes. Read carefully verse 54. The Bible has a song for all seasons, and a psalm for all places.
6. Darkness: "in the night" (verse 55). There is no night-light like the Word, enlightening and enlivening the heart.

IV. THAT THE FORM OF OUR COMFORT IS A TEST OF CHARACTER.

1. Some look to wealth: when their corn and their wine are increased, they say, "This is my comfort." They mind the main chance: they are worldly (Luke 12:19).
2. Some seek to dreams and visions, omens and fancies, impressions and presentiments: they are superstitious.

3. Some run to sin, drink, gaming, worldly company, dissipation, opium: they are wicked.

4. Some resort to their fellow men for advice and assistance: they are unwise, and will be disappointed (Jer. 17:5).
  - What is your comfort?
  - Has this blessed volume quickened you?
  - If so, look to it under all trials, for it will never fail you.

The Rev. E. Paxton Hood says, "When I visited one day, as he was dying, my beloved friend Benjamin Parsons, I said, "How are you today, sir?" He said, "My head is resting very sweetly on three pillows—infinite power, infinite love, and infinite wisdom." Preaching in the Canterbury Hall in Brighton, I mentioned this some time since; and, not many months after, I was requested to call upon a poor but holy young woman, apparently dying. She said, "I felt I must see you before I died. I heard you tell the story of Benjamin Parsons and his three pillows; and when I went through a surgical operation, and it was very cruel, I was leaning my head on pillows, and as they were taking them away, I said, 'Mayn't I keep them?' The surgeon said, 'No, my dear, we must take them away.' 'But,' said I, 'you can't take away Benjamin Parsons' three pillows: I can lay my head on infinite power, infinite love, and infinite wisdom.'"

"*My word*"—"The best relief that mourners have,
  It makes our sorrows blest;
  Our fairest hope beyond the grave,
  And our eternal rest."

"Speak to me now in Scripture language alone," said a dying Christian. "I can trust the words of God, but when they are the words of man, it costs me an effort to think whether I may trust to them."

  I would, when dying comforts fly,
  As much as when they present were,
  Upon my living joy rely:
  Help, Lord, for here I daily err.
  —*Ralph Erskine*

I was questioning my spiritual life, I who have so long been a preacher to others. I entered a little rustic assembly. An unlettered man preached the gospel, he preached it heartily; my tears began to flow; my soul leaped at the very sound of the Word of the Lord. What a comfort it was to me! How frequently have I thought of it since! The Word did revive me; my heart was not dead to its influence; I was one of those happy people who know the joyful sound. Assurance was bright in my soul—the Word had quickened me.

What energy a text will breathe into a man! There is more in one divine sentence than in huge folios of human composition. There are tinctures of which one drop is more powerful than large doses of the common dilutions. The Bible is the essence of truth; it is the mind of God, the wisdom of the Eternal. By every word of God men are made to live and are kept in life.

53

I will praise Thee with my whole heart: before the gods will I sing praise unto Thee. I will worship towards Thy holy temple, and praise Thy name for Thy lovingkindness and for Thy truth: for Thou hast magnified Thy word above all Thy name. In the day when I cried Thou answeredst me, and strengthenedst me with strength in my soul.

—Psalm 138:1-3

AVID was vexed with rival gods, as we are with rival gospels. Nothing is more trying to the soul of a true man than to be surrounded with vile counterfeits, and to hear these cried up, and the truth treated with contempt.

How will David act under the trial? For so should we act. Our text informs us. He will:

I. SING WITH WHOLE-HEARTED PRAISE. "I will praise thee with my whole heart: before the gods will I sing praise unto thee."

1. His song would openly show his contempt of the false gods: he would sing whether they were there or no. They were such nothings that he would not change his note for them.
2. It would evince his strong faith in the true God. To the teeth of the adversary he glorified Jehovah. His enthusiastic wholehearted song was better than denunciation or argument.
3. It would declare his joyful zeal for God: he sang to show the strong emotion of his soul. Others might be pleased in Baal; he greatly rejoiced in Jehovah.
4. It would shield him from evil from those about him; for holy song keeps off the enemy. Praise is a potent disinfectant. If called to behold evil, let us purify the air with the incense of praise.

II. WORSHIP BY THE DESPISED RULE. "I will worship toward thy holy temple."

1. Quietly ignoring all will-worship, he would follow the rule of the Lord, and the custom of the saints.

2. Looking to the Person of Christ, which was typified by the Temple. There is no singing like that which is directed towards the Lord Jesus, as now living to present it to the Father.

3 Trusting in the one finished Sacrifice, looking to the one Great Expiation, we shall praise aright.

4. Realizing God himself; for it is to God he speaks, "towards thy holy temple." Music which is meant for the ear of God is music indeed.

III. PRAISE THE QUESTIONED ATTRIBUTES. "I will praise thy name for thy loving kindness, and for thy truth."

1. Loving kindness in its universality.
   - Loving kindness in its specialty.
   - Grace in everything. Grace to me. Grace so much despised of Pharisees and Sadducees, but so precious to true penitents.
   - Concerning the grace of God, let us cling close to the doctrine and spirit of the gospel all the more because the spirit of the age is opposed to them.
2. Truth.
   - Historic accuracy of Scripture.
   - Absolute certainty of the gospel.
   - Assured truthfulness of the promise
   - Complete accuracy of prophecy.

It is ours in these evil days to hold to the infallible inspiration of the Word, and to affirm it in unmistakable terms. No wonder that men rush off to find an infallible church in Popery, or rely upon their own infallible reason, when once they doubt the plenary inspiration of the Bible.

IV. REVERENCE THE HONORED WORD. "Thou hast magnified thy word above all thy name."

God has magnified His sure word of testimony beyond all such revelations as we receive through creation and providence, though these declare God's name. The Gospel word is:

1. More clear. Words are better understood than nature's hieroglyphs.
2. More sure. The Spirit Himself sealing it.
3. More sovereign. Effectually blessing believers.
4. More complete. The whole of God is seen in Christ.
5. More lasting. Creation must pass away; the Word endures for ever.
6. More glorifying to God. Especially in the great Atonement.

V. PROVE IT BY PERSONAL EXPERIENCE. "In the day when I cried Thou answeredst me," etc.

He had used his knowledge of God derived from the Word:

1. By offering prayer. "I cried." What do men know of the bud, and grace of God and the virtue of His Word if they have never prayed?
2. By narrating the answer. "Thou answeredst me," etc. We are God's witnesses, and should with readiness, care, frequency, and courage testify what we have seen and known.
3. By exhibiting the strength of soul which was gained by prayer. This is good witness-bearing. Show by patience, courage, joy, and holiness what the Lord has done for your soul.
   - Our Lord is above all others.
   - Our joy in Him surpasses all other joy.
   - Therefore will we delight in Him and extol Him beyond measure.

Jottings

Singing unto Jehovah before the gods was good for David's own soul It is perilous to attempt a secret fidelity to God, it is so apt to degenerate into cowardice. A converted soldier tried at first to pray in bed, or in some secret corner, but he found it would not do; he must kneel down in the barrack-room before the others, and run the gauntlet of the men's remarks; for until he had done so he had not taken his stand and he felt no peace of mind. It is needful for our spiritual health that we come out distinctly upon the Lord's side.

The effect of whole-heartedness is very manifest. Even prejudiced persons put up with a great deal in a service when they see that those engaged in it are enthusiastic. "It was very singular," said one who attended a Revival Service, "and I should have laughed outright, only I saw the tears running down an old sailor's cheeks as he sung the hymn with all his might."

Observe carefully the little points in a divine command: worship "towards the holy temple." Nothing is little when God's will is concerned. I knew a youth who had wished to be baptized, but his friends kept him back. When he fell ill, he fretted because he had not confessed his Lord according to the Scripture. "But Isaac," said his mother, "you know baptism will not save you." "No, mother," he replied, "of course it will not, for I am saved. But when I see Jesus in heaven I should not like Him to say, 'Isaac, it was a very little thing I asked of you; did you not love Me enough to do it?'" It is the non-essentiality of the precept which makes it such an important test of obedience.

We do not intend to place Scripture on a lower level than science; on the contrary, we claim for it the chief place. By science the name and character of the Lord may be dimly read; but His Word is magnified above all other manifestations, for therein the revelation is more full and clear. Observations made by sunlight are not to be revised by moonlight glances: the reverse is the correct process. You tell me what you gather from my Father's works; but I have His mind in His own words, written with His own pen, and I prefer my information to yours.

54

I flee unto thee to hide me.
—Psalm 143:9

HAT a mercy it is for us all that David was not an untried man! We have all been enriched by his painful experience. He was

A man so various that he seemed to be
Not one, but all mankind's epitome.

May it not be a blessing to others that we also are tried? If so, ought we not to be right glad to contribute our quota to the benefit of the redeemed family?

David may be our example; let us flee unto God as he did. We shall profit by our foes if we imitate this prudent warrior in his habitual way of escaping from his enemies.

The great point is, however, not only to see what David did, but to do the like promptly, and constantly. What, then, is essential in order to our copying the man of God?

I. A PERCEPTION OF DANGER.

No man will flee if he is not afraid; there must be a knowledge and apprehension of danger, or there will be no flight.

1. Men perish in many instances because they have no sense of danger. The noxious air is not observed, the sunken reef is not seen, the train rushes to collision unwarned. Ignorance of danger makes the danger inevitable.
   - Men will dare to die without fear of hell.
   - Men will sin and have no dread of any ill consequences.
   - Men will play with an evil habit and will not believe in its power to enslave them.
   - Men will toy with a temptation and refuse to see how certain it is to lead them into actual wrong-doing.

2. Every man is really in danger. The sinner is asleep on the top of a mast. Young and old are both in jeopardy. Even the saints are in peril of temptation from many sources.

3. Some dangers are slowly perceived. Those connected with sweet sin, those which grow out of a boastful mind, those which are countenanced by the example of others, etc. The more dangerous the serpent, the less likely to be seen.

4. The spiritual man is led to perceive dangers by inward monitions, by a spiritual sensitiveness which is the result of devotion, by experience, by perceptible declensions, or by observing the effect of certain things upon others.

II. A SENSE OF WEAKNESS. No man will flee for hiding if he feel able to fight the matter through in his own strength.

1. We are all weak and unable to cope with sin.
2. Some think themselves mighty men of valor, but these are among the very weakest of the weak.
3. Past failure should teach us not to trust our own strength.
4. In a deep sense of weakness we are made strong; in fancied strength lies the worst form of weakness.

III. A PRUDENT FORESIGHT. "I flee unto thee to hide me."

1. He would not venture into the danger or wait till it overtook him; but he took time by the forelock and fled. Often this is the highest form of courage.
2. Escape through *fear* is admirable prudence. It is not a mean motive; for Noah, "moved by fear, prepared an ark "
3. While we *can* flee we should, for time may come when we shall be unable. David says, "I flee"; he means, "I am fleeing, I always do flee unto thee, my God."

   A man should not live like a beast, who sees no further than the meadow in which he feeds. He should foresee evil and hide himself; for this is common prudence (Prov. 22:3).

IV. A SOLID CONFIDENCE. "To thee to hide me. He was sure

1. That there was safety in God.
2. That he might flee to God.
3. That he might flee there and then.

V. AN ACTIVE FAITH. He did not lie passive, but aroused himself.
   This may be clearly seen

1. In his fleeing to God. Directness, speed, eagerness.
2. In his after-prayers. "Teach me to do thy will; lead me; quicken me." See verses following the text.
   - Expect your share of enemies, and prepare for them.
   - Secure your best friend. Be reconciled to Him in Christ Jesus
   - Make constant use of Him. Flee to Him at all times.

Feathers for Wings

From some sins there is no safety but in flight. Our French school book represented Mentor as saying to his pupil in the court of Calypso, "Fly, Telemaque; there remains no other mode of conquest but by flight!" "Flee youthful lusts"; they are not to be wrestled with, but fled from. Flight being thus needful, whither shall we flee but to our God? Who will so surely welcome, so securely defend, so permanently entertain? As the bird to its nest, and the coney to its rock, let us flee unto our God that we may be secure from every foe.

God's people often find by experience that the places of their protection are places of destruction. Well, when all other places fail, Christ will not fail. See how it was with David, Psalm 142:4–5. But when his hiding place at Ziklag was gone, yet his Savior was not gone; "He encouraged himself in the Lord his God" (1 Sam. 30:6). It is a mighty encouragement to believers that Christ is a hiding place: (1) he is a safe and strong hiding place (Isa. 33:16); Christ is a rock, and he that is in Christ is in the munitions of rocks; (2) he is a large hiding place; there is room enough for his elect; his skirt is large; (3) he is a hiding-place to the soul as well as to the body; (4) he hath undertaken to hide us; God hath committed all his elect to Christ, that He should hide them.— *Ralph Robinson*

Under the influence of great fear the most timid creatures have sometimes fled to men for security. We have heard of a dove flying into a lady's bosom to escape from a hawk, and even of a hare running to a man for shelter. The confidence of the feeble secures the guardianship of the strong. He would be brutal indeed who would refuse protection to such simple reliance. Surely, if in our need we fly into the bosom of our God, we may be sure that love and majesty will unitedly smile upon us. There can be no question of that man's security who challenges by his faith the protection of the God of love. "He has trusted me and I will not fail him" has been the resolve of many an honorable man; how much more will it be the determination of the Lord!

A little party assembled in a shepherd's house in Nithsdale to hear Mr. Peden expound the Word of God. While thus engaged, the bleating of a sheep was heard. The noise disturbed the little congregation, and the shepherd was obliged to go out and drive the sheep away. While so engaged, he lifted up his eyes and saw, at a distance, horse soldiers coming towards his cottage. He hastened back to give the alarm. All instantly dispersed and hid themselves. Mr. Peden betook himself to the Cleft of the Rock, the Gave of Garrickfells, and soon the clatter of horses' hoofs and the ring of armor told him that his foes were at hand. But safe in the Cleft he sat unmoved, and through an opening saw them gallop past, without any suspicion that he whose life they sought was so near. —*From "Sunday Readings," by James Large*

55

The way of the slothful man is as a hedge of thorns: but the way of
the righteous is made plain.

—Proverbs 15:19

T has been said that the shrewdness of the Scotch nation is owing
to the pretty general study of the Book of Proverbs in that country. Of this I am not a judge; but certainly, if carefully followed, the
Proverbs of Solomon make men wise for this world with a high
order of prudence. God would have his people wise. There is no credit in being
a fool, even if you have the grace of God in your heart. To me it seems a duty to
make as much of myself as I can, since I am a servant of the Lord: I do not want
everybody to think that all my Lord's children are short of wit. In meditating
upon this two-leaved proverb, we shall:

I. TAKE THE TEXT IN ITS TEMPORAL BEARINGS.

1. It is clear from the apposition that a slothful man is the opposite of righteous. Certainly he is so. His sins of omission abound. He breaks his
   word, he vexes others, Satan finds him mischief to do; he is, in fact, ready
   for every bad word and work.
2. It is not enough to be diligent unless we are righteous; for though the
   curse is to the idle, the blessing is not to the active, but to the righteous.
   It is diligence in the service of God, under the Holy Spirit, which wins the
   reward of God
3. A slothful man's way is not desirable: "A hedge of thorns."
   - It is difficult in his own apprehension: a rough and thorny road, and
     he cannot have too little of it. He would sooner look at it a month than
     run in it an hour.
   - It becomes really thorny ere long. His neglects hedge him up, involve
     him in difficulties, bring losses, and create hindrances.
   - It becomes painful: he is poor, mistrusted, harshly dealt with by weary
     creditors, and at last without a livelihood.
   - It becomes blocked up: he does not know where to turn; he cannot dig,
     and he tries begging. Laziness gets little pity, and charity itself repels it.
4. A righteous man's way is under a blessing.
   - It becomes plain as he proceeds in it diligently.
   - God makes it so.
   - He makes it so himself.
   - Other people become willing to aid him, or, at least, to trust him,
     employ him, and recommend him.

II. TAKE THE TEXT IN ITS SPIRITUAL BEARINGS.

1. The spiritual sluggard.
   - Takes the way of indifference, carelessness, indecision, and unbelief; and this, though it may seem easy, is as full of sorrow as a thorn-hedge is full of pricking points.
   - He will have his own way; and self-will and obstinacy are briar hedges indeed: besides, his frowardness provokes others to oppose him, and the thorns thicken.
   - He chooses the way of sin, and he soon finds it full of sorrows, difficulties, perplexities, entanglements, and snares.
   - By his evil ways, and the inevitable consequences of his sins, he is shut out from God and heaven.

2. The righteous man.
   His way is that of faith and obedience.
   - It has its impediments: these are swept away.
   - It is frequently mysterious; but it is cleared up.
   - It is sometimes hilly; but it is the King's highway,
     Wherein we are right.
     Wherein we are protected.
     Wherein we are secured of a blessed end.
   - Are you wonderfully easy in religion, taking things as they come, in a slovenly way? Then your way will soon become a hedge of thorns. Neglect is quite sufficient to produce an immense crop of thorns and briars.
   - Do you seek to be righteous? Do you love holiness? Do you know Christ as your Way? Then go on without fear; for your way will be made plain, and your end will be peace (Ps. 37:37).

Confirmations

"The way of the slothful man," the course which the sluggard taketh in going about his affairs, "is as a hedge of thorns," is slow and hard; for he goeth creeping about his business, yea, his fears and griefs prick him and stay him like thorns and briars. "But the path of the righteous is as a paved causeway." The order which the godly man taketh is most plain and easy, who so readily and lustily runneth on in the works of his calling as if he walked on a paved causeway. —*P. Muffet*

Who can tell the pains which lazy people take? the muddles into which they bring themselves? They are driven to falsehood to excuse their sloth, and one lie leads on to more. Then they scheme and plot, and become dishonest. I knew one who fell out with hard work, and soon he fell in with drink and lost his position. Since then, to earn a scanty livelihood he has had to work ten times as much as was required of him in his better days, and he has hardly had a shoe to his foot. Meanwhile, a simple, plodding man has gone onward and upward, favored, as he confesses, by Providence; but, best of all, upheld by his integrity and industry; to him there has been success and happiness. He works hard, but his lot is ease itself compared with the portion of the sluggard.

Nobody rides to heaven on a feather-bed. Grace has made a road to heaven for sinners, but it does not suit sluggards. Those who reach the Celestial City are pilgrims and not lie-a-beds. Neglect is a sure way to hell; but we must strive to enter in at the straight gate, and so run that we may obtain. If you let your farm alone it will be overrun with weeds, and if your heart be let alone it will be eaten up with sins. Nothing comes of sloth but rags and poverty here, and damnation hereafter. Let idlers in Zion note this.

It is wonderful how difficulties vanish from the path of the righteous! In traveling up the Rhine you appear to be landlocked, but as the steamer proceeds you perceive a clear passage; a sudden bend enables you to see the opening between the hills. The road of Israel seemed blocked at the Red Sea, and again at the Jordan; but as they were following the Divine Leader, he made a way for them through the waters. Old Roman roads are still visible which were thrown up along the sides of hills and across valleys; these were plain enough to be followed by the least familiar traveler: even so hath the Lord cast up the road-way of his people and they shall not miss it. "The way-faring man, though a fool, shall not err therein."

The spiritually negligent involve themselves in much sorrow. Neglecting prayer and other means of grace, they seek spiritual ease; but if they are God's children they do not find it, but sow for themselves abundant thorns of regret and depression. I know of a surety that the diligent Christian is the only happy Christian. True religion is above all other things a business which is not only worth doing but is worth doing well. High farming in the fields of the soul is the only farming which pays.

56

All the ways of a man are clean in his own eyes, but the Lord weigheth the spirits.

—Proverbs 16:2

OCCASIONALLY in seasons of collapse and disaster great discoveries are made concerning those who appeared to be commercially sound but turn out to be rotten. Then the whole machinery of financing is laid bare, and things which directors and managers have thought to be right have been seen to be utter robbery. All looked solid and substantial until the inevitable crash came, and then no man felt that he could trust his neighbor. No doubt these schemers thought their ways "clean," but the event discovered their dirty hands.

Spiritual failures of like kind occur in the church. Great reputations explode, high professions dissolve. Men readily cajole themselves into the belief that they are right, and are doing right. They misapply Scripture, misinterpret providence, and in general turn things upside down, but the inexorable judgment overtakes them. A weighing time comes, and their professions are exposed. Niagara is at the end of the fatal rapid of self-deception: the self-satisfied pretender descends with a plunge to sure destruction.

Let us practically consider some of the "ways" which appear to be "clean," but are not so, when the Lord comes to weigh the spirits.

I. THE WAYS OF THE OPENLY WICKED. Many of these are "clean" in their own eyes.

To effect this self-deception:
- They give pretty names to sin.
- They think ill of others, making them out to be much worse than themselves, and finding in this an excuse for themselves,
- They claim to have many admirable qualities, and fine points.
- They urge that if imperfect they cannot help it.
- They also seriously resolve to amend; but never do so.

Men do with themselves as financiers do with companies:
- They put down doubtful assets as certain property.
- They reckon expectations as receipts.
- They tear out pages from the account-book.
- They conceal damaging facts, and ruinous entanglements.
- They cook the accounts in all sorts of ways, and make groundless promises.

The Lord's trial will be thorough and decisive. He weighs with accurate balances and weights; and he looks not only to the open way but to the inner spirit.

II. THE WAYS OF THE GODLESS.
- These often boast that they are better than the religious.
- They pretend that their superior intellects prevent their being believers: they must doubt because they are clever.
- They extol regard to the second table of the Law as being far more important than any service rendered to God himself.
- They will not be held accountable for their creed, or be judged for rejecting a few crabbed dogmas.

But all these shall be weighed in the balances and found wanting.

III. THE WAYS OF THE OUTWARD RELIGIONIST. These seem "clean."
- His observance of ceremonies.
- His regular attendance at worship.
- His open profession of religion.
- His generosity to the cause, and general interest in good things.

Thus ministers, deacons, members, etc., may boast, and yet when the Lord weighs their spirits they may be castaways.

IV. THE WAYS OF THE COVETOUS PROFESSOR. His ways are specially "clean."
- His greed keeps him from expensive sins, and therefore he gives himself credit for self-denial.
- He stints the cause of God and the poor.
- He oppresses his workmen in their wages.
- He makes hard bargains, drives debtors to extremes, takes undue advantage, and is a skinflint to all around him.

The Lord says of him, "covetousness which is idolatry."

V. THE WAYS OF THE WORLDLY PROFESSOR. He thinks himself "clean."
Let him honestly consider whether he is "clean":
- In his secret life? In his private and hidden indulgences?
- In his pleasures and amusements?
- In his company and conversation ?
- In his forsaken closet, forgotten Bible, lukewarm religion, etc.

What a revelation when the weighing of his spirit comes!

VI. THE WAYS OF THE SECURE BACKSLIDER. He dreams that his way is "clean," when a little observation will show him many miry places:
- Decline in private prayer (Job 15:4).
- Sin gradually getting the upper hand (Jer. 14:10).
- Conversation scantily spiritual (Eph. 5:4)
- Scriptures little read (Hos. 8:12).
- Heart growing hard (Heb. 3:13).
- Religion almost destitute of life (Rev. 3:1).
- Pride cropping up in many directions (Deut. 8:14).

The Lord gives him a weighing in trial and temptation; then there follows an opening up of deceit and hypocrisy.

VII. THE WAYS OF THE DECEIVED MAN. He writes pleasant things for himself, and yet all the while he is a spiritual bankrupt.
- Failed in true faith in Jesus.
- Failed in real regeneration.

- Failed in heart-work and soul-service for the Lord.
- Failed for ever. *Will our hearer do this?*

Comparisons

How beautiful all things look when winter has bleached them! What a royal bed is to be seen in yonder corner! The coverlet is whiter than any fuller on earth could white it! Here might an angel take his rest, and rise as pure as when he reclined upon it. Pshaw! It is a dunghill, and nothing more.

All the ships that came into the harbor were claimed by one person in the city. He walked the quay with a right royal air, talked largely about owning a navy, and swaggered quite sufficiently had it been so. How came he to be so wealthy? Listen, he is a madman. He has persuaded himself into this folly, but in truth he has not a tub to call his own. What absurdity! Are not many the victims of even worse self-deception? They are rich and increased in goods according to their own notion; yet they are naked, and poor, and miserable.

"This must be the right way, see how smooth it is! How many feet have trodden it!" Alas, that is precisely the mark of the broad road which leadeth to destruction.

"But see how it winds about, and what a variety of directions it takes! It is no bigot's unbending line." Just so; therein it proves itself to be the wrong road; for truth is one, and unchanging.

"But I like it so much." This also is suspicious; for what an unrenewed man is so fond of is probably an evil thing. Hearts go after that which is like themselves, and graceless men love graceless ways

"Would you have me go that narrow and rough road?" Yes, we would; for it leadeth unto life; and though few there be that find it, yet those who do so declare that it is a way of pleasantness. It is better to follow a rough road to heaven than a smooth road to hell.

57

The Lord pondereth the hearts.
—*Proverbs 21:2*

 HE heart among the Hebrews is regarded as the source of wit, understanding, courage, grief, pleasure, and love. We generally confine it to the emotions, and especially the affections, and, indeed these are so important and influential that we may well call them the heart of a man's life.

Now *we* cannot read the heart, much less ponder or weigh it. We can only judge our fellow men by their actions; but of motive, and actual condition before God, we cannot form a true estimate, nor need we do so. This, however, the Lord can do as easily as a goldsmith judges silver and gold by weight. He knows all things, but he is pleased to show us the strictness of his examination by the use of the metaphor of weighing. He takes nothing for granted, he is not swayed by public opinion, or moved by loud profession; he brings everything to the scale, as men do with precious things, or with articles in which they suspect deception. The Lord's tests are thorough and exact. The shekel of the sanctuary was double that which was used for common weighings, so at least the Rabbis tell us; those who profess to be saints are expected to do more than others. The sanctuary shekel was the standard to which all common weights ought to be conformed. The law of the Lord is the standard of morals. The balances of God are always in order, always true, and exact.

I. THE WEIGHING OF HEARTS.

1. God has already performed it. Every man's purpose, thought, word, and action is put upon the scale at the first moment of its existence. God is not at any instant deceived.
2. The law under which we live daily weighs us in public and in private, and by our disobedience discovers the short weight of our nature, the defect of our heart.
3. Trials form an important order of tests. Impatience, rebellion, despair, backsliding, apostasy, have followed upon severe affliction or persecution.
4. Prosperity, honor, ease, success, are scales in which many are found wanting. Praise arouses pride, riches create worldliness, and a man's deficiencies are found out (Prov. 27:21).
5. Great crises in our own lives, in families, in religious thought, in public affairs, etc., are weights and scales. A man's heart can hardly be guessed at when all goes on steadily.
6. Truth is ever heart-searching. Some left Jesus when he preached a certain doctrine. Hearts are weighed by their treatment of the truth. When they refuse God's word, that word condemns them.
7. The moment after death, and specially the general judgment, will be heart-weighing times.

II. THE HEARTS WHICH ARE WEIGHED.

They greatly vary, but they may be divided roughly into three classes, upon which we will dwell, hoping that our hearers will judge themselves.

1. *Hearts which are found wanting at once.*
   - The natural heart. All who have been unchanged come under this; even "the good-hearted man at bottom."

- The double heart. Undecided, double-minded, false. "Their heart is divided, now shall they be found faulty" (Hos. 10:2).
- The heartless heart. No decision, energy, or seriousness. He is "a silly dove without heart" (Hos. 7:7).
- The perverse heart. Rebellious, willful, sinful.
- The unstable heart. Impressions forgotten, promises broken, etc.
- The proud heart. Self-righteous, confident, arrogant, defiant.
- The hard heart. Unaffected by love or terror. Obstinate. Resisting the power of the Holy Ghost.

2. *Hearts which turn out to be wanting on further weighing.*
- "Another heart," such as Saul had. A new phase of feeling, but not a new nature.
- A humbled heart, like that of Ahab when Elijah had prophesied his ruin. Humbled, but not humble; turned, but not turned from iniquity.
- A deceived heart. Thinks itself good, but is not.

3. *Hearts which are of good weight.*
- The trembling heart: penitent, afraid of sin, etc.
- The tender heart: sensitive, affectionate, longing.
- The broken heart: mourning, pining, humble, lowly.
- The pure heart: loving only that which is good and clean, mourning sin in itself and others, sighing for holiness.
- The upright heart: true, just, sincere, etc.
- The perfect heart: earnest, honest, resolute, consecrated, intent, united, etc.
- The fixed heart: resting firmly, abiding steadfastly, etc.
- Is your heart ready for the weighing? Have you no fear of the final trial? Is this confidence well founded
- Is Jesus enthroned therein by faith? If so, you need not fear any weighing.
- If not, what will you do when the King sets up the final scales?

Sundry Helps

Heaven's Sovereign saves all beings, but himself,
That hideous sight, a naked human heart.
—Young

In the reign of King Charles I., the goldsmiths of London had a custom of weighing several sorts of their precious metals before the Privy Council. On this occasion, they made use of scales, poised with such exquisite nicety, that the beam would turn, the master of the Company affirmed, at the two-hundredth part of a grain. Noy, the famous Attorney General, replied, "I shall be loath, then, to have all my actions weighed in these scales." "With whom I heartily concur," says the pious Hervey, "in relation to myself; and since the balances of the sanctuary, the balances in God's hand, are infinitely exact, oh what need have we of the merit and righteousness of Christ, to make us acceptable in his sight, and passable in his esteem."

> My balances are just,
>   My laws are equal weight;
> The beam is strong, and thou mayst trust
>   My steady hand to hold it straight.
> Were thine heart equal to the world in sight,
> Yet it were nothing worth, if it should prove too light.
>
> But if thou art asham'd
>   To find thine heart so light,
> And art afraid thou shalt be blam'd,
>   I'll teach thee how to set it right.
> Add to my law my gospel, and there see
> My merits thine, and then the scales will equal be.
>   —*Christopher Harvey, "Schola Cordis"*

In the mythology of the heathen, Momus, the god of fault-finding, is represented as blaming Vulcan, because in the human form, which he had made of clay, he had not placed a window in the breast, by which whatever was done or thought there might easily be brought to light. We do not agree with Momus, neither are we of his mind who desired to have a window in his breast that all men might see his heart. If we had such a window we should pray for shutters, and should keep them closed.

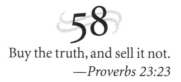

58

Buy the truth, and sell it not.
—*Proverbs 23:23*

HEN describing the pilgrims passing through Vanity Fair, Mr. Bunyan says: "That which did not a little amuse the merchandisers was, that these pilgrims set very light by all their wares; they cared not so much as to look upon them; and if they called upon them to buy, they would put their fingers in their ears and cry, 'Turn away mine eyes from beholding vanity'; and look upwards, signifying that their traffic was in heaven.

"One chanced, mockingly, beholding the carriage of the men, to say unto them, 'What will ye buy?' But they, looking gravely upon him, said, 'We buy the truth.'"

The true Christian is like the merchantman who sought goodly pearls: he sought them to buy them; he bought them with all that he had.

Let us carefully consider

I. THE COMMODITY: "the truth."

1. Doctrinal Truth. The Gospel. The three R's—Ruin, Redemption, and Regeneration. The doctrines of grace.
   • These are the genuine articles, but counterfeits are in the market. A gospel buyer must learn to discriminate, so as to reject
   • Salvation without Christ as God.
   • Pardon without an atoning sacrifice.
   • Life without the new birth.
   • Regeneration without faith.
   • Faith without works.
   • Safety without perseverance in holiness
2. Experimental Truth. The new birth and the heavenly life are real gems. But of these there are base imitations.
   • Discriminate between true religion and
   • Faith without repentance.
   • Talk without feeling.
   • Life without struggles.
   • Confidence without examination.
   • Perfection without humility.
3. Practical Truth. Truth as a matter of act and deed. Take care not to seem what you are not.
   • Never do what you are ashamed of.
   • Never be willfully ignorant of what you should know.

II. THE PURCHASE: "buy the truth." Here let us at once:

1. Correct an Error. Strictly speaking, truth and grace cannot be either bought or sold. Yet Scripture says, "Buy wine and milk without money and without price."
2. Expound the word. It is fitly chosen; for in order to be saved we should be ready to buy truth if it were to be bought:
   • To give up every sin, fulfill all righteousness, and give that which we have, if such were the price.
   • To be right with God by earnest watchfulness as much as if everything depended upon ourselves.

- To be ready to endure every test, make every search, etc.
- To run every risk, bear every cross, give up every worldly pleasure in order to be true to Jesus.

3. Paraphrase the Sentence.
   - Buy what is *truly* the Truth
   - Buy *all* the Truth
   - Buy *only* the Truth.
   - Buy the Truth *at any price.*
   - Buy *now* the Truth.

4. Give reasons for the Purchase.
   - It is in itself most precious.
   - You need it at this moment for a thousand useful purposes.
   - You will need it in time and in eternity.

5. Direct you to the Market.
   "Buy of Me," saith Christ.
   The Market-day is now on; "Come, buy."

6. Repeat the Text: "BUY the Truth."
   - Not merely hear about it.
   - Nor rest content with commending it to others.
   - Nor satisfied just to know about it.
   - Nor content with heartily wishing for it.
   - Nor be content with intending to buy it.
   - But, "Buy the Truth": down with the cash, conclude the bargain, secure the estate.

III. THE PROHIBITION: "sell it not." Purchase it as a permanent investment, not to be parted with.

- Some sell it for a livelihood; for respectability; for repute of being scientific and thoughtful; to gratify a friend; for the pleasure of sin; for nothing at all but mere wantonness; but you must hold to it as for life itself.
- Buy it at any price and sell it at no price.
- You still need it.
- It has well repaid you hitherto.
- You cannot better yourself by bartering it for the whole world.
- You are lost without it. Sell it not!

Hints to Buyers

Solomon bids us "buy the truth," but doth not tell us what it must cost, because we must get it though it be never so dear. We must love it both shining and scorching. Every parcel of truth is precious as the filings of gold; we must either live with it, or die for it. As Ruth said to Naomi, "Whither thou goest I will go, and where thou lodgest I will lodge, and nothing but death shall part thee and me" (Ruth 1:16–17); so must gracious spirits say, Where truth goes I will go, and where truth lodges I will lodge, and nothing but death shall part me and truth. A man may lawfully sell his house, land, and jewels, but truth is a jewel that exceeds all price, and must not be sold; it is our heritage: "Thy testimonies have I taken as a heritage for ever (Ps. 119:11). It is a legacy which our forefathers have bought with their blood, which should make us willing to lay down anything, and to lay out anything, that we may, with the- wise merchant in the gospel (Matt. 13:45) purchase the precious pearl, which is more worth than heaven and earth, and which will make a man live happy, die comfortably, and reign eternally. —*Thomas Brooks*

"Now, as I said, the way to the Celestial City lies just through this town where this lusty fair is kept; and he that would go to the City, and yet not go through this town, must needs go out of the world. The Prince of princes himself, when here, went through this town to His own country, and that upon a Fair-day too. Yea, and as I think, it was Beelzebub, the chief Lord of this Fair, that invited Him to buy of its vanities: yea, would have made Him Lord of the Fair, would he but have done him reverence as He went through the town; yea, because He was such a person of honor, Beelzebub had Him from street to street, and showed Him all the kingdoms of the world in a little time, that he might, if possible, allure that blessed One to cheapen and buy some of his vanities, but he had no mind to the merchandise, and therefore left the town, without laying out so much as one farthing upon these vanities. This Fair, therefore, is an ancient thing, of long standing, and a very great Fair." —*Bunyan*

59

My son, give me thine heart.
—*Proverbs 23:26*

 T is wisdom that here speaks. Wisdom is but another name for God, or, better still, for the Lord Jesus, who is incarnate wisdom. The request is for the heart, the affections, the center of our being. "Give me thine heart" is the first, the daily, the chief, the ultimate demand of the good Spirit.

I. LOVE PROMPTS THIS REQUEST OF WISDOM.

1. Only love will thus seek love. What cares indifference for the love of others? If it can serve its turn by their hands, their hearts may go where they choose.

2. Only for love would wisdom seek the hearts of such poor things as we are. What service can we render to him whom angels adore? What matters our love or hate to him?

3. Yet wisdom gains a son when the heart is given to it; for no one is a true son who does not love. "He that loveth is born of God."

4. If a son already, God's love bids us become yet more wise by a more complete yielding of the heart to God, to Christ, to wisdom. We cannot push this precept too far.

II. WISDOM PERSUADES US TO OBEY THIS LOVING REQUEST.
It is for our lasting good to love the Lord and his wisdom.

1. Evil lovers will seek us, and our hearts will be given to one or other. To our ruin or our ennobling the choice will be. He who has the heart has the man.

2. It is well to be engaged with the highest love that we may overcome the lower. God's servant cannot be Satan's slave.

3. It will please God for us to love him; a father is charmed with the love of his little child. What an honor, a heritage, a heaven to be allowed to love the Lord!

4. Nothing else can please him. Whatever we do without our hearts will grieve him; it will be an empty formality. Fish were never offered to God, for they could not come to the altar alive. The heathen reckoned it to be a fatal omen when the heart of the victim was not sound.

5. He deserves our heart, for he made it, he keeps it beating, he cheers it, he bought it, he prepares it for heaven; he gives heart for heart—his own love for ours.

6. There is no getting wisdom without giving the heart to it. God will not give himself to the heartless. Nothing can be done well unless the heart is thrown into it.

III. LOVE WOULD HAVE US OBEY THE REQUEST WISELY.
- At once–give God your heart. Delay is wicked and injurious.
- Freely–give God your heart; it cannot be done else. Force cannot compel love; the gift must be spontaneous.
- Altogether give God your heart. Half a heart is no heart. A divided heart is dead. "God is not the God of the dead."
- Once for all give him your heart, and let it remain in his keeping: for ever.
- Where is your heart now?
- What state is it in? Is it not cold, worldly, restless?
- Come and believe in Jesus, that you may receive power to become a son of God, and serve him with loving heart.

Choice Quotations

Of all the suitors which come unto you, it seems there is none which hath any title to claim the heart but God, who challengeth it of you, calling you by the name of a son (Mal. 1:6), as if he should say, Thou shalt give it to thy Father, which gave it to thee. Art thou my son? My sons give me their hearts, and by this they know that I am their Father, if I dwell in their hearts, for the heart is the temple of God (1 Cor. 6:16); therefore, if thou be his son, thou wilt give me thy heart.

Canst thou deny him anything, whose goodness created us, whose favor elected us, whose mercy redeemed us, whose wisdom converted us, whose grace preserved us, whose glory shall glorify us? Oh, "if thou knewest," as Christ said to the woman of Samaria, "If thou knewest who it is that saith unto thee" give me thy heart, thou wouldst say unto him, as Peter did when Christ would wash his feet (John 13:9), "Lord, not my feet only, but my hands and my head"; not my heart only, but all my body, and my thoughts, and my words, and my works, and my goods, and my life; take all that thou hast given. If ye ask me why you should give your hearts to God, I do not answer like the disciples which went for the ass and colt, "The Lord hath need" (Matt. 21:3), but you have need. If ever the saying were true (Acts 20:35), "It is more blessed to give than to take," more blessed are they which do give their hearts to God than they which take possession of the world. —*Henry Smith*

"My son, give me thine heart." For two reasons: Because, (1) unless the heart be given, nothing is given (Hos. 7:14; Matt.15:8–9); (2) if the heart be given, all is given (2 Chron. 30:13–20). —*Hugh Stowell*

No possible compromise. Now, most people think, if they keep all the best rooms in their hearts swept and garnished for Christ, that they may keep a little chamber in their heart's wall for Belial on his occasional visits; or a three-legged stool for him in the heart's countinghouse; or a corner for him in the heart's scullery, where he may lick the dishes. It won't do! You must cleanse the house of him, as you would of the plague, to the last spot. You must be resolved that as all you have shall be God's, so all you are shall be God's. —*John Ruskin*

"My guilt is damnable," exclaimed a humble saint, "in withholding my heart; because I know and believe his love, and what Christ has done to gain my consent—to what?—my own happiness." —*C. Bridges*

> Give thee mine heart? Lord, so I would,
> And there's great reason that 1 should,
>   If it were worth the having:
> Yet sure thou wilt esteem that good
> Which thou hast purchased with thy blood,
>   And thought it worth thy craving.
> Lord, had I hearts a million,

> And myriads in every one
>> Of choicest loves and fears;
> They were too little to bestow
> On thee, to whom I all things owe,
>> I should be in arrears.
>
> Yet, since my heart's the most I have,
> And that which thou dost chiefly crave,
>> Thou shalt not of it miss.
> Although I cannot give it so
> As I should do, I'll offer it though:
>> Lord, take it; here it is.
> —*Christopher Harvey, "Schola Cordis"*

It is said that during the persecution of the Papists by Queen Elizabeth, certain of the wealthy Catholics desired to save their lives by an open compliance with her intolerant laws, though they remained Romanists at heart. To their enquiry for direction it is reported that the Pope of that day replied, "Only let them give me their hearts, and they may for this time do as they are compelled to do." Whether the story is true or not, we may be sure that if the evil one can but keep the heart, he cares little what outward religion is practiced.

60

It is the glory of God to conceal a thing, but the honor of kings is to search out a matter.

—Proverbs 25:2

W E will first give the usual interpretation. It is God's glory to conceal many things and the honor of kings to search them out.

But this must be taken in a limited sense. It is not absolutely for God's glory to conceal, or why a revelation at all? Many things it would not be to his glory to conceal. Most mysteries are not so much concealed by any act of God, as hidden from their very nature and from our want of capacity to understand them. The Divine nature, the filiation of the Son of God, the complex person of Jesus, the procession of the Holy Ghost, the eternal decrees, and so forth, are not so much to be understood as believed.

But it is true that what is concealed it is for God's glory to conceal.

His eternal purpose as to individuals, who as yet abide in sin.

The future, and especially the day of the second coming.

The connecting link in doctrine between predestination and free agency, and a thousand other matters. These are concealed, and there is wisdom in the concealment; therefore, we need not wish to know.

But to me this seems not to be the meaning.

The antithesis is not complete. It is rather for wise men than kings to search out the secrets of nature and grace. Moreover, the following verse would not allow the antithetical sense.

We will therefore go upon another tack, and first ask, What things ought kings to search out? Here is the pith of the matter.

When justice is baffled, hoodwinked by bribes, or misled by prejudice, or puzzled by falsehood, it is to a king's damage, and dishonor, and he is bound to search the matter to the bottom. A magistrate's honor lies in the discovery of crime, but the glory of God lies in his graciously and justly hiding guilt from view.

With God no search is needful, for he sees all; his glory is to cover that which is plain enough to his eye, to cover it justly and effectually.

I. THAT IT IS GOD'S GLORY TO COVER SIN.

1. The guilt, aggravations, motives, and deceits of a life, the Lord is able to remove for ever by the atoning blood.
2. Sin which is known and confessed, he yet can cover so that it shall not be mentioned against us any more for ever.
3. He can do this justly through the work of Jesus.
4. He can do this without compensation from the offender himself, because of what the Substitute has done.
5. He can do this without any ill effect on others; no man will think that God connives at sin, seeing he has laid its punishment on Jesus.
6. He can do this without injury to the man himself. He will hate sin none the less because he escapes punishment; but all the more because of the love of the atoning Lamb.
7. He can do this effectually and for ever. Sin once put out of sight by the Lord shall never be seen again. Glorious Gospel, this, for guilty ones.

II. THIS SHOULD BE A GREAT ENCOURAGEMENT TO SEEKING SOULS.

1. Not to attempt to cover their own sin, since it is God's work to hide their iniquities, and they may leave it with him.
2. To give God glory by believing in his power to conceal sin, eves their own crimson sin.
3. To believe that he is willing to do it at this moment for them.
4 To believe at once, so as to have sin covered once for all.

III. THIS SHOULD BE A MIGHTY STIMULUS TO SAINTS.

1. To glorify God in covering their sin. Let them talk of pardon with exultation, and tell how the Lord casts sin behind his back, casts it into the depths of the sea, blots it out, and puts it where if it be sought for it cannot be found. Jesus "made an end of sin."
2. To aim at the covering of the sins of others by leading them to Jesus, that their souls may be saved from death.
3. To imitate the Lord in forgetting the sins of those who repent. We are to put away for ever of any wrong done to ourselves, and to treat converts as if they had not disgraced themselves aforetime. When we see a prodigal let us "bring forth the best robe and put it on him," that all his nakedness may be concealed and his rags forgotten.

Come and lay bare your sin that the Lord may conceal it at once.

Studs of Silver

Thomas Brooks discussing the question whether the sins of the saints shall be publicly declared at the judgment-day, argues that they will not. His fifth argument is this: It is the glory of a man to pass over a transgression: "The discretion of a man deferreth his anger; and it is his glory to pass over a transgression" (Prov. 19:11) or to pass by it, as we do by persons or things we know not, or would take no notice of. Now is it the glory of a man to pass over a transgression, and will it not much more be to the glory of Christ, silently to pass over the trans-gressions of his people in that great day? The greater the treasons and rebellions are that a prince passes over and takes no notice of, the more is it his honor and glory; and so doubtless, it will be Christ's in that great day, to pass over all the treasons and rebellions of his people, to take no notice of them, to forget them, as well as to forgive them.

The heathens have long since observed that in nothing man came nearer to the glory and perfection of God himself than in goodness and clemency. Surely if it be such an honor to man "to pass over a transgression," it cannot be a dishonor to Christ to pass over the transgressions of his people, he having already buried them in the sea of his blood. Again, said Solomon, "It is the glory of God to conceal a thing" (Prov. 25:2). And why it should not make for the glory of divine love to conceal the sins of the saints in that great day, I know not.

Of this truth we may say, what *Young* says of redemption:

> A truth so strange! 'twere bold to think it true;
> If not far bolder still to disbelieve

Mrs. Elizabeth Fry's labors amongst the female prisoners at Newgate owed much of their success to her tenderness in dealing with them. "I never ask their crimes, for we have all come short," was her quiet reproof to someone curious about a prisoner's offense.

German rationalists, discussing the sins of the patriarchs, were designated by *Dr. Duncan*: "Those Ham-like writers!" He often said, "Let us speak tenderly of the faults of the Old Testament saints."

There is no pardon so complete as that of God. He forgets as well as forgives. He restores to favor, and he does not think he has done enough when he withdraws his anger, for he manifests his love. An act of amnesty and oblivion has been passed concerning the believer's transgressions; neither can any of them be justly charged against him any more. The atonement makes it as just for God to pass by iniquity as it would have been to punish it. The wound is so healed that no scar remains. O Jehovah, who is a God like unto thee? In this glorious forgiveness none can compare with thee.

61

As cold waters to a thirsty soul, so is good news from a far country.
—*Proverbs 25:25*

 t is only on hot summer days that we can appreciate the illustration here employed; for we dwell in a well-watered country where thirst is readily assuaged. Yet we can imagine ourselves in the condition of Hagar, Ishmael, and Samson; or of a caravan in the desert; or of poor sailors in a boat upon the salt sea, dying for a draught of water.

When separated from friends by their journeying, or by our own, or when we have a trading interest in foreign ports, or a holy concern in missions, good news from a far country is eminently refreshing.

We shall use the text in three ways.

I. GOOD NEWS FOR SINNERS FROM GOD.

Sin put men into a far country, but here is the good news:

1. God remembers you with pity.
2. He has made a way for your return.
3. He has sent a messenger to invite you home.
4. Many have already returned, and are now rejoicing.
5. He has provided all means for bringing you home.
6. You may return at once. "All things are ready."

   If this good news be received, it will be exceedingly refreshing to thirsty souls. To others it will be commonplace.

II. GOOD NEWS FOR SAINTS FROM HEAVEN.

1. News does come from heaven. By the Spirit's application of the Word, and by the sweet whispers of Jesus' love.
2. To keep up this intercourse is most refreshing, and it is very possible; for Jesus delights to commune with us, the Father himself loveth us, and the Holy Spirit abideth with us for ever.
3. If for a while suspended, the renewal is sweeter than ever, even as cold water is doubly refreshing to a specially thirsty soul.
4. The news itself may thus be summarized:
   - The Father on the throne of Providence works all things for your good.
   - The Lord Jesus is interceding, preparing a place for you, and representing you before God.
   - He will shortly come in his glory.
   - Many like yourself are with him in the Father's house above.
   - You are wanted there: they cannot be a perfect family till you are brought home.
   - Receive this, and feel the attractions of heaven drawing you above the distractions of earth.

III. GOOD NEWS FOR HEAVEN FROM EARTH.

It gives joy to the home circle to hear that:
1. Sinners are repenting.
2. Saints are running their race with holy diligence.
3. Churches are being built up and the Gospel is spreading.
4. More saints are ripening and going home.

Let us accept the message of love and be happy in the Lord.

Let us tell the glad tidings to all around.

Scraps of News

The Hawaiian notions of a future state, where any existed, were peculiarly vague and dismal, and Mr. Ellis says that the greater part of the people seemed to regard the tidings of *ora loa ia Jesu* (endless life by Jesus) as the most joyful news they had ever heard, "breaking upon them," to use their own phrase, "like light in the morning." "Will my spirit never die? and can this poor weak body live again?" an old chieftain exclaimed, and this delighted surprise seemed the general feeling of the natives. —*From "Six Months in the Sandwich Islands," by Miss Bird*

Thirst is a blessed thing, if cold water be at hand; cold water is a blessed thing to those who thirst. Needy sinners get; a gracious Savior gives. When thirst drinks in cold water, when cold water quenches thirst, the giver and the receiver rejoice together. While the redeemed obtain a great refreshment in the act, the Redeemer obtains a greater; for himself was wont to say, "It is more blessed to give than to receive." —*W. Arnot*

The words remind us of the scanty intercourse in the old world between wanderers and the home they had left. The craving for tidings in such a case must be as a consuming thirst, the news that quenched it as a refreshing fountain. —*Speaker's Commentary*

Dr. Field, in his "Journey through the Desert," speaks of being upon Mount Sinai and writes, "Here in a pass between rocks under a huge granite boulder is a spring of water, which the Arabs say never fails. It was very grateful in the heat of the day, especially as we found snow in a cleft of the rocks, which, added to the natural coldness of the spring, gave us ice-water on Mount Sinai."

62

Thine own friend, and thy father's friend, forsake not.
—*Proverbs 27:10*

 MAN may have many acquaintances, but he will have few friends; he may count himself happy if he has one who will be faithful to him in time of trouble. If that person has also been kind to his father before him, he should never be slighted, much less alienated. Real friends are to be retained with great care, and, if need be, with great sacrifice. The wisdom of the world teaches this, and inspiration confirms it.

If we rise into a higher sphere, it is much more so. There we have one Friend—the Friend of sinners, who in infinite condescension has called us friends, and has shown that greatest of all love-laying down his life for his friends. To him we must cleave in life and death. To forsake him would be horrible ingratitude.

I. DESCRIPTIVE TITLE. "Thine own friend and thy father's friend."

1. "Friend": this implies kindness, attachment, help.
2. "Father's friend": one who has been faithful, unchanging, patient, wise, and tried, and this in the experience of our own father, on whose judgment we can depend. In many cases the best medical man you can have is the family physician, who knows your parents' constitutions as well as your own. The friend of the family should ever be a welcome guest.
3. "Thine own friend," with whom you have enjoyed converse, in whom you can safely place confidence, with whom you have common objects, to whom you have made private revelations.
4. Do not forget the other side of friendship: thou must be a friend to him whom thou callest thy friend. "He that hath friends must shew himself friendly."

In all these points our Lord Jesus is the best example of a friend, and it is well for us to set him in the forefront, as a "Friend that sticketh closer than a brother." "This is my beloved, and this is my friend."

II. SUGGESTIVE ADVICE. "Forsake not."

1. What it does not suggest. It gives no kind of hint that he will ever forsake us. Hath he not said, "I will never leave thee nor forsake thee"?
2. In what sense can we forsake him? Alas, some professed friends of Jesus become traitors, others follow afar off, grow cold, turn to the world, lose fellowship, do not defend his cause, etc.
3. What seasons tempt us to it? Both prosperity and adversity. Times of spreading heresy, worldliness, infidelity, etc.
4. What is the process of forsaking? Gradual cooling down leads on to utter turning away. By degrees we see his poor people despised, his doctrine doubted, his ways forgotten, his cause no longer aided, and at last, profession given up.
5. What are the signs of this forsaking? They can be seen in the heart, heard in the conversation, marked in the absence of zeal and liberality, and at length detected in actual sins.
6. What reasons cause forsaking? Pride, deadness of heart, neglect of prayer, love of the world, fear of man, etc.
7. What arguments should prevent it? Our obligations, his faithfulness, our vows, our danger apart from him, etc.
8. What in the end comes of such forsaking?
   All manner of evils follow, to ourselves, to his cause, to other friends, to the worldlings around us.

III. CONSEQUENT RESOLVE. I will cleave to him.

Let us cling to Jesus.
- In faith, resting alone in him.
- In creed, accepting his every teaching.
- In confession, declaring our loyalty to him.
- In practice, following his footsteps.
- In love, abiding in fellowship with him.

Forsake not Christ when he is persecuted and blasphemed.

Forsake him not when the world offers gain, honor, ease, as the price of your defection.

Forsake him not when all men seem to desert him, and the church is decaying and ready to die.

Good Words

He hath the substance of all bliss,
To whom a virtuous friend is given;
So sweet harmonious friendship is,
Add but eternity, you'll make it heaven.

—*John Norris*

Hewitson writes: "I think I know more of Jesus Christ than of any earthly friend." Hence one who knew him well remarked, "One thing struck me in Mr. Hewitson: he seemed to have no gaps, no intervals in his communion with God." —*G. S. Bowes*

The Prime Minister of Madagascar presiding at a missionary meeting, July 11th, 1878, said, "I don't like to speak about my own father here before you all, but I remember one young woman whom my father taught to read the Bible, and trained to be a Christian. When the persecution came again she was accused, convicted, and sentenced to death for being a Christian. She was brought here to be thrown over this rock, and at the last moment was offered her life if she would recant. But she refused, crying out, 'No, throw me over, for I am Christ's.'" —*Chronicle of the London Missionary Society*

We must not forsake our own friend, for that would be to forsake our second self; and we must not forsake our father's friend, for that would make us guilty of a double ingratitude of the basest sort that we can practice towards men. Our fathers' friends, if they are honest, are the best possessions that they can leave us; and if Naboth would not sell, for any price, the inheritance left him by his father, but kept it in spite of an Ahab and a Jezebel, till he was stoned, shall we show such irreverence to the memory of our fathers, as to give up, without any price, the most precious possessions which they have bequeathed us? Solomon carried on his father's friendly intercourse with Hiram, and spared a traitor to his crown and dignity, because he had shared with his father in all his afflictions. Rehoboam would have been a wiser and happier man if he had followed the example and precept of his father. —*Dr. G. Lawson*

Old family friends. I. Consider some of our father's old friends: (1) the Sabbath, (2) the Sanctuary, (3) the Savior, (4) the Scriptures. II. Consider some reasons for being true to them: (1) because of what they have done for those who are dear to us, (2) because of what they promise to do for us, (3) because of what they have already done for some of us. —*Biblical Museum*

One day the pulpit of the Rev. G. Cowie, of Huntley, was occupied by a minister who spoke as if the Holy Spirit was not needed either by saints or sinners. After the sermon, Mr. Cowie stood on the pulpit stairs, and said: "Sirs, haud in wi' your auld freen, the Holy Ghost; for if ye ance grieve him awa', ye'll nae get him back sae easy."

63

Whoso keepeth the fig tree shall eat the fruit thereof: so he that waiteth on his master shall be honored.

—Proverbs 27:18

HE general rule is that service brings reward. The man tended the
fig tree, and it bore him fruit: faithful service usually brings its recompense. Masters, if at all worthy of their position, will honor
those servants who do their duty to them.

I. CHRIST IS OUR MASTER.

1. Our sole master. We serve others, that we may serve him: we do not
   divide our service. "One is your master, even Christ."
2. Our choice Master. There is not such another in the universe.
3. Our chosen Master. We cheerfully take his yoke: to serve him is to us a
   kingdom. "I love my master (Exod. 21:5).
4. Our gracious Master: bearing with our faults, cheering us when faint,
   aiding us when weary, tending us in sickness, instructing us with
   patience, promising a great reward, etc.
5. Our life Master. Our ear is bored to his door-post: we are his to all eternity.

II. OUR BUSINESS IS TO SERVE HIM.

1. Expressed by the sense of *"keeping the fig tree."* We are to see to our Lord as
   a good body-servant watches over his master.
   - Remaining with him. Never quitting his side, or getting out of com-
     munion with him.
   - Defending him. Allowing none to speak against him, or to injure his
     honor while we have a tongue in our heads.
   - Guarding his interests. Making his cause our own, his business
     our business.
   - Cherishing his family. Loving the least of them, and laboring for the
     good of all.
   - Striving for his objects. Consecrating ourselves to carry out the grand
     purposes of our Lord, and laying aside everything which would hin-
     der us in this one pursuit.
2. Expressed by the words *"waiteth on his master."*
   - Waiting his word. "Speak, Lord; for thy servant heareth" (1 Sam.
     3:9; Ps. 85:8).
   - Seeking his smile. "Make thy face to shine upon thy servant" (Ps. 31:16).

- Depending upon him for strength "Give thy strength unto thy servant" (Ps. 86:16).
- Expecting the fulfillment of his promises. "Remember the word unto thy servant, upon which thou hast caused me to hope" (Ps. 119:49).
- Consecrated to his service—"body, soul, and spirit." Having no private ends (1 Chron. 12:18).
- Acquiescent in his will. Ready either to suffer or to labor as he may appoint (Luke 7:7-10).

The contrary of this is
- Self-seeking. Lusting after honor, wealth, ease, pleasure.
- Self-guiding: doing your own will, and yet pretending to serve the Lord.
- Self-applauding: robbing our Lord of the glory which belongs to him alone.

III. OUR SERVICE WILL BRING HONOR.

1. Among your fellow servants here below.
2. Even among enemies, who will be forced to admire sincerity and fidelity.
3. From our Lord, who will give us a sweet sense of acceptance even here below.
4. At the judgment-day, before the assembled universe.
5. Throughout eternity, among angels and glorified spirits.
   - Let us grieve that we have not served him better.
   - Let us repent if we have not served him at all.
   - Let us pray him to receive us into his service this day.

Concerning the Master

How sweetly doth *My Master* sound! *My Master!*
As ambergris leaves a rich scent
Unto the taster:
So do these words a sweet content,
An oriental fragrancy, *My Master.*

—*George Herbert*

Two aged ministers met one Saturday at a station in Wales as they were going to preach in their respective places on Sunday. "I hope," said Mr. Harris, of Merthyr, to Mr. Powell, of Cardiff, "I hope the Great Master will give you his face tomorrow." "Well, if he does not," replied Mr. Powell, "I will speak well of him behind his back."

Rutherford, speaking of how his Lord encouraged him with sweet fellowship while he was serving him, says in his quaint way, "When my Master sends me on his errands, he often gives me a bawbee for myself"; by which he meant that as sure as ever God employed him he gave him a penny for reward, as we do to boys who go upon our errands.

An old highlander, Hugh Chisholm, was one of the personal attendants of Prince Charles in his wanderings. Lord Monboddo was much attached to this interesting old man, and once proposed to introduce him to his table at dinner, along with some friends of more exalted rank. On mentioning the scheme to Mr. Colquhoun Grant, one of the proposed party, that gentleman started a number of objections, on the score that poor Chisholm would be embarrassed and uncomfortable in a scene so unusual to him, while some others would feel offended at having the company of a man of mean rank forced upon them. Monboddo heard all Mr. Grant's objections, and then assuming a lofty tone, exclaimed: "Let me relieve you, Mr. Grant: Hugh Chisholm has been in better company than either yours or mine!" The conscience stricken Jacobin had not another word to say. —*Memoir of Robert Chambers*

There will be a resurrection of credits, as well as of bodies. We'll have glory enough by-and-bye.—*Richard Sibbes*

A dog which follows anybody and everybody belongs to no one, and no one cares for it. The more it shows its devotion to its master the greater is the man's attachment to it. In domestic service we should not care to keep a body-servant who spent half his time in waiting upon another employer.

Old and faithful servants grow to look upon all their master's property as their own. One such said, "Here comes our carriage, and there are our dear children coming home from school!" Our Lord Jesus loves to see us feel a fellowship—a community of interests with himself. He makes such service to be its own reward, and adds heaven besides. He will not cast off his old servants, but he will grant them to be with him in his glory, as they have been with him in his humiliation.

64

The fear of man bringeth a snare: but whoso putteth his trust in the Lord shall be safe.

—*Proverbs 29:25*

 E have here a double proverb: each half is true by itself; and, put together, the whole is forcible and full of teaching. He who fears man is in great danger from that very fact; he who trusts in the Lord is in no danger of any sort; trusting in the Lord is the great antidote against the fear of man.

I. HERE IS A VERY COMMON EVIL. "The fear of man bringeth a snare."

1. It is thought by some to be a good; but it is in the best instance doubtful. Even virtue followed through dread of a fellow creature loses half its beauty, if not more.

2. It leads men into great sins at times, snaring them, and holding them like birds taken by a fowler. Aaron yielded to popular clamor and made the calf. Saul cared more to be honored among the people than to please the Lord. Pilate feared that a charge would reach Caesar, and so he violated his conscience. Peter denied his Master for fear of a silly maid.

3. It keeps many from conversion: their companions would ridicule, their friends would be annoyed, they might be persecuted, and so they are numbered with the "fearful, and unbelieving."

4. It prevents others avowing their faith. They try to go to heaven through a back door. Remember, "With the mouth confession is made unto salvation" (Rom. 10:10).

5. It lowers the dignity of good men. David was a poor creature before Achish, and even Father Abraham made but a poor figure when he denied his wife.

6. It holds some believers in equivocal positions. Illustrations are far too abundant. Men fail to carry out their principles for fear of men.

7. It hampers the usefulness of very many: they dare not speak, or lead the way, though their efforts are greatly needed.

8. It hinders many in duties which require courage. Jonah will not go to Nineveh because he may be thought a false prophet if God forgives that city. Galatian preachers went aside to false doctrine to be considered wise, etc.

9. It is the cause of weakness in the Church. It is cowardly, shameful, dishonorable to Jesus, idolatrous, selfish, foolish. It should not be allowed by any man in his own case.

II. HERE IS A VERY PRECIOUS SAFEGUARD. "Whoso putteth his trust in the Lord shall be safe."

Not slavish fear of man, but childlike trust in the Lord will be the protection of the believer.

1. The truster is safe from fear of man.
   - God is with us, therefore we are strong, and need not fear.
   - We are determined, and will not fear.
   - We pray, and lose our fear.
   - We prepare for the worst, and fear vanishes.

2. The truster is safe from the result of men's anger.
   - It often never comes. God restrains the persecutor.

- The loss which it inflicts if it does come is less than that which would be caused by cowardice.
- When we trust in God any such loss is joyfully borne.
- After all, what is there to fear? What can man do unto us? God being with us, our safety is perfect, continuous, eternal, even though the whole human race should besiege us.

III. HERE IS A VERY GLORIOUS DOCTRINE. We may take in the widest sense the doctrine of the second sentence, "Whoso putteth his trust in the Lord shall be safe":

- From the damning and conquering power of sin.   From the overcoming force of temptation.
- From the deadening effect of sorrow.
- From the destroying force of Satan.
- From death, and hell, and every evil
- From all injury which men can inflict.

Will you fear a worm, or trust your God?

Break the snare in which fear has entangled you.

Enter the palace of safety by the door of trust.

Warnings

The soul that cannot entirely trust God, whether man be pleased or displeased, can never long be true to him; for while you are eyeing man you are losing God, and stabbing religion at the very heart. —*Manton*

"*Fear of man.*" Grim idol—bloody-mouthed—many souls he has devoured and trampled down into hell! His eyes are full of hatred to Christ's disciples. Scoffs and jeers lurk in his face. The laugh of the scorner growls in his throat. Cast down this idol. This keeps some of you from secret prayer, from worshipping God in your family, from going to lay your case before ministers, from openly confessing Christ. You that have felt God's love and Spirit, dash this idol to pieces. Who art thou, that thou should'st be afraid of a man that shall die? "Fear not, thou worm, Jacob." "What have I to do any more with idols?" —*M'Cheyne*

The difficulties attending an open confession of Christ are the occasion of multitudes making shipwreck of their souls. In many hopeful characters, that Scripture, "the fear of man bringeth a snare," is verified. Cato and the philosophers of Rome honored the gods of their country though unbelievers in the superstitions of their country. Plato was convinced of the unity of God, but durst not own his convictions, but said, "It was a truth, neither easy to find, nor safe to own." Even Seneca, the renowned moralist, was forced by temptation to dissemble his convictions, of whom Augustus said, "He worshipped what himself reprehended, and did what himself reproved." At the interruption which was given to the progress of the Reformation by the return of the Papists to power, some, as they went to mass, would exclaim, "Let us go to the common error." Thus, conviction is not conversion where there is no confession of Christ. —*Salter*

One fire puts out another. Nothing so effectually kills the fear of man as abundance of the fear of God. Faith is an armor to the soul, and, clothed with it, men enter the thick of the battle without fear of wounds. Fear of man deadens conscience, distracts meditation, hinders holy activity, stops the mouth of testimony, and paralyzes the Christian's power. It is a cunning snare which some do not perceive, though they are already taken in it.

65

Where the word of a king is, there is power.
—*Ecclesiastes 8:4*

INGS were autocratic in Solomon's day. We may be glad that we are not under bondage to any absolute monarch, but enjoy the blessings of constitutional government. We are by no means slow to say to any one of our governors, "What doest thou?" And such a question, wisely put, is good both for him and for us.

God alone is rightfully sovereign without limit. He is King in the most absolute sense; and so it should be; for he is supremely good, wise, just, holy, etc.

As he is Maker of all, dominion over his creatures is a matter of natural right.

He has infinite power wherewith to carry out his royal will.

Even in his least word there is omnipotence.

Let us consider this:

I. TO EXCITE OUR AWE.

Let us carefully think of:

1. His creating word, by which all things arose out of nothing.
2. His preserving word, by which all things abide.
3. His destroying word, by which he will shake earth and heaven.
4. His word of prerogative by which he kills and makes alive.
5. His word of everlasting promise, which is our comfort.
6. His word of terrible threatening, which is our warning.
7. His word of prophecy and fore-ordination, which is a great deep, full of solemn teaching to the lowly in heart.

Who can stand before any of these without trembling adoration? Power attends them to the fullest degree, for each one is the word of a King.

II. TO ENSURE OUR OBEDIENCE.

1. No divine command is to be treated as non-essential, for it is the word of Jehovah, the King. See verses 2 and 3.
2. Each precept is to be obeyed at once, heartily, to the full, by every one, since the King commands.
3. His service must not be shunned, for that were to rebel against our Sovereign. Jonah did not find this succeed: for the Lord will not be trifled with, and will make runaways know that his arm is long.
4. Disobedience is to be repented of. If we have fallen into sin, let the King's word have a gracious power to subdue us to hearty grief.

III. TO INSPIRE OUR CONFIDENCE.

1. That he is able to give to the penitent, pardon; for he has promised in his word to do so.
2. That he will give to the believing, power to renew their lives. "He sent his word, and healed them" is true, spiritually.
3. That he will give to the tempted, power to overcome temptation. God ensures the believer's victory over every assault of Satan through the word. This weapon Jesus used in the wilderness.
4. That he will give to the suffering, power to endure with patience, and to gather profit from the trial.
5. That he will give to the dying, hope, peace, beatific vision, etc. One word from the Lord of life robs death of its sting.

IV. TO DIRECT OUR CHRISTIAN EFFORT.

1. In all we do we should respect the King's word. Churches should own Christ's headship, obey his laws, and acknowledge no other lawgiver. This would be a source of power, as the opposite is the cause of weakness.
2. We must look nowhere else for power. Education, oratory, music, wealth, ceremonialism are weakness itself, if depended on.
3. We must rely upon the word of our King as the instrument of power whenever we seek to do works in his name.
   - Preach it: for nothing else will break hard hearts, comfort the despairing, beget faith, or produce holiness.
   - Plead it in prayer: for the Lord will surely keep his own promises, and put forth his power to make them good.
   - Receive it into our mind and heart: for where divine truth is treasured, there will be a wealth of spiritual power.
   - Practice it: for none can gainsay a life which is ordered according to the precepts of the Lord. An obedient life is full of a power before which men and devils do homage.

4. We shall see its power in various ways.

- Gathering congregations. After all, the many do not go to listen to mere human teachings, but the cross attracts everywhere
- Gaining true converts. No conversion is worth anything unless it is wrought by the word of truth.
- Keeping such converts to the end. The incorruptible seed alone produces an incorruptible life.
- Order is created and preserved in the church by God's word.
- Saints are instructed, edified, sanctified, and fed by the word.
- Love, joy, peace, and every grace are begotten and fostered by the word.
- Read much the royal word.
- Speak more than ever the King's word, which is the gospel of peace.
- Believe in the word of King Jesus, and be bold to defend it.
- Bow before it, and be patient and happy.

Experiences

No language ever stirs the deeps of my nature like the Word of God; and none produces such a profound calm within my spirit. As no other voice can, it melts me to tears, it humbles me in the dust, it fires me with enthusiasm, it fills me with felicity, it elevates me to holiness. Every faculty of my being owns the power of the sacred Word: it sweetens my memory, it brightens my hope, it stimulates my imagination, it directs my judgment, it commands my will, and it cheers my heart. The word of man charms me for the time; but I outlive and outgrow its power; it is altogether the reverse with the Word of the King of kings: it rules me more sovereignly, more practically, more habitually, more completely every day. Its power is for all seasons: for sickness and for health, for solitude and for company, for personal emergencies and for public assemblies. I had sooner have the Word of God at my back than all the armies and navies of all the great powers; ay, than all the forces of nature; for the Word of the Lord is the source of all the power in the universe, and within it there is an infinite supply in reserve.

Believers know the life-giving power of the Word, for they can say, "Thy word hath quickened me"; and its life-sustaining power, for they live "by every word that proceedeth out of the mouth of God"; and its power against sin, for they can say, "Thy word have I hid in my heart, that I might not sin against thee."

"His word was with power" in Capernaum of old, and it will be with the same power in any place nowadays. His word cannot fail; "it shall not return void; it shall prosper." Therefore, when our "words fall to the ground," it only proves that they were not his words. —*Miss Havergal*

66

I am the Rose of Sharon, and the Lily of the valleys.
—*Song of Solomon 2:1*

ERE we have the Bridegroom praising himself, and this is a thing to be considered with careful attention.

This self-praise is not tainted with pride: such a fault could not find a place in the lowly Jesus. His egoism is not egotism. He does not commend himself for his own sake, but for our sakes He sets himself forth in glowing terms because:

- In condescension he desires our love. What a poor thing it is for him to care about! Yet he thirsts after it.
- In wisdom he uses the best way to win our love.
- In tenderness he deigns to describe himself that we may be encouraged by his familiarity in praising himself to us. This is one of the most effectual proofs of lowliness.
- Of necessity he describes himself, for who else can describe him? "No man knoweth the Son, but the Father" (Matt. 11:27).
- Moreover, he here states a fact which else might not be believed, seeing he makes himself so common a flower of earth, so graciously a joy for men, that all may have him.

We will not take up your time by trying to discover what flowers these may have been in the eastern flora: we may select those most like them in our own western land, and do our Lord no wrong.

I. THE EXCEEDING DELIGHTFULNESS OF OUR LORD.

He compares himself, not only, as in other places, to needful bread, and refreshing water, but to lovely flowers. In Jesus there are all delights as well as all necessaries.

1. He is now all that he ever was, for his "I am" runs through all eternity in unabated force.
2. He is in himself the delight of men. He speaks not of offices, gifts, works, possessions, but of himself. "I am."
3. He is delightful to the eye of faith, even as flowers are to the bodily sight. What more beautiful than roses and lilies?
4. He is delightful in the savor which comes of him. In him is a delicious, varied, abiding fragrance.
5. In all this he is the choicest of the choice: the rose—yea, Sharon's rose: the lily—yea, the most delicious lily of the valleys. There is none like him. He is indeed "a plant of renown."

Yet blind men see no color, and men without scent perceive no odor in the sweetest flowers; and carnal men see no delights in, Jesus. Roses and lilies require eyes and light ere they can be appreciated, and to know Jesus we must have grace and gracious dispositions. He says, "I am the Rose of Sharon"; and so he is essentially; but the grave question is, "Is he this to you?" Yes or no?

II. THE SWEET VARIETY OF HIS DELIGHTFULNESS.

1. Of the rose, majesty: of the lily, love.
2. Of the rose, suffering: of the lily, purity.
3. Of both a great variety: all the roses and all the lilies, all the beauties of heaven and earth meet in Jesus.
4. Of both the very essence. Of all the creatures, all the excellences, virtues, and blessings, which may be found in them, come from Jesus, and abide in Jesus without limit. Many eyes are wanted to spy out the whole of Christ. No eye, nor all eyes, can see all that lies in his varied perfections.
5. Of all these a perfect proportion, so that no one excellence destroys another. He is all a rose should be, and yet not the less perfect as a lily.

Hence he is suitable to all saints, the joy of all, the perfection of beauty to each one.

III. THE EXCEEDING FREENESS OF HIS DELIGHTFULNESS.

1. Meant to be plucked and enjoyed as roses and lilies are.
2. Abundant as a common flower. He is not as a rare orchid, but as the anemones which covered Sharon's plains, and as the lilies which abounded in all the valleys of Palestine.
3. Abiding in a common place, as roses in Sharon, and lilies in the valleys, where every passer-by was free to gather according to his own sweet will. Not found on inaccessible steeps, or within guarded enclosures, Jesus is out in the open: a flower of the common. This is a leading idea of the text. Those who desire Christ may have him.
4. Scattering fragrance, not over a room or a house, but far and wide, perfuming every wandering wind.
5. Yet roses and lilies fail to set forth our Beloved, for his is unfading virtue. They are soon withered, but "He dieth no more."

In all things look for Jesus. See him in primroses and daisies.

In Jesus look for all things of beauty and sweetness: lilies and roses are in him.

Listen much to Jesus, for he can tell you most about himself; and, coming at first hand, it will be surely true, and come with great force and unction. Hearken, and hear him say, "I am the Rose of Sharon."

Observations

"I am the Rose of Sharon, and the Lily of the Valleys"; words most seemly in the lips of the Lord Jesus Christ, in whom it is not robbery from others, but condescension and grace, to commend himself to the sons of men. "I am meek and lowly," would be the utterance of pride in Gabriel, but it is humility in Jesus, who has stooped that he might become meek and lowly. "I am the true Vine," "I am the good Shepherd," etc., are the expressions alike of truth and grace, and so here. —*A. Moody Stuart*

Not to flowers which only the rich and great can possess, but to those easily obtainable, does he liken himself; for always did he stoop to the lowliest, arid the common people ever heard him gladly. His presence on earth never failed to bring comfort to the needy, and refreshment to the downcast spirit, just as sweet odors float around roses and lilies, and minister solace to the organ of smell, while their fair forms and rich and delicate colors gratify the eye. —*H. K. Wood, in "The Heavenly Bridegroom and His Bride"*

We believe there can be little doubt that the rose is really intended by the Hebrew word. Even if in the general sense it should mean but a *flower*, we should still infer that, when applied in a particular sense, it means a rose, for this would be according to the usage of the East. Thus, the Persian word *gul* describes a flower in general, and the rose *par excellence*. This suffices to show the estimation in which the rose is held in the East. In the Persian language, particularly, there is perhaps no poem in which allusions to it, and comparisons drawn from it, do not recur even to repletion. . . . The extreme fragrance and beauty of the rose in some parts of Western Asia have attracted the notice of many travelers. It is also cultivated, not merely as a garden plant for pleasure, but in extensive fields, from the produce of which is prepared that valued and delicious perfume called rose-water. The size of the rose trees, and the number of the flowers on each, far exceed in the rose districts of Persia, anything we are here accustomed to witness. —*Pictorial Bible*

67

It was but a little that I passed from them, but I found him whom my soul loveth: I held him, and would not let him go, until I had brought him into my mother's house, and into the chamber of her that conceived me.

—*Song of Solomon 3:4*

HE first position is *"I passed from them."* We must go beyond the fellowship of the best of men, and commune with him whom our soul loveth. Our love must lead to action: *"I sought him."* Those who love Jesus seek his presence with an agony of desire.

After this seeking, we read at first, *"I found him not."* Sad, but needful disappointment. But this lasts not for ever; we soon come into the region of our text, where everything is bright with sunlight. Three flashes of delight follow each other: *"I found him"; "I held him"; "I brought him."* May these be our joyous experience! To that end let us muse upon them and pray the Holy Spirit to help us.

I. "I FOUND HIM": or, love in fellowship.

1. I was inquiring for him.
2. I had got beyond all men and means, and could not be contest with any but himself.
3. I beheld his person. He drew near in his Word and ordinances. I perceived him by the Spirit. Faith saw him clearly.
4. I was assured of his presence. My heart felt peculiar influences operating upon it. It was a time of love.
5. I knew him to be mine. There were no doubts and fears. He was "my Beloved," and I was all his own.
6. I was filled with content. I looked for no one else, for in finding him I had found my all for earth and heaven.
   - Do we know what this blessed finding means'
   - If not, let us never rest till we do.

II. "I HELD HIM": or, love in possession.

1. By my heart's resolve, determining never to lose him again.
2. By my tearful pleas, entreating him not to mane me wretched by withdrawing I pleaded:
   - My joy in his society.
   - My need of his gracious protection.
   - My love to him, which made me hunger for him.
   - His love to me, which surely would not let him leave me.
3. By making him my all in all. He stays where he is prized, and I set him on a high throne in my spirit.
4. By renouncing all other loves, sins, idols, etc. He is jealous, and I kept myself altogether for him.
5. By a simple faith: for he is pleased with trust; and dwells where he is rested in.
6. By his own power. "I would not let him go," because I held him by his promise, and by the power which it gave me.

If you have Jesus, hold him.

He is willing to be constrained. See how often, in his life on earth, "they constrained him," and he yielded to their will.

III. "I BROUGHT HIM": or, love in communication.

The love of Jesus creates in our hearts love to our fellow-believers for their Redeemer's sake.

The church of God is our mother: the holy assembly is her chamber, where we were born unto God, and nurtured in his fear. We are to labor to promote communion with Christ among those who are our brethren, taking Jesus with us whensoever we go up to the gatherings of the faithful.

This we should do:

1. By our own spirit: communing with Jesus before we go to public worship, and going there with him in our company.

    We shall always find him in the church if we take him in our hearts to its hallowed services.

2. By our words: we should so speak as to set forth Jesus, and promote fellowship with him. Alas, how many speak controversially, or without savor, or with carnal oratory wherein is no room for the Beloved! Oh, for a crucified style of speech!

3. By our prayers we should bring him into the assembly; ay, bring him into society where hitherto he has been unknown. The world also was once our mother. Oh, that we could introduce the Lord Jesus into her chambers, that he might reign and rule there! "Thy Kingdom come." By loving violence we will constrain him to come with us in his presence and power.

    - See what the church needs!—Christ in her midst.
    - See how he is likely to come!—he must be brought
    - See what must first be done!—he must be held.
    - See who alone can do this!—those who have found him.
    - Yet see, also, who may find him!—all who love him, and seek him.
    - Are we among the number?

Further Suggestions

Hold him by not offending him. First, by sloth. When the soul turns sleepy or careless, Christ goes away. Secondly, by idols. You cannot hold two objects. Thirdly, by being unwilling to be sanctified. Fourthly, by an unholy house. "I brought him into my mother's house." Remember to take Christ home with you, and let him rule in your house. If you walk with Christ abroad but never take him home, you will soon part company for ever.—*McCheyne*

"I found him"; I, a man, found the Lord of Glory; I, a slave to sin, found the great Deliverer; I, the child of darkness, found the Light of life; I, the uttermost of the lost, found my Savior and my God; I, widowed and desolate, found my

Friend, my Beloved, my Husband. Go and do likewise, sons and daughters of Zion, and he will be found: of you; for "then shall ye find when ye search with all your heart."

But we have another mother, and other brethren, in the human family from which we are sprung. The Church has the first, not the only claim on our affections; the perishing world has its right to a large share of our pity and our prayers. Comparatively, it is not hard for us to bring Jesus into the Church, which is his mother's house as well as ours. But the world hates Christ, has nothing in common with him, is aware that he rightfully claims the dominion, is sensitively jealous of the claim, and lives with its doors barred against him night and day. No criminal keeps so vigilant a watch against the officers of justice, no lonely widow makes her gates so fast against the midnight robber, no miser spurns so haughtily the beggar from his door, as the unrenewed heart keeps watch and ward against the entrance of Jesus, and scornfully sends him away when he asks for a lodging in the soul. To introduce him, therefore, into this home of our mother is a work demanding effort, watchfulness, patience. There is much to provoke him to turn away; we must plead with him, hold him, and not let him go; and with our mother's children we must also plead with "the soft tongue that breaketh the bone," for they are offended with us as well as with him. So sought and prevailed the Bride of the Lamb, till she brought her own Beloved into the midst of her mother's children, by whom she had been herself so hardly entreated, requiting evil with good. Have you attempted this? Are you engaged in the effort now? If not, rise and commence such a work of faith and labor of love on behalf of the lost. —*A. Moody Stuart*

68

Turn away thine eyes from me, for they have overcome me.
—*Song of Solomon 6:5*

 UCH of our life's business consists in overcoming evil, but here we have to deal with overcoming him who is perfect good.

It is not to be supposed that there is any opposition in the heavenly Bridegroom, nor any unwillingness to be overcome by his bride: no, it is the loving heart of Jesus which is readily overcome by the love of his chosen one.

Let us learn from this most remarkable exclamation:

I. THAT LOOKING UPON HIS CHURCH HAS OVERCOME THE HEART OF THE LORD JESUS.

1. He left heaven to be one with her. He could not bear to see her ruin, but left his Father that he might share her lot.
2. He died to redeem her: "found guilty of excess of love."
3. His delight is in her now; she is lovely in his sight.
4. His eternal joy is to spring from her: he will see in her the result of his death-agony: "he will rest in his love."

Jesus is so overcome that he still gives all that he is, and has, yea, and his own self, to his beloved.

II. THAT THE EYES OF HIS CHOSEN STILL OVERCOME THE LORD JESUS.

Because his eyes are full of love, therefore is he overcome by our eyes when we are:

1. Looking up in deep repentance
   • At first seeking for pardon.
   • At times when we pine for restoration from backsliding.
   • Whenever we are struggling to maintain fellowship, and mourning our breaches of it.
   • Whenever we groan under inbred sin, and would be free from it.
2. Looking at him by faith for salvation.
   • At first, by a desperate act, daring to glance with feeble hope.
   • Afterwards, in simplicity, day by day gazing at his wounds.
   • In deep distress still hoping on, and never removing our eyes.
3. Looking for all things to his love alone.
   • When in sore trouble, patiently submitting.
   • When in humble hope, quietly waiting.
   • When under severe tests, firmly believing.
   • When in full assurance, joyfully expecting.
4. Looking in prayer.
   • In personal trouble, like Jacob, pleading the promise, and saying, "I will not let thee go." The Lord says, "Let me go."
   • In holy compassion pleading for others, like Moses, to whom the Lord said, "Let me alone."
5. Looking in rapturous, restful love.
   • He is altogether lovely, and all mine: my eyes swim with tears of delight as they gaze on him, and thus they overcome him.
   • My heart burns with love to him, and I adore him; and this wins everything from him.
6. Looking in sacred longing for his appearing.
   • Pining for a personal revelation of himself to me by his Spirit.
   • Most of all, sighing for his speedy coming in the glory of the Second Advent. He replies, "Behold, I come quickly!"

Oh, the power of a spiritual man with Jesus!

Oh, the power of a church with heaven! The Lord will deny nothing to the prayer of his elect.

III. THAT IF THE CHURCH WOULD BUT LOOK TO HER LORD MORE SHE WOULD OVERCOME THE WORLD MORE.

To overcome the Lord is the greater thing, and when this is done, the church may well go forth conquering and to conquer all that is less than her Lord. The eyes of the church should be set on Jesus, and then she would overcome. If we were—

1. Weeping for dishonor done to him, he would see this, and retrieve our defeat.
2. Depending on him for our strength, our faith would give us victory through Jesus' love.
3. Obediently following his commands, he would then feel it right to give honor to his own truth, and to reward obedience to his own precepts.
4. Confidently expectant of victory, Jesus would make bare his arm for us. Faith's eyes calmly watching, or flashing with exultant expectancy, would be as flames of fire to the foe.
5. Eagerly pleading for his interposition, our tearful, earnest eyes would soon succeed with our gracious God.

See the secret of strength. Look to Jesus, and overcome.

Let us lament our infrequent use of this conquering weapon.

Now for a long and loving look at the Bridegroom of our souls.

Help us, O Holy Spirit, to whom our eyes owe their sight!

Hints

Who has not felt the power of the eye? The beggar looked so imploringly that we gave him alms; the child's eye so darkened with disappointment that we indulged his desire; the sick man gazed so sadly at our departure that we turned back, and lengthened our visit. But the eyes of those we love master us. Does a tear begin to form? We yield at once. We cannot endure that the beloved eyes should weep. Our Lord uses this figure to most encouraging purpose. The weeping eyes of prayer move the loving heart of Jesus. Matthew Henry says, "Christ is pleased to borrow these expressions of a passionate lover to express the tenderness of a compassionate Redeemer, and the delight he takes in his redeemed, and in the workings of his own grace in them."

We read in Matthew 15 that the Lord Jesus said to the Canaanitish woman, "O woman, great is thy faith; be it unto thee even as thou wilt." He seems to surrender at discretion, conquered by that faith which he had himself put into her heart. Now, faith is the eye of the soul, and here is an instance of the eyes overcoming the Lord. We cannot vanquish him with the works of our hands, or the eloquence of our lips; but we can win the victory by the pleadings of our eyes, those eyes, which are as the eyes of doves, seeing afar, the eyes of true faith.

Some devout persons find it a profitable exercise to bow the knee, and to look up. Using few words, they commune through a long, upward, pleading glance. One only cried, "My God," and at another timer "God be merciful to me, a sinner"; and yet he came forth from his closet as one who had bathed in heaven.

"Have you a glimpse of Christ now that you are dying?" was the question asked of an old Scottish saint, who, raising himself, made the emphatic reply, "I'll hae none o' your glimpses now that I am dying, since that I have had a full look at Christ these forty years gane." —*Annals of the Early Friends*

69

Come now, and let us reason together, saith the Lord: though your sins be as scarlet, they shall be as white as snow; though they be red like crimson, they shall be as wool.

—*Isaiah 1:18*

THE sinful condition of men is terrible in the extreme. This is set forth vividly in previous verses of the chapter. They are altogether alienated from their God.

God himself interposes to produce a change. The proposal of peace is always from his side.

He urges that a conference be held at once, "Come, and let us reason together."

That conference is to be held at once: "Come now," for the danger is too great to admit of a moment's delay. God is urgent; let us not procrastinate.

In our text we have:

I. AN INVITATION TO A CONFERENCE.

Sinful men do not care to think, consider, and look matters in the face; yet to this distasteful duty they are urged.

If they reason, they rather reason against God than together with him; but here the proposal is not to discuss, but to treat with a view to reconciliation. This also ungodly hearts decline.

1. They prefer to attend to ceremonial observances. Outward performances are easier, and do not require thought.
2. Yet the matter is one which demands most serious discussion, and deserves it; for God, the soul, heaven, and hell are involved in it. Never was wise counsel more desirable.
3. No good can come of neglecting to consider it. It is one of those matters which will never drift the right way of itself.

4. It is most gracious on the Lord's part to suggest a conference. Kings do not often invite criminals to reason with them.

5. The invitation is a pledge that he desires peace, is willing to forgive, and anxious to set us right.

6. The appointment of the immediate present as the time for the reasoning together is a proof of generous wisdom. "Just as thou art," come to God in Christ, just as he is. Love invites thee in all thy sin and misery.

II. A SPECIMEN OF THE REASONING ON GOD'S PART.

1. The one main ground of difference is honestly mentioned, "though your sins be as scarlet." God calls the most glaring sinners to come to him, knowing them to be such.

2. This ground of difference God himself will remove, "they shall be as white as snow." He will forgive, and so end the quarrel.

3. He will remove the offense perfectly, "as snow—as wool."
   - He will remove for ever the guilt of sin.
   - He will discharge the penalty of sin.
   - He will destroy the dominion of sin.
   - He will prevent the return of sin.

4. He explains by his own Word how this is done.
   - Free forgiveness obliterating guilt
   - Full atonement averting punishment.
   - Regeneration by the Spirit breaking the power of sin.
   - Constant sanctification forbidding its return.
   - See, then, the way of your return to God made easy.
   - Consider it carefully, and talk with God about it at once.

III. THIS SPECIMEN REASONING IS AN ABSTRACT OF THE WHOLE ARGUMENT.

Each special objection is anticipated.

1. The singular greatness of your sins, "red like crimson." This is met by a great atonement, which cleanses from all sin.

2. The long continuance of your sins. Cloth dyed scarlet has lain long in the dye vat. The blood of Jesus cleanses at once.

3. The light against which your sins were committed. This puts a glaring color upon them. But "all manner of sin and blasphemy shall be forgiven unto men."

4. The grieving of the Holy Spirit. Even this is removed by Jesus.

5. The failure of your attempts to whiten your soul. Crimson and scarlet cannot be removed by the art of man; but the Lord saith, "I have blotted out thy sins."

6. The despair which your sins create: they are so glaring that they are ever before you, yet they shall be washed out by the blood of the Lamb of God, which taketh away the sin of the world.

- Come now. Your minister pleads with you on God's behalf.
- Can it be right to slight God's invitation?
- What harm can come of a conference with him?
- Must it not be right to be reconciled with your Maker?
- What if this day should see you made "white as snow"?

Enforcements

A husband and wife had parted, and had been for years separated. He on several occasions entreated her to meet him, and talk over their differences with a view to reconciliation. She steadily declined an interview, and would not enter upon the subject of their alienation. Are you surprised when we add that the fault from the beginning lay with her? You cannot doubt that the sin of their continued division was her's alone. The parable is easy to be interpreted.

Certain scarlet cloth is first dyed in the grain, and then dyed in the piece; it is thus double-dyed. And so are we with regard to the guilt of sin; we are double-dyed, for we are all sinners by birth, and sinners by practice. Our sins are like scarlet, yet by faith in Christ they shall be as white as snow: by an interest in Christ's atonement, though our offences be red like crimson, they shall be as wool; that is they shall be as white as the undyed wool. —*"Friendly Greetings"*

When a dye enters into the very substance of the stuff, how can it be removed? Our own laundresses, by continually removing common stains, at length destroy the fabric of our linen; but what is to be done where art, and labor, and time have mingled the color and the cloth into one? With man this may be impossible, but not with God. When a man has taken up sin into him, till it is as much himself as his black skin is part and parcel of the Ethiopian, yet the Lord can put the sin away as thoroughly as if the Negro became a fair Caucasian. He takes the spots out of human tigers, and leaves not one of them.

Consider how the Tyrian scarlet was dyed; not superficially dipped, but thoroughly drenched in the liquor that colored it, as thy soul in custom of sinning. Then was it taken out for a time and dried, put in again, soaked and sodden the second time in the vat; called therefore twice-dyed; as thou complainest thou hast been by relapsing into the same sin. Yea, the color so incorporated into the cloth, not drawn over, but diving into the very heart of the wool, that, rub a scarlet rag. On what is white, and it will bestow a reddish tincture upon it; as, perchance, thy sinful practice and precedent have also infected those which) were formerly good, by thy badness. Yet such scarlet sins, so solemnly and substantially colored, are easily washed white in the blood of our Savior.
—*Thomas Fuller*

70

O house of Jacob, come ye and let us walk in the light of the Lord!

—Isaiah 2:5

H that the literal "house of Jacob" would walk in the light of Jehovah by acknowledging Jesus, who is the Dayspring from on high! Alas, they refuse the light, for the veil is upon their hearts! Let us pray for the ingathering of the tribes of Israel. Surely "it shall come to pass in the last days" (verse 2).

We will treat at this time of the spiritual Israel, even of the children of God at this hour.

I. HERE IS AN INVITATION. "Come ye, and let us walk in the light of Jehovah."

It is singular that the people of Jehovah should need such an invitation, for it seems natural that they should live in him, rejoice in him, and learn of him, seeing he is their own God.

It is a still more singular invitation in that it comes from the nations to the house of Jacob. The word of the Lord goes forth from Jerusalem, converts the nations, and then returns to the people from whom it first came. The parallel is found when the invitation comes to those of us who are believers:

1. From those to whom we have ministered. How it rewards and encourages us to hear such a call from those who once refused the invitations of the gospel! When there is a move among the dry bones, we hope for the best results.
2. From new converts, who in their burning zeal urge on older saints, and thus create joy, and hint a gentle rebuke.
3. From saints bent on mutual edification. "Come ye, and let us." Here are willing brethren calling to others who are equally willing. Would God we had more of this!

Such invitations as these are healthy signs. We should encourage their production by mutual intercourse upon holy things.

II. LET US ACCEPT THIS INVITATION. "Let us walk in the light of the Lord."

- No other light is comparable to it; especially for the Lord's own people. Jehovah should be the light of Jacob.
- No other walking is so safe, so gladsome.
- No other people are so able to walk in the light of God: their eyes are opened, their feet are strengthened, their hearts are purified, their actions suit the day.

1. In this light we find certainty for the mind.
   - Reason makes guesses, or confesses that she knows nothing.
   - Fanaticism dotes on dreams and superstitions.
   - Human authority blunders.
   - Revelation alone is sure, infallible, unalterable. All other light darkness when compared with it.
2. In this light we find rest for the conscience.
   - We see Jesus, his blood, and the perfect pardon which it procures.
   - We see his perfect righteousness covering us, and making us comely before God.
3. In this light we find direction for the judgment.
   - We see sin, love, providence, the future, etc. in their true colors, and know how to act in reference to them.
   - We learn to know the right way, and the wise course.
   - We discover the hidden snares, and are led to avoid them
4. In this light we find delight for the soul.
   - In the purposes of the Lord. "Predestined to be conformed to the image of his Son."
   - In our personal condition in Christ. "Complete in him."
   - In the dealings of our Father's hand. "All things work together for good to them that love God," etc.
   - In the struggling which goes on within, which as a symptom of grace yields us comfortable hope.
   - In the future of death and eternity, which else would distress us.
5. In this light we find communion for the heart.
   - We see God, and feel perfect peace.
   - We see grace within, and enjoy full assurance.
   - We see Jesus, and are in conscious union with him.
   - We feel the Spirit of God, and are workers with him.
   - We see the saints, and delight in their graces.

Beloved hearers, may the Holy Spirit lead you:
   - To enter into the light of God.
   - To remain in it, walking therein quietly from day to day.
   - To make progress in it, walking onward toward perfection.

Come ye, and let us even now walk together in this light.

It shines perpetually, and we are the children of light.

Living in it here will prepare us for enjoying it in all its glorious brightness, where "the Lamb is the light."

Oil for the Light

A weary and discouraged woman, after struggling all day with contrary winds and tides, came to her home, and flinging herself into a chair, said: "Everything looks dark, dark."

"Why don't you turn your face to the light, aunty dear?" said a little niece who was standing near.

The words were a message from on high, and the weary eyes were turned toward him who is the Light and the Life of men, and in whose light alone we see light.

A man who looks toward the light sees no shadow; a man who walks toward the light leaves darkness behind him. People get in darkness by fuming away from the light. They hide in obscure comers; they bury themselves in nooks where the rays of the Sun of Righteousness cannot reach them; they close their blinds and shutters, and wonder that they have no light.

A house may be dark, but it is not the fault of the sun. A soul may be dark, but it is not because the Light of the world does not shed beams abroad. He that followeth Christ "shall not walk in darkness, but shall have the light of life." But if our deeds are evil, we shall turn away from God, and love darkness rather than light; while if we are willing to be reproved, corrected, and guided in the right way, we shall find that "light is sown for the righteous, and gladness for the upright in heart." Walking in the light, as Christ is in the light, we have fellowship with the Father, and the blood of Jesus Christ, his Son, cleanseth us from all sin. —*The Boston "Christian"*

It is worth noting how plants and trees turn to the light; how bleached vegetation becomes if it be shut up in darkness. The utter dark is dreadful to men, it may even be felt, so does it press upon the mind. The dimness of a foggy day depresses many spirits more than trouble or pain. The cry of the sick man, "Would God it were morning!" is the groan of all healthy life when gloom surrounds it. What then can be said, if there be light, and we refuse it? He must have ill work on hand who loves the darkness. Only bats, and owls, and unclean and ravenous things are fond of the night. Children of light walk in the light, and reflect the light.

"Where the sun does not enter, the physician must"; so say the Italians, and their witness is true. Sunlight has not only a cheering but a health-giving influence. Along the Riviera, invalids owe everything to the sun; and when it is gone, they shrink into their own rooms. Chambers to which his warmth does not come are at a discount: the light is essential to restoration as well as to enjoyment.

71

I will also command the clouds that they rain no rain upon it.
—*Isaiah 5:6*

AIN essential for growth of seed and fruit, and its withdrawal for a length of time a terrible temporal judgment, especially in hot climates.

The spiritual rain of the Holy Spirit's influence essential to a spiritual life, in its beginning, growth, ripening, perfecting.

Its withdrawal the last and most terrible of judgments. (See whole verse.)

Especially is it a mark of anger for clouds to be overhead, and yet to drop no rain: to have the means of grace, but no grace with the means

Let us consider:

I. WHAT IT MEANS.

1. Ministers allowed to preach, but without power.
2. Ordinances celebrated, but without the benediction of the Lord.
3. Assemblies gathered, but the Lord not in the midst.
4. The Word read, but with no application to the heart.
5. Formality of prayer kept up, but no pleading with God
6. The Holy Ghost restrained, and grieved.

This has been the case full often, and may be again with any church or person if sin be tolerated after warning. Is it so in the present assembly, or with any one in it?

The clouds, ordained to rain, are commanded not to do so; commanded by God himself, with whom is the key of the rain; commanded altogether to withhold their refreshing showers. There is no necessary connection between outward ordinances and grace; we may have clouds of the first, and no drops of the second.

II. WHAT IT INVOLVES.

1. No conversions, for these are by the Spirit.
2. No restorations of backsliders. Withered plants are not revived when there is no rain.
3. No refreshing of the weary: comfort and strength come not except by the dew of heaven.
4. No spiritual activities. Lukewarmness reigns through routine unto death. The workers move like persons walking in their sleep.
5. No holy joys, delights, triumphs.

As everything pines when there is no rain, so do all good things suffer when there is a spiritual drought.

Nothing can make up for it.

Nothing can flourish without it.

III. HOW IT MANIFESTS ITSELF.

A parched season spiritually has its own signs in the individual.

1. The soul experiences no benefit under the Word.
2. The man feels glutted with the gospel, and wearied with it.
3. He begins to criticize, carp, cavil, and despise the Word.
4. Soon he is apt to neglect the hearing of it.
5. Or he hears and perverts the Word, either to boasting, to ridicule, to controversy, or to ill-living.
   - It is a horrible thing when that which should be a savor of life unto life becomes a savor of death unto death, when even the clouds refuse to rain.
   - Is it so with any one of us?

IV. HOW IT CAN BE PREVENTED.

Let us humbly use the means without putting our trust in them, and then let us:

1. Confess our ill-desert. The Lord might justly have withheld his grace from us.
2. Acknowledge our dependence upon the heavenly showers of spiritual influence.
3. Pray incessantly, till, like Elias, we bring down the rain.
4. Look alone to Jesus. "He shall come down like rain."
5. Value the least sign of grace, watching for it as the prophet did from the top of Carmel, till he saw the little cloud arise from the sea.
6. Use the blessing more diligently when it returns, bringing forth fruit unto God.

Let this act as an *incentive to gratitude* to those who are wet with showers of blessing.

And as a *warning* to those who are losing their interest in the gatherings of the Sabbath.

Anecdotes and Aphorisms

God's grace can save souls without any preaching: but all the preaching in the world cannot save souls without God's grace. —*Benjamin Beddome*

The hearer sometimes complains that there is no food for his soul; when the truth is that there is no soul for the food. —*Joseph Parker*

Every preacher must have felt that in certain places his labor is in vain. For some cause unknown to him, there is no response to his appeals, no fruit of his teaching. I knew a place from which Mr. Whitefield was chased away, and it was said of it that ever since there appeared to be a blight upon it; and indeed it seemed so. I have seen churches acting wrongly, and becoming withered from that time. On the other hand, we feel when there is dew about, and we know when there is a sound of abundance of rain. I have preached at times with the absolute certainty of success because a grace-shower was on saint and sinner, on preacher and people.

In a newspaper we met with the following:

"There was an old turnpike-man, on a quiet country road, whose habit was to shut his gate at night, and take his nap. One dark, wet midnight I knocked at his door, calling, 'Gate, gate!' 'Coming,' said the voice of the old man. Then I knocked again, and once more the voice replied, 'Coming.' This went on for some time, till at length I grew quite angry, and jumping off my horse, opened the door, and demanded why he cried 'Coming' for twenty minutes, and never came. 'Who is there?' said the old man, in a quiet, sleepy voice, rubbing his eyes 'What d'ye want, sir?' Then awakening, 'Bless yer, sir, and ax yer pardon, I was asleep; I gets so used to hearing 'em knock, that I answer "coming" in my sleep, and take no more notice about it.'"

Thus may the ministry accomplish nothing because the habitual hearer remains in a deep sleep, out of which the Spirit of God alone can awaken him. When the secret influence from heaven ceases to spear to the heart, the best speaking to the ear avails little.

72

What shall one then answer the messengers of the nation? That the Lord hath founded Zion, and the poor of his people shall trust in it.

—*Isaiah 14:32*

 ᴛ is clear that Zion attracts attention. The messengers of the nations inquire concerning her.

The church excites attention by:
- The peculiarity of her people.
- The speciality of her teaching.
- The singularity of her claims.
- The greatness of her privileges.

It is so good a thing to have this attention excited, that one should be ever ready to give an answer, for this is the way by which the truth is spread in the earth.

Oh that all nations would send messengers to inquire concerning our King, and his reign! Perhaps they will when we are what we ought to be, and are ready to answer their inquiries.

I. WHAT DO THE MESSENGERS ASK?

They come as the ambassadors from Babylon to see everything. They ask questions, as did the Queen of Sheba. Concerning Zion, or the church, they ask:

1. What is her origin (Ps. 78:68–69)?
2. What is her history (Ps. 87:3)?
3. Who is her King (Ps. 99:2)?
4. What is her charter (Gal. 4:26.)?
5. What are her laws (Ezek. 43:12)?
6. What is her treasure (Ps. 147:12–14; Rev. 21:21)?
7. What is her present security (Ps. 48:13)?
8. What is her future destiny (Ps. 102:16)?
   - There is nothing about Zion which is unworthy of their inquiry.
   - There is nothing about Zion which is closed against inquiry.

II. WHY DO THEY ASK?

1. Some from mere contempt. "What do these feeble Jews?" They would see the nakedness of the land. Perhaps when they know more their contempt will evaporate.
2. Some from idle curiosity. Yet many who come to us from that poor motive are led to Christ. Zaccheus comes down from his tree as he did not go up.
3. Some from hearty admiration. They inquire, "What is thy Beloved more than another beloved?" They have seen his star, and are come to worship, asking, "Where is he?"
4. Some from a desire to become citizens. How can they be initiated? What is the price of her franchise? What will be required of her burgesses? Is there room for more citizens?
   - They are wise thus to ask, and count the cost.
   - Men can hardly remain indifferent when the true Church of God is near them: for some reason or another they will inquire.

III. WHY SHOULD THEY BE ANSWERED?

1. It may silence their cavils.
2. It may win them to God.
3. It will do us good to give a reason for the hope that is in us.
4. It will glorify God to tell of what his grace has done for his church and of what it is prepared to do.
   - The answers should be prudently suited to the inquirer.
   - They should be clear, bold, truthful, and joyous.
   - We should think before we give an answer. "What shall one answer?"
   - Our manner in answering should be gracious (1 Pet. 3:15).

- The answer should refer rather to God than to ourselves: it is so in the text now before us.

IV. WHAT SHOULD BE THE ANSWER?

1. That God is all in all to his church—"The Lord hath."
2. That her origin is from him—"The Lord hath founded Zion."
3. That his people are poor in themselves, and rely upon another. It is a city to which the poor flee for refuge, as many fled to the cave of Adullam who were in debt and discontented
4. That their trust is in the foundation which the Lord hath laid.
5. That we resolve to abide in that trust—"The poor of his people shall trust in it."

If you ungodly ones would only ask the righteous concerning their hope, it would be well.

If you godly ones would tell inquirers your experience, it might do great good. "That we may seek him with thee" (Song of Sol. 6:1).

Incentives

Visiting a vaulted passage in the palace of Nero, at Rome, we were shown certain frescoes upon the roof. To exhibit these a candle was lifted up upon a telescopic rod, and then moved along from picture to picture. Let the candle stand for the believer, and let him be willing to be so elevated in life as to shine upon those high mysteries of our holy faith which else had never been perceived by other men. Eminent saints in the past have served such a purpose: their lives have cast a light upon priceless truths, which else had been forgotten.

If a man should ask me, after I have recovered from an illness, by what means I had been healed, should I not tell him with pleasure? To monopolize such information would be monstrous. The church of Christ is not a close borough, or a club with exclusive rules. Its walls are for inclusion, not for exclusion; its gates shut out no refugees who would enter. All that we know we are glad to tell, for all that there is to tell is glad tidings to our fellow men.

A young Kaffir, who was brought to England to be educated for mission-work in his own country, when taken to St. Paul's Cathedral, gazed up into the dome for some time as if lost in wonder, and when at length he broke silence, it was to ask, "Did man make this?" Those who obtain a view of the grandeur and glory of the spiritual temple may ask a similar question. We can tell them that its "Builder and Maker is God."

Inquirers should be answered. It is never well to be dumb to attentive ears. As some one has wisely said, "we shall have to give an account of idle silence, as well as of idle speech."

Our testimony should be bright and cheerful. The dismal tale some tell of trials and temptations is not likely to fetch home the prodigal from the far country:

such lean and discontented followers will never make anybody say, "How many hired servants of my Father have bread enough, and to spare!" —*Mark Guy Pearse*

To the matter of the safety of the church, through the presence of the Lord, we may apply the following dialogue between a heathen and a Jew: "After the Jews returned from captivity, all nations round about them being enemies to them, a heathen asked a Jew how he and his countrymen could hope for any safety; 'Because,' saith he, 'every one of you is as a silly sheep compassed about with fifty wolves.' 'Ay, but,' saith the Jew, 'we are kept by such a Shepherd as can kill all these wolves when he pleases, and by that means preserve his sheep.'" —*Thomas Brooks*

73

A man shall be as an hiding place from the wind, and a covert from the tempest.

—*Isaiah 32:2*

OD's best blessings to men have usually come by men. When our Lord ascended on high, he received gifts for men, and these gifts were men (Ps. 68:18; Eph. 4:8, 11).

Immense boons have come to nations by kings like David, prophets like Samuel, deliverers like Gideon, lawgivers like Moses.

But what are all good men put together compared with THE MAN, Christ Jesus?

We are now to view him as our shield against ten thousand ills: the hiding place and covert of his people.

Let us consider that:

I. THIS LIFE IS LIABLE TO STORMS.

1. Mysterious hurricanes within, which cause the most dreadful confusion of mind. Winds, whose direction is uncertain, shaking everything, creating unrest and distraction. Frequently no definite cause can be assigned for them; the cause may be constitutional, or physical, or circumstantial.
2. Overwhelming tempests of spiritual distress on account of sin, wrong desire, conscious declension, unbelief, etc.
3. Fierce blasts of temptation, insinuation, suggestion, denunciation, etc., from Satan.
4. Wild attacks from human enemies, who taunt, slander, threaten, etc. David was wont to use this refuge. He says, "I flee unto thee to hide me" (Ps. 143:9).

5. Trying gales of temporal losses, bereavements, and other afflictions.

6. Above all, the storm of divine anger when we have grieved the Holy Spirit, and lost communion with God.

> None of these winds and tempests are we able to bear: our only safety lies in getting out of them by finding a shelter where God has provided it (Isa. 25:4; 26:20; Ps. 32:7).

II. FROM THESE STORMS THE MAN CHRIST JESUS IS OUR HIDING PLACE.

1. As truly man.
   - Sympathizing with us, and
   - Bringing God near to us.
2. As more than man, ruling every tempest, covering every feeble traveler, as within the cleft of a rock.
3. As Substitutionary Man, interposing, breasting the storm for us, hiding us by being weather-beaten himself.
4. As Representative Man, more than conqueror, and glorified.
   - In him we are delivered from divine wrath.
   - In him we are covered from Satan's blasts.
   - In him we dwell above trial by happy fellowship with him.
   - In him we are victors over death.
5. As Ever-living Man: we live because he lives, and thus we defy the tempest of death (John 14:19).
6. As Interceding Man. He says, "I have prayed for thee," when Satan is seeking to destroy any one of us (Luke 22:32).
7. As the Coming Man. We dread no political catastrophes, or social disruptions, for "he must reign." The end is secured: "Behold, he cometh with clouds" (Rev. 1:7).

III. LET US SEE TO IT THAT WE TAKE SHELTER IN THE MAN.

1. Let him stand before us, interposing between us and the punishment of sin. Hide behind him by faith.
2. Let him daily cover us from all evil, as our Shield and Protector (Ps. 119:114).
3. Let us enter into him more and more fully, that we may be more hidden, that he may be more known to us, and that we may have a fuller sense of security.

O you that are out of Christ, the tempest is lowering! Come to this covert; hasten to this hiding place!

He is an effectual shelter, tried and proved

He is an open refuge, available now, for you.

He is a capacious hiding-place: "Yet there is room." As in Adullam all David's army could hide, so is Jesus able to receive hosts of sinners.

He is an eternal covert: our dwelling-place throughout all generations.

He is an inviting shelter, because he is Man, and therefore has compassion towards men, and a joy in their salvation.

Instances and Instructions

Well do I remember being caught in the mistral at Hyeres, when it blew with unusual fury; it not only drove clouds of dust with terrible force, but boughs of trees, and all sorts of light material were propelled with tremendous force. One wondered that a tree remained upright, or a fence in its place. What a joy it was to hide behind a solid wall, and under its shelter to run along till we were safe within doors! Then we knew in some measure the value of a hiding-place from the wind. But what is that to a cyclone, which tears down houses, and lifts ships upon the dry land? Friends who have lived abroad have startled us with their descriptions of what wind can be, and they have made us cease to wonder that a hiding-place should be greatly prized by dwellers in eastern lands.

> The tempest's awful voice was heard;
> O Christ, it broke on thee!
> Thy open bosom was my ward,
> It braved the storm for me.
> Thy form was scarred, thy visage marred;
> Now cloudless peace for me.
> —*Sacred Songs and Solos*

I creep under my Lord's wings in the great shower, and the waters cannot reach me. Let fools laugh the fools' laughter, and scorn Christ, and bid the weeping captives in Babylon to sing them one of the songs of Zion. We may sing, even in our winter's storm, in the expectation of a summer's sun at the turn of the year. No created powers in hell, or out of hell, can mar our Lord's work, or spoil our song of joy. Let us then, be glad and rejoice in the salvation of our Lord, for faith had never yet cause to have tearful eyes, or a saddened brow, or to droop or die. —*Samuel Rutherford*

A shelter is nothing if we stand in front of it. The main thought with many a would-be Christian is his own works, feelings, and attainments: this is to stand on the windy side of the wall by putting self before Jesus. Our safety lies in getting behind Christ, and letting him stand in the wind's eye. We must be altogether hidden, or Christ cannot be our hiding place.

Foolish religionists hear about the hiding place, but never get into it. How great is the folly of such conduct! It makes Jesus to be of no value or effect. What is a roof to a man who lies in the open, or a boat to one who sinks in the sea?

Even the Man Christ Jesus, though ordained of God to be a covert from the tempest, can cover none but those who are in him. Come then, poor sinner, enter where you may; hide in him who was evidently meant to hide you, for he was ordained to be a hiding place, and must be used as such, or the very aim of his life and death would be missed.

74

A man shall be . . . as rivers of water in a dry place.
—*Isaiah 32:2*

 UR Lord Jesus is nearest and dearest to us as Man. His manhood reminds us of:

- His incarnation, in which he assumed our nature.
- His life on earth, in which he honored our nature.
- His death, by which he redeemed our nature.
- His resurrection, by which he upraised our nature.

Consider the Word made flesh, and you have before you "rivers of water." "It pleased the Father that in him should all fullness dwell."

Though manhood seems to be a dry place, a salt and barren land, yet in the case of this Man it yields rivers of water, numberless streams, abounding with refreshment.

Let us learn from the simile before us:

I. THAT NATURE'S DROUGHT DOES NOT HINDER CHRIST'S COMING TO MEN.

1. He came into the dry place of a fallen, ruined, rebellious world.
2. He comes to men personally, notwithstanding their being without strength, without righteousness, without desire, without life.
3. He flows within us in rivers of grace, though the old nature continues to be a dry and parched land.
4. He continues the inflowing of his grace till he perfects us, and this he does though decay of nature, failure, and fickleness prove us to be as a dry place.

"Where sin abounded, grace did much more abound."

II. THAT NATURE'S DROUGHT ENHANCES THE PRECIOUSNESS OF CHRIST.

1. He is the more quickly discovered; as rivers would be in a desert.

2. He is the more highly valued; as water in a torrid climate.

3. He is the more largely used; as streams in a burning wilderness.

4. He is the more surely known to be the gift of God's grace. How else came he to be in so dry a place? Those who are most devoid of merit are the more clear as to God's grace.

5. He is the more gratefully extolled. Men sing of rivers which Flow through dreary wastes.

III. THAT NATURE'S DROUGHT IS MOST EFFECTUALLY REMOVED BY CHRIST.

Rivers change the appearance and character of a dry place. By our Lord Jesus appearing in our manhood as Emmanuel, God with us:

1. Our despair is cheered away.

2. Our sinfulness is purged.

3. Our nature is renewed.

4. Our barrenness is removed.

5. Our trials are overcome.

6. Our fallen condition is changed to glory.

The desert of manhood rejoices and blossoms as the rose now that the Man Christ Jesus has appeared in it

IV. THAT OUR OWN SENSE OF DROUGHT SHOULD LEAD US THE MORE HOPEFULLY TO APPLY TO CHRIST.

He is rivers of water in a dry place. The dry place is his sphere of action. Nature's want is the platform for the display of grace.

1. This is implied in our Lord's offices. A Savior for sinners. A Priest who can have compassion on the ignorant, etc.

2. This is remembered in his great qualifications. Rivers, because the place is so dry. Full of grace and truth, because we are so sinful and false. Mighty to save, because we are so lost, etc.

3. This is manifested by the persons to whom he comes. Not many great or mighty are chosen. "I came not to call the righteous, but sinners to repentance." He calls "the chief of sinners." In every case the rivers of love flow into a dry place.

4. This is clear from the object which he aimed at, namely, the glory of God, and the making known of the riches of his grace. This can be best accomplished by working salvation where there is no apparent likelihood of it, or, in other words, causing rivers to water dry places.

Come to Jesus, though your nature be dry, and your case hopeless.

Come, for there are rivers of grace in him.

Come, for they flow at your feet, "in a dry place."

Come, if you have come before, and are just now in a backsliding condition.

The Lord Jesus is still the same; the rivers of mercy in him can never be dried up.

Christ never seems empty to any but those who are full of themselves. He is dry to those who overflow with personal fullness, but he floods with his grace all who are dried up as to all self-reliance.

Rivulets

It is my sweetest comfort, Lord,
And will for ever be,
To muse upon the gracious truth
Of thy humanity.
—*Edward Caswall*

Men that have dry land spare no cost, refuse no pains, to bring rivulets of waters through it, that it may be moistened. It will, they know, in a little time, quit all their cost, and recompense all their labor. Oh, that men would be as careful that their dry hearts might be watered! —*Ralph Robinson*

The claims of Jesus Christ upon our gratitude and devotion are such that we gladly borrow language from any that may help us to utter his praise. Thus Dr. Marsh adopted Pope's lines, altering only the last words:

Not bubbling waters to the thirsty swain,
Not rest to weary laborers, faint with pain,
Not showers to larks, not sunshine to the bee,
Are half so precious as thy love to me—

My Savior.

With what joy do travelers through the Bayuda desert come within sight of the Nile! While toiling over the burning sand they have dreamed of rivers, and the mirage mocks them with the image of their day dream. The fiction enchants them because the fact would be so delightful What must it be actually to drink of the stream after terrible hours of thirst? Hindus worship their rivers as gods, so precious do they conceive them to be. Do you wonder that the gratitude of the ignorant should take such a form? What would their hot country be without them? What would our hearts, our lives, our present, our future, be without Christ? What would be the outlook of the age—what the prospect of our nation—what the destiny of the world, without the Lord Jesus?

What we want in Christ, we always find in him. When we want nothing, we find nothing. When we want little, we find little. When we want much, we find much. But when we want everything, and get reduced to complete nakedness and beggary, we find in Christ God's complete treasure-house, out of which come gold and jewels to enrich us, and garments to clothe us in the richness and righteousness of the Lord. —*Sears*

75

Behold, for peace I had great bitterness: but thou hast in love to my soul delivered it from the pit of corruption: for thou hast cast all my sins behind thy back.

—Isaiah 38:17

 ERE is the case of a man who, as far as mortal help was concerned, was a dead man, and yet prayer prevailed for his recovery, and the lengthening of his life.

He records his experience for the glory of God, for his own refreshment, and for our encouragement.

In our deep depressions we have the same God to help us.

Hezekiah sets before us in this verse:

I. HEALTHFUL BITTERNESS. "For peace I had bitter bitterness" *(margin)*.

1. He had been in peace. Probably this had brought with it a dangerous state, in which the mind became carnally secure, self-contented, stagnant, slumbering, careless, worldly.
2. He underwent a change. It was sudden and surprising—"Behold." It broke up all his peace, and took the place of it.
3. His new state was one of emphatic sorrow—"Bitterness." "Great bitterness." In bodily condition and in mental emotion he tasted the wormwood and the gall. Read previous verses, and see how he mourned.
4. It wrought his health. "So wilt thou recover me" (verse 16).
   - It led him to repentance for the past. He speaks of "my sins."
   - It brought him to his knees in prayer.
   - It revealed his inward decline, and weakness of grace.
   - It made him put away his defilements.
   - It deepened his faith in God. "The Lord was ready to Save me" (verse 20).
5. Peace came back again, and with it songs of joy.

If any are now drinking the bitter cup, let them be of good cheer, for there is a cup of salvation in God's hand.

II. DELIVERING LOVE. "In love to my soul thou hast delivered it."

In its first meaning we see recovery from sickness, but it intends much more: upon the surface lies benefit to his soul.

Let us observe:

1. The deed of love. "Thou hast loved my soul from the pit" *(margin)*.

   The Lord delivers the soul from the pit of hell, of sin, of despair, of temptation, of death. He alone can do this.

2. The love which performed the deed.
- Love suggested and ordained it.
- Love actually performed it by its own hands. "In love to my soul thou hast loved it from the pit."
- Love breaks the heart, and binds it up.
- Love sets us free, and then holds us captive.
- We are by love loved out of sorrow, rebellion, despondency, coldness, and weakness. Acknowledge this heartily.
- Measure this love by your demerit, your danger, your present complete safety, and by the greatness of the Deliverer, and what the delivery cost him.
- Treasure this love, and sing of it all the days of your life.

III. ABSOLUTE PARDON. "Thou hast cast all my sins behind thy back."

1. This was the cause of his restored peace. He was burdened while sin remained, but when that was gone, peace returned.
2. This removed the whole burden. "Sins"; "my sins"; "all my sins."
3. This involved effort on God's part. "Thou hast cast." We remember the more than herculean labors of Jesus, who has hurled our load into the bottomless deep.
4. This is wonderfully described. "Behind thy back"; this is:
- The place of desertion. God has gone from our sin never to return to it. He has left it for ever, and it will never cross his path again, for he never moves backward.
- The place of forgetfulness: he will not remember it any more.
- The place of nonentity: nothing is behind the back of God.

Therefore we will *tell* others our story, as Hezekiah has told us his. Let us seek out one or more who will hear us with attention.

"Therefore we will *sing* my songs to the stringed instruments" (verse 20). At this hour let us lift up the voice of gratitude.

Enlargements

Thomas Bilney, the martyr, after his submission to the Papacy, being brought again to repentance, was, as Latimer reports, for a time inconsolable. "His friends dared not suffer him to be alone day or night. They comforted him as they could, but no comforts would serve; and as for the comfortable places of Scripture, to bring them to him was as though a man should run him through the heart with a sword."

Now friend, give me your answer: Is it best to see sin and guilt *now*, while you may see a Savior also; or to see sin and a judge hereafter, but no Savior? Sin you shall see, as we say, in spite of your teeth, will you, nil you. Oh, then, let me see sin and guilt *now*; Oh, *now,* with a sweet Savior, that I may have this woeful sight past when I come to die. —*Giles Firmin*

"Thou hast cast," etc. These last words are a borrowed speech, taken from the manner of men, who are wont to cast behind their backs such things as they have no mind to see, regard, or remember. A gracious soul hath always his sins before his face: "I acknowledge my transgressions, and my sin is ever before me"; and therefore no wonder if the Lord cast them behind his back. A father soon forgets and casts behind his back those faults that the child remembers and hath always before his eyes, so cloth the Father of spirits. —*Thomas Brooks*

I have read somewhere of a great divine (I think it was åcolampadius), who being recovered from a great sickness, said, "I have learned! under this sickness to know *sin* and *God*." Did he not know these before? Doubtless he could preach good sermons concerning God and sin; but the Spirit, it seems, in that sickness, taught him these otherwise than he knew them before. —*Giles Firmin*

Some of the pits referred to in the Bible were prisons; one such I saw at Athens, and another at Rome. To these there were no openings except a hole at the top, which served for both door and window. The bottoms of these pits were necessarily in a filthy and revolting state, and sometimes deep in mud. Isaiah speaks of "the pit of corruption," or putrefaction and filth. —*John Gadsby*

Dr. Watts, from his early infancy to his dying day, scarcely ever knew what health was; but however surprising it may appear, he looked on the affliction as the greatest blessing of his life. The reason he assigned for it was, that, being naturally of a warm temper, and an ambitious disposition, these visitations of divine providence weaned his affections from the world, and brought every passion into subjection to Christ. This he often mentioned to his dear friend, Sir Thomas Abney, in whose house he lived many years. —*John Whitecross*

76

Look unto me, and be ye saved all the ends of the earth: for I am God, and there is none else.

—*Isaiah 45:22*

 HE nations have been looking to their idols for all these weary centuries, but in vain.

Many of them are looking to their boasted philosophies, and still in vain.

False religions, politics, alliances, theories, organizations, men all will be in vain to save the nations.

They must look to God: the God of all the families of the earth.

Happy are we that we live in a time when God's command to the nations is proclaimed abroad. Be it ours to spread the saving truth, and bid men look and live.

The same principle applies to individuals If they would be saved they must look to the Lord.

If you, oh hearer, would be saved, here is the only method—"Look."

I. WHAT MEANS THIS WORD "LOOK" IN REFERENCE TO GOD?

It includes many things; as for instance:

1. Admit his reality by looking to him. Consider that there is a God, and enthrone him in your mind as a real Person, the true God, and your Lord. Let the Invisible God be to you as real as that which you see with your eyes.

2. Address yourself to him by prayer, thanksgiving, thought, obedience, reverence, etc., looking to him so as to know him, and recognize his presence.

3. Acknowledge that from him only salvation can come. Regard him as the only possible Savior. "There is none else."

4. Anticipate that HE will bless you: look for his interposition.

5. Abide alone in HIM for salvation. Keep your eyes fixed on him, as the Morning Star of your day.

II. FOR WHAT PART OF SALVATION ARE WE THUS TO LOOK?

For every part of it from beginning to end.

1. Pardon. This must be God's act, and it can only come through the atonement which he has provided in Christ Jesus.

2. Preparation for pardon, namely, life, repentance, faith. Grace must prepare us for more grace.

3. Renewal of heart is the Holy Ghosts work: look to him for it. Regeneration must be of the Lord alone.

4. Sustenance in spiritual life is of the Lord alone. All growth, strength, fruit, must be looked for from him.

5. Daily succor in common things is as much a divine gift as great deliverances. Our look should be constant, and it should comprise expectancy for time as well as eternity.

Any one matter left to self would ruin us altogether.

III. WHAT IS OUR ENCOURAGEMENT TO LOOK?

1. His command. He bids us look, and therefore we may look.

2. His promise. He says, "look, and be saved," and he will never run back from his own word.

3. His Godhead. "For I am God." All things are possible to him: his mercy is equal to our salvation, his glory will be manifest thereby.

4. His character, as "a just God and a Savior" (see verse 21). This combination is seen by those who know the cross, and it is full of hope to sinners.

5. His broad invitation: "all the ends of the earth." Each seeking soul may be sure that he is included therein.

Who will refuse so simple an act as to look?

IV. WHAT IS THE BEST TIME IN WHICH TO LOOK?

Look now, at this very moment.

1. The command is in the present tense: "Look unto me."
2. The promise is in the same tense: "and be ye saved." It is a fiat, like "light be." It takes immediate effect.
3. Your need of salvation is urgent: you are already lost.
4. The present time is yours, no other time is yours to use; for the past is gone, and the future will be present when it comes.
5. Your time may soon end. Death comes suddenly. Age creeps on us. The longest life is short.
6. It is the time which God chooses: it is ours to accept it.

This is a great soul-saving text: give earnest heed to it

All who have obeyed it are saved: why should you not at once be saved? This is the one command: "Look! Look!"

Stories and Brevities

A striking example of prayer unto "gods that cannot save" is given by Miss Isabella Bird, who describes a service in a Buddhist temple in Japan, when a popular priest preached to a vast congregation on future punishment, *i.e.*, the tortures of the Buddhist hells. When he concluded, the people, slightly raising the hands on which the rosaries were wound, answered with the roar of a mighty response, "Eternal Buddha, save!"

To this text, under God, I owe my own deliverance from despair. An explanation of the work of Jesus, given by a humble, unlettered lay preacher, was followed by a direct appeal to me. "Young man, you are miserable, and you will never be happy unless you obey this message. Look! Look!" I did look, and in that instant lost my crushing load of guilt. It was all clear to me. Jesus had taken the sins of all believers. I believed, and knew that he had taken mine, and therefore I was clear. The matchless truth of the substitution of the divine Lord for me was light and liberty to my soul. A look saved me, and for my present salvation I have no other resort but still to look. "Looking unto Jesus" is a motto both for penitent and preacher, for sinner and saint. —*C. H. S.*

There is an affecting story of a celebrated literary man, Heinrich Heine, who was prematurely disabled by disease, and utterly heart-sick and weary. In one of the art palaces of Paris there is the famous statue called the Venus of Milo, the bewitching goddess of pleasure, which, by the rude accident of time, has lost both her arms, but still preserves much of her supreme, enchanting beauty. At the feet of this statue Heine cast himself down in remorse and despair, and, to use his own words, "There I lay a long time, and wept so passionately that a stone must have had compassion on me. The goddess looked down compassionately upon me, but she was helpless to console me. She looked as if she would say—'See you not that I have no arms, and that therefore I can give you no help?'" So, vain and useless is it to look to any for spiritual help and comfort, except to him of whom it is declared, "Behold, the Lord's hand is not shortened, that it cannot save."

Some divines would need a week in which to tell you what you are to do to be saved: but the Holy Ghost only uses four letters to do it. Four letters, and two of them alike—"Look!"

Be not like the man, in the Interpreter's house, whose eyes were fixed on the ground where he was raking together straws and dust, and who would not look up to him who was offering him a celestial crown. Look up! Look up!

77

And even to your old age I am he; and even to hoar hairs will I carry you: I have made, and I will bear; even I will carry, and will deliver you.

—Isaiah 46: 4

 HE doctrine of the text is the unchanging nature of God, and the constancy of his kindness towards his people in providence and grace.

We need scarcely prove the unchanging nature of God's dealings with his people, during the short period of mortal life, when:

- In nature we see many things unchanged during seventy or eighty years: sun, ocean, rocks, etc.
- We see his Word and gospel to be still the same.
- Prayer, praise, communion, and holy service are the same.
- Our experience is similar to that of saints in the olden time.
- Especially we remember that the very nature of God places mutability beyond the range of supposition.

Of the Lord's dealings in providence and grace it is scarcely necessary to prove the immutability, when we remind you:

- That the mercies of one age are in the main identical with those of another; and the promises are altogether unaltered.
- That holy men are ready to testify to the faithfulness of God, and that both now and in the past the witnesses to his divine truth and immutability are many.

- That divine strength is not dependent on man's weakness; divine love is not changed by man's demerits; and divine truth is not affected by lapse of years.
- That the completion of the body of Christ requires the preservation of all the saints, and therefore the Lord must abide the same to every one of them.

Yet without doubt "old age" has its peculiarities, which do but serve to evidence the firmness of God's grace.

I. IT HATH ITS PECULIAR MEMORIES.
1. It remembers many joys, and it sees in them proofs of love.
2. It remembers many visits to the house of sickness, and it recollects how the Lord cheered its desolate chamber.
3. It remembers many trials in its loss of friends, and its changes of condition, but it sees HIM to have been ever the same.
4. It remembers many conflicts with temptation, doubt, Satan, the flesh, and the world; but it remembers how HE covered its head in the day of battle.
5. It remembers its own many sins; and it is not forgetful how man, professors have made shipwreck of faith; but it clearly sees covenant faithfulness in its own preservation.
    All our recollections are unanimous in their testimony to an unchanging God.

II. IT HATH ITS PECULIAR HOPES.
It has now few things to anticipate; but those few are the same as in younger days, for the covenant abides unaltered.
1. The Ground of its hope is still Jesus, and not long service.
2. The Reason of its hope is still faith in the infallible Word.
3. The Preservation of its hope is in the same hands.
4. The End of its hope is still the same heaven, the same crown of life and blessedness.
5. The Joy of its hope is still as bright and cheering as before.

III. IT HATH ITS PECULIAR SOLICITUDES.
Cares are fewer, for business is curtailed, and the needs which remain only serve to show that God is the same.
1. The Body is infirm, but grace makes amends for the departed joys of youth, health, and activity.
2. The Mind is weaker, the memory less retentive, and the imagination less vivid; but gracious doctrines are more sweet than ever, and eternal verities sustain the heart.

3. Death is nearer, but then Heaven is nearer too. Earth may be less lovely, but the home-country is dearer, since more loved ones have entered it, and have left us fewer ties to earth.

4. Preparation by Examination is now more imperative, but it is also more easy, since repetition has removed its difficulties, faith has more constancy, and tried promises afford richer comfort.

All these prove God the same.

IV. IT HATH ITS PECULIAR BLESSEDNESS.

Deprived of certain enjoyments, age is enriched with others.

1. It has a long experience to read, proving the promise true.
2. It has less wavering in its doctrines, *knowing* now what once it only guessed.
3. It has less to fear in the future of life, seeing the way is shorter.
4. It has more divine unveilings of the celestial regions, for it is now in the land Beulah.
5. It has less business on earth, and more in heaven, and hence it has an inducement to be more heavenly-minded

Here is divine love made manifest as still the same.

V. IT HATH ITS PECULIAR DUTIES.

These are proofs of divine faithfulness, since they cause men to bring forth fruit in old age. They are:

1. Testimony to the goodness of God, the unchangeableness of his love, and the certainty of his revelation.
2. Comfort to others who are battling, assuring them they will come off safely.
3. Warning to the wayward: such warning coming with tenfold force from the aged saint.
4. And frequently we may add:
   Instruction, since the old man's experience has opened up many a mystery unknown before.

From the whole we gather:

- A *lesson* to the young to make this God their God, since he will never forsake his people.
- A *solace* for men in middle life to persevere, for they shall still be carried in the arms of grace.
- A *song* for the aged, concerning undying love and unchanging mercy. With mellowed voice let it be sung.

To the Point

Dr. O.W. Holmes says, "Men, like peaches and pears, grow sweet a little while before they begin to decay." This is true; but Christian men should be sweet from the hour that they are renewed in heart. Yet even then maturity brings a special mellowness.

Of the Christian it has been said, "The decay, and wasting, and infirmities of old age will be, as Dr. Guthrie called these symptoms of his own approaching death, only 'the land-birds, lighting on the shrouds, telling the weary mariner that he is nearing the desired haven.'"

It is a favorite speculation of mine that, if spared to sixty, we then enter on the seventh decade of human life, and that this, if possible, should be turned into the Sabbath of our earthly pilgrimage, and spent Sabbatically, as if on the shores of an eternal world, or in the outer courts, as it were, of the temple that is above, the tabernacle that is in heaven. —*Dr. Chalmers*

78

The children which thou shalt have, after thou hast lost the other, shall say again in thine ears, The place is too strait for me: give place to me that I may dwell. Then shalt thou say in thine heart, Who hath begotten me these, seeing I have lost my children, and am desolate, a captive, and removing to and fro? and who hath brought up these? Behold, I was left alone; these, where had they been?

—*Isaiah 49:20–21*

 HOPEFUL mood becomes the church of God, for the memories of the past, the blessings of the present, and the promises of the future are full of good cheer.

"All the promises do travail with a glorious day of grace."

The church lives, progresses, conquers by her faith; let her abandon despondency, as her weakness, her sin, her greatest hindrance.

The prophet, to remove all fear, reminds us that:

I. IN THE CHURCH THERE ARE DECREASES. "I have lost my children," etc. This is frequently the bitter cry of a church.

1. Death invades the house of God and takes away those who were its pillars and ornaments. But those who depart go to swell the chorus of heaven.
2. Providence takes away useful persons by removal or by excessive occupation which keeps them from holy service. The removed ones go to build up the church elsewhere: those who are lawfully detained by business are still doing the Lord's will.

3. Sin causes some to backslide, wander away, or become inactive. But they go from us because they are not of us.

This decrease is painful, and it may go sofar that a church may feel itself to be "desolate" and "left alone." Yet the Lord has not forgotten his church, for he is her Husband.

II. IN THE CHURCH WE SHOULD LOOK FOR INCREASE. "The children which thou shalt have."

Let us not be absorbed in lamenting losses; let us rejoice by faith in great gains which are surely coming.

1. Increase is needful, or what will become of the church?
2. Increase is prayed for, and God hears prayer.
3. Increase can only come through God, but he will give it, and be glorified by it.
4. Increase is promised in the text, and in many other Scriptures.
5. Increase is to be labored for with agony of heart. "As soon as Zion travailed, she brought forth children."

III. IN THE CHURCH INCREASE OFTEN CAUSES SURPRISE.

So narrow are our hearts, so weak our faith, that we are amazed when conversions are numerous

1. Because of the time: "Behold, I was left alone."
2. Because of their number: "Who hath begotten me these?"
3. Because of their former character: "These, where had they been?" They were not after all so very far off.
   • Some of them were quite near to us and near to the kingdom, in the family, school, class, congregation, inquiry-room.
   • Others were far off in irreligion, and open sin.
   • Others were opposed through rationalism, superstition, or self-righteousness.
4. Because of their good nurture: "Who hath brought up these?"
5. Because of their eagerness and courage. "Shall say again in thine ears, The place is too strait for me."
6. Because of their constancy. "Give place to me that I may *dwell*."
   They come to remain.

Where had they been? Say rather, "Where had *we* been?" that we had not long ago looked after them, and welcomed them.

IV. IN THE CHURCH INCREASE SHOULD BE PREPARED FOR.

We make ready for the coming of children. Is the church an unnatural mother? Will she not welcome newborn souls?

We must prepare for an increase:

1. By intense united prayer for it.
2. By the preaching of the gospel, which is the means of it.
3. By every form of Christian effort which may lead to it.
4. By enlarging our bounds: "The place is too strait for me." To provide a larger audience chamber may be a true act of faith.
5. By welcoming all true-born children of God: who say, each one, "give place to me that I may dwell."

Oh, for a triumphant faith that the little one shall become a thousand!
Oh, for grace to act upon such faith at once!
"Believe great things; attempt great things; expect great things."

Notes

My observation leads me to believe that, where churches are duly careful in the admission of members, they will find that their best converts come in flocks. My impression is that, when very few come forward, everybody leans towards a less exact judgment than in times when many are forthcoming. Bad fish are more likely to be taken home when fish are scarce than when they are plentiful; for then the fisherman feels more free to make a rigid selection. I say nothing about the severity or laxity of a church in receiving members, but it is incidental to human nature that when we are in a revival we become more guarded, and in dull times we are more apt to look at a convert with a hope which is rather eager than anxious. Thus I account for what I believe to be a fact, that rare converts are frequently bare converts; and that the best sheep come to us in flocks.

Dr. Judson, the devoted missionary to Burmah, during his visit to Boston, was asked, "Do you think the prospect bright of the speedy conversion of the heathen?" "As bright," he replied, "as the promises of God."

Monday, December 22, 1800—Creesturo, Gokol and his wife, and Felix Carey gave us their experience tonight. Brother C. concluded in prayer after we had sung, "Salvation, oh, the joyful sound!" Brother Thomas is almost mad with joy. —*Diary of the Rev. W. Ward, of Serampore*

"I am inclined to think that a single soul is never born again, apart from the tender concern and anxiety of some creaturely heart or hearts. . . . Probably Saul was converted in answer to the prayers of the disciples at Damascus."—*John Pulsford*

Dr. Isaac Barrow, when a lad, was most unpromising. Such was his misconduct, and so irreclaimable did he seem, that his father, in despair used to say that "if it pleased God to remove any of his children, he wished it might be his son Isaac." What became of the other and more hopeful children of the worthy linen-draper, we cannot tell; but this unworthy son lived to be the happiness and pride of his father's old age, to be one of the most illustrious members of the university to which he belonged, and one of the brightest ornaments of the church of which be became a minister.

79

Wherefore, when I came, was there no man? when I called, was there none to answer? Is my hand shortened at all, that it cannot redeem? or have I no power to deliver? behold, at my rebuke I dry up the sea, I make the rivers a wilderness: their fish stinketh, because there is no water, and dieth for thirst. I clothe the heavens with blackness, and I make sackcloth their covering.

The Lord God hath given me the tongue of the learned, that I should know how to speak a word in season to him that is weary: he wakeneth morning by morning, he wakeneth mine ear to hear as the learned. The Lord God hath opened mine ear, and I was not rebellious, neither turned away back. I gave my back to the smiters, and my cheeks to them that plucked off the hair: I hid not my face from shame and spitting.

—Isaiah 50:2-6

 HERE was no one to take up the divine challenge: no one to answer for guilty man. To the call of God for one who could save, there was no answer but the echo of his voice.

See who it is that comes to rescue man! Jehovah interposes to save; but he appears in a special manner.

The Lord himself draws the portrait. View it with solemn attention.

I. BEHOLD THE MESSIAH AS GOD!

1. He comes in fullness of power. "Is my hand shortened at all?"
2. His power to save is equal to that with which he destroys. Let Egypt be the instance: "I dry up the sea," etc.
3. His power is that which produces the phenomena of nature. "I clothe the heavens with blackness."
4. This should excite deep gratitude, that he who rebukes the sea was himself rebuked; he who clothes the heavens with blackness was himself in darkness for our sake.
5. This should excite confidence; for he is evidently Lord of the sea and the sky, the dark and the gloom.

II. BEHOLD HIM AS THE APPOINTED TEACHER!

1. Instructed and endowed: "the Lord hath given me the tongue of the learned." He knows, and he imparts knowledge.
2. Condescending to the needy: "to him that is weary."

3. Watchful of each case: "that I should know how to speak a word in season." This is a rare gift: many speak, and perhaps speak in season, but have not learned the right manner.

4. Constantly in communion with God: "he wakeneth morning by morning." "He that hath sent me is with me."

Should we not be heartily attentive to his teachings? "I will hear what God the Lord will speak."

III. BEHOLD HIM AS THE SERVANT OF THE LORD!

1. Prepared by grace: "he wakeneth mine ear to hear." He spoke not his own words, but those which he had heard of his Father.

2. Consecrated in due form: "hath opened mine ear," boring it to the door-post. This was publicly done in his baptism, when in outward symbol he fulfilled all righteousness.

3. Obedient in all things: "I was not rebellious." In no point did Jesus refuse the Father's will, not even in Gethsemane.

4. Persevering through all trials: "neither turned away back." He did not relinquish the hard task, but set his face as a flint to carry it through.

5. Courageous in it all: as we see in the verse following our text.

What a model for our service! Consider him, and copy him.

IV. BEHOLD HIM AS THE PEERLESS SUFFERER!

1. His entire submission; his back, his cheeks, his hair, his face.

2. His willing submission: "I gave my back to the smiters." "I hid not my face."

3. His lowly submission, bearing the felon's scourge, and the utmost of scorn: "shame and spitting."

4. His patient submission. Not a word of reproach, or resentment.

Grace had taught him effectually, and he suffered perfectly.

It may bring out important truths very vividly if we make combinations of the four subjects which have come before us.

- Place the first and the last together: the God and the Sufferer. What condescension! What ability to save!
- Place the two middle terms together: the Teacher and the Servant, and see how sweetly he serves by teaching, and teaches by serving.
- Put all together, and let the blended characters ensure ardent affection, obedient reverence, and devout delight.

A Golden Lecturer's Word

I imagine myself placed in the world at the time when the Christ was expected, commissioned to announce to it that God was about to send his own Son, having endowed him with "the tongue of the learned." What excitement in all the schools of philosophy! What gatherings of the sages of the earth! What expectations of the discoveries with which science was about to be enriched! "Now," say they, "shall long-hidden secrets be revealed: now shall we penetrate the laboratories of nature, and observe all those processes of which, at present, we see only the results. For what purpose can the tongue of the learned have been given to a Divine Person, if not that he may expound mysteries to the world, that he may tell us what the wise have been unable to detect, and the studious labored in vain to unfold?"

But this Divine Person shall speak for himself to the assembled throng of philosophers and sages. "Yes, the Lord God hath given me the tongue of the learned; and I have descended that I might speak with that tongue to every nation of the earth. But he hath not: given me the tongue that I might tell how stars and planets roll, or settle the disputes of the wise. He hath not given me the tongue that I should know how to speak a word to you, ye disputers of this world; but simply that I should know how to speak a word in season to him that is weary." Oh, how fallen are the expectant countenances of philosophers and sages! "Is this all?" they exclaim. "Was it only for this that the tongue of the learned was bestowed? Does this require, or can this employ, the tongue of the learned?"

Nay, men of science, turn not angrily away. With all your wisdom you have never been able to do this. The weary have sought to you in vain. They have found no "word in season," no word of comfort and sustainment; and why then should you be indignant at the province here assigned to "the tongue of the learned"?

What tongue but "the tongue of the learned" could speak "a word in season" to a world oppressed with this universal weariness? The tongue must be one which could disclose the mysteries of the Godhead, prove the immortality of the soul, and be charged with intelligence as to the pardon of sin, and the mode of reconciliation between man and his Maker: things into which angels had in vain striven to look. —*Condensed from Henry Melvill*

80

For the Lord God will help me; therefore shall I not be confounded: therefore have I set my face like a flint, and I know that I shall not be ashamed.

—*Isaiah 50:7*

HERE was no flint in the heart of Jesus, but there was much in his face. He was as resolute as he was submissive. Read verse 6 and this verse together—"I hid not my face from shame and spitting. . . . I have set my face like a flint." Gentleness and resolve are married.

In Luke 9:51, we read, "he steadfastly set his face to go to Jerusalem." In our Lord there was no turning aside, though none helped him, and every one hindered him. He was neither confounded by thoughts within his own soul, nor rendered ashamed by the scorn of others.

Let us consider our Lord's stern resolution thus:

I. HIS STEADFAST RESOLVE TESTED.

He declared his determination in the language of our text, and by many an ordeal this declaration was justified. He was tried:

1. By the offers of the world. They would make him a king. His triumphant ride into Jerusalem proved how easily he could have become a popular leader. By a little compromise he might have won an enthusiastic following as a religious teacher.
2. By the persuasions of friends. Peter rebuked him. All the disciples marveled at his determination. His relatives sought a very different career for him. Many yield to well-meaning friends; but Jesus set his face like a flint.
3. By the unworthiness of his clients.
   - He that ate bread with him betrayed him.
   - His disciples forsook him and fled.
   - The whole race conspired to put him to death.
4. By the bitterness which he tasted at his entrance upon his great work as a substitutionary sacrifice. Gethsemane, the betrayal, the false accusation, the mockery: these were sharp commencements, and many have shrunk when the fire has begun to kindle upon them; but Jesus stood firm.
5. By the ease with which he could have relinquished the enterprise.
   - Pilate would have released him had Jesus pleaded.
   - Legions of angels would have come to his rescue.
   - He might himself have come down from the cross.
   - He was not held to his work by inability to quit it, but only by that love which is strong as death. He said, "If it be possible, let this cup pass from me": the impossibility lay in his resolve to redeem his people.
6. By the taunts of those who scoffed.
   - The people: "Let us see whether Elias will come to save him."
   - The priests, etc.: "If he be the King of Israel," etc.
   - The thieves: "If thou be Christ, save thyself and us."
Strong men have been overcome by ridicule; but not so Jesus.
7. By the full stress of the death-agony.
   The pain, thirst, fever, fainting, desertion, death: none of these moved him from his invincible resolve.

II. HIS STEADFAST RESOLVE SUSTAINED.

As man, our Lord owed his glorious steadfastness to several things, and he gives us in the text two "therefores." It was due:

1. To his divine schooling (see verse 4).
2. To his conscious innocence. "I know that I shall not be ashamed" (see verse 5).
3. To the joy that was set before him. He would overcome for his people. "Who will contend with me?" (see verse 8).
4. Specially to his unshaken confidence in the help of the Lord God. We have this both in the text and in verse 9.

   Even to his cry of "It is finished" he never flinched, but held to his grand purpose.

III. HIS STEADFAST RESOLVE IMITATED.

1. Our purpose must be God's glory, as his was.
2. Our education must be God's teaching, as his was.
3. Our life must combine active and passive obedience, as his did (see verses 5 and 6).
4. Our strength must lie in God, as his did.
5. Our path must be one of faith, as his was. Note verse 10, and its remarkable connection with the whole subject.
6. Our resolve must be carefully made, and steadily carried out till we can say, "It is finished," in our manner and degree.

Close with a warning to the men of this world from verse 11.

The ungodly must have present light, from earth, from a fire of their own kindling, from mere momentary sparks.

Their resolve will end in eternal regrets; they shall lie down as for the night; their bed shall be sorrow; they shall never rise from it.

Addenda

A secret divine support was rendered to the human nature of our Redeemer; for the great work in which he was engaged required abundant strength. One has well said that "it would have broken the hearts, backs, and necks of all the glorious angels in heaven, and all the mighty men upon earth, had they engaged in it." Upon the Father's aid the Lord Jesus relied, according to our text; and this enabled him to contemplate the tremendous woes of the passion with a resolve of the most steadfast kind. Faith in God is the best foundation for a firm resolution, and a firm resolution is the best preparative for a great undertaking. There is nothing so hard but that it can be cut by that which is harder: against his hard labor our Lord set his harder determination. His face was as a flint; you could not turn him to leave his work, nor melt him to pity himself. He was set upon it: he must die because he must save his people; and he must save his people because he loved them better than himself.

The saints endeavor to imitate the strong resolve of their Lord to yield themselves up. For instance, a Scottish peasant, dying as a martyr on the scaffold, said, "I came here to die for Christ, and if I had as many lives in my hand as I have hairs on my head, I would lay them all down for Christ."

Oh, what a sea of blood, a sea of wrath, of sin, of sorrow and misery, did the Lord Jesus wade through for your internal and eternal good! Christ did not plead, "This cross is too heavy for me to bear; this wrath is too great for me to lie under; this cup, which hath in it all the ingredients of divine displeasure, is too bitter for me to sup off, how much more to drink the very dregs of it!" No, Christ stands not upon this; he pleads not the difficulty of the service, but resolutely and bravely wades through all, as the prophet shows. Christ makes nothing of his Father's wrath, the burden of your sins, the malice of Satan, and the rage of the world, but sweetly and triumphantly passes through all. Ah, souls, if this consideration will not raise up your spirits above all the discouragements that you meet with, to own Christ and his service, and to stick and cleave to Christ and his service, I am afraid nothing will! A soul not stirred by this, not raised and lifted up by this, to be resolute and brave in the service of God, notwithstanding all dangers and difficulties, is a soul left of God to much blindness and hardness. —*Thomas Brooks*

81

With his stripes we are healed.
—*Isaiah 53:5*

 HAT a chapter! A Bible in miniature. The Gospel in its essence.

When our subject brings us near to the passion of our Lord, our feelings should be deeply solemn, our attention intensely earnest.

Hark, the scourge is falling! Forget everything but *"his stripes."*

We have each one a part in the flagellation: we wounded him, for certain; is it as certain that "with his stripes *we are healed*"?

Observe with deep attention:

I. THAT GOD HERE TREATS SIN AS A DISEASE.

Sin is a great deal more than a disease, it is a willful crime; but the mercy of our God leads him to consider it under that aspect, in order that he may deal with it in grace.

1. It is not an essential part of man as he was created: it is abnormal, disturbing, and destructive.
2. It puts the faculties out of gear, and breaks the equilibrium of the life forces, just as disease disturbs the bodily functions.

3. It weakens the moral energy, as disease weakens the body.

4. It either causes pain, or deadens sensibility, as the case may be.

5. It frequently produces visible pollution. Some sins are as defiling as the leprosy of old.

6. It tends to increase in the man, and it will prove fatal before long.

Sin is a disease which is hereditary, universal, contagious, defiling, incurable, mortal. No human physician can deal with it. Death, which ends all bodily pain, cannot cure this disease: it displays its utmost power in eternity, after the seal of perpetuity has been set upon it by the mandate: "He that is filthy, let him be filthy still."

II. THAT GOD HERE DECLARES THE REMEDY WHICH HE HAS PROVIDED.

Jesus is his Son, whom he freely delivered up for us all.

1. Behold the heavenly medicine: the stripes of Jesus in body and in soul. Singular surgery, the Healer is himself wounded, and this is the means of our cure!

2. Remember that these stripes were vicarious: he suffered in our stead.

3. Accept this atonement, and you are saved by it.
   • Prayer begs for the divine surgery.
   • Belief is the linen cloth which binds on the plaster.
   • Trust is the hand which secures it to the wound.
   • Repentance is the first symptom of healing.

4. Let nothing of your own interfere with the one medicine. You see the proper places of prayer, faith, and repentance; do not misuse them, and make them rivals of the "stripes." By the stripes of Jesus we are healed, and by these alone.

One remedy, and only one, is set forth by God. Why seek another?

III. THAT THIS DIVINE REMEDY IS IMMEDIATELY EFFECTIVE.

To the carnal mind it does not appear to touch the case.

But those of us who have believed in the stripes of Jesus are witnesses to the instant and perfect efficacy of the medicine, for we can speak from experience, since "We are healed."

1. Our conscience is healed of its smart: eased but not deadened.

2. Our heart is healed of its love of sin. We hate the evil which scourged our Well-Beloved.

3. Our life is healed of its rebellion. We are zealous of good works.

4. Our consciousness assures us that we are healed. We know it, and rejoice in it. None can dispute us out of it.

Application

1. Friend, *you are by nature in need of healing.*
   - You do not think so: this disease affects the mind, and breeds delusions.
   - You ridicule such teaching: your disease leads to madness.
   - You oppose it. Thus do the sick refuse medicine, and the insane hate their friends.
2. Friend, *you are either healed or sick.*
   - Do you not know which is your condition?
   - You ought to know. You may know.
3. *Why are you not healed?*
   There is power in the remedy, for you, for you now.
4. *If you are healed, behave accordingly.*
   - Quit diseased company.
   - Do a healthy man's work.
   - Praise the Physician, and his singular surgery.
   - Publish abroad his praises.

Suggestive Paragraphs

The Balsam-tree sheds its balm to heal the wounds of those that cut it; and did not our blessed Savior do the like? They mock him, and he prays for them; they shed his blood, and he makes it a medicine for their healing; they pierce his heart, and he opens therein a fountain for their sin and uncleanness. Was it ever heard, before or since, that a physician should bleed, and thus heal his patient; or that an offended prince should die to expiate the treasons of his rebellious subjects?

Our heavenly Balsam is a cure for all diseases. If you complain that no sins are like yours, remember that there is no salvation like Christ's. If you have run the complete round of sin, remember that the blood of Jesus Christ cleanseth from *all* sin. No man ever perished for being a great sinner, unless he was also an unbelieving sinner. Never did a patient fail of a cure who accepted from the great Physician the balm of his atoning blood.

See how Christ, whose death was so bitter to himself, becomes sweetness itself to us. Rejection was his, but acceptance is ours; the wounding was his, but the healing is ours; the blood was his, but the balm is ours; the thorns were his, but the crown is ours; the death was his, but the life is ours; the price was his, but the purchase is ours. There is more power in Christ's blood to save than in your sin to destroy. Do but believe in the Lord Jesus, and thy cure is wrought.
—*Modernized from Spurstows "Spiritual Chymist"*

The Hebrew word here, and the Greek word the Apostle Peter uses in his quotation of this passage which we render "stripes" (1 Pet. 2:24), denote properly the marks which stripes or wounds leave upon the body, or as we say, *scars*. The scars in his hands, feet, and side, and perhaps other marks of his many wounds, remained after his resurrection. And John saw him, in vision, before the throne, as "a Lamb as it had been slain." All these expressions and representations, I apprehend, are designed to intimate to us that, though the death of the Messiah is an event long since past, yet the effects and benefits are ever new, and to the eye of faith are ever present. How admirable is this expedient, that the wounds of one, yea, of millions, should be healed by beholding the wounds of another! Yet, this is the language of the gospel: "Look, and live!" "Look unto me, and be ye saved!" Three great wounds are ours, guilt, sin, and sorrow; but by contemplating his weals, or scars, with an enlightened eye, and by rightly understanding who was thus wounded, and why, all these wounds are healed.

You who live by this medicine, speak well of it. Tell to others, as you have opportunity, what a Savior you have found. It is usual for those who have been relieved, in dangerous and complicated diseases, by a skillful physician, to commend him to others who are laboring under the like maladies. We often see public acknowledgments to this purpose. If all the persons who have felt the efficacy of a dying Savior's wounds, apprehended by faith, were to publish their cases, how greatly would his power and grace be displayed! —*John Newton*

He cures the mind of its blindness, the heart of its hardness, the nature of its perverseness, the will of its backwardness, the memory of its slipperiness, the conscience of its benumbedness, and the affections of their disorder, all according to his gracious promises (Ezek. 36:26–27). —*John Willison*

Trajan, it is said, rent his clothes to bind up his soldiers' wounds. Christ poured out his blood to heal his saints' wounds, and tears his flesh to bind them up. —*Gurnall*

Dr. Cheyne was an eminent as well as a pious physician; but he was supposed to be severe in his regimen. When he had prescribed, and the patient began to object to the treatment, he would say, "I see you are not bad enough for me yet." Some are not bad enough for Christ yet—we mean, in their own apprehension; but when they find and feel that they are entirely lost, and have no other help or hope, they will cordially acquiesce in his recommendations, however mysterious, however humbling, however trying. —*Jay*

Four travelers, not very well acquainted with the cross-road over which they were journeying, began to look out for a finger-post. Soon after this, one of them cried out, "I think I can see one yonder in the distance"; and "I believe that I can see it too, about half-a-mile off," rejoined another; and "I am almost certain that I can see it," added a third, "it stands up higher than the hedges." "Well, well," said the fourth, "you may be right, or you may be wrong; but we had better make the best of our way to it, for while we keep at such a distance, whether it be a finger-post or not, it will be of little use to us."

Now I want you all to draw near to the Savior of sinners, and not to be satisfied with "thinking," or "believing," or being "almost certain," that he is your Redeemer; I want you to see him as your Savior, as distinctly as you can see the sun in the skies, and to break out with all the conviction and fervency of Thomas, the Apostle, "My Lord, and my God!" —*George Mogridge*

82

For a small moment have I forsaken thee; but with great mercies will I gather thee. In a little wrath I hid my face from thee for a moment; but with everlasting kindness will I have mercy on thee, saith the Lord thy Redeemer. For this is as the waters of Noah unto me: for as I have sworn that the waters of Noah should no more go over the earth; so have I sworn that I would not be wroth with thee, nor rebuke thee.

—Isaiah 54:7–9

HIS text is the property of all believers. Their title to it is seen at the end of the chapter (verse 17). Let them not fail to enjoy it. It follows upon the prophecy of their Lord's great griefs (Isa. 53). We are never so able to believe a great promise as when we have been at the cross.

The people of God are often greatly tried, and their griefs are sometimes spiritual, and more deep than those of the wicked.

Their grand comfort lies in this, that in all their afflictions there is no penal wrath, no great indignation, no final judgment from the Lord.

We shall speak upon:

I. THE LITTLE WRATH AND ITS MODIFICATIONS.

The Lord calls it "a little wrath," and speaks of the time of its continuance as "a moment," "a small moment."

1. Our view of it differs from the Lord's. To us it appears to be an utter forsaking, and the hiding of his face forever.
   - We are too foolish, too agitated, too unbelieving, to judge aright.
   - God's view is truth itself, therefore let us believe it.
2. The time of it is short. What is less than "a small moment"?
   - As compared with eternal love.
   - When looked back upon in after years of holy peace.
   - In reality it only endures for a little while.
   - It will soon be over if we repent and pray.
3. The recompense is great. Jehovah vows to give "mercies," many, divine, everlasting, great, effectual: "with great mercies will I gather thee."

4. The wrath itself is little. A Husband's wrath, a Redeemer's wrath, a Pitier's wrath; wrath occasioned by holy love.

5. The expression of it is not severe.
   - Not set my face against thee; nor change my mind.
   - But hide my face, and that only for a moment.
   - Thus God views the matter of our chastisement, seeing the end from the beginning.

6. It is quite consistent with eternal love. This love will endure forever, is present during the little wrath, is the cause of the wrath, and will continue unchanged forever.

   The chastened child is none the less loved.

7. It does not change our relationship to the Lord. He is still our Redeemer (verse 8), and we are still the redeemed of the Lord.

Our duty is to grieve because of the Lord's anger; to be humbled and sanctified by it; but not to faint, or despair under it.

II. THE GREAT WRATH AND OUR SECURITY AGAINST IT.

1. The wrath of God against his people can no more break out upon them than can Noah's flood return to go over the earth. That flood has not returned during these many centuries, and it never will. Seed-time and harvest continue, and the bow is in the cloud. We have no dread of another universal deluge of water, nor need believers fear a return of divine wrath (enlarge on verse 9).

2. The great flood of wrath has broken forth once for all. On our Lord it has burst, and thus it has been ended forever. "Christ hath redeemed us from the curse of the law, being made a curse for us" (Gal. 3:13). "As far as the east is from the west, so far hath he removed our transgressions from us" (Ps. 103:12). "Who is he that condemneth? It is Christ that died" (Rom. 8: 34). "The iniquity of Israel shall be sought for, and there shall be none; and the sins of Judah, and they shall not be found" (Jer. 50:20). This is real, true, effectual, eternal atonement.

3. We have the oath of God that it shall not return: "so have I sworn that I would not be wroth with thee, nor rebuke thee." In a way of punishment there shall not even be a hard word uttered—"nor rebuke thee."

4. We have a covenant of peace as sure as that made with Noah, and of a higher order, for it is made with Jesus our Lord.

5. We have pledges of immutable, immovable mercy: "the mountains and the hills" (verse 10). These may depart and be removed, but never the kindness of the Lord.

6. All this is spoken to us by Jehovah the Merciful: "saith the Lord that hath mercy on thee."

How wicked it is to doubt and distrust!
How safe is the condition of the covenanted ones!
How glorious is our God of everlasting kindness!
How careful should we be that we do not grieve him!

Cheering Words

Ah, Zion's daughters! do not fear
The cross, the cords, the nails, the spear,
The myrrh, the gall, the vinegar;

For Christ, your loving Savior, hath
Drunk up the wine of God s fierce wrath;
Only there's left a little froth,

Less for to taste, than for to show
What bitter cups had been your due,
Had he not drunk them up for you.

—Herrick

The darkness of sorrow has often been shown to be but "the shadow of God's wing as he drew near to bless."

We cannot have fertilizing showers on the earth without a clouded heaven above. It is thus with our trials.

O Lord! let me have anything but thy frown; and anything with thy smile. *—R. Cecil*

A learned minister, attending an aged Christian in humble life, when in his last illness, remarked that the passage in Hebrews 13:5, "I will never leave thee, nor forsake thee," was much more emphatic in the original language than in our translation, inasmuch as it contained no fewer than five negatives in proof of the validity of the divine promise, and not merely two, as it appears in the English version; intending by this remark, to convey to him that, in consequence of the number of negatives, the promise was expressed with much greater force in the original language than in the English. The man's reply was very simple and striking: "I have no doubt, sir, that you are quite right, but I can assure you that if God had only spoken *once*, I should have believed him just the same."

83

Let the wicked forsake his way, and the unrightous man his thoughts: and let him return unto the Lord, and he will have mercy upon him.

—*Isaiah 55:7*

HIS is the great chapter of gospel invitation. How free! How full! How plain and pressing are the calls to receive grace!

Yet the necessity of repentance, in its most practical form, is not cast into the background. Turning, or conversion, is insisted on.

- Gospel provisions are presented freely (verses 1 and 2).
- A Savior is provided and proclaimed (verses 3 and 4).
- Saved nations are absolutely promised to him (verse 5).
- Men are encouraged to seek and find the Lord (verse 6).

But the call to conversion follows close after, and is intended to be the necessary inference from all that preceded it. Men must return to God: his very mercy makes it imperative.

Very earnestly, therefore, let us turn our thoughts to:

I. THE NECESSITY OF CONVERSION.

The text makes this clear, but it may also be inferred from:

1. The nature of God. How can a holy God wink at sin, and pardon sinners who continue in their wickedness?
2. The nature of the gospel. It is not a proclamation of tolerance for sin, but of deliverance from it. It contains no single promise of forgiveness to the man who goes on in his iniquity.
3. The facts of the past. No instance has occurred of pardon given to a man while obstinately persisting in his evil way. Conversion always goes with salvation.
4 The needs of society. It would be unsafe to the common-weal of the universe to show mercy to the incorrigible offender. Sin must be punished, or else virtue will perish.
5. The well-being of the sinner himself requires that he should quit his sin, or feel its penalty. To be favored with a sense of divine pardon, while obstinately abiding in sin, would confirm the man in sin; and sin itself is a worse evil than its penalty.
6. The work of the Holy Spirit would be set aside, for he is the Sanctifier.
7. The design of our Lord Jesus would be overborne, for he comes to save *from* sin.

8. The character of heaven requires that a sinner's nature be renewed, and his life purged, ere he can enter the holy place where God, and holy angels, and perfect saints abide.

"Except ye be converted, and become as little children, ye shall not enter into the kingdom of heaven" (Matt. 18:3).

II. THE NATURE OF CONVERSION.

1. It deals with the life and conduct. The man's "way."
- His natural way; that into which he runs when left to himself.
- His habitual way; to which he is accustomed.
- His beloved way; wherein his pleasures lie.
- The general way; the broad road in which the many run.

This, our text says, he must "forsake." He must have done with sin, or he will be undone. It will not suffice for him to:
- Own that it is wrong;
- Profess to be sorry for following it;
- Resolve to leave it, and end in resolve; or,
- Move more cautiously in it.

No, he must forsake it, altogether, at once, and forever.

2. It deals with the "thoughts." A man must forsake:

His unscriptural opinions, and self-formed notions:
- About God, his law, his gospel, his people.
- About sin, punishment, Christ, self, etc.

His contemplations, so far as they lead him:
- To find pleasure in evil;
- To indulge in conceit and self-sufficiency; or,
- To harbor wrong thoughts of God.

His evil resolves:

To continue in sin, to delay repentance, to be a free thinker, to be his own master, to defy God, etc.

Such thoughts are to be forsaken; he must flee from them.

3. It deals with the man in reference to God. "Let him return *unto the Lord*."

It bids him cease from pride, neglect, opposition, distrust, disobedience, and all other forms of alienation from the Lord. He must turn and return; wandering no further, but coming home.

III. THE GOSPEL OF CONVERSION.

1. A sure promise is made to it "He will have mercy upon him."
2. Divine power is exercised to effect it. "Turn thou us unto thee, O Lord, and we shall be turned" (Lam. 5:21). A man converts when grace converts him.

3. It is itself promised to faith in Jesus (Acts 5:31; 13:38–39).

4. The pardon which comes with it is the result of a full atonement, which renders the pardon abundant, just, safe, and easy of belief to the awakened conscience.

Oh, that the sinner would consider the need of a total change of *thought* within, and *way* without! It must be thorough and radical or it will be useless.

Total and terrible ruin must ensue if you continue in evil.

May this hour see the turning-point in your life's course! God saith, "Let him return." What doth hinder you?

A Story

William Burns was preaching one evening, in the open-air, to a vast multitude. He had just finished, when a man came timidly up to him, and said, "O Sir! will you come and see my dying wife?" Burns consented; but the man immediately said, "Oh! I am afraid when you know where she is you won't come." "I will go wherever she is," he replied. The man then tremblingly told him that he was the keeper of the lowest public-house in one of the most wretched districts of the town. "It does not matter," said the missionary, "come away." As they went, the man, looking up in the face of God's servant, said earnestly, "O Sir! I am going to give it up at the *term*." Burns replied, "There are no *terms*, with God." However much the poor trembling publican tried to get Burns to converse with him about the state of his soul, and the way of salvation, he was unable to draw another word from him than these: "There are no *terms* with God." The shop was at last reached. They passed through it in order to reach the chamber of death. After a little conversation with the dying woman, the servant of the Lord engaged in prayer, and while he was praying the publican left the room, and soon a loud noise was heard, something like a rapid succession of determined knocks with a great hammer. Was this not a most unseemly noise to make on such a solemn occasion as this? Is the man mad? No. When Burns reached the street, he beheld the wreck of the publican's sign-board strewn in splinters upon the pavement. The business was given up for good and all. The man had in earnest turned his back on his low public house, and returned to the Lord, who had mercy upon him, and unto our God, who abundantly pardoned all his sins. Nothing transpired in his afterlife to discredit the reality of his conversion.
—*William Brown, in "The Joyful Sound"*

84

Let him return unto the Lord, and he will have mercy upon him; and to our God, for he will abundantly pardon.

—Isaiah 55:7

HE prophet is setting forth the mission of Jesus (verses 4 and 5). Straightway he makes an appeal to sinners, for Jesus comes to sinners. He proclaims pardon to them, for this Jesus brings: his coming is as the morning, bedewing the earth with delight.

The call is practically to faith and repentance; immediate, frank, spiritual, complete.

The inducement presented is an abundant free-grace pardon: "he will abundantly pardon."

There is no more likely argument wherewith to persuade souls.

I. LET US CONTEMPLATE THE ABUNDANCE OF DIVINE PARDON.

We may do so the better if we consider:

1. The abundance of the attribute from which it springs. All the attributes of God are infinite and harmonious, but we are told that "God is love," and this is not said of justice, or power. "Thy mercy is great above the heavens" (Ps. 108:4). "The earth, O Lord, is full of thy mercy" (Ps. 119:64). "His mercy endureth forever" (Ps. 136).

2. The abundance of the objects of the pardon. From the days of Adam until now God has pardoned multitudes among all nations, classes, and ages.
   • We quickly lose patience when many offend, but it is not so with our God. "Thou hast forgiven this people from Egypt even until now" (Num. 14:19).

3. The abundant sins which are pardoned. Who can count the thoughts, words, and deeds which are pardoned?
   • These repeated ad nauseam (Isa. 43:24; Rev. 3:16).
   • Sins against law and gospel, light and love, in youth and old age.
   • Yet these God removes, like the countless locusts blown away by the wind, or as the drops of dew exhaled by the sun.

4. The abundant sin of the sins which are pardoned.
   • Some sins are planned and deliberated on, and each plotting and devising entails sin.
   • Some are a spider's nest, swarming with many sins.
   • Some are proud, wanton, cruel, blasphemous, impudent.
   • Some are repeated, aggravated, and persisted in.
   • Yet the intensified venom of epitomized sin the Lord removes.

5. The abundant means of pardon.
- The atonement of his Son, and his righteousness.
- The infinite merit of the ever-living Advocate.
- The Holy Spirit ever present to apply gospel provision
6. The abundant ease of the terms of pardon.
- No hard conditions of penance or purgatory.
- Only ask and have; repent and trust.
- Even the repentance and faith required are also given.
7. The abundant fullness of the pardon.
- It covers all sin, past, present, and to come.
- It is most effectual, and sure.
- It is perpetual, and irreversible.
- It is accompanied with imputed righteousness. Pardon washes, and justification clothes and beautifies.
8. The abundant blessings which attend it.
- Liberation from spiritual prison, legal bonds, etc.
- Freedom from the reigning power of inbred sin.
- Adoption into the heavenly family.
- Acceptance so full that we may challenge accusers.
- Employment in services of trust.
- Communion with the thrice-holy God.
- Reception of answers to our prayers, as true and certain as if we were perfectly pure.
- Ultimate admission into glory itself with the perfect ones.

II. LET US CONSIDER ITS PROPER INFERENCES, and these shall furnish the practical conclusion of our discourse.

1. Then there is no room for despair. If the Lord only pardoned now and then, it were well to seek his favor even on the bare chance of obtaining it; but now let us return unto him in sure and certain hope of pardon.
2. Then there is a loud call to repent, for who would offend so good, so kind a Lord? Let our relentings be kindled, since he is so forward to promise us pardon.
3. Here is a special call to the greatest sinners, since abundant mercy is most appropriate to their case: and no less should the less guilty come, since there must be room for them.
4. Such a much-forgiving God deserves to be much loved, and the lives of the pardoned should prove that to whom much is forgiven, the same loveth much.
5. If such mercy be slighted, we may be sure it will entail great wrath.

Inviting Sounds

That sin which is not too great to be forsaken, is not too great to be forgiven.

Mercy in us, it is no more than a drop; but in God it is an ocean: in us it is no more than a little stream; in God it is a springing and flowing fountain. A spring continually runs, an ocean is never drawn dry. What is a little sparkle of fire, if it fall into the main sea? The same are the sins of a penitent person when dealt with by the mercy of God. —*Thomas Horton*

One of the captive followers of the Duke of Monmouth was brought before James the Second. "You know it is in my power," said the king, "to pardon you." "Yes," said the man, who well knew his cruel character, "but it is not in your nature." However unwise this answer was, its truth was soon seen. Happily, we know that God has not only the power but the disposition to show mercy. "Also, unto thee, O Lord, belongeth mercy."

Mr. Fleming, in his "Fulfilling of the Scriptures," relates the case of a most hardened sinner who was put to death in the town of Ayr. It pleased the Lord to bring him to repentance when in prison, and so full was his assurance of pardoning mercy that, when he came to the place of execution, he could not help crying out to the people, under the sense of pardon, "Oh, he is a great Forgiver! He is a great Forgiver!" and he added, "Now hath perfect love cast out fear. I know God hath nothing to say against me, for Jesus Christ hath paid all; and those are free whom the Son makes free."   *G. S. Bowes*

Lord, before I commit a sin, it seems to me so shallow that I may wade through it dry-shod from any guiltiness; but when I have committed it, it often seems so deep that I cannot escape without drowning. Thus I am always in extremities: either my sins are so small that they need not any repentance, or so great that they cannot obtain thy pardon. Lend me, O Lord, a reed out of thy sanctuary, truly to measure the dimension of my offenses. But O! as thou revealest to me more of my misery, reveal also more of thy mercy; lest, if my wounds, in my apprehension, gape wider than thy tents (plugs of lint), my soul run out at them. If my badness seem bigger than thy goodness but one hair's breadth, but one moment, that is room and time enough for me to run to eternal despair. —*Thomas Fuller*

85

Who are these that fly as a cloud, and as the doves to their windows?
—Isaiah 60:8

N the days when the Lord shall visit his church, multitudes will come to seek him.

It is a great blessing when they do so; a matter for admiring praise.

They will come from far to learn of Jesus, flying in a straight line, as pigeons when they return to their homes.

Jesus is the great attraction, and when he is faithfully lifted up, men will hasten to him in flocks, flying like clouds before a gale.

Yet will it astonish those who see it, and they will ask questions such as those which follow.

I. WHO ARE THESE CONVERTS THAT THEY SHOULD BE SO MANY?

"As a cloud."

The answers are many and easy.

1. Are not sinners many?
2. Is not Christ's redemption great?
3. Are not his blessings attractive?
4. Shall Satan have the pre-eminence in numbers at the last? We cannot think it will be so.
5. Is not the Spirit of God able to draw many?
6. Is not heaven great, and is there not room for hosts of souls?

Naturalists tell us of vast clouds of pigeons in America. Oh, to see such a cloud of converts!

II. WHO ARE THEY THAT THEY SHOULD FLY?

Why are they in such eager haste as to speed like doves when coming homeward to their cotes?

This also is plain.

1. They are in great danger.
2. Their time is very short.
3. They are driven by a great wind. The Spirit, like a heavenly breath, impels souls to seek salvation.
4. They are moved by strong desire: a great hunger is on them to reach their home, where they shall be fed and housed.

Doves fly straight, swiftly, surely. They neither linger nor loiter, but hasten home.

III. WHO ARE THEY THAT THEY SHOULD FLY TOGETHER?

They fly in such a flock that they appear like a cloud: why is this?

1. They are all in one common danger.
2. They have no time to quarrel while seeking safety.
3. They have one common object: they seek one Savior.
4. They are wafted by the same heavenly wind. The Spirit works in each according to his own will.
5. They find comfort in each other's society.
6. They hope to live together forever above.

IV. WHO ARE THEY THAT THEY SHOULD FLY THIS WAY?

They are doves, and so they come to their usual abodes in the clefts of the rock or to the openings of the dove-house.

1. Seeking safety in Jesus, from the hawks which pursue them.
2. Desiring rest in his love, for they are wearied, and find no other rest for the soles of their feet.
3. Finding a home in his heart. Swallows go to another home in winter, but saints abide in Christ forever.
4. Their companions are there: doves congregate, and so do saved sinners love fellowship with each other.
5. Their young are there. "The swallow hath found a nest for herself, where she may lay her young" (Ps. 84:3). Believers love to have their children housed in Christ.
6. Their food is there. Where else can we find provender?
7. Their all is there. Christ is all.

V. BUT WHO ARE THEY INDIVIDUALLY?

1. Some are our own children.
2. Some are from the Sabbath-school.
3. Some are old hearers, who were gospel-hardened.
4. Some are quite strangers, outsiders.
5. Some are backsliders returning.
6. Some are those whom we sought in prayer, and personal address.

Dear hearer, are you one of them?

Have you not reason to fly from the wrath to come?

Fly first to Jesus, and then without delay hasten to his church.

Feathers

This text has been well illustrated by *Morier*. "In the environs of the city (Ispahan), to the westward, near Zainderood, are many pigeonhouses, erected at a distance from habitations. They are large, round towers, rather broader at the bottom than at the top, and crowned by conical spiracles, through which the pigeons descend. The interior resembles a honey-comb, pierced with a thousand holes, each of which forms a snug retreat for a nest. The extraordinary flights of pigeons, which I have seen upon one of these buildings, afford perhaps a good illustration of the passage. The great numbers, and the compactness of the mass, literally looked like a cloud at a distance, and obscured the sun in their passage." What gives an additional value to this illustration is the probability that similar dove-houses were in use among the Hebrews, for they certainly were so among their Egyptian neighbors. —*Kitto's Pictorial Bible*

God's children love communion and fellowship one with another, that they may mutually be comforted and edified in faith: "they fly like a cloud, and as doves to their windows"; that is, to the house or church of God. —*Benjamin Keach*

Those that are weak want supply and support from others. Nature teacheth this lesson. The weakest creatures amongst fish, or fowls, or beasts, go usually in flocks and companies. —*G. Swinnock*

Birds of a feather flock together.

Everybody knows that large flocks of pigeons assemble at the stroke of the great clock in the square of St. Mark, Venice. Believe me, it is not the music of the bell which attracts them, they can hear that every hour. They come, Mr. Preacher, for food, and no mere sound will long collect them. This is a hint for filling your meeting house; it must be done, not merely by that fine, bell-like voice of yours, but by all the neighborhood's being assured that spiritual food is to be had when you open your mouth. Barley for pigeons, good sir; and the gospel for men and women. Try it in earnest, and you cannot fail; you will soon be saying, "Who are they that fly as a cloud, and as doves to their windows?" —*From "Feathers for Arrows," by C. H. Spurgeon*

A writer in "Nature" states that the small birds, that are unable to fly the three hundred and fifty miles across the Mediterranean Sea, are carried over on the backs of cranes When the first cold weather comes, the cranes fly low, making a peculiar cry. Little birds of every species fly up to them, while the twittering of those already settled may be distinctly heard. But for this provision, many species of small birds would become extinct. So, many converts that are young and feeble need much assistance in seeking Christ. Let those that are strong help the weaker ones in their spiritual flight.

86

Return, thou backsliding Israel, saith the Lord. . . . Turn, O backsliding children, saith the Lord. . . . Return, ye backsliding children, and
I will heal your backslidings.

—Jeremiah 3:12, 14, 22

ᴛ is a fearful thing that a believer should backslide.
- Such mercy has been shown to him.
- Such love has been enjoyed by him.
- Such prospects lie before him.
- Such comfort is sacrificed by his backsliding.

It is a wretched business for the man himself, since by it nothing is gained,
and everything is endangered.

It is injurious to the whole church to which the backslider belongs.

It is mischievous to the outside world.

What is the immediate duty of the backslider? the immediate remedy for
his backsliding?

One word sums it up, and it is God's word, *"Return."*

Let us earnestly note:

I. WONDER AWAKENED BY THE CALL.

There would seem to be many reasons why the Lord should not invite the
backslider to return. We will follow the guidance of the chapter, which will richly repay a careful exposition.

1. The usual jealousy of love. Note the terrible imagery of verse 1. A wanton adulteress is allowed to return to her husband.
2. The abundance of the sin: "Thou hast polluted the land" (verse 2). The
   very earth felt the leprosy of the idolatry.
3. The obstinate continuance in evil, notwithstanding chastisements (verse
   3). "Thou refusedst to be ashamed."
4. The refusal of tender persuasion. "Wilt thou not?" etc. (verse 4).
5. The perversion of mercy. God did not reserve his anger forever, and they
   sinned the more because of his long-suffering (verse 5).
6. The warnings which had been despised. Judah saw Israel doomed, and
   yet followed her evil ways (verses 6–11). It is a great increase of iniquity
   when we perceive the suffering which it causes others, and yet persevere
   in it ourselves.

Is it not marvelous that God should be so full of mercy as to bid such
revolters return, and repeat the exhortation again and again?

II. MEMORIES AROUSED BY THE CALL.

Does it not remind you of other days?

1. When you first came to Jesus.
2. When you were happy with other believers.
3. When you could teach and warn others.
4. When you began to go aside, a little.
5. When you have sinned grievously through this backsliding.

Indulge these memories till they affect your heart.

III. REASONS URGED FOR OBEYING THE CALL.

1. It is God himself who utters it. Twice we read, "saith the Lord."
2. Anger will be removed: "I will not cause mine anger to fall upon you" (verse 12).
3. Love continues: "I am married unto you" (verse 14).
4. Healing will be given: "I will heal your backslidings" (verse 22).

Each verse yields its own forcible argument,

IV. DIRECTIONS GIVEN TO MAKE OBEDIENCE TO THE CALL EASY.

1. "Only acknowledge thine iniquity" (verse 13). What a simple matter!
2. Lament the evil: "Weeping and supplications" (verse 21). Do you not mourn your sin even now?
3. Own the sad result. "We lie down in our shame," etc. (verse 25).
4. Trust in God for restoration: "Truly in the Lord our God is the salvation of Israel" (verse 23).
5. Heartily renew allegiance: "Behold, we come unto thee; for thou art the Lord our God" (verse 22).

These things, carefully and immediately attended to, will restore the fallen to their first estate. "Return! Return!" saith the Lord.

Oh, that the Holy Ghost may lead them to it!

V. PROMISES MADE TO THOSE ANSWERING TO THE CALL.

Such shall obtain:

1. Special guidance: "I will bring you to Zion" (verse 14).
2. Suitable food: "Feed you with knowledge" (verse 15).
3. Spiritual insight (see verses 16 and 17).
4. Childlike spirit: "Thou shalt call me, 'My father'" (verse 19).

The whole subject needs pressing upon all believers, for we may have already backslidden more than we are aware.

Upon the conscious backslider the three-fold call should be pressed, "Return!" "Turn!" "Return!"

Turns of Expression

There is a play upon words, or rather upon senses, in the original, "Return, ye backsliding children," more literally, "Turn, ye turned-away sons, and I will heal your turnings," as in Hosea 14:4.

God invites and does not drive; he here exchanges threats for promises. God will "heal," not simply receive his children. God alone can heal their apostasies. Man repents of sin, but God cures it. It is our part to turn from evil, God's to destroy that evil. Sin is washed out, not by tears of penitence, but by the blood of Christ. The healing is of the apostasies themselves, not simply of their painful effects Christ saves from sin. —*The Pulpit Commentary*

I was weary of a cold heart towards Christ, and his sacrifice, and the work of his Spirit—of a cold heart in the pulpit, in secret prayer, and in study. For fifteen years previously I had felt my heart burning within, as if going to Emmaus with Jesus. On a day ever to be remembered by me, as I was going from Dolgelly to Machynlleth, and climbing up towards Cadair Idris, I considered it to be incumbent upon me to pray, however hard I felt my heart, and however worldly the frame of my spirit was. Having begun in the name of Jesus, I soon felt as it were the fetters loosening, and the old hardness of heart softening, and, as I thought, mountains of frost and snow dissolving, and melting within me. This engendered confidence in my soul in the promise of the Holy Ghost. I felt my mind relieved from some great bondage: tears flowed copiously, and I was constrained to cry out for the gracious visits of God, by restoring to my soul the joy of his salvation. —*Christmas Evans*

I am sometimes downright staggered at the exceeding riches of his grace. How Christ can go on pardoning day after day, and hour after hour; sometimes I feel almost afraid to ask, for shame. —*A. L. Newton*

> Man-like is it to fall into sin,
> Fiend-like is it to dwell therein,
> Christ-like is it for sin to grieve,
> God-like is it all sin to leave.
> 　　　　　　—*Longfellow*

> Yet sovereign mercy calls, "Return!"
> 　Dear Lord, and may I come?
> My vile ingratitude I mourn—
> 　O take the wanderer home!
> 　　　　　　—*Steele*

87

But I said, How shall I put thee among the children, and give thee a pleasant land, a goodly heritage of the hosts of nations? and I said, Thou shalt call me, My father; and shalt not turn away from me.
—*Jeremiah 3:19*

 AN thinks lightly of sin; but not so the Lord.
Man thinks lightly of grace; but not so the Lord.
Man trifles where God wonders.
Man forgets where God considers.

The text may be viewed as written with a note of interrogation (?) or a note of exclamation (!).

Let us treat it somewhat in that blended fashion.

I. HERE IS A DIFFICULT QUESTION.

Many knotty questions are involved in it.

1. As to the holy Lord. "How shall *I* put thee among the children?" How, in consistency with justice and purity, shall the Holy One place in his family persons of such character? They have forgotten, despised, forsaken, rejected, and insulted their God and can he treat them as if they had loved and obeyed?

2. As to the unholy person. "How shall I put *thee* among the children?" Shalt thou be adopted after being:
   - A rebel so set on mischief, willfully disobeying?
   - A sinner so open, so presumptuous, so obstinate?
   - A desperado so profligate, profane, and persecuting?
   - A criminal "condemned already" by thine unbelief?

   Such persons do obtain mercy, but how is it done?

3. As to the family. "How shall I put thee *among the children*?"
   - What will the children say? "A fine brother, certainly!"
   - What will the world say? Will not observers exclaim, "See what characters are received into the household of God!" May it not even seem like trifling with iniquity? May not the wicked hope for impunity in their sinning?
   - What can I myself say to justify such a course? How shall I make this appear to be the act of the Judge of all the earth?

4. As to the inheritance: "and give thee *a pleasant land, a goodly heritage*?" Is not this too good for such?
   - Shalt thou have peace and happiness below?
   - Shalt thou have all that my favored children enjoy?
   - Shalt thou be admitted into heaven?

   It is a question which none but the Lord would ever have thought of.

He himself asked it long ago, as if to let us see that it was no small matter which he proposed.

He himself answered the question, or it had been unanswerable.

II. HERE IS A WONDERFUL ANSWER.

1. It is from God himself, and is therefore a perfect answer.
2. It is in the divine style: "Thou shalt" and "thou shalt not." Omnipotence speaks, and grace reveals its unconditional character.
3. It is concerning a divine work. God himself puts sinners among his children, and none beside can do it.
   - The Lord infuses a new spirit—a filial spirit.
   - This spirit expresses itself by a new call: "My Father."
   - This creates new bonds: "and shalt not turn away from me."
4. It is effectual for its purpose.
   - Those who heartily cry "My Father" may safely be put among the children.
   - Those who do not turn away from their father must be children. Servants go, but sons abide.

Thus the wisdom of our gracious God, by regeneration and adoption, answers the difficult question.

III. HERE, WITHOUT QUESTION, IS A MATCHLESS PRIVILEGE

We are put among the children.

1. We are indeed made children of God, and joint-heirs with Christ.
2. We are as much loved as the children.
3. We are treated as the children.
   - We are forgiven as a father forgives his children.
   - We are clothed, fed, and housed as children.
   - We are taught, ruled, and chastened as children.
   - We are honored and enriched as children.
4. We are placed under filial obligations:
     To love, honor, obey, and serve our Father.

This should be regarded as a high honor, and not as a burden.

Let us admire the grace which puts us into the family.

Let us enjoy the privileges which this secures to us.

Let us act as loving children should do.

Extracts

God seems, as it were, to be at a stand. "How shall I act so as to save these sinners, and yet not wrong myself?" This should greatly humble us for our sins. As if a child should do much evil, and bring himself into grievous troubles, so that if his tender father would help him he must be put to abundance of difficulties, and is fain to beat his brains, and laboriously study how he shall contrive to save his poor, foolish child from utter undoing. Now, if the child has any ingenuousness in him, he will not think, "My father's anxiety is no great matter, so long as I am delivered"; but he will cry, "Alas, this will break my heart! What troubles have I brought my father into! I cannot bear to think of it!" It should be thus with us in reference to our God, who in this text speaketh after the manner of men. —*Jeremiah Burroughs*

In the second century, Celsus, a celebrated adversary of Christianity, distorting our Lord's words, complained, "Jesus Christ came into the world to make the most horrible and dreadful society; for he calls sinners, and not the righteous; so that the body he came to assemble is a body of profligates, separated from good people, among whom they before were mixed. He has rejected all the good, and collected all the bad." "True," said Origen, in reply, "our Jesus came to call sinners—but to repentance. He assembled the wicked—but to convert them into new men, or rather to change them into angels. We come to him covetous, he makes us liberal; lascivious, he makes us chaste; violent, he makes us meek; impious, he makes us religious."

Regeneration is not a change of the old nature, but an introduction of a new nature. Not "Ishmael changed," but "Isaac born," is the son of the promise.

Whom God adopts, he anoints; whom he makes sons, he makes saints. —*Watson*

One of my parishioners at East Hampton, converted after having lived, through three or four revivals, to the age of fifty, and having given up hope, used to exclaim for several weeks after his change, "Is it I? Am I the same man who used to think it so hard to be converted, and my case so hopeless? Is it I? Is it I? Oh, wonderful!" —*Dr. Lyman Beecher*

88

They have refused to return.
—*Jeremiah 5:3*

HERE is about all men the primary evil of sin.

This is greatly increased by a refusal to return to their allegiance.

This is intensified by the rejection of pressing invitations.

I. WHO HAVE REFUSED TO RETURN?

1. Those who have said as much. With unusual honesty or presumption, they have made public declaration that they will never quit their sinful ways.
2. Those who have made a promise to repent, but have not performed it.

3. Those who have offered other things instead of practical return to God: ceremonies, religiousness, morality, and the like.

4. Those who have only returned in appearance. Formalists, mere professors, and hypocrites offer the counterfeit for the genuine; and thus in a veiled manner really refuse to repent.

5. Those who have only returned in part. Hugging some sins while hanging others is a wretched method of continuing rebellion while feigning submission.

II. WHAT THIS REFUSAL UNVEILS.

1. An intense love of sin. Suppose the prodigal had refused to leave the famine-stricken country, it would have proved his insane attachment to those with whom he had spent his substance.

2. A want of love to the great Father, who bids them return.

3. A disbelief of God: they neither believe in what he has revealed concerning the evil consequences of their sin, nor in what he promises as to the benefit of returning from it.

4. A despising of God: they reject his counsel, his command, and even himself.

5 A resolve to continue in evil. This is their proud ultimatum, "they have refused to return."

6. A trifling with serious concerns. They are too busy, too fond of gaiety, etc. There is time enough yet. There is no need to be so earnest. No doubt things will come right. Thus, they treat God's command as a light matter.

III. WHAT DEEPENS THE SIN OF THIS REFUSAL?

1. When correction brings no repentance.

2. When conscience is violated, and the Spirit of God is resisted. Repentance is seen to be right, but yet refused: duty is known but declined.

3. When repentance is known to be the happiest course, and yet it is obstinately neglected against the plainest reasons.

4. When this obstinacy is long-continued and is persevered in against convictions and inward promptings.

5. When vile reasons are at the bottom: such as secret sins, which the sinner dares not confess or quit; or the fear of man, which makes the mind cowardly.

IV. WHAT IS THE REAL REASON OF THIS REFUSAL?

1. It may be ignorance, but that can be only in part, for it is plainly a man's duty to return to his Lord. No mystery surrounds this simple precept: "Return."

2. It may be self-conceit: perhaps they dream that they are already in the right road.

3. It is at times sheer recklessness. The man refuses to consider his own best interests. He resolves to be a trifler; death and hell and heaven are to him as toys to sport with.
4. It is a dislike of holiness. That lies at the bottom of it: men cannot endure humility, self-denial, and obedience to God.
5. It is a preference for the present above the eternal future.

Oh, do not refuse the reasonable request to return when God tenderly invites you to come to himself! Is it not right? Is it not wise?

Life or death hangs on your choice! Why will you die?

Let a sweet consent be given. Say, "I will arise, and go unto my Father." You will never regret obedience to such a suggestion.

What is the riotous living of the far country compared with the joy of your Father's house?

From the cross the Lord Jesus calls on you to return. Hasten home!

Morsels

The door of heaven shuts from below, not from above. "Your iniquities have separated," saith the Lord. —*Williams, of Wern*

Lord Byron, a short time before death, was heard to say, "Shall I sue for mercy?" After a long pause, he added, "Come, come, no weakness; let's be a man to the last!"

The reason why a wicked man doth not turn unto God is not because he cannot (though he cannot), but because he will not. He cannot say at the day of judgment, "Lord, thou knowest I did my best to be holy, but I could not." The man that had not on a wedding-garment could not say, "Lord, I was not able to get one." But he was "speechless" —*W. Fenner*

89

Ask for the old paths, where is the good way, and walk therein, and ye shall find rest for your souls.

—*Jeremiah 6:16*

 T is the distinguishing feature of the good old way that in it we find rest for our souls. This is one of the tokens by which we may discern the false from the true.

- Rest was the promise of the Savior. "I will give you rest."
- Rest is the point in which the law failed. Moses could not lead the people into Canaan, neither can the works of the law conduct us into the rest of God.

- Rest has been enjoyed by believers, and it is now enjoyed by them.
- Rest is never found apart from the gospel, and faith in Jesus.
- Rest comes not from wealth, health, honor, or any other earthly thing.

I. IN "THE GOOD WAY" WE FIND REST IF WE WALK THEREIN.

We walk by faith in the gospel way, and are rested.

1. The way of pardon by an atonement gives rest to the conscience.
2. The way of believing the Word as a little child gives rest to the understanding.
3. The way of trusting our affairs with God gives rest to the mind.
4. The way of obedience to divine commands gives rest to the soul.
5. The way of communion with Christ gives rest to the heart.

It is no little matter which can rest the desires, the fears, the regrets, the questionings, of our manhood; but gospel doctrines, promises, and precepts, and the gospel spirit accomplish this.

II. REST FOUND BY WALKING IN "THE GOOD WAY" IS GOOD FOR THE SOUL.

Some forms of rest rust and injure the soul; but this does not.

1. It brings satisfaction, but not self-satisfaction.
2. It brings a sense of safety, but does not lead to presumptuous sin
3. It creates content, but also excites desires for progress.
4. It removes legal fears, but supplies superior motives for holiness.

It is actually beneficial to a man to walk in the good way, for as a saved believer his possession of salvation:

- Supplies him with an answer to the bribes of Satan; for what can Satan offer which could be preferable to assured salvation?
- Sets him free from personal anxiety, and thus enables him to serve the Lord without distraction, since he is himself saved.
- Engenders intense love to his Savior for his completed work.
- Excites him to holy imitation of his heavenly Father, who is so gracious as to afford rest to the weary.

III. REST OF THIS KIND SHOULD BE ENJOYED NOW.

It is so enjoyed by many of us, and it is a grievous error when it is not the case with all real Christians.

1. You should be in the way, know that you are there, and try to keep to the very middle of the road. Truly believe in Jesus, and perfect rest must come. "Therefore, being justified by faith, we have peace with God" (Rom. 5:1).
2. You should have no doubt that the way is good, and that it is the way of the Lord. This is the assurance of understanding.

3. You should lay aside all anxious care because "he careth for you."
4. You should feel an intense satisfaction in Jesus. You will do so unless you live at a distance from him, and so miss his presence and smile. A present Christ is a well of delight.
5. You should indulge the largest anticipations concerning your future blessedness, both in time and in eternity.

We challenge Romanists, sacramentarians, selfjusticiaries, and the like, to say that they have any rest. Rome does not promise it even to her own votaries, either in this world or in the world to come; but goes on saying her masses for the repose of the souls of her own departed cardinals, who evidently are not at rest. If her most eminent divines go to purgatory, where do the common people go?

We invite all the laboring and laden to come and try the Lord Jesus, and see if he does not rest them at once, and forever.

We bear our own willing testimony to the sweetness, safety, perpetuity, and truthfulness of the rest of faith.

Way-Marks

It is called "the good way." It is not the easy way: the idle and the foolish ask for that, but it is not worth seeking for, since it leads poverty and perdition. Neither is it the popular way, for few there be that find it. But it is the good way, made by a good God, in infinite goodness to his creatures; paved by our good Lord Jesus, with pains and labors immeasurable; and revealed by the good Spirit to those whose eternal good he seeks. It is the way of holiness, of peace, of safety, and it leads to heaven. Is it not good? It has been traversed by the best of men since time began, and the unclean do not pass over it. It is good at its commencement, for at its entrance men are born again; it is good in its continuation, for they are righteous who hold on their way; and it is good in its termination, for it leads to perfection, to bliss, to God himself.

In this good old way you shall find rest if you have never enjoyed it before; traveling you shall rest, as certain birds are said to rest upon the wing. Joy shall be upon your head, peace shall prepare the place of your feet. It is wisdom's dominion, and concerning her we read, "Her ways are ways of pleasantness, and all her paths are peace." Rest for the conscience comes to those who enter God's way of salvation; rest of heart arises out of their love to him who is the Way; rest of brain from their acceptance of his teaching; rest of desire from their satisfaction with his person-in a word, the soul rests in all its powers and faculties. Nor does it alone rest in the present; the future is guaranteed beyond all fear. —C. H. S.

Here there is a well-beaten track under our feet. Let us keep it. It may not be quite the shortest way; it may not take us through all the grandeur and sublimity which bolder pedestrians might see: we may miss a picturesque waterfall, a remarkable glacier, a charming view: but the track will bring us safe to our quarters for the night. —Dr. Dale

Dr. Judson once sent for a poor Christian convert, who was about to engage in something which he feared would not be for her spiritual good. "Look here," he said, snatching a ruler from the table, and tracing a not very straight line upon the floor; "here is where you have been walking You have made a crooked track, to be sure-out of the path half the time; but then you have kept near it, and not taken to new roads; and you have, to a certain extent, grown in grace. And now here you stand. You know where this path leads. You know what is before you: some struggles, some sorrows, and finally, eternal life, and a crown of glory. But to the left branches off another very pleasant road, and along the air floats, rather temptingly, a pretty bubble. You do not mean to leave the path you have walked in fifteen years; you only want to step aside, and catch the bubble, and think you will come back again; but you never will." The solemn warning was not given in vain.

90

Can the Ethiopian change his skin?
—Jeremiah 13:23

 EREMIAH had spoken to these people, and they would not hear; he had wept over them, and they would not consider. Even God's judgments had failed to move them, and he came to the conclusion that they were incorrigible, and could no more improve than a black man could become white.

Jeremiah's figure was most probably suggested to him by the Ethiopians in the king's court, one of whom attended more to him than his countrymen ever did (Jer. 38:7–13). Persons of color were no doubt more notable among an exclusive people like the Jews than they would be among us.

I. THE QUESTION AND ITS ANSWER. *"Can the Ethiopian change his skin?"* The expected reply is, "He cannot do so."

The outward impossibility is the Ethiopian's changing the color of his own skin: a physical experiment never yet accomplished.

The inward impossibility is a change of heart and character by one "accustomed to do evil."

Can he—will he—change himself? Never.

The difficulty in the sinner's case lies:

1. In the thoroughness of the operation. The Ethiopian can wash, or paint; but he cannot change that which is part and parcel of himself. A sinner cannot change his own nature.
2. In the fact that the will is itself diseased by sin. The man cannot do good, for he has no mind to it, no wish that way. In man's will lies the essence of the difficulty: he cannot means that he does not will to have it done. He is morally unable.
3. In the strength of habit. Use is second nature. Practice in transgression has forged chains, and bound the man to evil.
4. In the pleasure of sin, which fascinates and enslaves the mind.
5. In the appetite for sin, which gathers intensity from indulgence. Drunkenness, lechery, covetousness, etc., are a growing force.
6. In the blindness of the understanding, which prevents men from seeing the evil of their ways, or noting their danger. Conscience is drugged into a deep sleep, out of which the man cannot arouse himself.
7. In the growing hardness of the heart, which becomes more stolid and unbelieving every day, till nothing affects it.
8. In the evident fact that outward means prove ineffectual: like "sope" and "nitre" on a negro, they fail to touch the living blackness.

For all these reasons we answer the question in the negative: sinners can no more renew themselves than Ethiopians can change their skins.

Why then preach to them?

It is Christ's command, and we are bound to obey. Their inability does not hinder our ministry, for power goes with the word.

Why tell them that it is their duty to repent?

Because it is so: moral inability is no excuse: the law is not to be lowered because man has grown too evil to keep it.

Why tell them of this moral inability?

To drive them to self-despair, and make them look to Christ.

II. ANOTHER QUESTION AND ANSWER. *Can the Ethiopian's skin be changed?* Or, can the sinner be made anew?

- This is a very different affair, and in it lies the door of hope for men.
- Assuredly the Lord can make a black man white.
- The greatest sinner can be transformed into a saint.
- The grounds for so believing are many.

Here are a few of them:

1. All things are possible with God (Matt. 19:26).
2. The Holy Spirit has special power over the human heart.
3. The Lord Jesus has determined to work this wonder, and for this purpose he came into this world, and died, and rose again. "He shall save his people from their sins" (Matt. 1:21).

4. Many such jet-black sinners have been totally changed: among ourselves there are such and in all places such may be found.

5. The gospel is prepared with that end. It does more than change the skin; for it affects the head, the heart, the understanding, the conscience, the motives, the desires, the hopes, the fears; and through these, the whole conduct, so that those who were accustomed to do evil become expert in doing good.

6. God has made his church long for such transformations, and prayer has been offered that they may now be wrought. Will not the Lord hear us?

Herein lies hope for the most inveterate sinner.
- Not in the bath of baptism;
- Nor in the scalding tears of remorse;
- Nor in the medicine of vows and pledges;
- But in his word of power, who doeth great wonders of grace.

Chips

Dirt contracted may be washed off, but we cannot alter the natural color of a hair (Matt. 5:36), much less of the skin; and so impossible is it, morally impossible, to reclaim and reform these people. —*Matthew Henry*

If it were possible for those who have been for ages in hell to return to the earth (and not to be regenerated), I firmly believe that, notwithstanding all they have suffered for sin, they would still love it, and return to the practice of it. —*John Ryland*

The Christian sects in Syria appear to consider a true case of Druze conversion to Christianity as out of the question. "The wolf's whelps," they say, "are not tamed." The conversion of many sinners appears equally impossible, and yet how many such triumphs of grace are recorded as that which John Newton described in himself: "I was a wild beast on the coast of Africa once, but the Lord Jesus caught me, and tamed me, and now people come to see me as they would go to look at the lions in the Tower."

O endless misery!
I labor still, but still in vain,
The stains of sin I see
Are woaded all, or dy'd in grain.
There's not a blot will stir a jot,
For all that I can do.
There is no hope in fuller's sope,
Though I add nitre too.

I many ways have tried,
Have often soak'd it in cold fears;
And when a time I spied,
Pour'd upon it scalding tears:
Have rins'd and rubb'd, and scrap'd and scrubb'd
And turn'd it up and down;
Yet can I not wash out one spot;
It's rather fouler grown.

Can there no help be had?
Lord, thou art holy, thou art pure:
Mine heart is not so bad,
So foul, but thou canst cleanse it, sure
Speak, Blessed Lord, wilt thou afford
Me means to make it clean?
I know thou wilt: thy blood was spilt.
Should it run still in vain?
—*Christopher Harvey, in "Schola Cordis"*

91

Return ye now every one from his evil way, and make your ways and
your doings good.

—*Jeremiah 18:11*

THIS is the voice of mercy, anxious about each individual.

Justice might slay the sinner in his sin; but mercy would slay the
sin, and spare the sinner.

Yet it is the voice of holiness, opposed to each man's special evil
way; and claiming of each man an acceptable life. The Lord Jesus has not come
to be the Minister of sin, but the Destroyer of it.

Let us hear each one for himself on this occasion, for have we not every one
some evil way of his own?

It is Jehovah's voice, and concerning its message we enquire:

I. WHAT? *"Return."*

This includes three things:

1. Stop! Stand still! Go not a foot further in your evil way.
2. Turn round! Face towards God, holiness, heaven, etc.

3. Hasten back! Practically move in the right way, and continue in that good course which is the reverse of your present one.

II. WHEN? "Return ye *now*."

1. Every step makes so much more to retrace.
2. Every step makes it more difficult to return.
3. Further wandering will be wanton and willful; a presumptuous rejection of the warning which is now so earnestly given.
4. Never again may you have an opportunity to return.
   - There is nothing certain about life save its uncertainty.
   - Joy is being lost by this procrastination; you are missing present peace of mind.
   - God is robbed of your service, and you cannot make up the loss.
   - Man is being injured by your example.

Every reason pleads for now, but for delay there is no excuse.

III. WHO? "Return ye now *every one*."

The personality of the call to each hearer of it is necessary, for:
1. Each man has his own peculiar way of sin.
2. Each man is apt to think of his neighbor's sin more than his own.
3. Each man needs a special effectual call ere he will turn.
4. Each man is now lovingly invited to return.

IV. FROM WHAT? "From *his evil way*."

"We have turned every one to his own way" (Isa. 53:6). This way of your own you are to return from:
   - Your own personal sin.
   - Your constitutional sin.
   - Your most frequent sin.

To many it will be important to be able to discover this favorite sin.
1. It is that into which you are most easily led.
2. It is that which has already been most indulged by you.
3. It is that about which you are most irritated if you are rebuked concerning it. Darling sins must not be touched, or their fond friends grow angry.
4. It is that for which you give up other sins; a covetous person will not be extravagant, a hypocrite will deny himself, etc.
5. It is that with which you are most loth to part.
6. It is that on which you spend most money, energy, etc.

From such a darling sin each man must turn.

V. TO WHAT? "*Make your ways and doings good*."

Negative religion is not enough, there must be positive goodness.

1. Your general habits or ways must be made good as a whole.
2. Your *ways* in reference to yourself.
3. Your *doings* towards both God and man.
Personal examination of the utmost importance.
Practical repentance an absolute necessity.

Yet how difficult is the way back. To descend into sin is easy, but to retrace your steps, this is the work, this is the labor.

Only by faith in the Lord Jesus can it be accomplished, a look at his cross breeds more repentance than anything in the world besides.

To those who believe in Jesus, he will send the Holy Spirit to lead them in the way everlasting.

Explanatory

There are two things proper to a man that *returneth*: first, to go a way clean contrary to the way he went before; secondly, to tread out and obliterate his former steps. . . . First, I say, he must go a way clean contrary to his former way. Many men think that the way to hell is but a little out of the way to heaven, so that a man in a small time, with small ado, may pass out of the one into the other; but they are much deceived: for as sin is more than a stepping aside, *viz.*, a plain, a direct going away from God; so is repentance, or the forsaking of sin, more than a little coasting out of one way into another. Crossings will not serve; there is no way, from the road of sin to the place we seek, but to go quite back again the way we came. The way of *pleasure* in sin must be changed for *sorrow* for the same. He that hath superstitiously worshipped false gods must now as devoutly serve the true; the tongue that hath uttered swearings, and spoken blasphemies, must as plentifully sound forth the name of God in prayer and thanksgiving; the covetous man must become liberal; the oppressor of the poor as charitable in relieving them; the calumniator of his brother a tender guarder of his credit; in fine, he that hated his brother before must now love him as tenderly as himself. —*Joseph Mede*

"*Now*," thou resolvest, "I will hereafter look to it better than I have done before." Alas, this will for hereafter is no will! First: because it is only to shuffle off the willing of the present. The heart is unwilling to obey, and therefore it puts off the commandment to the future, not for any desire that it hath to do it hereafter, but only because it is unwilling to do it for the present; like a man that is unwilling to lend. "I'll lend you hereafter," says he, only because he would shuffle off lending at all. Secondly: this will for hereafter is no will, because it goes without God's will. God's will is *now*; thine is *hereafter*. "He that will not when he may, when he would he shall have 'Nay.'" Take heed lest when thou wouldst fain be pardoned, and criest, "Lord, open to me," thou dost find thyself too late. —*William Fenner*

A missionary in India, addressing the natives on the question of sin, asked, "What say your own shasters?

> 'I a sinner, you a sinner, sinners every one;
> *Sinless*—none are found who dwell beneath the sun.'"

(1) He that leaves not all sin; (2) He that leaves sin only outwardly; (3) He that leaves sin because he cannot commit it; (4) He that leaves sin out of sinister respects; (5) He that leaves one sin for another; (6) He that leaves sin but for a time; (7) He that leaves sin, but does not endeavor to subdue it; (8) He that so turns from sin as not to turn to God—has not had complete repentance. —*Clarkson*

Many would kill the adder, and spare the viper; as in Hudibras, they:

> Compound for sins they are inclined to,
> By damning those they have no mind to.
> —*C. H. S.*

92

Call unto me, and I will answer thee, and shew thee great and might things, which thou knowest not.

—*Jeremiah 33:3*

 HIS is a prison word: let those who are spiritually in prison prize it. This was the second time the Lord had spoken to the prophet while in the dungeon. God leaves not his people because of their being in ill odour with the world, nor even when they are put into prison. Nay, rather, he doubles his visits when they are in double trouble.

The first prison-word was a trial of Jeremiah's faith by *obedience*: he was to redeem the field at Anathoth; and this he did.

This second word tested his faith by *prayer*, and we doubt not that he endured the test, for in after days he saw great and mighty things, even as the Lord had promised.

The text belongs to every afflicted servant of God.

It encourages him in a threefold manner:

I. TO CONTINUE IN PRAYER. "Call unto me!"

1. Pray, though you have prayed. See previous chapter at 16th verse and onward.
2. Pray concerning your present trouble. In Jeremiah 32:24, the prophet mentions "the mounts" which were raised against Jerusalem, and in verse 4 of this chapter the Lord answers on that very point.

3. Pray, though you are still in prison after prayer. If deliverance tarries, make your prayers the more importunate.

4. Pray, for the word of the Lord comes to you with this command.

5. Pray, for the Holy Spirit prompts you, and helps you.

We need this precept because of our backwardness, forgetfulness, want of spirituality, and tendency to unbelief

This precept is sent to us because of the Lord's wisdom, love, and condescending thoughtfulness for our welfare.

II. TO EXPECT ANSWERS TO PRAYER. " I will answer thee, and shew thee."

Usually the promise is to "hear" us: but when we are in trouble the promise is special: "I will answer thee."

The Lord will answer us because:

1. He has appointed prayer, and made arrangements for its presentation and acceptance. He could not have meant it to be a mere farce: that were to treat us as fools.

2. He prompts, encourages, and quickens prayer; and surely he would never mock us by exciting desires which he never meant to gratify. Such a thought well nigh blasphemes the Holy Ghost, who indites prayer in the heart.

3. His nature is such that he must hear his children.

4. He has given his promise in the text; and it is often repeated elsewhere: he cannot lie or deny himself.

5. He has already answered many of his people, and ourselves also.

We know that the only limit to the prevalence of prayer is our heavenly Father's wise and loving will; which, to his loving children, is really no limit whatever. Let us ask in faith, and look up in hope.

III. TO EXPECT GREAT THINGS AS ANSWERS TO PRAYER. "I will shew thee great and mighty things."

Read the previous chapter from verse 18, and learn from it that we are to look for things:

1. Great in counsel: full of wisdom and significance.

2. Mighty in work: revealing might, and mightily effectual.

3. New things to ourselves, fresh in our experience, and therefore surprising. We may expect the unexpected.

4 Divine things: "I will shew thee." These are enumerated in the verses which follow the text, even to the end of the chapter; such as these:

- Health and cure (verse 6).
- Liberation from captivity (verse 7).
- Forgiveness of iniquity (verse 8).
- See how prayer increases the knowledge of those who know best.

- See how saints may advance in experience by calling unto God.
- See how sufferers may win unexpected deliverances.
- See how workers may achieve surprising marvels.
- See how seekers may find more than they dare expect,

Further Encouragements

Many years ago, the late Duchess of Gordon called on good Harrington Evans, and said, "I have just five minutes, but I could not leave town without calling to say 'good-bye'!" "Five minutes," said Mr. Evans, with that solemn and impressive manner by which he was distinguished; "five minutes! Then pray! Pray! Pray! Good morning." "I felt so struck with these words," said the Duchess to a friend, "that I could not forget them; and, as I thought on them, I was led to study prayer, as a means of grace as well as an act of worship, and ever after my chief work in the Lord's service became the promotion of prayer-meetings."

A young engineer was being examined, and this question was put to him: "Suppose you have a steam-pump constructed for a ship, under your own supervision, and know that everything is in perfect order, yet, when you throw out the hose, it will not draw; what should you think?" "I should think, sir, there must be a defect somewhere." "But such a conclusion is not admissible; for the supposition is that everything is perfect, and yet that the pump will not work." "Then, sir," replied the student, "I should look over the side of the ship to see if the river had run dry." Even so it would appear that if true prayer is not answered the nature of God must have changed.

God's praying people get to know much more of his mind than others; like as John, by weeping, got the book opened; and Daniel, by prayer, had the king's secret revealed unto him in a night vision. *"Bene orasse, est bene studuisse,"* said Luther; who, as he had much communion with God by prayer, so holy truths were daily more and more made known unto him, he knew not how or which way, as himself said. —*Trapp*

Sir Walter Raleigh one day asking a favor from Queen Elizabeth, the latter said to him, "Raleigh, when will you leave off begging?" To which he answered, "When your Majesty leaves off giving." Ask great things of God. Expect great things from God. Let his past goodness make us "instant in prayer." —*New Cyclopædia of Illustrative Anecdote*

Thomas Brooks, alluding to the old classical myth of Daedalus, who, being imprisoned in the island of Crete, made wings for himself, by which he escaped to Italy, says, "Christians must do as Daedalus, who, when he could not escape by a way upon earth went by a way of heaven." Holy prayers are the wings of the soul's deliverance.

The dungeon of the Mamertine, where a probable tradition declares that Paul was for a while confined, is entered through a round hole in the floor of another dungeon above. The uppermost apartment is dark enough, but the lower one is darkness itself, so that the apostle's imprisonment was of the severest kind. We noticed, however, a strange fact—in the hard floor there is a beautiful fountain of clear crystal water, which doubtless was as fresh in Paul's day as it is now; of course the Papists believe the fountain to be miraculous; we who are not so credulous of traditions rather see in it a symbol full of instruction: there never was a dungeon for God's servants which was without its well of consolation. —*C. H. S.*

93

Let Jerusalem come into your mind.
—*Jeremiah 51:50*

HE captives in Babylon are charged to remember Jerusalem:
- Because the temple of their God was there;
- To keep them from settling down in Babylon;
- To make them long for the holy city; and
- To keep them prepared to return to it.

There are equally good reasons for our remembering the New Jerusalem.

We are too apt to forget our spiritual citizenship, and hence we will meditate on our text under two aspects.

I. THERE IS A JERUSALEM HERE BELOW WHICH SHOULD COME INTO OUR MIND.

The church of the living God is our holy city, the city of the Great King, and we should have it in mind:

1. To unite with its citizens. We should join with them in open profession of faith in Christ, in Christian love and mutual help, in holy service, worship, communion, etc.
2. To pray for its prosperity. Whenever it is well with us in prayer, we should let the cause of God be on our mind. Our window, like that of Daniel, should be opened towards Jerusalem.
3. To labor for its advancement. We should remember it in the allotment of our money, the use of our time, the employment of our talents, the exercise of our influence, etc.
4. To prefer its privileges above earthly gain. We ought to consider these privileges in our choice of our residence, occupation, etc. With many professors this is a very small matter.
5. To act consistently with her holy character. We must not dishonor the place of our citizenship. God's people must not degrade his name and cause by living in sin.

6. To lament its declensions and transgressions. Remember how our Lord wept over Jerusalem, and Paul wept over enemies in the churches (Luke 19:41; Phil. 3:18).

Oh, that all Christians took a deeper interest in the church of God!

It were well if into all our joys and sorrows the cause of God were interwoven like a thread of gold. He is a poor patriot who forgets his country, and he is no Christian who does not bear the church upon his heart

II. THERE IS A JERUSALEM ABOVE WHICH SHOULD COME IN OUR MIND.

1. Let the believer's thoughts often go thither, for Jesus is there, our departed brethren are there, our own home is there, and thither our hopes and desires should always tend.

   It should be upon our minds:
   - In our earthly enjoyments, lest we grow worldly.
   - In our daily trials, lest we grow despondent.
   - In our associations, lest we idolize present friendships.
   - In our bereavements, lest we grieve inordinately.
   - In old age, that we may be on the watch for the home-going
   - In death, that visions of glory may brighten our last hours.
   - In all seasons, that our conversation may be in heaven

2. Let the unconverted permit such thoughts to come into their mind, for they may well enquire of themselves thus:
   - What if I never enter heaven?
   - Shall I never meet my godly relatives again?
   - Where then must I go?
   - Can I hope that my present life will lead me to heaven?
   - Why am I not taking the right path?
   - Unbelievers perish: why am I one of them? Do I wish to perish?
   - How can I hope to enter heaven if I do not so much as think about it, or the Lord who reigns in it?

Such thoughts will come to our minds if we will let them.

Shall we not open the door of our minds at once, and let the heavenly visitors enter and abide?

Reminders

The undying love of the Jews for their Fatherland, and their ineradicable desire to return to it, are displayed in an affecting manner on the day of atonement, which is still observed by them with great solemnity. The services of the day close with the beseeching shout, "when next year comes, may we all be in Jerusalem!" We could almost make this prayer our own as we think of the "Jerusalem above."

I have been endeavoring to establish amongst us what are called "Aaron and Hur Societies," i.e., little collections of four or five or more persons, who meet before service on Sabbath morning, to spend an hour in prayer for a blessing on the minister and the ordinances. They began on New Year's Day, and we seemed to have an immediate answer, for the meeting was unusually solemn, and we have reason to hope that the word was not preached in vain. —*Dr. Payson*

> My soul shall pray for Zion still,
>   While life or breath remains;
> There my best friends, my kindred dwell;
>   There God my Savior reigns.
>   —*Watts*

The church of God should come into our minds as spontaneously as the recollection of our wife or mother. When we look at a map of any country, we should think of how the cause of God prospers in that region. If we make a profit in business, one of our first thoughts should be—"now I can do something more for the work of the Lord." When the newspaper is read, it should be in relation to the progress of the kingdom of God. This one thing should tinge all other things with its own color, and draw all other thoughts into its net. The cause of Christ should be an all-absorbing maelstrom, into which all our thoughts and pursuits should be drawn. A man of one idea sees the universe by the light of it, and he who loves the church of God with all his heart will do the same. How can we say, "Lord, remember me," to Christ in heaven, if we do not remember his church on earth?

It may be a sin to long for death, but I am sure it is no sin to long for heaven. —*Matthew Henry*

Blessed are the homesick, for they shall come at last to the Father's house. —*Heinrich Stillings*

John Eliot was once on a visit to a merchant, and finding him in his counting house, where he saw books of business on the table, and all his books of devotion on the shelf, he said to him, "Sir, here is earth on the table, and heaven on the shelf. Pray don't think so much of the table as altogether to forget the shelf."

"Here I sit the whole day with the visage of the church ever before me, and the passage 'Why hast thou made all the sons of men in vain?' How horrible a form of God's anger is that abominable kingdom of the Roman Antichrist! I abhor my own hardness of heart that I am not dissolved in tears, and that I do not weep fountains of tears for the slain sons of my people. But is there no one to arise, and cleave to God, and make himself a wall for the house of Israel in this last day of his wrath? God have mercy on us! Wherefore, be thou meanwhile instant as a minister of the Word, and fortify the walls and towers of Jerusalem till they shall assail thee." —*From a Letter to Melancthon, written by Luther, at the Castle of the Wartburg*

94

I will settle you after your old estates, and will do better unto you than at your beginnings: and ye shall know that I am the Lord.

—Ezekiel 36:11

HEN other nations fall they rise no more, but to the covenanted people future still remains.

Even the land given by covenant has an entailed blessing on it, for these words are to the "mountains of Israel."

To hypocrites and formalists an end cometh; but true children of God rise again after decays and declensions. As saith the prophet, "Rejoice not against me, O mine enemy: when I fall, I shall arise; when I sit in darkness, the Lord shall be a light unto me" (Mic. 7:8).

A greater blessing than that which they have lost may yet be granted to restored wanderers.

The text contains a great promise. Oh, that we may enjoy it!

I. WHAT WAS THERE SO GOOD IN OUR BEGINNINGS?

As Israel's land in the beginning flowed with milk and honey, so our first estate had a singular richness about it. Oftentimes, in looking back, we sing:

> Where is the blessedness I knew
> When first I saw the Lord?
> Where is the soul-refreshing view
> Of Jesus, and his Word?

1. We enjoyed a vivid sense of free and full forgiveness.
2. We had a delicious proof of the joy of true religion.
3. We gained repeated victories over sinful inclinations, and outward temptations; and this made us jubilant in Christ.
4. We felt great delight in prayer, the Word, communion, etc.
5. We abounded in zeal and service, and the joy of the Lord was our strength.
6. We were in our first love, and everything was lively, intense, hopeful, wonderful, to our humble, happy mind. We were simplehearted and confiding, had not yet found out the imperfections of our brethren, and were too humble to look for them. We have not gained much by losing that confidence if in its room we have received suspicion.

We read of the "first ways of David" (2 Chron. 17:3). We are bidden to do our "first works" (Rev. 2:5).

II. CAN WE ENJOY SOMETHING BETTER THAN OUR BEGINNINGS?

Assuredly we shall if the Lord will fulfill this promise; and that he is sure to do if we walk more closely with him.

1. Our faith will be stronger, more steadfast, and intelligent.
2. Our knowledge will be fuller and deeper.
3. Our love will be more constant, practical, enduring.
4. Our prayer will be more prevalent.
5. Our usefulness will be more extended, more abiding.
6. Our whole being will be more mature.

We are to shine more and more unto the perfect day (Prov. 4:18).

Growth in grace brings with it many good things.

III. HOW CAN WE SECURE THIS BETTERNESS?

There must be a re-settlement according to our old estates in our own souls, and then there will be a renewed settlement by the act of God.

1. We must return to our first simple faith in Jesus.
2. We must quit the sins which alienated us from God.
3. We must be more thorough, and earnest.
4. We must seek after closer fellowship with Christ.
5. We must more resolutely strive to advance in divine things.

Admire the liberality of our God! He promises to do better unto us than at our beginnings. What more can he do?

See the constancy of his love-how he maintains ancient settlements, and restores old estates! Covenant heritages are entailed upon their holders by the unchanging grace of God.

Mark with what tenderness he woos us to return to his fellowship: he draws, he allures, he wins by greatness of love!

Let us, in the power of his Holy Spirit, return to him!

Doors of Hope

God's dealings with his people are best at last; they may have much kindness and mercy in the morning, but they shall have more in the evening. "I will settle you after your old estates," etc. The Jews had the best wine at last; they had milk and honey before, but the feast of fat things full of marrow, and of wines on the lees well-refined, were at the latter end of their day given in; they had Christ and the Gospel at last. Abraham had much of the world at first, and his Isaac afterward. "God blessed the latter end of Job more than his beginning." Simeon in his latter days saw Christ, and had him in his arms. —*Wm. Greenhill*

No instance of backsliding can be more aggravated than that of the apostle Peter, and yet no recovery was more signal. While that stands upon record, no traitor to his Lord and Master is justified in saying, "The door of hope is closed against my return." The Scriptures contain several instances in which the lamentable and disgraceful lapses of God's people are shown to be followed by their recovery and restoration. Frequently such characters, after they have been corrected and chastened of the Lord, have risen to stations of great eminence in his church. David in the Old Testament, and Peter in the New, while both illustrating the shame and sorrow of a backsliding state, stand forth as monuments of that sovereign grace which can forgive the penitent wanderer, and once more infuse into his heart the "peace that passeth all understanding." —*Leifchild*

Fractures well cured make us more strong. —*Herbert*

The joy of conversion is great:

> Earth has a joy unknown to heaven,
> The new-born peace of sins forgiven!
> Tears of such pure and deep delight,
> Ye angels! never dimmed your sight:

but there are wondrous joys as yet unknown to the inexperienced soul, and concerning which the most advanced believer has to sing:

> I have a heritage of joy
> That yet I must not see:
> The hand that bled to make it mine,
> Is keeping it for me.

✔Those that will not return to the duties they have neglected, cannot expect to return to the comforts they have lost. —*G. S. Bowes*

He is a skillful physician indeed who, finding a man sorely afflicted, not only succeeds in restoring him to health, but actually causes him to be better than he was before, dealing with his medicine, not only with the disease which caused pain, but with some other which lay deeper, but had scarcely been perceived by the patient. Such is the medicine of mercy. Thus graciously doth God deal with repenting sinners. He must be worse than a brute beast who would turn this into an argument for sinning. A true child of God feels the water standing in his eyes when he thinks of such superabounding love.

95

And I will multiply the fruit of the tree, and the increase of the field, that ye shall receive no more reproach of famine among the heathen. Then shall ye remember your own evil ways, and your doings that were not good, and shall loathe yourselves in your own sight for your iniquities, and for your abominations.

—Ezekiel 36:30–31

 HE day of manifested mercy is to be the day of hearty repentance. *"Then."* When God loads you with benefits you shall loathe yourselves.

The Lord speaks as one who is supreme in the region of free agency, and able to work his will with human minds: "Then *shall ye*," etc.

His processes of grace are such as, in the nature of things, lead up to the end which he proposes.

He declares that he will conquer by love—love so wonderful that the objects of it must of necessity yield to its power, and change their minds and their conduct.

Repentance is wrought in the heart by a sense of love divine.

This sets repentance in its true light, and helps us to meet a great many mistakes which have darkened this subject. Many are kept from Christ and hope by misapprehensions of this matter. They have:

I. MISTAKEN IDEAS OF WHAT REPENTANCE IS.

They confound it with:

1. Morbid self-accusation, which is the fruit of dyspepsia, or melancholy, or insanity. This is an infirmity of mind, and not a grace of the Spirit. A physician may here do more than a divine.
2. Unbelief, despondency, despair: which are not even a help to repentance, but tend rather to harden the heart.
3. Dread of hell, and sense of wrath: which might occur even to devils, and yet would not cause them to repent. A measure of this may go with repentance, but it is no part of it.
4. Satanic temptations. These are by no means like to repentance, which is the fruit of the Spirit.
5. A complete knowledge of the guilt of sin; which even advanced saints have not yet obtained.
6. Entire abstinence from all sin—a consummation devoutly to be wished, but by no means included in repentance.

It is a hatred of evil, a sense of shame, a longing to avoid sin, wrought by a sense of divine love.

II. MISTAKEN IDEAS OF THE PLACE WHICH REPENTANCE OCCUPIES.

1. It is looked upon by some as a procuring cause of grace, as if repentance merited remission: a grave error.
2. It is wrongly viewed by others as a preparation for grace; a human goodness laying the foundation for mercy, a meeting of God half way; this is a deadly error.
3. It is treated as a sort of qualification for believing, and even as the ground for believing: all which is legality, and contrary to pure gospel truth.
4. Others treat it as the argument for peace of mind. They have repented so much, and it must be all right. This is to build our confidence upon a false foundation.

Repentance attends faith, and is a precious gift of the Spirit of God.

III. MISTAKEN IDEAS OF THE WAY IN WHICH IT IS PRODUCED IN THE HEART.

It is not produced by a distinct and immediate attempt to repent.

Nor by strong excitement at revival meetings.

Nor by meditating upon sin, and death, and hell, etc.

But the God of all grace produces it:

1. By his free grace, which by its action renews the heart (verse 26).
2. By bringing his great mercy to our mind.
3. By making us receive new mercy (verses 28–30).
4. By revealing himself and his methods of grace (verse 32).

Every gospel truth urges repentance upon the regenerate. Election, redemption, justification, adoption, eternal love, etc., are all arguments for loathing every evil way.

Every gospel privilege makes us loathe sin: prayer, praise, the reading of Scripture, the fellowship of saints, the table of the Lord, etc.

Every gospel hope puriles us from sin, whether it be a hope for more grace in this world, or for glory in the next.

Oh, that we might feel the touch of love, and weep ourselves away for having grieved our Lord! This would work in us a revenge against all our sins, and lead us to entire consecration to our holy Lord.

Rectifications

There are no arguments like those that are drawn from the consideration of the great and glorious things Christ hath done for you; and if such will not take with you, and win upon you, I do not think the throwing of hell-fire in your faces will ever do it. —*Thomas Brooks*

The Roman Catholic definition of penitence is not a bad one, though they draw bad conclusions from it—*"Confessio oris, contritio cordis, satisfactio vitæ"*— that is, for true repentance there should be confession with the mouth, grieving in the heart, and amendment made for our faults as far as possible in our life. —*Richard Glover*

Repentance—the tear dropped from the eye of faith.

God's loving-kindnesses and mercies do work more with sinners than his judgments do. All the time the Jews were in Babylon, their hearts were never so affected for their sins as after God brought them out, settled them in Canaan, and showed much love unto them; then they should remember their evil ways, before they minded them not; then they should loathe themselves. Mercies in Zion are more efficacious with sinners than judgments in Babylon; God's favor melts hard hearts sooner then the fire of his indignation; his kindness is very penetrative, it gets into the hearts of sinners sooner than his threats and frowns; it is like a small soaking rain, which goes to the roots of things, whereas a dashing rain runs away, and does little good. It was David's kindness that brake the heart of Saul (1 Sam. 24); and it is God's kindness which breaks the hearts of sinners. The milk and honey of the gospel affect the hearts of sinners more than the gall and wormwood of the law; Christ on Mount Zion brings more to repentance than Moses on Mount Sinai. —*William Greenhill*

Cowper, the poet, in his own memoirs of his early life, describes the time when he reflected on the necessity of repentance. "I knew that many persons had spoken of shedding tears for sin; but when I asked myself whether the time would ever come when I should weep for mine, it seemed to me that a stone might sooner do it. Not knowing that Christ was exalted to give repentance, I despaired of ever attaining it." A friend came to his bed-side, and declared to him the gospel. He insisted on the all-atoning efficacy of the blood of Jesus, and his righteousness for our justification. "Then," says Cowper, "while I heard this part of his discourse, and the Scriptures on which he founded it, my heart began to burn within me; my soul was pierced with a sense of my bitter ingratitude to so merciful a Savior; and those tears, which I thought impossible, burst forth freely."

"Some people," says Philip Henry, "do not wish to hear much of repentance, but I think it so necessary that, if I should die in the pulpit, I wish to die preaching repentance; and if out of the pulpit, practicing it."

96

But the miry places thereof and the marishes thereof shall not be healed; they shall be given to salt.

—Ezekiel 47:11

HE prophet saw in vision the flow of the life-giving river, and marked its wonderful and beneficial effects.

Let the chapter be read, and a brief abstract of it be given.

The prophet also observed that here and there the river carried no blessing: there were marshes which remained as barren as ever.

I. THERE ARE SOME MEN WHOM THE GOSPEL DOES NOT BLESS.

1. It stagnates in them: they hear in vain; learn but do not practice; feel but do not decide; resolve but do not perform.
2. It mingles with their corruptions, as clear water with the mire of the marshes. They see with blinded eye, understand in a carnal manner, and receive truth but not in the power of it.
3. It becomes food for their sins, even as rank sour grass is produced by the stagnant waters of "miry places."
   - Their unbelief makes mysteries into apologies for infidelity.
   - Their enmity is stirred by the sovereignty of grace.
   - Their impenitence takes liberties from grace, and makes excuses out of divine mercy.
   - Their carnal security feeds on the fact of having heard the gospel.
4. It makes them worse and worse. The more rain, the more mire.
   - The more grace misused, the more wicked the heart.
   - The more unsanctified knowledge, the greater the capacity for evil.
   - The more false profession, the more treachery.

II. SOME OF THESE WE HAVE KNOWN.

These marshes are at no great distance. They constitute an eye-sore, and a heart-sore, near at hand.

1. The talkative man, who lives in sin: flooded with knowledge, but destitute of love: fluent expression but no experience.
2. Those critics who note only the faults of Christians, and are quick to dwell on them; but are false themselves.
3. Those who receive orthodox truth, and yet love the world.
4. Those who feel impressed and moved, but never obey the word. They delight to hear the gospel, and only the gospel, and yet they have no spiritual life.

5. Those who are mere officials, and attend to religion in a mechanical manner. Judas is both treasurer and traitor, apostle and apostate. His descendants are among us.

III. SUCH PERSONS ARE IN A TERRIBLE PLIGHT.

Their condition is more than commonly dreadful.

1. Because they are not aware of it: they think it is well with them.
2. Because the ordinary means of blessing men have failed in their case. That which is a river of life to others is not so to them.
3. In some instances the very best means have failed. A special river of gracious opportunity has flowed down to them, but its streams have visited them in vain.
4. No known means now remain: "What shall I do unto thee?" What more can be hoped for from the economy of mercy?
5. Their ruin appears certain: they will be given over; left to themselves, to be barren marshes.
6. Their ruin is as terrible as it is sure: much like that of the cities of the plain—given to salt; only their doom will be less tolerable than that of Sodom and Gomorrah.

IV. FROM THESE WE MAY LEARN.

1. A lesson of warning, lest we ourselves be visibly visited by gracestreams, and yet never profit thereby.
2. A lesson of arousing, lest we rest in ordinances, which in themselves are not necessarily a saving blessing.
3. A lesson of gratitude: if we are indeed healed by the life-river, let us bless the effectual grace of the Lord our God.
4. A lesson of quickening to ministers and other workers, that they may look well to the results of their labor, and not be making marshes where they wish to create fields rich with harvest.

Apropos

No persons appear less likely to be saved than your religious unbelievers. They wear an armor of proof. You cannot tell them anything new and striking, their heads are helmeted with religious knowledge; you cannot touch their hearts, for they wear the breast-plate of gospel-hardening. They bow assent to every truth, and yet believe nothing; they attend to every religious observance, and yet have no religion. No other suit of plate armor is one half so effective for warding off the strokes of truth as that which is forged in the arsenals of religion. I have more hope of an avowed infidel than of a gospel-proof hearer. — *C. H. S*

Either the waters came not to these marshes; or if they did, they refused them, and so were given to salt, made like Sodom, barren and accursed. Some places have not the waters of the sanctuary, the doctrine of the gospel, and they are barren, and perish for want of the same, as Tyre and Sidon. Other places have them, and because they are impenitent, and will not receive the truth with the love of it, because they will not drink in these waters, therefore they are given to salt, they are barren, and must perish. So it was with Capernaum and Jerusalem (Matt. 11:23; 23:37–38); and so is it with many places in this nation, I fear. —*William Greenhill*

Certain persons are to be met with, at revival services, who are the first to enter the inquiry-room, but when full inquiry is made about their history it will be found that they are old practitioners, and have under gone conversion of a sort many times before. These are the plague and disgrace of a religious awakening. Easily affected, their piety itself is an affectation: they are not exactly hypocrites, but yet there is so little depth in them that they are next door to it. We heard of one who had been healed of lameness, so he said, but within a few days he took to his crutches again, and thereby cast grave doubt upon the professed healer. Even thus do these wretched converts raise a cry against admirable movements. They are a sort of people whom even the gospel does not bless— marshes, which even the river of life does not fertilize.

Who is the most miserable man on earth, and whither shall we go to seek him? Not to the tavern; not to the theater; not even to the brothel; but to the church! That man, who has sat, Sabbath after Sabbath, under the awakening and affecting calls of the gospel, and has hardened his heart against these calls, he is the man whose condition is the most desperate of all others. "Woe unto thee, Chorazin! woe unto thee, Bethsaida! And thou, Capernaum, which art exalted to heaven, shalt be thrust down to hell." —*Richard Cecil*

The Latins used to say, "The corruption of what is best is the worst of all things."

Of all compounds of human weakness and depravity, the most repulsive is a bonfire of religious cant, which is all feeling and no principle, all talk and no character, all prayer and no life, all Sunday and no weekday. Ye whited sepulchers!" "Ye generation of vipers!" The holiest of men join the indignant outcry of the world against such nauseating hypocrisy. That is a wise and always timely petition of the Church of England: "From the deceits of the world, from the crafts of the devil, good Lord, deliver us!" —*Austin Phelps*

97

His thoughts troubled him.
—*Daniel 5:6*

o many men *thinking* is an unusual employment.

Yet it is a distinction of man that he can think.

No wonder that when thought is forced on some men they are troubled.

This trouble from thought is salutary: by it conviction and conversion may come; and, in any case, troubled thought is as the sounding of the tocsin, arousing the mind, and warning the soul.

Let us think of Belshazzar, and of ourselves. Of us, too, it may have been said, "His thoughts troubled him." We must be in a bad way if we dare not face our own thoughts about ourselves. What must God's thoughts of us be?

I. IT DID NOT APPEAR LIKELY THAT HIS THOUGHTS WOULD TROUBLE HIM.

1. He was an irresponsible and reckless monarch. He came of a fierce nation, and was born of a father who had been punished for his haughty spirit.
2. He had hardened his heart with pride (verses 22 and 23). Daniel said, "thou hast lifted up thyself against the Lord of heaven."
3. He was drinking wine, and it had worked upon him (verse 2).
4. He was rioting in gay company: "his princes, his wives, and his concubines." Such comrades as these usually chase all thought away, and help their leader in his recklessness.
5. He was venturing far in profanity (verse 3); daring to abuse the sacred vessels, in his banquets, as an expression of his contempt for Israel's God, whom he despised in contrast with his "gods of gold, and of silver, of brass, of iron, of wood, and of stone." Perhaps he had mentioned these in detail as the gods who had triumphed; at any rate, the prophet brings them forward with detestation in verse 4.

No man is rendered wise or thoughtful by the wine-cup.

No man is out of the reach of the arrows of God.

No conscience is so dead that he cannot arouse it.

Many other men in far lower positions exhibit equal pride of station and success; this is stimulated in much the same manner, and exhibited with much the same contempt for the things of God.

A parallel is easily drawn between Belshazzar and other proud ones.

II. YET WELL MIGHT HIS THOUGHTS TROUBLE HIM.

1. For what he saw was appalling: "fingers of a man's hand over against the candlestick" (verse 5).

    God sometimes gives men warnings which they must notice.

2. For what he could not see was suggestive. Where was the hand?

    • Where was the writer? What had he written? What did it mean? A terrible mystery was involved in his vision.

    • God gives men hints of something behind, which is yet to appear

3. For what he had done was alarming.

    • His own past flashed before him. His cruel wars, oppressions, blasphemies, and vices.

    • What he knew of his father's career increased his terror.

    • What he had himself failed to do came before him: "The God in whose hand thy breath is, and whose are all thy ways, hast thou not glorified" (verse 23).

    • What he was then in the act of doing startled him. He was wantonly defying Jehovah, the God of Israel.

See *him* trembling before whom all trembled.

He has drunk a strange draught out of those holy cups.

III. AND MIGHT NOT YOUR THOUGHTS TROUBLE SOME OF YOU?

1. You are careless, riotous, fond of feasts, given to much wine. Does wantonness ever end well?

2. You are prosperous. Are not beasts fattened for the slaughter?

3. You are trifling with holy things. You neglect, or ridicule, or use without seriousness the things of God. Will this be endured? Will not the Lord be provoked to avenge this contempt?

4. You mix with the impure. Will you not perish with them?

5. Your father's history might instruct you, or at least trouble you.

6. The sacred writing "over against the candlestick" is against you.

    Read the Holy Scripture, and see for yourself.

7. Specially, you have been weighed in the balances, and found wanting.

    Conscience beholds the scales in the hand of the infallible Judge.

Take heed that you do not fall into Belshazzar's condition, to whom Daniel gave no counsel, but simply interpreted the sentences which sealed his doom.

As yet we dare preach the gospel to you, and we do. God's thoughts are above your thoughts. He bids you repent of sin, and believe in his Son Jesus; and then your thoughts will cease to trouble you.

Thoughts and Facts

Such mystery of iniquity within,
That we must loathe our very thoughts, but for the cure
He hath devised—the blessed Tree
The Lord hath shown us, that, cast in, can heal
The fountain whence the bitter waters flow.
Divinest remedy
Whose power we feel,
Whose grace we comprehend not, but we know.

—Miss Havergal

Conscience, from inaction, is like a withered arm in the souls of many; but the Lord of conscience will one day say to it, "Be thou stretched forth, and do thine appointed work."

As the ant-hill, when stirred, sets in motion its living insects in every direction, so the conscience of the sinner, disturbed by the Spirit, or judgments of God, calls up before its vision thousands of deeds which fill the soul with agony and woe. *—McCosh*

The Duke of Wellington once said that he could have saved the lives of a thousand men a year, had he had chaplains, or any religious ministers. The uneasiness of their minds reacted on their bodies, and kept up continual fever, once it seized upon their frames. It is our blessed office to tell of One who can "minister to a mind diseased," whose grace can deliver from "an evil conscience," and through whom all inward fear and trouble are removed.

Charles IX of France, in his youth, had humane and tender sensibilities. The fiend who had tempted him was the mother who had nursed him. When she first proposed to him the massacre of the Huguenots, he shrunk from it with horror: "No, no, madam! They are my loving subjects." *Then* was the critical hour of his life. Had he cherished that natural sensitiveness to bloodshed, St. Bartholomew's Eve would never have disgraced the history of his kingdom, and he himself would have escaped the fearful remorse which crazed him on his death-bed. To his physician he said in his last hours, "Asleep or awake, I see the mangled forms of the Huguenots passing before me. They drip with blood. They make hideous faces at me. They point to their open wounds, and mock me. Oh, that I had spared at least the little infants at the breast!" Then he broke out in agonizing cries and screams. Bloody sweat oozed from the pores of his skin. He was one of the very few cases in history which confirm the possibility of the phenomenon which attended our Lord's anguish in Gethsemane. That was the fruit of resisting, years before, the recoil of his youthful conscience from the extreme of guilt. *—Austin Phelps*

98

Now therefore, O our God, hear the prayer of they servant, and his supplications, and cause thy face to shine upon thy sanctuary that is desolate, for the Lord's sake.

—Daniel 9:17

HIS true-hearted man lived not for himself. Daniel was a fervent lover of his country.

He had been personally faithful, and in consequence he had been honored, but he did not rest content with personal ease.

He had visions of God, but he was not visionary.

He had searched and studied, but now he prayed. Supplication should ever be the outcome of our meditation.

His prayer is instructive to us.

It suggests our fervent entreaties for the church of God in these days.

I. THE HOLY PLACE. "Thy sanctuary."

The temple was typical, and for our edification we shall read the text as if the spiritual house had been meant. There are many points in the type worthy of notice, but these may suffice:

1. The temple was unique; and as there could only be one temple for Jehovah, so there is but one church.
2. The temple was "exceeding magnifical"; and in the eyes of God, and of holy beings, the church is the house of God's glory.
3. The temple was the fabric of wisdom. King Solomon built it; and of the church we may say, "a greater than Solomon is here."
4. The temple was the result of great cost and vast labor: so was the church builded by the Lord Jesus at a cost which can never be estimated.
5. The temple was the shrine of God's indwelling.
6. The temple was the place of his worship.
7. The temple was the throne of his power: his word went forth from Jerusalem; there he ruled his people, and routed his foes.

The church of Jesus Christ in the latter day shall be more accurately the anti-type of the temple, as the present church is of the tabernacle in the wilderness.

II. THE EARNEST PRAYER. "Cause thy face to shine upon thy sanctuary that is desolate."

1. It rose above all selfishness. This was his one prayer, the center of all his prayers.

2. It was the child of thought (verse 2).
- He had thought over the sins, calamities, prospects of his people.
- Such prayers show the way in which a man's mind is running, and are more full of force than unprepared expressions.
3. It cast itself upon God. "O our God."
4. It was a confession that he could do nothing of himself. Honest men do not ask God to do what they can do themselves.
5. It asked a comprehensive boon. "Cause thy face to shine."
This would mean many things which we also implore for the church of God:
(1) Walls rebuilt and securely standing.
(2) Ministers in their places, faithful in their service.
(3) Worship presented with acceptance.
(4) Truth proclaimed in its clearness. God's face cannot shine upon falsehood or equivocation.
(5) Holiness displayed in its beauty. Where the holy God is smiling, his servants are holy.
(6) Delight in fellowship: the saints walking with God.
(7) Power in testimony. When God is pleased, his word is mighty, and all holy endeavors are prospered.
6. It asked needful things.
- For the church; unity, life, purity, power, joy, etc.
- For the world; enlightenment and conversion. A desolate church is a defeated church.
- For ourselves; edification. We cannot prosper in soul when Zion languishes.
- For our children; salvation. Our sons and daughters are not likely to be saved in a desolate church.
7. It asked with a mighty plea: "For the Lord's sake."

III. THE CONSISTENT CONDUCT. This is suggested by such a prayer.
1. Let us consider the state of Zion (verse 23). Let us form a careful estimate of the condition of true religion.
2. Let us lay it earnestly to heart. Whether for joy or sorrow, let the condition of the church concern us deeply.
3. Let us do all we can for her, or our prayer will be a mockery.
4. Let us do nothing to grieve the Lord; for all depends upon his smile. "Cause thy face to shine."
5. Let us pray much more than we have done. Let each one of us be a Daniel.

Incitements

During the troubles times of Scotland, when the Popish court and aristocracy were arming themselves to suppress the Reformation in that land, and the cause of Protestant Christianity was in imminent peril, late on a certain night John Knox was seen to leave his study, and to pass from the house down into an enclosure to the rear of it. He was followed by a friend, when, after a few moments of silence, his voice was heard as if in prayer. In another moment the accents deepened into intelligible words, and the earnest petition went up from his struggling soul to heaven, "O Lord, give me Scotland, or I die!" Then a pause of hushed stillness, when again the petition broke forth, "O Lord, give me Scotland, or I die!" Once more all was voiceless and noiseless, when, with a yet intenser pathos the thrice-repeated intercession struggled forth, "O Lord, give me Scotland, or I die!" And God gave him Scotland, in spite of Mary and her Cardinal Beatoun; a land and a church of noble loyalty to Christ and his crown.

"At the time the Diet of Nuremburg was held," says *Tholuck*, "Luther was earnestly praying in his own dwelling; and at the very hour when the edict, granting full toleration to all Protestants, was issued, he ran out of his house, crying out, 'We have gained the victory'."

The church may be sick, yet not die. Die it cannot, for the blood of an eternal King bought it, the power of an eternal Spirit preserves it, and the mercy of an eternal God shall crown it. —*Thomas Adams*

Prayer was a universal habit among the heathen people of Samoa, and they manifested considerable intelligence in their conception of prayer. For example, when on their boatjourneys, those who were sitting as passengers in the boat were expected to pray for those who were plying the paddles. The passengers would repeatedly thank the rowers in these words: "Thanks for your strong strokes"; to which the rowers immediately made answer, "Thanks for your intercessory prayers," recognizing, it will be seen, the principle that their power to ply the paddles was dependent upon the prayers of the passengers. —*The Congregationalist*

99

Therefore, behold, I will hedge up thy way with thorns, and make a
wall, that she shall not find her paths.

And she shall follow after her lovers, but she shall not overtake
them; and she shall seek them, but shall not find them: then shall she
say I will go and return to my first husband; for then was it better
with me than now.

—Hosea 2:6–7

 HIS is a parenthesis of mercy in a passage of threatening. It relates
to a people to whom the Lord was united by bonds of covenant
love, who had, nevertheless, been faithless and rebellious. Strangely
enough, it begins with a *"therefore"*; and the logic of it lies in the
immutable resolve of the unchanging God never to renounce his covenant, nor
utterly to cast away his chosen; as, also, in his unchangeable determination to
win them to himself.

The words might still be spoken in reference to the chosen but sinning
people of God.

Let us note carefully:

I. THE STUBBORN CHARACTER OF MANY SINNERS.

This appears in their case, as in that of Israel, in several ways:

1. Ordinary means have missed their aim. The details are given in previous
   verses; and then we read "therefore": showing that because of former failures the Lord is about to try further measures.
2. Extraordinary means are now to be used, and attention is called to their
   speciality by the word "behold." God's wonderful ways of grace prove the
   wonderful obstinacy of sinners.
3. Even these means are to fail. Providence uses strange ways, like making
   hedges and walls; and yet for a while the sinner defeats the gracious
   design. "She shall follow after her lovers," etc. Men will leap hedges, and
   scale walls, to get at their darling sins.
4. Only divine power can overcome the hardened one. God saith, "I will",
   and adds "she shall not", and "she shall"; proving that the omnipotence
   of love had now entered the lists, and intended to conquer the rebellious
   and obstinate transgressor. God himself must personally interpose, or
   none will turn to him.

What sinners those must be whom neither hedge nor wall will stop unless
God be there also in omnipotence of grace!

II. THE MEANS WHICH GOD USES TO RECLAIM THEM.

These, when used by God himself, become effectual, though they would have accomplished nothing of themselves.

1. Sharp afflictions: "I will hedge up thy way with thorns." Many are checked, and made to think by being made to smart. Travelers tell us of the "wait-a-bit thorn," which puzzles the most cautious walker. When in full pursuit of evil, the Lord can bring the sinner to a pause.

2. Insurmountable difficulties: "and make a wall." The lord of love places effectual stoppages in the road of those whom he means to save: if men break down hedges, his persevering love builds walls, so that they may find it hard to persevere in sin.

3. Blinding perplexities: "she shall not find her paths." He can make the ways of sinful pleasure to be difficult and bewildering, till even the broad road seems to be barricaded.

4. Utter failures: "she shall follow after, but not overtake." We know persons with whom nothing is going right; even the utmost diligence in their case fails to secure prosperity: and all because their ways are not pleasing to God, and he means to bring them out of them. Such men hunt after sinful success, but it flees from them.

5. Bitter disappointments: "she shall seek them, but shall not find them." Pleasure shall be no longer found by them even in those amusements where once it danced around them.

These severe chastenings are frequently made useful in the early days of religious impression: they are the ploughing before the sowing.

III. THE BLESSED RESULT WHICH IS AT LAST ATTAINED.

The wandering, wanton spirit is led to return to her God.

1. Remembrance aroused: "it was better with me."

2. Confession of sad loss extorted: "then was it better with me *than now*." She thinks upon happier times, now that her days are clouded over.

3. Resolution formed: "I will go and return."

4. Affection stirred: "I will return to my first husband."

   - She owns the bands of love; she sorrows that she has strained them so terribly.
   - When the matter has come so far, the sad breach is healed, the work of reclaiming love is done.
   - Let us turn to the Lord before he uses thorns to stop us.
   - If already hedged up, let us consider our ways.
   - In any case, let us by faith turn to Jesus, and rest in him.

Cuttings

"I will hedge up thy way."—There is a twofold hedge that God makes about his people. There is the hedge of protection, to keep evil from them; and the hedge of affliction, to keep them from evil. The hedge of protection you have in Isaiah 5:5, where God threatens that he "will take away the hedge" from his vineyard; and it is said of Job, that God had "hedged him about." But the hedge here meant is the hedge of affliction. "I will hedge up thy way," that is, I will bring sore and heavy afflictions upon you to keep you from evil.

When a husbandman sees passengers make a path in his ground where they ought not, and so spoil the grass or the corn, he lays thorns in the way that they cannot go into his corn; or if they do, they shall go with some pain and trouble: "so," saith God, "I will hedge up thy way with thorns." —*Jeremiah Burroughs*

Consider the good effects of a wounded conscience, privative for the present, and positive for the future. First, privative; this heaviness of thy heart (for the time being) is a bridle to thy soul, keeping it from many sins it would otherwise commit. Thou that now sittest sad in thy shop, or standest sighing in thy chamber, mightest perchance at this time be drunk, or wanton, or worse, if not restrained by this affliction. God saith to Judah, "I will hedge up thy way with thorns," namely, to keep Judah from committing spiritual fornication. A wounded conscience is a hedge of thorns; but this thorny fence keeps our wild spirits in the true way, which otherwise would be straggling; and it is better to be held in the right road with briars and brambles than to wander on beds of roses in a wrong path which leads to destruction. —*Thomas Fuller*

A popular and successful young minister in America became entangled in the meshes of infidelity, left the pulpit, joined an infidel club, and derided the name he had preached to others as the Savior of the world. But he sickened, and came to his death-bed. His friends gathered round him, and tried to comfort him with their cold and icy theories, but in vain. The old thought came back to him—the old experience came before him. He said, "Wife, bring me my Greek Testament." Upon his bed he turned to the fifteenth chapter of the First Epistle to the Corinthians. When he had finished the chapter, great tears of joy rolled down his cheeks. He closed the Book, and said, "Wife, back again at last upon the old rock to die."

100

Therefore, behold, I will allure her, and bring her into the wilderness, and speak comfortably unto her.

—Hosea 2:14

N the former part of the chapter we find words of accusation and threatening most justly uttered towards a guilty nation. In this second portion we come to a passage of unmixed grace. The person dealt with is the same, but she is dealt with under another dispensation, even that covenant of grace of which we find an abstract in verse 23.

God, intending to deal with his sinful people in love, speaks words which are of the most extraordinary tenor.

I. HERE IS, FOR HIS DEEDS OF LOVE, A REASON BEYOND ALL REASON.

The text begins with "therefore." God always has a reason.

The context describes the grossest sin, and how should God find a reason there?

1. God finds a reason for grace where there is none. Why else did he bless Israel, or any one of us?
2. God makes a reason which overrides all other reasons. Because his people will persist in being so evil, he will display more love till he wins them from their wanderings.
3. God creates a reason *for* out of reasons against. "She forgat me, saith the Lord. Therefore I will allure her" (see all preceding verses). The great sin which is in itself a reason for judgment is by divine grace turned into an argument for mercy.
4. God justifies his own reasoning with men by a reason. According to the margin, "I will speak to her heart," is the promise of the text, and the Lord gives a *"therefore"* for it. He has a gracious reason for reasoning with us in love.

The sovereign grace of God had chosen his people, and his immutable love resolves to win this people to itself, *therefore* it sets about the work.

II. HERE IS A METHOD OF POWER BEYOND ALL POWER. "I will allure her."

1. Allurement of love surpasses in power all other forces.
   It appears that other methods had been used, such as:
   - Affliction with its thorny hedge (verse 6).
   - Instruction with all its practical application (verse 8).
   - Deprivation even of necessaries (verse 9).
   - Exposure of sin beyond all denial (verse 10).
   - Sorrow upon sorrow (verses 11 and 12).
   - The sweet allurement of tenderness would succeed where these failed,
2. Allurement of love overcomes the will to resist.
   Assaulted we defend, allured we yield.
3. Allurement of grace has many conquering weapons.
   - The person, work, offices, and love of Jesus lead men captive.
   - The freeness and abundance of divine pardon vanquish opposition.

- The grace and truth of the covenant defy resistance.
- The adoption and inheritance so graciously bestowed subdue the heart by overwhelming force of gratitude.
- The sense of present peace, and the prospect of future glory, allure us beyond all things.

III. HERE IS A CONDITION OF COMPANY BEYOND ALL COMPANY.

1. She is made to be alone. Free from tempting, distracting, or assisting company. All her lovers far from her. Her hope in them is gone.
2. Alone with God. He becomes her trust, desire, aim, love.
3. Alone as in the wilderness. Illustrate by Israel, who, in the wilderness, knew the Lord as Deliverer, Guide, Guard, Light, Manna, Physician, Champion, central Glory, and King.
4. Alone for the same purpose as Israel, for training, growth, illumination, and preparation for the promised rest: above all that the' might be the Lord's own separated ones.

IV. HERE IS A VOICE OF COMFORT BEYOND ALL COMFORT. "And speak comfortably to her."

1. Real comfort is given to souls alone with God. The divine speech is applied to the heart, and so its comfort is understood and appropriated, and effectually touches the affections.
2. Abundant comfort is bestowed, received, and acknowledged:
   - By renewed gratitude: "she shall sing there as in the days of her youth" (verse 15).
   - By a more confiding spirit: "thou shalt call me Ishi," etc. (verses 16 and 17).
   - By an established peace (verse 18).
   - By a clearer revelation of eternal love (verses 19 and 20).
   - By a surer sense of the eternal future and its marriage-union of endless bliss; for betrothal prophesies marriage.

Now let all this be known and felt, and we are sure the heart is won: there can be no revolting after this.

Let the prayer of each one of us be:

> O heavenly love, my heart subdue,
> I would be led in triumph too;
> Allured to live for God alone,
> And bow submissive at his throne

Jottings

When God's free grace has pitched upon its object, it often solicits that soul in its own peculiar way: I mean that grace woos and wins by its own graciousness, it conquers not by arms but by allurement. Have you not seen a mother allure her child to run into her bosom with the promise of a kiss? Have you never heard the little birds alluring their mates with rapturous song? Know you not the way of love by which it wins its victories? If so, you also understand why the beloved one is to be spoken with in the wilderness. Love is shy, and shuns the crowd: solitude is her element. When a soul is made to be alone with God, it shall hear many things which for the present could not be spoken to it. Speaking to the heart is reserved for retirement; it were not meet to display the secrets of divine communion to a mingled concourse. Understand, therefore, O lonely one, why thou art made to be one by thyself; and now surrender thy heart to the sacred allurements of sovereign grace! —C. H. S.

Some years ago an affecting incident was reported in reference to the ex-Empress Charlotte, an Austrian princess, whose husband was for a short time Emperor of Mexico. In the year 1867 he was shot by the revolutionists, and his unhappy widow became the victim of melancholy madness, which her physicians gave up all hope of curing. As in similar cases, she returned to the tastes and habits of childhood, one of which was a passion for flowers, and she spent most of her time over them. Their attractiveness for her was touchingly manifested on the occasion in question, when, having eluded the watch of her attendants, she had fled from the castle. When overtaken it was found impossible to induce her to return, except by the use of means which would certainly have proved hurtful. One of her physicians happily bethought himself of her intense affection for flowers; and by showing them from time to time before her, she was gradually lured on her way back to her home. May not this story be taken as an illustration of the way in which God allures wandering souls back to himself by the invitations and promises of the gospel?

101

I will have mercy upon her that had not obtained mercy; and I will say to them which were not my people, Thou art my people; and they shall say, Thou art my God.

—*Hosea 2:23*

As he saith also in Osee, I will call them my people, which were not my people; and her beloved which was not beloved. And it shall come to pass, that in the place where it was said unto them, Ye are not my people; there shall they be called the children of the living God.

—*Romans 9:25–26*

E accept the supreme authority of Holy Scripture: every word of it is truth to us.

Yet we attach special weight to words which are the personal utterance of the Lord God; as in this case, where God himself is the Speaker, in the first person.

Still more are we impressed when a divine message is repeated; as in this instance, where Paul writes, "As he saith also in Osee."

God "saith" still what he said long ago.

Come then, anxious souls, and hear the story of God's grace to his chosen, in the hope that he may do the like for you.

Observe with attention, concerning the Lord's people:

I. THEIR ORIGINAL STATE: "not obtained mercy—not my people."

1. They not only were not "beloved," but *they were expressly disowned*. It was said unto them, ye are not my people." Their claim, if they made any, was negatived.
   - This is the worst case that can be: worse than to be left alone.
   - This, conscience, providence, and the Word of God all appear to say to men who persist in sin.
2. They had no approval of God.
   - They were not numbered with his people.
   - They were not "beloved," in the sense of the love of complacency.
3. They had not in the highest sense "obtained mercy."
   - For they were under providential judgment.
   - That judgment had not become a blessing to them.
   - They had not even sought for mercy.
4. They were the types of a people who as yet:
   - Have felt no application of the blood of Jesus;
   - Have known no renewing work of the Spirit;
   - Have obtained no relief by prayer; perhaps have not prayed;
   - Have enjoyed no comfort of the promises;
   - Have known no communion with God;
   - And possess no hope of heaven, or preparation for it.

It is a terrible description, including all the unsaved.

It is concerning certain of such that the unconditional promise is made in the text: "I will call them my people." Who these are shall be seen in due time by their repentance and faith, which shall be wrought in them by the Spirit of God. There are such people, and this fact is our encouragement in preaching the gospel, for we perceive that our labor will not be in vain.

II. THEIR NEW CONDITION: "Thou art my people."

1. Mercy is promised: "I will have mercy upon her that had not obtained mercy." This is absolutely free.
2. A divine revelation is pronounced: "I will say, Thou art my people."
   - This is done by the Spirit of God in the heart.
   - This is supported by gracious dealings in the life.
3. A hearty response shall be given: "they shall say, Thou art my God." The Holy Ghost will lead them to this free acceptance.
   - As a whole, they will say this with one voice.
   - Each individual will say it for himself in the singular, "Thou."
4. A declaration of love shall be made: "I will call her beloved, which was not beloved" (Rom. 9:25). Love shall be enjoyed.
5. This shall be perceived by others: "There shall they be called the children of the living God."

   Their likeness to God shall make them to be called the children of God, even as the peacemakers in Matthew 5:9.

Thus every blessing shall be theirs surely, personally, everlastingly.

Reflections arising from all this:

- We must give up none as hopeless; even though they be marked out by terrible evidence to be not the people of God.
- None may give up themselves in despair.
- Sovereign grace is the ultimate hope of the fallen.
- Let them trust in a God so freely gracious, so omnipotent to save, so determined to bring in those whom it seemed that even he, himself, had disowned, whom everybody had abandoned as not the people of God.

Notabilia

"Have you ever heard the gospel before?" asked an Englishman, at Ningpo, of a respectable Chinaman, whom he had not seen in his mission-room before.

"No," he replied, "but I have *seen* it. I know a man who used to be the terror of his neighborhood. If you gave him a hard word, he would shout at you, and curse you for two days and nights without ceasing. He was as dangerous as a wild beast, and a bad opium-smoker; but when the religion of Jesus took hold of him, he became wholly changed. He is gentle, moral, not soon angry, and has left off opium. Truly, the teaching is good!" —*Word and Work*

It will give a kind of exaltation to the saint's happiness to look down upon that moral depth from which he was taken. A man on the edge of a precipice, *at night*, cannot clearly see it; but when the morning dawns, he will be able to see the danger he has been in. So the saint cannot, while on earth, conceive the depth of sin from which he has been raised; but he will be able to measure it by the light of heaven, and he may go down ages before he comes to the place where he once was: and then to think what *he is*—how deep once, but how high now—it will augment the sense of happiness and glory—and then to recollect *who* has been the cause—and every time he looks down at what he was, it will give greater emphasis to the ascription, "Unto him that loved us, and washed us from our sins in his own blood, and hath made us kings and priests unto God and his Father: to him be glory and dominion for ever and ever." —*John Foster*

The announcement made by Brownlow North to his old friends of his sudden change, whether orally or in writing, created no small sensation among them. Some thought he had gone out of his mind, others thought it was a temporary impression or excitement, and that it would soon pass off; and this was specially the case with those of them who were acquainted with his previous convictions, and temporary reformation, while, in some of the newspapers, it was even said, after he began his public work, that the whole thing was done for a wager, and that he had taken a bet to gather a certain number of thousands or tens of thousands of hearers in a given time. So little do carnal men understand the workings of the Spirit of God, even when they see the most striking and manifest proofs of it. —*From Brownlow North's Life-story, by Reverend K. Moody-Stuart, M.A.*

102

For they have sown the wind, and they shall reap the whirlwind: it hath no stalk: the bud shall yield no meal: if so be it yield, the strangers shall swallow it up.

—Hosea 8:7

IFE is a seed time. Of all men it may be said, "they have sown." Prudent men put the question, "What will the harvest be?"

The hope of harvest is the joyful encouragement of the righteous. The certainty of harvest should be a solemn warning to the godless.

It is well to follow worldly lives to their issues that we may avoid them. Here we see what evil seed will produce.

I. THE RESULT OF CERTAIN SOWINGS WILL BE TERRIBLE. "They have sown the wind, and they shall reap the whirlwind."

The sowing was careless, or mischievous, or changeable; and the harvest was of the same reckless, ruthless, mingled character, only terribly intensified. Wind grew into whirlwind.

1. Vicious men sow their wild oats, and we need not say what they reap.
   The debauched, drunken, and profligate are around us, bearing

already in their own persons the first-fruits of the fearful harvest of transgression.

2. Oppressors in a nation are sure to be repaid with revolt, bloodshed, etc., as may be seen in the French Revolution, and many other dreadful historical incidents. Wars bring an awful harvest of poverty and death. Oh, that our nation would cease to be so eager for the fray!

3. Immoral theories go far beyond their original intent. The speculation was an airy nothing, but the outcome is a whirlwind, breaking down all that is built up.

4. Heresies in the church also lead to unexpected evils. Apparently trifling errors grow to grievous evils. The use of a symbol develops into idolatry. A little laxity increases into absolute immorality. Small disputes lead on to heart-burnings and divisions.

5. Tolerance of sin in a family is a fruitful source of overwhelming evil. See the case of Eli. Mind it is not your own.

6. Toleration of sin in yourself. Occasional indulgence becomes habit, and habit is as the Simoom of the desert, before which life expires, and hope is swept away. Even allowable acts may grow into dangerous excess.

Let no man think that he can measure, much less limit, the consequences of sin as to himself, his family, the church, or the world. When once the winds are up, who can still them?

II. THE RESULT OF SOME SOWINGS IS MANIFEST FAILURE. "It hath no stalk."

The seed feebly tries to grow, but it comes to nothing.

1. Self-conceit vainly endeavors to produce a reputation.

2. Self-righteousness strives unsuccessfully to obtain salvation.

3. Human wisdom idly struggles to make a new gospel.

4. Mere idlers and talkers affect to be useful, but it is a delusion. What appears to be accomplished soon vanishes away. Great talk, but "no stalk."

5. He who spends his life without faith in Christ, and obedience to his will, may dream of a happy future, but he will be deceived: "it hath no stalk"

Wherefore do men live for folly, and dote on vanity?

III. THE RESULT OF MANY SOWINGS IS UNSATISFACTORY. "The bud shall yield no meal."

"The devil's meal is all bran," so they say, and it is true.

1. The man lived for pleasure, and found satiety.

2. He lived for fame, and gathered vanity.

3. He lived for self, and found misery.

4. He lived by his own works and religiousness, but reaped no peace of mind, and no real salvation.

IV. THE RESULT OF MANY SOWINGS IS PERSONAL DISAPPOINT-
MENT. "If so be it yield, the strangers shall swallow it up."

1. The man spends his life as a common toiler, who earns much for his master, but nothing for himself, and this is a poor result if there be no higher object in life.
2. He invents, devises, and commences, but another gains the profit.
3. He heapeth up riches, and knoweth not who shall gather them. His heirs forget him, and strangers swallow up his savings without gratitude.

Without God, nothing is wise, or strong, or worth the doing.

Only to live unto God is a wise sowing.

May the Lord destroy utterly all our sowings to the flesh, lest we reap corruption (Galations 6:8)!

May the Lord Jesus supply us with good seed, and bless us in the sowing! Oh, for a consecrated life!

Incidents

An Eastern apologue tells us of Abdallah, to whom an evil spirit came at first as a fly, sipping an atom of syrup. He did not drive away the creature, and to his surprise it increased to the size of a locust. Being further indulged, the creature went on growing, and made such rapid increase that it became an enormous monster, devoured his substance, and in the end murdered him, leaving in the garden, where it slew its victim, a footprint six cubits long. Thus does sin grow upon men, till it becomes a giant habit, and slays them.

Augustine tells us of a young man who thought that the devil had made flies, and such like tiny things. By the influence of this apparently insignificant error, he was led on, step by step, till in the end he ascribed everything to Satan, and ceased to believe in God. Thus does error sow the wind, and reap the whirlwind. Scrupulous correctness of faith is as much a duty as careful practice in morals.

David Hume, the historian, philosopher, and skeptic, spent his life in traducing the Word of God. In his last moments he joked with those around him; but the intervals were filled up with sadness. He wrote, "I am affrighted and confounded with the forlorn solitude in which I am placed by my philosophy. When I turn my eye inward, I find nothing but doubt and ignorance. Where am I, and what? I begin to fancy myself in the most deplorable condition imaginable, environed in the deepest darkness." —*New Cyclopedia of Anecdote*

The history of the Rev. Caleb Colton, M.A., the author of "Lacon," may serve as a striking illustration of the truth of our text. He was a clergyman at Tiverton, popular and clever, but very fond of field-sports. One day, however, a friend suddenly expired while uttering most impious language. The awe-struck minister abjured dogs and guns, and vowed to live henceforth for his sacred calling. For months his preaching was earnest, but at the end of that time he resumed the sporting life. He had, moreover, acquired a love for gambling. A presentation to the vicarage of Kew and Petersham brought him to London, and while numbers were reading with delight his "Lacon; or, Many Things in Few Words; addressed to those who think," the wretched author was sitting far into the night among swindlers. His passion for play involving him in pecuniary difficulties, he was forced to abscond, and his living was declared void. After leading a vagabond life, he perished by his own hand at Fontainebleau in 1832.

103

Their heart is divided; now shall they be found faulty.
—*Hosea 10:2*

 SRAEL, as a nation, divided its allegiance between Jehovah and Baal, and so became good for nothing, and was given up to captivity.

God has made one heart in man, and the attempt to have two, or to divide the one, is in every case injurious to man's life.

A church divided into parties, or differing in doctrine, becomes heretical, or contentious, or weak and useless.

A Christian, aiming at another object besides his Lord's glory, is sure to spend a poor, unprofitable life. He is an idolater, and his entire character will be faulty.

A seeker after Christ will never find him while his heart is hankering after sinful pleasures, or self-righteous confidences: his search is too faulty to be successful.

A minister, aiming at something else besides his one object, whether it be fame, learning, philosophy, rhetoric, or gain, will prove to be a very faulty servant of God.

In any case this heart-disease is a dire malady. A broken heart is a blessing; but a divided heart is a mortal malady.

Let us seriously consider:

I. THE DISEASE. "Their heart is divided."

This evil is to be seen:

1. In their idea of their state: they say they are "miserable sinners," but they believe themselves to be exceedingly respectable.
2. In the ground of their trust: they profess faith in Christ, and yet they rely upon self: they try to mix grace and works.
3. In the aim of their life: God and mammon, Christ and Belial, heaven and the world.
4. In the object of their love. It is Jesus and some earthly love. They cannot say "Jesus only."

5. In the decision of their will. They are never settled; they halt between two opinions; they do not know their own mind: they have two minds, and so no mind at all.

The disease complained of is in the central fountain of life, and it affects every part of their manhood. It is fearfully common, even in those who make a loud profession. If not cured it will end fatally, and perhaps suddenly, as heart disease is very apt to do.

II. THE EVIL EFFECT OF IT. "Now shall they be found faulty."

In all sorts of ways the fault will show itself.

1. God is not loved at all when not wholly loved.
2. Christ is insulted when a rival is admitted.
3. No grace reigns within the soul if the heart be not wholly won.
4. The life limps and halts when it has not a whole heart behind it.
5. Before long the man goes over entirely to the wrong side.

This secret evil must sooner or later prove the whole profession to be faulty from beginning to end. It will be an awful thing if this be never discovered till death is close at hand.

III. ATTEMPTS AT A CURE.

Let it be seriously considered by the double-hearted man:

1. That he condemns himself by yielding so much of his heart to God. Why any if not all? Why go this way at all, if not all the way?
2. That his salvation will require all his thought and heart; for it is no tri-fling matter. "The kingdom of heaven suffereth violence" (Matt. 11:12). The righteous scarcely are saved (1 Pet. 4:18).
3. That the blessing he seeks is worthy of all his soul and strength.
4. That Jesus gave his whole heart to our redemption, and therefore it is not consistent for us to be half-hearted.
5. That all potent beings in the universe are undivided in heart.
   - Bad men are eager for their pleasure, gains, etc.
   - The devil works evil with his whole power.
   - Good men are zealous for Christ.
   - God is earnest to bless.
6. That faith in Christ is an act of the whole heart, and therefore a divided heart is not capable of saving faith, and consequently shuts itself off from the Savior.

From this time forward pray that you may have an undivided heart.

Read, hear, pray, repent, believe with your whole heart, and you shall soon rejoice with all your heart.

Helps toward Application

A minister in Brooklyn was recently called upon by a business man, who said to him, "I come, sir, to inquire if Jesus Christ will take me into the concern as a sleeping partner." "Why do you ask?" said the minister. "Because I wish to be a member of the firm, and do not wish anybody to know it." The reply was: "Christ takes no sleeping partners."

Some talk that the devil hath a cloven foot; but whatever the devil's foot be, to be sure his sons have a cloven heart: one half for God, the other half for sin; one half for Christ, the other half for this present world. God hath a corner in it, and the rest is for sin and the devil. —*Richard Alleine*

As to the evil of being neither one thing nor the other, one finds an illustration in the waterways of Southern China, which in wintertime are quite useless for purposes of commerce. The temperature is most tantalizing, for it is neither cold enough to freeze the canals, so that the ice would be able to bear traffic; nor warm enough to thaw them, so that they could be navigable by boats.

Some great king or potentate, having a mind to visit his imperial city, the harbinger is ordered to go before, and mark out a house suitable to entertain his majesty's retinue. The prince will only come to a house where he may dwell alone: if he cannot have the whole house, he will go elsewhere. The herald findeth one house where the master desireth to entertain the king, but he must have but one small chamber, wherein to lodge his wife and children. The herald will not accept his offer. Then he entreats the benefit of some by-place, to set up a trunk or two, full of richer goods than ordinary. "No," says the harbinger, "it cannot be; for if your house were as big again as it is, it would be little enough to entertain the king and all his royal train." So it is that every man's body is a temple of God, and his heart the sanctum sanclorum of that temple. His ministers are sent out into the world to inform us that Christ is coming to lodge there, and that we must clear the rooms, that this great King of glory may enter in. God will have the whole heart, the whole mind, the whole soul—and all will be too little to entertain him, and the graces of his Holy Spirit which are attendant on him. "Let it be neither mine nor thine; divide it": was the voice of a strange woman (1 Kings 3:26), and such is that of the present world; but God will take nothing by halves: he will have the whole heart or nothing. —*John Spencer*

On one occasion, when a former ruler of Montenegro was supposed to have received the offer of peace and a sum of money if he would acknowledge himself a vassal of the Porte, it is said that the chief men of the people waited on him to remind him that he was at perfect liberty to take service with the Sultan, but that no servant of the Sultan could be Gospodar of the Black Mountaineers. —*Travels in the Sclavonic Provinces of Turkey*

104

Sow to yourselves in righteousness, reap in mercy; break up your fallow ground: for it is time to seek the Lord, till he come and rain righteousness upon you.

—*Hosea 10:12*

HAT should we think of a farmer who allowed his finest fields to lie fallow year after year?

Yet men neglect their souls; and besides being unprofitable, these inward fields become full of weeds, and exceedingly foul.

You see to everything else, will you not see to your souls?

It is God who calls you to break up the fallow ground of your uncultivated heart, and he waits to aid you therein.

Regard attentively the argument which he uses: "for it is time to seek the Lord." Thus, God reasons with you. To this he adds instructions which deserve our best attention.

I. WHEN IS IT TIME? "It is time."

1. In the very first hour of responsibility it is none too soon.
2. At the present it is late, but not too late. "It is time."
3. When chastening has come, seek the Lord instantly; for now it is high time, "lest a worse thing come unto thee" (John 5:14).
4. Before trial comes, let mercy and gentleness lead to gratitude. Why should we need to be flogged to our God (Isa. 1:5)?
5. Have you not sinned long enough? May not the time past suffice for us to have served the flesh (1 Pet. 4:3)?
6. When you assume great responsibilities, and enter on a new stage of life—married, made a master, a father, etc. (1 Chron. 22:19).
7. When God's Spirit is specially at work, and therefore others are saved (Acts 3:19).
   • When you yourself feel holy stirrings in your conscience, and hope in your heart (Ps. 27:8; 2 Sam. 5:24).
   • When the gospel is aimed at you by an earnest minister or friend.

II. WHAT IS THE PECULIAR WORK? "to seek the Lord."

1. To draw nigh unto God; seeking him in worship, prayer, etc. (Ps. 105:4).
2. To ask pardon at his hands through the atonement of Jesus (Isa. 55:6).
3. To obtain the blessings connected with the new birth (John 1:12–13).
4. To live for his glory: seeking his honor in all things (Matt. 6:33).

III. HOW LONG SHALL THIS BE DONE? "Till he come and rain righteousness upon you."

1. Until the blessing of righteousness be obtained: "till he come."
2. Until it be plenteously received: "rain righteousness."
3. Until your soul is saturated: "rain righteousness upon you."

Suppose a pause between the seeking and the blessing, do not look in some other direction, but seek the Lord still.

- What else can you do (John 6:68)?
- Is not God a Sovereign? May he not give when he pleases?
- Even now some rain of grace falls on you. Be thankful for it.
- Is it not worth waiting for this grace of life?
- It is sure to come. He will come, and will not tarry (Heb. 10:37).

IV. WHAT WILL COME OF IT?

1. He will come. This is implied in the expression "till he come." God's coming in grace is all you need.
2. He will come in righteousness. You need purity and holiness, and he will bring these with him.
3. He will come in abundance of grace meeting your obedient sowing. Mark the precept, "Sow in righteousness." Then note the promise, "and rain righteousness upon you."
4. In consequence of the Lord's coming to you in righteousness, you shall "reap in mercy." With joy you shall gather the fruits of his love; not because of your own righteousness, but because of his righteousness, which he rains upon you; not as merit, but as mercy.

Come then, and seek the Lord at this very hour!

If thou wouldst find him, he is in Christ. Believe, and thou hast found him, and righteousness in him (Rom. 3:22).

Quickeners

While Christ calls, it is not too late to come. Dost thou object—"Is there not a set day, which, if sinners neglect, the door is shut?" I answer; There is truth in this; but yet there is no day but a sinner ought to come in it. Though thou mayest think the day of Christ's acceptance to be over, yet is not the day of thy submission over. Thy time to be subject to the divine precept is not over while thou livest. Thou art still under the command, and bound to yield obedience to God whatever he biddest thee do. . . . So long as God calls thee, the day is not over. This should encourage thee to come at once, driven by duty, and drawn by grace. —*Ralph Robinson*

Sir Thomas More, whilst he was a prisoner in the Tower, would not so much as suffer himself to be trimmed, saying that there was a controversy betwixt the king and him for his head, and till that was at a happy end, he would be at no cost about it. Let us but scum off the froth of his wit, and we may make a solemn use of it; for certainly all the cost we bestow upon ourselves, to make our lives pleasurable and joyous to us, is but mere folly, till it be decided what will become of the suit betwixt God and us, what will be the issue of the controversy that God hath against us, and that not for our heads, but for our souls, whether for heaven or hell. Were it not, then, the wisest course to begin with making our peace; and then we may the sooner lead a happy life? It is said, "He who gets out of debt grows rich." Most sure it is that the pardoned soul cannot be poor; for as soon as peace is concluded, a free trade is opened between God and the soul. If once pardoned, we may then sail to any port that lies in God's dominions, and be welcome. All the promises stand open with their treasures, and say, "Here, poor soul, take in full lading of all precious things, even as much as thy faith can bear and carry away I" —*John Spencer*

A little maiden stood trembling, weeping, timidly knocking at the door of a minister's library. "Come in," said a cheerful voice. The door handle slowly turned, and there she stood, sobbing with emotion. "What is the matter, my dear child?" said the sympathizing pastor. *"Oh, sir,"* was the reply, *"I have lived seven years without Jesus!"* She had just been celebrating her seventh birthday. —*The British Messenger*

> Moments seize;
> Heaven's on their wing: a moment we may wish,
> When worlds want wealth to buy.
>
> —*Young*

Thomas Fuller says, "God invites many with his golden scepter whom he never bruises with his rod of iron." If the invitations of his grace were more freely accepted, we should often escape the chastisements of his hand. Oh, that men did but know that a time of health, and happiness, and prosperity is as fit a season as can be for seeking the Lord! Indeed, any hour is a good time in which to seek the Lord, so long as it is present with us. He who would be wise will find no better day in the calendar for casting away folly than that which is now with him. But let no man trifle with time, for in an instant the die may be cast, and then it is written concerning the ungodly, "I also will laugh at your calamity, and mock when your fear cometh" (Prov. 1:26).

105
I will be thy King.
—*Hosea 13:10*

 HIS was God's declaration to Israel, meeting a great want, and saving the people from a great burden. They were to be spared the expense and danger arising from a human monarch, and to find government and headship in God himself.

This did not content their unspiritual nature, and they desired a king, like the nations around them. By this desire they angered the Lord, and missed a great privilege.

To us the Lord presents the same privilege in a high spiritual sense, and if we are wise we shall accept it.

I. THE CRAVING OF NATURE. *"Give me a king."*

We do not go into the political question of the right or wrong of monarchy in the abstract: that would be too vexed a discussion, and unsuitable for our present engagement. We are quite content with the form of government of our own land.

But we speak morally and spiritually of individual need.

Man was happy in the garden while God was his King; but when he became a rebel against the King of kings, he was forced to accept another lord.

"Give me a king" is:

1. The cry of weakness. Man needs some one to look up to.
2. The sigh of distress. In straits he sighs for the wise and the strong to counsel and succor him.
3. The prayer of thoughtfulness.
   - Anarchy of soul is terrible; each passion fights for mastery.
   - A kingless, aimless life is misery. Idleness is hard work: the purposeless are unhappy.
   - King Self is a poor, mean, despicable despot, foolish and feeble.
   - The World is a cruel and ungrateful master.
4. The desire of experience.
   - Folly proved makes us desire a Lawgiver.
   - Danger felt makes us long for a Protector.
   - Responsibility weighing upon us makes us sigh for a Superior, who will undertake to choose our way, and direct us in it.

II. THE ROYAL ANSWER OF GRACE. "I will be thy King."

1. Eminently condescending. Our God comes to rule over:
   - A ruined, bankrupt, desolated realm.
   - Torn to pieces by contending pretenders.
   - Surrounded by mighty and relentless enemies.
   - Full of unruly members.
   - Nothing but infinite love could prompt him to assume such a throne, or to wear a crown which cost him so dear. "Behold your King!"
2. Abundantly satisfactory; for:
   - He has power to subdue every inward rebel.
   - He has a character worthy of dominion. It is a great honor to submit to such a Prince.
   - He has more than the wisdom of Solomon to arrange every matter.
   - He has goodness to bless, and he is as ready as he is able to make his reign a period of happiness, peace, and prosperity.
   - He has love with which to command affectionate obedience.
3. Infinitely consoling:
   - To be protected by his omnipotence.
   - To be ruled by absolute perfection.
   - To be governed by a King who can neither be defeated, nor die, nor abdicate, nor change.
   - To find in God far more of greatness and goodness than could be dreamed of as existing in the best of earthly sovereigns.
4. Gloriously inspiring:
   - To live and die for such a Leader.
   - To claim possession of human hearts for such a Benefactor.
   - To have such an Example for obedient imitation.
   - To be for ever linked with a Potentate so majestic.

III. THE DELIGHT OF LOYALTY. Our answer to the promise of the text is this: "Thou art my King, O God" (Ps. 44:4).

If we unreservedly accept our King—
1. We look to see and share his glory ere long (Isa. 33:17).
2. We expect present deliverances (Ps. 44:4).
3. We repose in delicious confidence in the wisdom, goodness, ant immutability of all his arrangements.
4. We seek to extend his dominions (Matt. 6:10).
5. We glory in his name with unspeakable delight. His history is our meditation, his promise is our sustentation, his honors are our glory, and his person is our adoration. His throne is our haven and our heaven. He, himself, is all our salvation, and all our desire (2 Sam. 23:5).

Pleas for Homage

Is Jesus in very deed and truth my King? Where is the proof of it? Am I living in his kingdom of "righteousness, and peace, and joy in the Holy Ghost" now? (Rom. 14:17). Am I speaking the language of that kingdom? Am I following "the customs of the people" (Jer. 10:3) which are not his people? or, do I "diligently learn the ways of his people"? (Jer. 7:16). Am I practically living under the rule of his laws? Have I done heart-homage to him? Am I bravely and honestly upholding his cause, because it is his, not merely because those around me do so? Is my allegiance making any practical difference to my life today? —*Miss Havergal*

God is the ultimate foundation of all human society; without him you can neither cement nor govern society. The mad attempt, if you remember, was made in France. The governing council decreed that there was no God. What was the result? Anarchy, confusion, license, bloodshed, terror. Robespierre, one of the leading spirits of the Revolution, had to declare to his comrades in conclave assembled, "If there be no God, we must make one—we cannot govern France without him." —*J. Cynddylan Jones*

What, then, shall we render for this inestimable favor, in taking us to be his subjects? Oh, let us offer him not only the tenths of our labors, but the first fruits of our affections: let us open not only the doors of our lips, but the gates of our hearts, that the King of glory may come in. And when thou vouchsafest, O my Lord, to come with thy high majesty under my low roof; and to work a miracle, by having that greatness, which the world containeth not, contained in a little corner of my breast; vouchsafe also to send thy grace for the harbinger of thy glory!

Possess me wholly, O my Sovereign! Reign in my body, by obedience to thy laws; and in my soul, by confidence in thy promises: frame my tongue to praise thee, my knees to reverence thee, my strength to serve thee, my desires to covet thee, and my heart to embrace thee. —*Sir R. Baker, on "The Lord's Prayer"*

The Lord in our text assumes the throne, not so much by the election of his subjects as by his election of them; and the act is not an ascent to a higher dignity than that which he naturally possesses, but a descent of love to a position which is for our gain rather than his own. He comes to us with this sweet willingness to reign over us, and it is our wisdom joyfully to accept the infinite privileges of his endless dominion.

106

Rend your heart, and not your garments, and turn unto the Lord you God.

—Joel 2:13

XPLAIN the oriental custom of rending robes. People were ready enough to use the outward signs of mourning when, as in the present instance, locusts appeared to devour their crops, or when any other judgment threatened them.

They failed in mourning *as to the Lord*, and in rendering spiritual homage to his chastising rod. Hence the language of the text.

Let us revolve in our minds:

I. THE GENERAL DOCTRINE THAT TRUE RELIGION IS MORE INWARD THAN OUTWARD.

The expression "Rend your heart, and not your garments," casts somewhat of a slur upon the merely outward.

1. This respects forms and ceremonies of men's devising. These are numerous and vain. "Not your garments" may in their case be treated in the most emphatic manner. Will-worship is sin.
2. It bears also upon ordinances of God's own ordaining if practiced without grace, and relied upon as of themselves effectual.

Among good things which may become unprofitable we may mention:

- The regular frequenting of a place of worship.
- The practice of family prayer in one's own home.
- The reading of Holy Scripture.
- The holding of an orthodox creed.
- The practice of private prayer.
- The attendance upon sacraments.

All these good things should have their place in our lives; but they do not prove saint-ship: since a sinner may practice them all, after a sort. The absence of a true heart will make them all vain.

II. THE FURTHER DOCTRINE THAT MAN IS MORE INCLINED TO THE OUTWARD OBSERVANCE THAN TO INWARD MATTERS.

Hence he needs no exhortation to rend his garments, though that act might in certain cases be a fit and proper expression of deep repentance, and holy horror for sin.

Man is thus partial to externals:

1. Because he is not spiritual, but carnal by nature.

2. Because the inward is more difficult than the outward, and requires thought, diligence, care, humiliation, etc.

3. Because he loves his sin. He will rend his robes, for they are not himself; but to rend off his beloved sins is like tearing out his eyes.

4. Because he cares not to submit to God. Law and gospel are both distasteful to him; he loves nothing which necessitates the obedience of his heart to God.

Many throng the outer courts of religious observance who shun the holy place of repentance, faith, and consecration.

III. THE PARTICULAR DOCTRINE THAT HEART-RENDING IS BETTER THAN ANY EXTERNAL ACT OF PIETY.

1. Heart-rending should be understood. It is:
   - To have the heart broken, contrite, tender, sensitive.
   - To have the heart grieving over past evils.
   - To have the heart rent away from sin, as by holy violence.
   - To have the heart torn with holy horror and indignation in the presence of temptation. The sight of sin should rend the heart, especially when it is seen by the light of the cross.

2. Heart-rending is to be preferred to external observances, for:
   - These are not commanded for their own sakes.
   - They are good or evil as the heart may be.
   - Their observance may co-exist with sin, even with great sin.
   - Outward signs may even be Antichrists keeping us from Christ.
   - They can never supply the place of Jesus himself.

3. Heart-rending should be practiced. "Rend your hearts."
   - This would need a great tug. Can a man rend himself?
   - This drives us to look to a higher power.
   - This is met only by Jesus. Looking to him whom we have pierced, our hearts are rent.
   - This, when fully done, leaves us at his feet, who alone "heareth the broken in heart, and bindeth up their wounds."

Ad Rem

An old Hebrew story tells how a poor creature came one day to the Temple, from a sick bed, on tottering limbs. He was ashamed to come, for he was very poor, and he had no sacrifice to offer; but as he drew near he heard the choir chanting, "Thou desirest not sacrifice; else would I give it: thou delightest not in burnt-offerings. The sacrifices of God are a broken spirit: a broken and a contrite heart, O God, thou wilt not despise." Other worshippers came, pressed before him, and offered their sacrifices; but he had none. At length he prostrated himself before the priest, who said, "What wilt thou, my son? Hast thou no offering?" And he replied, "No, my father, for last night a poor widow and her children came to me, and I had nothing to offer them but the two pigeons which were ready for the sacrifice." "Bring, then," said the priest, "an ephah of fine flour." "Nay, but, my father," said the old man, "this day my sickness and poverty have left only enough for my own starving children; I have not even an ephah of flour." "Why, then, art thou come to me?" said the priest. "Because I heard them singing, 'The sacrifices of God are a broken spirit.' Will not God accept my sacrifice if I say, 'Lord, be merciful to me, a sinner'?" Then the priest lifted the old man from the ground, and he said, "Yes, thou art blessed, my son; it is the offering which is better than thousands of rivers of oil." — *"The World of Proverb and Parable," by E. Paxton Hood*

If this hypocrisy, this resting in outward performances, was so odious to God under the law, a religion full of shadows and ceremonies, certainly it will be much more odious under the gospel, a religion of much more simplicity, and exacting so much the more sincerity of heart, even because it disburdens the outward man of the performances of legal rights and observances. And therefore, if we now, under the gospel, shall think to delude God Almighty, as Michal did Saul, with an idol handsomely dressed instead of the true David, we shall one day find that we have not mocked God, but ourselves; and that our portion among hypocrites shall be greater than theirs. — *William Chillingworth*

As garments to a body, so are ceremonies to religion. Garments on a living body preserve the natural warmth; put them on a dead body and they will never fetch life. Ceremonies help to increase devotion; but in a dead heart they cannot breed it. These garments of religion upon a holy man are like Christ's garments on his own holy body; but joined with a profane heart, they are like Christ's garments on his crucifying murderers. — *Ralph Brownrig*

Rending the clothes was a common and very ancient mode of expressing grief, indignation, or concern; and as such is frequently mentioned in the Scriptures. . . . It is said that the upper garment only was rent for a brother, sister, son, daughter, or wife, but all the garments for a father or mother. Maimonides says that the rents were not stitched up again till after thirty days, and were never sewed up well. There is no law which enjoins the Jews to rend their clothes; yet in general they so far think it requisite to comply with this old custom as to make a slight rent for the sake of form. — *Pictorial Bible*

107

Thus he shewed me: and behold, the Lord stood upon a wall made by a plumbline, with a plumbline in his hand.

—Amos 7:7

HE metaphors of Amos are very forcible, though homely and simple. He was God-taught; or, as men say, self-taught. Let his vision come before us, as though we saw it ourselves.

What the Lord had done was according to rule: "he stood upon a wall made by a plumbline." His past dealings are just and true.

The Lord continues to use the same infallible rule: wherever he is, he has a plumbline in his hand.

The plumb of lead falls in a straight line, and therefore the line is the best test as to whether a wall is truly perpendicular. The plumbline shows whether it bows outward, or inclines inward. It never flatters, but by its own certainty of truth it reveals and condemns all deviations from uprightness: such is the judgment of the Most High.

We shall treat the plumbline as the emblem of truth and right.

I. A PLUMBLINE IS USED IN BUILDING.

In all that we build up, we must act by the sure rule of righteousness.

1. In God's building it is so.
   - He removes the old walls when tested by the plumbline, and found faulty. Truth requires the removal of falsehood.
   - He builds in truth and reality. Sincerity is his essential
   - He builds in holiness and purity.
   - He builds to perfection according to the rule of right.
2. In our own life-building it should be so.
   - Not haste, but truth should be our object.
   - Not according to the eye of man, but according to fact.
   - We should build by the Word; in God's sight; after Christ's example; by the Spirit; unto holiness. Only thus shall we be using the plumbline.
3. In our building of the church it should be so.
   - Teaching the Scriptures only in all things.
   - Preaching nothing but the gospel.
   - Laying sinners low by the law, and exalting the grace of God.
   - Leading men to holiness and peace by the doctrines of truth.
   - Exercising discipline that the church may be pure.

II. A PLUMBLINE IS USED FOR TESTING.

That which is out of the upright is detected by the plumbline, and so are men tested by the truth.

1. We may use it:
   - On the wall of self-righteousness, conceit, boasting, etc.
   - On the wall of careless living.
   - On the wall of trust in ceremonials.
   - On the wall of reliance upon merely hearing the gospel.
   - On the wall of every outward profession.
2. God uses it in this life. He tests the hearts of men, and tries their doings. They are often detected in the act of deception. Time also proves them, and trials test them.
3. He will use it at the last.
4. Let us use it on ourselves.

Are we born again? Are we without faith, etc.? Are we without holiness? Or is the work of the Spirit to be seen in us?

III. A PLUMBLINE WILL BE USED FOR DESTROYING.

Strict justice is the rule of God's dealing on the judgment-seat.

The same rule will apply to all.

1. Even the saved will be saved justly through our Lord Jesus, and in their case every sin will be destroyed, and every trace of evil will be removed before they enter heaven.
2. No one will be condemned who does not deserve it. There will be a trial, with witnesses, and pleadings, and an infallible Judge. The righteous are saved by sovereignty, but the wicked are condemned by righteousness alone.
3. Not a pain will be inflicted unjustly.
   - Differences will be made in the cases of the condemned.
   - There will be the strictest justice in each award.
   - Every circumstance will be taken into account.
   - Knowledge or ignorance will increase or abate the number of stripes (Luke 7:47–48).
4. Rejecters of Christ will find their doom intolerable, because they, themselves, will be unable to deny its justice (Luke 19:27). The lost know their misery to be deserved.
5. Since every sentence will be infallible, there will be no revision. So impartial and just will be each verdict that it shall stand for ever (Matt. 25:46).

Are we able to endure the test of the plumbline of perfect truth?

Suppose it to be used of God at this moment.

Will it not be wisest to look to Jesus, that we may have him for a foundation, and be built up in him?

Sayings and Sentences

The question "What is truth?" was proposed at a Deaf and Dumb Institution, when one of the boys drew *a straight line*. "And what is falsehood?" The answer was a crooked line. —*G. S. Bowes*

That will be a wretched day for the church of God when she begins to think any aberration from the truth of little consequence. —*J. H. Evans*

Whitefield often affirmed that he would rather have a church with ten men in it right with God, than one with five hundred at whom the world would laugh in its sleeve. —*Joseph Cook*

Livingstone, as a missionary, was anxious to avoid a large church of nominal adherents. "Nothing", he wrote, "will induce me to form an impure church. 'Fifty added to the church' sounds well at home, but if only five of these are genuine, what will it profit in the Great Day?" —*Blaikie*

> Set thine heart upright, if thou wouldst rejoice,
> And please thyself in thine heart's pleasing choice:
> But then be sure thy plumb and level be
> Rightly applied to that which pleaseth me.
> —*Christopher Harvey*

Sinners on earth are always punished less, and in hell never more, than their iniquities deserve. —*Benjamin Beddome*

It is said of the Areopagites, in Athens, that their sentence was so upright that none could ever say he was unjustly condemned of them. How much more true is this of the righteous judgment of God, who must needs therefore be justified, and every mouth stopped! —*Trapp*

When a building is noticed to bulge a little, our builders hasten to shore it up with timbers; and before long the surveyor bids them take it down. Should we not see great changes in our churches if all the bowing walls were removed? Yet this would be no real loss, but in the Lord's sight an actual gain to the City of God.

When a man is afraid of self-examination, his fear is suspicious. He who does not dare to apply the plumbline to his wall may rest assured that it is out of perpendicular. A sincere man will pray, "Lord, let me know the worst of my case." It is far better to suffer needless distress than to be at ease in Zion, and then perish of the dry-rot of self-deceit.

108

The pride of thine heart hath deceived thee.
—Obadiah 1:3

 HIS is true of all proud persons, for pride is self-deceit.

There may be proud persons in this congregation. Those who are sure that they have no pride are probably the proudest of all. Those who are proud of their humility are proud indeed.

The confidence that we are not deceived may only prove the completeness of the deception under which we labor.

In considering the case of the Edomites, and the pride of their hearts, let us look to ourselves that we may profit withal.

I. THEY WERE DECEIVED.

The prophet mentions certain matters in which they were deceived.

1. As to the estimate formed of them by others. They thought themselves to be had in honor, but the prophet says, "Thou art greatly despised" (see verse 2).

    You might not be pleased if you knew how little others think of you; but if you think little of others you need not wonder if you are yourself greatly despised, for "with what measure ye mete, it shall be measured to you again" (Matt. 7:2).

2. As to their personal security. They felt safe, but were near their doom. "Who shall bring me down?" "I will bring thee down, saith the Lord" (verses 3 and 4). Dwelling in their rock-city of Petra was no real security to them: neither may any one of us think himself proof against misfortune, sickness, or sudden death.

3. As to their personal wisdom. They talked of "The wise man out of Edom" (verse 8); but the Lord said, "There is none understanding in him" (verse 7).

    Those who know better than the Word of God know nothing.

4. As to the value of their confidences. Edom relied on alliances, but these utterly failed. "The men that were at peace with thee have deceived thee" (verse 7). Rich relatives, influential friends, tried allies—all will fail those who trust in them.

II. THEIR OWN PRIDE DECEIVED THEM.

1. In each of the points mentioned above, pride lay at the bottom of their error.

2. In every way pride lays a man open to being deceived.

- His judgment is perverted by it: he cannot hold the scales.
- His standard is rendered inaccurate: his weights are false.
- His desires invite flattery, and his folly accepts it.

3. In every case a proud man is a deceived man: he is not what he thinks himself to be; and he is blind to that part of his character which should cause him to be humble.

4. In spiritual cases it is emphatically so.

   The self-righteous, self-sufficient, perfectionists, etc., are all deceived by the pride of their hearts.

III. THIS PRIDE LED THEM INTO EVIL WAYS.

1. They were full of defiance. "Who shall bring me down to the ground?" This self-asserting spirit provokes hostility and leads to wars and fighting and all manner of emulations and contentions.

2. They were destitute of compassion. "Thou stoodest on the other side" (see verses 9–12).

   Those of kindred race were being slain, and they had no pity. Pride is stony-hearted.

3. They even shared in oppression (see verses 13 and 14). This is not unusual among purse-proud religionists. They are not slow to profit by the nurseries of God's poor people.

4. They showed contempt of holy things. "Ye have drunk upon my holy mountain" (verse 16). God will not have his church made into a tavern, or a playhouse: yet something like this may be done even now by proud hypocrites and formalists.

IV. THESE EVIL WAYS SECURED THEIR RUIN.

1. Their defiance brought enemies upon them.

2. Their unkindness was returned into their own bosom. Verse 15 shows the *lex talionis* in action.

3. Their contempt of God made him say, "there shall not be any remaining of the house of Esau" (verse 18).

How different the lot of despised Zion! (see verses 17 and 21)

Let us seek him who in Zion is above all others "the Savior."

Hating all pride, let us humbly rest in him.

Then we shall not be deceived, for Jesus is "the Truth."

Warnings

There is something intensely amusing, according to our notions, in the name which the Eskimo bestow upon themselves. It appears they call themselves the "Innuit"—that is, "the people" *par excellence*.

Stranger, henceforth be warned; and know that pride,
Howe'er disguised in its own majesty,
Is littleness: that he who feels contempt
For any living thing, hath faculties
Which he has never used; that thought with him
Is in its infancy.

—Wordsworth

If a man is a perfectionist, and thinks he is sinless, it is a proof not that he is better, but only that he is blinder, than his neighbors. *—Richard Glover*

When a proud man thinks best of himself, then God and man think worst of him; all his glory is but like a vapor, which climbeth as though it would go up to heaven, but when it comes to a little height, it falls down again, and never ascends more. So Adam thought that the fair apple should make him like his Maker, but God resisted his pride, and that apple made him like the serpent that tempted him with it. Absalom thought that rebellion would make him a king, but God resisted his pride, and his rebellion hanged him on a tree. *—Henry Smith*

The Venetian ambassador wrote of Cardinal Wolsey: "I do perceive that every year he groweth more and more in power. When I first came to England, he used to say, "*His Majesty* will do so and so"; subsequently, he said, "*We* shall do so and so"; but now he says, "*I* shall do so and so." But history records how Wolsey's pride went before destruction, and his haughty spirit before a fall.

Napoleon Buonaparte, intoxicated with success, and at the height of his power, said, "I make circumstances." Let Moscow, Elba, Waterloo, and St. Helena, that rocky isle where he was caged until he fretted his life away, testify to his utter helplessness in his humiliating downfall. *—J. B. Gough*

As God hath two dwelling-places, heaven and a contrite heart, so hath the devil—hell and a proud heart. *—T. Watson*

109

And Jonah began to enter into the city a day's journey, and he cried, and said, Yet forty days, and Nineveh shall be overthrown.

—Jonah 3:4

The men of Nineveh shall rise in judgment with this generation, and shall condemn it: because they repented at the preaching of Jonas; and, behold, a greater than Jonas is here.

—Matthew 12:41

UR Lord never lost patience with an audience, and never brought railing accusation against any man: his rebuke was well deserved.

Nineveh under Jonah was indeed a reproof to the Jerusalem of our Lord's day, for the Jews, though favored with his divine ministry, did not repent, but wickedly crucified the Messenger of peace.

Might not our Lord rebuke the unbelievers of our day in the same way? Is not Nineveh a reproach to England?

Let us see.

The men of Nineveh repented, and turned to God; and yet:

I. THEIR CALLS TO REPENTANCE WERE NOT MANY.

Many unbelievers have been warned and entreated times without number, and yet they remain impenitent; but:

- Nineveh enjoyed no privileges: it was in heathen darkness.
- Nineveh heard but one prophet; and he was none of the greatest, or most affectionate.
- Nineveh heard that prophet only once; and that was an open-air sermon, very short and very monotonous.
- Nineveh had heard no word of good tidings; she heard the thunder of the law, but nothing else.

Yet the obedience to the warning was immediate, universal, practical, and acceptable, so that the city was spared.

II. THE MESSAGE OF THE PROPHET WAS NOT ENCOURAGING.

1. He proclaimed no promise of pardon.
2. He did not even mention repentance; and consequently he held out no hope to the penitent.
3. He foretold a crushing and final doom: "Nineveh shall be overthrown." His message began and ended with threatening.
4. He mentioned a speedy day: "yet forty days."

Yet out of this dreadful message the people made a gospel, and so acted as on it to find deliverance; while to many of us the rich, free, sure promise of the Lord has been of no force through our unbelief.

Those who heard the teaching of Jesus were, like ourselves, highly favored, for "never man spake like this Man"; and, like us, they were grievously guilty in that they repented not.

III. THE PROPHET HIMSELF WAS NO HELPER TO THEIR HOPE.

Jonah was no loving, tender pastor, anxious to gather the lost sheep.

1. He disliked the ministry in which he was engaged, and no doubt discharged it in a hard, harsh manner.

2. He uttered no word of sympathetic love, for he had none in his heart. He was of the school of Elijah, and knew not the love which burned in the heart of Jesus.
3. He offered no prayer of loving pity.
4. He was even displeased that the city was spared.

Yet these people obeyed his voice, and obtained mercy through hearkening to his warnings. Does not this rebuke many who have been favored with tender and loving admonitions? Certainly it rebuked those who lived in our Lord's day, for no two persons could afford a more singular contrast than Jonah and our Lord.

Indeed, a "greater," better, tenderer than Jonah was there.

IV. THE HOPE TO WHICH THE NINEVITES COULD REACH WAS SLENDER.

It was no more than, "Who can tell?"
1. They had no revelation of the character of the God of Israel.
2. They knew nothing of an atoning sacrifice.
3. They had received no invitation to seek the Lord, not even a command to repent.
4. Their argument was mainly negative.
    Nothing was said against their repenting.
    They could not be the worse for repenting.
5. The positive argument was slender.
    The mission of the prophet was a warning: even a warning implies a degree of mercy: they ventured upon that bare hope, saying, *Who can tell?*

Have we not all at least this much of hope?
Have we not far more in the gospel?
Will we not venture upon it?

Monitions

I saw a cannon shot off. The men at whom it was leveled fell flat on the ground, and so escaped the bullet. Against such blows, falling is all the fencing, and prostration all the armor of proof. But that which gave them notice to fall down was their perceiving of the fire before the ordnance was discharged. Oh! the mercy of that fire, which, as it were, repenting of the mischief it had done, and the murder it might make, ran a race, and out-stripped the bullet, that men (at the sight thereof) might be provided, when they could not resist to prevent it! Thus every murdering-piece is also a warning-piece against itself.

God, in like manner, warns before he wounds; frights before he fights "Yet forty days, and Nineveh shall be overthrown." Oh, let us fall down before the Lord our Maker! Then shall his anger be pleased to make in us a daily pass-over, and his bullets leveled at us must fly above us. —*Thomas Fuller*

"I have heard," says Mr. Daniel Wilson, in a sermon of his, "of a certain person whose name I could mention, who was tempted to conclude his day over, and himself lost; that, therefore, it was his best course to put an end to his life, which, if continued, would but serve to increase his sin, and consequently his misery, from which there was no escape; and seeing he must be in hell, the sooner he was there the sooner he should know the worst; which was preferable to his being worn away with the tormenting expectation of what was to come. Under the influence of such suggestions as these, he went to a river, with a design to throw himself in; but as he was about to do it, he seemed to hear a voice saying to him, 'Who can tell,' as if the words had been audibly delivered. By this, therefore, he was brought to a stand; his thoughts were arrested, and thus began to work on the passage mentioned: '*Who can tell?* (Jon. 3:9) viz., What God can do when he will proclaim his grace glorious. *Who can tell* but such an one as I may find mercy? or what will be the issue of humble prayer to heaven for it? *Who can tell* what purposes God will serve in my recovery?' By such thoughts as these, being so far influenced as to resolve to try, it pleased God graciously to enable him, through all his doubts and fears, to throw himself by faith on Jesus Christ, as able to save to the uttermost all that come to God by him, humbly desiring and expecting mercy for his sake, to his own soul. In this he was not disappointed; but afterwards became an eminent Christian and minister: and, from his own experience of the riches of grace, was greatly useful to the conversion and comfort of others." *Religious and Moral Anecdotes*

110

For the inhabitant of Maroth waited carefully for good: but evil came down from the Lord unto the gate of Jerusalem.

—*Micah 1:12*

HE village of the bitter spring (for such is probably the meaning of the name Maroth) experienced a bitter disappointment.

The more eager and patient their careful waiting, the more distasteful the draught of evil which they were compelled to drink.

Their trust in man proved to be vain, for the Assyrian swept over them, and stopped not till he reached the gate of Jerusalem, where Hezekiah's faith in God made the enemy pause and retreat.

Let us consider, as suggested by the text:

I. SAD DISAPPOINTMENTS. "waited carefully for good: but evil came."

Disappointments come frequently to the sanguine, but they also happen to those who wait—wait carefull, and expect reasonably.

1. Disappointments are often extremely painful at the time.
2. Yet could we know all the truth, we should not lament them.
3. In reference to hopes of several kinds they are certain. As for instance, when we expect more of the creature than it was ever meant to yield us, when we look for happiness in sin, when we expect fixity in earthly things, etc.
4. In many cases disappointments are highly probable. Conceited hopes, groundless expectations, speculations, etc.
5. In all cases they are possible. "There's many a slip 'twixt the cup and the lip."
6. They should be accepted with manly patience.
7. They may prove highly instructive, teaching us:
   - Our fallibility of judgment.
   - The uncertainty of sublunary things.
   - The need of reserve in speaking of the future (James 4:14).
   - The duty of submitting all our projects to the divine will.
8. They may be greatly sanctified.
   - Sometimes they have turned the current of a life.
   - They are intended to wean us from the world.
   - They tend to make us prize more the truthfulness of our God, who fulfills the desire of them that fear him.
   - They bring us precious things which can only come of experience.
   - They save us from unknown evils which might ruin us.

II. STRANGE APPOINTMENTS.

The text tells us, "evil came down from the Lord."

1. The expression must not be misunderstood. God is not the author of moral evil. It is the evil of sorrow, affliction, calamity that is here meant.
2. It is nevertheless universally true. No evil can happen without divine permission. "I make peace, and create evil" (Isa. 45:7).
3. Some evils are distinctly from the Lord. "This evil is of the Lord" (2 Kings 6:33).
   - For testing men, and making their true character to be known,
   - For chastening the good (1 Chron. 21:7).
   - For punishing the wicked (Gen. 6:5–7; 19:24–25).
4. Hence such evils are to be endured by the godly with humble submission to their heavenly Father's will.
5. Hence our comfort under them: since all evils are under divine control, their power to injure is gone.
6. Hence the antidote for our disappointments lies in the fact that they are God's appointments.

III. EXPECTATIONS WHICH WILL NOT END IN DISAPPOINTMENT.

1. Hopes founded on the promises of God (Heb. 10:23).
2. Confidence placed in the Lord Jesus (1 Pet. 2:6).
3. Desires presented in believing prayer (Matt. 21:22).
4. Harvest hopes in connection with sowing seed for the Lord (Ps. 126:5–6).
5. Expectations in falling asleep in Jesus (1 Thess. 4:14).

Is your life embittered by disappointment?

Cast the cross into the bitter water, and it will become sweet.

Gatherings

During the period when lotteries were unhappily allowed to flourish in this country, a gentleman, looking into the window of a lottery office in St. Paul's Churchyard, discovered to his joy that his ticket had turned up a £10,000 prize. Intoxicated with this sudden accession of wealth, he walked round the church-yard, to consider calmly how he should dispose of his fortune. On again, in his circuit, passing the lottery office, he resolved to take another glance at the charming announcement in the window, when, to his dismay, he saw that a new number had been substituted. On inquiry, he found that a wrong number had at first been posted by mistake, and that after all he was not the holder of the prize. His chagrin was now as great as his previous pleasure had been. —*W. Haig Miller's "Life's Pleasure Garden"*

It is wise, when we are disappointed in one thing, to set over against it a hopeful expectancy of another, like the farmer who said, "If the peas don't pay, let us hope the beans will." Yet it would be idle to patch up one rotten expecta-tion with another of like character, for that would only make the rent worse. It is better to turn from the fictions of the sanguine worldling to the facts of the believer in the Word of the Lord. Then, if we find no profit in our trading with earth, we shall fall back upon our heart's treasure in heaven. We *may* lose our gold, but we can never lose our God. The expectation of the righteous is from the Lord, and nothing that comes from him shall ever fail.

I knew one who had made an idol of his daughter, and when she sickened and died, he was exceedingly rebellious, and the result was that he died himself. Expectations which hang upon the frail tenure of a human life may fill our cup with wormwood if we indulge them. Could this father have owned the Lord's hand in the removal of his child, and had he beforehand moderated his expec-tations concerning her, he might have lived happily with the rest of his family, and have been an example of holy patience. —*C. H. S.*

Who has not muttered "Marah" over some well in the desert which he strained himself to reach, and found to be bitterness? Have you found no salt waters where you thought to find sweetness and joy? Love, beauty, the world's bright throngs, marriage, home, the things which once wooed you, and promised to slake the thirst of your soul for happiness, are they all Elims, sweet springs and palms? Oh, what fierce murmurings of "Marah" have I heard from hearts wrung with anguish, from souls withered and blasted by a too fond confidence in anything or any being but God! Believe it, no man, with a man's heart in him, gets far on his wilderness way without some bitter soul-searching disappointment; happy he who is brave enough to push on another stage of the journey, and rest in Elim, where there are twelve springs, living springs of water, and threescore and ten palm trees. —*I. B. Brown*

Disappointments in favorite wishes are trying, and we are not always wise enough to remember that disappointments in time are often the means of preventing disappointments in eternity. —*William Jay*

111

Even of late my people is risen up as an enemy.
—Micah 2:8

 HEN men are in trouble they are apt to blame God. But the blame lies with themselves. "Are these his doings?" (verse 7). Does the good Lord arbitrarily cause sorrows? No, they are the fruit of sin, the result of backsliding.

The Lord here answers Israel's complaint *of him* by a deeply truthful complaint *of them*.

They should not have wondered that they suffered, for they had become enemies to God, and thus enemies to themselves.

I. LET US LISTEN TO THE GRIEVOUS CHARGE.

There is a deep pathos about this as coming from the God of love.

1. They were his own people. "My people." God has enemies enough without his own beloved ones becoming such. It is horrible ingratitude and treachery for the chosen to rebel.
2. They had risen up "as an enemy." Faithless friends wound keenly, and are often more bitter than other antagonists. For favored ones to rise up as foes is cruel indeed.
3. They had lately done this: "even of late,"—"yesterday," in the margin. The sin is fresh, the wound is bleeding, the offense is rank. A fit of willfulness was on them.
4. They had done this wantonly (see latter part of verse). They picked a quarrel with One who is "averse from war." God would have our love, yet we turn against him without cause.

How far may this indictment lie against us?

II. LET US HEAR THE MORE GRIEVOUS EVIDENCE BY WHICH THE CHARGE IS SUBSTANTIATED.

Taking the words "my people" as referring to all professing Christians, many of them "rise up as an enemy" from the fact of:

1. Their separation from their Lord. "He that is not with me is against me" (Matt. 12:30). They walk not in communion with him, neither are they diligent in his service, nor careful in obedience, nor consecrated to his cause.

2. Their worldliness. By this the Lord's jealousy is moved, for the world is set up as his rival in the heart. "The friendship of the world is enmity with God" (James 4:4).

3. Their unbelief, which stabs at his honor, his veracity, his immutability (1 John 1:10). A man cannot treat another more maliciously than by calling him a liar.

4 Their heresies, fighting against his revealed truth. It is wretched work when the church and its ministers oppose the gospel. It is to be feared that this is by no means uncommon in these degenerate days.

5. Their unholiness. Unholy professors are, *par excellence*, "the enemies of the cross of Christ" (Phil. 3:18).

6. Their lukewarmness: by which they sicken their Savior (Rev. 3:16), grieve his Spirit (Eph. 4:30), encourage sinners in sin (Ezek. 16:54), and discourage seekers.

By these, and other miserable courses of action, those who should be the friends of God are often found to be "risen up as an enemy."

III. LET US HEARKEN TO MOST GRIEVOUS WARNINGS.

No good can possibly come of opposition to the Lord; but the most painful evils will inevitably ensue.

1. In the case of true Christians, there will come to them heavy chastisements and humiliations. If we walk contrary to the Lord, he will walk contrary to us (Lev. 26:23–24).

2. With these will come the keenest regrets, and agonies of heart. It may be pleasant to go down By-path Meadow, but to return to the King's highway will cost many a groan and tear.

3. In the case of mere professors, there will soon come abandonment of profession, immorality, seven-fold wickedness, etc.

4. To such may also come special punishments, which will make them a terror to the universe of God.

Be anxious to be truly reconciled to God by the blood of Jesus.

Abide in peace with God by yielding to his Spirit.

Increasingly love and honor him, that no root of bitterness may ever spring up between him and you.

Home-Thrusts

It is not, perhaps, that we are determinably his enemies, but his love is so great that he feels very keenly the slightest swerving of our hearts from him. So much so that he that is not with him is against him, he that turns aside from his friendship is felt to be "an enemy." —*From "Wounded in the House of his Friends," by F. M.*

Sin will cause repenting work, even for the children of God. The sins of the wicked pierce Christ's side, but the sins of the godly plunge the spear into his heart.

Carlyle, speaking of the changes made by time, says, "How tragic to me is the sight of old friends; a thing I always really shrink from!" Sin has made still more painful changes in some once numbered amongst the friends of God.

Pharnaces, the son of Mithridates, the king of Pontus, sending a crown to Caesar at the time he was in rebellion against him, he refused the present, saying, "Let him first lay down his rebellion, and then I will receive his crown." There are many who set a crown of glory upon the head of Christ by a good profession, and yet plant a crown of thorns upon his head by an evil conversation. —*Secker*

After poor Sabat, an Arabian, who had professed faith in Christ by the means of the labors of the Rev. H. Martyn, had apostatized from Christianity, and written in favor of Mohammedanism, he was met at Malacca by the late Rev. Dr. Milne, who proposed to him some very pointed questions, in reply to which, he said, "I am unhappy! I have a mountain of burning sand on my head. When I go about, I know not what I am doing!" It is indeed an evil thing and bitter to forsake the Lord our God. —*Bate's Cyclopaedia*

Blow, blow, thou winter wind,
Thou art not so unkind
   As man's ingratitude;
Thy tooth is not so keen,
Because thou art not seen,
   Although thy breath be rude.

Freeze, freeze thou bitter sky,
Thou cost not bite so nigh
   As benefits forgot:
Though more the waters warp,
Thy sting is not so sharp
   As friend remembered not.
         —*Shakespeare*

112

Oh my people, what have I done unto thee? and wherein have I wearied thee? testify against me.

—Micah 6:3

HIS is a portion of Jehovah's pleading with his people.

He has called upon the mountains and the strong foundations of the earth to hear the suit between him and Israel.

Far be it from us to trifle when God has a controversy with us, for to him it is a matter of deep solemnity. In condescending grace he makes much of the affection of his people, and he will not lose it without effort.

We have before us:

I. A PITEOUS EXCLAMATION. "O my people!"

Is it not remarkable that such language should be used by the Eternal God?

1 It is the voice of solemn earnestness.

2. It is the cry of sorrow. The interjection is wet with tears.

3. It is the appeal of love. Love injured, but living, pleading, striving, entreating.

4. It is the language of desire. Divine love yearns for the reconciliation of the rebel; it pines to have his loyal affection

The Lord calls a revolted nation "my people" still. Grace is stronger than sin. Eternal love is not founded upon our merits.

II. A PAINFUL FACT. "Wearied thee."

Israel acted as if they were tired of their God.

1. They were weary of his name. Baal and Ashtaroth had become the fashion, and the living God was despised.

2. They were weary of his worship. The sacrifice, the priest, the holy place, prayer, praise, etc.; all these were despised.

3. They were weary of obedience to his laws, though they were right, and just, and meant for their good.

4. They were weary of his restraints: they desired liberty to ruin themselves by transgression.

The parallel between ourselves and Israel lies upon the surface.

In the following points, and many more, certain professors prove their weariness of God:

- They give up nearness of communion.
- They abandon preciseness of walking.
- They fail in fullness of consecration.
- They cool down from intensity of zeal.

- They lose the full assurance of faith, and other joys.
- And all this because they are in reality weary of their God

This is a sorrow of sorrows to the great heart of love.

III. A PATIENT ENQUIRY. "What have I done unto thee?" etc.

Amazing love! God himself puts himself upon trial.

1. What single act of God could induce us to forsake his way? "What have I done unto thee?"
2. What continuous way of the Lord could have caused us weariness? "Wherein have I wearied thee?"
3. What testimony of any kind can we bear against God? "Testify against me."

No answer is possible except the most unreserved confession that the Lord has done us no ill.

The Lord is goodness itself, and unmingled kindness.

- He has not wearied us with demands of offering.
- He has not burdened us with austerities.
- He has not tired us with monotonies.
- He has not denied us rest, but has even commanded it.

If wearied with our God, it is:

- Because of our foolish waywardness.
- Because of our fickle fancy.
- Because of our feeble love to himself and holiness.
- Or because we have misunderstood his commands.

By all that God has already done for us, let us cling to him.

By the superlative excellence of Jesus, let us be bound to him.

By the sacred power of the Holy Ghost, may we be kept loving to the end.

Quotations

Now there is one thing to which we need to call the attention of backsliders; and that is—that the Lord never forsook them; but that they forsook him! The Lord never left them; but they left him! And this, too, without a cause! He says, "What iniquity have your fathers found in me, that they are gone far from me?" Is not God the same to-day as when you came to him first? Has God changed? Men are apt to think that God has changed; but the change is with them. Backslider, I would ask you, "What iniquity is there in God, that you have left him, and gone far from him?"

Love does not like to be forgotten. You mothers would break your hearts if your children left you, and never wrote you a word, or sent any momento of their affection for you: and God pleads over backsliders as a parent over loved ones who have gone astray; and he tries to woo them back. He asks, "What have I done that you should have forsaken me?" The most tender and loving words to be found in the whole of the Bible are from Jehovah to those who have left him without a cause. —D. L. Moody

Let those tempted to depart from the Lord remember the answer of Christian to Apollyon, when the latter sought to persuade him to turn back, and forsake his Lord: "O thou destroying Apollyon, to speak truth, I like his service, his wages, his servants, his government, his company, and country, better than thine; and, therefore, leave off to persuade me further: I am his servant, and I will follow him."

Polycarp, being required by an infidel judge to blaspheme Christ, made him this witty and devout answer: "Eighty-six years have I lived, neither did he once harm me in any one thing; why, then, should I blaspheme my God, which hath neither hindered me nor injured me?" We cannot charge our God with any wrong, our gracious Lord with any hardness, injury, or unkindness towards us; but must always, with Polycarp, acknowledge his exceeding bounty and unspeakable goodness. —*Richard Meredeth*

"*O my people, what have I done unto thee?*" or, rather, what have I not done to do thee good? "O generation, see ye the word of the Lord," and not hear it only; was ever anything more evidencing and evincing than what I now allege? "Have I been a wilderness unto Israel, a land of darkness?" (Jer. 2:31). May I not well say unto you, as Themistocles did to his ungrateful countrymen, "What? are ye weary of receiving so many benefits from one man?" But say, What hurt have I ever done you? and wherein have I wearied you, or been troublesome to you? unless it be by daily loading you with lovingkindnesses (Ps. 68:19), and bearing with your provocations? Forgive me that injury (2 Cor. 12:13). —*Trapp*

"*O my people,*" etc. If subjects quit their allegiance to their prince, they will pretend, as the ten tribes did when they revolted from Rehoboam, that his yoke is too heavy for them; but can you pretend any such thing? *What have I done to you* that is unjust or unkind? *Wherein have I wearied you* with the impositions of service, or the exaction of tribute? *Have I made you to serve with an offering?* (Isa. 43:23). —*Matthew Henry*

113

The Lord is good, a strong hold in the day of trouble; and he knoweth them that trust in him.

—*Nahum 1:7*

 ERE we come upon an island in Nahum's stormy lake. All is calm in this verse, though the whole context is tossed with tempest. The text is full of God, and brims over with his praise.

I. GOD HIMSELF. "Jehovah is good."

1. Good in himself essentially and independently.

2. Good eternally and unchangeable.

3. Good in each person: Father, Son, and Holy Ghost.

4. Good in all his acts of grace.

5. Good in all former acts of providence.

6. Good in his present act, be it what it may.

7. Good for a stronghold: to be trusted in trouble.

8. Good to his own people, who find their goodness in him.

Let us praise him as good in the most emphatic and unlimited sense. Whoever else may or may not be good, we know that the Lord is good. Yea, "there is none good but one, that is, God" (Matt. 19:17).

II. GOD TO US. "A strong hold in the day of trouble."

1. Under special circumstances our resort.

   The day of trouble, when trial is special and vehement.

   The *day* of trouble: temporary, but yet long enough to last through our life unless the Lord prevent.

   The day of *trouble*: when within, without, around, there seem to be only care, and fear, and want, and grief.

2. Securing our safety at all times: for a stronghold is always strong, even when there is no immediate war.

3. Maintaining our peace. Within the walls of a castle men walk at ease, for they are shut in from enemies.

4. Defying our foes, who dare not attack such a fortress.

5. Abiding for ever the same: always a sure refuge for the needy.

Let us run to him, as the poor people of the open country fly to the walled towns in the time of war.

III. GOD WITH US. "He knoweth them that trust in him."

The term "he knoweth them" includes:

1. His intimate acquaintance with their persons, conditions, etc.

2. His tender care to supply all their necessities.

3. His divine approval of them. To others he says, "I know you not" (Luke 13:25).

4. His loving communion with them, which is the best proof that they are known to him, and are his beloved friends.

5. His open acknowledgment: he owns them now, and will confess them before assembled worlds (Rev. 3:5).

Let us believe in the goodness of the Lord even when we cannot discern it with the eye of sense.

Let us fly to his protection when storms of trouble fall.

Let us confide in his loving care when hunted by our enemies.

Let us take care that we rely upon him, in Christ Jesus, for salvation.

Testimonies

The only place of safety in this world is the one in which we are sure to meet God, and to be "under the shadow of his wing." The Bible sets forth, in grand metaphor, this idea, by speaking of a "fortress into which the righteous runneth, and is safe"; and of "a strong tower," and of "the shadow of a great rock." When we were in the Yosemite Valley, lately, our driver told us of a series of terrific earthquakes, which visited the valley several years ago. The few inhabitants who dwelt there were thrown out of their beds in the night. Frail cottages were overturned. Loose rocks were hurled down from the precipices into the valley. These shocks were repeated for several days until the people were panic-stricken and ready to despair. "What did you do?" we inquired. The driver (pointing to the mighty and immovable rock, El Capitan, which rises for three thousand feet on the south side of the valley, and has a base of three solid miles) replied: "We determined to go and camp under old *Capitan*; for if that ever moved we knew the world would be coming to an end." —*Dr. Cuyler*

Tamar may disguise herself, and walk in an unaccustomed path, so that Judah may not know her; Isaac, through the dimness of his sight, may bless Jacob, and pass over Esau; want of time may make Joseph forget, or be forgotten of, his brethren; Solomon may doubt to whom of right the child belongeth; and Christ may come to his own, and not be received: but the Lord knoweth them that are his, and his eye is always over them. Time, place, speech, or apparel cannot obscure or darken his eye or ear. He can discern Daniel in the den; and Job, though never so much changed, on the dung-hill. Let Jonah be lodged in the whale's belly, Peter be put into a close prison, or Lazarus be wrapped in rags, or Abel rolled in blood, yet can he call them by name, and send his angels to comfort them. Ignorance and forgetfulness may cause love and knowledge to be estranged in the creature, but the Lord is not incident to either, for his eye, as his essence, is everywhere; he knoweth all things. —*Spencer's "Things New and Old"*

A safe stronghold our God is still,
    A trusty shield and weapon;
He'll help us clear from all the ill
    That hath us now o'ertaken.
The ancient Prince of hell
    Hath risen with purpose fell;
Strong mail of craft and power
    He weareth in this hour,
On earth is not his fellow.
With force of arms we nothing can,

> Full soon were we down-trodden;
> But for us fights the proper Man,
>   Whom God himself hath bidden.
> Ask ye, "Who is this same?"
>   Christ Jesus is his name,
> The Lord Zebaoth's Son,
>   He and no other one
> Shall conquer in the battle.
>   —*Martin Luther*

Many talk of trusting God when indeed they know nothing of real faith. How are we to know who is, and who is not, a believer? This question is hard to answer in times of prosperity, but not in the day of trouble: then the true truster is calm and quiet in his God, and the mere pretender is at his wits' end. Our text seems to hint as much. Everybody can find a bird's nest in winter when the trees are bare, but the green leaves hide them; so are believers discovered by adversity. One thing, however, should never be forgotten: whether we know believers or not, God knows them. He does not include one hypocrite in the number, nor exclude one sincere truster, even though he be of little faith. He knows infallibly, and universally. Does he know me, even me, as one of those who trust in him? The Lord knoweth them that are his, and they know him as their stronghold. Have I such knowledge?

114

I will stand upon my watch, and set me upon the tower, and will watch to see what he will say unto me, and what I shall answer when I am reproved. And the Lord answered me, and said, Write the vision, and make it plain upon the tables, that he may run that readeth it. For the vision is yet for an appointed time, but at the end it shall speak, and not lie: though it tarry, wait for it; because it will surely come, it will not tarry. Behold, his soul which is lifted up is not upright in him: but the just shall live by his faith.
—*Habakkuk 2:1–4*

 HE promise of God tarried, and the ungodly triumphed.
Here was the old problem of David in another form. "Wherefore lookest thou upon them that deal treacherously?" (Hab. 1:13) is but a repetition of "I was envious at the foolish, when I saw the prosperity of the wicked" (Ps. 73:3).

This same problem occurs to ourselves, and this text may help us.

Observe with understanding:

I. THE SENSE IN WHICH THERE IS A DELAY IN THE PROMISE.

It is not every apparent delay which is real. Our time and God's time are not measured upon the same dial.

1. Each promise will bide its due season for fulfillment: "For the vision is yet for an appointed time."
2. Each promise in the end will prove true: "At the end it shall speak, and not lie."
3. Each promise will repay our waiting: "Though it tarry, wait for it."
4. Each promise will really be punctual to its hour: "It will surely come, it will not tarry."

The word of the Lord is as true to the time as to the thing.

To him its time of ripening is short: only to us is it long.

II. THE ATTITUDE OF A BELIEVER WHILE THE PROMISE DELAYS.

We should watch for the appearing of the Lord in fulfillment of his promise, and should be prepared to receive reproof as well as blessing.

The prophet took up:

1. A determined and thoughtful attitude: "I will stand, and set me."
2. An attentive attitude: "and will watch to see what he will say unto me." He is engrossed in this one pursuit: he only desires to be taught of the Lord.
3. A patient attitude: "I will set me upon the tower." It is as if he had been set as a sentinel, and would remain at his post.
4. A solitary position if need be. He speaks of himself alone.
5. A humble and submissive frame of mind: "what I shall answer when I am reproved."

In all respects the man of God is ready for his Lord.

The delay is evidently a blessing to him.

The blessing will be the greater when it comes.

III. THE WORK OF THE LORD'S SERVANT WHILE THE PROMISE DELAYS.

1. By faith see the vision. Realize the fulfillment of the divine word in your own soul. "Watch to see what he will say."
2. Declare it as certain: record it in black and white, as a fact not to be questioned. "Write the vision upon tables."
3. Declare it plainly, so that the runner may read it.
4. Declare it practically, so that he that readeth may run in consequence of it.
5. Declare it permanently: write down the matter for a record to be referred to: engrave it on tablets for perpetuity.

Sham faith prudently declines to mention her expectations.

It is deemed presumptuous, fanatical, and imprudent to be positive that God will keep his promise; and still more to say so.

The real believer thinks not so, but acts with the Lord's promises as he would deal with engagements made in business by honest men: he treats them as real, and would have others do the like.

IV. THE DIFFERENCE SEEN IN MEN WHEN THE DELAY OF THE PROMISE TESTS THEM.

1. The graceless man is too proud to wait on God as the Lord's servant will do. "His soul is not upright in him."
   - He is himself dishonest, and so suspects his God.
   - This prevents his finding comfort in the promise.
2. The just man believes the word of a holy God. He waits serenely, in full assurance; and He lives in the highest sense by his faith.

"My soul, wait thou only upon God" (Ps. 62:5).

What can he do who has no faith in his Maker? (Heb. 11:6)

From Our Tablets

It was a custom among the Romans for the public affairs of every year to be committed to writing by the *pontifex maximus*, or high priest, and published on a table. They were thus exposed to public view, so that the people might have an opportunity of being acquainted with them. It was also usual to hang up laws approved and recorded on tables of brass in their market-places, and in their temples, that they might be seen and read (*Tacitus*). In like manner, the Jewish prophets used to write, and expose their prophecies publicly on tables, either in their own houses, or in the temple, that every one that passed by might go in and read them. —*Burder*

> And though it linger till the night,
>   And round again till morn,
> My heart shall ne'er mistrust thy might,
>   Nor count itself forlorn.
> Do thus, O ye of Israel's seed.
>   Ye of the Spirit born indeed;
> Wait for your God's appearing!
>   —*Martin Luther*

Good old Spurstow says that "some of the promises are like the almond tree— they blossom hastily in the very earliest spring; but," saith he, "there are others which resemble the mulberry tree—they are very slow in putting forth their leaves." Then what is a man to do, if he has a mulberry-tree promise, which is late in blossoming? Why, he is to wait till it does blossom; since it is not in his power to hasten it. If the vision tarry, exercise the precious grace called patience, and the appointed time shall surely bring you a rich reward. —*C. H. S.*

God's promises are dated, but with a mysterious character; and, for want of skill in God's chronology, we are prone to think God forgets us; when, indeed, we forget ourselves in being so bold as to set God a time of our own, and in being angry that he comes not just then to us. —*Gurnall*

If we were more humble, we should be more patient. A beggar, who is worn with hunger, will wait at the rich man's gate for many an hour with the hope of getting broken victuals; but my lord, who is in no need, will soon be gone if the door does not open to his knock. We have kept the Lord waiting long enough, and we need not wonder if he tries our faith and patience by apparent delays. In any case, let us settle this in our hearts, that he must and will fulfill his promises. Our text shows us a punctual God, a patient waiter, and a published confidence; but it finishes up with a proud unbeliever. Or, if you will, it is man uttering a brave resolve, and the Lord answering to his faith; reasons presented to patient faith, and rebukes to impatient pride.

115

Behold, his soul which is lifted up is not upright in him: but the just shall live by his faith.

—*Habakkuk 2:4*

ELAY of deliverance is a weighing of men. Suspense is very trying, and constitutes a searching test.

This divides men into two classes by bringing out their real character.

The proud and the just stand out in relief: the uplifted and the upright are far as the poles asunder; and the result of trial in the two cases is as different as death from life.

The tarrying of the promise:

I. REVEALS A GREAT FAULT. "his soul which is lifted up."

The man is impatient, and will not endure to wait. This is pride full-blown, for it quarrels with the Lord, and dares to dictate to him.

1. It is very natural to us to be proud. So fell our first father, and we inherit his fault.

2. Pride takes many shapes, and among the rest this vainglorious habit of thinking that we ought to be waited on at once.

3. In all cases pride is unreasonable. Who are we that God should make himself our servant, and take his time from our watch?

4. In every case pride is displeasing to God, and specially when it interferes with the sovereign liberty of his own grace. Shall he be dictated to in the matter of his own love? "Nay but, O man, who art thou that repliest against God?" (Rom. 9:20).

II. BETRAYS A SAD EVIL. "his soul is not upright in him."

1. He does not know the truth. His mind is out of the perpendicular, his knowledge is incorrect, and his judgment is mistaken. He puts "bitter for sweet, and sweet for bitter" (Isa. 5:20).

2. He does not seek the light. His heart is not upright: the affections are perverted. He has a bias towards conceited views of self, and does not wish to be set right (Obad. 1:3).

3. His whole religion is warped by his false mood of heart and mind. The very soul of the man is put out of order by his vanity.

4 He will not endure the test of waiting; he will sin in his haste to be delivered; he will rush from God to other confidences; he will show by his life that his real self is not right with God.

III. DISCOVERS A SERIOUS OPPOSITION.

He grows tired of the gospel, which is the sum of the promises, and he becomes averse to the exercise of the faith which it requires.

His pride makes him reject salvation by grace through faith in Jesus.

1. He is too great to consider it.

2. He is too wise to believe it.

3. He is too good to need it.

4. He is too advanced in "culture" to endure it.

Most of the objections to revealed truth arise from a mind thrown out of balance by pride of intellect, or pride of purse, or pride of heart.

IV. DIRECTS US TO A PLEASING CONTRAST.

1. The man who is really just is truly humble. The text implies a contrast in this respect between the proud and the just.

2. Being humble, he does not dare to doubt his God, but yields to his word an implicit faith.

3. His faith keeps him alive under trial, and conducts him into the joys and privileges of spiritual life.

4 His life conquers the trial, and develops into life eternal.

The Believer has the blessing promised, and truly lives while he lives.

The Unbeliever misses the blessing, and is dead while he lives.

What folly to refuse faith because of pride, and so to miss eternal life and all its felicities!

Quotations

"I think it is decidedly unscriptural to fix any time with God for his doing anything. The times and seasons the Father hath put in his own hand. The Man Christ Jesus has asked for the heathen, and he *will* get them, but he has waited eighteen hundred years already, and has told us that as Man he knows nothing of the 'when.' Pray on, and believe; you *shall* reap." —*From a letter of Brownlow North to a Christian worker*

Strange that the mortal, who cannot believe in the healing power of the sparkling Jordan, will often willingly go down to the muddiest creek of Abana and Pharpar! —*Edward Garrett*

As the first step heavenward is humility, so the first step hellward is pride. Pride counts the gospel foolishness, but the gospel always shows pride to be so. Shall the sinner be proud who is going to hell? Shall the saint be proud who is newly saved from it? God had rather his people fared poorly than live proudly. —*Mason*

Poverty of spirit is the bag into which Christ puts the riches of his grace. —*Rowland Hill*

We must be emptied of self before we can be filled with grace; we must be stripped of our rags before we can be clothed with righteousness; we must be unclothed that we may be clothed; wounded, that we may be healed; killed, that we may be made alive; buried in disgrace, that we may rise in holy glory. These words, "Sown in corruption, that we may be raised in in corruption; sown in dishonor, that we may be raised in glory; sown in weakness, that we may be raised in power," are as true of the soul as of the body. To borrow an illustration from the surgeon's art: the bone that is set wrong must be broken again, in order that it may be set aright. I press this truth on your attention. It is certain that a soul filled with self has no room for God; and like the inn at Bethlehem, crowded with meaner guests, a heart pre-occupied by pride and her godless train, has no chamber within which Christ may be born in us "the hope of glory." —*Guthrie*

A heart full of pride is but a vessel full of air; this self-opinion must be blown out of us before saving knowledge be poured into us. Humility is the knees of the soul, and to that posture the Lamb will open the book; but pride stands upon tip-toes, as if she would snatch the book, and unclasp it herself. The first lesson of a Christian is humility; and he that hath not learned the first lesson is not fit to take out a new. —*Thomas Adams*

But for pride, the angels, who are in hell, should be in heaven (Jude 6); but for pride, Nebuchadnezzar, who is in the forest, should be in his palace (Dan. 4); but for pride, Pharaoh, who lies with the fishes, should be with his nobles (Exod. 14); no sin hath pulled so many down as this, which promised to set them up. Of all the children of pride, the Pope is the father, which sitteth in the temple of God, and is worshipped as God (2 Thess. 2:4). . . . But for pride, the Pharisees would have received Christ as gently as his disciples; but for pride, Herod would have worshipped Christ as humbly as the shepherds; but for pride, our men would go like Abraham, and our women like Sarah, as they would be called their children; but for pride, noblemen would come to church as well as the people; but for pride, gentles would abide reproof as well as servants; but for pride, thou wouldst forgive thy brother, and the lawyers should have no work. —*Henry Smith*

116

Behold, his soul which is lifted up is not upright in him: but he just shall live by his faith.
                                        —*Habakkuk 2:4*

For therein is the righteousness of God revealed from faith to faith: as it is written, The just shall live by faith.   —*Romans 1:17*

But That no man is justified by the law in the sight of God, it is evident: for, The just shall live by faith.   —*Galations 3:11*

Now the just shall live by faith: but if any man draw back, my soul shall have no pleasure in him.   —*Hebrews 10:38*

 HEN the Spirit of God frequently repeats himself, he thereby appeals for special attention.

A doctrine so often declared must be of the first importance.

A doctrine so often declared should be constantly preached.

A doctrine so often declared should be unhesitatingly received by each one of our hearers.

I. WE WILL TREAT THE FOUR TEXTS AS ONE.

The teaching is clear. "The just shall live by his faith."

1. Life is received by the faith which makes a man just.

   • A man begins to live by a full acquittal from condemnation, and from penal death, so soon as he believes in Jesus.

- A man begins to live as one raised out of spiritual death so soon as he has faith in the Lord Jesus Christ.

No form of works, or profession, or knowledge, or even of natural feelings, can prove him to be an absolved and quickened man; but faith does this.

2. Life is sustained by the faith which keeps a man just.

- He who is forgiven and quickened lives ever afterwards as he began to live—namely, by faith. Neither his feelings, nor devotions, nor acquirements ever become his trust: he still looks out of himself to Jesus. He is nothing except so far as he is a believer.
- He lives by faith as to all the forms of his life:
  > As a child, and as a servant;
  > As a pilgrim progressing, and as a warrior contending;
  > As a pensioner enjoying, and as an heir expecting.
- He lives by faith in every condition:
  > In joy and in sorrow; in wealth and in poverty;
  > In strength and in weakness; in laboring and in languishing; in life and in death.
- He lives best when faith is at its best, even though in other respects he may be sorely put to it. He lives the life of Christ most blessedly when most intensely he believes in Christ.

Hearty belief in God, his Son, his promises, his grace, is the soul's life, neither can anything take its place. "Believe and live" is a standing precept both for saint and sinner. "Now abideth faith" (1 Cor. 13:13).

II. WE WILL TREAT THE FOUR TEXTS SEPARATELY.

If we read with precision, we shall see that Scripture contains no repetitions. The context gives freshness of meaning to each apparent repetition.

1. Our first text (Hab. 2:4) exhibits faith as enabling a man to live on in peace and humility, while as yet the promise has not come to its maturity. While waiting, we live by faith, and not by sight.
   - We are thus able to bear up under the temporary triumphs of the wicked. See the first chapter of Habakkuk's prophecy.
   - We are thus preserved from proud impatience at delay.
   - We are thus filled with delight in confident expectation of good things to come.

2. Our second text (Rom. 1:17) exhibits faith as working salvation from the evil which is in the world through lust. The chapter in which it stands presents an awful view of human nature, and implies that only faith in the gospel can bring us life in the form of:
   - Mental enlightenment of life as to the true God (Rom. 1:19–23).
   - Moral purity of life (Rom. 1:24 ff.).
   - Spiritual life and communion with that which is divine and holy.

- Naturally men are dead and corrupt. The law reveals our death (Rom. 3:10–20); but the gospel imparts spiritual life to those who receive it by faith.

3. Our third text (Gal. 3:11) exhibits faith as bringing to us that justification which saves us from the sentence of death.

Nothing can be plainer, more positive, more sweeping than this declaration that no man is justified before God except by faith. Both the negative and the positive are plain enough.

4. Our fourth text (Heb. 10:38) exhibits faith as the life of final perseverance.
- There is need of faith while waiting for heaven (verses 32–36).
- The absence of such faith would cause us to draw back (verse 38).
- That drawing back would be a fatal sign.
- That drawing back can never occur, for faith saves the soul from all hazards, keeping its face heavenwards even to the end.

What can you do who have no faith?

In what other way can you be accepted with God?

On what ground can you excuse your unbelief in your God?

Will you perish sooner than believe him?

Breviates

The Jews in the Talmud have the saying, "The whole law was given to Moses at Sinai, in six hundred and thirteen precepts." David, in the fifteenth Psalm, brings them all within the compass of eleven. Isaiah brings them to six (Isa. 33:15); Micah to three (Mic. 6:8); Isaiah, again, to two (Isa. 56); Habakkuk to this one, "The just shall live by his faith." —*Lightfoot*

The soul is the life of the body. Faith is the life of the soul. Christ is the life of faith. —*Flavel*

> Inscribed upon the portal from afar
> Conspicuous as the brightness of a star,
> Legible only by the light they give
> Stand the soul-quickening words—Believe and Live.
>
> —*Cowper*

To believe God is not a little thing: it is the index of a heart reconciled to God, and the token of true spirituality of mind; it is the essence of true worship, and the root of sincere obedience. He who believes his God in spite of his sins, does him more honor than cherubim and seraphim in their continual adoration. A little thing faith! How is it then that unbelief is so great a crime that it is marked out for reprobation as the one damning evil which shuts men out of heaven? Despise not faith lest you despise God. Whatever else you put in the second place, give faith the lead; it is not a vain thing, for it is your life.

117

Seek ye the Lord, all ye meek of the earth, which have wrought his judgment; seek righteousness, seek meekness: it may be ye shall be hid in the day of the Lord's anger.

—*Zephaniah 2:3*

 HERE is a "may be" about all temporal things; and in pleading for them we ask with much diffidence.

Yet we may plead confidently when our appeal is made to God in the day of his anger. Then our need is pressing: it is for our life that we are pleading, and the Lord is very gracious in our extremities.

In spiritual things we may draw encouragement from the faintest sign of hope when it proceeds from God: "it may be ye shall be hid."

The seeking for refuge, here commanded, is directed only to the meek and righteous; but it is our joy to proclaim a hiding place for the guilty, and to bid them seek the Lord even on the least encouragement.

The three seekings commanded are:

- "Seek the Lord"; or, repent and trust in Jehovah.
- "Seek righteousness." Directed as it is in the text to those who are already righteous, it bids them persevere in righteousness
- "Seek meekness." Spoken to the meek, it bids them bow even more humbly before the chastening hand of God.

But our point is this: that we may seek the Lord upon the faintest encouragement. There are strong inducements and large promises; but if we cannot grasp these we may come even with a "may be."

I. IN MANY A RECORDED INSTANCE "MAY BE" HAS PROMPTED AND JUSTIFIED A RIGHT ACTION.

From the cases which we will mention lessons may be learned.

1. A "may be" led Jonathan to attack the garrison of the Philistines (1 Sam. 14:6). "It may be that the Lord will work for us: for there is no restraint to the Lord to save by many or by few." This should nerve saints for holy enterprises.

2. A "may be" cheered David when Absalom rebelled, and Shimei cursed (2 Sam. 16:12). "It maybe that the Lord will look on mine affliction." Let us hope in God in our darkest hours.

3. A "may be" induced the lepers to visit the Syrian camp (2 Kings 7:4). Their desperate venture should be laid to heart by those who are in like condition. They can but perish in any case; let them seek the Lord, and try whether he does not save.

4. A "may be," diluted with an "if so be," moved the afflicted to humble himself. See Jeremiah's Lamentations 3:29. Let no tried soul refuse the like hope.

5. A "may be," in the form of "Who can tell?" brought all Nineveh to repentance (Jon. 3:9).

If others have acted so vigorously upon such slender encouragement, may not we, when dreading the ruin of our souls, act with like decision and hopefulness? If we fly to Jesus by childlike faith, there is more than a "may be" that the result will be happy.

II. IN THE INSTANCE OF A SINCERE SEEKER THE "MAY BE" HAS UNUSUAL STRENGTH.

There is every probability of the penitent obtaining salvation if we:

1. Consider the gracious nature of our God (Mic. 7:18).
2. Consider the glorious work of Christ for sinners (1 Tim. 1:15).
3. Consider the mercy they have already received. "It is of the Lord's mercies that we are not consumed" (Lam. 3:22).
4. Consider the number and character of those who have been saved. (Rev. 5:9; 7:9; 1 Cor. 6:11).
5. Consider the omnipotence of the Holy Spirit (John 3:8).
6. Consider the glory which is to be the Lord's at the last: surely it will come by saving souls, and saving many of them.

III. BUT IN THE SEEKERS CASE HE HAS FAR MORE TO GO UPON THAN A MERE "MAY BE."

There are innumerable sure promises in the Word of God, and these are made to:

- Repentance (Prov. 28:13; Isa. 55:7).
- Faith (Mark 16:16; John 3:18; Acts 16:31).
- Prayer (Matt. 7:7; Acts 2:21).

Let these promises be studied, and their encouragement accepted by immediate compliance with their requirements.

- Consider that God foresaw all events when he made these promises, and accordingly he has not made them in error.
- Consider that he cannot withdraw his promise.
- Consider that he is the same as when he made the promise, and so in effect makes it again every day.
- Consider that it will be a crime to doubt the Lord our God, and an act of reverence to believe him. Venture now upon the bare promise of God, who cannot lie (Titus 1:2).

O sinner, seek the Lord!

He comes to you in Christ Jesus. Look to him at once, and live.

Cheering Words

Possibly ye may be hid from punishment, probably ye shall escape sorrow: but pardon of sin ye shall be sure of; mitigation also of sorrow, if not prevention of it. Saved ye shall be, or more gently handled, or so inwardly calmed, that ye shall be able to call your souls to rest when others are at their wits' ends. You shall be safe under the cover of God's wings, and in the hollow of his hand; when others, that are without God in the world, shall be as a naked man in a storm, as an unarmed man in the field of battle, or as a ship at sea without an anchor, subject to dash and split against rocks and quicksands. —*Trapp*

Dr. John Duncan was once heard thus addressing a beggar-woman in Edinburgh—"Now, you'll promise me that you'll seek: but mind, seeking will not save you, yet it is your duty; and if you seek you'll find,. and finding will save you."

Our hope is not hung upon such untwisted thread as "I imagine so', or, 'it is likely"; but the cable, the strong rope of our fastened anchor is the oath and promise of him who is eternal verity; our salvation is fastened with God's own hand, and Christ's own strength, to the strong stake of God's unchanging nature. —*Rutherford*

How long a beggar will wait, and how eagerly he will plead, although he has no promise of an alms, but only the bare chance of winning a penny from a passer-by! How laboriously will fishers cast their nets again and again, though nothing has been taken as yet, and their only encouragement is the possibility that fish may come that way! How desperately will men dive into the sea with the expectation of finding pearls in oyster-shells, encountering fierce monsters of the deep with the uncertain hope of being enriched! And will not men draw near to God when their outlook is so much more bright, their expectation so much more justifiable? As for me, I will lay down my sick soul at Christ's feet, in sure and certain belief that he will heal me, and then I will follow him whithersoever he goeth, in calm assurance that he will lead me to his eternal kingdom and glory. —*C. H. S.*

118

She obeyed not the voice; she received not correction; she trusted not in the Lord; she drew not near to her God.

—Zephaniah 3:2

WHEN the Lord is judging men he does not spare those who are called his people: Moab and Ammon and Nineveh are visited, and Jerusalem is not spared.

There are sins which outsiders cannot commit, such as those of the text. When peculiar privileges only create peculiar sins, they will be followed by peculiar punishments.

The offenses mentioned in this verse are to be found in nations, churches, and individuals unto this day: and in a measure among God's own people.

I. IN THE TEXT WE PERCEIVE FOUR MANIFEST SINS.

1. We will make upon them, as a whole, four observations.
   - Sins of omission are sure to exist where there are sins of commission. Jerusalem is said to be "filthy and polluted," and then these omissions are recited.
   - Sins of omission rank with the blackest of offenses. Consider the context, and see with what fearful crimes omissions are catalogued, as if to mark their vileness.
   - Sins of omission go in clusters. "She obeyed not." "She received not instruction." "She trusted not." "She drew not near to her God." How many foul birds may dwell in one nest! One sin never goes alone.
   - Sins of omission are none the less when they are mainly spiritual. Such are those mentioned in the text, and they are cited among crimes of deepest dye.
2. We will note each one of the four separately.
   - They heard God speak, but they took no heed. This included rebellion, hardness of heart, presumption, and defiance of the Lord; and all this after solemn warnings, great instruction, and tender invitation.
   - They felt correction, but were not instructed. This involved greater persistence in rebellion, and still more obduracy of heart.
   - They were unbelieving and distrustful, and relied upon idols, and not upon the Lord. Unbelief is a master-sin.
   - They had no communion with their God. "Her God" implies existence of covenant-relationship, in name at least; but there was no worship, love, or service.

These four sins abound around us, and among us.

Inattention, Obstinacy, Unbelief, and Aversion to God are all common.

They involve men in misery in this life, and in eternal ruin in the world to come. Are they not destroying some of you?

II. IN THE TEXT WE SPY OUT FOUR HIDDEN ENCOURAGEMENTS TO SEEK BETTER THINGS.

Let those who confess their sin look at the text with hope, for it is clear that:
1. God does speak to men. He may speak to us again.
2. God corrects for our good. It is meant for instruction, not for destruction (see the margin).
3. God would have us trust him. He would not blame us for not trusting if we were not permitted to trust him.

4. God would have us draw near to him. Else it were not mentioned as our sin that we do not draw near to him.

All this applies to us at this day.

Still the Lord is in the midst of us, reading our inmost souls.

Let us lay our sins to heart, and seek his face through Christ Jesus.

A Few Small Fishes

Remember, O my soul, the fig tree was charged, not with bearing noxious fruit, but no fruit. —*Thomas Fuller*

The last words that Archbishop Usher was heard to say were these: "Lord, forgive my sins, especially my sins of omission."

Sins of commission are usual punishments for sins of omission. He that leaves a duty may soon be left to commit a crime. —*Gurnall*

No sin is ever alone. Dr. Macdonald says, "There is no fault that does not bring its brothers and sisters and cousins to live with it."

Oh, how rare it is to find a soul still enough to hear God speak! —*Fenelon*

Grace turns the serpent into a rod; but sin turns the rod into a serpent. The former turns poison into a remedy; but the latter turns the remedy into poison. —*Benjamin Beddome*

Sorrow is sent for our instruction, just as we darken the cages of birds when we would teach them to sing. *Jean Paul Richter*

119

Then said Haggai, If one that is unclean by a dead body touch any of these, shall it be unclean? And the priests answered and said, It shall be unclean.

Then answered Haggai, and said, So is this people, and so is this nation before me, saith the Lord; and so is every work of their hands; and that which they offer there is unclean.

—*Haggai 2:13–14*

 HE prophet makes the priests witness against themselves and the people. This was a powerful means of forcing home the truth.

It is clear from verse 12 that the mere bearing of a holy thing did not enable the bearer to communicate consecration.

But the priests owned that the touch of an unclean person did communicate uncleanness.

What a picture! An unclean person making everything unclean wherever he laid his hand! He could not move without spreading defilement on all sides.

Such were the erring people of Haggai's day in the judgment of their God, and he never judges too severely.

Such are sinful men at this day.

I. THE TERRIBLE UNCLEANNESS. *Here we keep to our text.*

For a New Testament exposition, read Titus 1:15.

1. Common things are polluted by men of unclean nature.

   Nothing is common or unclean naturally; for every creature of God is good (1 Tim. 4:4). But in diverse ways the things of ordinary life are made to be unclean:
   - By making gods of them, saying, "What shall we eat?" etc.
   - By excess in the use of them. By gluttony, drunkenness, etc.
   - By excess in the keeping of them. A miser's goods are accursed.
   - By ingratitude concerning them. Then they remain unblessed.

2. Holy things are polluted by men of unclean nature.
   - They use the gospel as an excuse for sin.
   - They offer prayer in solemn mockery.
   - They make praise into a musical performance.
   - They turn the sacraments into hypocrisy or worse.
   - There is nothing so holy but that sin can defile it.

3. Good works are polluted when they come from evil men: "so is every work of their hands."
   - They can be charitable for ostentation.
   - They can he religious to be seen of men.
   - They can be sternly righteous in order to be revenged.
   - They can be humble to gain their ends.

4. Sacrifices are polluted when offered by unclean men: "and that which they offer there is unclean."
   - Their public thanksgivings are a falsehood.
   - Their solemn fasts are a mere comedy.

What a wretched condition is he in who even in his holiest acts is defiling everything! He may well pause and humble himself before God, for the more he does in his present state the more does he defile.

Sin has cast a serpent's trail over the whole universe, making the creation itself subject to vanity. What does man touch which he does not degrade and pollute? Here is a wide field for thought, and abundant cause for humiliation.

II. THE ALL-SUFFICIENT REMEDY. *Here we go beyond our text.*

In Numbers 19, we have the type of the great remedy, and a fuller account of the uncleanness which it removed.

In the rites used for purifying the unclean:

1. There was a sacrifice (Num. 19 :2-4): "A red heifer without spot." This must be slain. Without shedding of blood there is no remission of sin (Heb. 9:22).
2. There was a burning (verses 5 and 6). Sin is hateful, and we must see it to be such; it must be burned without the camp.
3. There was a water of separation. Having been purged with blood of sacrifice, we must be sprinkled with water of sanctification.
4. There was an application with hyssop. Faith must receive the cleansing. "Purge me with hyssop and I shall be clean."
5. This must cleanse our whole nature (see verse 19). There was a washing of the whole man and his garments.

All that this type intended may be found:
- In the water and the blood which flowed from the side of our Lord; manifesting the doubly cleansing power of his sacrifice: and
- In the efficacious work of the Holy Spirit.

See, O sinner, your need of cleansing before you attempt anything.

Before this, nothing you are, or have, or do, is clean before God.

After this, all things shall be holy to you.

See to this cleansing at once, and all else will follow in due course.

Vivacities

"My friends say everywhere that I am not a Christian. I have just given them the lie direct by performing my Easter devotions (mes paques) publicly, thus proving to all my lively desire to terminate my long career in the religion in which I was born, and I have fulfilled this important act after a dozen attacks of consecutive fever, which made me fear I should die before I could assure you of my respect and my devotion." —*Voltaire, to Madame Du Barri* (What a specimen of polluted holy things!)

Those whose devotions are plausible, but whose conversation is wicked, will find their devotions unable to sanctify their enjoyments, but their wickedness prevailing to pollute them.

When we are employed in any good work, we should be jealous over ourselves, lest we render it unclean by our corruptions and mismanagement. —*Matthew Henry*

Diogenes, standing beside a foul bath, was heard to exclaim, "Where shall those be washed who wash here?" When even the religious duties of men are defiled, what hope can they have of making themselves clean? Those who turn prayer into a mockery, and sacraments into a show, have turned medicine into poison; and how shall they be healed?

A child has taken an infectious disease. He comes to fondle you, and you push him away. He moves the furniture, and you command him to take his hands off. He must be shut up, and kept from contact with the household. Suppose he persists in leaving his room, and joining with the rest of the family. No matter how kind his motive, he is doing wrong, and acting mischievously. The more industriously he works about the house, and runs to and fro, the more does he spread the disorder. The household work which he does would be well enough if he were but in health: as it is, his every movement is a danger, and his best endeavors are perilous. The child must be healed before he can do real good in the family: while he is infected he pollutes all that he touches, and injures all whom he approaches. Oh, that unconverted men were wise enough to see that what they need, at first, is not so much work to do, as cleansing from pollution, in order that they may be able to do good works.

At one of the Ragged-schools in Ireland, a clergyman asked the question, "What is holiness?" After some pause, a poor Irish convert, in dirty, tattered rags, jumped up, and said, "Plaise your Riverence, it's to be clane inside." —*G. S. Bowes*

120

For who hath despised the day of small things?
—*Zechariah 4:10*

 REAT numbers of persons do despise "the day of small things." If they were wise, they would not do so; for it is not wise to despise anything, and to despise a thing because it is small is great folly.

A small thing may be greatly good, or terribly evil; and in neither case would it be prudent to despise it.

It is usually God's way to begin his great works with a day of small things
- Thus it is seen that there is nothing in the means themselves.
- Thus the divine power is more fully displayed.
- Thus faith is exercised, and made to learn many lessons

Why should men despise what God ordains?

Who are those persons who dare act thus contemptuously? They are not entitled to give themselves such airs: yet they dare to do so.

They show their contempt in various ways.
- They affect pity for such feebleness (Neh. 4:2).
- They decry, and find fault (1 Sam. 17:28).
- They sneer, and ridicule (Matt. 8:5; Acts 17:18).
- They leave alone, with silent neglect (Acts 5:8).

It is a sad pity when this contempt is poured upon a beginner in grace, for it may cause him sad distress and discouragement.

Our object at this time is to reprove those who despise the earlier and weaker works of grace in the soul. True it is "the day of small things," but this is to be rejoiced in, and is not to be despised.

Let us commune with:

I. THOSE WHO DESPISE OTHERS WHO ARE IN THE DAY OF SMALL THINGS.

1. Do you not know that there are babes in grace, and that these are true children of God? Do you doubt that evident fact?
2. Were you not once such little ones yourselves? If you never were, who are you to despise your betters?
3. Were not the greatest of the saints once very feeble? Would you have acted thus to them?
4. May not the strong be glad at times to be as sure of salvation as these little ones? Why despise those whom you may yet envy?
5. Does not our Lord care tenderly for the lambs? (Isa. 40:11).
6. Has He not threatened all proud despisers? (Matt. 18:6).

Who then dares despise the day of small things?

Who are those who are so wicked? They are the proud, the ignorant, the thoughtless, the unfeeling, the profane, and such like.

II. THOSE WHO DESPISE THE DAY OF SMALL THINGS IN THEMSELVES.

1. They will frequently fail to notice and nurture thoughts and feelings which would lead them to Christ.
2. They cannot believe that salvation can come by ordinary means, or through their present knowledge end emotions: these are too small in their esteem, they crave for signs and wonders.
3. Therefore they endeavor to kill their own thoughtfulness at its birth, and quench the spark of desire before it can become a flame. Yet these despised things might have led on to salvation.
4. If they would nurture their weak desires, and feeble resolves, and faint beliefs, and trembling hopes, good would come of them.
5. No doubt many think ill of their own condition when God thinks well of them. They judge that little faith, and little life, and little strength are useless; but the Lord thinks not so.

It is wise to look away, both from small things and great things, to Jesus. Let us see his day, and be glad (John 8:56).

Let us trust in his finished work, and rejoice in his continued work.

"Rejoice, and see the plummet in the hand of Zerubbabel" (see context).

III. THOSE WHO DO NOT DESPISE THE DAY OF SMALL THINGS.

1. Hopeful pastors. We are looking out for gracious signs, and are more apt to be misled by our sanguine hopes than to fall into the opposite fault of despising the day of small things.
2. Anxious parents. They long to see buds of grace in their children. The smallest signs of spiritual life would charm them.
3. Wise soul-winners. They rejoice to see "first the blade."
4. Jesus himself. He loves the little ones (Mark 10:14).

Come ye to him, all ye trembling souls!

Multum in Parvo

When the boy began to draw portraits upon his slate, and to sketch with charcoal, the great artist was in him in embryo. It was not every eye that could perceive his budding genius, but he who did so, and encouraged the youth to pursue art as his vocation, found a life-long satisfaction in having helped him. Had he sneered at the young draughtsman, he would have lived to see his folly; but now he takes pleasure in every triumph of the renowned painter. Some such joy, only of a higher and more spiritual order, will be yours if you stimulate early piety, and teach the tender heart the way to peace and holiness. To repress desires which are heavenward, because they are attended with something of childishness, is wicked cruelty: prune the vine of its wild shoots, but do not uproot it. Foster and nurture even the tiniest sign of grace. "Destroy it not; for a blessing is in it" (Isa. 65:8).

FEEBLEMIND.—I do not yet know all the truth; I am a very ignorant Christian man; sometimes, if I hear some rejoice in the Lord, it troubles me because I cannot do so too. It is with me as it is with a weak man among the strong, or as with a sick man among the healthy, or as a lamp despised." He that is ready to slip with his feet is as a lamp despised in the thought of him that is at ease" (Job. 7:5). So that I know not what to do.

GREATHEART.—But, brother, I have it in commission to comfort the feeble-minded, and to support the weak. You must needs go along with us; we will wait for you, we will lend you our help, we will deny ourselves of some things, both opinionative and practical, for your sake; we will not enter into doubtful disputations before you, we will be made all things to you rather than you shall be left behind (Rom. 14; 1 Cor. 8; 4:22). —*Bunyan's "Pilgrim's Progress"*

One afternoon, I noticed a young lady at the service, whom I knew to be a Sunday School teacher. After the service, I asked her where her class was. "Oh," said she, "I went to the school, and found only a little boy, and so I came away." "Only a little boy!" said I; "Think of the value of one such soul! The fires of a Reformation may be slumbering in that tow-headed boy; there may be a young Knox, or a Wesley, or a Whitefield in your class." —*D. L. Moody*

The little lichen imperceptibly deposits the first layer of soil upon barren rocks in mid-ocean, from which grow up all the luxuriant wealth and beauty of the spice-island. Ferns have seeds so extremely diminutive that for a long time it was doubted if they existed at all. Yet such a seed, altogether invisible to the naked eye, floats on long journeys through the air, and falls on some lichen-covered island, where it immediately fructifies, and covers the place with vegetation.

The moss is but a very little plant, yet when its seeds fall on deep, swampy, treacherous morasses, they grow up, and bind the ground together with such bands that it becomes quite safe to pass over—building, in fact, a broad and durable bridge. "Throughout creation the grandest and most complicated ends are obtained by the employment of the simplest means." —*James Neil, in "Rays from the Realms of Nature"*

121

Speak unto all the people of the land, and to the priests, saying, When ye fasted and mourned did ye at all fast unto me, even to me? And when ye did eat, and when ye did drink, did not ye eat for yourselves, and drink for yourselves?

—Zechariah 7:5–6

 HE acceptableness of religious duties must not be taken for granted. We should ask searching questions about them, for the Lord himself does so. It behooves hearers to be very attentive to close personal inquiries as to their holy things.

During long years, "even those seventy years," pious observances may have been kept up, and yet there may have been no virtue in them.

This fact makes it wise for us all to question ourselves, for we may have been habitual religionists, and yet may also never have done any thing as "unto the Lord."

Two reflections rise before our mind:

I. RELIGIOUS OBSERVANCES SHOULD BE UNTO THE LORD. "Did ye at all fast unto me, even to me?"

1. They should be attended to out of respect to his command. Ceremonies which are not of his ordaining are mere will-worship. We partake of ordinances, not because of custom, or church rule, but "unto the Lord" (Rom. 14:6).

2. They should be carried out with a dependence upon God's grace to make them useful to us, for outward forms are nothing of themselves. Unless the Spirit of God apply them to us, they are empty buckets drawn up from a dry well (John 6:63).

3. They should be fulfilled with such an eye to God as their nature and meaning suggest: as for instance, in fasting there should be sorrow towards God for having grieved him; and in holy feasting the joy must not be carnal, but "joy in the Lord."

4. They should be accompanied with that spiritual understanding without which they are mere play-acting in the sight of God. There must be the true fasting, which is abstinence from sin; and the true feasting, which is the reception of Christ with joy.

5. They should be attended to with a view to glorifying God in them. For this end come we to baptism, communion, praise, etc.

If these things are not done unto the Lord, what are they but the rites of atheism?—or a sort of witchcraft, a repetition of incantations, genuflection, and the like? (Isa. 66:3).

II. RELIGIOUS OBSERVANCES MAY BE UNTO OURSELVES. "Did not ye eat for yourselves, and drink for yourselves?"

They are so most clearly:

1. When the spiritual element is absent. Then even in the Sacred Supper there is nothing more than mere eating and drinking, as in the case of the Corinthian church. How generally have religious festivals become mere excuses for banqueting!

2. When the ordinance is attended to because it brings personal credit. Motives of custom, respectability, or dignity, may lead men even to the table of the Lord. This is eating for ourselves.

3. When the outward observance is used as a means of pacifying the conscience, and taken as a spiritual opiate. Without drawing near to God, the man feels easier because he has performed a bit of pious ritual. This is eating and drinking for ourselves.

4. When outward ritual is practiced in the hope that we shall be saved thereby. The motive is religious selfishness, and the act must be unacceptable.

5. When there is no intent to please God therein: for as the intent is, such is the act; and when there is no intent toward God, the whole matter falls short of acceptance with God.

See how vain are the religious performances of unbelievers. Read verses 1 to 3 of this chapter.

Let us come to Jesus, who is the sum and substance of all fasts, and feasts, and all else of right observance.

Let us live as unto the Lord (Rom. 14:8).

Striking Paragraphs

If, after thou hast heard so many masses, matins, and even-songs, and hast received holy bread and holy water, and the bishop's blessing, or the cardinal's, or the pope's, thou wilt be more kind to thy neighbor, and love him better, and be more obedient to thy superiors, more merciful and ready to forgive; if thou dost more despise the world, and art more athirst for spiritual things, then do such things increase grace. *If not, they are a lie. —Tyndale*

A certain king would build a cathedral, and, that the credit of it might be all his own, he forbade anyone to contribute to its erection in the least degree. A tablet was placed in the side of the building, and on it his name was carved as the builder. But one night he saw in a dream an angel, who came down, and erased his name; and the name of a poor widow apt peered in its stead. This was three times repeated, when the enraged king summoned the woman before him, and demanded, "What have you been doing, and why have you broken my commandment?" The trembling widow replied, "I loved the Lord, and longed to do something for his name, and for the building up of his church. I was forbidden to touch it in any way, so in my poverty I brought a wisp of hay for the horses that drew the stones." Then the king saw that he had labored for his own glory, but the widow for the glory of God, and he commanded that her name should be inscribed upon the tablet. —*Cyclopaedia of Illustrative Anecdotes*

In no part of the great universe is any being fervently *devout by accident*. Everywhere, even in heaven, creatures are devout from purpose, design, endeavor. Eminently is this true on earth; no man ever *happened* to be religious. *Dr. Stoughton, in "Lights of the World"*

A story which needs careful telling, and then may be most useful: There is an Eastern story of a Sultan who overslept himself, so as not to awaken at the hour of prayer. So the devil came, and waked him, and told him to get up and pray. "Who are you?" said the Sultan. "Oh, no matter!" replied the other; "my act is good, is it not? No matter who does the good action, so long as it is good." "Yes," replied the Sultan, "but I think you are Satan. I know your face; you have some bad motive." "But," said the other, "I am not so bad as I am painted. I was an angel once, and still keep some of my original goodness." "That's all very well," replied the sagacious and prudent Caliph, "but you are the tempter: that's your business; and I wish to know why you want me to get up and pray." "Well," said the devil, with a flirt of impatience, "if you must know, I will tell you. If you had slept and forgotten your prayers, you would have been sorry for it afterwards, and penitent; but if you go on as now, and do not neglect a single prayer for ten years, you will be so satisfied with yourself that it will be worse for you than if you had missed one sometimes, and repented of it. God loves your fault mixed with penitence more than your virtue seasoned with pride."

> What is all righteousness that men devise,
> What—but a sordid bargain for the skies?
> But Christ as soon would abdicate his own,
> As stoop from heaven to sell the proud a throne.
> —*Cowper*

122

As for thee also, by the blood of thy covenant I have sent forth thy prisoners out of the pit wherein is no water. Turn you to the strong hold, ye prisoners of hope: even today do I declare that I will render double unto thee.

—Zechariah 9:11–12

 ET us commence our meditation with the description of our Lord which is given us in verses 9 and 10.

Here we see his kingdom, his character, his power to save, his lowliness, the weapons of his conquest: "speak peace unto the heathen"; and the ultimate extent of his dominion: "to the ends of the earth."

Because of him, and through him, there is mercy for the oppressed and troubled ones in Zion: "as for thee also" (verse 11).

This is a wonderful text for those who are in the lowest possible state of mind. May the Lord make it a blessing to them!

Our subjects of thought shall be:

I. CONDITION OF THE SORROWING ONES. "Prisoners in the pit wherein is no water."

They are described as:

1. Prisoners: bound, freedom gone, unable to do as they would, in the power of another, miserable.
2. Prisoners in a pit: escape impossible, darkness intolerable, fate unavoidable, present discomfort terrible.
3. Prisoners in a pit wherein is no water: comfortless, and likely to perish of thirst. They find no comfort in sin, nor indeed in anything else. They are, however, though less comfortable, all the less likely to be drowned when there is no water. Comfort in sin is deadly: the absence of that comfort is hopeful.

Thus are many oppressed souls helplessly in the power of despair till the Lord comes to rescue them.

II. CAUSE OF THEIR DELIVERANCE. "I have sent forth thy prisoners."

1. The Lord Omniscient spies them out in their dungeon, and he knows whose prisoners they are.
2. He has the power and the right to set free prisoners. Who can shut up those whom he delivers?
3. He sends them forth from the pit. He grants life, light, and liberty to them. Their feet are free, and they are on free soil.

4. He sends them forth by "the blood." By the expiation made for sin before God. By the peace created in the conscience of the penitent.

5. He sends them forth by what is called "the blood of thy covenant"—the covenant made between Zion and her King.

Let a soul once know the blessedness of "the covenant," and the sealing power of "the blood," and it is a prisoner no longer.

III. COURSE COMMENDED TO THE DELIVERED ONES. "Turn you to the strong hold, ye prisoners of hope."

They are out of the pit of despair, but not "out of the wood" of trouble: they have hope of salvation, but they need salvation itself.

It will be their wisdom:

1. To make hope their characteristic. When they feel like prisoners, let them hope, and so become "prisoners of hope."
2. To make Christ their Stronghold.
3. To turn to him every day, and all the day.
4. To turn to him specially when they feel like prisoners.

When a man is freed from death and despair, he is still to come to Jesus more and more. "To whom coming," etc. (1 Pet. 2:4).

IV. COMFORT GIVEN TO THOSE WHO TURN TO THE STRONG-HOLD. "Even today do I declare that I will render double unto thee."

1. God is speedy in his comforts to those who turn to Jesus. "Even today do I declare."
2. God is abundant in his mercy: "I will render double unto thee."
   - The double of your trouble (Job 13:10).
   - The double of your expectation (Isa. 67:7).
   - The double of your attainments: "grace for grace" (John 1:16).
   - The double of your largest faith (Eph. 3:20).
3. God is consoling in his promise; for it is:
   - Plain: "I declare."
   - Present: "Even today do I declare."
   - Positive: "I declare that I will."
   - Personal: "I will render unto thee."

Let us glorify the Lord for lifting us out of the pit.

Let us glorify the Lord Jesus for being our Stronghold.

Let us glorify the Lord for that double portion which he allots us.

Free Thoughts

Here God the Father speaks to Christ with relation to some covenant between them both; and what covenant can that be but the covenant of redemption? All the temporal, spiritual, and eternal deliverances which we enjoy, they swim to us through the blood of that covenant that is passed between the Father and the Son. By virtue of the same blood of the covenant, wherewith we are reconciled, justified, and saved, were the Jews delivered from their Babylonish captivity. The Babylonish captivity, thralldom, and dispersion, was that waterless pit, that dirty dungeon, that uncomfortable and forlorn condition, out of which they were delivered by virtue of the blood of the covenant; that is by virtue of the blood of Christ, figured by the blood that was sprinkled upon the people, and by virtue of the covenant confirmed thereby (Exod. 24:8; Ps. 74:20; Heb. 13:20). Look, as all the choice mercies, the high favors, the noble blessings, that the saints enjoy, are purchased by the blood of Christ; so they are made sure to the saints by the same blood; "by the blood of thy covenant I have sent forth thy prisoners." Whatever desperate distresses, and deadly dangers, the people of God may fall into, yet they are "prisoners of hope," and may look for deliverance by the blood of the covenant. —*Thomas Brooks*

With what gratitude and joy should these intimations of hope be received by those who are naturally in so miserable a condition ! It is a celebrated story that, when Titus Flamininus, at the public games, proclaimed the liberty of Greece, after it had been conquered by the Romans, the auditors were at first lost in a silent amazement, and then burst out into one continued shout for two hours together, *"Liberty! Liberty!"* Methinks such joy, and greater than this, should appear amongst miserable sinners when these proclamations for liberty are made. And are they not now made? Have I not been telling you, from the Word of God, that though you were condemned under the righteous sentence of the law, through a Redeemer that sentence may be reversed, your souls may be restored to life and happiness? Have I not been proving that, though Satan held you in a dark captivity, yet by the law of the great Redeemer you may be rescued from his hands, and made more than conquerors through him? Have I not told you that, notwithstanding the painful and the fruitless struggle which you have hitherto had with the feebleness and corruptions of a depraved nature, you may still receive those communications of the Spirit which will purify and strengthen you, and enable you to perfect holiness in the fear of God? . . . Prisoners of hope, will you despair? —*Dr. Doddridge (sermon on this text)*

123

I have mercy upon them: and they shall be as though I had not cast them off: for I am the Lord their God, and will hear them.

—Zechariah 10:6

HE manner in which hope can come to sinners: "I have mercy upon them." Mercy abides in the heart of God even after the hope of it has left the human bosom.

The token that God's mercy is coming, and that it is indeed come, is prayer. "Behold he prayeth" is the sure indication of coming deliverance (Acts 9:11).

God had observed prayer in them, for he said, "I will hear them."

The result of mercy's coming is exceedingly delightful: "They shall be as though I had not cast them off."

This promise may be applied:

I. IN GENERAL, TO ALL PENITENT SINNERS.

God's mercy in many ways restores men to their lost position: and in some senses even to their pristine condition before the fall.

1. The forgiveness of sin, and justification by faith, make them as accept able as if they had never transgressed.

2. The renovation of nature, by the regenerating work of the Holy Ghost, creates in them as pure an inner life as Adam ever had.

3. Restoration to paradise. Even now we dwell with God in a blessed state, for the Lord hath raised us to the heavenlies in Christ.

4. Redemption from the curse. The curse is clean gone forever, through him who was made a curse for us (Gal. 3:13) The anger of God is removed from us forever.

5. Engagement in service. We are honorably employed, and could not have been more so had we never sinned.

6. Communion with God. This we enjoy as truly as unfallen humanity could have done. Indeed, the Spirit of God dwells in the regenerate, and this is not said of Adam.

7. Eternal life. We are preserved from penal death. As Jesus lives so must we (John 14:19). There is no fear that we shall eat and die, for the Lord has given us eternal life, and we shall never perish (John 10:28).

The further working out of the likeness between the state of the saved and that of Adam in the garden, may be made highly instructive.

II. IN PARTICULAR, TO PENITENT BACKSLIDERS. Only return unto God, and live in his fear, and you shall enjoy all the blessedness of your best spiritual state.

You shall again enjoy:

1. The complete removal of your guilt, and shall have no more consciousness of sin; thus shall you return to rest of soul.
2. Renewed joy, as in the days of your first love.
3. Restored purity of heart, as in the times before you wandered.
4. Fresh communion with God, and guidance from his Holy Spirit. Is not this your cry, "Take not thy Holy Spirit from me? (Ps. 51:11)
5. New usefulness. You shall teach transgressors the pardoning ways of Jehovah (Ps. 51:13).
6. Restoration to the church, from which you may have been excluded. Your brethren will rejoice over you, and so will your God.
7. Future upholding. You shall watch against temptation all the more earnestly, and so you shall stand the more firmly through grace. God can make use of your unhappy fall to teach you many precious lessons.

Suppose this invitation to turn unto the Lord should be refused:

- It will be a wanton rejection of generous love.
- There can never be a fairer offer.
- This will increase the uneasiness of a guilty conscience.
- This will lead to the fear that the refuser is not one of the Lord's chosen.

But we hope better things of you, and things which accompany salvation, though we thus speak. We are jealous lest you miss the day of grace.

At once confess your sin, and humbly plead the word of the Lord, "I have mercy upon them."

Then cry out in prayer, for it is written, "I will hear them."

Then, in faith in the name of Jesus, hang upon the promise, "They shall be as though I had not cast them off."

By the mercy of God, we entreat you to seek his face at once, with true heart, and resolute importunity.

Selections

The fall is a greater mystery than the Redemption. He who has had experience of the one may well accept the revelation of the other. —*C. Vaughan*

> Now thou hast avenged
> Supplanted Adam, and, by vanquishing
> Temptation, hast regain'd lost Paradise,
> And frustrated the conquest fraudulent.
> He never more henceforth will dare set foot
> In Paradise to tempt; his snares are broke:

For, though that seat of earthly bliss be fail'd,
A fairer Paradise is founded now
For Adam and his chosen sons, whom thou,
A Savior, art come down to reinstall,
Where they shall dwell secure, when time shall be,
Of Tempter and temptation without fear.

—Milton

The end of the gospel is life and perfection. . . . It is to make us partakers of the image of God, in righteousness and true holiness. . . . God himself cannot make me happy, if he be only without me; unless he give me a participation of himself and his own likeness unto my soul. —*Cudworth*

He raised me from the deeps of sin,
The gates of gaping hell,
And fixed my standing more secure
Than 'twas before I fell.

—Watts

A man upon the way, having accidentally lost his purse, is questioned by his fellow-traveler where he had it last. "Oh!" says he, "I am confident that I drew it out of my pocket when I was in such a town, at such an inn." "Why, then!" says the other, "there is no better way to have it again than by going back to the place where you last had it." This is the case of many a man in these loose, unsettled times; they have lost their love to Christ, and his truth, since their corn and wine and oil have increased; since outward things are in abundance added unto them they have slighted the light of God's countenance. When they were poor and naked of all worldly comfort, then they sought God's face both early and late, and nothing was more dear and precious unto them than the truth of Christ. What, then, is to be done to recover this lost love to Christ? Back again, back again directly where you last had it! Back to the sign of the broken and contrite heart! There it was that you drew it out into good words and better works; and though it be since lost in the crowd of worldly employments, there and nowhere else, you shall be sure to find it again. —*Spencer's "Things New and Old"*

124

And I will strengthen them in the Lord; and they shall walk up and down in his name, saith the Lord.

—Zechariah 10:12

NLARGE upon the reference of the text and of the whole chapter to the Lord's ancient people, the Jews.

They are so much forgotten, and so often persecuted, and so generally despised, that we do well to think upon the prophecies of a glorious future, which the Lord God has spoken concerning them.

But the heritage of the natural and typical Israel belongs, in its spiritual meaning, to the spiritual Israel; and this promise is ours.

To those who lament their weakness the promise of the text is peculiarly cheering.

I. DIVINE STRENGTHENING PROMISED. "I will strengthen them in the Lord."

1. It is painfully needed. We are naturally weak as water.
   - After soul-sickness we are sadly feeble.
   - In the presence of great labors we feel our weakness.
   - We want strength for watching, walking, working, and warring.
2. It is freely promised. See also verse 6.
   - Justice might have left us to ourselves.
   - Tender love observes our need.
   - Infinite power abundantly supplies it.
3. It is divinely bestowed: "*I will strengthen them.*" Hence it is—
   - Certain in accomplishment.
   - Honorable in reception. How ennobling to receive strength immediately from the Lord Jehovah!
   - Unlimited in communication, if we have but faith to receive it.
4. It is gradually received. We go from strength to strength.
   - By use of the means of grace: prayer, communion with God, spiritual exercise, experience, etc.
   - By the silent operations of the Holy Ghost.
   - By the growth of each holy grace, and the increase of life within.
5. It is delightfully perceived.
   An excellent illustration is that of a sick man recovering strength. As in his case, so in ours:
   - Appetite returns: we relish the Word.
   - Difficulties vanish: burdens grow light, etc.
   - Employment is desired: strength pines for exercise.
   - Expansive views are obtained. We walk abroad with delight, and leave the narrow chamber in which a sickly soul is shut up.
   - Pleasure is enjoyed, and gratitude is excited.
6. It is sufficiently continued.
   - God continues to strengthen us day by day.
   - He increases our strength as it is required.

- He makes *his* strength more and more apparent in our weakness, till we know no power but *his.*

II. CHRISTIAN ACTIVITY PREDICTED. "They shall walk up and down in his name."
1. They shall enjoy ease—implied in walking up and down.
2. They shall possess freedom: it is the gait of liberty.
3. They shall be active for the Lord, in varied forms of service.
4. They shall persevere in such activity, walking up and down; and evermore crying joyously, "Onward and Upward!"
5. They shall consecrate that activity with care: "they shall walk in his name"—doing all in the name of the Lord Jesus.

Sick souls shall exhibit the activities of convalescence when the Lord imparts strength to them. Those who are recovering from sickness know how happy such a condition usually is.

III. BOTH BLESSINGS GUARANTEED.
1. Here is the divine "I will" of omnipotent grace.
2. Here is the divine "they shall" of consecrated free-agency.
3. Here is the divine "saith the Lord" of infallible faithfulness.

All these united make our text a glorious one.

Are you sick, sorry, weak? This sacred text is for you.

See where your strength lieth! Look to the Strong for strength.

Believe in Jesus to obtain it! He is ready to bestow it.

When you have it—use it abundantly! Help the weak, bear the burdens of others, serve the Lord with gladness, and glorify God.

Words of a Great Preacher
Sir Walter Scott relates in his autobiography that, when he was a child, one of his legs was paralyzed, and when medical skill failed, a kind uncle induced him to exert the muscles of the powerless limb by drawing a gold watch before him on the floor, tempting him to creep after it, and thus keeping up and gradually increasing vital action and muscular force. So God deals with us in our spiritual childhood, and the weakness of our faith. How weak our efforts; how slow our movements! But spiritual vitality is elicited, developed, strengthened by those efforts and movements, slow and weak as they are.

Every man needs *strength.* We ask for daily bread: and we ask for it as a means of renewing our strength. We have as much need to ask for strength, as for deliverance from evil, and for the forgiveness of our trespasses. There are certain things to be done, certain things to be endured, and things to be resisted, which can be performed, and borne, and stood against, only by power of a certain kind, and by that power in a certain degree. Nor is strength needful merely for doing and for suffering. It is also necessary for enjoyment. Weakness is so much less of life. The feeble live but in a low degree.

Lack of strength is more serious than lack of any kind of outward possession. A weak rich man is in a far worse position than a strong poor man; and the strong poor man is really the wealthier. Weakness lessens work, reduces enjoyment, and greatly aggravates suffering of any kind. In many instances, moreover, it is the cause of wickedness—leading directly to transgression, and exposing the individual to fierce and exceedingly dangerous temptations. So that, as a means of preserving ourselves against sin, we should ask daily for strength.

Every man needs strength; but no man has within him strength equal to the demands that are made upon him. He requires *strengthening*.

The Christian is no exception to this rule. He needs strength. His conversion was not translation to inactivity, to ease, and to unbroken quiet. His work is not the ceaseless singing of psalms while he reclines upon green pastures, and sits beside still waters. There are times when he lies down in green pastures; but he lies down wearied; and he lies down that he may rise again a stronger man, to enter upon fiercer battles, and to do harder work. We rest, not for resting's sake, but that we may work again.

Brethren, a Christian's strength can come only by his being strengthened. There is not within the man, as a man, nor within him as a Christian, any stock or store of strength given him at the commencement of his life. Day by day, stage after stage, first as a babe, then as a young man, and then as a father in Christ, does the man need strengthening. And what a glorious thing it is that, instead of our resources being given to us at the beginning of our Christian life, they are supplied to us as we need them. Does not this arrangement keep us in close communion with the Father of our spirits, and with the Source of all energy and wisdom? So that the very application to God, apart from the things which application always secures, tends to strengthen you. —*Samuel Martin*

125

And I will pour upon the house of David, and upon the inhabitants of Jerusalem, the spirit of grace and of supplications: and they shall look upon me whom they have pierced, and they shall mourn for him, as one mourneth for his only son, and shall be in bitterness for him, as one that is in bitterness for his firstborn.

—*Zechariah 12:10*

OTE the remarkable change of persons: "look upon me" and "mourn for him." Such changes indicate unity and distinctness; and afford us a hint as to the Unity of the Godhead, and the Trinity of the Persons.

He who speaks is Jehovah, "which stretcheth forth the heavens" (see verse 1), and yet he says "me, whom they have pierced."

It is Jehovah-Jesus who is pierced, and pours out the Spirit of grace.

It is a marvel that Jesus should be crucified when the Jewish law required stoning; and that, when crucified, the Roman soldier, though ignorant of the prophecy, should pierce him with his spear.

The conversion of the Jews is here promised: they will be converted to a crucified Christ.

They, by their unbelief and hatred, were guilty of his death: let us pray that they may be saved by it right speedily.

Our text reveals their way of repentance, and this must also be ours.

Evangelical sorrow for sin is to be our subject at this time.

We shall remark that:

I. IT IS CREATED BY THE HOLY SPIRIT. "I will pour upon the house of David and upon the inhabitants of Jerusalem, the spirit of grace and of supplications."

1. It is not produced by mere conscience, nor by terror, nor by the use of a form of penitence; much less by music, pictures, etc.
2. It comes as a gift of grace: "I will pour." The understanding is enlightened, the heart renewed, etc., by a distinct act of the Spirit of God, sent forth by the Father.
3. It is attended by prayer: "grace and of supplications." In this differing from remorse, which never prays.
4. It is continuous, for it comes with abiding things, such as the fountain opened (see next chapter); and it flows from an abiding source, for the Spirit of grace and of supplications abides in the saints.

II. IT IS CAUSED BY LOOKING TO JESUS. "They shall look upon me, whom they have pierced."

It cannot, therefore, prepare for that look: we look to Jesus as we are, and the look makes penitents of us.

1. We see the horrible hatred which sin bears toward purity, for it slew the Holy One, and that when he was arrayed in the most lovely and attractive form.
2. We see its ingratitude to love. Sin repays infinite compassion with inveterate hate, and therefore crucifies Jesus.

3. We see its abhorrence of God. It would slay him if it could, and it did so in effect. Sin is Deicidal in intent and tendency.

4. We see that such is the terrible guilt of our sin that nothing but an infinite sacrifice could atone for it.

5. We see that we have entered into the sin of Calvary by our conduct towards the Lord Jesus in our rejecting and resisting him and his cause! We have repeated the crime of the cross.

III. IT IS THE CHIEF OF SORROWS. "They shall mourn for him, as one mourneth for his only son."

1. Comparable to a terrible parental agony, for an only son, or for a first-born child: both very special sources of grief.

2. Comparable also to the national mourning for Josiah (see verse 11).

Never nation sustained greater loss than Judah when it lost Josiah, and the people showed it by the national lamentation. Such is a penitent's sorrow at the death of Jesus.

3. It is personal and private (see verses 12–14).

4. It is spreading and social. "The land shall mourn" (verse 13).

IV. IT IS NOT IN ITSELF THE CLEANSING FOR SIN.

By it we confess the crime, but cannot thereby remove it. Conviction is a glass to show our spots, not a bath to cleanse them.

1. It acknowledges our need of the fountain; but it is not itself a fountain of cleansing.

2. It goes with the saving look to Jesus, but it is no rival to it.

3. It leads away from self, and even from its own self.

4. It leads to Jesus: we mourn for him; and this linking us with Jesus is most operative upon our hearts.

Come, bleeding heart, and look to Jesus for healing!

Come, hard heart, and look to Jesus for brokenness!

Come, careless heart, for tile sight of Jesus may arrest even thee!

NOTE: *For variety, Spurgeon added a second outline on the same text.*

126

They shall be in bitterness for him.
—*Zechariah 12:10*

HEN the Jews receive Jesus as Messiah, they shall look upon him as pierced and slain: and the first result will be bitter repentance. It is the same with us. Of all sights, a sight of Jesus crucified is the sweetest; but at the same time it causes bitterness.

I. OUR FIRST SIGHT OF CHRIST BRINGS BITTERNESS.

1. For not having known his preciousness before. What a loss!
2. For having slighted such love so long. What crime upon crime!
3. From fear lest he should not be ours after all. This causes a bitter pang, an anxious grief of soul.
4. Sin, its greatness, and its effects, are seen in his cruel death; and this makes us deplore our guilt, and his woes.
5. The wrath of God, its justice and terribleness, are also seen at the cross, and we tremble.
6. Dread of never being forgiven, and a sense that we can never forgive ourselves, are mingled in one bitter draught.

II. OUR CONTINUED SIGHT OF CHRIST WORKS IN US THROUGHOUT LIFE A MEASURE OF THE SAME BITTERNESS.

1. His great love, when better known, brings deeper grief for sin.
2. It inspires a direr dread of grieving him.
3. It creates a deeper regret for our present unworthiness.
4. It inspires a greater horror at man's rejection of him, while we see thousands around us perishing by that madness.
5. It promotes a more overwhelming sympathy with Jesus in his striving against the evil which he died to destroy.

III. THIS BITTERNESS HAS MOST GRACIOUS EFFECTS.

1. It works great hatred of sin, and a tender and careful avoiding of it.
2. It makes Christ very sweet.
3. It makes worldly joys and temptations tasteless.
4. It removes the bitterness of affliction, pain, and death.
5. It prevents the sinful bitterness of anger, etc., at persecution.
6. It has an unutterable sweetness in it. We come to relish repentance, and to feel a pleasure in lowly grief for Jesus.

Nails

I see the crowd in Pilate's hall, I mark their wrathful mien;
   Their shouts of "Crucify!" appall, with blasphemy between,
And of that shouting multitude I feel that I am one;
   And in that din of voices rude, I recognize my own.

I see the scourges tear his back I see the piercing crown,
   And of that crowd who smite and mock I feel that I am one;
Around yon cross, the throng I see, mocking the Sufferer's groan,
   Yet still my voice it seems to be—as if I mocked alone.

'Twas I that shed the sacred blood, I nailed him to the tree,
   I crucified the Christ of God, I joined the mockery;
Yet not the less that blood avails to cleanse away my sin,
   And not the less that cross prevails to give me peace within.

We must nail our sins to the cross of Christ, fasten them upon the tree on which he suffered. Sin will begin to die within a man upon the sight of Christ on the cross, for the cross of Christ accuses sin, shames sin, and by a secret virtue destroys the very heart of sin. We must use sin as Christ was used when he was made sin for us; we must lift it up, and make it naked by confession of it to God; we must fasten the hands and feet of it by repentance, and pierce the heart of it by godly sorrow. —*Byfield*

Now, to make and keep the heart soft and tender, the consideration of Christ's dolorous passion must needs be of singular use and efficacy; as the sight of Caesar's bloody robes greatly affected the people of Rome, "and edged them on to revenge his death. —*Trapp*

   I am no preacher, let this hint suffice—
   The cross once seen is death to every vice;
   Else he that hung there suffered all his pain,
   Bled, groan'd, and agonized, and died, in vain.
                    —*Cowper*

Newton's hymn, "In evil long I took delight," describes the experience of one who was brought to repentance and salvation by the sight of Christ crucified.

It is a sweet saying of one of old, "Let a man grieve for his sin, and then joy for his grief." —*Thomas Brooks*

127

And the land shall mourn, every family apart; the family of the house of David apart, and their wives apart; the family of the house of Nathan apart, and their wives apart; The family of the house of Levi apart, and their wives apart; the family of Shimei apart, and their wives apart; All the families that remain, every family apart, and their wives apart.

—Zechariah 12:12-14

RUE repentance is attended with mourning It may not in itself be sorrow, but a repentance which did not include sorrow for sin would be a mere presence. It is a change of mind, and that change involves sorrow for the past.

We have need to stand in doubt of that repentance which hath no tear in its eye, no mourning in its heart.

Even when Christ is clearly seen, and pardon is enjoyed, mourning for sin does not cease; say rather, it is both deepened and purified.

This mourning has one special characteristic that it is personal, the act of each individual, and the act of the individual apart from any of his fellows. Its watchword is "apart."

I. THE INDIVIDUALIZING EFFECT OF SORROW FOR SIN. Observe the man, times in which we here have the word "apart."

1. It is seen even when that mourning is universal. "The land shall mourn, every family apart." The widest spread of grace will not diminish its power over each separate person.

2. It will be seen in the separation of one family from another when the mourning is common, and most families repent. How much more when only a few households worship God!

3. It is seen in the distinction between family and family even when both fear the Lord. Each family has its peculiar sin, and a speciality must be made in the confession of each one.

   - The royal family: or rich: influential: "the family of the house of David apart."
   - The prophet's family: the family at the manse: "the family of the house of Nathan apart."
   - The priest's family: the family of the church-officer, or the teacher, etc.: "the family of the house of Levi apart."
   - The ordinary family: the household of the trader, workman, etc.: "the family of Shimei apart."

Each family has its neglected duties, evil habits, differences, unconverted members, besetments, etc.

4. It is seen in the individualizing of those nearest akin: "and their wives apart." These are one flesh; but when their hearts are made flesh, each one mourns alone.

Common sin in husbands and wives should be mourned in common; holy joy, and holy grief, and much of devotion should be united; but in seeking the Lord by repentance each one must come alone.

This personality of holy grief has been stigmatized as morbid, self-conscious, and eelfish; but those who thus speak are strangers to spiritual facts, and cavil for the mere sake of caviling.

II. HOW DOES THIS INDIVIDUALITY SHOW ITSELF?

Of course, from the nature of things, it differs in each case, but:

1. Each individual sees most his own sin: he is alone as to *character*.
2. Each individual desires to be alone as to *place*. No matter where, whether at the bedside, or in the field, or in the barn: but solitude is desired, and must be obtained.
3. Each individual has his own *time*. At once the penitent must mourn, whether it be morning, noon, or night: he cannot be timed by regulation.
4. Each individual has his own *manner*. Some are silent; others cry aloud. One weeps, another cannot literally do so, and is all the more sad. One feels broken in heart, another laments his hardness, etc.
5. Each individual has his own *secret*. None can enter into it even if they would do so. Each mourner has a secret hidden away in his own soul, and he cannot reveal it to men.

III. HOW DO WE ACCOUNT FOR THIS INDIVIDUALITY?

1. In part it is accounted for by a natural and justifiable shame, which prevents our confessing all our sins before another.
2. The heart desires to come to God himself, and the presence of a third person would be an interruption.
3. The man is conscious that his guilt was all his own, and as he disassociates everyone else from it, he instinctively comes to God apart, and solely on his own account.
4. This is the sign of sincerity. Sham piety talks about religion as, national, and delights to display itself in the assembly, or in the street; true godliness is of the heart, and being "in spirit and in truth," it is deeply personal.
5. This is the mark of spiritual life with its individual emotions, needs, struggles, desires, regrets, confessions, etc. No two living men are quite alike outwardly, and certainly none are so inwardly: therefore, before the Lord they must exhibit a separate personal existence.

Practice much self-examination; minute, and searching.

Realize the fact that you must die apart, and, in a sense, be judged, and sentenced apart. Never forget your own individuality. You must have Christ for yourself, and be born again yourself, or you are lost.

Go forth and bless all the world when you are yourself prepared for such work. Light your own torch, or you cannot enlighten others. There is no selfishness in seeking to be made unselfish, and that is what grace alone can do for you.

Personalities

Let the question of eternity have a monopoly in you. It is an intensely personal question; but instead of making you selfish, it will expand your heart. He who has never felt for his own soul cannot feel for another's. —*Brownlow North*

Personal private faults must be privately confessed. It is not meet a wife should know all the bosom-sins of him in whose bosom she lieth. Perchance being now offended for not hearing her husband's prayers, she would be more offended if she heard them. Nor hath she just cause to complain, seeing herein Nathan's wife is equal with Nathan himself; what liberty she alloweth is allowed her, and she may, as well as her husband, claim the privilege privately and apart, to pour forth her soul unto God in her daily devotions. Yet man and wife, at other times, ought to communicate in their prayers, all others excluded —*Thomas Fuller*

The question "Guilty?" or "Not Guilty?" must be put to each prisoner separately, and each one must answer to his name, and put in his personal plea. Should a pardon be granted, it must bear the individual's name, and it must be issued distinctly *to him*, or it will be a document of no value to him. In every case, the guilt and the pardon must have a personal bearing: but how hard it is to make a man see this! Oh, that we could preach in the "thou and thee" style, and could make each hearer feel that we were as personal as Nathan when he said, "Thou art the man!" If our hearers will not cry, "Lord, is it I?" we must go to them with the word, "I have a message from God unto thee."

128

I have loved you, saith the Lord, Yet ye say, Wherein hast thou loved us?
—*Malachi 1:2*

ISRAEL under Malachi was in a captious, querulous condition; his brief prophecy is full of unbelieving questions, in which man seems bent upon having the last word with God.

The text might be treated as bearing upon our own favored nation, for God has been very gracious to Britain, and Britain is sadly ungrateful.

We prefer to consider Israel as the type of the election of grace.

It occurs even to the chosen, when grace runs low, to fall into an ill humor, and to appear beaten down, depressed, and full of sullen unbelief. This is a very wretched state of affairs.

With this state of heart we deal.

I. GOD'S LOVE DECLARED. *"I have loved you, saith the Lord."*

To every believer the special love of God is declared in the Scriptures, and to that love the text refers. This is clear if we observe the words, which follow:"Was not Esau Jacob's brother? saith the Lord: yet I loved Jacob, and I hated Esau." This is the precise language used by Paul when speaking of the election of grace (Rom. 9:13).

To every believer this love has been shown in:

1. Election in Christ Jesus from of old.
2. Covenant engagements made by Christ on his behalf.
3. Accomplished Redemption by the Lord Jesus.
4. Regeneration and the gift of eternal life in Christ Jesus.
5. Pardon of sin, justification by faith, adoption, sanctification, etc.
6. Preservation to this hour, and promise for all future time.

This is a scanty list of the ways by which the Lord has said to each regenerate soul,"I have loved you."

Do we not remember times of love when this was personally sealed upon our hearts by the Holy Spirit?

Even now the Lord speaks thus to his redeemed by his Word, and by his Spirit. Do they not hear it? Are they not touched with so gracious and condescending an avowal of love?

II. GOD'S LOVE QUESTIONED. "Yet ye say, Wherein hast thou loved us?"

This is a shocking and disgraceful thing; but, alas, it indicates a condition of heart which has been seen far too frequently.

Such a question has been asked:

1. Under great afflictions in which there seemed no relief. Petulantly the sorrowing one has questioned divine love.
2. In sight of the prosperous wicked in their day of pride many a poor despised believer has rashly doubted the special love of God.
3. In times of grievous doubt as to one's personal salvation, and under heavy temptations of Satan, the same doubt has arisen.
4. Alas, this has also happened when, immersed in worldliness, the man for the time has lost all sight and sense of spiritual things, and has treated distinguishing love as though it were a fiction!

This is a grievous wounding of the Lord of love.

It pours despite upon amazing mercy.
It exposes the questioner to fearful peril.

III. GOD'S LOVE CONSIDERED.

When we solemnly turn, and meditate upon these things, we see:

1. Love lamenting. Is God to be thus treated? Shall he mournfully cry, "I have loved you. Yet ye say, Wherein hast thou loved us?"
2. Love entreating. Does not each accent say, "Return to me"?
3. Love abounding. Our question shames us. God loves us in ten thousand ways; loves us so as to be patient even when we wickedly question his love.
4. Love conquering. We bow at Jehovah's feet with shame, and yield our heart's best love in return for his love.

Come, ye cast down ones, leave your sullen questionings!

Run into his arms, and receive the *quietus* of all your fears.

Love-Notes

A child has willfully disobeyed. For this offense he has been chastised, and confined to his own room. He is very sullen and obstinate, and his father reasons with him, and tells him with tears that he is greatly grieved with him, and feels wounded by the ingratitude which he receives after all his love. The boy angrily replies that he does not believe in his father's love: if he loved him, why did he whip him, and send him to bed? This would be a very rebellious speech; but it would be pitched in the same key as our text. It would also set forth the spirit which is often seen in Christians when they measure the Lord's love by their temporal circumstances, and ask in rebellion whether their poverty, their pains, and their persecutions are fit fruits of divine favor. The Lord knows how foolish we are apt to be when our soul is vexed with bitter anguish, and therefore he does not destroy us for our presumption, but he patiently reasons with us that he may bring us to a better mind.

If it would be marvelous to see one river leap up from the earth full-grown, what would it be to gaze upon a vast spring from which all the rivers of the earth should at once come bubbling up, a thousand of them born at a birth? What a vision would it be! Who can conceive it? And yet the love of God is that fountain, from which all the rivers of mercy, which have ever gladdened our race—all the rivers of grace in time, and of glory hereafter—take their rise. My soul, stand thou at that sacred fountainhead, and adore and magnify for ever and ever God, even our Father, who hath loved us. —*C. H. S.*

What is more tender than a mother's love
To the sweet infant fondling in her arms?
What arguments need her compassion move
To hear its cries, and help it in its harms?

> Now, if the tenderest mother were possessed
> Of all the love within her single breast
> Of all the mothers since the world began,
> 'Tis nothing to the love of God to man.
> —*John Byrom*

A very tender parent had a son, who, from his earliest years, proved headstrong and dissolute. Conscious of the extent of his demerits, he dreaded and hated his parent. Meanwhile, every means was used to disarm him of these suspicions, so unworthy of the tenderness and love which yearned in his father's bosom, and of all the kindness and forbearance which were lavished upon him. Eventually the means appeared to be successful, and confidence, in a great degree, took the place of his ungenerous suspicions. Entertained in the family as one who had never trespassed, he now left his home to embark in mercantile affairs, and was assured that if in any extremity he would apply to his parent, he should find his application kindly received. In the course of years it fell out that he was reduced to extremity; but, instead of communicating his case to his parent, his base suspicion and disbelief of his tenderness and care again conquered him, and he neglected to apply to him. Who can tell how deeply that father's heart was rent at such depravity of feeling? Yet this is the case of the believer, who, pardoned and accepted, yet refuses to trust his heavenly Parent, throws away his filial confidence, and with his old suspicions stands aloof in sullen distrust. Oh, how is God dishonored by this sinful unbelief! —*Salter*

Dr. Chalmers used to say that "As soon as a man comes to understand that 'God is love,' he is infallibly converted."

129

But unto you that fear my name shall the Sun of righteousness arise with healing in his wings; and ye shall go forth, and grow up as calves of the stall.

—*Malachi 4:2*

THERE is one grand distinction among men—"him that serveth God, and him that serveth him not." See last verse of previous chapter.

Fearing God is the mark which distinguishes man from man far more than wealth, rank, or nationality.

The coming of Christ is a calamity or a blessing to men according to their character.

What a change of figures! To the wicked, *"an oven"!* (see verse 1). To God fearing men, a *"Sun"!*

Our text was fulfilled at our Lord's first coming.

It awaits a far larger fulfillment at his second coming.

It is always true as a general principle, and it is felt to be true when the Lord Jesus spiritually draws near to his people.

I. LET US THINK OF OUR LORD AS THE SUN.

1. He is the center of the whole system of grace.
2. He is to us the Grand Attraction, and Holdfast, keeping us in our places, as the sun keeps the planets in their orbits.
3. He is the source of all good. His beams are righteousness: all that emanates from him is good: all good emanates from him; even as all light and heat come, directly or indirectly, from the sun.
4. He is without variableness or shadow of turning (James 1:17). In himself he is forever the same, shining on without ceasing.
5. To us he has his risings, and his settings. If for a while we are in the shade, let us look for his arising.
6. To those who fear him not he never rises, for they are blind, and know no day, and see no light.

What the world would be without the sun, that should we be without our Lord. Can we conceive the gloom, the death, etc.?

II. LET US ENJOY THE BLESSINGS WHICH HE SCATTERS.

1. What light of knowledge, what warmth of love, what radiance of joy we receive from him! Let us walk in it.
2. What health he gives! Healing for the sick, health for the strong.
   - Every sunbeam is medicinal, every word of Christ is life.
   - The earlier we come to Christ the better: his rising is attended with sparkling dews of joy.

The more we commune with him the better: let us bask in the sunlight.

3. What liberty he brings ! "Ye shall go forth."

When the sun has reached a certain point in his annual course, the cattle which have been stalled are led forth to the mountain pastures; so the Lord Jesus sets his people free, and they go forth:
   - To enjoy spiritual privileges.
   - To perform spiritual duties.
   - To reach spiritual attainments.
   - To carry abroad spiritual influences.

4. What growth he fosters!: "and grow up as calves of the stall."

When the Lord Jesus is with his people:
   - They are abundantly fed.

- They are comfortably housed.
- They are regularly tended.
- They advance rapidly to maturity.

A heart which communes with Jesus possesses a freshness of youth, an ease of life, and other advantages, which admirably fulfill the comparison of "calves of the stall."

As all this comes of fearing the Lord, let us be diligent in worship, careful in obedience, and reverent in spirit.

As all this comes through our Lord Jesus, let us abide under his sweet influences, and never move out of his sunshine into that far off country, where the Arctic winter is never cheered by the Sun of righteousness.

We have not to make a Sun, or move the Sun, or buy the Sun; but only to step into the free and blessed sunshine. Why do we hesitate?

Why do we not by faith pass from darkness into his marvelous light?

Sunbeams

The late Mr. Robinson, of Cambridge, called upon a friend just as he had received a letter from his son, who was surgeon on board a vessel then lying off Smyrna. The son mentioned to his father that every morning, about sunrise, a fresh gale of air blew from the sea across the land, and, from its wholesomeness and utility in clearing the infected air, this wind is always called *the Doctor.* "Now," says Mr. Robinson, "it strikes me that the prophet Malachi, who lived in that quarter of the world, might allude to this circumstance when he says that 'the Sun of righteousness shall arise *with healing in his wings.*' The Psalmist mentions 'the wings of the wind,' and it appears to me that this salubrious breeze, which attends the rising of the sun, may be properly enough considered as the wings of the sun, which contain such healing influences, rather than the beams of the sun, as the passage has been commonly understood." —*Burder's "Oriental Customs"*

There is a beautiful fable of the ancient mythology, to the effect that Apollo, who represents the sun, killed a huge poisonous serpent by arrows surely aimed, and shot from afar. It intimates that sunbeams, darted straight from heaven, destroy many deadly things that crawl upon the ground, and so make the world a safer habitation. The parable is, in this respect, a stroke of truth, and it coincides with a feature of the eternal covenant. Light from the face of Jesus, when it is permitted to stream right into a human heart, destroys the noisome things that haunt it, as Apollo's arrows slew the snake. —*W. Arnot*

In all the departments of vegetable, animal, moral, and spiritual life, light stands out as the foremost blessing and benefit which God confers. In physical existence this is especially true. Thousands die for lack of light. No vigorous vegetable life, no healthy animal life, can long exist without light. The pestilence "walketh in darkness".... Sir James Wylie, late physician to the Emperor of

Russia, attentively studied the effects of light as a curative agent in the hospital of St. Petersburg, and he discovered that the number of patients who were cured in rooms properly lighted was four times that of those confined in dark rooms. These different results are due to the agency of light, without a full supply of which plants and animals maintain but a sickly and feeble existence. Light is the cheapest and best of all medicines. Nervous ailments yield to the power of sunshine. Pallid faces grow fresh and ruddy beneath its glow. The sun's rays have wonderful purifying power. —*H. L. Hastings*

"Heaven be praised! I have once more seen the sun," said Dr. Hayes, in his record of the experience of a certain Arctic day, when he, with others had visited a point from which they could see the sun come up for the first time from his long winter isolation. "Off went our caps with simultaneous impulse, and we hailed this long-lost wanderer of the heavens with loud demonstrations of joy."

A man scoffingly asked, "What advantage has a religious man over any one like myself? Does not the sun shine on me as on him, this fine day?" "Yes," replied his companion, a pious laborer, "but the religious man has two suns shining on him at once—one on his body, the other on his soul." —*The Biblical Treasury*

130

If thou be the Son of God.
—*Matthew 4:3*

 HERE is no sin in being tempted; for the perfect Jesus "was in all points tempted like as we are" (Heb. 4:15).

Temptation does not necessitate sinning; for of Jesus, when tempted, we read, " yet without sin."

Not even the worst forms of it involve sin: for Jesus endured without sin the subtlest of temptations, from the evil one himself.

It may be needful for us to be tempted:
- For test. Sincerity, faith, love, patience, are thus put to proof.
- For growth. Temptation develops and increases our graces.
- For usefulness. We become able to comfort and warn others.
- For victory. How glorious to overcome the arch-enemy!
- For God's glory. He vanquishes Satan by feeble men.

Solitude will not prevent temptation.
- It may even aid it. Jesus was tempted in the wilderness.
- Nor will fasting and prayer always keep off the tempter; for these had been fully used by our Lord.

Satan knows how to write prefaces: our text is one.

- He began the whole series of his temptations by a doubt cast upon our Lord's Sonship, and a crafty quotation from Scripture.
- He caught up the echo of the Father's word at our Lord's baptism and began tempting where heavenly witness ended.
- He knew how to discharge a double-shotted temptation, and at once to suggest doubt and rebellion; this was such: "If thou be the Son of God, command," etc.

I. THE TEMPTER ASSAILS WITH AN "IF."

1. Not with point-blank denial. That would be too startling. Doubt serves the Satanic purpose better than heresy.
2. He grafts his "if" on a holy thing. He makes the doubt look like holy anxiety concerning divine Sonship.
3. He ifs a plain Scripture. "Thou art my Son" (Ps. 2:7).
4. He ifs a former manifestation. At his baptism God said, "This is my beloved Son." Satan contradicts our spiritual experience.
5. He ifs a whole life. From the first Jesus had been about his Father's business; yet after thirty years his Sonship is questioned.
6. He ifs inner consciousness. Our Lord knew that he was the Father's Son; but the evil one is daring.
7. He ifs a perfect character. Well may he question us, whose faults are so many.

II. THE TEMPTER AIMS THE "IF" AT A VITAL PART.

1. At our sonship.
   - In our Lord's case he attacks his human and divine Sonship.
   - In our case he would make us doubt our regeneration.
2. At our childlike spirit. He tempts us to cater for ourselves. "Command that these stones be made bread."
3. At our Father's honor. He tempts us to doubt our Father's providence and to blame him for letting us hunger.
4. At our comfort and strength as members of the heavenly family.
   - By robbing us of our sonship, he would leave us orphans, and consequently naked, poor, and miserable.
   - Thus he would have us hindered in prayer. How could we say, "Our Father" if we doubted our sonship (Matt. 6:9)?
   - Thus he would destroy patience. How can we say, "Father, thy will be done," if we are not his sons (Luke 22:4)?
   - Thus he would lay us open to the next shot, whatever that might be. Doubt of sonship leaves us naked to the enemy.

III. THE TEMPTER SUPPORTS THAT "IF" WITH CIRCUMSTANCES.

1. You are alone. Would a Father desert his Child?
2. You are in a desert. Is this the place for God's Heir?
3. You are with the wild beasts. Wretched company for a Son of God!
4. You are hungry. How can a loving Father let his perfect Son hunger?

Put all these together, and the tempter's question comes home with awful force to one who is hungry, and alone.

When we see others thus tried, do we think them brethren? Do we not question their sonship, as Job's friends questioned him? What wonder if we question ourselves!

IV. WHEN OVERCOME, THE TEMPTER'S "IF" IS HELPFUL.

1. As coming from Satan, it is a certificate of our true descent.
   * He only questions *truth*: therefore we are true sons.
   * He only leads *sons* to doubt their sonship; therefore we are sons.
2. As overcome, it may be a quietus to the enemy for years.
   * It takes the sting out of man's questionings and suspicions; for if we have answered the devil himself we do not fear men.
   * It puts a sweetness into all future enjoyment of OUR FATHER.
3. As past, it is usually the prelude to angels coming and ministering to us, as in our Lord's case. No calm is so deep as that which follows a great storm (Mark 4:39).

Friend, are you in such relation to God that it would be worth Satan's while to raise this question with you?

Those who are not heirs of God are heirs of wrath.

Selections

What force there is often in a single monosyllable! What force, for instance, in the monosyllable "If," with which this artful address begins! It was employed by Satan, for the purpose of insinuating into the Savior's mind a doubt of his being in reality the special object of his Father's care, and it was pronounced by him, as we may well suppose, with a cunning and malignant emphasis. How different is the use which Jesus makes of this word "if" in those lessons of Divine instruction and heavenly consolation, which he so frequently delivered to his disciples when he was on earth! He always employed it to inspire confidence; never to excite distrust. Take a single instance of this: "If God so clothe the grass of the field, which today is, and tomorrow is cast into the oven, shall he not much more clothe you, O ye of little faith?" What a contrast between this divine remonstrance and the malicious insinuation of the great enemy of God and man! —*Daniel Bagot*

God had but one Son without corruption, but he had none without temptation. Such is Satan's enmity to the Father, that the nearer and dearer any child is to him, the more will Satan trouble him, and vex him with temptations. None so well-beloved as Christ; none so much tempted as he. —*Thomas Brooks*

Satan did not come to Christ thus, "Thou art not the Son of God"; or "That voice which gave thee that testimony was a lie or a delusion." No, he proceeds by questioning, which might seem to grant that he was the Son of God, yet withal might possibly beget a doubt in his mind. —*Richard Gilpin*

Oh, this word "if"! Oh, that I could tear it out of my heart! O thou poison of all my pleasures! Thou cold icy hand, that touches me so often, and freezes me with the touch! *"If! If!"* —*Robert Robinson*

131

And he saith unto them, follow me, and I will make you fishers of men.

—*Matthew 4:19*

ONVERSION is most fully displayed when it leads converts to seek the conversion of others: we most truly follow Christ when we become fishers of men.

The great question is not so much what we are naturally, as what Jesus makes us by his grace: whoever we may be of ourselves, we can, by following Jesus, be made useful in his kingdom.

Our desire should be to be men-catchers; and the way to attain to that sacred art is to be ourselves thoroughly captured by the great Head of the College of Fishermen. When Jesus draws us we shall draw men.

I. SOMETHING TO BE DONE BY US. "Follow me."

1. We must be separated to him, that we may pursue his object.
   - We cannot follow him unless we leave others (Matt. 6:4).
   - We must belong to him, that his design may be our design.
2. We must abide with him, that we may catch his spirit.
   The closer our communion with Christ, the greater our power with souls. Near following means full fellowship.
3. We must obey him, that we may learn his method.
   - Teach what he taught (Matt. 28:20).
   - Teach as he taught (Matt. 11:29; 1 Thess. 2:7).
   - Teach such as he taught, namely, the poor, the base, children, etc.
4. We must believe him, that we may believe true doctrine.
   - Christ's own teaching catches men; let us repeat it.
   - Faith in Jesus on our part is a great force to beget faith.

5 We must copy his life, that we may win his blessing from God; for God blesses those who are like his Son.

II. SOMETHING TO BE DONE BY HIM. "I will make you."
Our following Jesus secures our education for soul-winning.
1. By our following Jesus he works conviction and conversion in men; he uses our example as a means to this end.
2. By our discipleship the Lord makes us fit to be used.
   • True soul-winners are not self-made, but Christ-made.
   • The making of men-catchers is a high form of creation.
3. By our personal experience in following Jesus he instructs us till we become proficient in the holy art of soul-winning.
4. By inward monitions he guides us what, when, and where to speak.
   These must be followed up carefully if we would win men.
5. By his Spirit he qualifies us to reach men.
   The Spirit comes to us by our keeping close to Christ.
6. By his secret working on men's hearts he speeds us in our work.
   He makes us true fishers by inclining men to enter the gospel net.

III. A FIGURE INSTRUCTING US. "Fishers of men."
The man who saves souls is like a fisher upon the sea.
1. A fisher is dependent and trustful.
2. He is diligent and persevering.
3. He is intelligent and watchful.
4. He is laborious and self-denying.
5. He is daring, and is not afraid to venture upon a dangerous sea.
6. He is successful. He is no fisher who never catches anything.

See the ordination of successful ministers. They are made, not born: made by God, and not by mere human training.

See how we can partake in the Lord's work, and be specimens of his workmanship: "Follow me, and I will make you."

Hooks

I love your meetings for prayer, you cannot have too many of them: but we must work while we pray, and pray while we work. I would rather see a man, who has been saved from the gulf below, casting life-lines to others struggling in the maelstrom of death, than on his knees on that rock thanking God for his own deliverance; because I believe God will accept action for others as the highest possible expression of gratitude that a saved soul can offer. —*Thomas Guthrie*

Ministers are fishers. A busy profession, a toilsome calling, no idle man's occupation, as the vulgar conceive it, nor needless trade, taken up at last to pick a living out of. Let God's fishermen busy themselves as they must, sometimes in preparing, sometimes in mending, sometimes in casting abroad, sometimes in drawing in the net, that they may "separate the precious from the vile," etc. (Jer. 15:19; Matt. 13:48); and no man shall have just cause to twit them with idleness, or to say they have an easy life. —*John Trapp*

The minister is a fisherman. As such he must fit himself for his employment. If some fish will bite only by day, he must fish by day. If others will bite only by moonlight, he must fish for them by moonlight. —*Richard Cecil*

I watched an old man trout fishing the other day, pulling them out one after another briskly. "You manage it cleverly, old friend," I said. "I have passed a good many below who don't seem to be doing anything." The old man lifted himself up, and stuck his rod in the ground. "Well, you see, Sir, there be three rules for trout-fishing, and 'tis no good trying if you don't mind them. The first is, Keep *yourself* out of sight; and the second is, Keep yourself farther out of sight; and the third is, Keep yourself farther still out of sight. Then you'll do it." "Good for catching men, too," thought I. —*Mark Guy Pearse*

> Lord, speak to me, that I may speak
>   In living echoes of thy tone:
> As thou hast sought, so let me seek
>   Thy erring children, lost and lone.
>
> O lead me, Lord, that I may lead
>   The wandering and the wayward feet;
> O feed me, Lord, that I may feed
>   Thy hungering ones with manna sweet.
>
> O strengthen me, that while I stand
>   Firm on the Rock, and strong in thee,
> I may stretch out a loving hand
>   To wrestlers with the troubled sea
>
> O teach me, Lord, that I may teach
>   The precious things thou dost impart;
> And wing my words, that they may reach
>   The hidden depths of many a heart.
>   —*F. R. Havergal*

The best training for a soul-saving minister is precisely that which he would follow if his sole object were to develop the character of Christ in himself. The better the man, the more powerful will his preaching become. As he grows like Jesus, he will preach like Jesus. Given like purity of motive, tenderness of heart, and clearness of faith, and you will have like force of utterance. The direct road to success in saving souls is to become like the Savior. The imitation of Christ is the true art of sacred rhetoric. —*C. H. S.*

Mr. Jesse relates that certain fish give preference to bait that has been perfumed. When the prince of evil goes forth in quest of victims, there does not need much allurement added to the common temptations of life to make them effective. Fishers of men, however, do well to employ all the skill they can to suit the minds and tastes of those whom they seek to gain. —*G. McMichael*

132

Not every one that saith unto me, Lord, Lord, shall enter into the kingdom of heaven; but he that doeth the will of my Father which is in heaven. Many will say to me in that day, Lord, Lord, have we not prophesied in they name? And they name have cast out devils? And in they name done many wonderful works? And then will I profess them, I never knew you: depart from me, ye that work iniquity.

—*Matthew 7:21-23*

NE of the best tests of everything is how it will appear in the moment of death, in the morning of resurrection, and at the day of judgment. Our Lord gives us a picture of persons as they will appear "in that day."

Riches, honors, pleasures, successes, self-congratulations, etc., should all be set in the light of "that day."

This test should especially be applied to all religious professions and exercises; for "that day" will try these things as with fire.

The persons here depicted in judgment-light were not gross and open sinners; but externally they were excellent.

I. THEY WENT A LONG WAY IN RELIGION.

1. They made an open profession. They said, "Lord, Lord."
2. They undertook Christian service, and that of a high class: they habitually prophesied and worked miracles.
3. They had obtained remarkable success.
   Devils had owned their power.
4. They were noted for their practical energy.
   - They had done *many* wonders: they were active in many ways.
   - They had done wonders. Astonished everybody.
5. They were diligently orthodox.
   They did everything in the name of Christ. The words "Thy name" are mentioned three times.

II. THEY KEPT IT UP A LONG WHILE.

1. They were not silenced by men.

    No one discovered their falsehood, or detected their inconsistency.

2. They were not openly disowned by the Lord himself during life.

3. They were not made a laughing-stock by being left to use the holy name without result (Acts 19:13-17).

    Devils were cast out.

4. They expected to enter the Kingdom, and they clung to that false hope to the last.

    They dared to say, "Lord, Lord," to Christ himself, at the last.

III. THEY WERE FATALLY MISTAKEN.

1. Their tongue was belied by their hand They said, "Lord, Lord," but did not do the will of the Father.

2. They used the name which is named by disciples, but did not possess the nature of obedient servants (Luke 6:46).

3. They prophesied, but did not pray.

4. They cast out devils, but the devil was not cast out of them.

5. They attended to marvels, but not to essentials.

6. They wrought wonders, but were also workers of iniquity.

IV. THEY FOUND IT OUT IN A TERRIBLE WAY.

They had the information from the mouth of him whom they called Lord. Here let us carefully notice:

1. The solemnity of what he said. "I never knew you." He had been omitted from their religion. What an oversight!

2. The terror of what it implied: they must depart from all hope, and continue for ever to depart.

3. The awful truth of what he said. They were utter strangers to his heart. He had not chosen them, nor communed with them, nor approved them, nor cared for them.

4. The solemn fixedness of what he said. His sentence would never be recalled, altered, or ended. It stood, "depart from me."

Brethren, the Lord cannot say to some of us that he does not know us, for he has often heard our voices, and answered our requests.

He has known us:

- In repentance, seeking mercy, and receiving it.
- In gratitude, blessing his gracious name.
- In adversity, looking for his aid, and enjoying it.
- In reproach, owning his cause under ridicule.
- In difficulty, seeking help and safety under his wing.
- In love, enjoying happy fellowship with him.

In these and many other ways he knows us.

Professors, does Jesus know you? The church knows you, the school knows you, the world knows you; does Jesus know you?

Come unto him, ye strangers, and find eternal life in him

Warnings

In many simple works God is more seen than in wonderful works. The Pharisee at heaven's gate says, "Lord, I have done many wonderful works in thy name"; but, alas, has he ever made the Lord's name wonderful? —*T. T. Lynch*

Pollok describes the hypocritical professor as:

> The man that stole the livery of heaven
> To serve the devil in.

I knew you well enough for "black sheep," or, rather, for reprobate goats: I knew you for hirelings and hypocrites, but I never knew you with a special knowledge of love, delight, and complacency. I never acknowledged, approved, and accepted of your persons and performances (Ps. 1:6; Rom. 11:2). —*John Trapp*

Not "I once knew you, but cannot own you now;" but "I *never* knew you;—as real penitents, suppliants for pardon, humble believers, true followers." —*E. R. Conder*

Note our Lord's open confession before men and angels, and specially to the men themselves: "I never knew you." I knew about you; I knew that you professed great things; but you had no acquaintance with me; and whatever you knew about me, you did not know *me*. I was not of your company, and did not know you. Had he once known them, he would not have forgotten them.

Those who accept his invitation, "Come unto me," shall never hear him say, "Depart from me." Workers of iniquity may now come to the Savior for mercy; but if they set up a hope of their own, and ignore the Savior, he will bid them depart to endure the rigors of his justice. Is it not striking that preachers, casters-out of devils, and doers of wonders, may yet be workers of iniquity? They may work miracles in Christ's name, and yet have neither part nor lot in him. —*C. H. S.*

"Depart *from me*,"—a fearful sentence, a terrible separation. "From me," said Christ, that made myself man for your sakes, that offered my blood for your redemption. "From me," that invited you to mercy, and you would not accept it. "From me," that purchased a kingdom of glory for such as believed on me, and have resolved to honor their heads with crowns of eternal joy. "Depart from me:" from my friendship, my fellowship, my paradise, my presence, my heaven. —*Thomas Adams*

133

And Jesus saith unto him, I will come and heal him.
—*Matthew 8:7*

Say in a word, and my servant shall be healed.
—*Luke 7:7*

HE centurion who cared for the religious welfare of the people, and built them a synagogue, had also a heart of compassion for the sick. It is well when public generosity is sustained by domestic kindness.

This servant was his boy, and perhaps his slave; but he was dear to him. A good master makes a good servant.

It is well when all ranks are united in sympathy: captain and page are here united in affection.

The master showed his affection by seeking help. Heart and hand should go together. Let us not love in word only.

It is well that the followers of Jesus should be ready to help all sick folk; and that healing should be still associated with prayer to Jesus.

Mark the growing manifest faith of the centurion, and the growing manifestation of Jesus.

- Centurion sends elders with request to "come and heal." Jesus will come and heal.
- Centurion comes himself asking for "a word." Jesus gives the word, and the deed is done.

We see in this passage a miracle in the physical world, and are thereby taught what our Lord Jesus can do in the spiritual world.

Let us imitate the centurion in seeking to Jesus about others.

We learn from the narrative:

I. THE PERFECT READINESS OF CHRIST.

1. He did not debate with the elders of the Jews, and show the weakness of their plea: "He was worthy" (Luke 7:4–5).
2. He cheerfully granted their request, although it was needless for him to come. "Then Jesus went with them" (Luke 7:6).
3. He did not raise a question about the change which the centurion proposed, although he was already on the road (Luke 7:6).
4. He did not suspect the good man's motive, as some might have done. He read his heart, and saw his true humility.
5. He did not demur to the comparison of himself to a petty officer. Our Lord is never captious; but takes our meaning.

6. He promptly accepted the prayer and the faith of the centurion, gave the boon, and gave it as desired.

Our Lord's love to sinners, his forgetfulness of self, his willingness to please us, and his eagerness to fulfill his own mission, should encourage us in prayer to him for ourselves and others.

II. THE CONSCIOUS ABILITY OF CHRIST.

1. He is not puzzled with the case. It was singular for the servant to be at once paralyzed and tormented; but whatever the disease may be, the Lord says, "I will come and heal him."
2. He is not put in doubt by the extreme danger of the servant. No, he will come to him, though he hears that he is stricken down. and is utterly prostrate.
3. He speaks of healing as a matter of course.
   His coming will ensure the cure: "come and heal."
4. He treats the method of procedure as of no consequence.
   He will come or he will not come, but will "say in a word"; yet the result will be the same.
5. He wonders more at the centurion's faith than at the cure.
Omnipotent grace moves with majestic ease.
We are worried and fretted, but the Lord is not.
Let us thus be encouraged to hope.

III. THE ABIDING METHOD OF CHRIST.

He is accustomed to heal by his Word through faith; Signs and wonders are temporary, and answer a purpose for an occasion; but both faith and the Word of the Lord are matters for all time.

Our Lord did not in the case before us put in a personal appearance, but spoke, and it was done; and this he does in our own day.

1. This is coming back to the original form of working in creation.
   It is apparently a greater miracle than working by visible presence; at any rate, the means are less seen.
2. This method suits true humility. We do not demand signs and wonders; the Word is enough for us (Luke 7:7).
3. This pleases great faith; for the Word is faith's chosen manifestation of God. It rejoices more in the Word than in all things visible (Ps. 119:162).
4. This is perfectly reasonable. Should not a word of command from God be enough? Mark the centurion's reasoning (Matt. 8:9).
5. This is sure to succeed. Who can resist the divine fiat? In our own case, all we need is a word from the Lord.
6. This must be confidently relied on for others. Let us use the Word, and pray the Lord to make it his own word.

Henceforth, let us go forward in his name, relying upon his Word!

Insertions

Had the centurion's roof been heaven itself, it could not have been worthy to be come under of him whose word was almighty, and who was the Almighty Word of his Father. Such is Christ confessed to be by him that says, "only say the word." None but a divine power is unlimited: neither has faith any other bounds than God himself. There needs no footing to remove mountains, or devils, but a word. Do but say the word, O Savior, my sin shall be remitted, my soul shall be healed, my body shall be raised from dust, and both soul and body shall be glorified. —*Bishop Hall*

"I have been informed," says Hervey, "that when the Elector of Hanover was declared by the Parliament of Great Britain successor to the vacant throne, several persons of distinction waited upon his Highness, to make timely application for valuable preferments. Several requests of this nature were granted, and confirmed by a kind of promissory note. One gentleman solicited the Mastership of the Rolls. Being indulged in his desire, he was offered the same confirmation which had been vouchsafed to other successful petitioners; upon which he seemed to be overcome by grateful confusion and surprise, and begged that he might not put the royal donor to such unnecessary trouble, protesting that he looked upon His Highness's word as the best ratification of his suit. With this compliment the Elector was not a little pleased. 'This gentleman,' he said, 'treats me like a king; and, whoever is disappointed, he shall certainly be gratified.'"

Our Lord can cure either by coming or by speaking. Let us not dictate to him the way in which he shall bless us. If we were permitted a choice, we ought not to select that method which makes most show, but that in which there is least to be seen and heard, yet most to be admired. Comparatively, signs and wonders show less of him than his bare Word, which he has magnified above all his name. Marvels dazzle, but the Word enlightens. That faith which sees least, sees most, and that which has no eyes at all for the visible has a thousand eyes for the invisible. Lord, come in thy glory, and bless me, if such be thy will; but if thou wilt stay where thou art, and bless me only through thy will and Word, I will be as well content, and even more so if this method the more honors thee! —*C. H. S.*

134

And as Jesus passed forth from thence, he saw a man, named Matthew, sitting at the receipt of custom: and he saith unto him, follow me. And he arose, and followed him.

—*Matthew 9:9*

ATTHEW is here writing about himself. Note his modesty in the expression "a man, named Matthew," and in his omission of the fact that the feast mentioned in verse 10 was held in his own house.

The story is placed immediately after a miracle, as if to hint that Matthew's conversion was a miracle.

There are points of similarity between the miracle and the conversion.

Matthew was spiritually palsied by his sins, and his money-making; hence he needed the divine command, "Arise, and walk."

There may be points of likeness also between Matthew's personal story and our own. These may be profitably considered.

I. HIS CALL SEEMED ACCIDENTAL AND UNLIKELY.

- Jesus had often been at Capernaum, which he had selected to be "his own city"; and yet Matthew remained unsaved. Was it likely that he would now be called? Had not his day of grace closed?
- Jesus was about other business; for we read, "as Jesus passed forth from thence." Would he now be likely to call Matthew?
- Jesus left many other persons uncalled; was it not highly probable that the tax-gatherer would be passed by?
- Yet Jesus called to himself this "man, named Matthew," while many another man had no such special call.
- "He saw a man, named Matthew," for he foresaw him.
- He knew him, for he foreknew him.

In all which there is a parallel between Matthew and ourselves.

II. HIS CALL WAS ALTOGETHER UNTHOUGHT OF AND UNSOUGHT.

1. He was in a degrading business. None but the lowest of the Jews would care to gather taxes for the Roman conqueror. His discipleship would bring no honor to the Lord Jesus.
2. He was in an ensnaring business. The publicans usually made a personal profit by extorting more than was due. He was not paying away, but sitting "at the receipt of custom; and this is a pleasing exercise." Money is bird-lime to the soul.
3. He would not have dared to follow Jesus even if he had wished to do so. He felt himself to be too unworthy.
4. He would have been repulsed by the other disciples had he proposed to come without the Lord's open invitation.
5. He made no sign in the direction of Jesus. No prayer was offered by him, nor wish expressed towards better things.

The call was of pure grace, as it is written, "I am found of them that sought me not."

III. HIS CALL WAS GIVEN BY THE LORD, WITH FULL KNOWLEDGE OF HIM.

Jesus "saw a man, named Matthew," and called him.

1. He saw all the evil that had been in him, and was yet there.
2. He saw his adaptation for holy service, as a recorder and penman.
3. He saw all that he meant to make of him.
4. He saw in him his chosen, his redeemed, his convert, his disciple, his apostle, his biographer.

The Lord calls as he pleases, but he sees what he is doing. Sovereignty is not blind; but acts with boundless wisdom.

IV. HIS CALL WAS GRACIOUSLY CONDESCENDING.

- The Lord called "a man, named Matthew,"—that was his best.
- He was a publican—that may not have been his worst.
- He allowed such a sinner to be his personal attendant; yea, called him to that honor, saying," Follow *me*."
- He allowed him to do this immediately, without putting him into quarantine. He was to follow the Lord there and then.

V. HIS CALL WAS SUBLIMELY SIMPLE.

1. Few were the words: "Follow me."
   It is very tersely recorded, " He saw . . . he saith . . . he arose."
2. Clear was the direction: "Follow me."
3. Personal was the address: "He saith *unto him*."
4. Royal was the command: "He saith."

VI. HIS CALL WAS IMMEDIATELY EFFECTUAL.

1. Matthew followed at once. "He arose' and followed him."
2. He followed spiritually as well as literally. He became a sincere, devout, earnest, intelligent disciple.
3. He followed wholly: bringing his voice and his pen with him.
4. He followed growingly, more and more.
5. He followed ever after, never deserting his Leader.
   What a call was this! None could have given it but the Lord.

VII. HIS CALL WAS A DOOR OF HOPE FOR OTHERS.

1. His salvation encouraged other publicans to come to Jesus.
2. His open house gave opportunity to his friends to hear Jesus.
3. His personal ministry brought others to the Savior.
4. His written gospel has convinced many, and will always do so.

Are *you* up to your neck in business? Are you "sitting at the receipt of custom?" Yet may a call come to you at once. It does come.

Hear it attentively, rise earnestly, and respond immediately.

Good Words

God often calls men in strange places. Not in the house of prayer, not under the preaching of the Word; but when all these things have been absent, and all surrounding circumstances have seemed most adverse to the work of grace, that grace has put forth its power. The tavern, the theater, the ballroom, the gaming-house, the race-course, and other similar haunts of worldliness and sin, have sometimes been the scenes of God's converting grace. As an old writer says: "Our calling is uncertain in respect of place, for God calls some from their ships, and some from their shops; some from under the hedges, and others from the market; so that, if a man can but make out unto his own soul that he is certainly called, the time when and the place where matter little."

How I now loved those words that spake of a Christian's calling! As when the Lord said to one, "Follow me"; and to another, "Come after me." Oh! thought I, that he would say so to me: how gladly would I run after him! I could seldom read of any that Christ did call, but I presently wished, "Would I had been in their clothes! Would I had been born Peter, or John!" I often thought, "Would I had heard him when he called *them*, how would I have cried, 'O Lord, call me also!'" But I feared he would not call me. —*John Bunyan*

We read in classic story how the lyre of Orpheus enchanted with its music, not only the wild beasts, but the very trees and rocks upon Olympus, so that they moved from their places to follow him; so Christ, our heavenly Orpheus, with the music of his gracious speech, draws after him those less susceptible to benign influences than beasts and trees and stones, even poor, hardened, senseless, sinful souls. Let him but strike his golden harp, and whisper in thy heart, "Come, follow me," and thou, like another Matthew, shalt be won.

135

He was moved with compassion on them.
—*Matthew 9:36*

 HE expression is very strong (εσπλαγχνισθη). All that was within him was stirred by the sight which he beheld. He was full of emotion, and showed it in his whole person.

His yearning compassions gathered around (περι) the people.

- Exhibit the picture of Jesus under strong emotion.
- This is a portrait of him as he appeared on many occasions.
- Indeed, the words before us might sum up his entire life.

Let us behold his compassion as manifested in:

I. THE GREAT TRANSACTIONS OF HIS LIFE.

1. The Eternal Covenant, in its conception, arranging, provisions, etc., is full of compassion to men.
2. The Incarnation of our Lord shows matchless compassion.
3. His living in the flesh among men declares it.
4. His bearing the death penalty is the highest fruit of it.
5. His intercession for sinners proves its continuance.

This is a wide subject. In every act of his grace the Lord of love manifests tender pity to men.

II. THE SPECIAL INSTANCES RECORDED BY THE EVANGELISTS.

1. In Matthew 15:32, we see a fainting crowd, hungry, etc.
   - A crowd is a sad sight: a crowd, when faint, is far more so.
   - Such crowds are perishing in our cities today.
2. In Matthew 14:14, the sick are most prominent in the throng.
   - Jesus lived in a vast hospital, himself suffering, as well as healing, the diseases of men.
   - None can tell how deep is his pity for suffering humanity.
3. In the case mentioned in the text, he saw an ignorant, neglected, perishing crowd.
   - The sorrows, dangers, and sins of spiritual ignorance are great.
   - The Lord Jesus is the Shepherd of the unshepherded.
4. In Matthew 20:34, we see the blind. Jesus pities spiritual blindness.
   Dwell upon the interesting details of the two blind men.
5. In Mark 1:41, we see the leper. Christ pities sin-polluted men.
   Jesus compassionated the man who said "If thou wilt, thou canst."
6. In Mark 5:19, we have the demoniac. Jesus pities tempted souls.
   - The man out of whom he cast a legion of devils was to be dreaded, but the Lord gave him nothing but compassion.
   - He pities rather than blames those sore vexed by the devil.
7. In Luke 7:13, we meet with the widow of Nain. The bereaved, the widow and fatherless are specially near to the heart of Jesus.

These instances should encourage similar cases to hope in our Lord.

III. THE FORESIGHTS OF COMPASSION.

Knowing our ignorance, needs, sorrows the Lord Jesus has provided beforehand for our wants:

1. The Bible for our guidance and comfort.
2. The minister to speak as man to man, tenderly, experimentally.
3. The Holy Spirit to comfort us, and help our infirmity, in prayer, etc.
4. The mercy-seat as our constant resort.
5. The promises to be our perpetual food.

6. The ordinances to help our memories, and make truth vivid to us.
The whole system reveals a most compassionate Savior.

IV. OUR PERSONAL RECOLLECTIONS PROVE THIS COMPASSION.

Let us remember how tenderly he dealt with us.
1. He tempered our convictions with intervals of hope.
2. He ended them ere they drove us to despair.
3. He has moderated our afflictions, and sustained us under them.
4. He has taught us, as we have been able to bear it. "I have many things to say unto you, but ye cannot bear them now."
5. He has put us to graduated tasks.
6. He has returned to us in love after our backslidings.
Let us trust in this divine mercifulness for ourselves.
Let us commend it to those around us
Let us imitate it in dealing compassionately with our fellows.

Touches for the Portrait

The literal translation is "All his bowels were agitated, and trembled with sympathy and compassion." The ancients believed the bowels to be the seat of sympathy, or mercy. The Greek word used here to denote compassion is the most expressive that human language is capable of employing, insomuch that our version utterly fails to convey the vastness and fullness of the meaning of the original. —Dr. Cumming

Compare the impression produced upon Xerxes by the sight of his enormous army. "His heart swelled within him at the sight of such a vast assemblage of human beings; but his feelings of pride and pleasure soon gave way to sadness, and he burst into tears at the reflection that in a hundred years not one of them would be alive."

How a tender-hearted mother would plead with a judge for her child ready to be condemned! Oh, how would her bowels work; how would her tears trickle down; what weeping rhetoric would she use to the judge for mercy! Thus, the Lord Jesus is full of sympathy and tenderness (Heb. 2:17), that he might be a merciful High Priest Though he hath left his passion, yet not his compassion. An ordinary lawyer is not affected with the cause he pleads, nor doth he care which way it goes; profit makes him plead, not affection. But Christ intercedes feelingly; and that which makes him intercede with affection is, it is his own cause which he pleads in the cause of his people. —Thomas Watson

"Five hundred millions of souls," exclaimed a missionary (many years ago), "are represented as being unenlightened! I cannot, if I would, give up the idea of being a missionary, while I reflect upon this vast number of my fellow-sinners, who are perishing for lack of knowledge. 'Five hundred millions' intrudes itself upon my mind wherever I go, and however I am employed. When

I go to bed, it is the last thing that recurs to my memory; if I awake in the night, it is to meditate on it alone; and in the morning it is generally the first thing that occupies my thoughts."

We may suppose that there was nothing in the external appearance of these multitudes which, to the common eye, would indicate their sad condition. We may suppose that they were "well-fed and well-clad," and that their hearts, under the influence of numbers, as is generally the case, were buoyant with pleasurable excitement; that good humor sunned their countenances, and enlivened their talk, and that—both to themselves, and to the ordinary spectator—they were a happy folk. But he, who seeth not as man seeth, looked down through the superficial stream of pleasurable excitement which now flowed and sparkled, and saw—What? Intellect enslaved, reason blinded, moral faculties benumbed, souls faint and lost, *"scattered abroad as sheep having no shepherd." —David Thomas*

136

What I tell you in darkness, that speak ye in light: and what ye hear in the ear, that preach ye upon the housetops.

—Matthew 10:27

USEFULNESS is the great desire of our souls if we are disciples of Jesus. We believe that it will most surely be attained by our making known the gospel. We have full faith in "the foolishness of preaching."

We feel that we have need to receive that gospel personally from the Lord himself, or we shall not know it so as to use it aright.

We must not run till we are prepared. This verse describes, and by implication promises, the needful preparation of heart. Our Lord will speak in our ear: he will commune with us in solitude.

I. AN INVALUABLE PRIVILEGE. The disciple is associated very nearly with his Lord, and received into closest fellowship with him.

We see before us three important matters.

1. We are permitted to realize our Lord's presence with us personally.
    He is still on speaking terms with us: still is he our Companion in the night, our Friend in solitude.
2. We are enabled to feel his word as spoken to us.

- Immediately: "*I* tell *you*." Personal contact.
- Forcefully: "in the ear." Not as thundered from Sinai, but as whispered by "a still, small voice." Still, very effectually.

3. We are privileged to receive such communications again and again: "I tell you . . . ye hear."
   - We need precept upon precept, line upon line.
   - Our Lord is willing to manifest himself to his own day by day.
   - We shall be wise to make occasions for hearing his voice in solitude, meditation, prayer, communion, etc.
   - We shall do well to use occasions of the Lord's own making such as the Sabbath, sickness, the night-watches, etc.
   - We need for a thousand reasons this private tuition, this personal communication with our Commander-in-chief.

II. A PREPARATORY PROCESS. We do not rightly perceive what we have to make known till Jesus personally imparts his holy teaching to our inmost hearts.

We see by reason of personal contact with our Lord:
1. Truth in its personality; living, acting, feeling; for he is "the way, the truth, and the life." Truth is no theory or phantom in Christ. Substantial truth is spoken by him.
2. Truth in its purity is found in him, in his written teaching, and in that which he speaks to the heart. Truth from man is mixed and adulterated; from Jesus it is unalloyed.
3. Truth in its proportions; he teaches all truth, in its true relations. Christ is no caricaturist, partisan, or politician.
4. Truth in its power. It comes strikingly, persuasively, convincingly, omnipotently from him. It quickens, and sustains.
5. Truth in its spirit. His words are spirit, life, love.
6. Truth in its certainty. "Verily, verily," is his motto.
7. Truth in its joyfulness. He speaks delight unto the soul. The truth in Jesus is glad tidings.

See the advantage of studying in Christ's College.

III. THE CONSEQUENT PROCLAMATION. What Jesus has told us alone in the dark we are to tell out openly in the light.

Courting publicity, we are to preach "upon the housetops."

What is this message which we have heard in the ear?

We bear our willing witness that:
1. There is peace in the blood of Jesus.
2. There is sanctifying power in his Holy Spirit.
3. There is rest in faith in our Lord and God.

4 There is safety in conformity to our great Exemplar.

5. There is joy in nearness to Jesus our Lord.

As we hear more we will tell more.

Oh, that men would receive our earnest testimony!

Will not you receive it who hear us at this present hour?

Private Pencillings

Claus Hames, one of the most useful preachers in Germany, once met a friend to whom he told how many times daily he was obliged to speak. His friend presently asked, "But, Friend Hames, if thou hast so much to say, when art thou still? And when does the Spirit of God speak to thee?" That simple question so impressed Hames that he resolved from that time to devote a portion of each day to retirement and silent study.

"How is it?" said a Christian man to his companion, as they were both returning from hearing the saintly Bramwell, "How is it that Brother Bramwell always tells us so much that is new?" The companion answered, "Brother Bramwell lives so near the gates of heaven that he hears a great many things which the rest of us do not get near enough to hear." —*J. H. Hitchens*

Of a certain preacher it was said: "He preaches as if Jesus Christ were at his side. Don't you see how every now and then he turns around as if he were saying, 'Lord Jesus, what shall I say next?'"

> Take my lips, and let them be
> Filled with messages from thee.
> —*F. R. Havergal.*

> Then sorrow touched by thee grows light,
>   With more than rapture's ray;
> As darkness shows us worlds of light
>   We never saw by day.
> —*Thomas Moore*

Men learn in suffering what they teach in song.

Possessors of divine truth are eager to spread it. "For," as Carlyle says, "if new-got gold is said to burn the pockets till it be cast forth into circulation; much more may new-found truth."

A servant was desired by his master to carry a present of fish to a friend, and to do it as quickly as possible. In all haste the man seized a basket, and set out; but when he reached his journey's end he became a laughing-stock, for he had forgotten the fish: his basket was empty Teacher! Preacher! let not the like happen to thee.

Often in the South of France have I needed to have a fire lighted; but I have found little or no comfort from it when my wish has been granted. The dwellers in that mild region build their fireplaces so badly that all the heat goes up the chimney. No matter how big the blaze, the hearth only seems to warm itself. Thus many professors of our holy faith would seem to get grace, and light, and pious feeling for themselves only: their heat goes up their own chimney. What is told them in the dark they keep in the dark, and that which is spoken in their ear never blesses any other ear. —*C. H. S.*

137

But the very hairs of your head are all numbered.
—*Matthew 10:30*

 ow considerate of our fears is the Lord Jesus! He knew that his people would be persecuted, and he sought to cheer them.

In how sweet and homely a way he puts things! He deigns to speak about the hairs of our head. Here is a proverb, simple in words, but sublime in sense.

We think we see four things in this sentence.

I. FORE-ORDINATION. The text may be read, "have all been numbered." It is of the past as well as of the present.

1. Its extent. Predestination extends to everything.
   - All the man; his being as a whole is foreknown. "In thy book all my members were written" (Ps. 139:16).
   - All that concerns him is foreknown; even to his hair, which may be shorn from him without damage to life or health.
   - All that he does; even the least and most casual thought, or act.
   - All that he undergoes. This may affect his hair so as to change its color; but every hair blanched with sorrow is numbered.
2. Its source. The counting is done by the Lord.
3. Its lessons. Jesus mentions this fore-ordination for a purpose:
   - To make us brave under trial.
   - To teach us to be submissive.
   - To help us to be hopeful.
   - To induce us to be joyful.
4. Its influence. It ennobles us to be thus minutely predestinated.
      If God arranges even our hairs, we are honored indeed.
To be the subject of a divine purpose of grace is glorious.

II. KNOWLEDGE. We are known so well as to have our hairs counted.

Concerning this divine knowledge let us note:

1. Its character.
   - Minute. "The very hairs of your head."
   - Complete. The whole man, spirit, soul, and body, is thus most assuredly well known to the Omniscient Lord.
   - Pre-eminent. God knows us better than we know ourselves, or than others know us; for neither we nor they have numbered the hairs of our head.
   - Tender. Thus a mother values each hair of her darling's head.
   - Sympathetic. God enters into those trials, those years, and those sicknesses which are registered in a man's hair.
   - Constant. Not a hair falls from our head without God.
2. Its lessons.
   - Concerning consecration, we are taught that our least precious parts are the Lord's and are included in the royal inventory. Let us not use even our hair for vanity.
   - Concerning prayer. Our heavenly Father knoweth what things we have need of. We do not pray to inform him of our case.
   - Concerning our circumstances. These are before the divine mind, be they little or great. Since trifling matters like our hairs are catalogued by Providence, we are assured that greater concerns are before the Father's eye.

III. VALUATION. The hairs of our head are counted because valued.

These were poor saints who were thus highly esteemed.

The numbering mentioned in the text suggests several questions.

- If each hair is valued, what must their heads be worth?
- What must their bodies be worth?
- What must their souls be worth?
- What must they have cost the Lord, their Redeemer?
- How can it be thought that he will lose one of them?
- Ought we not greatly to esteem them?
- Is it not our duty, our honor, our joy to seek after such of them as are not yet called by grace?

IV. PRESERVATION. The hairs of their head are all numbered, because they are to be preserved from all evil.

1. From the smallest real loss we are secured by promise. "There shall not a hair of your head perish" (Luke 21:18).
2. From persecution we shall be rescued. "Fear not them" (Matt. 10:28).
3. From accident. Nothing can harm us unless the Lord permits.

4. From necessity. You shall not die of hunger, or thirst, or nakedness. God will keep each hair of your head.

5. From sickness. It shall sanctify rather than injure you.

6. From death. In death we are not losers, but infinite gainers.
Resurrection will restore the whole man.
Let us for ourselves trust, and not be afraid.
Let us set a high value upon souls, and feel an earnest love for them.

Pins

"*Hairs*"—of which ye yourselves are heedless. Who cares for the hairs once dragged out by a comb? A hair is a proverbial expression for an utter trifle. —*John Albert Bengel*

If God numbers their hairs, much more does he number their heads, and take care of their lives, their comforts, their souls. This intimates that God takes more care of them than they do of themselves. They who are solicitous to number their money, and goods, and cattle, yet were never careful to number their hairs, which fall, and are lost, and they never miss them: but God numbers the hairs of his people, and not a hair of their head shall perish (Luke 21:18). Not the least hurt shall be done them, but upon a valuable consideration: so precious to God are his saints, and their lives and deaths! —*Matthew Henry*

> There are who sigh that no fond heart is theirs,
> None loves them best—Oh! vain and selfish sigh!
> Out of the bosom of His love He spares—
> The Father spares the Son, for thee to die:
> For thee He died—for thee He lives again:
> O'er thee He watches in His boundless reign.
>
> Thou art as much His care, as if beside
> Nor man nor angel lived in Heaven or earth:
> Thus sunbeams pour alike their glorious tide
> To light up worlds, or wake an insect's mirth
> They shine and shine with unexhausted store—
> Thou art thy Savior's darling—seek no more.
> —*John Keble*

An Italian martyr, in the sixteenth century, was most cruelly treated in the prisons of the Inquisition. His brother, who with great difficulty obtained an interview with him, was deeply affected by the sight of his sufferings. "My brother," said the prisoner, "if you are a Christian, why do you distress yourself thus? Do you not know that a leaf cannot fall to the ground without the will of God? Comfort yourself in Christ Jesus, for the present troubles are not to be compared with the glory to come."

If pestilence stalk through the land, ye say "This is God's doing";
Is it not also his doing when an aphis creepeth on a rosebud?—
If an avalanche roll from its Alp, ye tremble at the will of Providence;
Is not that will concerned when the sear leaves fall from the poplar?

—*Martin F. Tupper*

138

Ye that taketh not his cross, and followeth after me, is not worthy
of me.

—*Matthew 10:38*

EFORE his crucifixion, our Lord has a foresight of it, and does not
hesitate to realize himself as bearing his cross.

With equal prescience he foresees each true disciple receiving
and taking up his own personal cross. He sees none exempted.

Picture to the mind's eye a procession led by the cross-bearing Jesus, and
made up of his cross-bearing train. This is not a pageant, but a real march of
suffering. It reaches through all time.

The chief requirement of a disciple is to follow Jesus in all things, in cross-
bearing as in all else.

Cross-bearing is trying, laborious, sorrowful, humiliating.

Cross-bearing is inevitable to the follower of Jesus. We are bound to take up
our cross or give up all idea of being Christians.

Let us obediently inquire:

I. WHAT IS MY PECULIAR CROSS? "He that taketh not his cross."

1. It may be the giving up of certain pleasures or indulgences.
2. It may be the endurance of reproach and unkindness, or remaining in
   poverty and obscurity for the good of others.
3. It may be the suffering of losses and persecutions, for Christ's sake.
4. It certainly means the consecrating of all to Jesus: the bowing of my whole
   self beneath the blessed burden of service with which he honors me.
5. It also includes the endurance of my heavenly Father's will with patience,
   acquiescence, and thanksgiving.

My cross is well, wisely, kindly, and surely chosen for me by my Lord.
It is only meet that I should be made like my Lord in bearing it.

II. WHAT AM I TO DO WITH IT? "Taketh . . . followeth after me."

1. I am deliberately to take it up.

- Not to choose a cross, or pine after another form of trial.
- Not to make a cross, by petulance and obstinacy.
- Not to murmur at the cross appointed me.
- Not to despise it, by callous stoicism, or willful neglect of duty.
- Not to faint under it, fall beneath it, or run from it.

2. I am boldly to face it. It is only a wooden cross after all.
3. I am patiently to endure it, for I have only to carry it a little way.
4. I am cheerfully to resign myself to it, for my Lord appoints it.
5. I am obediently to follow Christ with it. What an honor and comfort to be treading in his steps! This is the essential point.

It is not enough to bear a cross, we must bear it after Jesus.

I ought to be thankful that I have only to bear it, and that it does not bear me. It is a royal burden, a sanctified burden, a sanctifying burden, a burden which gives communion with Christ.

III. WHAT SHOULD ENCOURAGE ME?

1. Necessity: I cannot be a disciple without cross-bearing.
2. Society: better men than I have carried it.
3. Love: Jesus bore a far heavier cross than mine.
4. Faith: grace will be given equal to the weight of the cross.
5. Hope: good to myself will result from my bearing this load.
6. Zeal: Jesus will be honored by my patient endurance.
7. Experience: I shall yet find pleasure in it, for it will produce in me much blessing. The cross is a fruitful tree.
8. Expectation: glory will be the reward of it. No cross, no crown.

Let not the ungodly fancy that theirs is a better lot: the Psalmist says, "many sorrows shall be to the wicked."

Let not the righteous dread the cross, for it will not crush them: it may be painted with iron colors by our fears, but it is not made of that heavy metal; we can bear it, and we will bear it right joyously.

Nails

When Alexander the Great marched through Persia, his way was stopped with ice and snow, insomuch that his soldiers, being tired out with hard marches, were discouraged, and would have gone no further, which he perceiving, dismounted his horse, and went on foot through the midst of them all, making himself a way with a pickax; whereat they all being ashamed, first his friends, then the captains of his army, and, last of all, the common soldiers, followed him. So should all men follow Christ their Savior, by that rough and unpleasant way of the cross that he hath traversed before them. He having drunk unto them in the cup of his passion, they are to pledge him when occasion is offered; he having left them an example of his suffering, they are to follow him in the selfsame steps of sorrow. —*John Spencer*

The cross is easier to him who takes it up than to him who drags it along. —*J. E. Vaux*

We are bid to take, not to make our cross. God in his providence will provide one for us. And we are bid to take it up; we hear nothing of laying it down. Our troubles and our lives live and die together. —*W.Gurnall*

> Must Jesus bear the cross alone,
> And all the church go free?
> No, there's a cross for every one,
> And there's a cross for me.

"No man," said Flavel, "hath a velvet cross."

As an old Yorkshire working man, a friend of mine, said, "Ah! it is blessed work cross-bearing when it's tied on with love." —*Newman Hall*

Welcome the cross of Christ, and bear it triumphantly; but see that it be indeed Christ's cross, and not thine own. —*Wilcox*

Christ's cross is the sweetest burden that ever I bore; it is such a burden as wings are to a bird, or sails to a ship, to carry me forward to my harbor. —*Samuel Rutherford*

Whatever the path is, Christ is there, and to be with him is joy enough for any creature, whether man or angel. He does not send us to walk in a dreary, desolate road. He does not say, "Go ye," pointing to a lonely way in which he is not to be found; he says, "Come after me," so that we need not take a single step where his footprints cannot be seen, and where his presence may not still be found. If the sharp flints cut our feet, they have wounded his before. If the darkness gathers thickly here and there, it was a denser gloom that surrounded him. If ofttimes we must stand and fight, it was through fiercer conflicts that he passed. If the cross is heavy to our shoulder, it is light when compared with the one he bore. "Christ leads me," said Baxter, "through no darker room than he went through before." If the road were a thousand times rougher than it is, it would be well worth while to walk in it for the sake of walking with Christ there. Following Jesus means fellowship with Jesus, and the joy of that fellowship cannot be told. —*P.*

139

Come unto me, all ye that labor and are heavy laden, and I will give you rest. Take my yoke upon you, and learn of me; for I am meek and lowly in heart: and ye shall find rest unto your souls. For my yoke is easy, and my burden light.

—*Matthew 11:28-30*

ESUS had first taught the solemn truth of *human responsibility* (verses 20–24), and afterwards he had joyfully proclaimed in prayer the doctrine of *election*: now he turns to give a free and full invitation to those who are needing rest. These three things are quite consistent and should be found in all Christian preaching.

Remember who he is who thus invites men to come to him.

The Son of the Highest, the revealer of God *then* and *now*; he bids men draw near to himself without fear, and rest in such nearness.

The Savior ever living, having once died, is waiting to receive and save all who will come to him; and such he will bless with rest.

In our Lord's gracious invitation you note:

I. A CHARACTER WHICH DESCRIBES YOU.

1. Laboring, "all ye that labor," in whatever form.
   - In the service of formal religion, in the attempt to keep the law, or in any other way of self-justification.
   - In the service of self to get gain, honor, ease, etc.
   - In the service of the world to discover, invent, legislate, etc.
   - In the service of Satan, lust, drink, infidelity, etc.
2. Laden. All who are "heavy laden" are called.
   - Laden heavily because weary, vexed, disappointed; despairing.
   - Laden with sin, guilt, dread, remorse, fear of death.
   - Laden with care, anxiety, greed, ambition, etc.
   - Laden with sorrow, poverty, oppression, slander, etc.
   - Laden with doubt, temptation, conflict, inner faintness, etc.

II. A BLESSING WHICH INVITES YOU.

1. Rest to be given. "I will give you rest."
   - To the conscience, by atonement and pardon.
   - To the mind, by infallible instruction and establishment.
   - To the heart a rest for love. Jesus fills and contents the heart.
   - To the energies, by giving an object worth attaining.
   - To the apprehensions, assuring that all things work for good.
2. Rest to be found. "Ye shall find rest unto your souls."
   - This is rest upon rest, deepening, settling.
   - This is rest which comes of conquered passion, desire, etc.
   - This is rest which comes of being fully consecrated to the Lord.

How such rest would cheer you, strengthen you, save you!

How it would counteract the labors and the loads!

III. A DIRECTION TO GUIDE YOU.

1. "*Come* unto me."

- Come to a person, to Jesus, the living Savior and Example.
- Come at once, Jesus is ready now. Are you?
- Come *all* who labor and are loaded. None will be refused.
- Come laden, with your burdens on your hearts, and "I will give you rest." Come as you are. Come by faith.

2. "*Take* my yoke upon you."
   - Be obedient to my command.
   - Be willing to be conformed to me in service and burden-bearing.
   - Be submissive to the afflictions which I may lay upon you.

3. "*Learn* of me."
   - You do not know; but must be content to learn.
   - You must not cavil; but have a mind to learn.
   - You must learn by heart, and copy my meekness and lowliness.

IV. AN ARGUMENT TO PERSUADE YOU.

You wish to be like your Lord in restfulness and service; then come end learn of him, and remember that he is:

1. A lowly Teacher: bearing with failure, repeating his lessons, assisting the disciple, restoring the fallen.
2. Laying no heavy burden. "My yoke is easy," etc.
3. Giving rest by the burden which he causes you to bear: "Take my yoke . . . and ye shall find rest."

Magnets

The immediate occasion of the invitation, with its deep earnestness of pity and sympathy, was found, I doubt not, in the outward appearance of the crowd actually surrounding Jesus. Probably by this time it was about sunset. After a day of exhausting toil for our Savior himself; the workman from the field, the busy trader, the fisher with his nets, the slave with his burden, the rich man with his heavier burden of care, the gray-haired sinner stooping under the weight of years, and inly burdened with remorse and fear—these, and such as these, met the Savior's eye, which read their hearts; but in them he saw represented our toiling, suffering world, and uttered a voice of invitation meant to reach, and destined yet to reach, all mankind. "*I will give you rest.*" Rest for the burdened conscience, in pardon; for the unquiet intellect, in truth; for the aching thirsty heart, in divine love; for the care-fretted spirit, in God's providence and promises; for the weary with sorrow and suffering, in the present foretaste, and shortly in the actual enjoyment of "his rest." —*E. R. Conder*

"Come," saith Christ, "and I will give you rest." I will not *show* you rest, nor barely *tell* you of rest, but I will *give* you rest. I am faithfulness itself, and cannot lie, I *will* give you rest. I that have the greatest power to give it, the greatest will to give it, the greatest right to give it, come, laden sinners, and *I* will give you rest. Rest is the most desirable good, the most suitable good, and to you the greatest good. Come, saith Christ, that is, believe in me, and I will give you rest; I will give you peace with God, and peace with conscience: I will turn your storm into an everlasting calm; I will give you such rest, that the world can neither give to you nor take from you. —*Thomas Brooks*

Lord, thou madest us for thyself, and we can find no rest till we find rest in thee! —*Augustine*

A poor English girl, in Miss Leigh's home in Paris, ill in body and hopeless in spirit, was greatly affected by hearing some children singing "I heard the voice of Jesus say." When they came to the words, "weary, and worn, and sad," she moaned, "That's me! That's me! What did he do? Fill it up, fill it up!" She never rested until she had heard the whole of the hymn which tells how Jesus gives rest to such. By-and-by she asked, "Is that true?" On being answered, "Yes," she asked, "Have you come to Jesus? Has he given you rest?" "He has." Raising herself, she asked, "Do you mind my coming very close to you? May be it would be easier to go to Jesus with one who has been before than to go to him alone." So saying, she nestled her head on the shoulder of her who watched, and clutching her as one in the agony of death, she murmured, "Now, try and take me with you to Jesus." —*The Sunday at Home*

There are many heads resting on Christ's bosom, but there's room for yours there. —Samuel Rutherford

NOTE: *For variety, Spurgeon added another outline on a portion of the same text*

140

Come unto me, all ye that labor and are heavy laden, and I will give you rest.

—*Matthew 11:28*

 HIS text is often preached from, but never too often, since the sorrows with which it deals always abound, and the remedy is always effective.

This time we purpose to view it from our Lord's side.

He entreats the weary to come to him. He beseeches them to learn of him. He not only receives those who come, but begs them to come. What is this desire which burns in his bosom? And whence comes it?

Let us carefully consider:

I. WHO IS HE?

1. One who has been rejected, yet he cries "Come unto me."

2. One whose rejection involves us in fearful guilt, yet he is ready to forgive, and to bestow rest upon us if we come.

3. One who knows his Father's purpose, but fears not to give a pressing invitation to all who labor and are heavy laden.

4. One who has all power to receive such as come, and to give rest to them all. This is no vain invitation saying more than it means.

5. One who as the Son of God is infinitely blessed, and yet finds new joy in giving rest to poor restless men.

II. WHOM DOES HE CALL AND WHY?

1. Laborers, with more than they can do: disquieted, unhappy.
   These he calls to himself that he may give them rest, and cause them to find rest.

2. Heavy laden ones, with more than they can bear: oppressed, sorrowful, ready to die.

3. The poor and illiterate who need to be taught.

4. The spiritually burdened, who much need a helping hand, and can only find it in him.

III WHAT CAUSES HIS DESIRE FOR THEM?

Not his own need of them.

Not their personal worthiness.

Nor aught that they are or can ever be. But:

1. He has a love to our race. "My delights were with the sons of men" (Prov. 8:31). He would have these resting with himself.

2. He is himself a man, and knows the needs of men.

3. He has done so much to buy us rest that he would fain give it to us.

4. He delights to do more and more for us: it is his joy to give good things to men.

5. He knows what our ruin will be unless we find rest in him.

6. He knows what our bliss will be if we come unto him.

IV. HOW THEN SHALL WE TREAT THIS CALL?

1. It is very earnest, let us heed it.

2. It is very simple, let the poorest seize upon it.

3. It exactly suits us. Does it not suit you?

4 It is very gracious, let us accept it.

Echoes

The most condescending affections that ever he discovered, the most gracious invitations that ever he made, were at those times when he had a sense of his glory in a particular manner, to show his intention in his possessing it.

When he spake of all things delivered to him by his Father, an invitation to men to come unto him is the use he makes of it (Matt. 11:27–28). If this be the use he makes of his glory, to invite us, it should be the use we should make of the thoughts of it, to accept his proffer. A nation should run to him because he is glorified. —*Stephen Charnock*

"Come unto me," is the invitation of this Blessed One, so intensely human, though so gloriously divine, "Unto me," in whose arms little children were embraced, on whose bosom a frail mortal lay: "unto me," who hungered, thirsted, fainted, sorrowed, wept, and yet whose love, and grief, and pains, and tears, wore the expression of emotions felt in the mighty heart of God. —*Caird*

> Lord, I have invited all,
> And I shall
> Still invite, still call to thee:
> For it seems but just and right
> In my sight,
> Where is all, there all should be.
> —*George Herbert*

It runs thus—you to me, and I to you. Here is a double communion set up. This is all to our advantage, and to the display of our Lord's great graciousness. We come, and therein he obtains the company of a beggar, a leper, a patient, a repulsive rebel: this is no gain to anything in him except his pity. But surely he expects something of us to reward him for receiving us? By no means. We are to come to him, not that we may give him something, but that he may give everything to as. What a Lord is this!

141

And immediately Jesus stretched forth his hand, and caught him, and said unto him, O thou of little faith, wherefore didst thought doubt?

—*Matthew 14:31*

 ur Lord did not question the doubter till he had saved the sinker. His rebukes are always timely.

The question was not only well deserved as a rebuke, but it was specially instructive, and no doubt it proved useful in after years.

When the grace of faith is really present, doubt has to answer for itself, and to die if it cannot defend itself.

Oh, that it may die in us at once!

We will put the question of our text to the two great classes of men.

I. WHEREFORE DOST THOU DOUBT, O CHRISTIAN?

1. *Let us mention some supposedly valid reasons.*
   - Can you quote past experience of broken promises?
   - Is the present evil beyond the power of Omnipotence?
   - Are the promises abolished? Are the purposes of grace annulled?
   - Has God himself changed? Is his mercy clean gone for ever?

None of these supposable reasons have any existence.

2. *Let us hear your actual reasons; if you dare state them.*
   - My sense of guilt is peculiarly deep and clear.
   - My inbred sin has risen upon me with terrible fury.
   - My failures justify despair when viewed by the side of other men's attainments, and my own obligations.
   - My trials are so peculiar, so fierce, so long, so varied.
   - My heart fails me. I can bear up no longer.
   - My fears predict greater evils still, and threaten ultimate ruin.

Many such insufficient reasonings becloud the mind; and it may be wisdom to look them in the face, and so dissipate them.

3. *Let us view these reasonings from other standpoints.*
   - How would you have viewed them when first you believed?
   - How did you view former trials when they came in your way; and how do you view them now that you have overcome them?
   - What do you think of your trials when you are lying in Jesus' bosom—assured of his love?
   - How do you speak of them when you are instructing others?
   - How will they appear to you when you get to heaven?

Jesus is now near you. How can you take such gloomy views of things in his presence?

4. *Shall we hint at the true reasons of your doubting?*
   - You were self-confident, and that confidence has failed you.
   - You looked too much to things seen by the light of sense; and now that it is dark, you are in consequence troubled.
   - You took your eye off from your Lord.
   - Perhaps you neglected prayer, watching, repentance, etc.

When you find out the real reason of your doubt, cry for pardon, and seek to the Holy Spirit to restore faith, and set you right.

II. WHEREFORE DOST THOU DOUBT, O SINNER?

The Lord's hand is stretched out to save sinking sinners.

Do not distrust the power of Jesus to save you from sinking.

1. *Let us suppose good reasons for your doubting.*
  - Have others believed and perished?
  - Have you yourself tried faith in Jesus, and found it vain?
  - Has the blood of Jesus lost its power?
  - Has the Holy Spirit ceased to comfort, enlighten, renew?
  - Is the gospel abrogated? Is God's mercy dean gone for ever?

None of these can be answered in the affirmative.

2. *Let us hear your apparent reasons.*
  - Your sins are great, numerous, aggravated, and singular.
  - You cannot think that salvation is for you.
  - You have refused the gospel call so long.
  - Your heart is so dreadfully hard and unfeeling.

None of these are sufficient reasons for doubting Almighty love.

3. *Let us learn the way to deal with such unreasonable doubting.*
  - Repent of it, for it dishonors the power and promise of the Father, the blood of Jesus, and the grace of the Holy Spirit.
  - End it, by simply believing what is so surely true.
  - Run as far as possible the other way. Believe up to the hilt.

In every case, let us be sure that to believe God is sanctified common-sense and to doubt him is an extravagance of folly.

Modern Instances

Mr. Haslam has reported a conversation between two poor aged Christians to the following effect: "Oh!" said the husband, who was evidently the weaker vessel, "I've got so little faith, I do get these 'ere doubts so much." "Yes," added the wife, "and ye keeps them, Peter, and brings them to me."

Though the providence of God may be exceedingly dark, the language of faith is, "The Lord is ready to save." If you look into your past experience, you will find that God has done great things for you. Is it not true that nine-tenths of all the difficulty you have anticipated have never come to pass at all? I have great sympathy with Billy Bray, whose wife said to him, when he came home, having given all his money away, "I never saw such a man in my life. Thee'lt go and look after other people's wives and children, and help them, and thee own wife and children may starve." Billy, with great force, said, "Well, woman, thee'st never starved yet;" and that was the fact, for there she stood, a living witness to his word. —*Henry Varley*

Good old Mr. Crisp, :who had been President of the Baptist College at Bristol for fifty years, was towards the end of his life fearful that his faith would fail. Being reminded of the passage, "He that spared not his own Son, but delivered him up for us all, how shall he not with him also freely give us all things?" He said, after repeating and dwelling on the last words, "No, it would be wrong to doubt; I cannot, I dare not, I will not doubt!" —*S. A. Swaine, in "Faithful Men"*

> When darkness long has veiled my mind,
>   And smiling day once more appears,
> Then, my Redeemer! then I find
>   The folly of my doubts and fears.
>
> I chide my unbelieving heart;
>   And blush that I should ever be
> Thus prone to act so base a part,
>   Or harbor one hard thought of thee.
>   —*Cowper*

Certain persons think that doubting is a needful part of Christian experience, but it is by no means the case. A child may have a deep experience of its father's love, and yet it may never have known a doubt of him. All the experience of a Christian is not Christian experience. If many Christians are despondent, it is no reason why I must be: it is rather a reason why I should watch against it. What if many sheep suffer from the fly; am I to be anxious to have my fleece fly-blown in order to be like them? Never doubt the Lord till you have cause for it; and then you will never doubt him as long as you live.

142

And he went out about the third hour, and saw others standing idle in the marketplace, and said unto them; Go ye also into the vineyard, and whatsoever is right I will give you. And they went their way.
                                        —*Matthew 20:3-4*

THE reason for employing these people must have been gracious. Surely the good man could have waited till the next morning; but he charitably chose to employ the needy ones at once. He did not need laborers, but the poor men needed their pennies.

Certainly it is sovereign grace alone which leads the Lord God to engage such sorry laborers as we are.

Let us inquire:

I. HOW MAY THE LORD BE SAID TO GO OUT?

1. Inasmuch as the impulse of grace comes first in every case, and none go into the vineyard till he calls them.
2. Inasmuch as there are times of revival, when the Lord goes forth by the power of his Spirit, and many are brought in.

3. Inasmuch as there are times of personal visitation with most men when they are specially moved to holy things.

II. WHAT IS THE HOUR HERE MENTIONED?

It represents the period between 25 and 35 years of age, or thereabouts.

1. The dew of youth's earliest and best morning hour is gone.
2. Habits of idleness have been formed by standing in the market place so long. It is harder to begin at the third hour than at the first. Loiterers are usually spoiled by their loafing ways.
3. Satan is ready with temptation to lure them to his service.
4. Their sun may go down suddenly, for life is uncertain. Many a day of life has closed at its third hour.
5. Fair opportunity for work yet remains; but it will speedily pass away as the hours steal round.
6. As yet the noblest of all work has not been commenced; for only by working for our Lord can life be made sublime.

III. WHAT WERE THEY DOING TO WHOM HE SPOKE? "Standing idle in the market place."

1. Many are altogether idling in a literal sense. They are mere loafers and *dilottanti*, with nothing to do.
2. Many are idle with laborious business—industrious triflers, wearied with toils which accomplish nothing of real worth.
3. Many are idle because of their constant indecision. Unstable as water they do not excel (James 1:6).
4. Many are idle though full of sanguine intentions; but as yet their resolves are not carried out.

IV. WHAT WORK WOULD THE LORD HAVE THEM DO?

He would have them work by day in his vineyard.

1. The work is such as many of the best of men enjoy.
2. The work is proper and fit for you.
3. For that work the Lord will find you tools and strength.
4. You shall work with your Lord, and so be ennobled.
5. Your work shall be growingly pleasant to you.
6. Your work shall be graciously rewarded at the last.

V. WHAT DID THEY DO IN ANSWER TO HIS CALL? "They went their way."

May you, who are in a similar time of the day, imitate them!

1. They went at once. The parable indicates immediate service.
2. They worked with a will.
3. They never left the service, but remained till night.

4. They received the full reward at the day's end.

Let us pray the Lord to go out among our young men and women.

Let us expect to see such come into the church, and let us guide them in their work, for they come into the vineyard to labor.

Let us inquire if some will come *now.*

Spades

Have you never thought with extreme sadness of the many men and women upon our earth whose lives are useless? Have you never reflected upon the millions of people who waste in nothingness their thoughts, their affections, their energies, all their powers, which frivolity dissipates as the sand of the desert absorbs the water which is sent upon it from the sky? These beings pass onward, without even asking themselves toward what end they journey, or for what reason they were placed here below. —*Eugene Bersier*

All activity out of Christ, all labor that is not labor in his church is in his sight a *"standing idle."* —*Archbishop Trench*

A good minister, now in heaven, once preached to his congregation a powerful sermon, founded upon the words of Christ, "Why stand ye here all the day idle?" The sermon did good to many, among whom was a lady who went to the minister the next day, and said, "Doctor, I want a spade." We should be happy to put spades into the hands of all our idle friends. There are Sunday school spades, Mission room spades, Tract-distribution spades, Sick-visitation spades, etc., etc. Who will apply for them? —*Home Evangel*

> What can I do the cause of God to aid?
>   Can powers so weak as mine
>   Forward the great design?
> Not by young hands are mighty efforts made.
>
> Not mighty efforts, but a willing mind,
>   Not strong, but ready hands
>   The vineyard's Lord demands;
> For every age fit labor he will find.
>
> Come, then, in childhood, to the vineyard's gate;
>   E'en you can dress the roots,
>   And train the tender shoots—
> Then why in sloth and sin contented wait?
>
> To move the hardened soil, to bend and lift
>   The fallen branch, to tread
>   The winepress full and red,
> These need a stronger arm, a nobler gift;

But all can aid the work. The little child
  May gather up some weed,
  Or drop some fertile seed,
Or strew with flowers the path which else were dark and wild.

—*J. H. Clinch*

"Are you not wearying for the heavenly rest?" said Whitefield to an old minister. "No, certainly not!" he replied. "Why not?" was the surprised rejoinder. "Why, my good brother," said the aged saint, "If you were to send your servant into the fields, to do a certain portion of work for you, and promised to give him rest and refreshment in the evening, what would you say if you found him languid and discontented in the middle of the day, and murmuring, 'Would to God it were evening?' Would you not bid him be up and doing, and finish his work, and then go home, and enjoy the promised rest? Just so does God require of you and me that, instead of looking for Saturday night, we do our day's work in the day."

143

Then saith he to his servants, the wedding is ready, but them which were bidden were not worthy. Go ye therefore into the highways and as many as ye shall find, bid to the marriage. So those servants went out into the highways, and gathered together all as many as they found, both bad and good; and the wedding was furnished with guests.

—*Matthew 22:8-10*

 HE grand design of God is to make a marriage for his Son.

Our Lord Jesus has espoused his Church, and there must be a feast at the wedding. Is it not meet that it should be so?

A feast would be a failure if none came to it, and therefore the present need is that the wedding be "furnished with guests."

I. THE FIRST INVITATION WAS A FAILURE.

This is seen in Jewish history.

Among Gentiles, those to whom the gospel invitation specially comes are, as a rule, unwilling to accept it.

Up to this hour, children of godly parents, and hearers of the word,. many of them refuse the invitation for reasons of their own.

The invitation was refused:

1. Not because it involved suffering, for it was a wedding feast to which they were bidden.
2. Nor because there were no adequate preparations: "The wedding is ready."
3. Nor because the invitations were not delivered, or were misunderstood: they "were bidden."
4. But because they were not fit for the high joy.
   - They were not loyal to their King.
   - They were not attached to his royal Son.
   - They were not pleased with his noble marriage.
   - They were wrapped up in self-interest.
   - They were cruel to well-intentioned messengers.
5. Therefore they were punished with fire and sword.
   - But this destruction was no wedding feast for the King's Son
   - This punishment was no joy to the King.

Love must reign: mercy must be glorious; Christ must reveal his grace; otherwise he has no joy of his union with mankind.

Therefore:

II. THE COMMISSION WAS ENLARGED.

1. Disappointment must arouse activity and enterprise—"Go ye."
2. Disappointment suggests change of sphere—"into the highways."
3. A wide invitation is to be tried—"as many as ye shall find, bid."
4. A keen outlook is to be kept—"as many as ye shall find."
5. Publicity is to be courted—"went out into the highways."
6. Small numbers—ones and twos— are to be pressed in.

This is said to have been the result of the anger of the King.

So good is the Lord that his wrath to despisers works good for others.

III. THE NEW MISSION WAS FULFILLED.

The particulars of it will be suggestive for ourselves at this present era.

1. The former servants, who had escaped death, went out again.
2. Other servants, who had not gone at first, entered zealously into the joyful but needful service.
3. They went in many directions—"into the highways."
4. They went out at once. Not an hour could be left unused.
5. They pointed all they met to one center.
6. They welcomed all sorts of characters—"as many as they found."
7. They found them willing to come. He who sent the messengers inclined the guests: none seem to have refused.

This blessed service is being carried on at this very hour.

IV. THE GREAT DESIGN WAS ACCOMPLISHED.

1. The King's bounty was displayed before the world.
2. His provision was used. Think of grace and pardon unused!
3. The happiness of men was promoted: they feasted to the full.
4. Their grateful praise was evoked. All the guests were joyful in their King as they feasted at his table.
5. The marriage was graced.
6. The slight put upon the King's Son, by the churls who refused to come, was more than removed.
7. The quality of the guests most fully displayed the wisdom, grace, and condescension of the Host.

The whole business worked for the highest glory of the King and his Son. Amen! So let it be among us!

Wedding-Cards

The wicked, for the slight breakfast of this world, lose the Lamb's supper of glory (Rev. 19:9); where these four things concur, that make a perfect feast: A good time, eternity; a good place, heaven; a good company, the saints; good cheer, glory. —*Thomas Adams*

The devil does not like field-preaching; neither do I. I love a commodious room, a soft cushion, a handsome pulpit; but where is my zeal if I do not trample all these under foot in order to save one more soul. —*John Wesley*

> "Call them in"—the Jew, the Gentile;
> Bid the stranger to the feast;
> "Call them in"—the rich, the noble,
> From the highest to the least:
> Forth the Father runs to meet them,
> He hath all their sorrows seen;
> Robe, and ring, and royal sandals,
> Wait the lost ones: "Call them in."
> —*Sacred Songs and Solos*

From hedges and lanes of conscious nakedness and need, the marriage festival is furnished with guests. To the poor the gospel is preached, and the poor in spirit gladly listen, whether they are clothed in purple or in rags. —*William Arnot*

We might do better if we went further afield. Our invitations to Christ, which fall so feebly on the ears of those who regularly hear us, would be welcomed by those to whom we never deliver them. We are fools to waste time in the shallows of our churches and chapels when the deep outside teems with waiting fishes. We need *fresh* heaters: the newer the news to any man, the more likely is he to regard it as good news. Music hall work, outdoor preaching, and house-to-house visitation have virgin soil to deal with, and there is none like it.

Invite the oft-invited—certainly; but do not forget that those who have never been invited as yet cannot have been hardened by refusals. Beggars in the highways had never been bidden to a marriage-feast before; and so, when they were surprised with an invitation, they raised no questions, but gladly hastened to the banquet.

144

They that were ready went in with him to the marriage; and the door was shut.

—Matthew 25:10

URING the waiting period, the virgins seemed much alike, even as at this day one can hardly discern the false professor from the true.

When the midnight cry was heard the difference began to appear, as it will do when the Second Advent approaches.

When the Bridegroom was actually come, they were finally divided.

Let us prayerfully consider:

I. THE READY AND THEIR ENTRANCE.

1. What is this readiness? "They that were ready."
   - It is not a fruit of nature. None are ready to enter the marriage feast of glory while they are in an unregenerate condition.
   - It must be a work of grace; since we are unable to make ourselves fit for the vision of God, and the glory of Christ is too bright for us to be naturally fit to share in it.
   - It should be our daily concern. He who is ready for the marriage feast is ready to live, and ready to die—ready for anything.
   - It mainly consists in a secret work wrought in us:
     In being reconciled to God by the death of his Son.
     In being regenerated, and so made meet for glory.
     In being anointed with the Spirit, and fitted for holy service.
     In being quickened into a high and holy fellowship with God.
     In being delighted with God, and so being ready to enjoy him.
   - It should be our present inquiry whether we are now "ready."
     Some make no profession, never pray, nor praise.
     Others make profession, but neither love, nor trust; they have lamps, but no oil with which to keep them burning.
2. What is this entrance? A going in unto glory to be for ever with the Lord (1 Thess. 4:17).

- Immediate. "They that were ready *went in*." No sooner was the Bridegroom come, than they went in. Love brooks no delays.
- Intimate. They "went in *with him*." This is the glory of heaven, and the crown of its joys, that we go into them with Jesus, who remains our constant Companion therein.
- Joyous. "They went in with him *to the marriage*."
- Personal. "*They* went in"— each one entered for herself.
- Eternal. "The door was shut"—to shut them in for ever.
- "He shutteth, and no man openeth" (Rev. 3:7).
- Actual. In all the marriage-festival each one of the wise virgins had a share: indeed, they enjoyed more than appears in the parable, for they were brides, as well as maids of honor.

What a world of meaning lies in that abundant entrance which will be ministered to all the faithful! (2 Pet. 1:11).

II. THE UNREADY AND THEIR EXCLUSION.

1. What is this unreadiness?
   - It was the absence of a secret essential; but that absence was consistent with much apparent preparation.

      These persons had the name and character of virgins.
      They had the lamps or torches of true bridesmaids.
      They were companions of the true virgins.
      They acted like the true; in their virtues and in their faults.
      They awakened as the true did, startled by the same cry.
      They prayed also, after a fashion—"give us of your oil."
   - Yet were they never ready to enter in with the King.
   - They had no heart-care to be found ready, hence flaming external lamps, but no hidden internal oil.
   - They had no faith-foresight; they had not provided for the probable waiting, and the late coming.
   - They played the fool with Christ's wedding-feast, not thinking it worth the purchase of a little oil, but going to it with torches which would inevitably go out in smoke.
   - They put off till night what should have been done at once.
2. What is this exclusion?
   - It was universal to all who were not ready.
   - It was complete: "the door was shut"—shut for those without quite as surely as for those within.
   - It was just; for they were not ready, and so slighted the King.
   - It was final. Since the fatal news that the door was shut, no news has come that it has been opened, or that it ever will be.

What if the cry were heard at this moment, "Behold he cometh"?
As yet the door is not shut. Be ready ere it closes.

Flashes from the Lamps

"Uncle Ned," a colored Baptist of the South, was talking with his former master's son. "Child," said the old man solemnly, "yer talk is too highfalutin' for me; but de Bible is plain as A-B-C, whar it says yer got ter 'pent and be baptizen, or yer will be damned. Ise erfeared, fact I knows, yer's not dun nuther. 'Member, honey, ther Scripture says, 'keep yer lamp trum an' er burning, an' yer ile-can full to pour in it.'" "Now, Uncle Ned," was the evasive reply, "I hope you don't think my Lamp is without oil, do you?" "Child, 'tain't even got no wick in it. Fac' is, Ise erfeared *yer ain't even got a lamp*," muttered the old Negro, as he mournfully shambled off.

The poet Cowper tells us that, when under conviction of sin, he dreamed that he was walking in Westminster Abbey, waiting for prayers to begin. "Presently I heard the minister's voice. and hastened towards the choir. Just as I was upon the point of entering, the iron gate under the organ was flung in my face, with a jar that made the Abbey ring. The noise awakened me; and a sentence of excommunication from all the churches upon earth could not have been so dreadful to me as the interpretation which I could not avoid putting upon this dream."

Have you not felt a fainting of heart, and a bitterness of spirit, when, after much preparation for an important journey, you have arrived at the appointed place, and found that the ship or train, by which you intended to travel, had gone with all who were ready at the appointed time, and left you behind? Can you multiply finitude by infinitude? Can you conceive the dismay which will fill your soul if you come too late to the closed door of heaven, and begin the hopeless cry, "Lord, Lord, open to us"? —*William Arnot*

A lady, who heard Whitefield, in Scotland, preach upon the words, "And the door was shut," being placed near two dashing young men, but at a considerable distance from the pulpit, witnessed their mirth; and overheard one say, in a low tone, to the other, "Well, what if the door *be* shut? Another will open." Thus they turned off the solemnity of the text. Mr. Whitefield had not proceeded far when he said, "It is possible there may be some careless, trifling person here to-day, who may ward off the force of this impressive subject by lightly thinking, 'What matter if the door be shut? Another will open.'" The two young men were paralyzed, and looked at each other. Mr. Whitefield proceeded: "Yes; another *will* open. And I will tell you what door it will be: it will be the door of the bottomless pit!—the door of hell!—the door which conceals from the eyes of angels the horrors of damnation!"

145

And when they had platted a crown of thorns, they put it upon his head, and a reed in his right hand: and they bowed the knee before him, and mocked him, saying, Hail, King of the Jews!

—*Matthew 27:29*

 HE shameful spectacle! What element of scorn is lacking! Roman soldiers mocking a supposed rival of Caesar are sure to go to the utmost lengths in their derision.

Jesus himself is a victim so novel in his gentle weakness that they set no bounds to their scorn.

The spectacle is as cruel as it is derisive. Thorns and rough blows accentuate mockeries and scoffs.

Roman legionaries were the brutalized instruments of a race noted for its ignorance of all tenderness; they wrought cruelties with a singular zest, being most at home in amusements of the most cruel kind.

Let us go into the Hall of the Praetorian guard, and watch with our Lord in the hour of his mockery.

I. HERE LEARN A LESSON FOR YOUR HEART.

In the Lord of glory thus made the center of cruel scorn:

1. See what sin deserved. It is all laid on him.
   - Ridicule for its folly. It should be despised for its mad rebellion against the omnipotent will of the great King.
   - Scorn for its pretensions. How dared it propose to usurp dominion over hearts and lives which belonged alone to God?
   - Shame for its audacity. It dared defy the Eternal to battle. Oh, wretched, braggart sin!

2. See how low your Savior stooped for your sake.
   - He is made the Substitute for foolish, sinful man; and is treated as such.
   - He is scoffed at by soldiers of the meanest grade.
   - He is made a puppet for men who play the fool.

3. See how your Redeemer loved you.
   He bears immeasurable contempt, bears in silence, bears to the bitter end; and all for love of his people.

4. See the grand facts behind the scorn.
   - He is a King in very surety. They said, "Hail, King!" and he is indeed the King whom all shall hail.
   - He is glorified by conquering earth's sorrow: he is crowned with thorns. What a glorious diadem! No other coronet ever betokened such a conquest.

- He rules by weakness: a reed is his scepter. What a glory to be able to reign, not by force of arms, but by patience and gentleness!
- He makes men bow the knee: real homage is his; he reigns, whether men will have it so or not.
- He is the true Monarch of the Jews. In him the dynasty of David endures for ever, and Israel has hope of glory.

5. See that you honor and love him in proportion to this shame and mockery.
   - Bernard used to say, "The more vile Christ hath made himself *for* us, the more dear he ought to be *to* us."
   - Can you ever reach so great a height?

II. HERE LEARN A LESSON FOR YOUR CONSCIENCE.

1. Jesus may still be mocked.
   - By deriding his people. "Saul, Saul, why persecutest thou me?" Men mock the Master in the servant.
   - By contemning his doctrine. Many do this who affect to admire his character. This is the peculiar sin of the present age.
   - By resolves never fulfilled. Sinners vow, but never pay; confess faults, and cling to them. This is to insult the Lord.
   - By beliefs never obeyed. It is common to pretend to a belief which never affects the life, mocking great truths by acting contrary to them.
   - By professions never justified. May not many a church member be guilty of putting the Lord to an open shame in this fashion?

2. If guilty of mocking him, what shall you do?
   - Do not despair, but confess and lament your sin.
   - Do not give all up for lost. Believe and live.
   - Do not repeat the sad offense. Repent, and quit the crime.
   - Do not abide in sullen silence. Honor him whom you once despised.

3. What shall you do in any case?
   - Crown him with love.
   - Scepter him with obedience.
   - Bow the knee of worship.
   - Proclaim him King by your personal testimony.

Ye sinners, destroy the sins which grieved your Savior!

Ye saints, defy all the contempt of the world for his sake!

Laments and Honors

Whither, O whither, dost thou stoop, O thou co-eternal Son of thine eternal Father? Whither dost thou abase thyself for me? I have sinned, and thou art punished; I have exalted myself, and thou art dejected; I have clad myself with shame, and thou art stripped; I have made myself naked, and thou art clothed with robes of dishonor; my head hath devised evil, and thine is pierced with thorns; I have smitten thee, and thou art smitten for me; I have dishonored thee, and thou, for my sake, art scorned; thou art made the sport of men, for me that have deserved to be insulted by devils! —*Bishop Hall*

Christ's head hath sanctified all thorns; his back, all furrows; his hands, all nails; his side, all spears; his heart, all sorrows that can ever come to any of his children. —*Samuel Clark, in "The Saint's Nosegay"*

Here we see our King receiving the best homage the world would give him. His robe was some old cloak of purple. Behold his crown, platted of thorns! His coronation is performed by a ribald soldiery. His scepter is a reed; his homage is given by the knee of scorn; his proclamation by the mouth of ridicule. How then can we expect honor for ourselves?

Let us never despise the weak, or scoff at brethren who may appear singular, or oppress any man of woman born. Haply we may be following the act of these Praetorians, and may be insulting saints more like to Jesus than we are ourselves. To be ridiculed may give us communion with the Lord Jesus, but to ridicule others will place us in fellowship with his persecutors. —*C. H. S.*

During the last moments of a gracious lady, speech had left her; but she managed to articulate the word "Bring." Her friends, in ignorance of her meaning, offered her food, but she shook her head, and again repeated the word "Bring." They then offered her grapes, which she also declined, and, for the third time uttered the word "Bring." Thinking she desired to see some absent friends, they brought them to her: but again she shook her head; and then, by a great effort, she succeeded in completing the sentence:

> "Bring forth the royal diadem,
> And crown Him Lord of all;"

and then passed away to be with Jesus. —*Newman Hall*

146

And as they went to tell his disciples, behold, Jesus met them, saying, All hail. And they came and held him by the feet, and worshipped him. They said Jesus unto them, Be not afraid; go tell my brethren that they go into Galilee, and there shall they see me.

—*Matthew 28: 9–10*

 ᴀʟʟ that concerns our Lord after his resurrection is calm and happy. A French writer calls the forty days on earth, "the life of Jesus Christ in glory": truly it was glory as full as earth could then bear.

His tomb was empty, and consequently the disciples' grieves would have been over had they fully understood what that vacant grave meant.

Then was their choicest time for living fellowship with their risen Lord, and he did not fail to grant them the privilege on many memorable occasions.

Since our Lord is risen, we also may have happy communion with him.

These are days in which we may expect him to manifest himself to us spiritually, as he did for forty days to the disciples corporeally.

Let us not be satisfied unless it is often said of us, "Jesus met them."

I. IN THE WAY OF SERVICE JESUS MEETS US. "As they went to tell his disciples, behold, Jesus met them."

1. He may come at other times, as he did to those who visited the sepulcher, to those walking out to Emmaus, to others fishing, and to the eleven assembled for mutual consolation.
2. He is likeliest to come when we are doing his work, since:
   - We are then most awake, and most able to see him.
   - We are then in special need of him.
   - We are then most in accord with him.
3. But come when Jesus may, it will be a blessed visitation, worthy to be prefaced by a "Behold!" Oh, that he would come now!

II. WHEN JESUS MEETS US, HE HAS EVER A GOOD WORD FOR US.

The fittest motto for resurrection fellowship is "All hail!"

1. A word of salutation. He is not ashamed to call us brethren, and welcome us with "All hail!"
2. A word of benediction. He wishes us well, and expresses his hearty, sacred desire by the words "All hail!"
3. A word of gratulation. He was glad to see these women, he gave them glad tidings, he bade them be glad, he made them glad, he was glad with them, saying, "All hail!"
4. A word of pacification. He afterwards said, "Be not afraid"; but this was virtually contained in his "All hail!" His presence can never mean us harm; it ever works us health.

III. WHEN JESUS MEETS US, IT BECOMES US TO AROUSE OURSELVES.

We ought at such times to be like the disciples, who were:

1. All alive with hopeful energy. "They came." In eager haste they drew near to him. What life it would put into preachers and hearers if the Lord Jesus would manifestly appear unto them! Dullness flees when Jesus is seen.
2. All aglow with happy excitement. They "held him by the feet,"—hardly knowing what they did, but enraptured with the sight of him.
3. All ardent with reverent love. They "worshipped him." What heartiness they threw into that lowly adoration!

4. All amazed at his glory. They were prostrate, and began to fear.
5. All afraid lest they should lose their bliss. They grasped him, and held him by the feet.

IV. FROM SUCH A MEETING WE SHOULD GO ON A FURTHER ERRAND.

1. We must not plead spiritual absorption as an excuse for inactivity, but we must "go" at our Lord's bidding.
2. We must seek the good of others because of their relation to our Lord. He says, "tell *my brethren*."
3. We must communicate what our Lord has imparted—"go tell."
4. We must encourage our brethren by the assurance that joy similar to ours awaits them—"there shall *they* see me." Thus shall we best realize and retain the choice benefits of intercourse with the Lord. Not only for ourselves, but mainly for the benefit of others, are we to behold our Lord.
   - Let us go to holy work hoping to meet Jesus as we go.
   - Let us go to more holy work when we have met him.
   - Let us labor to "abide in him," looking for his promised appearing and exhorting others to do the same.

Illustrative

It is said that a venturesome diplomatist once asked the Emperor Nicholas who was the most distinguished of His Majesty's subjects. According to report, the Czar replied that the most distinguished Russian was he whomsoever the Emperor honored by speaking to him. Royal vanity dictated that reply, but we speak "words of truth and soberness" when we say that the most distinguished of men is he whom the Lord of hosts honors by admitting to communion with himself. "Speak, Lord; for thy servant heareth."

> In vain thou strugglest to act free,
> I never will unloose my hold;
> Art thou the Man that died for me?
> The secret of Thy love unfold.
> Wrestling, I will not let thee go,
> Till I Thy name, Thy nature know.
> —*Charles Wesley*

There is a striking legend illustrating the blessedness of performing our duty at whatever cost to our own inclination. A monk had seen a beautiful vision of our Savior, and in silent bliss he was gazing upon it. The hour arrived at which it was his duty to feed the poor at the convent gate. He would fain have lingered in his cell to enjoy the vision; but, under a sense of duty, he tore himself away from it to perform his humble service. When he returned, he found the blessed vision still waiting for him, and heard a voice, saying, "Hadst thou staid, I would have gone. As thou hast gone, I have remained."

It is a blessed thing to go forth with the Master's message after having seen him; it is delightful to meet him on the way when we are going to tell his disciples; and it is inexpressibly pleasant to find him in the assembly bearing witness with us. To go *from* the Lord, *for* the Lord, *with* the Lord is such an agreeable combination that it cannot be described, but must be personally experienced. The Lord Jesus is by no means niggardly in his converse with his people: he meets us as often as we are fit to be met, and oftener; and he uses such familiarities as could never have been expected had they not been already enjoyed. Who would have dreamed of his saying "All hail!" if he had not himself selected the term? —*C. H. S.*

A good theme might be found in the words of the message recorded in our text. Jesus prepares his messengers by saying "Be not afraid." Those who bear tidings for him should be calm and happy. He calls his disciples by a sweet name "my brethren"; invites them to meet him; appoints a well-known trysting-place; and promises to be there. Whatever else they had begun to do, they must make this their chief business, to be at Galilee to commune with him, to put themselves at his disposal, and to receive his commission. —*C. H. S.*

147

And he said unto them, Take heed what ye hear: with what measure ye mete, it shall be measured to you: and unto you that hear shall more be given.

—Mark 4:24

I N these days we have many instructions as to preaching; but our Lord principally gave directions as to hearing. The art of attention is as difficult as that of homiletics.

The text may be viewed as a note of *discrimination*.. Hear the truth, and the truth only. Be not indifferent as to your spiritual meat, but use discernment (John 4:1; Job 12:2).

We shall use it as a note of *arousing*. When you do hear the truth, give it such attention as it deserves. Give good heed to it.

I. HERE IS A PRECEPT. "Take heed what ye hear."

The previous verse is, "If any man have ears to hear, let him hear;" that is— use your ears well and to the best purpose.

1. Hear with discrimination, shunning false doctrine(John 10:5).

2. Hear with attention; really and earnestly hearing (Matt. 13:23).

3. Hear for yourself, with personal application (1 Sam. 3:9).

4. Hear retentively, endeavoring to remember the truth.

5. Hear desiringly, praying that the Word may be blessed to you.

6. Hear practically, obeying the exhortation which has come to you.

This hearing is to be given, not to a favorite set of doctrines, but to the whole of the Word of God (Ps. 119:128).

II. HERE IS A PROVERB. "With what measure ye mete, it shall be measured to you."

In proportion as you give yourself to hearing, you shall gain by hearing.

This is practically illustrated in the result of preaching.

1. Those who have no interest in the Word find it uninteresting.

2. Those who desire to find fault find faults enough.

3. Those who seek solid truth learn it from any faithful ministry.

4. Those who hunger find food.

5. Those who bring faith receive assurance.

6. Those who come joyfully are made glad.

But no man finds blessing by hearing error.

Nor by careless, forgetful, caviling hearing of the truth.

III. HERE IS A PROMISE. "Unto you that hear shall more be given."

You that hear shall have:

1. More desire to hear.

2. More understanding of what you hear.

3. More convincement of the truth of what you hear.

4. More personal possession of the blessings of which you hear.

5. More delight while hearing the glorious gospel.

6. More practical benefit therefrom.

God giveth more to those who value what they have.

For practical application let us say:

- *Hear*. It is your wisdom to know what God says.
- *Hear well*. God's teaching deserves the deepest attention. It will repay the best consideration.
- *Hear often*. Waste no Sabbath, nor any one of its services. Use weekday lectures and prayer meetings.
- *Hear better*. You will grow the holier thereby. You will find heavenly joy by hearing with faith.

Hear! Hear!

What care I to see a man run after a sermon if he cozens and cheats as soon as he comes home? —*John Selden*

A heart-memory is better than a mere head-memory. It were better to carry away a little of the life of God in our souls than if we were able to repeat every word of every sermon we ever heard. —*De Sales*

Ebenezer Blackwell was a rich banker, a zealous Methodist, and a great friend of the Wesleys. "Are you going to hear Mr. Wesley preach?" said one to Mr. Blackwell. "No," he answered, "I am going to hear God; I listen to him, whoever preaches; otherwise I lose all my labor."

Once-a-day hearers, represented by a Perthshire landlord, were pithily rebuked by Mr. Walker, the minister of Muthill. The landowner, meeting the minister on Monday, explained to him that he had not been hearing him at the second service on the previous day, as he could not *digest* more than one sermon. "I rather think," said Mr. Walker, "the appetite is at fault rather than the digestion."

Alas, the place of hearing is the place of sleeping with many a fine professor! I have often observed that those that keep shops can briskly attend upon a twopenny customer, but when they come themselves to God's market, they spend their time too much in letting their thoughts wander from God's commandments, or in a nasty, drowsy way. The head, also, and hearts of most hearers, are to the Word as the sieve is to water: they can hold no sermons, remember no texts, bring home no proofs, produce none of the sermon to the edification and profit of others. —*John Bunyan*

Some can be content to hear all pleasant things, as the promises and mercies of God; but judgments and reproofs, threats and checks, these they cannot brook; like unto those who, in medicine, care only for a pleasant smell or appearance in the remedy, as pills rolled in gold, but have no regard for the efficacy of the physic. Some can willingly hear that which concerns other men and their sins, their lives and manners, but nothing touching themselves or their own sins; as men can willingly abide to hear of other men's deaths, but cannot abide to think of their own. —*Richard Stock*

If verse 23 exhorts us to hear, verse 24 exhorts us to look to that which we do hear, and use it rightly. "Take heed what ye hear," means "Look after it as you would look after money that you have received." Learning a truth is not the end, but the beginning. After it is learnt, it is to be applied, kept, obeyed. And it would appear from the next sentence that, unless it is shared with others, we can neither get it nor keep it for ourselves. "With what measure ye mete, (understand, 'mete out your light,') it shall be measured unto you: and more shall be given unto you" (*Revised Version*). To learn the truth of God you need to listen, but you need to tell it to another as well. The meaning of this passage is brought out in the words of the old Rabbi: "Much have I learnt from my tutors; more from my companions; but most of all from my pupils." The more light you give another, the more you get yourself. You get a better grip of truth by pondering it with the wish to impart it. The love, which imparts what you have, opens your heart to receive something still higher. It is true, not only in regard to money, but to knowledge, and all power of help, that "There is that scattereth, and yet increaseth; and there is that with-holdeth more than is meet, but it tendeth to poverty." He is a dull teacher that does not learn by all he teaches. Rejoice in your work; it is worth doing well, for it is the best way of learning. —*Richard Glover*

148

But when he saw Jesus afar off, he ran and worshipped him.

—*Mark 5:6*

But when he was yet a great way off, his father saw him, and had compassion, and ran, and fell on his neck, and kissed him.

—*Luke 15:20*

 HESE two texts have a measure of apparent likeness: the man runs to Jesus from afar, and the Father runs to the prodigal from afar.

They do, however, as much illustrate the difference as the likeness of our action towards the Lord, and the Lord's action towards us.

From the two together a blended lesson may be learned.

I. THE SINNER'S PLACE. "Afar off." Jesus is afar off in the sinner's apprehension, and the sinner is in very deed far off from God.

1. As to character. What a difference between the demoniac and the Lord Jesus: between the prodigal son and the great Father!
2. As to knowledge. The demoniac knew Jesus, but knew little of his love. The prodigal knew little of his Father's great heart.
3. As to hope. The man possessed of a devil had no hope of recovery, or but a faint one, and that hope the demons tried to extinguish. The prodigal only hoped to be received as a hired servant: he felt that his sins had put him far away from the true position of a son.
4. As to possession. The demoniac had no hold upon the Savior; on the contrary, he cried, "What have I to do with thee?" The prodigal thought he had lost all claim to his Father, and therefore said, "I am no more worthy to be called thy son."

Immeasurable is the distance between God and a sinner: it is wide as the gulf between sin and holiness, death and life, hell and heaven.

II. THE SINNER'S PRIVILEGE. "He saw Jesus."

This much you, who are most under Satan's influence, are able to see concerning Jesus: you know that:

1. There is such a Person. He is God and man, the Savior.
2. He has done great things.
3. He is able to cast out the powers of evil.
4. He may cast them out from you and deliver you.

III. THE SINNER'S WISEST COURSE. "He ran and worshipped him."

The demoniac was all in confusion, for he was under contending influences: his own spirit and the evil spirit strove together.

He ran towards Jesus, and worshipped him; and yet in the same breath he cried, "What have I to do with thee?" Thus are sinners tossed about.

But it is the sinner's wisest course to run to Jesus, for:
1. He is the Son of the Most High God (John 1:34).
2. He is the great enemy of our enemy, the devil (Heb. 2:14).
3. He is abundantly able to drive out a legion of devils.
4. He can cause us to be clothed, and in our right mind.
5. He permits us even now to draw near and worship him.
It was the prodigal's wisdom to hasten to his Father.
Like arguments may be easily found in his case.

IV. THE SECRET OF HOPE FOR SINNERS. "His Father saw him."

1. The returning sinner was seen from afar by omniscience.
2. He was recognized as a son is known by his Father.
3. He was understood, beloved, and accepted by his Father.
This is the basis of hope for lost ones: not so much what *they* can see, as the fact that the Lord of love and grace sees them in all their sin and misery.

V. THE ACTION OF THE SINNER'S FATHER. He "ran, and fell on his neck, and kissed him."

1. Here was great tenderness—"his Father saw him, and had compassion."
2. Here was great swiftness—"and ran."
3. Here was great condescension—he "ran, and fell on his neck."
4. Here were great love and mercy—"and kissed him."
The Father's running made an end of the son's fears, and brought; swift realization of joyful acceptance.
Let us run to our Savior, and our Father.
Let us rejoice that our Savior and our Father run to meet us.

Running Comments

A needle will move towards a magnet when once a magnet has moved near to it. Our heart manifests a sweet willingness towards salvation and holiness when the great and glorious goodwill of the Lord operates upon it. It is ours to run to Jesus as if all the running were ours; but the secret truth is that the Lord runs towards us, and this is the very heart of the business. —*C. H. S.*

The mother, as she sits in her house, hears a little one shriek, and knows the voice, and cries out, "Oh! 'tis my child!" Away she throws all she hath in her hands, and runs to her babe. Thus God takes the alarm of his children's cry. "I heard Ephraim bemoaning himself," saith the Lord; his cry pierced God's ear, and his ear affected his bowels, and his bowels called up his power to the rescue of him. —*William Gurnall*

God will pardon a repentant sinner more quickly than a mother would snatch her child out of the fire. —*Vianney*

When either God or man is strongly moved, the pace is running. A soul in distress runs to Jesus: God in compassion runs to meet returning wanderers. A slow pace evidences an unwilling heart; hence delay to repent is a deadly sign. With sin within thee, Christ before thee, time pressing thee, eternity awaiting thee, hell beneath thee, heaven above thee; O sinner, thou mayest well run! It is the pace of one hunting after the game he desires, one anxious to win a prize, one escaping the avenger of blood. He that would have heaven must run for it. —*C. H. S.*

A father, whose affluence was considerable, mourned over a reckless son, whose misconduct brought shame upon himself and his family. From home the prodigal went into another country, and for years he was lost to his relatives. A chance occurring, the sorrowing parent sent by a friend this message, should he meet his boy, *"Your father loves you still."* The bearer long sought him in vain. At last he saw him enter a house of vice, and called him; and there, at a late hour of evening, he delivered this message. The dissolute gambler's heart was touched. The thought that his father still loved him, and wished to forgive him, broke the spell of Satan. He abandoned profligacy, and returned to his father. Oh, the power of such a message of inalienable love from God! —*The Preacher's Commentary*

149

And cried with a loud voice, and said, What Have I to do with thee, Jesus, thou Son of the most high God? I abjure thee by God, that thou torment me not.

—*Mark 5:7*

HE coming of Jesus into a place puts all into commotion.

The gospel is a great disturber of sinful peace.

Like the sun among wild beasts, owls, and bats, it creates a stir. In this case, a legion of devils began to move.

I. THE DEVIL CRIES OUT AGAINST THE INTRUSION OF CHRIST.

"What have I to do with thee?"

1. Christ's nature is so contrary to that of the devil that war is inevitable as soon as Jesus comes upon the scene.
2. There are no designs of grace for Satan, and, therefore, as he has nothing to hope for from Jesus, he dreads his coming.
3. He wishes to be let alone; for thoughtlessness, stagnation, and despair suit his plans.
4. He knows his powerlessness against the Son of the Most High God, and has no wish to try a fall with him.
5. He dreads his doom: for Jesus will not hesitate to torment him by the sight of good done, and evil overcome.

II. MEN UNDER THE DEVIL'S INFLUENCE CRY OUT AGAINST THE INCOMING OF CHRIST BY THE GOSPEL.

1. Conscience is feared by them: they do not wish to have it disturbed, instructed, and placed in power.
2. Change is dreaded by them; for they love sin, and its gains, and pleasures, and know that Jesus wars with these things.
3. They claim a right to be let alone: this is their idea of religious liberty. They would not be questioned either by God or man.
4. They argue that the gospel cannot bless them.
   - They expect nothing from it, for they do not know its rich benedictions, or the power of sovereign, almighty grace.
   - They think themselves too poor, too ignorant, too busy, too sinful, too weak, too involved, and perhaps too aged, to receive any good from the gospel.
5. They view Jesus as a tormentor, who will rob them of pleasure, sting their consciences, and drive them to obnoxious duties.

Therefore they cry out, "What have we to do with thee?"

III. SOBER MEN CAN ANSWER THESE OUTCRIES.

They endeavor to answer the question; "What have I to do with thee?" They remember a fact, and make an inquiry.

1. I have to do with him inevitably.
   - He has come to save, and I am responsible for accepting or refusing his grace.
   - I am his creature, as he is the Son of God, and he has power over me, and a right to my obedience.
   - I am under his rule, and he will judge me at the last day.
2. Has he to do with me graciously?
   - He has to do with me by the gospel which he has sent me.

- He has abundantly much to do with me if he has wrought in me repentance, faith, prayer, etc.
- He has everything to do with me if he has bestowed on me pardon, peace, sanctification, etc.

IV. MEN SAVED FROM SATAN RAISE AN OPPOSITE CRY.

According to the instance before us in the narrative:

1. They beg to sit at Jesus' feet, clothed, and in their right mind.
2. They ask to be with him always, and never to cease from personal attendance upon him.
3. They go at his bidding, and publish abroad what great things Jesus has done for them.
4. Henceforth they have nothing to do but to live for Jesus, and for him alone.

Come, ye despisers, and see yourselves as in a looking glass!

Look until you see yourselves transformed.

Cases in Point

Conversion is feared as a great danger by natural men, lest the promises put them on the pain and labor of godliness; for men do flee nothing but that which they apprehend as evil, dangerous, and so the true object of fear. Now, when Felix and Agrippa were both upon the wheel of the great Potter, I cannot say that conversion formally was begun, yet materially it was. The one trembled, and so was afraid and fled, and did put Paul away till another time. He saw the danger of grace (Acts 24:25–26), and fled from it. The other said that he was half a Christian (but it was the poorer half), and "he arose, and went aside" (Acts 24:28,30–31). "Their eyes they have closed; lest at any time they should see with their eyes, and hear with their ears, and should understand with their heart, and should be converted, and I should heal them" (Matt. 13:15). In which words it is evident that conversion is feared as an evil.

A wretch once jested that he was once in danger to be catched, when a Puritan preacher, as he said, "was preaching with divine power, and evidence of the Spirit of God." —*Samuel Rutherford*

It is said that Voltaire, being pressed in his last moments to acknowledge the Divinity of Christ, turned away, and said feebly, "For the love of God don't mention that Man—allow me to die in peace!"

A number of young men were sitting together in a country store one evening, telling what they did not believe, and what they were not afraid to do. Finally, the leader in the group remarked that, so far as he was concerned, he would be willing at any time to sign away all his interest in Christ for a five dollar bill. "What did I understand you to say?" asked an old farmer, who happened to be in the store, and who had overheard the remark. "I said that for five dollars I would sign away all my interest in Christ, and so I will." The old farmer, who had learned to know the human heart pretty well, drew out his leather wallet, took there from a five dollar bill, and put it in the storekeeper's hand. Then calling for ink and paper, he said: "My young friend, if you will just step to the desk now, and write as I direct, the money is yours." The young man took the pen, and began: "In the presence of these witnesses, I, A____ B____, for the sum of five dollars received, do now, once for all, and for ever, sign away all my interest—" Then he dropped the pen, and with a forced smile, said: *"I take it back, I was only fooling."* That young man did not dare to sign that paper. Why? He had an accusing conscience. He knew that there was a God. He believed in religion. He meant to be a Christian some time. And so do you, reader. Notwithstanding your apparent indifference, your trifling conduct, your boasting speech, you would not today for ten thousand dollars sign away, if such a thing were possible, your interest in Jesus Christ. You do not desire or expect to lose heaven. —*The Congregationalist (American)*

150

And he cometh to Bethsaida; and they bring a blind man unto him, and besought him to touch him. And he took the blind man by the hand, and led him out of the town; and when he had spit on his eyes, and put his hands upon him, he asked him if he saw ought. And he looked up, and said, I see men as trees, walking. After that he put his hands again upon his eyes, and made him look up: and he was restored, and saw every man clearly.

—*Mark 8:22–25*

EN arrive at Christ by different processes: one is found by Christ himself, another comes to him, another is borne of four, and this blind man is led. This matters little, so long as we do come to him.

The act of bringing men to Jesus is most commendable.

- It proves kindly feeling.
- It shows practical faith in the power of Jesus.
- It is thus an act of true wisdom.
- It is exceedingly acceptable to the Lord and is sure to prove effectual when the person himself willingly comes.

In this case there was something faulty in the bringing, since there was a measure of dictation as to the method in which the Lord should operate.

I. IT IS A COMMON WEAKNESS OF FAITH TO EXPECT THE BLESSING IN A CERTAIN FIXED WAY. "They besought him to touch him."

The Lord has his usual ways, but he is not bound to them. Yet too often we think and act as if he were so.

1. We dream that deliverance from trouble must come in one way.
2. We look for sanctification either by afflictions or by ecstasies.
3. We hope for salvation only by one form of experience.
4. We look to see others converted in one fashion of feeling only, or by some one favorite ministry.
5. We expect a revival to take the stereotyped shape.

II. WHILE OUR LORD HONORS FAITH, HE DOES NOT DEFER TO ITS WEAKNESS.

- He did not consent to work in the prescribed manner.
- He touched, but no healing came; and thus he proved that the miracle was not attached to that special form of operation.
- He did nothing to the blind man before their eyes; but led him out of the town. He would not indulge their observation, or curiosity.
- He did not heal him instantly, as they expected.
- He used a means never suggested by them—"spit on his eyes," etc.

When he did put his hands on him, he did it twice, so that, even in compliance with their wish, he vindicated his own freedom.

1 Thus he refused to foster the superstition which limited his power.
2. Thus he used a method more suited to the case.
3. Thus he gave to the people larger instruction.
4. Thus he displayed to the individual a more personal care.

The like happens in each distinct conversion: its specialty is justified in a multitude of ways.

III. WHILE OUR LORD REBUKES THE WEAKNESS OF FAITH, HE HONORS FAITH ITSELF.

1. The blind man had consented to be led to Jesus, and Jesus leads him further. He refuses none because their coming to him has been less their own spontaneous act than yielding to the persuasion of others.
2. His friends had asked for sight, and the Lord gave sight. If we have praying faith, he will keep pace with it.
3. The man and his friends had exhibited confidence in him, and he gave them even more than they expected. If we can confide, we shall receive.
4. The cure was perfect, and the method used displayed the completeness of it. Jesus gives perfect gifts to imperfect faith.

Faith ever honors the Lord, and therefore the Lord honors *it*.

If faith were not thus rewarded, Jesus himself would suffer dishonor.

He who has faith shall surely see; he who demands signs shall not be satisfied.

Let us forever have done with prescribing methods to our Lord.

Jesus will surely heal those who believe in him; he knows the best method; and he is to be trusted without reserve.

Examples

This case, and that of the deaf and stammering man brought to Christ in Decapolis, have many points of resemblance. In both, those who brought the diseased to Jesus prescribed to him the mode of cure. Was it for the purpose of reproving and counteracting the prejudice which connected the cure with a certain kind of manipulation, on the part of the curer, that Jesus, in both instances, went so far out of his usual course, varying the manner of his action so singularly that, out of all his miracles of healing, these two stand distinguished by the unique mode of their performance? It is certain that, had Jesus observed one uniform method of healing, the spirit of formalism and superstition, which lies so deep in our nature, would have seized upon it, and linked it, inseparably, with the divine virtue that went out of him, confounding the channel with the blessing it conveyed. As we ponder the life of our Redeemer, dwelling particularly on those parts of it—such as his institution of the sacraments—in which food might have been furnished upon which the spirit of formalism might have fed, more and more do we admire the pains evidently taken to give to that strong tendency of our nature as little material as possible to fasten on. —*Dr. Hanna*

Is the sick man the doctor, that he should choose the remedy? —*Madame Swetchine*

John Newton's hymn is a case in point. We quote a verse or two:

> I asked the Lord that I might grow
>> In faith, and love, and every grace;
> Might more of His salvation know,
>> And seek, more earnestly, His face
> I hoped that in some favored hour,
>> At once He'd answer my request;
> And, by His love's constraining power,
>> Subdue my sins, and give me rest.
> Instead of this He made me feel
>> The hidden evils of my heart,
> And let the angry powers of hell
>> Assault my soul in every part

Thus did infinite wisdom answer his prayer in a way which he had never dreamed of, and yet it was the right way, as he confessed.

So apt are people, as in the case of Naaman, to settle in their own minds the method of the work of grace, that it is hard to overcome their preconceptions. I met with one young woman, before whom I set the way of salvation by faith alone. She was long in accepting, or even understanding it; and when she did grasp it, and the joy of it filled her heart, she exclaimed, with surprise, "I never thought that people could find peace in this way." "Why not?" I asked her, and she replied very energetically, "I always believed that one must almost go to hell to get to heaven. My father was so full of despair that they locked him up in the asylum for six months, and then at last he got religion." —*C. H. S.*

151

And Straightway the father of the child cried out, and said with tears, Lord, I believe; help though mine unbelief.

—*Mark 9:24*

ERE was a man fully aroused to anxiety, prayer, and the use of means, and yet his desire was not at once granted to him.

Even so, many are in earnest about their souls, and yet do not immediately find conscious salvation.

This drives them to yet deeper grief.

Perhaps this father's case may help them to understand their own.

His child was not cured, but even appeared to be worse than ever.

Yet the matter came to a happy issue through the power of our Lord Jesus Christ.

Let us note the case carefully, and observe:

I. THE SUSPECTED DIFFICULTY.

1. The father may have thought it lay with the disciples.
   - Yet alone they could never have done anything.
   - Had their Lord been with them, they could have done everything.
   - The main difficulty was not with the disciples, though it was partly there.
2. He probably thought that the case itself was well-nigh hopeless.
   - The disease was:
     So fitful and mysterious.
     So terribly violent and sudden in its attacks.
     So deep-seated, and of such long continuance.
     So near to utterly destroying life.
   - But, after all, it is not our own case, or the case of those for whom we plead, which presents any unusual impediment to divine power. The Lord delights to work impossibilities.

3. He half hinted that the difficulty might lie with the Master. "If thou canst do anything, have compassion on us, and help us."
- "If thou canst." Had he seen the transfiguration, he would have known the *power* and glory of the Lord.
- "Have compassion." Could he have read the Lord's heart, he would have felt sure that the Savior's *pity* was already aroused.

Rest assured, O anxious heart, that the difficulty of your case lies alone in your want of faith!

II. THE TEARFUL DISCOVERY. "He said with tears, Lord, I believe; help thou mine unbelief."

The Lord Jesus repudiated the insinuation that there was any question as to his power, and cast the "if" back upon the father with "If thou canst believe." Then:

1. The man's little faith discovered his unbelief.
2. He was distressed and alarmed at the sight of his own unbelief.
3. He turned his thoughts and prayers in that direction. It was now not so much "Help my child," as "Help my unbelief."
4. He became deeply sensible of the sin and danger of unbelief.
    Let us look in the same direction personally, and we shall see that unbelief is an alarming and criminal thing; for it doubts:
    The power of Omnipotence.
    The value of the promise of God.
    The efficacy of Christ's blood.
    The prevalence of his plea.
    The almightiness of the Spirit.
    The truth of the gospel.

In fact, unbelief robs God of his glory in every way, and therefore it cannot receive a blessing from the Lord (Heb. 11:6).

III. THE INTELLIGENT APPEAL. "Lord, I believe; help thou mine unbelief."

In his great perplexity he cries to Jesus only.
1. On the basis of faith—"Lord, I believe."
2. With confession of sin—"mine unbelief."
3. To One who knows how to help in this matter—"Lord, help."
4. To One who is himself the best remedy for unbelief—"help thou."
    Unbelief is overcome when we fly to Jesus, and consider:
    The majesty of his divine nature.
    The tenderness of his humanity.
    The graciousness of his offices.
    The grandeur of his atonement.
    The glorious object of his work.

Come to Jesus with any case, and in every case.

Come with your little faith and with your great unbelief, for in this matter also he can help as none other can.

Helps

There is no sin which may not be traced up to unbelief. —*Mason*

"*Lord, I believe,*" etc. This act of his, in putting forth his faith to believe as he could, was the way to believe as he would. —*Trapp*

A young man, in the seventeenth century, being in deep distress of mind, applied to Dr. Goodwin for advice and consolation. After he had laid before him the long and black list of sins that troubled his conscience, the doctor reminded him that there was one blacker still, which he had not named. "What can that be, sir?" he despondently asked. "The sin," replied the doctor, "I refer to is that of refusing to believe in Christ Jesus as a Savior." The simple word banished the anxious one's guilty fears.

There was once a good woman who was well known among her circle for her simple faith, and her great calmness in the midst of many trials. Another woman, living at a distance, hearing of her, said, "I must go and see that woman, and learn the secret of her holy, happy life." She went; and accosting the woman, said, "Are you the woman with the great faith?" "No," replied she, "I am not the woman with the great faith; but I am the woman with a little faith in the great God."

> O help us, through the prayer of faith,
>   More firmly to believe;
> For still the more Thy servant hath,
>   The more shall he receive.
>   —*Milman*

A friend complained to Gotthold of the weakness of his faith, and the distress this gave him. Gotthold pointed to a vine, which had twined itself around a pole, and was hanging loaded with beautiful clusters, and said, "Frail is that plant; but what harm is done to it by its frailty, especially as the Creator has been pleased to make it what it is? As little will it prejudice your faith that it is weak, provided only it be sincere and unfeigned. Faith is the work of God, and he bestows it in such measure as he wills and judges right. Let the measure of it which he has given you be deemed sufficient by you. Take for pole and prop the cross of the Savior, and the Word of God; twine around these with all the power which God vouchsafes. A heart sensible of its weakness, and prostrating itself continually at the feet of the divine mercy, is more acceptable than that which presumes upon the strength of its faith, and falls into false security and pride. Can you suppose that the sinful woman, who lay and wept at the Lord's feet, was less approved than the swelling and haughty Pharisee?" —*Christian Scriver*

152

And Jesus stood still, and commanded him to be called. And they call the blind man, saying unto him, be of good comfort, rise; he calleth thee. And he casting away his garment, rose, and came to Jesus.

—*Mark 10:49–50*

HIS man is a picture of what we would fain have every seeker of Christ to become.

In his lonely darkness, and deep poverty, he thought and became persuaded that Jesus was the Son of David.

Though he had no sight, he made good use of his hearing. If we have not all gifts, let us use those which we have.

I. HE SOUGHT THE LORD UNDER DISCOURAGEMENTS.

1. No one prompted his seeking.
2. Many opposed his attempts. "Many charged him that he should hold his peace" (vs. 48).
3. For a while he was unheeded by the Lord himself.
4. He was but a blind beggar, and this alone might have checked some pleaders.

Let our hearers imitate his dogged resolution.

II. HE RECEIVED ENCOURAGEMENT.

This came from our Lord's commanding him to be called.

There are several kinds of calls which come to men at the bidding of our Lord Jesus. There is the:

1. Universal call. Jesus is lifted up that all who look to him may live (John 3:14–15). The gospel is preached to every creature.
2. Character call. To those who labor, and are heavy-laden. Many are the gospel promises which call the sinful, the mourning, the weary to Jesus (Isa. 4:7; Matt. 11:28; Acts 2:38–39).
3. Ministerial call. Given by the Lord's sent servants, and so backed by his authority (Acts 13:26,38–39; 16:31).
4. Effectual call. Sent home by the Holy Spirit. This is the calling of which we read, "whom he called, them he also justified" (Rom. 8:30).

III. BUT ENCOURAGEMENT DID NOT CONTENT HIM; HE STILL SOUGHT JESUS.

To stop short of Jesus and healing would have been folly indeed.

1. He arose. Hopefully, resolutely, he quitted his begging posture.
   In order to salvation we must be on the alert and in earnest.
2. He cast away his garment, and every hindrance. Our righteousness, our comfortable sin, our habit—anything, everything we must quit for Christ.
3. He came to Jesus. In the darkness occasioned by his blindness, he followed the Savior's voice.
4. He stated his case. "Lord, that I might receive my sight!"
5. He received salvation. Jesus said unto him, "Thy faith hath made thee whole." He obtained perfect eyesight; and in all respects he was in complete health.

IV. HAVING FOUND JESUS, HE KEPT TO HIM.

1. He used his sight to see his Lord.
2. He became his avowed disciple (See verse 52).
3. He went with Jesus on his way to the cross, and to the crown.
4. He remained a well-known disciple, whose father's name is given.

This man came out of cursed Jericho: are there not some to come from our slums and degraded districts?

This man at best was a beggar, but the Lord Jesus did not disdain his company. He was a standing glory to the Lord, for every one would know him as the blind man whose eyes had been opened.

Let seeking souls persevere under all drawbacks. Do not mind those who would keep you back. Let none hinder you from finding Christ and salvation.

Though blind, and poor, and miserable, you shall yet see, and smile, and sing, and follow Jesus.

Encouragements

"And command him to be called." By this circumstance he administered reproof and instruction: reproof, by ordering those to help the poor man who had endeavored to check him: instruction, by teaching us that, though he does not stand in need of our help, he will not dispense with our services; that we are to aid each other; that though we cannot recover our fellow creatures, we may frequently bring them to the place and means of cure. —*William Jay*

> Sad one, in secret, bending low,
> A dart in thy breast that the world may not know,
> Striving the favor of God to win—
> Asking his pardon for days of sin;
> Press on, press on, with thy earnest cry,
>   "Jesus of Nazareth passeth by."
>   —*Mrs. Sigourney*

"And he, casting away his garment, rose, and came to Jesus." I remember once reading these words on a memorial tablet in a country church. Inscriptions on tombstones are often unsatisfactory, and scriptural quotations upon them most inappropriate; but this one was as suitable as it was singular. The squire of the village, a High Church man, and an ardent sportsman, had late in life come under the influence of Christian friends, who brought him to a knowledge of the gospel; and to him the words of the Evangelist were applied. They were very suggestive. They told of pride, and worldly pursuits, and self-righteousness, of all to which the man had clung for a lifetime, cast away that he might come to the Savior. For a sinner saved in life's last hours a better epitaph could hardly have been chosen. I admired the piety that compared the rich man lying there to the poor blind beggar of the gospel story; the once highly esteemed garment of personal righteousness to the beggar's worthless robe; and that expressed the one hope and refuge of the soul in Christ by the words "he came to Jesus." It reminded me of the lines on William Carey's tomb:

> A guilty, weak, and helpless worm,
> On thy kind arms I fall;
> Be Thou my strength and righteousness.
> My Jesus and my all.
>
> —P.

Success in this world comes only to those who exhibit determination. Can we hope for salvation unless our mind is truly set upon it? Grace makes a man to be as resolved to be saved as this beggar was to get to Jesus, and gain his sight. "I must see him," said an applicant at the door of a public person. "You cannot see him," said the servant; but the man waited at the door. A friend went out to him, and said, "You cannot see the master, but I can give you an answer." "No," said the unfortunate pleader, "I will stay all night on the doorstep, but I will see the man himself. He alone will serve my turn." You do not wonder that, after many rebuffs, he ultimately gained his point: it would be an infinitely greater wonder if an importunate sinner did not obtain an audience from the Lord Jesus. If you must have grace, you shall have it. If you will not be put off, you shall not be put off. Whether things look favorable, or unfavorable, press you on till you find Jesus, and you shall find him. —C. H. S.

153

And when Jesus saw that he answered discreetly, he said unto him, Thou art not far from the kingdom of God.

—*Mark 12:34*

HE kingdom of God is set up among men.

Those who are in it are:
- Quickened with divine life. "He is not the God of the dead, but the God of the living" (verse 27).
- Received under the reign of grace (Rom. 5:21).
- Obedient to the law of love (1 John 4:7).
- Favored with divine privileges (Matt. 6:33; Luke 12:32).
- Raised to special dignities (Rev. 1:6).
- Indulged with peculiar happiness (Matt. 25:34).

Those who are outside of it are in some respects on a level.

But in other regards, some are "far off," and others "not far."

The scribe in the narrative was on the borders of the kingdom.

Of such a character we will now treat.

I. WHAT ARE ITS MARKS?

1. Truthfulness of spirit.
   - This man was candid as a student of the law.
   - This man was honest as a teacher of the law.
   - This man was fair as a controversialist.
   - A spirit of general uprightness, sincerity, and fairness, is a great moral advantage.
2. Spiritual perception. This scribe must have spoken with great discretion, or the Lord Jesus would not have taken such special notice of his reply. He saw:
   - More than a Papist, who makes everything of ceremonies.
   - More than a mere doctrinalist, who puts head-knowledge above heart-experience and holiness.
   - More than a moralist, who forgets the love of the heart.
3. Acquaintance with the law.
   - Those who see the unity, and yet the breadth and spirituality of the law's demands are in a hopeful condition.
   - Still more, those who perceive that their own lives fall short of those demands, and grieve on that account.
4. Teachableness, which this man clearly exhibited, is a good sign; especially if we are willing to learn truth, although its advocate is unpopular.
5. A sense of need of Christ, which did not appear in the case of this scribe, but is seen in many who attend the ministry.
6. A horror of wrongdoing, and of impurity of every kind.
7. A high regard for holy things, and a practical interest in them.
8. A diligent commencement of prayer, Bible reading, meditation. regular hearing of the word, and other gracious habits.

There are other signs, but time would fail us to mention more.

Many of these appear, like blossoms on a tree, but they disappoint the hopes which they excite.

II. WHAT ARE ITS DANGERS?

No man is safe till he is actually in the kingdom: the borderland is full of peril. There is the danger:

1. Lest you slip back from this hopefulness.
2. Lest you rest content to stop where you are.
3. Lest you grow proud and self-righteous.
4. Lest you proceed from being candid to become indifferent.
5. Lest you die ere the decisive step be taken.

III. WHAT ARE ITS DUTIES?

Though your condition is not one in which to rest, it is one which involves you in many responsibilities, since it is a condition of singular privilege.

1. Thank God for dealing so mercifully with you.
2. Admit with deep sincerity that you need supernatural help for entrance into the kingdom.
3. Tremble lest that decisive and saving step be never taken.
4. Decide at once through divine grace. Oh, for the Spirit of God to work effectually upon you!
   - What a pity that any should perish who are so near!
   - What horror to see such hopeful ones cast away!
   - How fatal to stop short of saving faith!

Expostulations

Among those who have turned out to be the most determined enemies of the gospel are many, who once were so near to conversion, that it was a wonder that they avoided it. Such persons seem ever after to take vengeance upon the holy influence which had almost proved too much for them. Hence our fear for persons under gracious impressions; for, if they do not now decide for God, they will become the more desperate in sin. That which is set in the sun, if it be not softened, will be hardened. I remember well a man, who, under the influence of an earnest revivalist, was brought to his knees, to cry for mercy, in the presence of his wife and others; but never afterwards would he enter a place of worship, or pay attention to religious conversation. He declared that his escape was so narrow that he would never run the risk again. Alas, that one should graze the gate of heaven, and yet drive on to hell! —C. H. S.

Some are in the suburbs of the city of refuge. I warn you against staying there. Oh, what pity is it that any should perish at the gates of salvation for want of another step!

He that makes but one step up a stair, though he be not much nearer to the top of the house, yet he has stepped from the ground, and is delivered from the foulness and dampness of that. So, he that taketh the first step of prayer by truly crying, "O Lord, be merciful unto me!" though he be not established in heaven, yet he has stepped from off the world, and the miserable comforts thereof. —*Dr. Donne*

A Christian minister says, "When, after safely circumnavigating the globe, *The Royal Charter* went to pieces in Moelfra Bay, on the coast of Wales, it was my melancholy duty to visit and seek to comfort the wife of the first officer, made by that calamity a widow. The ship had been telegraphed from Queenstown, and the lady was sitting in the parlor expecting her husband, with the table spread for his evening meal, when the messenger came to tell her he was drowned. Never can I forget the grief, so stricken and tearless, with which she wrung my hand, as she said, 'So near home, and yet lost!' That seemed to me the most terrible of human sorrow. But, ah! that is nothing to the anguish which must wring the soul which is compelled to say at last, 'Once I was at the very gate of heaven, and had almost entered in, but now I am in hell!'"

I remember a man coming to me in great distress of soul, and his case made a deep impression upon my mind. He was a man-of-war's man, with all the frankness of a British tar, but, alas: also, with a sailor's fondness for strong drink. As we talked and prayed together, the tears literally rained down the poor fellow's weather-beaten face, and he trembled violently. "Oh, sir," he exclaimed, "I could fight for it!" Truly, if salvation could have been obtained by some deed of daring, he would have won it. He left me without finding peace, and the next day he went back drunk, to join his ship; and I have never heard of him since. —*J. W. H.*

154

And they came to a place which was name Gethsemane.
—*Mark 14:32*

UR Lord left the table of happy fellowship, and passed over the brook Kedron, so associated with the sorrows of David (2 Sam. 15:23).

He then entered into the garden, named Gethsemane, not to hide himself from death, but to prepare for it by a season of special prayer.

Gethsemane was our Lord's place of secret prayer (John 18:1–2).

If *he* resorted to his closet in the hour of trial, we need to do so far more.

In his solitary supplication he was oppressed with a great grief, and overwhelmed with a terrible anguish.

It was a killing change from the cheerful communion of the Supper to the lone agony of the garden.

Let us think with great solemnity of the olive garden where the Savior sweat as it were great drops of blood.

I. THE CHOICE OF THE SPOT.

1. Showed his serenity of mind, and his courage.
   - He goes to his usual place of secret prayer.
   - He goes there though Judas knew the place.
2. Manifested his wisdom.
   - Holy memories there aided his faith.
   - Deep solitude was suitable for his prayers and cries.
   - Congenial gloom fitted his exceeding sorrow.
3. Bequeathed us lessons.
   - In a garden, Paradise was lost and won.
   - In Gethsemane, the olive-press, our Lord himself was crushed.
   - In our griefs, let us retreat to our God in secret.
   - In our special prayers, let us not be ashamed to let them be known to our choicer friends, for Jesus took his disciples with him to his secret devotions in Gethsemane.

II. THE EXERCISE UPON THE SPOT.

Every item is worthy of attention and imitation.

1. He took all due precautions for others.
   He would not have his disciples surprised, and therefore bade them watch. So should we care for others in our own extremity. The intensity of his intercourse with God did not cause him to forget one of his companions.
2. He solicited the sympathy of friends.
   We may not despise this; though, like our Lord, we shall prove the feebleness of it, and cry, "Could ye not watch with me?"
3. He prayed and wrestled with God.
   - In lowliest posture and manner (see verse 35).
   - In piteous repetition of his cry (see verses 36 and 39).
   - In awful agony of spirit even to a bloody sweat (Luke 22:44).
   - In full and true submission (Matt. 26:42,44).
4. He again and again sought human sympathy, but made excuse for his friends when they failed him (see verse 38). We ought not to be soured in spirit even when we are bitterly disappointed.
5. He returned to his God, and poured out his soul in strong crying and tears, until he was heard in that he feared (Heb. 5:7).

III. THE TRIUMPH UPON THE SPOT.

1. Behold his perfect resignation. He struggles with "if it be possible," but conquers with "not what I will, but what thou wilt." He is our example of patience.

2. Rejoice in his strong resolve. He had undertaken, and would go through with it (Luke 9:51; 12:50).
3. Mark the angelic service rendered. The blood-stained Sufferer has still all heaven at his call (Matt. 26:53).
4. Remember his majestic bearing towards his enemies.
   - He meets them bravely (Matt. 26:55).
   - He makes them fall (John 18:6).
   - He yields himself, but not to force (John 18:8).
   - He goes to the cross, and transforms it to a throne.

We, too, may expect our minor Gethsemane.
We shall not be there without a Friend, for he is with us.
We shall conquer by his might, and in his manner.

In Memoriam

The late Rev. W. H. Krause, of Dublin, was visiting a lady in a depressed state, "weak, oh, so weak!" She told him that she had been very much troubled in mind that day, because in meditation and prayer she had found it impossible to govern her thoughts, and kept merely going over the same things again and again. "Well, my dear friend," was his prompt reply, "there is provision in the gospel for that too. Our Lord Jesus Christ, when *his* soul was exceeding sorrowful, even unto death, three times prayed, and spoke *the same words*." This seasonable application of Scripture was a source of great comfort to her.

> Gethsemane, the olive-press!
> (And why so called let Christians guess.)
> Fit name, fit place, where vengeance strove,
> And griped and grappled hard with love.
> —*Joseph Hart*

"My will, not thine, be done," turned Paradise into a desert. "Thy will, not mine, be done," turned the desert into Paradise, and made Gethsemane the gate of heaven. —*E. ae Pressensé*

An inscription in a garden in Wales runs thus:

> In a garden the first of our race was deceived,
> In a garden the promise of grace he received,
> In a garden was Jesus betrayed to his doom,
> In a garden his body was laid in the tomb.

There will be no Christian but what will have a Gethsemane, but every praying Christian will find that there is no Gethsemane without its angel. —*Thomas Binney*

The Father heard; and angels, there,
Sustained the Son of God in prayer,
In sad Gethsemane;
He drank the dreadful cup of pain—
Then rose to life and joy again.
When storms of sorrow round us sweep,
And scenes of anguish make us weep;
To sad Gethsemane
We'll look, and see the Savior there,
And humbly bow, like Him, in prayer.

—*S. F. Smith*

"And there appeared an angel unto him from heaven, strengthening him."—What! The Son of God receives help from an angel, who is but his creature? Yes. And we learn thereby to expect help and comfort from simple persons and common things, when God pleases. All strength and comfort come from God, but he makes creatures his ministers to bring it. We should thank both them and him. —*Practical Reflections on every verse of the Holy Gospels, by a Clergyman*

There is something in an olive-garden, on a hillside, which makes it most suitable for prayer and meditation. The shade is solemn, the terraces divide better than distance, the ground is suitable for kneeling upon, and the surroundings are all in accord with holy thoughts. I can hardly tell why it is, but often as I have sat in an olive-garden, I have never been without the sense that it was the place and the hour of prayer. —*C. H. S.*

And when he thought thereon, he wept.
—*Mark 14:72*

 REPENTANCE is wrought by the Spirit of God. But he works it in us by leading us to think upon the evil of sin. Peter could not help weeping when he remembered his grievous fault.

Let us at this time:

I. STUDY PETER'S CASE, AND USE IT FOR OUR OWN INSTRUCTION.

1. He considered that he had denied his Lord.
   - Have we never done the like?
   - This may be done in many ways.
2. He reflected upon the excellence of the Lord whom he had denied.

3. He remembered the position in which his Lord had placed him, making him an apostle and one of the first of them.

Have we not been placed in positions of trust?

4. He bethought him of the special intercourse which he had enjoyed. He and James and John had been most favored (Matt. 17:1–13; 27:36–46; Mark 5:37–43).

Have not we known joyous fellowship with our Lord?

5. He recollected that he had been solemnly forewarned by his Lord.

Have we not sinned against light and knowledge?

6. He recalled his own vows, pledges, and boasts. "Although all shall be offended, yet will not I" (verse 29).

Have we not broken very earnest declarations?

7. He thought upon the special circumstances of his Lord when he had so wickedly denied him.

Are there no aggravations in our case?

8. He revolved in his mind his repetitions of the offense, and those repetitions with added aggravations: his lie, his oath, etc.

We ought to dwell on each item of our transgressions, that we may be brought to a more thorough repentance of them.

II. STUDY OUR OWN LIVES, AND USE THE STUDY FOR OUR FURTHER HUMILIATION.

1. Think upon our transgressions while unregenerate.
2. Think upon our resistance of light, and conscience, and the Holy Spirit before we were overcome by divine grace.
3. Think upon our small progress in the divine life.
4. Think upon our backslidings and heart-wanderings.
5. Think upon our neglect of the souls of others.
6. Think upon our little communion with our Lord.
7. Think upon the little glory we are bringing to his great name.
8. Think upon our matchless obligations to his infinite love.

Each of these meditations is calculated to make us weep.

III. STUDY THE EFFECT OF THESE THOUGHTS UPON OUR OWN MINDS.

1. Can we think of these things without emotion?
   - This is possible; for many excuse their sin on the ground of their circumstances, their constitution, their company, their trade, their fate: they even lay the blame on Satan, or some other tempter. Certain hard hearts treat the matter with supreme indifference.
   - This is perilous. It is to be feared that such a man is not Peter, but Judas: not a fallen saint, but a son of perdition.

2. Are we moved by thoughts of these things?
- There are other reflections which may move us far more.
  Our Lord forgives us, and numbers us with his brethren.
  He asks us if we love him, and he bids us feed his sheep.
- Surely, when we dwell on these themes, it must be true of each of us: "When he thought thereon, he wept."

Recollections

Peter's recollection of what he had formerly heard was another occasion of his repentance. We do not sufficiently consider how much more we need recollection than information. We know a thousand things, but it is necessary that they should be kept alive in our hearts by a constant and vivid recollection. It is, therefore, extremely absurd and childish for people to say, "You tell me nothing but what I know." I answer, you forget many things; and, therefore, it is necessary that line should be upon line, and precept upon precept. Peter, himself, afterwards said, in his Epistles, "I will not be negligent to put you always in remembrance of these things, though ye know them." We are prone to forget what we do know; whereas we should consider that, whatever good thing we know is only so far good to us as it is remembered to purpose. —*Richard Cecil*

Peter falls dreadfully, but by repentance rises sweetly; a look of love from Christ melts him into tears. He knew that repentance was the key to the kingdom of grace. At once his faith was so great that he leaped, as it were, into a sea of waters to come to Christ; so now his repentance was so great that he leaped, as it were, into a sea of tears, for that he had gone from Christ. Some say that, after his sad fall, he was ever and anon weeping, and that his face was even furrowed with continual tears. He had no sooner taken in poison but he vomited it up again, ere it got to the vitals; he had no sooner handled this serpent but he turned it into a rod, to scourge his soul with remorse for sinning against such clear light, and strong love, and sweet discoveries of the heart of Christ to him.

Clement notes that Peter so repented that, all his life after, every night when he heard the cock crow, he would fall upon his knees, and, weeping bitterly, would beg pardon for his sin. Ah! souls, you can easily sin as the saints, but can you repent with the saints? Many can sin with David and Peter, who cannot repent with David and Peter, and so must perish for ever. —*Thomas Brooks*

Cowper describes the time when he reflected on the necessity of repentance. "I knew that many persons had spoken of shedding tears for sin; but when I asked myself, whether the time would ever come, when I should weep for mine, it seemed to me that a stone might sooner do it . . . Not knowing that Christ was exalted to give repentance, I despaired of ever attaining it." A friend came to his bedside, and declared to him the gospel. He insisted on the all-atoning efficacy of the blood of Jesus, and his righteousness for our justification. "While I heard this part of his discourse, and the Scriptures on which he founded it, my heart began to burn within me; my soul was pierced with a sense of my bitter ingratitude to so merciful a Savior; and those tears, which I thought impossible, burst forth freely." —*Cowper's "Memoirs of his Early Life"*

Nothing will make the faces of God's children more fair than for them to wash themselves every morning in their tears. —*Samuel Clark*

The old Greeks thought that memory must be a source of torture in the next world, so they interposed between the two worlds the waters of Lethe, the river of forgetfulness; but believers in Christ want no river of oblivion on the borders of Elysium. Calvary is on this side, and that is enough. —*Alexander Maclaren*

156

And she went and told them that had been with him, as they mourned and wept.

—*Mark 16:10*

ARK is graphic: he paints an interior like a Dutch artist.

We see a choice company: "them that had been with him."

We know many of the individuals, and are interested to note what they are doing, and how they bear their bereavement.

We see:

I. A SORROWING ASSEMBLY. "As they mourned and wept"

What a scene! We behold a common mourning, abundantly expressed by tears and lamentations.

They mourned:

1. Because they had believed in Jesus, and loved him; and therefore they were concerned at what had happened.
2. Because they felt their great loss in losing him.
3. Because they had seen his sufferings and death.
4. Because they remembered their ill-conduct towards him.
5. Because their hopes concerning him were disappointed.
6. Because they were utterly bewildered as to what was now to be done, seeing their Leader was gone.

In considering the death of Jesus, there is just cause for mourning.

Let us intelligently mourn for him, since our sins occasioned his woes and death.

II. A CONSOLING MESSENGER. Mary Magdalene came and told them that Jesus had risen, and had appeared unto her.

Concerning this ministry, we note:

1. She was one of themselves. The witnesses to our Lord's resurrection were such as his disciples, and, indeed, all the world, might safely trust. They were not strangers, but individuals well known to those who heard them.
2. She came with the best of news. She declared that Jesus was indeed risen. The resurrection of our divine Lord:
   - Removes the cause of our sorrow.
   - Assures us of tile help of a living Redeemer (John 14:19).
   - Secures our own personal resurrection (1 Cor. 15:23).
   - Brings us personal justification (Rom. 4:25).
3. She was not believed.
   - Unbelief is apt to become chronic: they had not believed the Lord when he foretold his own resurrection, and so they do not believe an eyewitness who reported it.
   - Unbelief is cruelly unjust: they made Mary Magdalene a liar, and yet all of them esteemed her.

III. A REASSURING REFLECTION.

1. We are not the only persons who have mourned an absent Lord.
2. We are not the only messengers who have been rejected.
3. We are sure beyond all doubt of the resurrection of Christ.
   - The evidence is more abundant than that which testifies to any other great historical event.
   - The apostles so believed it as to die as witnesses of it.
   - They were very slow to be convinced, and therefore that which forced *them* to believe should have the like effect upon the most careful of *us*.
4. We have thus the most ample reason for joy concerning our Lord.

Let us not think too mournfully of our Lord's passion.

Let us not be too mournful about anything, now that we know that we have a living Savior for our Friend.

Memoranda

In the famous picture-gallery of Bologna, there is a striking picture by Domenichino, representing an angel standing beside the empty cross, from which the body of Christ has just been removed. He holds in his hand the crown of thorns, that had just fallen from the august Sufferer's brow; and the expression that passes over his face, as he feels with his finger the sharpness of one of the protruding thorns, is full of meaning. It is a look of wonder and surprise. To the pure, unstained, immortal nature of the angel, all that suffering is a profound mystery. The death of Christ was equally a mystery to his disciples. —*Hugh Macmillan*

A sorrow is none the less sharp because it is founded upon a mistake. Jacob mourned very bitterly for Joseph, though his darling was not torn in pieces, but on the way to be lord over all Egypt. Yet while there is of necessity so much well-founded sorrow in the world, it is a pity that one unnecessary pang should be endured, and endured by those who have the best possible grounds for joy. The case in the text before us is a typical one. Thousands are at this day mourning and weeping who ought to be rejoicing. Oh, the mass of needless grief! Unbelief works for the father of lies in this matter, and works misery out of falsehood among those who are not in truth children of sadness, but heirs of light and joy. Rise, faith, and with thy light chase away this darkness! And if even thou must have thy lamp trimmed by a humble Mary, do not despise her kindly aid.

157

We have seen strange things today.
—Luke 5:26

 HE world is aweary, and longs for something novel.

The greatest stranger in the world is Jesus; and, alas, he is the least seen, and the least spoken of by the most of men!

If men would come and watch him, they would see strange things.

His person, his life, his death, his teaching, are full of strange things.

What he is now doing has as much as ever the element of strangeness and wonder about it.

I. MARK THE STRANGE THINGS OF THAT PARTICULAR DAY.

1. Power present to heal doctors! (verse 17).
2. Faith reaching down to the Lord from above! (Verse 19).
3. Jesus pardoning sin with a word (verse 20).
4. Jesus practicing thought-reading (verse 22).
5. Jesus making a man carry the bed which had carried him (Verse 25).

II. MARK THE STRANGE THINGS OF CHRIST'S DAY.

1. The Maker of men born among men. The Infinite an infant.
2. The Lord of all serving all.
3. The Just One accused, condemned, and sacrificed for sin.
4. The Crucified rising from the dead.
5. Death slain by the dying of the Lord.

These are but incidents in a life which is all strange and marvelous.

III. MARK THE STRANGE THINGS SEEN BY BELIEVERS IN THEIR DAY WITHIN THEMSELVES AND OTHERS.

1. A self-condemned sinner justified by faith.

2. A natural heart renewed by grace.
3. A soul preserved in spiritual life amid killing evils, like the bush which burned with fire and was not consumed.
4. Evil made to work for good by providential wisdom.
5. Strength made perfect in weakness.
6, The Holy Ghost dwelling in a believer.
7. Heaven enjoyed on earth.

These are a small number out of a host of strange things.

Life never grows stale to a companion of Jesus.

Do you find it becoming so, and are you a believer?

Seek the conversion of your family, and your neighborhood.

Seek to know more of Jesus at work among men.

This will cause you to see stranger and stranger things, till you see the strangest of all with Christ in glory.

Wonders

Wonder at the work of God is natural, justifiable, commendable. He is a God of wonders. It is right to say of the Lord's doing, "It is marvelous in our eyes." We are to talk of all his wondrous works; but this must be in the spirit of devout admiration, not in the spirit of suspicion and doubt. A holy, grateful wonder should be indulged to the full; but a cold, skeptical wonder should be resisted as a suggestion from Satan. Faith accounts all things possible with God; it is unbelief that incredulously marvels at the work of his hand.

Guthrie, of Fenwick, a Scotch minister, once visited a dying woman. He found her anxious about her state, but very ignorant. His explanation of the gospel was joyfully received by her, and soon after she died. On his return home, Guthrie said, "I have seen a strange thing today—a woman whom I found in a state of nature, I saw in a state of grace, and left in a state of glory."

In a manuscript by an old Scotch minister, in the early part of the last century, there is a remarkable account of the conversion of Lord Jeddart, who had been famous for his recklessness in sin, and of the astonishment it caused among Christian people. A little after his conversion, and before the thing was known, he came to the Lord's table. He sat next a lady who had her hands over her face, and did not see him till he delivered the cup out of his hand. When she saw that it was Lord Jeddart, who had been so renowned for sin, she fell a-trembling terribly for very amazement that such a man should be there. He noticed it, and said, "Madam, be not troubled: the grace of God is free!" This calmed the lady; but when we consider what sort of man Lord Jeddart had been, we can account for her surprise.

When I get to heaven, I shall see three wonders there: the first wonder will be to see many people there whom I did not expect to see; the second wonder will be to miss many people whom I did expect to see; and the third and greatest wonder of all will be to find myself there. —*John Newton*

Wonders of grace to God belong,
Repeat His mercies in your song.
—*Dr. Watts*

158

At his feet.
—*Luke 7:38*

RIENTALS are demonstrative, and in their devotions they pay greater attention to bodily posture than we do. Let us be the more careful of the posture of our souls.

It is interesting to consider our posture towards our Lord.

He bears us on his heart (Song of Sol. 8:6), in his bosom (Isa. 40:11), in his hand (Isa. 49:2; 51:16), on his shoulders (Luke 15:5).

But yet "at his feet " is our most usual place.

I. IT IS A BECOMING POSTURE.

The posture is admirable for many reasons.

1. As he is divine, let us pay him lowliest reverence.
2. As we are sinful, let us make humble confession.
3. As he is Lord, let us make full submission.
4. As he is All in All, let us manifest immovable dependence.
5. As he is infinitely wise, let us wait his appointed time.

The best are at his feet joyfully, bowing before him.

The worst must come there, whether they will or no.

II. IT IS A HELPFUL POSTURE.

1. For a weeping penitent (Luke 7:38).
   - Our humility will help penitence.
   - Our lowly submission will bring assurance.
   - Our full obeisance will prepare for service.
2. For a resting convert (Luke 8:35).
   - In such a position devils are driven out, and no longer rule us.
   - In such a position they are kept off, and cannot return.
   - In such a position we give the best proof of being in our right mind.
3. For a pleading intercessor (Luke 8:41).

- We plead best when we are lowliest.
- We may be rulers of the synagogue, but when our heart is breaking we find most hope "at his feet."

4. For a willing learner (Luke 10:39). Mary "at his feet" showed:
  - A lowly sense of personal ignorance.
  - A believing acceptance of the Lord's teaching.
  - A hopeful uplooking to him.

5. For a grateful worshipper (Luke 17:16).
  - So the healed leper expressed his thanks.
  - So angels adore, giving him thanks, while bending low.
  - So would our hearts bow in unutterable gratitude.

6. For a saint beholding his Lord's glory (Rev. 1:17).
  - Overwhelmed, humbled, overjoyed, exhausted with excess of ecstasy.
  - Come, then, and submit to Jesus, and bow at his feet.
  - He is so worthy: pay him all reverence.
  - He has received from you so much despite: kiss his feet.
  - He will so freely forgive: this may well cause you to bow in the dust before him.
  - He will give you such joy: in fact, no joy excels that of full submission to his blessed sway.

III. IT IS A SAFE POSTURE.

1. Jesus will not refuse us that position, for it is one which we ought to occupy.
2. Jesus will not spurn the humbly submissive, who in self-despair cast themselves before him.
3. Jesus will not suffer any to harm those who seek refuge at his feet.
4. Jesus will not deny us the eternal privilege of abiding there.

Let this be our continual posture—"at his feet."

- Sorrowing or rejoicing; hoping or fearing;
- Suffering or working; teaching or learning;
- In secret or in public; in life and in death.

> Oh, that I might for ever sit
> With Mary at the Master's feet.

Clippings

In order that the mats or carpets, which are hallowed by domestic prayer, may not be rendered unclean by any pollution of the streets, each guest, as he enters a house in Syria or Palestine, takes off his sandals, and leaves them at the door. He then proceeds to his place at the table. In ancient times, as we find throughout the Old Testament, it was the custom of the Jews to eat their meals sitting. cross legged—as is still common throughout the East—in front of a tray placed on a low stool, on which is set the dish containing the heap of food, from which all help themselves in common. But this custom, though it has been resumed for centuries, appears to have been abandoned by the Jews in the period succeeding the captivity. Whether they had borrowed the recumbent posture at meals from the Persians, or not, it is certain, from the expressions employed, that, in the time of our Lord, the Jews, like the Greeks and Romans, reclined at banquets, upon couches placed round tables of much the same height as those now in use. We shall see, hereafter, that even the Passover was eaten in this attitude. The beautiful, and profoundly moving incident, which occurred in Simon's house, can only be understood by remembering that, as the guests lay on the couches which surrounded the tables, their feet would be turned towards any spectators who were standing outside the circle of bidden guests. —*Archdeacon Farrar*

Artabanus, one of the military officers of the Athenians, was applied to by a certain great man, who told him that he desired an audience of the king. He was answered that, before it was granted, he must prostrate himself before him, for it was a custom of the country for the king to admit no one to his presence who would not worship him. That which was an arrogant assumption in an earthly king is a proper condition of our approach to the King of kings. Humility is the foundation of our intercourse with him. We must bow before his throne. No sinner who is too proud to yield obedience to this law may expect any favors from his hands. —*Handbook of Illustration*

When the Danish missionaries, stationed at Malabar, set some of their converts to translate a catechism, in which it was asserted that believers become the sons of God, one of the translators was so startled that he suddenly laid down his pen, and exclaimed, "It is too much. Let me rather render it, 'They shall be permitted to kiss his feet.'" —*G. S. Bowes*

The Rev. Mr. Young was, one stormy day, visiting one of his people, an old man, who lived in great poverty, in a lonely cottage, a few miles from Jedburgh He found him sitting with the Bible open on his knees, but in outward circumstances of great discomfort, the snow drifting through the roof, and under the door, and scarcely any fire on the hearth. "What are you about today, John?" was Mr. Young's question on entering. "Ah! sir," said the happy saint, "I'm sitting under his shadow, wi' great delight." —*The Christian Treasury*

The end of all Christian preaching is to cast the sinner trembling at the feet of mercy. —*Vinet*

> Low at Thy feet my soul would lie.
> Here safety dwells, and peace divine;
> Still let me live beneath Thine eye,
> For life, eternal life, is Thine.
> —*Anne Steele*

159

"Tell me, therefore, which of them will love him most?"
—*Luke 7:42*

 T is right for us to desire to be among the most loving servants of the Lord Jesus. It would be an interesting question concerning a company just joining the church—"Which of them will love him most?"

How can we reach this point? How can we love him most?

We would love him as did the penitent who washed his feet with tears: whence shall come such eminence of love?

The passage before us may help us to a conclusion on that point.

I. WE MUST FIRST BE SAVED IN THE SAME MANNER AS OTHERS.

The road to eminence in love is just the plain way of salvation, which all who are in Christ must travel. There is no new gospel of the higher life, and there need be no singularity of dress, abode, or vow, in order to attain the greatest heights of love.

1. All are in debt; we must heartily own this to be our own case.
2. None have anything to pay; we must confess this, without reserve, as being our own personal condition.
3. The loving Lord forgives in each case: personally we have exceeding great need of such remission. We must feel this.
4. In each case he forgives frankly, or without any consideration or compensation: it must be so with us. We must accept free grace and undeserved favor.
5. Out of this arises love. By a sense of free grace we begin to love our Lord; and in the same way we go on to love him more.

The more clear our sense of sinnership, and the more conscious our obligation to free grace, the more likely are we to love much.

II. WE MUST AIM AT A DEEP SENSE OF SIN.

1. It was the consciousness of great indebtedness which created the great love in the penitent woman. Not her sin, but the consciousness of it, was the basis of her loving character.
2. Where sin has been open and loud, there ought to be this specially humbling consciousness; for it would be an evidence of untruthfulness if it were not manifest (1 Cor. 15:9).
3. Yet is it frequently found in the most moral, and it abounds in saints of high degree. In fact, these are the persons who are most capable of feeling the evil of sin, and the greatness of the love which pardons it (1 John 1:8).

4. It is to be cultivated. The more we bewail sin the better, and we must aim at great tenderness of heart in reference to it.

In order to cultivate it we must seek to get:

- A clearer view of the law's requirements (Luke 10:26,27).
- A fuller idea of God's excellences, especially of his holiness (Job 42:5–6).
- A sharper sense of sin's tendencies in ourselves, towards God, and towards men; and also a more overwhelming conviction of its dreadful punishment (Rom. 7:13; Ps. 51:3–4; John 5:28–29).
- A deeper consciousness of the love of God to us (1 John 3:1–2).
- A keener valuation of the cost of redemption (1 Pet. 1:18–19).
- A surer persuasion of the perfection of our pardon will also help to show the baseness of our sin (Ezek. 16:62–63).

By these means, and all others, we must endeavor to keep our conscience active, that our heart may be sensitive.

III. THIS WILL LEAD TO A HIGHLY LOVING CARRIAGE TOWARDS OUR LORD.

We shall so love him as to behave like the penitent in the narrative.

1. We shall desire to be near him, even at his feet.
2. We shall make bold confession, and shall do this at all risks, honoring him before gainsayers, and doing so though it may cause others to make unkind remarks.
3. We shall show deep humility, delighting even to wash his feet.
4. We shall exhibit thorough contrition, beholding him with tears.
5. We shall render earnest service; doing all that lies in our power for Jesus, even as this woman did.
6. We shall make total consecration of all that we have: our tears, our eyes, our choicest gifts, our hearts, ourselves, etc.

Thus shall we reach the goal we desire.

A company of those who "love him most", dwelling in any place, would give a tone to the society around them.

We have enough of head-workers; now for heart-lovers.

Why should we not aim to be among the closest followers of our Lord, loving most, and living specially consecrated lives?

Experimental Remarks

A spiritual experience which is thoroughly flavored with a deep and bitter sense of sin is of great value to him that hath had it. It is terrible in the drinking, but it is most wholesome in the bowels, and in the whole of the afterlife. Possibly much of the flimsy piety of the day arises from the ease with which men reach to peace and joy in these evangelistic days. We would not judge modern converts, but we certainly prefer that form of spiritual exercise which leads the soul by the way of Weeping cross, and makes it see its blackness before it assures it that it is "clean every whit." Too many think lightly of sin, and therefore lightly of a Savior. He who has stood before his God, convicted, and condemned, with the rope about his neck, is the man to weep for joy when he is pardoned, to hate the evil which has been forgiven him, and to live to the honor of the Redeemer by whose blood he has been cleansed.

Many of the most eminent of the saints were, before conversion, ringleaders in sin: instances will suggest themselves to all readers of church history. We naturally expect that a remarkable conversion should show itself by special fruits; we very properly doubt it if it does not. A virulent rebel, when he returns to his Lord, is bound to be valiant as well as loyal; for he remembers that he not only owes fealty to his Lord by nature, but he owes that life a second time to his Prince's clemency. Those who were once far gone in sin ought always to be found in the thick of the battle against sin. Bold blasphemers ought to be enthusiasts for the honor of their Lord when they are washed from their iniquities. As they say reclaimed poachers make the best game-keepers, so should the greatest sinners be the raw material out of which the Lord's transforming grace shall create great saints.

The Christian mentions a reminiscence of that saintly man, Mr. Pennefather. One day a member of his household knocked at the door of his study, and when at length it was opened, the good man was in tears. Being anxiously asked the cause, he replied, "My sins! my sins!" The sensitiveness of that holy soul, its quickened estimate of sin, its reverent conception of God's righteousness, which the tearful exclamation manifested, commend his memory to our love and veneration. All who knew him loved him as a living manifestation of the seven beatitudes.

I have heard say that the depth of a Scotch loch corresponds with the height of the surrounding mountains. So deep thy sense of obligation for pardoned sin, so high thy love to him who has forgiven thee. —*C. H. S.*

Love to the Savior rises in the heart of a saved man in proportion to the sense which he entertains of his own sinfulness on the one hand, and of the mercy of God on the other. Thus the height of a saint's love to the Lord is as the depths of his own humility: as this root strikes down unseen into the ground, that blossoming branch rises higher in the sky. —*William Arnot*

160

And it came to pass, that, when Jesus was returned, the people gladly received him: for they were all waiting for him.

—*Luke 8:40*

ESUS went to those who refused him in the land of Gadara; and there he saved one, to show the freeness and sovereignty of his grace.

He then quitted the inhospitable country, to show that he forces himself on none. Wisdom abandons those who refuse her counsels (Prov. 1:24). Those whom the Lord has chosen shall be willing in the day of his power (Ps. 110:3).

In the Revised Version we read, "The multitude welcomed him."

When Jesus is waited for and welcomed, he delights to come.

He is not waited for by all in our congregations; so that we may ask the question of our present hearers—Do you welcome Christ? Let it be answered by each one this day.

I. A BEAUTIFUL SIGHT. "They were all waiting for him."

This waiting may be seen in several different forms.

1. A gathered congregation, waiting in the place where prayer is wont to be made. Want of punctuality, and irregular attendance, often show that Jesus is not waited for.
2. A praying company, an earnest church, looking for revival, and prepared to cooperate in labor for it. Some churches do not wait for the Lord's presence, and would not be ready for him if he were to come.
3. A seeking sinner, sighing for mercy, searching the Scriptures, hearing the Word, inquiring of Christians, constantly praying, and thus "waiting for him."
4. A departing saint, longing for home: saying, like Jacob, "I have waited for thy salvation, O Lord" (Gen. 49:18).
5. An instructed church, looking for the Second Advent (Rev. 22:17).

It is good for the eyes to behold such sights.

II. A SURE ARRIVAL. "Jesus was returned."

We are quite sure that our Lord will graciously appear to those who are "all waiting for him," since:

1. His Spirit is there already, making them wait (Rom. 8:23).
2. His heart is there, in sympathy with them, longing to bless them.
3. His work is there. He has brought them into that waiting condition, and now he has found a sphere wherein to display his grace to saints and sinners.
4. His promise is there, "Lo, I am with you always" (Matt. 28:20).
5. His custom is to be there. His delights are still with the sons of men (Prov. 8:31).

What countless blessings his coming will bring!

III. A HEARTY WELCOME. "The people gladly received him."

1. Their fears made him welcome.

They feared lest he might have gone for ever from them (Ps. 77:7).

2. Their hopes made him welcome.

They trusted that now their sick would be cured, and their dead would be raised.

3. Their prayers made him welcome.

Those who pray that Jesus may come are glad when he comes.

4. Their faith made him welcome.

Jairus now looked to have his child healed (verse 41).

5. Their love made him welcome.

When our heart is with him, we rejoice in his appearing.

6. Their care for others made him welcome.

Jesus never disappoints those who wait for him.

Jesus never refuses those who welcome him.

Jesus is near us now: will you not open the doors of your hearts to receive him (Rev. 3:20)?

Hearty Welcome

A congregation cannot be said to welcome the Lord Jesus unless they are all there, which requires *punctuality*; unless they have come with design to meet him, which implies prayerful *expectancy*; unless they are ready to hear from him, which involves *attention*; and unless they are resolved to accept his teaching, which demands *obedience*.

When the inhabitants of Mentone desired a visit from the Prince of Savoy, they made a way for him over the mountains. Hills were tunneled, and valleys bridged, that the beloved sovereign might receive the welcome of his subjects. If we would really welcome the Lord Jesus, we must make a road for him by abasing our pride, elevating our thoughts, removing our evil habits, and preparing our hearts. Never did a soul cast up a highway for the Lord, and then fail to enjoy his company. —*C. H. S.*

161

And she had a sister call Mary, which also sat at Jesusí feet, and heard his word.

—*Luke 10:39*

 HE family at Bethany was highly favored by being permitted to entertain our Lord so often.

They all appreciated the privilege, but Mary made the wisest use of it.

Martha sought to serve the Lord with her very best.

Mary was full of love to Jesus, as we know by her anointing him, and therefore she also would serve him with her very best.

She did so by attending to his words.

She was a wise and saintly woman, and our Lord commended her chosen method of service.

It will be safe, therefore, for us to follow her example.

Let us learn from the woman who sat as a learner at the feet of our Lord, and thus taught us to choose the good part.

Here we see:

I. LOVE AT LEISURE. "Which also sat at Jesus feet."

When the evening comes on, and all the members of the family are around the fireside, then love rests and communes, forgetting all care, happily at home, oblivious of the outside world, and of time itself.

Like Mary:
- We would feel ourselves quite at home with Jesus our Lord.
- We would be free from worldly care—leaving all with Jesus.
- We would even be free from the care of his service, the battle for his Kingdom, and the burden of the souls committed to our charge.
- We would sweetly enjoy the happy leisure which he provides for us, as we muse upon the rest-giving themes which he reveals so clearly, and makes so true to us.
- His work for us, finished, accepted, abidingly effectual, and perpetually overflowing with priceless blessings.
- His great gifts received, which are greater than those to come.
- All other needful and promised benedictions of grace, sure to come in due season (Rom. 8:32).
- All our future, for time and for eternity, safe in his dear hands.
- Let us, without fear, enjoy leisure with Jesus—leisure, but not laziness—leisure to love, to learn, to commune, to copy.
- Leisure in a home where others are cumbered (verses 40–42).
- Leisure to sit, and to sit in the most delightful of all places

II. LOVE IN LOWLINESS. "At Jesus' feet."

In this lowliness let each one personally copy Mary.

Say unto yourself, "I choose the feet of Jesus to be my place."

Let me be:

> Not a busy housewife and manager, which any one may be, and yet be graceless; but:

1. A penitent, which is an acknowledgment of my unworthiness.
2. A disciple, which is a confession of my ignorance.
3. A receiver, which is an admission of my emptiness.

This posture befits me when I think of what I was, what I am, what I must be, what my Lord is, and what he is to me.

Let me bless his condescending love, which permits me this bliss.

III. LOVE LISTENING. "And heard his word."

She could not have heard if she had not been at leisure to *sit*, nor if she had not been lowly, and chosen to sit *at his feet*.

Be it ours to hear that love-word which says, "Hearken, O daughter, and consider" (Ps. 45:10).

- Listening to what Jesus says in his Word, in his creation, in his providence, and by his Spirit in our soul.
- Listening to the tones and accents with which he emphasizes and sweetens all that he says.
- Listening to himself. Studying *him*, reading his very heart.
- Listening, and not obtruding our own self-formed thoughts, notions, reasonings, questionings, desires, and prejudices.
- Listening, and forgetting the observations and unbeliefs of others.
- Listening, and bidding all cares lie still, that they may no more disturb the reverent silence of the heart.

How sweet! How instructive! How truly "the good part"!

IV. LOVE IN POSSESSION.

She had obtained her Lord, his love, his presence, his word, his fellowship, and she sat there *in full enjoyment* to delight her soul with that which she had so joyfully lighted upon.

She had in this one thing supplied her soul's necessity, and so she sat down *in perfect satisfaction*.

She had her Lord's promise that she should not be robbed of it, and she sat down *in full assurance*, to be happy in her possession.

Her Lord's promise assured her that she should not lose the good part, which she had chosen:

- By a cold word from her Lord.
- By the angry expostulation of her sister.
- By any future affliction, or temptation, or occupation.
- Nor even by death itself.

Now, then, she rests *in resolute constancy*: she has reached her *ultimatum*: she will go no further than her Lord and his word.

Oh, to be more with Jesus! This is true life.

Oh, to hear Jesus more! This is true service.

Oh, to love Jesus more! This is true treasure.

Oh, to abide with Jesus, and never dream of going beyond him! This is true wisdom.

Quiet Morsels

Behold Mary, all reverence, all attention, all composure, feeding on the doctrine of eternal life—she "sat at Jesus' feet." She wisely and zealously improved the opportunity given her for the good of her soul. "This is my summer, my harvest: let me redeem the time." —*Jay*

Mary sitteth to hear the word, as Christ used to sit when he preached the word (Matt. 5; Luke 14; John 8); to show that the word is to be preached and heard with a quiet mind. In a still night, every voice is heard, and when the body is quiet, the mind most commonly is quiet also. . . .When our minds are quiet, we are fit to deal with heavenly matters; therefore the doctors conferred sitting in the temple, and God delighteth to deal with us when we are most in private; he appeared to Abraham sitting in the door of his tent (Gen. 18). The Holy Ghost came down upon the Apostles, and filled all the house where they were sitting (Acts 2). The eunuch, sitting in his chariot, was called and converted by Philip's preaching (Acts 8). —*Henry Smith*

Whether shall we praise more, Mary's humility, or her docility? I do not see her take a stool and sit by him, or a chair and sit above him; but, as desiring to show her heart was as low as her knees, she sits at his feet. She was lowly set, and richly warmed with his heavenly beams. The greater submission, the more grace. If there be one hollow in the valley lower than another, thither the waters gather. —*Bishop Hall*

Dr. Chalmers' complained: "I am hustled out of my spirituality."

> At the feet of Jesus, list'ning to His word;
> Learning wisdom's lesson from her loving Lord;
> Mary, led by heav'nly grace,
> Chose the meek disciple's place.
> At the feet of Jesus is the place for me;
> There a humble learner would I choose to be.
> —*Sacred Songs and Solos*

162

What man of you, having an hundred sheep, if he lose one of them, doth not leave the ninety and nine in the wilderness, and go after that which is lost, until he find it? And when he hath found it, he layeth it on his shoulders, rejoicing. And when he cometh home, he calleth together his friends and neighbors, saying unto them, rejoice with me; for I have found my sheep which was lost.

—*Luke 15:4–6*

HE love of Jesus is not mere sentiment; it is active and energetic.

It is prevenient love, going after sheep that have no notion of returning to the fold from which they have wandered.

It is engrossing, making him leave all else: making one lost one to be of more present importance than ninety and nine.

It sets him upon resolute, determined, persevering search.

Let us behold our great Shepherd:

I. IN THE SEARCH. "Until he find it."

Mark him well, as, with his eyes, and heart, and all faculties, he goes "after that which is lost."

1. No rejoicing is on his countenance. He is anxious for the lost.
2. No hesitation is in his mind. Despite the roughness of the way, or the length of the time, or the darkness of the night, he still pursues his lost one.
3. No anger is in his heart. The many wanderings of the sheep cost him dear, but he counts them as nothing, so that he may but find it.
4. No pausing because of weariness. Love makes him forget himself, and causes him to renew his strength.
5. No giving up the search. His varied non-successes do not compel him to return defeated.

Such must our searches after others be.

We must labor after each soul until we find it.

II. AT THE CAPTURE. "When he hath found it."

Mark the Shepherd when the sheep is at last within reach.

1. Wanderer held. How firm the grip! How hearty! How entire!
2. Weight borne. No chiding, smiting, driving; but a lift, a self-loading, an easing of the wanderer.
3. Distance traveled. Every step is for the Shepherd.
   - He must tread painfully all that length of road over which the sheep had wandered so wantonly.
   - The sheep is carried back with no suffering on its own part.
4. Shepherd rejoicing to bear the burden.
   - The sheep is so dear that its weight is a load of love.
   - The Shepherd is so good that he finds joy in his own toil.
5. Sheep rejoicing, too. Surely it is glad to be found of the Shepherd, and so to have its wanderings ended, its weariness rested, its distance removed, its perfect restoration secured.

III. IN THE HOME-BRINGING. "When he cometh home."

Mark well the end of the Shepherd's toil and care: he does not end his care till he has brought the stray one "home."

1. Heaven is home to Christ.
2. Jesus must carry us all the way there.
3. The Shepherd's mission for lost souls is known in glory, and watched with holy sympathy: in this all heavenly ones are "his friends and neighbors."
4. Jesus loves others to rejoice with him over the accomplishment of his design. "He calleth together his friends." See how they crowd around him! What a meeting!
5. Repentance is also regarded as our being brought home (verse 7). "I have found" refers to the repenting sinner, and it is a finding which secures salvation, or angels would not rejoice over it.
6. One sinner can make all heaven glad (verses 7 and 10.)

Let us learn a lesson from each of the three pictures which we have looked upon:

Of perseverance till souls are saved.

Of patience with souls who are newly found.

Of encouragement in expectation of the gathering into glory of those for whom we labor on behalf of Jesus.

Sheep Tracks

One evening in 1861, as General Garibaldi was going home, he met a Sardinian shepherd lamenting the loss of a lamb out of his flock. Garibaldi at once turned to his staff, and announced his intention of scouring the mountain in search of the lamb. A grand expedition was organized. Lanterns were brought, and old officers of many a campaign started off, full of zeal, to hunt the fugitive. But no lamb was found, and the soldiers were ordered to their beds. The next morning, Garibaldi's attendant found him in bed, fast asleep. He was surprised at this, for the General was always up before anybody else. The attendant went off softly, and returned in half-an-hour. Garibaldi still slept. After another delay, the attendant awoke him. The General rubbed his eyes, and so did his attendant, when he saw the old warrior take from under the covering the lost lamb, and bid him convey it to the shepherd. The General had kept up the search through the night, until he had found it. Even so doth the Good Shepherd go in search of his lost sheep until he finds them. —*The Preachers' Monthly*

Christ a Shepherd.—He is the Good Shepherd that laid down his life for the sheep (John 10:11); the Great Shepherd that was brought again from the dead (Heb. 13:20); the Chief Shepherd who shall appear again (1 Pet. 5:4); the Shepherd and Bishop of souls (1 Pet. 2:25); he is the Shepherd of the sheep, who gathers the lambs with his arm, and carries them in his bosom (John 10; Isa. 40:11); the Shepherd of Israel (Ezek. 34:23); Jehovah's Shepherd (Zech.13:7). —*John Bate*

Why doth he not drive the sheep before him, especially seeing it was lively enough to lose itself? First, because, though it had wildness more than enough to go astray, it had not wisdom enough to go right. Secondly, because probably the silly sheep had tired itself with wandering. "The people shall weary themselves for very vanity" (Hab. 2:13). Therefore the kind Shepherd brings it home on his own shoulders. —*Thomas Fuller*

Yam Sing, on his examination for membership on experience before the Baptist Church, San Francisco, in response to the question, "How did you find Jesus?" answered, "I no find Jesus at all; he find me." He passed.

A little boy, in a Chinese Christian family at Amoy, wishing to make a profession of religion, was told that he was too young to be received into the church. He replied, "Jesus has promised to carry the lambs in his bosom. I am only a little boy; it will be easier for Jesus to carry me." —*The Sunday-School Teacher*

163

And when Jesus came to the place, he looked up, and saw him, and said unto him, Zacchaeus, make haste, and come down; for today I must abide at thy house.

—Luke 19:5

UR Savior for the first time invited himself to a man's house.

Thus he proved the keeness and authority of his grace. "I am found of them that sought me not" (Isa. 65:1).

We ought rather to invite him to our houses.

We should at least cheerfully accept his offer to come to us.

Perhaps at this hour he presses himself upon us.

Yet we may feel ourselves quite as unlikely to entertain our Lord as Zacchaeus seemed to be. He was a man:

- In a despised calling—a publican, or tax collector.
- In bad odor with respectable folk.
- Rich, with the suspicion of getting his wealth wrongly.
- Eccentric, for else he had hardly climbed a tree.
- Excommunicated because of his becoming a Roman tax gatherer.
- Not at all the choice of society in any respect.

To such a man Jesus came; and he may come to us even if we are similarly tabooed by our neighbors, and are therefore disposed to fear that he will pass us by.

I. LET US CONSIDER THE NECESSITY WHICH PRESSED UPON THE SAVIOR TO ABIDE IN THE HOUSE OF ZACCHAEUS.

He felt an urgent need of:

1. A sinner who needed and would accept his mercy.
2. A person who would illustrate the sovereignty of his choice.
3. A character whose renewal would magnify his grace.
4. A host who would entertain him with hearty hospitality.
5. A case which would advertise his gospel (verses 9 and 10).

There was a necessity of predestination which rendered it true, "Today I must abide at thy house."

There was a necessity of love in the Redeemer's gracious heart.

There was also a necessity in order to the, blessing of others through Zacchaeus.

II. LET US INQUIRE WHETHER SUCH A NECESSITY EXISTS IN REFERENCE TO OURSELVES.

We can ascertain this by answering the following questions, which are suggested by the behavior of Zacchaeus to our Lord:

1. Will we receive him this day? "He made haste."
2. Will we receive him heartily? "Received him joyfully."
3. Will we receive him whatever others say? "They all murmured."
4. Will we receive him as Lord? "He said, Behold, Lord."
5. Will we receive him so as to place our substance under the control of his laws (verse 8)?

If these things be so, Jesus must abide with us.

He cannot fail to come where he will have such a welcome.

III. LET US FULLY UNDERSTAND WHAT THAT NECESSITY INVOLVES.

If the Lord Jesus comes to abide in our house:

1. We must be ready to face objections at home.
2. We must get rid of all in our house which would be objectionable to him. Perhaps there is much there which he would never tolerate.
3. We must admit none who would grieve our heavenly Guest. His friendship must end our friendship with the world.
4. We must let him rule the house and ourselves, without rival or reserve, henceforth and for ever.
5. We must let him use us and ours as instruments for the further spread of his kingdom.

Why should we not today receive our Lord?

There is no reason why we must not.

There are many reasons why we must do so at once.

Lord, issue your own mandate, and say, "I must."

Noteworthy Passages

Had our Savior said no more but "Zacchaeus, come down," the poor man would have thought himself taxed for his boldness and curiosity: it were better to be unknown than noted for misbehavior. But how the next words comfort him: "For today I must abide at thy house!" What a sweet familiarity was here! as if Christ had been many years acquainted with Zacchaeus, whom he now first saw. Contrary to custom the host is invited by the guest, and called to an unexpected entertainment. Well did our Savior hear Zacchaeus' heart inviting him, though his mouth did not: desires are the language of the spirit, and are heard by him that is the God of spirits. —*Bishop Hall*

Now, Christ begins to call Zacchaeus from the tree to be converted, as God called Adam from among the trees of the garden to be judged (Gen. 3:8–9). Before, Zacchaeus was too low, and therefore was fain to climb; but now he is too high, and therefore he must come down. —*Henry Smith*

164

And he took bread, and gave thanks, and brake it, and gave unto them, saying, This is my body which is given for you: this do in remembrance of me. Likewise also the cup after supper, saying, This cup is the new testament in my blood, which is shed for you.

—*Luke 22:19–20*

ERE we have full directions for observing the Lord's Supper.

You see what it was, and how it was done.

The directions are plain, clear, definite.

It will not be right to do something else; we must "this do."

Nor this for another purpose; but "this do in remembrance of me."

This command raises a previous question: Do you know him? He who does not know him cannot remember him.

This being premised, let us observe that:

I. THE MAIN OBJECT OF THE SUPPER IS A PERSONAL MEMORIAL.

"In remembrance *of me.*" We are to remember not so much his doctrines, or precepts, as his person.

Remember the Lord Jesus at this Supper:

1. As the trust of your hearts.
2. As the object of your gratitude.
3. As the Lord of your conduct.
4. As the joy of your lives.
5. As the Representative of your persons.
6. As the Rewarder of your hopes.

Remember what he was, what he is, what he will be.

Remember him with heartiness, concentration of thought, realizing vividness, and deep emotion.

II. THE MEMORIAL ITSELF IS STRIKING.

1. Simple, and therefore like himself, who is transparent and unpretentious truth. Only bread broken, and wine poured out.
2. Frequent—"as oft as ye drink it," and so pointing to our constant need. He intended the Supper to be often enjoyed.
3. Universal, and so showing the need of all. "Drink ye all of it." In every land, all his people are to eat and drink at this table.
4. His death is the best memory of himself, and it is by showing forth *his death* that we remember *him*.
5. His covenant relation is a great aid to memory; hence he speaks of: "The new covenant in my blood." We do not forget Adam, our first covenant-head; nor can we forget our second Adam.
6. Our *receiving* him is the best method of keeping him in memory; therefore we eat and drink in this ordinance.

No better memorial could have been ordained.

III. THE OBJECT AIMED AT IS ITSELF INVITING.

Since we are invited to come to the holy Supper that we may remember our Lord, we may safely infer that:

1. We may come to it, though we have forgotten him often and sadly. In fact, this will be a reason for coming.
2. We may come, though others may be forgetful of him. We come not to judge *them*, but to remember him ourselves.
3. We may come, though weak for aught else but the memory of his goodness.
4. It will be sweet, cheering, sanctifying, quickening, to remember him; therefore let us not fail to come.

Let us at the sacred table quit all other themes.

Let us not burden ourselves with regrets, resolves, etc.

Let us muse wholly and alone on him whose flesh is meat indeed, whose blood is drink indeed (John 6:55).

Testimonies

Our Lord Jesus has his own memorials of us, even as he has given us a memorial of himself. The prints of the nails constitute forget-me-nots of a peculiarly personal and abiding kind: "Behold, I have graven thee upon the palms of my hands" (Isa. 49:16). By these marks he sees what he has already suffered, and he pledges himself to do nothing apart from those sufferings, for his hands, with which he works, are pierced. Since he thus bears in his hands the marks of his passion, let us bear them on our hearts.

Frequently to me the Supper has been much better than a sermon. It has the same teaching power, but it is more vivid. The Lord is known of us in the breaking, of bread, though our eyes have been holden during his discourse. I can see a good meaning in the saying of Henry III. of France, when he preferred the Sacrament to a sermon: "I had rather see my Friend than hear him talked about." I love to hear my Lord talked about, for so I often see him, and I see him in no other way in the Supper than in a sermon; but sometimes, when my eye is weak with weeping, or dim with dust, that double glass of the bread and wine suits me best. —*C. H. S.*

"*This do in remembrance of me.*" (1) This command implies a knowledge of himself. To remember, we must first know. It is no use saying to a man born blind, "Remember the sunshine." (2) It reveals the love of Christ. Why should he care about our remembering him? Dying voices have said to some of us, "Think of me sometimes; don't forget me." It is the very nature of love to want to be remembered. (3) It implies a tendency to forget. God never founds a needless institution. It is a sin that we do not remember Christ more. We should thankfully use every help to memory. —*Outline of an Address by Dr. Stanford*

At school we used certain books called "Aids to Memory." I am sure they rather perplexed than assisted me. Their utility was equivalent to that of a bundle of staves under a travelerís arm: true, he might use them one by one to walk with, but in the meantime he carried a host of others which he would never need. But our Savior was wiser than all our teachers, and his remembrancers are true and real aids to memory. His love-tokens have an unmistakable language, and they sweetly win our attention. —*C. H. S.*

If a friend gives us a ring at his death, we wear it to keep up the memory of our friend; much more, then, ought we to keep up the memorial of Christ's death in the sacrament. —*Thomas Watson*

> In mem'ry of Thy cross and shame (1 Cor. 9:23–26),
> I take this Supper in Thy name;
> This juice of grape, and flour of wheat,
> My outward man doth drink and eat.
> Oh, may my inward man be fed
> With better wine and better bread!
> May Thy rich flesh and precious blood
> Supply my spirit's daily food! (John 6:54).
> I thank Thee, Lord, Thou diedst for me:
> Oh, may I live and die to Thee! (Rom. 14:7–10).
> —*A. A. Rees.*

165

I am among you as he that serveth.
—*Luke 22:27*

INGULAr fact with regard to the apostles. They were at the same time troubled with two questions: "Which of them should be accounted the greatest?" and "Which of them should betray his Master?"

Where humility should have abounded ambition intruded.

Of the evil of self-seeking our Lord would cure the apostles.

The remedy which he used was his own conduct (John 13:12–17).

If he made himself least, they must not strive to be greatest.

May this example be blessed to us also!

Let us attentively note:

I. OUR LORD'S POSITION. "I am among you as he that serveth."

1. In the world our Lord was not one of the cultured few on whom others wait. He was a workingman, and in spirit he was *servus servorum*, servant of servants (Mark 10:45).

2. In the circle of his own disciples he was one that served. Where he was most Master he was most servant.
   • He was like a shepherd, servant to the sheep.
   • He was like a nurse, servant to a child.

3. In the celebration of the Supper, our Lord was specially among them "as he that serveth," for he washed his disciples' feet.

4. In the whole course of his life, Jesus on earth ever took the place of the servant, or slave.
   • His ear was bored by his entering into covenant. "Mine ears hast thou digged, or pierced" (Ps. 40:6 *margin*; Exod. 21:6).
   • His office was announced at his coming, "Lo, I come to do thy will!" (Ps. 40:7; Heb. 10:5–9).
   • His nature was fitted for service: he "took upon him the form of a servant" (Phil. 2:7).
   • He assumed the lowest place among men (Ps. 22:6; Isa. 53:3)
   • He cared for others, and not for himself. "The Son of man came not to be served but to serve" (Mark 10:45).
   • He laid aside his own will (John 4:34; 6:38).
   • He bore patiently all manner of hardness (1 Pet. 2:23).

II. THE WONDER OF IT. That he should be a servant among his own servants.

The marvel of it was rendered the greater:

1. As he was Lord of all by nature and essence (Col. 1:15-19).
2. As he was superior in wisdom, holiness, power, and in every other way, to the very best of them (Matt. 8:26, 27; John 14:9).
3. As he was so greatly their Benefactor (John 15:16).
4. As they were such poor creatures, and so unworthy to be served.

How could it be that they suffered themselves to be served of him?

How could it be that he endured to serve them?

III. THE EXPLANATION OF IT.

We must look for this to his own nature.

1. He is so infinitely great (Heb. 1:2-4).
2. He is so immeasurably full of love (John 15:9; 1 John 3:16).

Because of these two things he condescended so marvelously.

IV. THE IMITATION OF IT.

Let us copy our Lord:

1. In cheerfully choosing to fulfill the most lowly offices.
2. In manifesting great lowliness of spirit, and humility of bearing (Eph. 4:1-3; Phil. 2:3; 1 Pet. 5:5).
3. In laying ourselves out for the good of others. Let self-sacrifice be the rule of our existence (2 Cor. 12:15).
4. In gladly bearing injustice rather than break the peace, avenge ourselves, or grieve others (1 Pet. 2:19-20; 3:14).
5. In selecting that place in which we receive least, and give most; choosing to wait at table rather than to sit at meat.

Does not the text rebuke our pride?

Does it not arouse our adoring love?

Does it not lead us to gird up our loins to serve the brethren?

Concerning Service

When the son of Gamaliel was married, Rabbis Eliezer, Joshuah, and Zadig were invited to the marriage-feast. Gamaliel, though one of the most distinguished men among the Israelites, himself waited on his guests, and pouring out a cup of wine, handed it to Eliezer, who politely refused it. Gamaliel then handed it to Joshuah. The latter accepted it. "How is this, friend Joshuah?" said Eliezer, "shall we sit and permit so great a man to wait on us?" "Why not?" replied Joshuah, "a man even greater than he did so long before him. Was not our father Abraham a very great man? Yet even he waited upon his guests, as it is written, 'and he (Abraham) *stood by them whilst they were earing.'* Perhaps you may think he did so because he knew them to be angels; no such thing. He supposed them to be Arabian travelers, else he would neither have offered them water to wash their feet, nor viands to allay their hunger. Why, then, shall we prevent our kind host from imitating so excellent an example?" "I know," exclaimed Rabbi Zadig, "a Being still greater than Abraham, who doth the same. "Indeed," continued he, "how long shall we be engaged in reciting the praises of created beings, and neglect the glory of the Creator? Even he, blessed be his name, causes the winds to blow, the clouds to accumulate, and the rain to descend! He fertilizes the earth, and daily prepares a magnificent table for his creatures. Why, then, shall we hinder our kind host, Gamaliel, from following so glorious an example?" —*Hebrew Tales*

An old woman in Glencroe, visited by William McGavin, was found seated in bed, which, contrary to usual experience in the district, was scrupulously clean.

"You are an old servant of Christ, I understand," said he.

"Servant of Christ!" she responded, "Na, na; I'm naething pit a pair sinner. It's nine-and-forty years syne he pegan tae serve me."

"Serve you; how?"

"Dae ye no ken that?" she replied. "In the hoose o' Christ the Maister serves a' the guests. Did he no' himsel' say, 'I'm amang ye as ane that serveth'? When he brocht me hame tae himsel' he then pegan tae serve me, an' he ha' served me ere syne. Nane ere compleened o' Christ pein' a pad servant!"

"Well, but I hope you are a servant for all that. In the state of glory his servants serve him; and what is perfected there must begin here."

" That's a' fery true. I ken that I'm under his authority, pit somehoo I dinna like tae think much aboot servin' Christ. It gi'es me nae comfort." —*The Sword and the Trowel*

Why is it that so many professed Christians "feel above" undertaking humble work for God and humanity? We have heard of a minister of Christ complaining that his station was "beneath his talents!" As if the soul of a beggar were beneath the genius of a Paul! Some are unwilling to enter a mission-school, or to distribute tracts through a poor district, strangely forgetting that their divine Master was himself a missionary. Have such never learned that the towel wherewith Jesus wiped his disciples' feet outshone the purple that wrapped Caesar's limbs? Do they not know that the post of honor is the post of service?" My seat in the Sunday school is higher than my seat in the Senate," said an eminent Christian statesman. —*Dr. Cuyler*

166

Then said Jesus, Father, forgive them; for they know not what they do.

—*Luke 23:34*

ET us go to Calvary to learn how we may be forgiven; and then let us linger there to learn how we may forgive. There shall we see what sin is, as it murders the Lord of love; and see also how almighty mercy prevailed against it.

As we behold our Lord nailed to the cross, and hear his first words upon the tree, let us watch, and learn, and love.

I. WE SEE THE LOVE OF JESUS ENDURING.

- To the closing act of human malice.
- To the utmost endurance of shame (Phil. 2:8; Heb. 12:2).
- To the extreme limit of personal suffering (Ps. 22:1-18).

We see not alone patience that bears without complaint, but love that labors to bestow benefits upon its enemies.

II. WE SEE THAT LOVE REVEALING ITSELF.

- Love can use no better instrument than prayer.
- Love, when in a death-agony, still prays.
- Love thus brings heaven to the succor of those for whom it cares.
- Love thus, to the highest, blesses its object.

To this present our Lord Jesus continues to bless the people of his choice by continually interceding for them (Rom. 8:34; Heb. 7:25).

This is his daily prayer for us.

III. WE SEE FOR WHAT THAT LOVE PRAYS.

- Forgiveness is the first, chief, and basis blessing.
- Forgiveness from the Father can even go so far as to pardon the murder of his Son.
- Forgiveness is the great petition of our Lord's sacrifice.

Love admits that pardon is needed, and it shudders at the thought of what must come to the guilty if pardon be not given.

IV. WE SEE HOW THE LOVING JESUS PRAYS.

- For his wanton murderers in the very act.
- For their full and immediate forgiveness.
- For no other reason except their ignorance; and this plea grace alone could suggest or accept.

Are there any so guilty that Jesus would refuse to intercede for them?

V. WE SEE HOW HIS PRAYER BOTH WARNS AND WOOS.

- It warns, for it suggests that there is a limit to the possibility of pardon.
- Men may so sin that there shall remain no plea of ignorance; nay, no plea whatever.

• It woos, for it proves that if there be a plea, Jesus will find it.

Come and trust your ease in his hands; he will draw out his own brief, and invent his own arguments of love.

VI. WE SEE HOW HE INSTRUCTS FROM THE CROSS.
• He teaches us to put the best construction on the deeds of our fellowmen, and to discover mitigating circumstances when they work us grievous ill.
• He teaches us to forgive the utmost wrong (Mark 11:25).
• He teaches us to pray for others to our last breath (Acts 7:59–60).

That glorious appeal to the divine Fatherhood, once made by the Lord Jesus, still prevails for us.

Let the chief of sinners come unto God with the music of "Father, forgive them," sounding in their ears.

Commendations and Recommendtions

It is well to suppose ignorance when we suffer wrong. A cruel letter came to me in my illness, but I hoped the writer did not know how depressed I was; a gossip repeated a silly slander, but I always believed that she thought it was the truth; an individual intentionally grossly insulted me, but I mistook it for a rough jest. In every case I have found it to my own comfort to believe that there must have been a mistake; besides, it makes it much easier to remove any unpleasant feeling if all along you have treated it as an error of judgment, or a blunder, occasioned by want of better information. —*C. H. S.*

There is something in this plea that at first confounds me, and that makes me ask with reverence in what sense Christ used it. Surely ignorance is not the gospel plea. Ignorance gives no man a claim on God....We are not to say, "Being justified by ignorance, we have peace with God"—Ignorance is not innocence, it is often a sin; and one sin is no salvation from another.

The ignorance of Christ's enemies of what is involved in their capital crime brings them within the pale of mercy, and allows their pardon to be a possibility—a possibility on the ground which his cross supplies. Perhaps no mere men really know what they do in repudiating Christ. Satan knew what he did, and nothing has been said in our hearing of any gospel for him; but human sinners cannot fully know; and their ignorance, though it does not make sin sinless, leaves it pardonable. —*Charles Stanford*

Savior, thou couldst not but be heard! Those, who out of ignorance and simplicity thus persecuted thee, find the happy issue of thine intercession. Now I see whence it was that three thousand souls were converted soon after, at one sermon. It was not Peter's speech, it was thy prayer, that was thus effectual. Now they have grace to know and confess whence they have both forgiveness and salvation, and can recompense their blasphemies with thanksgiving. What sin is there, Lord, whereof I can despair of the remission? Or what offense can I be unwilling to remit, when thou prayest for the forgiveness of thy murderers and blasphemers? —*Bishop Hall*

> To do him any wrong was to beget
> A kindness from him; for his heart was rich,
> Of such fine mould, that if you sow'd therein
> The seed of Hate, it blossomed Charity.

It was a mark of true moral grandeur in the character of Phocion, that, as he was about to be put to death, when one asked him whether he had any commands to leave for his son, he exclaimed, "Yes, by all means, tell him from me to forget the ill-treatment I have received from the Athenians." Such a spirit of forgiveness, if it became a heathen, will much more become a disciple of the gentle and loving Christ, who, in his dying hour, prayed, "Father, forgive them; for they know not what they do." No one has a right to claim the Christian spirit who refuses to forgive a foe, and even cement his forgiveness by some act of self-denying love.

A great boy in a school was so abusive to the younger ones, that the teacher took the vote of the school whether he should be expelled. All the small boys voted to expel him except one, who was scarcely five years old. Yet he knew very well that the bad boy would continue to abuse him. "Why, then, did you vote for him to stay?" said the teacher. "Because, if he is expelled, perhaps he will not learn any more about God, and so he will become still more wicked." "Do you forgive him, then?" said the teacher. "Yes," said he, "father and mother forgive me when I do wrong; God forgives me too; and I must do the same." —*The Biblical Treasury*

167

And as they thus spake, Jesus himself stood in the midst f them, and saith unto them, Peace be unto you.

—*Luke 24:36*

 ROM what a man has been it is usually safe to infer what he is.

This is eminently the case with our Lord Jesus, since he is unchangeable. What he was to his disciples in the days of his flesh, he will be to his followers at this present hour.

We gather that he loves to reveal himself to his saints when they are assembled on the Sabbath-day, for he did so when on earth.

Let us consider the visit described in the text.

Uninvited, unexpected, undeserved, but most welcome was that visit.

Jesus stood in the center to be near to them all, and that he might assume the place which a leader should take among his followers.

I. WHEN HE APPEARED.

1. When they had been acting unworthily by fleeing from him at his betrayal, and deserting him at his trial.
2. When they were unprepared, and unbelieving, doubting his express promise, and refusing the testimony of his messengers.
3. When they greatly needed his presence, for they were like sheep without a shepherd.
4. When they were exercising the little life they had by coming together in loving assembly. So far they were doing well, and acting in a way which was likely to bring blessing.
5. When they were lamenting his absence, and thus proving their desire after him. This is an admirable means of gaining his presence.
6. When certain among them were testifying concerning him.

Are not *we* in a similar condition?

May we not hopefully look for our Lord's manifestation of himself?

II. WHAT HE SAID. "Peace be unto you."

1. It was a benediction: he wished them peace.
2. It was a declaration: they were at peace with God.
3. It was a fiat: he inspired them with peace.
4. It was an absolution: he blotted out all offenses which might have spoiled their peace.

The Lord by his Holy Spirit can calm our perturbed minds, relieve of all care, discharge from all sin, deliver from all spiritual conflict, and give to each one of us immediate and perfect peace.

III. WHAT CAME OF HIS APPEARING.

1. He banished their doubts. Even Thomas had to shake off his obstinate unbelief.
2. He revealed and sealed his love upon their hearts by showing them his hands and his feet.
3. He refreshed their memories. "These are the words which I spake unto you" (verse 44).
4. He opened their understandings (verse 45).
5. He showed them their position. "Ye are witnesses of these things" (verse 48).
6. He filled them with joy (John 22:20).

Has the Lord come into our midst during this service?

Has he breathed into our souls a special peace?

If so, let us wait a while, and further enjoy his company, and praise his condescending love.

If we do not feel that we have been thus favored, let us tarry behind, and further seek his face.

A special meeting for praise and prayer will be held during the next half-hour. O Lord Jesus, abide with us!

Ripples

The Master's greeting to the first company had been in the word "Rejoice!" (Matt. 28:9–10). His greeting to the second was in the phrase, "Peace be unto you!" And this he said twice over (John 20:19–21). We should keep in mind the difference between the first company and the second. The first was a small detachment of the general society, and consisted of women only. The second was the general society itself, including all the men; and all the men had in one moment of panic forsaken their Master. In that shameful moment even John had not been an exception. The women, when Christ met them, had been true, and were only conscious of grief; the men had not been true; and, besides their grief, were conscious of deep agitation and burning shame. He knew their thoughts. Like the young Hebrew in their national story, who, years after his brethren had cast him into a pit, then sold him for a slave, met them face to face again, he as their lord, they as his supplicants, but who, that they might not fall back blasted, gently discovered himself to them in the words, "I am Joseph, your brother," to the mention of his name eagerly adding the mention of his relation; so the Celestial Joseph, in discovering himself to those whom he had so grandly loved, but by whom he had been so basely forsaken, first sent forward by Mary the message, "Go tell my brethren," then followed up the message by personally appearing with these words on his lips—"Peace to you!"— words meant to dispel their fear, to kindle their tenderness, and to still the tempest within them. Brothers in Christ, this message was meant for our one whole family. —*Charles Stanford*

There are depths in the ocean, I am told, which no tempest ever stirs; they are beyond the reach of all storms, which sweep and agitate the surface of the sea. And there are heights in the blue sky above to which no cloud ever ascends, where no tempest ever rages, where all is perpetual sunshine, and nought exists to disturb the deep serene. Each of these is an emblem of the soul which Jesus visits; to whom he speaks peace, whose fear he dispels, and whose lamp of hope he trims. —*Tweedie*

In the life of Dr. John Duncan there is a touching passage, which relates how much he suffered from religious melancholy. His mental struggles were often very distressing, casting a shadow over his whole life and work. On one occasion, he went to his college-class in a state of extreme dejection. During the opening prayer, however, the cloud passed away. His eye brightened, his features relaxed, and before beginning his lecture he said, with pathetic sympathy, "Dear young gentlemen, I have just got a glimpse of Jesus."

We are the soldiers of Jesus Christ. Now, that which nerves the soldier's arm, and strengthens his heart, as he goes forth to battle, is not so much the multitude of the army of which he forms a part, as the character of the chief whom he is following. It is related that, in one of the Duke of Wellington's battles, a portion of the army was giving way, under the charge of the enemy, when he rode into the midst of them. A soldier called out in ecstasy, *"There's the Duke— God bless him! I'd rather see his face than a whole brigade;"* and these words, turning all eyes to their chief, so reassured his comrades that they repulsed the foe; they felt, he is beside us who was never defeated yet, and who will not be defeated now. A military friend, with whom I conversed on this subject, said that, though he had never heard the anecdote, he could well conceive it to be true: the presence of the distinguished General, he added, was at any time worth five thousand men. —*Tait on the Hebrews*

168

And he led them out as far as to Bethany, and he lifted up his hands, and blessed them.

—*Luke 24:50*

JESUS having spoiled the grave, and sanctified the earth, now purified the air as he passed through it on his way to heaven.

He arose to heaven in a manner worthy of special note. We will review a few points connected with his ascension.

1. The time he sojourned on earth after his resurrection, namely, forty days, sufficed to prove his identity, to remove doubts, to instruct his disciples, and to give them their commission.

2. The place from which he rose was a mountain, a mount where he aforetime had communed with them. This mount looked down on Bethany, his dearest earthly rest; and was near to Gethsemane, the place of his supreme agony.

3. The witnesses were enough in number to convince the candid, persons who had long been familiar with him, who could not be deceived as to his identity.

They were persons of character, of simplicity of nature, of ripe years, and of singularly cool temperament.

4. The scene itself was very remarkable.

- So unlike what superstition would have devised.
- So quiet—no chariot of fire and horses of fire.
- So majestic—no angels, nor other agents to lend imaginary splendor; but the Lord's own power and Godhead in sublime simplicity working all.

Our chosen theme at this time shall be the last posture in which our ascending Lord was seen.

I. HIS HANDS WERE UPLIFTED TO BLESS.

1. This blessing was no unusual thing. To stretch out his hands in benediction was his customary attitude. In that attitude he departed, with a benediction still proceeding from his lips.
2. This blessing was with authority. He blessed them while his Father acknowledged him by receiving him to heaven.
3. This blessing was so full that, as it were, he emptied his hands. They saw those dear hands thus unladen of their benedictions.
4. The blessing was for those beneath him, and beyond the sound of his voice: he scattered benedictions upon them all.
5. The blessing was the fit finis of his sojourn here: nothing fitter, nothing better, could have been thought of.

II. THOSE HANDS WERE PIERCED.

This could be seen by them all as they gazed upward.
1. Thus they knew that they were Christ s hands.
2. Thus they saw the price of the blessing. His crucifixion has purchased continual blessing for all his redeemed.
3. Thus they saw the way of the blessing: it comes from those human hands, through those sacrificial wounds.
4. A sight of those hands is in itself a blessing. By that sight we see pardon and eternal life.
5. The entire action is an epitome of the gospel. This is the substance of the matter—"hands pierced distribute benedictions." Jesus, through suffering and death, has power to bless us out of the highest heaven.

This is the last that was seen of our Lord.

He has not changed his attitude of benediction.

He will not change it till he shall descend in his glory.

III. THOSE HANDS SWAY THE SCEPTER.

His hands are omnipotent. Those very hands, which blessed his disciples, now hold, on their behalf, the scepter:
1. Of providence: both in small affairs and greater matters.
2. Of the spiritual kingdom: the church and all its work.
3. Of the future judgment, and the eternal reign.

Let us worship him, for he has ascended on high.
Let us rejoice in all the fruit of his ascension, to him, and to us.
Let us continue praising him, and proclaiming his glory.

Glimpses

What spot did Jesus select as the place of his ascension? He selected, not *Bethlehem*, where angel-hosts had chanted his praises; nor *Tabor*, where celestial beings had hovered around him in homage; nor Calvary, where riven rocks and bursting graves had proclaimed his Deity; nor the *Temple-court*, in all its sumptuous glory, where, for ages, his own Shekinah had blazed in mystic splendor: but he hallows afresh the name of a lowly village, *Bethany*; he consecrates a Home of Love. —*Dr. Macduff's "Memories of Bethany"*

The manner of Christ's ascension into heaven may be said to have been an instance of divine simplicity and sublimity combined, which scarcely has a parallel. While in the act of blessing his disciples, he was parted from them, and was carried up, and disappeared behind a cloud. There was no pomp; nothing could have been more simple. How can the followers of this Lord and Master rely on pomp and ceremony to spread his religion, when he, its Founder, gave no countenance to such appeals to the senses of men? Had some good men been consulted about the manner of the ascension, we can imagine the result. —*N. Adams*

This is no death-bed scene. "Nothing is here for tears." We are not at the close, but at the beginning of a life. There is no sign of mourning that a great career is over, that the lips of a great Teacher are for ever dumb; no ground for that melancholy question that twice rang in the ears of Elisha, "Knowest thou that the Lord will take away thy master from thy head to day? And he said, Yea, I know it; hold ye your peace." No; the scene before us is one of calm victory:

All the toil, the sorrow, done;
All the battle fought and won.

The earthly work of the Redeemer is over; the work which that short sojourn on earth was designed to inaugurate is now to begin. We are in the presence of One who said, "All power is given unto me in heaven and in earth"; and again, "Be of good cheer, I have overcome the world." —*Dr. Butler, Head Master of Harrow*

That wonderful hand of Christ! It was that same hand which had been so quickly stretched out to rescue Peter when sinking in Galilee's waves. It was that same hand which had been held in the sight of the questioning disciples on the third evening after they had seen it laid lifeless in the tomb. It was that same hand which incredulous Thomas must see before he would believe its risen power; it was that same hand which was extended to him not only to see, but to touch the nail-prints in its palm. It was that same hand which the disciples last saw uplifted in a parting blessing when the cloud parted him from them. It was only after ten days that they realized the fullness of blessing which came from that extended, pierced hand of Christ. Peter at Pentecost must have preached with that last sight of it fresh in his memory, when he said, "God hath made that same Jesus, *whom ye have crucified*, both Lord and Christ." That hand, with its nail-prints, knocks at the heart's door for entrance. That hand, with its deep marks of love, beckons on the weary runner in the heavenly way. —*F. B. Pullan*

169

The next day John seeth Jesus coming unto him, and saith, Behold
the Lamb of God, which taketh away the sin of the world.
—John 1:29

 LACES and times become memorable when linked with our Lord; hence we are told what was done at Bethabara on such a day, and what happened on "the next day."

Let us treasure holy memories with great care—especially memories of Jesus—times when we saw the Lord.

In the case before us the preacher was a notable man, and his theme more notable still. John the Baptist preaches Jesus.

We have here a model for every minister of Christ.

I. THE TRUE MESSENGER.

1. He is one who sees Jesus for himself. There was a time when John did not know the Christ, but in due time the Holy Spirit pointed him out (verse 33). The true herald of Jesus is like John:
   - He is on the lookout for his Lord's appearing.
   - He rejoices to preach Jesus as one whom he has himself seen and known, and still hopes to see.
   - He preaches him as come, and as coming.
2. He calls upon men to see Jesus. "Behold the Lamb of God."
   - This he does plainly and confidently.
   - This he does continually: it is his one message. John preached the same sermon "again the next day after" (verse 35).
   - This he does earnestly and emphatically. "Behold!"
3. He leads his own followers to Jesus. John's disciples heard John speak, and followed Jesus (verse 37).
   - He had enough force to induce men to be his followers.
   - He had enough humility to induce his followers to leave him for Jesus. This is the glory of John the Baptist.
   - He had enough grace to make him rejoice that it was so.

Our speech should make men go beyond ourselves to Christ. "We preach not ourselves, but Christ Jesus the Lord" (2 Cor. 4:5.)

4. He loses himself in Jesus.

- He sees the necessity of this "He must increase, but I must decrease" (John 3:30).
- He sees the propriety of this: he knows himself to be only the Bridegroom's friend, and not the Bridegroom (John 3:29).

Blessed is that minister of whom all these points can be asserted.

II. THE TRUE MESSAGE.

John's word was brief, but emphatic.

1. He declared Jesus to be sent and ordained "of God."
2. He declared him to be the one real, divinely-appointed sacrifice for sin— "the Lamb of God."
3. He declared him to be the only remover of human guilt—"which taketh away the sin of the world."
4. He declared him to be set forth as the object of faith—"Behold the Lamb." He exhorted his hearers to look at him with that look which saves.

The end of all ministries and ordinances is to bring men to look to Jesus. Both John, who ran before, and we, who run after, must point in the same direction.

III. THE TRUE RECEPTION OF THAT MESSAGE.

The conduct of John's disciples shows that our true wisdom concerning gospel testimony is:

1. To believe it, and so to acknowledge Jesus as our sin-removing sacrifice.
2. To follow Jesus (verse 37).
3. To follow Jesus, even if we be alone. These were the vanguard of the vast hosts who have since followed Jesus. They knew not what suffering it might involve, but went first and foremost.
4. To abide with Jesus (verse 39).
5. To go forth and tell others of Jesus (verse 40 and 41).

Here, then, is a lesson for those who preach. John s sermon was short, but full of Jesus, and effectual for soul-winning. Imitate him.

Here also is an example for those who have believed.

Here is a gospel for those who hitherto have not known the Savior.

Specialties

In 1857, a day or two before preaching at the Crystal Palace, I went to decide where the platform should be fixed; and, in order to test the acoustic properties of the building, cried in a loud voice, "Behold the Lamb of God, which taketh away the sin of the world." In one of the galleries, a workman, who knew nothing of what was being done, heard the words, and they came like a message from heaven to his soul. He was smitten with conviction on account of sin, put down his tools, went home, and there, after a season of spiritual struggling, found peace and life by beholding the Lamb of God. Years after, he told this story to one who visited him on his death-bed. —*C. H. S.*

Notice how simple the means, how grand the result! John simply declared, "Behold the Lamb of God." Here is no vehement appeal, no angry rebuke, no feverish, would-be impressive urging; it is a simple, earnest declaration of God's truth. What else have Christ's servants to do but to set forth the truth, the gospel, the will of God, as revealed in the person and work of Christ? How much more important to give all our energy and strength to this, than to the attempt of enforcing and applying, threatening and inviting, urging and pressing, in perorations thundering or melting! The truth itself thunders and melts, rouses and whispers, bruises and comforts; entering into the soul, it brings with it light and power. How calm and objective do Christ's sermons, and those of the apostles, appear! How powerful by the consciousness which pervades them: this is the truth of God, light from heaven, power from above! "Behold the Lamb of God." —*Adolph Saphir*

It is related of John Wesley that, preaching to an audience of courtiers and noblemen, he used the "generation of vipers" text, and flung denunciation right and left. "That sermon should have been preached at Newgate," said a displeased courtier to Wesley on passing out. "No," said the fearless apostle, "my text *there* would have been, 'Behold the Lamb of God, which taketh away the sin of the world.'"

Roger Clark, one of the English martyrs, when at the stake, cried out to the people, "Behold the Lamb of God, which taketh away the sin of the world." How suitable such a cry from a saint about to seal his testimony with his blood!

No *herald* could live long in the wilderness on locusts and wild honey, if he had not to tell of a man or an era nobler than himself, and brighter than his own twilight-hour. John lived more truly on the prophecy he proclaimed than on the honey and locusts. —*Dr. Parker*

A young telegraph operator was anxious about his soul. After a sleepless night, he went to his duties; while restless and absorbed in the thought of his being a sinner, he heard the click of his instrument, and, with great astonishment and emotion, spelt out this message: "From H. Windermere. To J. B. Warkworth. 'Behold the Lamb of God, which taketh away the sin of the world; in whom we have redemption, through his blood, even the forgiveness of sins.'"

This was sent as an answer to a letter from a young man, who also was seeking peace. It acted as a double blessing, showing to both operator and receiver the way of salvation.

170

Jesus saw Nathanael coming to him, and saith of him, Behold an Israelite indeed, in whom is no guile!

—John 1:47

 HIS is a chapter of "beholds." We are first to "Behold the Lamb of God," and then to behold a man of God.

Nathanael was simple, straightforward, honest, "an Israelite indeed."

In this he was not like his great progenitor, Jacob, who was a supplanter, and not a prince with God, till that memorable night when the angel wrestled with him, and withered his carnal strength. Then, in the weakness of that simplicity which laid hold upon the mighty One, Jacob became Israel (Gen. 27:36; 32:28).

A sincere and simple character was not common in our Lord's day.

It is despised by many at this day.

It was greatly appreciated by our Lord, who has the same character in perfection, and is truly called "the holy child Jesus."

This characteristic of guilelessness is:

I. A HAPPY SIGN IN A SEEKER.

We will illustrate this by Nathanael's procedure.

1. He is the sort of man to whom disciples like to speak. "Philip findeth Nathanael" (verse 45).
2. He is outspoken with his difficulties, and therefore his friends see how to meet them. "Can there any good thing come out of Nazareth?" (verse 46).
3. He is ready to apply the proper tests "Come and see" (verse 46).
4. He is honest in his use of those tests. Our Lord saw that Nathanael was no captious critic, nor idly-curious observer (verse 47).
5. He is open to conviction if fair evidence be supplied. As soon as our Lord proved his omniscience Nathanael believed (verse 48).
6. He is ready to make confession (verse 49).
7. He is prepared to proceed far in the school of Christ. The Lord promised him the sight of greater things because he was prepared to see them (verses 50 and 51).

An Israelite is the man to know "the King of Israel" (verse 49).

An Israelite is the man to understand the famous dream of the father of all Israelites (verse 51; Gen. 28:12).

II. A VITAL POINT IN A BELIEVER.

The truly upright man, and he only, can be a Christian.

1. A sense of pardon removes the temptation to guile: we cease to excuse ourselves when pardon is received (Ps. 51).
2. A reception of Christ as "the truth" causes guile to be hated.
3. A truthful assurance of the gospel prevents a hypocritical faith.
4. A complete consecration to the Lord puts an end to a double-minded life, and to all false aims and maxims.
5. A sense of the presence of God makes guile appear absurd.
6. A brave faith in God causes it to appear mean and cowardly.

III. A SURE PRODUCER OF OTHER QUALITIES.

1. It makes a man love his Bible. Nathanael was familiar with the law and the prophets.
2. It makes him pray. He is an Israelite (Gen. 32:28).
3. It leads him to be much alone. "Under the fig-tree" (verse 48).
4. It makes him wear his heart in his countenance. "Behold an Israelite indeed."
5. It prepares him to behold the pure and true glories of heaven.

Who among us is renowned for cleverness, craft, shrewdness, and the critical faculty in general?

Let him be afraid of the much-admired quality of cleverness.

The absence of simplicity is by no means a healthy sign.

Let us be true in any case, and may the Lord teach us his truth!

Mosaic

'Twas well Christ spake among plain men. Had the Scribes and the Pharisees heard him, had some men of these times heard him, they would have said that Christ purposed to define a fool. Who is not now a fool that is not false? He is rated as having but small wit that is not of great subtlety and great wiliness? Plainness is weakness, and solid sincerity stolid simplicity. No man is honest but for want of sense. Conscience comes only from a crazed brain. He hath no reach that cloth not overreach. Only to disguise is to be wise; and he is the profoundest that is the grandest counterfeit. Christ will have a serpent and a dove coupled together—wisdom and simplicity; and he bids, what God hath joined, that man should not sever. But the world dares uncouple them. Uncouple them? That's little; dares divorce them. In these days doves may not consort with serpents, nor singleness and sapience harbor in one heart. Certainly plain-dealing is a jewel; but the world dubs him a fool that useth it.

Hence it is that, nowadays, men dare not deal uprightly, lest their wit be called in question; they are afraid of honest plainness lest they be held for idiocy. Term one an honest man, you do discredit him. The name of fool is so disgraceful, one will rather be a villain than be called a fool. But here, God's Word, God's Wisdom, defines a true Israelite, by truth and plainness; he is one that hath no guile. —*Richard Clerke*

"Behold an Israelite indeed, in whom is no guile."—The expression would appear to be so distinct an allusion to the thirty-second Psalm as to amount to a quotation, and to imply that this guilelessness of spirit was not mere amiability, but was the fruit of forgiven sin. "Blessed is he whose transgression is forgiven, whose sin is covered (or atoned). Blessed is the man unto whom the Lord imputeth not iniquity, and in whose spirit there is no guile." Nathanael, if we may follow this clue, was no stranger to the spiritual meaning of atonement; no stranger, therefore, to the consciousness of sin which made its necessity felt. Pressed on the one hand by the sense of guilt, allured on the other by the provision of atonement in the temple sacrifices, he had been forced to earn his first title by wrestling in prayer with God for pardon; and, having prevailed, there had sprung up within the forgiven man the guileless spirit of childlike trustfulness in God, who had thus stooped to his prayer, and granted the benison he sighed for. He is in the happiest state of preparation for the personal knowledge of Christ, and we shall see with what fullness of faith he honors his Master al the first interview, uttering on the threshold of discipleship a confession more advanced than was made at the same point by any other of the twelve. —*C. A. Davis*

Nathanael was one of these true Israelites; he was in reality, as well as by profession, one of the people of God; and the evidence he gave of this was his freedom from guile. But our Savior does not say he has no guilt. A man may be freckled, or have spots, and not be painted. A Christian is not sinlessly pure he has many unallowed and bewailed infirmities, but guile he has not: he is no hypocrite. He does not in religion ascend a stage, to assume a character which does not belong to him. He is what he appears to be. There is a correspondence between his professions and actions, his meanings and his words. He is upright in his dealings with himself, in his dealings with his fellow-creatures, and in his dealings with his God. He is all of a piece. He is the same alone as in company; the same in his own house as in the house of God; the same in prosperity as in adversity. —*William Fay*

The clearer the diamond, the more it sparkles; the plainer the heart is, the more it sparkles in God's eye. What a commendation did Christ give Nathanael—"Behold an Israelite indeed, in whom is no guile!" —*Thomas Watson*

171

Now Jacob's well was there. Jesus therefore, being wearied with his journey, sat thus on the well; and it was about the sixth hour.

—John 4:6

ANY things may well remind us of our Lord.

Chiefly may we think of him when we see a well or a weary peasant resting at noon.

How truly human was Jesus! To him a long walk brought weariness; his weariness needed rest; to rest he "sat thus on the well."

How worn was his humanity! He was more weary than the disciples.

- He had a greater mental strain than they.
- He had a weariness that they knew not of.

His self-denials were even then remarkable.

- He would in all points be made like unto his brethren.
- He would not exempt himself from fatigue.
- He would not work a miracle for his own refreshment.
- He would not refuse to bear heat, thirst, exhaustion.

He has thus made himself able to sympathize with:

- The traveler who rests by the roadside.
- The laborer who is worn-out with toil.
- The sufferer who feels pain in bone and flesh.
- The poor man who must rest on a cold stone, and look for refreshment to the public fountain.
- The weary mind, oppressed by life's long way, which has no luxurious comfort prepared for it, but finds a measure of repose in the simple arrangements of nature.

Reading this text, let it set a picture before you, and:

I. LET YOUR CONSCIENCE DRAW A SPIRITUAL PICTURE OF YOUR WEARIED SAVIOR.

1. He is wearied with our sins (Isa. 43:24).
2. He is wearied with our formal worship (Isa. 1:14).
3. He is wearied with our errings through unbelief (Ps. 95:10).
4. He is wearied with our resistance of his Spirit (Isa. 63:10).
5. He is wearied with our cavillings and rebellions (Mal. 2:17).

Perhaps we have specially wearied the Lord, as we read in Amos 2:13, where singular provocations are mentioned.

That is a grave question asked by the prophet Isaiah, "Will ye weary my God also" (Isa. 7:13)?

II. LET YOUR CONSCIENCE DRAW A SPIRITUAL PICTURE OF YOUR WAITING SAVIOR.

1. He waits for comers to the well: he seizes on all occasions to bless, such as affliction, the hearing of the Word, the recurrence of a birthday, or even the simplest event of life. Men have other errands; they come to the well only to draw water, but the Lord meets them with his greater errand.

2. He waits for the most sinful; she that had had five husbands.

3. He waits to enlighten, convince, convert.

4. He waits to accept, and to commission.

5. He waits to begin by one convert the ingathering of a great harvest of souls, as in the case of the Samaritans.

How long he has waited for some of you!

At how many points has he been on the outlook for you!

Is he not waiting for you at this very hour?

Will you not yield to his patient love?

III. LET YOUR PENITENCE DRAW ANOTHER PICTURE.

Alter the position of the character.

1. Be yourself weary of your sinful way.

2. Sit down on the well of your Lord's gracious ordinances.

3. Wait and watch till your Savior comes.

4. Ask him to give you to drink, and, in so doing, give him to drink for this is his best refreshment.

5. Drink yourselves of the living water, and then run to tell others.

Will you not do this at once?

May his Holy Spirit so direct you!

Musings

It was the hour of noon, and weary as he was with the long journey. possibly also with the extreme heat, our Lord sat "thus on the well." The expression in the original is most pathetically picturesque. It implies that the Wayfarer was quite tired out, and in his exhaustion flung his limbs wearily on the seat, anxious, if possible, for complete repose. —*Archdeacon Farrar*

When hard-working people sit down at midday for their few minutes of rest and refreshment, let them recall their Master's noonday rest at the well. He was tired, like we are, yet his rest was short, and his work scarcely broken. He was tired with seeking for us. Our stubborn hearts brought him all this way from heaven. He has long sought for our love, and hardly finds it. Think on this verse. With whom did Jesus find his portion in this life? Not with the great and luxurious, but with the common people, sharing their toils. —*Practical Reflections on the Gospels By a Clergyman*

While we sympathize with the bodily weariness of our Lord, it will be well to remember the soul-weariness which sin must have occasioned him. He hungered to bless men, and they refused the bread of life. He would have gathered them, but they would not be gathered. He must have been specially wearied with the ostentatious hypocrisy of the Pharisees, and the silly legalisms of the Scribes with their tithing of mint and anise. He was often wearied with the dogged unbelief of the Jews, and the provoking want of faith among his own disciples. The sin, the caviling, the slander, the selfishness, the hardness of heart of those about him, must have worn down his holy soul, and made him every day a Man of sorrows. Yet he never left the well, never refused to give the living water to a thirsting soul, never ceased to entreat men to come to him and drink. —*C. H. S.*

"*Jesus, therefore, being wearied*"—And in that he himself had suffered, he was the more able and apt to help this poor Samaritan. So the apostle bids us pity those in adversity, as being ourselves in the body, *i.e.*, the body of flesh and frailty, subject to like misery. —*Trapp*

When wearied, let us still be on the watch to do good. Wearied, and sitting on the well, our Lord is still in the attitude of observation. "I am never too tired to pray," said a minister, who, after a hard day's toil, found his host ready to excuse him from conducting family prayer. When God is blessing the Word, true ministers forget their fatigue, and hold on long into the night with inquirers. Alas! when the Holy Spirit has nothing to do with a man's heart, the man excuses himself from "making overtime," as I once heard a professor call it, when he quitted the room the instant the service was over. Another, in describing a minister, said, "Oh, he is so cold! He is one who thinks it is wrong to be too religious. He cannot endure zeal." Be it ours to show a more excellent way. Holy Brainerd, when he could not preach, because he was on his dying bed, called to him a little Indian boy, and tried to teach him his letters. Let us live soul-saving, and so let us die. —*C. H. S.*

172

The woman saith unto him, Sire thou hast nothing to draw with, and
the well is deep; from whence then hast though that living water?
—*John 4:11*

 UR Lord's object was to bring the woman to seek salvation of him. Our desire is the immediate conversion of all now present.

The Samaritan woman accepted the Savior upon the first asking.

Many of you have been invited to Jesus many times—will you not at last comply?

Our Lord aimed at her heart by plain teaching and home dealing—we will take the same course with our hearers.

When his interesting emblem failed to reach her, he fell to downright literalism, and unveiled her life. Anything is better than allowing a soul to perish.

I. WE WILL EXPOUND THE PRECEDING TEACHING.

The Lord had said to her, "If thou knewest the gift of God, and who it is that saith to thee, Give me to drink; thou wouldest have asked of him, and he would have given thee living water."

The figure was that of living water in contrast to the water collected in Jacob's well, which was merely the gatherings of the surrounding hills—land-water, not spring-water.

He meant to say that his grace is like water from a springing well.

- It is of the best and most refreshing kind.
- It is living and ministers life.
- It is powerful and finds its own way.
- It is abiding and is never dried up.
- It is abounding and free to all comers.

Furthermore, he intimated to the woman that:

1. He had it. There was no need of a bucket to draw with.
2. He had it to give.
3. He would have given it for the asking.
4. He alone could give it. It would be found in no earthly well.

II. WE WILL ANSWER THE QUESTION OF THE TEXT.

In ignorance the woman inquired, "Whence then hast thou that living water?"

We can at this time give a fuller reply than could have been given when our Lord sat on the well.

He has now a boundless power to save, and that power arises:

1. From his divine nature, allied with his perfect humanity.
2. From the purpose and appointment of God.
3. From the anointing of the Holy Ghost.
4. From his redeeming work, which operated for good even before its actual accomplishment, and which is in full operation now.
5. From the power of his intercession at the Father's right hand.
6. From his representative life in glory. Now all power is delivered into his hand (Matt. 28:18).

III. WE WILL DRAW CERTAIN INFERENCE FROM THE ANSWER.

1. Then he is still able to bless. Since he has this living water only from his unchanging self, he therefore has it now as fully as ever.
2. Then he needs nothing from us. He is himself the one sole Fountain, full and all-sufficient forever.
3. Then we need not fear exhausting his fullness.
4. Then at all times we may come to him, and we need never fear that he will deny us.

Drops

When we see a great volume of water issuing from a spring, it is natural that we should enquire—whence does it come? This is one of the mysteries of nature to most people. Job speaks of "the springs of the sea", and hints that none can find them out. But where are the springs of salvation? Whence comes the river, yea, the boundless ocean of divine grace? All fullness is in Jesus, but how came it there? He gives drink to all who come to him; whence has he this inexhaustible supply? Are not these questions worth asking? Must not the reply be instructive to ourselves, and glorifying to our Lord? Come, then, and let us borrow the language of this Samaritan woman, and talk with our Lord.—*C. H. S.*

When I have ridden through London, I have been overwhelmed with the greatness of the supply which must daily be necessary to feed its millions, and have wondered that a famine has not at once set in. But when I have seen the markets and the storehouses, and have thought of the whole earth as eager to obtain a sale for its produce in our vast metropolis, I have rested in content. I see whence the almost illimitable supplies are drawn, and my wonder henceforth is, not that the millions are fed, but that they should be able to consume such immeasurable quantities of food.

Thus, when I behold man's spiritual need, I marvel that it should ever be met; but when I behold the person and work of the Lord Jesus, my marvel ceases, and a new wonder begins. I wonder rather at the infinity of grace than at the power of sin.—*C. H. S.*

Speaking of Cairo, the author of "Ragged Life in Egypt" says, "Perhaps no cry is more striking, after all, than the short and simple cry of the water carrier. 'The gift of God' he says, as he goes along with his water-skin on his shoulder. It is impossible to hear this cry without thinking of the Lord's words to the woman of Samaria, 'If thou knewest the gift of God, and who it is that saith to thee, Give me to drink; thou wouldest have asked of him, and he would have given thee living water?' It is very likely that water, so invaluable, and so often scarce in hot countries, was in those days spoken of, as now, as 'the gift of God', to denote its preciousness; if so, the expression would be extremely forcible to the woman, and full of meaning."—*The Biblical Treasury*

How ready are men and women to go to this well and that well to drink water for the help and healing of bodily distempers, and to go many miles, and dispense with all other affairs, that they may be recovered of corporeal diseases: but how few enquire after the water of life, or leave all their secular business for the good and health of their immortal souls!—*Benjamin Keach*

"*The well is deep,*" the woman said to Jesus; and so it was. It took two and a half seconds from the time that the pebble was dropped, before we heard the splash in the water below. . . . Turning to the illustration before us—"*living water,*"—the meaning only dawned upon me when I visited the spot. Jacob's well, deep as it was, and cool as its waters doubtless were, was only an artificial well—a cistern for the collection of rain, and the drainage of the land. . . . In seasons of drought, this well must have been useless—it was a well, or cistern, not a spring.—*J. W. Bardsley*

The fountain of living waters is God himself (Jer. 2:13). "With thee is the fountain of life" (Ps. 36:9). It is not a mere cistern to hold; it is a pouring, running, living stream; nay, rather a fountain that springs up perpetually. We all know that a jet or fountain is produced by a head of water that presses down from a great elevation; and that, the higher the spring, the loftier and more powerful the jet, which, however, never surpasses the height of its source. Our spiritual life, "our well-spring of life", has its source in heaven: and it is heavenward that it rises, and it is content with no lower level. It came from God, and to God it will return.—*F. A. Malleson*

173

On the same day was the Sabbath.
—*John 5:9*

CHRIST healed men on all sorts of days. But Sabbaths were high days of grace. Six special cases of cures wrought on the Sabbath are recorded:

1. The evil spirit cast out (Luke 4:31–35).
2. The withered hand restored (Luke 6:6–10).
3. The crooked woman made straight (Luke 13:10–17).
4. The man with the dropsy cured (Luke 14:1–6).
5. The impotent man made whole (John 5:1–9).
6. The blind man's eyes opened (John 9:1–14).

As God rested on the Sabbath, and hallowed it; so as God it was rest to Jesus to heal, and thus he hallowed the day.

As man he also rested his heart, exercised a holy ministry, glorified God, and hallowed the day.

I. THESE CURES MEET MANY CASES.

1. Those under Satanic influence (Luke 4:31–35). Many are in this case at this hour.
2. Those conscious of spiritual inability (Luke 6:6–10).
3. Those bowed down with great distress, despondency, despair, etc. (Luke 13:10–17). This poor woman had been infirm for eighteen years.
4. Those smitten with mortal disease (Luke 14:1–6). This typifies the deadly character of sin, and represents the case of those upon whom is the dread of the second death.

5. Those altogether paralyzed (John 5:1–9). This man had been impotent for thirty-eight years. Some seem specially unable to feel, or do, or be what they should be. They are weak and irresolute, and though lying at the healing-pool, others step in before them, and they derive no benefit from the means of grace.
6. Those blind from birth (John 9:1–14). Many are in this condition. They see no spiritual truth, but abide in total darkness as to all gospel truth.

II. THESE CURES REPRESENT USUAL PROCESSES.

1. A word addressed to the devil. "Hold thy peace, and come out of him" (Luke 4:35). Satan feels the power of the Word of the Lord; but he cares for nothing else.
2. A word personal to the sufferer. "Stretch forth thy hand" (Luke 6:10). He was unable, and yet he was commanded; and he obeyed. This is the gospel method.
3. A word accepted as done. "Thou art loosed from thine infirmity" (Luke 13:12). Faith turns promise into fact, gospel-teaching into actual salvation.
4. Power without a word (Luke 14:4).
5. A word arousing and commanding. "Rise, take up thy bed, and walk" (John 5:8). Many are saved by being stirred up from long inactivity and lethargy.
6. A word associated with other means (John 9:6–7). The whole miracle is deeply instructive on this point.

In these varied forms and fashions, Jesus works on the Sabbath.

III. THESE CURES WERE BOTH IN AND OUT OF THE SYNAGOGUE.

1. There, and misbehaving (Luke 4:33).
2. There, and singled out from the crowd (Luke 6:8).
3. There, and called to Jesus. (Luke 13:12).
4. After the synagogue service. Luke 14:1).
5. Too feeble to get there (John 5:5).
6. Too poor to be there (John 9:8).

IV. THESE CURES WERE ALL UNSOUGHT.

This is one special feature about them all.

1. The possessed man entreated Christ to leave him alone (Luke 4:34).
2. The man with the withered hand did not think of cure (Luke 6:6).
3. The infirm woman did not hope for healing (Luke 13:11).
4. The man with the dropsy did not ask for the blessing (Luke 14:2).
5. The infirm man was too paralyzed to seek Christ (John 5:5).
6. It was an unheard of thing that the eyes of a man born blind should be opened, and therefore he did not expect it (John 9:32).

This also is the Sabbath; let us look to the Lord of the Sabbath.
Will he not this day bless those who are seekers?
Will he not bless those whom we bring to him?
Will he not bless those for whom we pray?

Sermon Bells

On Sunday heaven's gate stands ope;
Blessings are plentiful and rife,
More plentiful than hope.
— *George Herbert*

On his death-bed, Brainerd said: "I was born on a Sabbath-day; I have reason to hope I was new-born on a Sabbath-day; and I hope I shall die on this Sabbath-day."

Was it not meet that the Lord of the Sabbath should specially display his sovereignty upon that day? May we not now expect that, on the Lord's-day, the Lord of the day will magnify his own name, and make the day illustrious by his grace? The first day of the week was signalized by the giving of the light of nature, and it is most delightful that now it should be a chosen day for bestowing the light of grace. It is to us the Sabbath; should not the Lord give rest to wearied hearts upon that day? Men call it Sunday: we are happy when the Sun of righteousness then arises with healing in his wings. Of old the week's work was done, and then the Sabbath dawned; but now rest leads the way: we begin the week's work with the Sabbath rest, because we first find rest in Jesus, and then labor for him. Blessed is the Lord's-day when the Lord himself speaks rest in his own finished work, to those who otherwise would have labored in vain. — *C. H. S.*

Christ came not into the world merely to cast a mantle over us, and hide all our filthy sores from God's avenging eye, with his merits, and righteousness; but he came especially to be a chirurgeon and physician of souls, to free us from the filth and corruption of them, which are more grievous and burdensome, more noisome to a true Christian, than the guilt of sin itself. — *Cudworth*

Metaphor: Physicians come not to the sick until they are sent for; and though they come not far, yet expect to be paid for that, besides their physic. *Disparity*: Christ came to us, who sent not for him, which made him say, "I am sought of them that asked not for me; I am found of them that sought me not" (Isa. 65:1). The patients seek not first, come not first, to the Physician; but the Physician to the patients. "The Son of man is come to seek and to save that which was lost" (Luke 19:10); and, besides, he dearly paid all the charge of his long journey. — *Benjamin Keach*

174

Then the Jews sought him at the feast, and said, Where is he?
—*John 7:11*

ESUS went to the feast in secret, and the Jews sought him.

From differing motives they inquired for him, but they did inquire.

No man, having once heard of Jesus, can any longer remain indifferent to him: he *must* take some sort of interest in the Lord Jesus.

From many quarters comes the question, "Where is he?"

We will at this time:

I. CONSIDER THE WAYS IN WHICH THE QUESTION HAS BEEN ASKED.

1. Hate, ferociously desiring to slay him, and overthrow his cause. Herod was the type of this school.
2. Infidelity, sneeringly denying his existence, taunting his followers because his cause does not make progress (2 Pet. 3:4).
3. Timorous fear, sadly doubting his presence, power, and prevalence. "Where is he that trod the sea?" (Job 23:8–9).
4. Penitence, humbly seeking him that she may confess her sin, trust her Lord, and show her gratitude to him (Job 23:3).
5. Love, heartily pining for communion with him, and for an opportunity to serve him (Song of Sol. 3:3).
6. Fear, bitterly lamenting his absence, and craving his return.
7. Desire, ardently aspiring to meet him in his second advent, and to behold his glory (Rev. 22:20).

II. GIVE THE SAINTS' EXPERIMENTAL ANSWER.

1. He is at the mercy-seat when we cry in secret.
2. He is in the Word as we search the sacred page.
3. He is in the assemblies of his people, even with two or three.
4. He is at his table, known in the breaking of bread.
5. He is in the field of service, aiding, sympathizing, guiding, and prospering. In all things glorified before the eyes of faith.
6. He is in the furnace of trial, revealing himself, sanctifying the trial, bearing us through.
7. He is near us, yea, with us, and in us.

III. RETURN THE QUESTION TO YOU.

1. Is he at the bottom of your trust?
2. Is he at the root of your joys?
3. Is he on the throne of your heart?
4. Is he near you by constant converse?
5. Is his presence manifested in your spirit, your words, your actions?
6. Is he before you, the end of your journey, the terminus towards which you are daily hastening?

IV. ASK IT OF THE ANGELS.

They with one voice reply that the Lord Jesus Christ is:

1. In the bosom of the Father.
2. In the center of glory.
3. On the throne of government.
4. In the place of representation.
5. In the almoner of mercy.
6. Within reach of *you*, and of all needy sinners, who will now seek his face.

O come, let us go and find him!

We will hold no feast till he is among us.

Ana

Many years ago, there was a young man in Birmingham whom dissipation and excess had brought into a condition from which he endeavored to extricate himself by crime. The fear of detection, exposure, and ruin goaded him on to such a pitch of desperation, that he left his father's house resolutely bent on self-destruction. God's good providence led him through Bond Street; and, under some inexplicable impulse, he found himself sitting in the Baptist Chapel almost before he was aware. The minister, a Mr. Edmonds, was reading from the book of Job, occasionally throwing in some shrewd parenthetic remark. Coming to the following passage, the young man's attention was irresistibly arrested: "Behold, I go forward, but he is not there; and backward, but I cannot perceive him; on the left hand, where he doth work, but I cannot behold him: he hideth himself on the right hand, that I cannot see him" (Job 23:8–9). "Job, Job," the preacher cried entreatingly, "why don't you look upward?" These words were as nails fastened in a sure place, and the young man ever thanked God for the belief that he was unconsciously drawn by the Holy Spirit to enter that place, and that the preacher was impelled to the use of those words, to the end that his life might be redeemed from destruction, and crowned with loving-kindness and tender mercy.

"It befell me," says Henry Ward Beecher, "once to visit a friend, and to spend the night with him, in a manufacturing village in New England. I had never been in the place. I supposed that, when I arrived at the station, I should find a hack that could take me directly to the clergyman's residence. But it was an unusual train that I was on, and there were no hacks there; so I had to walk. The distance to the village was three miles; but before I reached it I had walked at least thirteen miles. I got there at a time of night when all sensible people were in bed. I knew nothing about the place, and did not know where to go. I could not see any church, or store, or hotel. I wandered about for nearly half-an-hour, and at the end of that time I knew no better where I was than I did when I began my search. I never felt so helpless as I did then. I realized what it was for a man, in his own country, and speaking his own language, to be utterly lost. I knocked at three or four houses, and received no response. I went to a house where I saw a light, and found the inmates quarreling. A minister seemed to be the last thing they knew anything about. I began to think I should be obliged to sleep out of doors. But, as I was shooting down a certain street, almost aimless, I saw a light; and on going to the house from which it proceeded, and ringing the bell, I found that it was the very house which I was seeking. I thought a great many profitable things that night. Among the rest, I thought that I was, for all the world, like men that I had seen trying to go about the streets of Jerusalem at night, with nobody to tell them the way, and with no chart of the city, who would turn first to the right, and then to the left, without seeming to have any object except that of finding a place where their souls could put up and rest. It is pitiful to see a man, whose mind is troubled, whose conscience is against him, and who yearns for spiritual rest, going hither and thither, up and down, saying, 'Have ye seen my Lord and Master? Can ye tell me where he tarries, whom my soul delights in?'"

Our glorious Master is always at home, but does not always hold his receptions in the same chamber. One while he will see us in his closet, and anon in his great hall. Today he meets us in the porch, and tomorrow in the innermost room. In reading the Bible I meet him in his library, in working for him I commune with him in the garden. When full of hope I walk with him on the housetop, at another time I wait for him in the secret places of the stairs. It is well to be in the parlor where he talks in sermons, or in his drawing-room where he converses in holy fellowship; but the best room of the house is that wherein he spreads his table, and makes himself to be our bread and wine. In any case, the one desire of our heart is to find him, and live upon him.—*C. H. S.*

175

So there was a division among the people because of him.
—*John 7:43*

EVEN when Jesus preached so sweetly his meek and loving doctrine there was a division among the people.

Even about himself there was a schism. We may not, therefore, hope to please everybody, however true may be our teaching, or however peaceful may be our spirit.

We may even dread the unity of death more than the stir of life.

To this day the greatest division in the world is *"because of him."*

I. THERE WAS A DIVISION AMONG NON-DISCIPLES.

We may view the parties formed in his day as symbolical of those in our own.

1. Some admitted none of his claims.
2. Others admitted a portion, but denied the rest.
3. Certain admitted his claims, but neglected to follow out the legitimate consequences of them.
4. A few became his sincere hearers, going as far with him as they had yet learned of him.

Let us view persons who have thoughts about Jesus with considerable hope. Though they blunder now, they may yet come right. Let us not frighten away the birds by imprudent haste.

Let us pray for those who deny his claims, and resist his kingdom.

Let us aid those who come a little way towards the truth, and are willing to go all the way if they can but find it.

Let us arouse those who neglect holy subjects altogether.

II. THERE WAS A DIVISION OF BELIEVERS FROM NON-BELIEVERS.

This is a great and wide difference, and the more clearly the division is seen the better; for God views it as very deep and all important.

There is a great division at this present hour:

1. In opinion: especially as to the Lord Jesus.
2. In trust: many rely on self; only the godly on Jesus.
3. In love. Differing pleasures and aims prove that hearts go after differing objects.
4. In obedience, character, and language.
5. In development, growth, tendency.
6. In destiny. The directions of the lines of life point at different places as the end of the journey.

This cleavage divides the dearest friends and relatives.

This is the most real and deep difference in the world.

III. YET WHEN FAITH COMES, UNITY IS PRODUCED.

There is unity among the people because of him.

1. Nationalities are blended. Calvary heals Babel.
   - Jews and Gentiles are one in Christ.
   - The near and the far-off as to spiritual things are brought nigh in him, who is the one and only center of grace and truth.
   - Believers of all nationalities become one church.
2. Personal peculiarities cease to divide.
   - Workers for Christ are sure to be blended in one body by their common difficulties.
   - Position, rank, and wealth give way before the uniting influence of grace.
3. Mental specialties feel the touch of unity.
   - Saints of varying creeds have an essential union in Christ.
   - Saints of all the changing ages are alike in him.
   - Saints of all styles of education are one in Jesus.
   - Saints in heaven will be many as the waves, but one as the sea

Ambitions, which else would disintegrate, are overcome, and laid at Jesus' feet.

Let us divide, if there be a division.

Let us closely unite, if there be real union in Christ.

Confirmations

Christ, who is properly the author of peace, is, on account of the wickedness of men, the occasion of discord.—*John Calvin*

There never lived any one who has so deeply moved the hearts of men as Jesus Christ has done. The greatest monarchs that ever reigned, the greatest warriors that ever fought, the greatest masters in art, or science, or literature, have never affected so many, and that to so great an extent, as Jesus of Nazareth has done. He has changed the course of the world's history, and made its condition almost inconceivably different from what it would have been but for his coming. His teachings are received by the foremost nations of the earth. Millions of men call themselves by his name. He occupies the highest place in the esteem and affection of multitudes. For his sake men have lived as none others were able or willing to live: for his sake they have died as none others could or would have died.

But in proportion to the faith, the veneration, the love with which Christ is regarded by a portion of mankind, are the unbelief, the contempt, and the hatred, which others display towards him. The poles are not more widely sundered than are the sentiments of men respecting Christ. There is nothing about which they are more completely at variance. Do you sing, "How sweet the name of Jesus sounds"? To this day the Jew curses that name, and the infidel brands it as the name of an impostor. Do you regard Christ as worthy of your warmest love? There are those who regard him with a passionate hate. Satan himself cannot be more bitterly hostile to Christ than some men are.—*P.*

The union of saints results from union with Christ, as the lodestone not only attracts the particles of iron to itself by the magnetic virtue, but by this virtue it unites them to one another.—*Richard Cecil*

I have seen a field here, and another there, stand thick with corn. A hedge or two has parted them. At the proper season the reapers entered. Soon the earth was disburdened, and the grain conveyed to its destined place, where, blended together in the barn or in the stack, it could not be known that a hedge once separated this corn from that. Thus it is with the church. Here it grows, as it were, in different fields; severed, it may be, by various hedges. By and by, when the harvest is come, all God's wheat shall be gathered into the garner, without one single mark to distinguish that once they differed in the outward circumstantiality of modes or forms.—*From "Parable, or Divine Poesy"*

Originating amongst the Jews, the Christian religion was regarded at first by great Rome as a mere Jewish sect, and shared alike in the impunity and the contempt with which that people were ever treated by their imperial masters. What did a Claudius or a Vespasian know, or care to know, of this new sect of Christians or Nazarenes, any more than of those other party names of Pharisee, Sadducee, Essene, Libertine, and the like? . . .Christ was then only "one Christus," and the controversies between his followers and the Jewish priests only one of those paltry squabbles to which that restless people were chronically subject. By and by, as the young church became strong, it began to make its existence and its presence felt in the world, and then it stood in its genuine character and distinctive spirit face to face with Rome. Once met, they instinctively recognized each the other as its natural and irreconcilable enemy, and straightway a war of deadliest hate began between them, which was from the first one of extermination, and could terminate only by the fall of the one or the other. There was no room in the world for Christ and Caesar, so one or the other must die.—*Islay Burns*

176

My word hath no place in you.
—*John 8:37*

 HERE the Word of Jesus ought at once to be received, it is often rejected. These Jews were Abraham's seed, but they had not Abraham's faith.

Jesus knows where his Word is received, and where it has no place. He declares that all else is unavailing: it was in vain that they were of the favored race if they did not admit the Savior's Word into their hearts.

The practical result appeared in their lives: they sought to kill Jesus.
Let us honestly consider:

I. WHAT PLACE THE WORD SHOULD HAVE IN MEN'S HEARTS.

The Word comes from Jesus, the appointed Messenger of God; it is true,
weighty, saving; and, therefore, it must have a place among those who hear it. It
ought to obtain and retain:

1. An inside place: in the thoughts, the memory, the conscience, the affections. "Thy Word have I hid in mine heart" (Ps. 119:11. See also Jer. 15:16; Col. 3:16).
2. A place of honor: it should receive attention, reverence, faith, obedience (John 8:47; Luke 6:46; Matt. 7:24–25).
3. A place of trust. We ought in all things to rely upon the sure Word of promise, since God will neither lie, nor err, nor change (Isa. 7:9; 1 Sam. 15:29; Titus 1:2).
4. A place of rule. The Word of Jesus is the law of a Christian.
5. A place of love. It should be prized above our daily food, and defended with our lives (Job. 23:12; Jude 3).
6. A permanent place. It must so transform us as to abide in us.

II. WHY IT HAS NO PEACE IN MANY MEN.

If any man be unconverted, let us help him to a reason applicable to his case.

1. You are too busy, and so you cannot admit it.
   • There is no room for Jesus in the inn of your life.
   • Think of it: "You are too much occupied to be saved"!
2. It does not come as a novelty, and therefore you refuse it.
   • You are weary of the old, old story.
   • Are you wearied of bread? of air? of water? of life?
3. Another occupies the place the Word of Jesus should have.
   • You prefer the word of man, of superstition, of skepticism.
   • Is this a wise preference?
4. You think Christ's Word too holy, too spiritual.
   This fact should startle you, for it condemns you.
5. It is cold comfort to you, and so you give it no place.
   This shows that your nature is depraved; for the saints rejoice in it.
6. You are too wise, too cultured, too genteel, to yield yourself to the government of Jesus (John 5:44; Rom. 1:22).
7. Is the reason of your rejection of the Word one of these?
   • That you are not in earnest?
   • That you are fond of sin?
   • That you are greedy of evil gain?
   • That you need a change of heart?

III. WHAT WILL COME OF THE WORD OF CHRIST HAVING NO PLACE IN YOU?

1. Every past rejection of that Word has involved you in sin.
2. The Word may cease to ask for place in you.
3. You may yourself become hardened, so as to decline even to hear that Word with the outward ear.
4. You may become the violent opponent of that Word, like these Jews.
5. The Word will condemn you at the last great day (John 12:48).

Let us therefore reason with you for a while.

Why do you not give place to it?

All that is asked of you is to give it place. It will bring with it all that you need.

Open wide the door, and bid it enter!

It is the Word of the Lord Jesus, the Savior.

It means your highest good, and will greatly bless you.

Common Places

Readers of this enlightened, gold-nugget generation can form to themselves no conception of the spirit that then possessed the nobler kingly mind. VERBUM DEI MANET IN ÆTERNUM was the epigraph and life motto which John the Steadfast had adopted for himself. The letters, V.D.M.I.Æ., were engraved on all the furniture of his existence, standards, pictures, plate, on the very sleeves of his lackeys, and I can perceive on his own deep heart first of all.—*Thomas Carlyle*

> O Book! Infinite sweetness! Let my heart
> Suck every letter, and a honey gain,
> Precious for any grief in any part;
> To clear the breast, to mollify all pain.
> —*George Herbert*

The only reason why so many are against the Bible, is because they know the Bible is against them.—*G. S. Bowes*

At one time the Malagasy did not know of any book except the Bible. There was a Creole trader, in Antananarivo, who had greatly offended some of the natives. They mobbed his house, they seized his property, and men were seen rushing in all directions, carrying away whatever they had been able to lay their hands upon. One man had got possession of the trader's ledger; and, holding it up aloft, he shouted at the top of his voice, "We have got the big Bible! We have got the big Bible!" It is to be feared that the trader's ledger is in too many cases his Bible.—*Mr. Cousins, of Madagascar*

The Bible has been expelled for centuries, by atheistic or sacerdotal hate, from the dwellings of many of the European nations. As a matter of course, the domestic virtues have declined; the conjugal relation is disparaged; deception and intrigue have supplanted mutual confidence; and society has become diseased to its very core. The very best thing we can do—the only thing which will be efficient—to arrest these evils, is to restore to those nations the Word of God; to replace in their houses that Bible of which they have been robbed. Only do for France and Italy, Belgium and Spain, Portugal and Austria, what has been attempted, and to a great extent accomplished, for our country; put a Bible in every family, and a mightier change will pass over Europe than can be effected by all the diplomacy of her statesmen, or all the revolutions projected by her patriots.—*The Leisure Hour*

The following anecdote, well told by Mr. Aitken, shows that, in some men, the Word has no place, even in their memories: "Only a short time ago, a friend of mine was preaching in one of our cathedral churches. As he was going to select for his text a prominent passage in one of the portions for the day, he thought it expedient to enquire of the clerk, 'What did the Canon preach from this morning?' The clerk became very pensive, seemed quite disposed to cudgel his brains for the proper answer; but, somehow or other, he really could not think of it just then. All the men of the choir were robing in the adjacent vestry, so he said that he would go and ask them. Accordingly, the question was passed round the choir, and produced the same perplexity. At length the sagacious clerk returned, with the highly explicit answer, 'It was upon the Christian religion, sir!' I think those good people must have needed a reminder as to how we should hear; don t you?"

177

Now we know that God heareth not sinners: but if any man be a worshipper of God, and doeth his will, him he heareth.

—John 9:31

 T is ill to wrench passages of the Bible out of their context, and treat them as infallible Scripture, when they are only the sayings of men.

By acting thus foolishly we could prove that there is no God (Ps. 14:1), that God hath forgotten his people (Isa. 49:14), that Christ was a wine-bibber (Matt. 9:19), and that we ought to worship the devil (Matt. 4:9).

This will never do. We must enquire who uttered the sentence before we begin to preach from it.

Our text is the saying of a shrewd blind man, who was far from being well instructed. It is to be taken for what it is worth; but by no means to be regarded as Christ's teaching.

The Pharisees evidently admitted the force of it, and were puzzled by it. It was good argument as against *them*.

This remark of the blind man is true or false as we may happen to view it.

I. IT IS NOT TRUE IN SOME SENSES.

We could not say absolutely that God heareth not sinners, for:

1. God does hear men who sin, or else he would hear no one: for there is not a man upon earth that sinneth not (1 Kings 8:46).

   Not a saint would be heard; for even saints are sinners.

2. God does sometimes hear and answer unregenerate men.
   - To show that he is truly God, and make them own it (Ps. 106:44).
   - To manifest his great compassion, whereby he even hears the ravens' cry (Ps. 147:9).
   - To lead them to repentance (1 Kings 21:27).
   - To leave them without excuse (Exod. 10:16–17).
   - To punish them, as when he sent quails to the murmurers (Num. 11:33), and gave Israel a king (1 Sam. 7:17), in his anger.

3. God does graciously hear sinners when they cry for mercy.
   - Not to believe this were to render the gospel no gospel.
   - Not to believe this were to deny facts. David, Manasseh, the dying thief, the publican, the prodigal, confirm this testimony.
   - Not to believe this were to deny promises. "Let the wicked forsake his way, and the unrighteous man his thoughts: and let him return unto the Lord, and he will have mercy upon him; and to our God, for he will abundantly pardon" (Isa. 55:7).

II. IT IS TRUE IN OTHER SENSES.

The Lord does *not* hear sinners as he hears his own people.

1. He hears no sinner's prayer apart from the mediation of our Lord Jesus (1 Tim. 2:5; Eph. 2:18).
2. He will not hear a wicked, formal, heartless prayer (Prov. 15:29).
3. He will not hear the man who willfully continues in sin, and abides in unbelief (Jer. 14:12; Isa. 1:15).
4. He will not hear the hypocrite's mockery of prayer (Job 27:9).
5. He will not hear the unforgiving (Mark 11:5, 26).
6. He will not hear even his people when sin is willfully indulged, and entertained in their hearts (Ps. 66:18).
7. He will not hear those who refuse to hear his Word, or to regard his ordinances (Prov. 28:9).
8. He will not hear those who harden their hearts against the monitions of his Spirit, the warnings of his providence, the appeals of his ministers, the strivings of conscience, and so forth.

9. He will not hear those who refuse to be saved by grace, or who trust in their own prayers as the cause of salvation.

10. He will not hear sinners who die impenitent. At the last he will close his ear to them, as to the foolish virgins, who cried, "Lord, Lord, open to us!" (Matt. 25:11)

One or two things are very clear and sure.

He cannot hear those who never speak to him.

He has never yet given any one of us a flat refusal.

He permits us at this moment to pray, and it will be well for us to do so, and see if he does not hear us.

Observations

Such is the mercy of our God that he will wink at many infirmities in our devotions, and will not reject the prayer of an honest heart because of some weakness in the petitioner. It must be a greater cause than all this that makes God angry at our prayers. In general it is sin. "We know that God heareth not sinners: but if any man be a worshipper of God, and doeth his will, him he heareth." "If I regard iniquity in my heart, the Lord will not hear me." It is our sins that block up the passage of our prayers. It is not the vast distance between heaven and earth, not the thick clouds, not the threefold regions, not the seven-fold orbs, not the firmament of heaven, but only our sins, that hinder the ascent of our prayers. "When ye make many prayers, I will not hear you." Why? "Because your hands are full of blood." God will have none of those petitions that are presented to him with bloody hands. Our prayers are our bills of exchange, and they are allowed in heaven when they come from pious and humble hearts; but if we be broken in our religion, and bankrupts of grace, God will protest our bills; he will not be won with our prayers.—*Thomas Adams*

> My words fly up, my thoughts remain below:
> Words, without thoughts, never to heaven go.
> —*Shakespeare*

God is "neither hard of hearing, nor hard of giving."

The blood of sheep and the blood of swine are both alike; yet the blood of swine was not to be offered, because it was the blood of swine: so the prayer of an unregenerate man may be as well framed, both for the petitions and for everything that is required immediately to a prayer, and yet not be accepted, because of the heart and person from whom it comes.—*Samuel Clark*

It is difficult to illustrate this truth, because, in human life, nothing ever takes place corresponding to what occurs when an impenitent sinner presumes to pray to God. To every government many petitions are presented, but never one by any who are in rebellion against its authority. It is universally recognized, that rebellion against any government of itself cuts off all right of petition to it.

So that, for an impenitent sinner to pray to God is one of the most unnatural and monstrous things that can be conceived of.

The fact that God is kind, good, bountiful, does not excuse the presumption of any impenitent sinner in praying to him. *That* only shows how inexcusable is his impenitence. For if God is good, kind, bountiful, why does he continue impenitent and rebellious?

The fact that he is in great need does not excuse the presumption or lessen the folly of an impenitent sinner in praying to God. It may be that his distress is the punishment of his sin; and for him in that case to pray to God for deliverance is as if a convicted thief were to petition Her Majesty's Government to release him, on the ground that he found it inconvenient and painful to work the treadmill. Or, it may be that his distresses are the means which God is employing for the very purpose of breaking down his obstinacy and impenitence: by them God is laying siege to his soul. But what rebellious city, besieged by the forces of the lawful government, would venture to ask aid from the government, on the ground that great distress prevailed in it, while all the time its inhabitants had not the slightest intention of surrendering to the government?—*The Preachers' Monthly*

178

I am the door: by me if any man enter in, he shall be saved, and shall go in and out, and find pasture.

—*John 10:9*

UR Lord sets himself forth very condescendingly.

The most sublime and poetical figures are none too glorious to describe him; but he chooses homely ones, which the most prosaic minds can apprehend.

A door is a common object. Jesus would have us often think of him.

A door makes a very simple emblem. Jesus would have the lowliest know him, and use him.

A door to a sheepfold is the poorest form of door. Jesus condescends to be anything, so that he may serve and save his people.

I. THE DOOR. In this homely illustration we see:

1. Necessity. Suppose there had been none, we could never have entered in to God, peace, truth, salvation, purity, or heaven.
2. Singularity. There is only one door; let us not weary ourselves to find another. Salvation is by entrance at that door, and at none other (Acts 4:12).

3. Personality. The Lord Jesus is himself the door. "I am the door," saith he; not ceremonies, doctrines, professions, achievements, but the Lord himself, our Sacrifice.

4. Suitability. He is suited to be the communication between man and God, seeing he unites both in his own person, and thus lies open both earthward and heavenward (1 Tim. 2:5).

5. Perpetuity. His "I am" is for all times and ages (Matt. 28:20). We can still come to the Father by him (John 14:6; Heb. 7:25).

II. THE USERS OF IT.

1. They are not mere observers, or knockers at the door, or sitters down before it, or guards marching to and fro in front of it.

   But they *enter* in by faith, love, experience, communion.

2. They are not certain persons who have special qualifications, such as those of race, rank, education, office, or wealth. Not lords and ladies are spoken of; but *"any man."*

3. They are persons who have the one qualification: they do *"enter in."* The person is "any man," but the essential distinction is entrance.

   • This is intended to exclude:

   Character previously acquired as a fitness for entrance.

   Feeling, either of grief or joy! as a preparation for admission.

   Action, otherwise than that of entering in, as a term of reception.

   • A door may be marked PRIVATE, and then few will enter.

   • A door which is conspicuously marked as THE DOOR is evidently meant to be used. The remarkable advertisement of "I am the door," and the special promises appended to it, are the most liberal invitation imaginable.

   • Come then, ye who long to enter into life!

III. THE PRIVILEGES OF THESE USERS.

They belong to all who enter: no exception is made.

1. Salvation. "He shall be saved." At once, forever, altogether.

2. Liberty. He "shall go in and out." This is no prison door, but a door for a flock whose Shepherd gives freedom.

3. Access. "Shall go in"—for pleading, hiding, fellowship, instruction, enjoyment.

4. Egress. "He shall go out"—for service, progress, etc.

5. Nourishment. "And find pasture." Our spiritual food is found through Christ, in Christ, and around Christ.

Let us enter: a door is easy of access; we shall not have to climb over some lofty wall.

Let us enter: it is a door for sheep, who have no wisdom.

Let us enter: the door is Jesus; we need not fear to draw nigh to him, for he is meek and lowly in heart.

Knockers

The work of the Reformation was thus described by Stern, a German statesman: "Thank heaven, Dr. Luther has made the entrance into heaven somewhat shorter, by dismissing a crowd of door-keepers, chamberlains, and masters of ceremony."

In olden times, cathedrals were regarded as places of sanctuary, where criminals and others might take refuge. Over the north porch of Durham Cathedral was a room, where two doorkeepers kept watch alternately, to admit any who at any time, either by day or by night, knocked at the gate, and claimed the protection of St. Cuthbert. Whoever comes to the door of our house of refuge, and at whatever time, finds ready admittance.

It is said that the ancient city of Troy had but one way of entrance. In whatever direction the traveler went, he would find no way to go into the city but the one which was legally appointed, and the only one which was used by those who went in and out. There is only one right way to the favor of God, to the family of God, to the presence of God in prayer, and, finally, to the city of God in eternity, and that one way is Christ. "I am the way," he declares, "and no man cometh unto the Father but by me."—*John Bate*

We cannot go abroad or return home without passing through an emblem of our Lord. So near as he is in the type, so near let him be in reality.

The sheep enters the fold at first by the door, and it remains in the fold because the door shuts it in. When the flock go forward, they proceed by way of the door; and when they return to their united rest, it is by the same passage. Take away the door from the fold, and the enemy would enter, or the flock would stray. A sheep-fold without a door would in effect be no fold at all.—*C. H. S.*

There are not half-a-dozen ways out of our sin and misery—not a choice of ways over the steep hills and desolate waste-places of this mortal life, so that by any of them we may reach heaven at last, but only one way.

But, if this is the only way, it is likewise a perfectly secure way. Via unica, via certa, is a Latin proverb in which this truth is stated very forcibly.—*Dean Howson*

Since Jesus glories that he is the door, let us not hesitate to use him in that capacity. Let us hasten to enter in by him into peace, life, rest, holiness. When we see it written up in large characters, THIS IS THE WAY, we do not fear that we shall trespass if we follow it. What is a way for, but to be followed? What is a door for, but to be passed through? Say that a door-way is never passed, and you have said that it is useless. Why not brick it up? It would be no honor to the Lord Jesus for sinners to be so in awe of him as never to come to God by him: but he delights in being evermore our way of access.—*C. H. S.*

179

And it was at Jerusalem the feast of the dedication, and it was winter. And Jesus walked in the temple in Solomon's porch.
—*John 10:22–23*

HE presence of Jesus brings into prominence:
- The place: "at Jerusalem, in the temple."
- The exact part of it: "Solomon's porch."
- The time—the season—the exact date: "it was winter."
- The proceedings: "it was the feast of the dedication."

The main feature in all history, and in all the events of a private life, is the presence or absence of Jesus.

At the time mentioned, the Lord Jesus walked manifestly among the people. We greatly desire his spiritual presence now.

I. WILL HE BE HERE? Will he be in our assembly?

The place may be a very Jerusalem; but will he be there? Our meeting place may be a temple; but will he be there. It may be a high day; but will the Lord be with us? It may be cold and wintry; but what of that if he be there? Our one eager inquiry is about his presence, and we feel sure that he will come, for:

1. We have invited him, and he will not refuse his friends.
2. We are prepared for him. We are waiting to welcome him.
3. We have great need of him, and he is full of compassion.
4. We have some of his brethren here among us, and these bring him with them: indeed, he is in them.
5. We have those here whom he is seeking. He seeks lost sheep, and such are here.
6. He has promised to come (Matt. 18:20).
7. Some declare that they have already seen him. Why should not others of us enjoy the same privilege?

II. WILL HE STAY? He will:

1. If we prize his company, and feel that we cannot live without it. We must by earnest prayer constrain him to abide with us (Luke 24:29).
2. If we love his truth, and delight to make it known.
3. If we obey his will, and walk in sincerity and holiness.
4. If we are diligent in his service and worship.
5. If we are united in love to him, to one another, and to poor sinners.
6. If we are humbly reverent, and sit at his feet in lowly confession. The proud he will never favor.
7. If we are jealously watchful.

III. WHAT WILL HE DO IF HE COMES?

1. He will walk among us, and observe what we are doing, even as he noticed those who went to the temple at Jerusalem.
2. He will grieve over the spiritual condition of many, even as he mourned over the ruin of Jerusalem.
3. He will wait to give audience to any who desire to speak with him.
4. He will teach by his servant; and his Word, whether received or rejected, will be with great authority and power.
5. He will this day explain to us the temple itself, by being himself the key to it.

   Think of Jesus, who is the temple of God (Rev. 21:22), in the temple, and then understand, by the light of his presence:
   - The temple (Heb. 9:11; Rev. 15:5).
   - The altar (Heb. 8:10; Rev. 8:3).
   - The Sacrifice (Heb. 9:28; 1 Cor. 5:7).
   - The shewbread (Heb. 9:2).
   - The veil (Heb. 10:20).
   - The ark and mercy-seat (Heb. 9:4–5; Rev. 10:19).
   - The Priest (Heb. 10:12).
6. He will to his own people reveal his love, as once the Lord's light shone above the mercy-seat.
7. He will take us where he always walks, but where there is no winter: to the New Jerusalem, to the temple, to a more beautiful building than Solomon's Porch (Rev. 21:10–11).

Expository

What is here called "Solomon's Porch", was, strictly speaking, not a porch at all in the English sense of the word, but one of the large open colonnades that surrounded the courts. . . . The whole length of the four sides of the outer court was three quarters of a mile. The eastern side was "Solomon's Porch." It was a vast gallery of columns in double rows. Each column, thirty-five feet high, consisted of one piece of white marble. The roof above was in panels of cedar-wood. The view, through the columns, eastward and outward, ranged across the valley over the Mount of Olives. The inward view was into the court itself, which was planted with trees, and where at festival times, there were crowds of people.

There is much solemnity in contemplating Jesus as he "walked" among the pillars of this famous colonnade; and it is interesting to compare this passage of the life of Jesus with a much earlier one recorded by the same Evangelist. We read, in the first chapter of John's Gospel, that Jesus was "walking"—in solitude—by the banks of the Jordan, while John the Baptist and two of his disciples looked on. Then, perhaps, the Lord was meditating on his great mission, on the beginning of his work, and on the calling of the first disciples which speedily followed in that place. Now, perhaps, he was meditating on the accomplishment of his work, on the destruction of Jerusalem and the Jewish temple, and on the doom of the Jewish people. The impression upon the mind is very serious when we think of Jesus, on either of these occasions, as walking in silence, either by the banks of the famous historical river, or in this colonnade of the temple, which, in another way, is equally famous in the sacred annals.—*Dean Howson's "Thoughts for Saints' Days"*

The Mohammedans have a saying, that, whenever two persons meet, there is always a third. The proverb refers to the presence of God.— *Professor Hoge*

As the sun is as ready to pour its radiance upon the daisy on a village common as upon the oaks in Windsor Park, so is Christ as willing to visit the heart of the poorest and feeblest as well as the richest and noblest of earth.—*Handbook of Illustration*

When Christ saith, "I will be with you," you may add what you will—to protect you, to direct you, to comfort you, to carry on the work of grace in you, and in the end to crown you with immortality and glory. All this and more is included in this precious promise.—*John Trapp*

180

Ye have heard how I said unto you, I go away, and come again unto you. If ye loved me, ye would rejoice, because I go unto the Father: for my Father is greater than I.

—*John 14:28*

 ESUS' love makes him use the disciples' love to himself as a comfort for themselves when they are distressed about his going away.

He appeals to the warmest feeling in their hearts in order to raise their spirits.

It is well when grace has put within us principles which are springs of consolation.

O blessed Master, thou speakest ever with a view to our joy!

From our text let us learn:

I. THAT WE SHOULD TRY TO SEE THINGS IN CHRIST'S LIGHT.

1. He sees the whole of things. He says not only, "I go away," but also, "I come again unto you."
2. He sees through things. He does not say, "I die," but he looks beyond, and says, "I go unto the Father."

3. He sees the true bearing of things. The events which were about to happen were in themselves sad, but they would lead to happy results. "If ye loved me, ye would rejoice."

To see facts in his light we must dwell with him, live in him, grow like him, and especially love him more and more.

II. THAT OUR LOVE SHOULD GO FORTH TOWARDS HIS PERSON.

"If ye loved *me*." All about him is amiable; but he himself is altogether lovely (Song of Sol. 5:16).

1. He is the source of all the benefits he bestows.
2. Loving him, we have him, and so his benefits.
3. Loving him, we prize his benefits the more.
4. Loving him, we sympathize in all that he does.
5. Loving him, we love his people for his sake.
6. Loving him, our love endures all sorts of rebuffs for his sake.
7. Loving him, the Father loves us (John 14:23).
8. Loving him, we are married to him. Love is the sure and true marriage-bond whereby the soul is united to Christ.

Love to a person is the most real of emotions.

Love to a person is the most influential of motives.

Love to a person is, in this case, the most natural and satisfying of affections.

III. THAT OUR SORROW OUGHT NOT TO PUT OUR LOVE IN QUESTION.

Yet, in the case of the disciples, our Lord justly said, "*If* ye loved me."

He might sorrowfully say the same to us:

1. When we lament inordinately the loss of creatures.
2. When we repine at his will, because of our severe afflictions.
3. When we mistrust his wisdom, because we are sore hampered and see no way of escape.
4. When we fear to die, and thus display an unwillingness to be with our Lord. Surely, if we loved him, we should rejoice to be with him.
5. When we complain concerning those who have been taken from us to be with him. Ought we not to rejoice that Jesus in them sees of the travail of his soul, and has his prayer answered, "Father, I will that they also, whom thou hast given me, be with me where I am" (John 17:4)?

IV. THAT OUR LOVE SHOULD MAKE US REJOICE AT OUR LORD'S EXALTATION, THOUGH IT BE OUR PERSONAL LOSS.

1. It was apparently the disciples' loss for their Lord to go to the Father; and we may think certain dispensations to be our loss:
   • When we are tried by soul-desertion, while Christ is magnified in our esteem.

- When we are afflicted, and he is glorified, by our sorrows.
- When we are eclipsed, and in the result the gospel is spread.
- When we are deprived of privileges for the good of others.
- When we sink lower and lower in our own esteem, but the kingdom of God comes with power.

2. It was greatly to our Lord's gain to go to his Father.
- Thus he left the field of suffering forever.
- Thus he reassumed the glory which he had laid aside.
- Thus he received the glory awarded by the Father.
- Thus he became enthroned for his church and cause.

It will be well for us to look more to our love than to our joy, and to expect our joy through our love.

It will be well for us to know that smallness of love may dim the understanding, and that growth in it may make us both wiser and happier.

In all things our Lord must be first. Yes, even in those most spiritual delights, about which it may seem allowable to have strong personal desires.

Striking Paragraphs

Observe that Christ does not say, "My Father *was* greater than I," in reference to his pre-existent glory; nor, "My father *will be* greater than I," in reference to the glory which he was to resume after his exaltation; but he uses a style of expression which shows that he refers to the *present* time—to the time of his humiliation in the flesh. The apostles had been expressing regret at the announcement of his immediate departure, and this passage contains a soft rebuke of the selfishness of their feelings. We may paraphrase it thus: "If ye really loved me on my own account—if the regard and affection you profess to entertain were purely disinterested in its nature—so far from evincing sorrow at the prospect of my departure, you would rejoice that I shall leave this state of temporary degradation; that I shall cease to be the Man of Sorrows, and acquainted with grief; that I shall resume that original and essential glory which I enjoyed with the Father from eternity. As long as I continue in my present state of humiliation, my Father is greater in glory than I; but when the days of my flesh shall terminate, I shall then be glorified with the Father's own self, with that glory which I had with him before the world was created." This is obviously the correct paraphrase of the passage; no other interpretation of the words, "For my Father is greater than I," could justify, or attach any force to, the interesting appeal which the Savior makes to the love and affection of his disciples.—*Dean Bagot*

Dr. John Duncan, having heard a sermon on the kingdom of heaven, in which the blessings of the new covenant were compared to a market, in which a man could buy everything needed for eternal life, met his friend, Dr. Moody Stuart, at the close of the service, and said to him, "Dear friend, when I heard of the good things that were offered in the market, I said to myself, I will marry the merchant, and they will all be mine."—*The Christian*

The author of a biographical sketch of the late Rev. W. Robinson, of Cambridge, says, "In one of my last conversations with him, I was referring to the sadness of seeing our good men die; and he turned to me with the well-known blaze in his eye, and emphasis of his voice, saying, 'I think it glorious.'"

A saint cares not how ill it goes with him so it goes well with Jesus Christ; he saith, as Mephibosheth to David, "Yea, let him take all, for as much as my lord the king is come again in peace unto his own house" (2 Sam. 19:30). So it may go well with God's name, Moses cares not though his be blotted out of the book of life; and, said John the Baptist, "He must increase, but I must decrease; this my joy, therefore, is fulfilled."—*Ralph Venning*

181

Arise, let us go hence.
—*John 14:31*

 E cannot be long in one stay. A voice ever sounds in our ear, "Arise, let us go hence."

Even when we have conversed on the sweetest themes, or have enjoyed the holiest ordinances, we have not yet come to our eternal abode; still are we on the march, and the trumpet soundeth. "Arise, let us go hence."

Our Lord was under marching-orders, and he knew it: for him there was no stay upon this earth.

Hear how he calls himself, and all his own, to move on, though bloody sweat and bloody death be in the way.

I. OUR MASTER'S WATCHWORD. "Arise, let us go hence."

By this stirring word:

1. He expressed his desire to obey the Father. "As the Father gave me commandment, even so I do. Arise, let us go hence."
   - He was not hindered by expected suffering.
   - He did not start back, though in that suffering there would be the special element of his Father's forsaking him.
   - He did not hesitate though death was in near prospect.
   - He was eager to do the will of the Father, and make all heaven and earth know how entirely he yielded himself to the Father.

2. He indicated his readiness to meet the arch enemy. "The prince of this world cometh. Arise, let us go hence."
   - He was prepared for the test. He "hath nothing in me."
   - He was eager to overthrow his dominion.
3. He revealed his practical activity. All through the chapter observe our Lord's energy. He is ever on the move. "I go. I will come again. I will do it. I will pray. Arise, let us go hence."
   - He prefers action to the most sacred rites, and so leaves the Supper-table with this word on his lips.
   - He prefers action to the sweetest converse. "I will not talk much with you. Arise, let us go hence."
4. He manifested his all-consuming love to us.
   - He was straitened till he had accomplished our redemption.
   - He could not rest in the company of his best-beloved till their ransom was paid.
   - He would not sit at God's right hand till he had felt the shame of the cross, and the bitterness of death (Heb. 12:2).

II. OUR OWN MOTTO. "Arise, let us go hence."
Ever onward, ever forward, we must go (Exod. 14:15).
1. Out of the world when first called by grace (2 Cor. 6:17).
   - How clear the call! How prompt should be our obedience!
   - Jesus is without the camp, we go forth unto him (Heb. 13:13).
   - We must arouse ourselves to make the separation. "Arise, let us go hence."
2. Out of forbidden associations, if, as believers, we find ourselves like Lot in Sodom. "Escape for thy life" (Gen. 19:17).
3. Out of present attainments when growing in grace (Phil. 3:13–14).
4. Out of all rejoicing in self. There we must never stop for a single instant. Self-satisfaction should startle us.
5. To work, anywhere for Jesus. We should go away from Christian company and home comforts, to win souls (Mark 16:15).
6. To defend the faith where it is most assailed. We should be prepared to quit our quiet, to contend with the foe (Jude 3).
7. To suffer when the Lord lays affliction upon us (2 Cor. 12:9).
8. To die when the voice from above calls us home (2 Tim. 4:6).
O sinner, where would you go if suddenly summoned?
O saint, what better could happen to you than to arise and go hence?

Trumpet Calls
It was well said once by a remarkable man, and the words are worth remembering, "Bear in mind that you are just then beginning to go wrong when you are

a little pleased with yourself because you are going right." Let us watch against this as a snare of Satan, and endeavor ever to maintain the apostolic attitude: "In lowliness of mind let each esteem other better than himself." And let me caution you not to make the mistake of supposing that this self-complacency can be effectually guarded against by a mere use of the recognized theological expressions duly ascribing all the merit and all the praise to God. These are too often merely the garments of spiritual pride, and by no means must they be mistaken for true humility.—*W. H. M. H. Aitken*

I heard a friend of mine, not long ago, relate an incident, which I will venture to repeat, as well as I remember it. He was having an earnest conversation, upon the necessity of full consecration, with a lady who professed to know Christ as her Savior, but shrank from yielding herself fully to him. At last she said, with more outspoken honesty, I am afraid, than many who mean exactly the same thing display, "I don't want to give myself right over to Christ; for, if I were to do so, who knows what he might do with me? For aught I know, he might send me out to China." Years had passed away when my friend received a most deeply interesting letter from this very lady, telling of how her long conflict with God had come to an end, and what happiness and peace she now felt in the complete surrender of herself to her Lord; and referring to her former conversation she said, "And now I am my own no longer, I have made myself over to God without reserve, and he is sending me to China."—*W. H. M. H. Aitken*

Pressed on all sides by the enemy, the Austrian General Melas sent a messenger to Suwarrow, asking whither he should "retire." Suwarrow wrote with a pencil, *"Forward."*

That pencil wrote a word immortal—a word which, in the memory and admiration of mankind, shall outlive a thousand boastful records on stoned marble—a word which no lapse of ages can erase.

The zealous are impatient of any hindrances. As Edmund Burke said to the electors of Bristol, "Applaud us when we run; console us when we fall; cheer us when we recover; but let us pass on—for God's sake, let us pass on!"

History tells us that, when the great Roman Catholic missionary— the apostle of the east—was lying on his dying bed, among the barbarous people whom he loved so well, his passing spirit was busy about his work, and even in the article of death, while the glazing eye saw no more clearly, and the ashen lips had begun to stiffen into eternal silence, visions of further conquests flashed before him, and his last word was *"Amplius,"*— onward. Brethren, let this be our motto, and our cry, "Onward." Until the last wandering sheep, far out upon the bleak mountainside, hears Christ's voice, and is gathered into his fold.—*A. H. Baynes*

We must be careful not to get out of the sound of the Master's voice. It is for us to watch and wait for his orders.

When adjutant of my regiment there were always orderlies on duty at the orderly room. In a garrison town, such as Dublin, I always had two. Their place was just outside the orderly-room door, within sound of my voice. They were watching and waiting for orders; they took letters, messages, etc. They were not always carrying messages, but they could not go away without my leave, and it was their duty to be always ready. They were doing their duty while watching and waiting, as much as when actually carrying a letter or message. So with the servant of Christ—"Blessed is the man that heareth me, watching daily . . . waiting at the posts of my doors."

A lady, who had been maid of honor to the Queen, said that it used to be her great delight to try and place herself near the Queen, that she might have the opportunity of doing any little service for her sovereign. —*From "Communion and Conflict," by Captain Dawson*

182

He saith unto the Jews, Behold your King!
—*John 19:14*

ILATE spake far more than he understood, and therefore we shall not confine ourselves to his meaning.

Everything concerning our Lord was more than ever full of meaning just then; the saying of Caiaphas, the fleeing of the disciples, the dividing of his garments, the soldier piercing his side, etc.

It was to the Jews that Jesus was brought forth, and by them he was rejected; yet was he distinctly declared to be their King.

The same is repeated at this day among those favored with special privileges; but whether they accept him or not, he is assuredly in some sense or other their King.

To the summons of the text the answer was mockery.

We would with deepest reverence draw near, and behold our King.

I. BEHOLD HIM PREPARING HIS THRONE.

1. He lays the foundation of it in his suffering nature.
2. He makes it a throne of grace by his atoning griefs.
3. He prepares access to it through his ability to have compassion on those who come to him, by partaking in all their sorrows.
4. He canopies and glorifies it by the shame to which he willingly and unreservedly yields himself.

Believe in the perpetuity of a throne thus founded.

II. BEHOLD HIM CLAIMING OUR HOMAGE.

He claims and wins our adoration:

1. By the right of supreme love.
2. By the right of complete purchase.
3. By the right of grateful consecration, which we heartily accord to him under a sense of loving gratitude.

Glory in rendering homage thus made due.

III. BEHOLD HIM SUBDUING HIS DOMINIONS.

1. Jews and Gentiles are won to obedience by beholding his sufferings for them.
2. This brings in his own elect everywhere.
3. This restores backsliders. They look to him whom they have wounded, and return to their allegiance.
4. This holds all his true servants captive: they glory in yielding their all to him who was thus put to shame for them.
5. This subdues all things unto him. By his cross and passion he reigns in heaven, earth, and hell.

Bow low before the scepter of his Cross.

IV. BEHOLD HIM SETTING FORTH THE PATTERN OF HIS KINGDOM.

He stands there the Prophet and the Type of his own dominion.

1. It is no earthly kingdom; the difference is palpable to all.
2. It is associated with shame and suffering, both on the part of the King and of his loyal subjects.
3. It is based on his love and self-sacrifice: this is his right of sovereignty, this his force of arms, this the source of his revenue.
4. It is made resplendent by his woes: these are the insignia and ornaments of his court; his glory even in heaven.

Glory only in the cross.

V. BEHOLD HIM PROVING THE CERTAINTY OF HIS KINGDOM.

1. Is he King there in his shame? Then, assuredly, he is King now that he has risen from the dead, and gone into the glory.
2. Is he King amid shame and pain? Then he is able to help us if we are in like case.
3. Is he King while paying the price of our redemption? Then, certainly, he is King now that it is paid, and he has become the author of eternal salvation.
4. Is he King at Pilate's bar? Then truly he will be so when Pilate stands at his bar to be judged.

Come hither, saints, and pay your accustomed worship!
Come hither, sinners, and adore for the first time!

Glimpses

It is far worse to despise a Savior in his robes than to crucify him in his rags. An affront is more criminal to a prince upon his throne than when he is disguised as a subject, and masked in the clothes of his servant. Christ is entered into glory after his sufferings; all who are his enemies must enter into misery after their prosperity: and whosoever will not be ruled by his golden scepter shall be crushed by his rod. —*Stephen Charnock*

Did Pilate hope to melt the Jewish heart to a sort of scornful pity? Did he think that they would turn away from so wretched an object, and be ashamed of having accused him of treason? Perhaps so. But he failed. The sorrows of Jesus do not of themselves overcome the hate of man; but this fact proves how desperately hardened his heart has become.

Given the Holy Spirit, there is nothing more likely to win men to Jesus than beholding him in his sorrows. Behold, O man, and see what thy sin has done, what thy Redeemer has borne, and what he claims of thee! Behold him not as another's, but as thine! Behold him not only as thy Friend, thy Savior, but thy King! Behold him, and at once fall at his feet, and own thyself his loving subject! —*C. H. S.*

"*Behold your King.*"—This is neither an impossible nor a delusive command. The eye that looks away up to Jesus *will* behold him now, and what shall we behold? The vision is all of beauty, and glory, and coronation *now*. The sorrow and the marred visage are past; and even when we behold him as the Lamb of God, it is the Lamb "in the midst of the throne" *now*.

O daughters of Zion, who gaze by faith upon Jesus our King, what do you see? Oh the music of the answers!—"We see Jesus crowned with glory and honor!" "Fairer than the children of men." "Beautiful and glorious!" "How great is his beauty!" "His countenance is as Lebanon, excellent as the cedars," and "as the sun shineth in his strength!" "Yea, he is altogether lovely!"—*Frances Ridley Havergal*

183

Jesus saith unto her, Woman, why weepest thou? Whom seekest thou?
—*John 20:15*

OMAN has had many reasons for weeping since the fall.

Jesus went to his death amid weeping women, and on his rising he met a little company of them.

The first words of a risen Savior are to a weeping woman.

He who was born of woman has come to dry up woman's tears.

Observe the wise method followed by the divine Consoler.

Magdalene is to state the reason of her weeping. "Why weepest thou?" Often sorrow vanishes when it is defined. It is wise to chase away mystery and understand the real cause of grief.

He helps her also by coming nearer to her grief in the second question: "Whom seekest thou?" She was seeking *him*.

He was himself the answer to his own inquiries.

In all cases Jesus is the most suitable Comforter and comfort.

Let us put this question, "Why weepest thou?" in two ways.

I. IS IT NATURAL SORROW?

1. Art thou bereaved? The risen Savior comforts thee; for:
   - He assures thee of the resurrection of the departed.
   - He is with thee, thy living Helper.
   - He sympathizes with thee, for he once lost his friend Lazarus; yea, he himself has died.
2. Are thy beloved ones sick? Sorrow not impatiently; for:
   - He lives to hear prayer for healing.
   - He waits to bless them if they are dying.
3. Art thou thyself sick? Be not impatient; for:
   - Jesus lives to moderate thy pains.
   - Jesus lives to sustain thy heart under suffering.
   - Jesus lives to give life to thy body, as he has done to thy soul.
4. Art thou poor? Do not murmur, for:
   - He lives, and is rich.
   - He would have thee find thine all in himself.
   - He will never leave thee nor forsake thee.
5. Art thou of a sorrowful spirit? Do not despond, but:
   - See where *his* sorrows have brought *him*.
   - See how he came to the sorrowful, and how he cometh still.
   - See what he does in his consoling ministry, and imitate him by cheering others.

Thus thou shalt thyself be comforted.

II. IS IT SPIRITUAL SORROW?

1. *Distinguish*. See whether it be good or ill. "Why weepest thou?"
   - Is it selfish sorrow? Be ashamed of it.
   - Is it rebellious? Repent of it.
   - Is it ignorant? Learn of Jesus, and so escape it.
   - Is it hopeless? Believe in God and hope ever.
   - Is it gracious? Then thank him for it.

2. *Declare.* Tell Jesus all about it. "Why weepest thou?"

Is it sorrow for others? He weeps with thee.
- Are loved ones abiding in sin?
- Is the church cold and dead?

Is it the sorrow of a seeking saint? He meets thee.
- Dost thou miss his presence?
- Hast thou grieved his Holy Spirit?
- Canst thou not attain to holiness?
- Canst thou not serve him as much as thou desirest?
- Do thy prayers appear to fail?
- Does thine old nature rebel?

Is it the sorrow of one in doubt? He will strengthen thee.
- Come to Jesus as a sinner.

Is it the sorrow of a seeking sinner? He will receive thee.
- Dost thou weep because of past sin?
- Dost thou fear because of thine evil nature?
- Art thou unable to understand the gospel?
- Dost thou weep lest thou grow hardened again?
- Dost thou mourn because thou canst not mourn?

He is before thee: believe in him, and weeping will end.

He accepts thee: in him thou hast all thou art seeking for.

Consolatory Thoughts

A Hindu woman said to a missionary, "Surely your Bible was written by a woman." "Why?" "Because it says so many kind things for women. Our pundits never refer to us, but in reproach."

"Woman, why weepest thou?" God and his angels take notice of every tear of our devotion. The sudden wonder hath not dried her eyes, nor charmed her tongue: she freely confesseth the cause of her grief to be the missing of her Savior: "They have taken away my Lord, and I know not where they have laid him." Alas! good Mary, how dost thou lose thy tears? Of whom dost thou complain but of thy best Friend? Who hath removed thy Lord but himself? Who but his own Deity hath taken away his human body out of the region of death? Neither is he now laid any more; he stands by thee whose removal thou complainest of. Thus many a tender and humble soul afflicts itself with the want of that Savior whom it hath, and feeleth not. —*Bishop Hall*

She turns away from the angels, like a Rachel who will not be comforted. But there is comfort in store for her, sorrow as she may. We have an example given us here of how only the Lord himself can suffice to comfort spirits like that of Mary Magdalene. The Lord sees the heart, and none shall weep for him in vain; but even the angels, gracious though their sympathy be, must leave the task of comforting the deepest sorrow to the Lord. —*Rudolf Stier*

The first words that ever Christ spake after his resurrection to them he appeared to were, "Woman, why weepest thou?" It is a good question after Christ's resurrection. What cause of weeping remains, now that Christ is risen? Our sins are forgiven, because he, our Head and Surety, hath suffered death for us; and if Christ be risen again, why weep we? If we be broken-hearted, humbled sinners, that have interest in his death and resurrection, we have no cause to grieve. — *Richard Sibbes*

"Good men weep easily," says the Greek poet; and the better any are, the more inclined to weeping, especially under affliction. As you may see in David, whose tears, instead of gems, were the ornaments of his bed; in Jonathan, Job, Ezra, Daniel, etc. "How," says one, "shall God wipe away my tears in heaven if I shed none on earth? And how shall I reap in joy if I sow not in tears? I was born with tears, and I shall die with tears; and why then should I live without them in this valley of tears?" —*Thomas Brooks*

Be not troubled, my soul. God has for thee something better than thy imaginings. It is with thee as with the women of Galilee. They sought only a dead form, and they found a living Lord. Thou also hast been too eager for the earthly form of thy hope's fulfillment. Has he promised that all things shall work together for thy good, and yet denied thee the comforts of the world? What then? Is his promise void? May it not be that thou hast found thy promise in the very region where it seems to have failed thee, in the privations and sorrows of life? What matter though thou hast lost the form, if thou hast found the sepulcher vacant? The loss is a gain, and the vacancy is fullness of joy. There are losses which mean nothing less than resurrection. I rise more by the discovery of my wants than by the discovery of my possessions ...O fragrance of the broken ointment box! O light of resurrection! Reached from human emptiness, I am enriched by the gain of thee. —*Dr. George Matheson*

184

Jesus saith unto her, Touch me not; for I am not yet ascended to my Father: but go to my brethren, and say unto them, I ascend unto my Father, and your Father; and to my God, and your God.

—John 20:17

THE lesson is to a soul brought into the conscious presence of the Lord.

Oh, to be in that condition!

Mary Magdalene had wept because of her Lord's absence, and longed to find him; and now she has her desire: he stands before her.

Oh, that we knew where we might find him (Job 23:3).

Her conduct in holding him by the feet was natural, and yet it was forbidden by a higher wisdom than that of mortal men.

I. THE CAUTION. "Touch me not."

1. We may blunder even in our closest fellowship, and may need a prohibition. We have never greater need of caution than in our nearest approaches to God. Courtiers must be most careful in the throne-room.
2. We may carnalize the spiritual.
   This has ever been a tendency with even the best of the saints; and it has misled many in whom affection has been stronger than intellect.
3. We may seek most passionately what is by no means essential.
   - The assurance of sense, by touch or otherwise: when the assurance of faith is far better, and quite sufficient.
   - The detaining of one who has no intention of going.
4. We may crave what were better further on.
   When we are raised to eternal glory we shall be able to enjoy what now we must not ask.
5. We may be selfish in our enjoyments.
   Staying to contemplate alone by ourselves, when we ought rather to bless others by publishing the blessed news (2 Kings 7:9).

II. THE MISSION. "Go to my brethren."

She would have preferred to stay, but Jesus bids her go.
1. This was better for her. Contemplation alone may degenerate into the sentimental, the sensuous, the impracticable.
2. This was better for them. They heard the best of news from the most trustworthy of informants.
3. This was unquestioningly done by this holy woman.
   - What she had seen she declared.
   - What she had heard she told.
   - Women are said to be communicative; and so there was wisdom in the choice.
   - Women are affectionate, and so persuasive; and therefore fit to bear such a tender message as we have now to consider.

III. THE TITLE. "My brethren."

Our Lord, of design, chose this title to comfort his sorrowing ones. They had so acted as almost to cease to be his followers, disciples, or friends; but brotherhood is an abiding relationship. They were:
1. His brethren, though he was about to ascend to his throne.
   - He was still a man, though no more to suffer and die.

- He still represented them as their risen Head.
- He was still one with them in all his objects and prospects.

2. His brethren, though they had forsaken him in his shame.
- Relationship abiding, for brotherhood cannot be broken.
- Relationship owned more than ever; since their sense of guilt made them afraid. He was a true Joseph to them (Gen. 14:4).
- Relationship dwelt upon, that they might be reassured.

Never let us omit the tender sweetnesses of the gospel, its courtesies, benedictions, and love-words, such as the "My brethren" of the text before us. If we leave out these precious words we shall mar the Master's message of grace.

IV. THE TIDINGS. "I ascend unto my Father, and your Father."

This message was meant to arouse and comfort them.

1. By the news of his departure they are to be aroused.
2. By the news of his ascension they are to be confirmed.
3. By his ascension to the common Father they are to be comforted with the prospect of coming there themselves. He is not going into an unknown country, but to his home and theirs (John 14:2).
4. By his ascent to God they are to be struck with solemn awe, and brought the more reverently to look for his presence among them.
- See how practical our Lord is, and how much he values the usefulness of his servants.
- Have we not something to tell?
- Whether man or woman, tell the Lord's brethren what the Lord hath told to *thee.*

Touches

It is this that men will labor after, and have labored for, even from the beginning of the world, to be too much addicted to the things of sight and sense. They will worship Christ, but they must have a picture before them. They will adore Christ, but they must bring his body down to a piece of bread. They must have a presence, and so, instead of raising their hearts to God and Christ in a heavenly manner, they pull down God and Christ to them. This the pride and base earthliness of man will do. And therefore saith Christ, "Touch me not" in that manner; it is not with me now as it was before. We must take heed of mean and base conceits of Christ. What saith Paul in 1 Corinthians 5:16? "Henceforth know we no man after the flesh: yea, though we have known Christ after the flesh, yet now henceforth know we him no more." Christ after the flesh was of such a tribe and of such a stature, and had such gifts and qualities. What is that to me? Christ is now Lord of lords and King of kings. He is glorious in heaven, and so I conceive of him. —*Richard Sibbes*

"Touch me not."—By which we are to understand, not that the Lord would have objected to this token of her affection, for we find that soon after the Lord made Thomas put his hand into his side (verse 25); but this was not the moment for Mary to be so employed. The Lord had a message to send by her to his disciples. It was time that they, as well as herself, should receive the joyful tidings of his resurrection; therefore he would first send her to them. *—Dr. Hawker*

To whom then dost thou send her? *"Go to my brethren."* Blessed Jesu! who are these? Were they not thy followers? Yea, were they not thy forsakers? Yet still thou stylest them thy brethren. O admirable humanity! O infinite mercy! How dost thou raise their titles with thyself? At first they were thy servants, and then thy disciples; a little before thy death they were thy friends; now, after thy resurrection, they were thy brethren. Thou that wert exalted infinitely higher from mortal to immortal, descendest so much lower to call them brethren who were before friends, disciples, servants. *—Bishop Hall*

While the going up of Elias may be compared to the flight of a bird which none can follow, the ascension of Christ is, as it were, a bridge between heaven and earth, laid down for all who are drawn to him by his earthly existence. *—Baumgarten*

185

Then saith he to Thomas, Reach hither thy finger, and behold my hands; and reach hither thy hand, and thrust it into my side: and be not faithless, but believing.

—John 20:27

ow struck must Thomas have been when his Lord addressed to him the very words which he had himself used! (See verse 25.) Jesus knows how to send the word home to us.

In the church of to-day we have many a Thomas—slow, suspicious, critical, full of doubts, yet true-hearted.

Thomas set his Lord a test, and thus tried his patience.

The Lord accepted the test, and so proved his condescension.

The proof sufficed for Thomas, and thus showed the Lord's wisdom.

Peradventure, certain among us would desire tests of some such sort.

To those we would earnestly say:

I. CRAVE NO SIGNS.

After the full proofs which Christ gave to his apostles, we need no more, and to look for further signs and evidences would be wrong. Yet some are demanding miracles, faith healings, visions, voices, impressions, transports, depressions, etc.

1. It is dishonoring to your Lord.
2. It is unreasonable, when the truth bears its own evidence.
3. It is presumptuous. How dare we stipulate for proof more than sufficient, or demand evidence of a sort which pleases our prejudices!
4. It is damaging to ourselves. Faith must be weak while we demand for it such proofs; and in this weakness lies incalculable mischief.
5. It is dangerous. We may readily be driven either into infidelity or super-stition, if we give way to this craving for signs.

Picture what Thomas could and would have become under the influence of his unbelief, had not his Lord interposed.

II. YET TURN TO CHRIST'S WOUNDS. Let these stand to you instead of signs and wonders.

Behold in these wounds:

1. The seals of his death. He did actually and truly die. How could he out-live that wound in his side?
2. The identification of his person as actually risen.
3. The tokens of his love. He has graven us upon the palms of his hands.
4. The ensigns of his conflict, of which he is not ashamed, for he displays them.
5. The memorials of his passion, by which he is manifested in glory as the Lamb that was slain (Rev. 5:6).

This should more than suffice you; but should doubt still linger:

III. USE SUCH EVIDENCES AS YOU POSSESS.

1. The sacred narrative of our Lord's life and death, if carefully studied, exhibits a singular self-evidencing power.
2. The regenerating and purifying result of faith in the great Lord is a fur-ther piece of evidence. "By their fruits ye shall know them" (Matt. 7:20).
3. The solace which faith yields in sorrow is good proof.
4. The strength it gives in the hour of temptation is further help.
5. The ardor of mind and elevation of aim, which faith in Jesus creates, are other experimental arguments.
6. The visitations of the Holy Spirit, in quickening the heart, reviving the spirit, and guiding the mind, are additional proofs. Thus the Holy Ghost bears witness to our Lord.
7. The actual enjoyment of fellowship with the Lord Jesus himself is the master key of the whole controversy. "We have known and believed" (1 John 4:16).

Does this seem an idle tale to you?

Should you not see cause for fear, if it be so?
Seek now to view those wounds believingly, that you may live.

Notes

For all thy rankling doubts so sore,
　Love thou thy Savior still
Him for thy Lord and God adore.
　And ever do his will.
Though vexing thoughts may seem to last,
Let not thy soul be quite o'ercast;
Soon will he show thee all his wounds, and say,
"Long have I known thy name—know thou my face alway."
—*Keble*

We learn here how prone we are to establish improper criteria of truth. How often do we judge of things exclusively by our experience, our reason, our senses! But what can be more foolish than this? To how small a distance do these powers extend? How many things are certainly true, the truth of which falls not within the compass of either! How many things can a man relate, which appear impossible to a child! Tell the inhabitant of the sultry climes, that, at a certain season of the year, water, which he has only seen in a fluid state, becomes solid, and hard enough to walk upon—and it will seem to him an idle tale: he has witnessed no such thing, and reasoning from what he knows, deems it incredible. If Thomas had constantly judged according to the rule he professed, how little could he have believed at all! . . . To believe no more than we can comprehend, or reduce to some of our modes of knowledge, is not to honor the authority of God at all; yea, it is a reflection upon his wisdom, and upon his veracity: upon his wisdom—as it he could tell us no more than we know; and upon his veracity—as if he were not to be trusted if he could. —*William Jay*

Skillful swimmers are not afraid to go above their depth, whereas young learners feel for the ground, and are loath to go far from the bank-side. Strong faith fears not when God carries the creature beyond the depth of his reason. "We know not what to do," said good Jehoshaphat, "but our eyes are upon thee" (2 Chron. 20). As if he had said, "We are in a sea of trouble beyond our own help, or any thought how we can wind out of these straits, but our eyes are upon thee. We dare not give up our case for desperate so long as there is strength in thine arm, tenderness in thy bowels, and truth in thy promise." Whereas weak faith, that is groping for some footing for reason to stand on, is taken up with how to reconcile the promise to the creature's understanding. —*William Gurnall*

186

Jesus saith unto him, Thomas, because thou hast seen me, thou hast believed: blessed are they that have not seen, and yet have believed.

—John 20:29

HOSE who saw and believed not, were far from being blessed.

Those who saw him, and believed, were undoubtedly blessed.

Those who have not seen, and yet have believed, are *emphatically* blessed.

There remains the superlative degree of blessedness in seeing Jesus face to face without need of believing in the same sense as now.

But for the present this is *our* blessedness, this is our place in the gospel history—we have not seen, and yet we have believed. What a comfort that so high a degree of blessedness is open to us!

I. DO NOT LET US DIMINISH THIS BLESSEDNESS.

1. Let us not diminish it by wishing to see.
   - By pining for some imaginary voice, or vision, or revelation.
   - By craving marvelous providences, and singular dispensations.
   - By hungering for despairs or transports.
   - By perpetually demanding arguments, and logical demonstrations.
   - By clamoring for conspicuous success in connection with the preaching of the word, and the missionary operations of the church.
   - By being anxious to believe with the majority. Truth has usually been with the minority.
2. Let us not diminish it by failing to believe.
   - Believe practically, so as to act upon our faith.
   - Believe intensely, so as to laugh at contradictions.
   - Believe livingly, so as to be simple as a child.
   - Believe continually, so as to be evenly confident.
   - Believe personally, so as to be assured alone, even if all others give the lie to the doctrines of the Lord.
   - Believe thoroughly, so as to find the rest of faith.

II. DO NOT LET US THINK THIS BLESSEDNESS UNATTAINABLE.

1. This blessedness is linked for ever with the faith which our Lord accepts; in fact, it is the appointed reward of it.
2. God deserves such faith of us. He is so true that his unsupported word is quite enough for faith to build upon. Can we only believe him as far as we can see him?

3. Thousands of saints have rendered, and are rendering, such faith, and are enjoying such blessedness at this moment. We are bound to have fellowship with them in like precious faith.

4. Hitherto our own experience has warranted such faith. Has it not?

5. Those of us who are now enjoying the blessed peace of faith can speak with great confidence upon the matter.

Why, then, are so many cast down? Why will they not believe?

III. DO NOT LET ANY OF US MISS IT.

The faith which our Lord described is exceedingly precious, and we ought to seek after it, for:

1. It is the only true and saving faith. Faith which demands sight is not faith at all; it cannot save the soul.

2. It is in itself most acceptable with God. Nothing is acceptable without it (Heb. 11:6). It is the evidence of the acceptance of the man and his works.

3. It is a proof of grace within: of a spiritual mind, a renewed nature, a reconciled heart, a new-born spirit.

4. It is the root principle of a glorious character.

5. It is exceedingly useful to others: in comforting the despondent, in impressing unbelievers, in cheering seekers, etc.

6. It enriches its possessor to the utmost, giving power in prayer, strength of mind, decision of character, firmness under temptation, boldness in enterprise, joy of soul, realization of heaven, etc.

Know *you* this faith?

Blessedness lies that way. Seek it!

Contributions

But why specially blessed? Because the Holy Spirit hath wrought this faith in their hearts. They are blessed in having a believing heart; they are blessed in the instrument of their belief, blessed in having an evidence that they are passed from death unto life: "whom, having not seen, ye love." It is more blessed to believe than to see, because it puts more honor upon God's word. It is more blessed, because it presents us with a more invariable object. He that can trust an unseen Savior may trust him in all circumstances: shut him up in a dungeon, separate from all sight and light, it matters not; for he has always a heart to believe unto righteousness, and his soul rests upon a rock that shall never be moved. The same faith that takes hold of an unseen, risen Savior, takes hold of every other truth in the gospel. —*Richard Cecil*

"With men," says Bishop Hall, "it is a good rule to try first, and then to trust; with God it is contrary. I will first trust him, as most wise, omnipotent, merciful, and try him afterwards."

By constant sight, the effect of objects seen grows less; by constant faith, the effect of objects believed in grows greater. The probable reason of this is that personal observation does not admit of the influence of the imagination in impressing the fact; while unseen objects, realized by faith, have the auxiliary aid of the imagination, not to exaggerate them, but to clothe them with living colors, and impress them upon the heart. Whether this be the reason or not, the fact is true that, the more frequently we see, the less we feel the power of an object; while the more frequently we dwell upon an object by faith, the more we feel its power. —*J. B. Walker*

Faith makes invisible things visible, absent things present, things that are very far off to be very near unto the soul. —*Thomas Brooks*

The region of unbelief is black with God's frown, and filled with plagues and wrath; but the region of faith is as the floor of heaven for brightness. Christ's righteousness shelters it, the graces of the Spirit beautify it, and the eternal smile of God comforts and glorifies it. —*Dr. Hoge*

It would grieve an indulgent father to see his own child come into court, and there bear witness against him and charge him of some untruth in his words, more than if a stranger should do it. The testimony of a child, though, when it is *for* the vindication of a parent, it may lose some credit in the opinion of those that hear it, upon the suspicion of partiality, yet, when *against* a parent, it seems to carry some more probability of truth than what another that is a stranger says against him. The band of natural affection with which the child is bound to his parent is so sacred that it will not be easily suspected. He cannot be supposed to offer violence to it, except upon the more inviolable necessity of bearing witness to the truth.

O think of this, Christian, again and again—by thy unbelief thou bearest false witness against God! And if thou, a child of God, speakest no better of thy heavenly Father, and presentest him with no fairer character to the world, it will be no wonder if it be confirmed in its hard thoughts of God, even to final impenitency and unbelief, when it shall see how little credit he finds with thee, for all thy great profession of love towards him and near relationship to him. —*William Gurnall*

187

Whom God hath raised up, having loosed the pains of death, because it was not possible that he should be holden of it.

—*Acts 2:24*

ur Lord felt the pains of death truly and really. His body was in very deed dead, yet there was no corruption.

- It was not needful: it could have borne no relation to our redemption.
- It would not have been seemly.
- It was not demanded by the law of nature; for he was sinless, and sin is the worm which causes corruption.

But from the pains of death his body was loosed by resurrection.

I. IT WAS NOT POSSIBLE THAT THE BANDS OF DEATH SHOULD HOLD OUR LORD.

He derived his superiority to the bondage of death:

1. From the command of the Father that he should have power to take his life again (John 10:18).
2. From the dignity of his human person.
   - As in union with Godhead.
   - As being in itself absolutely perfect.
3. From the completion of his propitiation.
   The debt was discharged; he must be freed.
4. From the plan and purpose of grace which involved the life of the Head as well as that of the members (John 14:19).
5. From the perpetuity of his offices.
   - "Priest for ever after the order of Melchizedek" (Heb. 6:20).
   - King—"Thy throne, O God, is for ever and ever" (Ps. 45:6).
   - Shepherd—"brought again from the dead" (Heb. 13:20).
6. From the nature of things, since without it we should have:
   - No assurance of our resurrection (1 Cor. 15:17).
   - No certainty of justification (Rom. 4:25).
   - No representative possession of heaven (Heb. 9:24).
   - No crowning of man with glory and honor, and exaltation of him over the works of God's hands.

II. IT IS NOT POSSIBLE THAT ANY OTHER BANDS SHOULD HOLD HIS KINGDOM.

1. The firm establishment of error shall not prevent the victory of truth. The colossal systems of Greek philosophy and Roman priestcraft have passed away ; and so shall other evil powers.
2. The scholarship of his foes shall not resist his wisdom. He baffled the wise in his life on earth; much more will he do it by his Holy Spirit (1 Cor. 1:20).
3. The ignorance of mankind shall not darken his light. "The poor have the gospel preached to them" (Matt. 11:5). Degraded races receive the truth (Matt. 4:16).

4. The power, wealth, fashion, and prestige of falsehood shall not crush his kingdom (Acts 4:26).
5. The evil influence of the world upon the church shall not quench the divine flame (John 16:33).
6. The rampant power of unbelief shall not destroy his dominion. Though at this hour it seems to bind the church in the bands of death, those fetters shall melt away (Matt. 16:18).

III. IT IS NOT POSSIBLE TO HOLD IN BONDAGE ANYTHING THAT IS HIS.

1. The poor struggling sinner shall escape the bonds of his guilt, his depravity, his doubts, Satan, and the world (Ps. 124:7).
2. The bondaged child of God shall not be held captive by tribulation, temptation, or depression (Ps. 34:19; Ps. 116:7).
3. The bodies of his saints shall not be held in the grave (1 Cor. 15:23; 1 Pet. 1:3–5).
4. The groaning creation shall yet burst into the glorious liberty of the children of God (Rom. 8:21).

Here is a true Easter hymn for all who are in Christ.

The Lord is risen indeed, and the happiest consequences must follow.

Let us rise in his rising, and walk at large in his loosing.

Free Thoughts

Christ being imprisoned for our debt, was thrown into the bands of death; but, divine justice being satisfied, it was not possible that he should be detained there, either by right or by force, for he had life in himself and in his own power, and had conquered the prince of death. —*Matthew Henry*

The Emperor Theodosius, having on a great occasion opened all the prisons, and released his prisoners, is reported to have said, "And now, would to God I could open all the tombs, and give life to the dead."

But there is no limit to the mighty power and royal grace of Jesus. He opens the prisons of justice, and the prisons of death with equal and infinite ease: he redeems not the soul only, but the body. —*Dr. Stanford*

188

Now when they heard this, they were pricked in their heart.

—*Acts 2:37*

ETER's sermon was not a fine display of eloquence. Neither was it a very pathetic plea. Nor was it a loud but empty cry of "Believe, believe!" It was simple, a plain statement, and a soberly earnest argument.

Its power lay in the truthfulness of the speaker, his appeal to Scripture, the concurrence of his witnessing brethren, and his own evident faith.

Above all, in the Holy Spirit who accompanied the word.

I. SAVING IMPRESSION IS A PRICK IN THE HEART.

To be cut to the heart is deadly (Acts 5:33); to be pricked in the heart is saving.

1. All true religion must be of the heart.
    Without this:
    • Ceremonies are useless (Isa. 1:13).
    • Orthodoxy of head is in vain (Jer. 7:4).
    • Profession and a constrained morality fail (2 Tim. 3:5).
    • Loud zeal, excited and sustained by mere passion, is useless.
2. Impressions which do not prick the heart may even be evil.
    • They may excite to wrath and opposition.
    • They may lead to sheer hypocrisy.
    • They may create and foster a spurious hope.
3. Even when such superficial impressions are good, they are transient; and when they have passed away, they have often hardened those who have felt them for a season.
4. They will certainly be inoperative. As they have not touched the heart, they will not affect the life.
    • They will not lead to confession and inquiry, nor
        to repentance and change of life,
        to glad reception of the word, nor
        to obedience and steadfastness.
    • Heart-work is the only real work.

II. WHAT TRUTHS PRODUCE SUCH A PRICK?

1. The truth of the gospel has often, by the power of the Holy Ghost, produced an indelible wound in minds skeptical and opposed.
2. A sense of some one specially startling sin has frequently aroused the conscience (2 Sam. 12:7).
3. Instruction in the nature of the law, and the consequent heinousness of sin, has been blessed to that end (Rom. 7:13).
4. The infinite wickedness of sin, as against the very being of God, is also a wounding thought (Ps. 51:4).
5. The exactness, severity, and terror of the judgment, and the consequent punishment of sin, are stirring thoughts (Acts 16:25-30).

6. The great goodness of God has led many to see the cruel wantonness of sin against him (Rom. 2:4).

7. The death of Christ as a Substitute has often been the means of revealing the greatness of the sin which needed such an atonement, and of showing the true tendency of sin in having slain One so good and kind (Zech. 12:10).

8. The abundant grace and love revealed in the gospel, and received by us are sharp arrows to wound the heart.

III. WHAT HAND MAKES THESE PAINFUL PRICKS?

1. The same hand which wrote the piercing truths also applies them.

2. He is well acquainted with our hearts, and so can reach them.

3. He is the Quickener, the Comforter, the Spirit helping our infirmities, showing to us the things of Jesus; his fruit is love, joy, peace, etc. We need not utterly despair when wounded by such a tender Friend.

4. He is a Spirit to be sought unto, who acts in answer to his people's prayers. We turn for healing to him who pricks.

IV. HOW CAN THESE PRICKS BE HEALED?

1. Only One who is divine can heal a wounded heart.

2. The only medicine is the blood of his heart.

3. The only hand to apply it is that which was pierced.

4. The only fee required is gladly to receive him.

Let us ask the question, "Men and brethren, what shall we do?"

Let us then obey the gospel, and believe in the Lord Jesus.

Pointed Passages

Conversion is a work of *argument*, for the judgment is gained by the truth. It is a work of *conviction*, for the awakened are pricked in their hearts. It is a work of *inquiry*, for they ask, "What must we do to be saved?" And, lastly, it is a work of *comfort*, for its subjects have received remission of sins, and the gift of the Holy Ghost. —*Joseph Sutcliffe*

Peter, standing up, said: "We heard from him whom we know that God has raised from the dead the promise of the Holy Ghost. He hath shed forth this; therefore let Jerusalem know assuredly that God hath made him Lord." I call that Peter's colossal "therefore." It is the strongest word in the first oration delivered in the defense of Christianity. The Holy Spirit was promised; he has been poured out; therefore, let those who receive him know that the power behind natural law—our Lord, who was, and is, and is to come—is now breathing upon the centuries as he breathed upon us symbolically. He hath shed forth this; therefore, let all men know assuredly that God hath made him Lord. When they who were assembled at Jerusalem at that time heard this *"therefore,"* they were pricked in the heart. —*Joseph Cook*

Heart-work must be God's work. Only the great heart-Maker can be the great heart-Breaker. —*Richard Baxter*

The Comforter came to convince the world. The Comforter! Does it seem a strange name to any of you, my brethren, for him who came on such an errand? Does it seem to you that, in convincing you of your sins, instead of comforting you, he must needs cover you with shame and confusion, and make you sink to the ground in unutterable anguish and dismay? No, dear brethren, it is not so. Those among you whom the Spirit has indeed convinced of sin, will avouch that it is not. They will avouch that, in convincing them of sin, he has proved that he is indeed the Comforter. If the conviction and consciousness of sin arises from any other source, then indeed it is enough to crush us with shame, and to harrow us with unimaginable fears. But when it comes from the Spirit of God, it comes with healing and comfort on its wings. Remember what the sin is, of which he convinces us—that we believe not in Christ. All other conviction of sin would be without hope; here the hope accompanies the conviction, and is one with it. If we have a deep and lively feeling of the sin of not believing in Christ, we must feel at the same time that Christ came to take away this along with all other sins. —*J. C. Hare*

When a man is wounded with a barbed arrow, the agonies he suffers will cause him to toss about in pain. But the harder he strives to release the weapon from his flesh, the more does it become entangled in his sinews, the wound becomes enlarged, and the torture is increased. When, by the power of the Holy Spirit, a man is wounded on account of sin, and the arrows of the Most High tear his soul, he frequently tries to pluck them out with his own hand, but finds that the misery becomes worse, and the inflaming wounds at last cause faintness and despair. Only the Good Physician knows how to relieve the pain without tearing and festering the spirit. —*Handbook of Illustration*

189

And beholding the man which was healed standing with them, they could say nothing against it.

—*Acts 4:14*

HE rulers and elders were opposed to Peter and John.

It is no new thing for the gospel to be opposed. Nor a strange thing for the great, the official, the powerful, and the influential to be foremost in such opposition.

The opposition of ungodly men is:

- Natural, seeing that the heart of man is depraved.
- Endurable, since our Lord and his apostles suffered it.
- Harmless, if we commit the case to God.
- Overruled for good by divine grace and wise providence.

The best and perhaps the only way to silence opposition is by exhibiting the blessed results which follow from the gospel.

Those who would say *anything* if they could, can say *nothing* of what they would, when they see before their eyes the cures wrought by the word of the Lord Jesus. "The man that was healed" is our best apologist. Better than Paley's "Evidences" or Butler's "Analogy" is the proof given by results.

I. THE GOSPEL IS VINDICATED BY ITS RESULTS.

1. On a broad scale in nations. England, the islands of the Pacific, Jamaica, Madagascar, etc.
2. In individual conversions from open sin. Some of the worst of men have become clear instances of the purifying power of the gospel.
3. In restoring to hope the comfortless and despairing. Very marvelous is its efficacy in the direction of healing mental maladies.
4. In elevating saints above selfish aims and designs, and inducing heroic consecrations. The biographies of gracious men and women are demonstrations of the divine power of the Word.
5. In sustaining character under fierce temptation. Wonderful is the preserving salt of grace amid surrounding putrefaction.
6. In holy and happy death-beds. These are plentiful throughout history, among all ranks; and they never fail to convince the candid.

Many another catalogue of results might be made.

Many a man is unable to be an infidel because of what he has seen in his mother, wife, or child.

II. GOSPEL-WORKS AND WORKERS MUST LOOK FOR LIKE VINDICATION.

Nowadays men ask for results; the tree must bear fruit, or the cry is, "Cut it down." We do not shrink from this test.

1. The minister must find in his converts a proof of his call, and a defense of his doctrines, methods, peculiarities, etc.
2. A society, college, or institution must stand or fall by its fruits.
3. The individual professor must abide the same test.
4. The church in any place, and the church on the largest scale, must be tried by similar methods.
5. Even our Lord himself loses or gains honor among men, according to the way his followers behave themselves.

III. THE GOSPEL AND ITS WORKERS DESERVE VINDICATION AT OUR HANDS. Those who are healed should boldly stand with Peter and John, as witnesses and fellow-workers

This suggests a series of practical questions:

1. Has it produced blessed results in us?
2. Have we come forward to stand with the preachers of it in evidence that it has wrought our cure? Are we continually witnessing to the truth and value of the Gospel of Christ?
3. Does the influence of the gospel upon us so continue and increase unto holiness of life as to be a credit to its influence?
4. Are there not points in our character which harm the repute of the gospel? Should not these be amended at once?
5. Could we not henceforth so live as more effectually to silence the opponents of the Word?

Let the Church plainly see that her converts are her best defense; they are, in fact, her reason for existence.

Let converts see the reason why they should come forward and declare their faith, and unite with the people of God.

Cases in Point

In the course of one of his journeys, preaching the word, Mr. Wesley went to Epworth. Having offered to assist the curate on the following day (Sunday), and his offer being refused, he took his stand upon his father's tombstone in the evening, and preached to the largest congregation Epworth had ever witnessed. This he did night after night. He preached also during his stay of eight days at several of the surrounding villages, where societies had been formed and a great work wrought among the people, and some of them had suffered for it. "Their angry neighbors," says Wesley, "had carried a whole wagon-load of these new heretics before a magistrate. But when he asked what they had done, there was a deep silence; for it was a point their conductors had forgotten. At length one said, 'They pretended to be better than other people, and prayed from morning to night;' and another said, 'They have *"convarted"* my wife. Till she went among them she had such a tongue! and now she is as quiet as a lamb!' 'Take them back, take them back,' replied the justice, and 'let them convert all the scolds in the town.'" —*Tyerman's Life of Wesley*

Lord Peterborough, more famed for his wit than for his religion, when he had lodged with Fenelon, the Archbishop of Canterbury, was so charmed with his piety and beautiful character, that he said to him at parting, "If I stay here any longer I shall become a Christian in spite of myself." —*G. S. Bowes*

A person who had expressed doubts whether the Negroes received any real advantage by hearing the gospel, was asked whether he did not think one, named Jack, was better for the preaching. He replied, "Why, I must confess that he was a drunkard, a liar, and a thief; but certainly now he is a sober boy, and I can trust him with anything; and since he has talked about religion I have tried to make him drunk, but failed in the attempt." —*Arvine*

Certain gentlemen waited upon Rev. Matthew Wilks to complain of the eccentricities of his discourses. Wilks heard them through, and then produced a long list of names. "There," said the quaint divine, "all those precious souls profess to have found salvation through what you are pleased to call my whims and oddities. Can you produce a similar list from all the sober brethren you have been so much extolling?" This was conclusive; they withdrew in silence.

The behavior of some professors has often given the wicked an opportunity to reproach religion. Lactantius reports that the heathen were wont to say, "The Master could not be good, when his disciples were so bad." The malice of sinners is such that they will reproach the rectitude of the law, for the obliquity of their lives who swerve from it. Oh that your pure life did but hang a padlock upon their impure lips! — *William Secker*

190

And at the second time Joseph was made known to his brethren.
—*Acts 7:13*

HERE is a plain parallel between Joseph and Jesus, his brethren and ourselves.

Certain classes of real seekers do not at once find peace; they go to Jesus after a fashion, and return from him as they went.

Our fear is that they may grow indifferent or despairing.

Our hope is that they will go again, and before long discover the great secret, and find food for their souls.

To this end we would follow the track of Joseph's story, and use it as an allegory for the benefit of the seeker.

I. THERE IS A SOMETHING WHICH YOU DO NOT KNOW.

The sons of Israel did not know Joseph. Like them:

1. You have no idea of who and what Jesus is. Power and pity blend in him. He is far more than he seems.
2. You view him only as great, lordly, unapproachable; a great and stern governor and tax-master.
3 You do not know that he is your brother, one with you in nature, relationship, and love.
4. You cannot conceive how he loves; he yearns to make himself known; his heart is swollen big with compassion.

5. You cannot guess what he will do for you; all that he is and has shall be at your disposal.

Picture the Israelitish shepherds in the presence of the exalted Egyptian prince, as he stands veiled in mystery, girded with power, and surrounded with honor. Little could they imagine that this was Joseph their brother.

II. THERE IS A REASON WHY AT YOUR FIRST GOING YOU HAVE NOT LEARNED THIS.

Joseph was not made known to his brethren on their first journey; nor have you yet found out Jesus, so as to know his love.

1. You have not looked for him. The sons of Jacob went to Egypt for corn, not for a brother. You are looking for comfort, etc., not for the Savior.
2. You have not yet felt your sin against Jesus, and he would bring you to repentance, even as Joseph brought his brethren to confess their great wrong.
3. You have not yet gone with your whole force. As the brothers left Benjamin at home, so have you left some faculty or capacity dormant, or chill, in your seeking for grace.
4. You will have a larger blessing through the delay; and the Lord Jesus will in the most seasonable hour reveal himself, as Joseph did. Till then he refrains.

III. THERE IS GREAT HOPE IN YOUR GOING AGAIN TO HIM.

Joseph's brethren made a great discovery *the second time*; you are in similar circumstances to them. Go a second time; for:

1. You must go or perish. There was corn only in Egypt, and there is salvation only in Christ.
2. Others have gone and speeded. All nations went to Egypt, and none were refused. Has Jesus cast out one?
3. You have lingered too long already, even as did Israel's sons.
4. A welcome awaits you. Joseph longed to see his brethren, and Jesus longs to see you.

IV. THERE ARE FORECASTS OF WHAT WILL HAPPEN IF YOU GO.

The story lends itself to prophecy. As the sons of Israel fared with Joseph, so shall you fare with Jesus.

1. You will tremble in his presence.
2. He will bid you draw near.
3. He will comfort you by revealing himself to you.
4. He will bless and enrich you and send you home rejoicing, to fetch all your family to him.
5. He will rule all the world for your sake, and you shall be with him, and be nourished by him.

Let us hasten to go to our Savior the second time.
Surely this is the season, for the Holy Ghost saith "to-day."

Line upon Line

You take it hard, that you are not answered, and that Christ's door is not opened at your first knock. David must knock often: "O my God, I cry by day, and thou hearest not, and in the night season I am not silent" (Ps. 22:2). The Lord's Church must also wait: "And when I cry and shout, he shutteth out my prayer" (Lam. 3:8). Sweet Jesus, the heir of all, prayed with tears and strong cries, once, "O my Father;" again, "O my Father;" and the third time, "O my Father," ere he was heard. Wait on; die praying; faint not.

It is good to have the heart stored with sweet principles concerning Christ and his love, so as to rest in hope though the Lord heareth not at the first. He is Christ, and therefore he will answer a sinner's cry ere long. It is but Christ's outside that is unkind. —*Samuel Rutherford*

A man who had long been seeking religion in a half-hearted way, one day lost his pocket-book. He said to his wife: "I know it is in the barn; I had it after I went there, and before I left it was gone. I am going back to find it; and find it I will, if I have to move every straw." Such seeking soon secured the prize, and enabled his wife so clearly to illustrate the way to seek Jesus, that the man soon found him also, and rejoiced in a full salvation.

The last time I preached upon the matter of decision in religion was in old Farwell Hall. I had been for five nights preaching upon the life of Christ. I took him from the cradle, and followed him up to the judgment hall, and on that occasion I consider I made as great a blunder as ever I made in my life. If I could recall my act I would give this right hand. It was upon that memorable night in October, and the Court House bell was sounding an alarm of fire, but I paid no attention to it. We were accustomed to hear the fire bell often, and it didn't disturb us much when it sounded. I finished the sermon upon "What shall I do with Jesus?" And I said to the audience, "Now, I want you to take the question with you and think over it, and next Sunday I want you to come back and tell me what you are going to do with it." What a mistake! It seems now as if Satan was in my mind when I said this. Since then I have never dared to give an audience a week to think of their salvation. If they were lost they might rise up in judgment against me. "Now is the accepted time." We went down-stairs to the other meeting, and I remember when Mr. Sankey was singing, and how his voice rang when he came to that pleading verse:

> To-day the Savior calls;
> For refuge fly.
> The storm of justice falls,
> And death is nigh.

After our meeting, on the way home, seeing the glare of flames, I said to my companion, "This means ruin to Chicago." About one o'clock, Farwell Hall went, soon the church in which I had preached went down, and everything was scattered. I never saw that audience again. My friends, we don't know what may happen to-morrow; but there is one thing I do know, and that is, if you take the gift of God, even Christ Jesus, you are saved. What are you going to do with him to-night? Will you decide now? —*D. L. Moody*

191

The witnesses laid down their clothes at a young man's feet, whose name was Saul.

—*Acts 7:58*

HE Holy Spirit records Stephen's martyrdom, but does not enter into details of his sufferings and death, as uninspired recorders would have been so apt to do.

The object of the Holy Ghost is not to indulge curiosity nor to harrow the feelings, but to instruct and move to imitation.

He tells us of the martyr's posture, "He kneeled down;" his prayer, "Lord, lay not this sin to their charge;" and his composure, "he fell asleep."

Upon each of these points, volumes might be written.

Our attention is now called to the incident of Saul's being present.

This supplies us with:

I. A SUGGESTED CONTRAST. Stephen and Saul.

These were both highly earnest, fearless men.

Yet at this time they were wide as the poles asunder.

1. Stephen spiritual; giving in his address great prominence to the spiritual nature of religion, and the comparative insignificance of its externals. See verses 48-50.

   Saul superstitious, worshipping form and ritual, full of reverence for the temple and the priests, and so forth.

2. Stephen, a humble believer in the Lord Jesus, saved by faith alone.

   Saul, a self-righteous Pharisee, as proud as he could live.

3. Stephen, defending and vindicating the gospel of Jesus.

   Saul, giving his countenance, his vote, his assistance in the persecution of the servant of the Lord Christ.

Inquire if a Saul is now present. Call him forth by name.

Have you been a *consenting* party to the persecution of good men?

Have you thus copied this young man Saul?

You do not object to making Christian men the theme of ridicule.

You smile when you hear such ridicule.

By your indecision in religion you aid and abet the adversary.

In these ways the witnesses lay down their clothes at your feet, and you are their accomplice.

Oh, that grace may yet convert you!

II. A SINGULAR INTRODUCTION TO TRUE RELIGION.

Many have been brought to God by means somewhat similar.

The young man, whose name was Saul, met with the religion of Jesus in the person of Stephen, and thus he saw it with the following surroundings:

1. The vision of a shining face.
2. The hearing of a noble discourse.
3. The sight of a triumphant death.

These did not convert Saul, but they made it harder for him to be unconverted, and were, no doubt, in after days thought of by him.

Let us so introduce religion to men, that the memory of its introduction may be worth their retaining.

III. A REMARKABLE INSTANCE OF THE LORD'S CARE FOR HIS CHURCH.

The apostolic succession was preserved in the church.

1. Stephen's death was a terrible blow to the cause; but at that moment his successor was close at hand.
2. That successor was in the ranks of the enemy.
3. That successor was far greater than the martyr, Stephen, himself.

There is no fear for the church; her greatest champions, though as yet concealed among her enemies, will be called in due time.

The death of her best advocates may assist in the conversion of others.

IV. A GRACIOUS MEMORIAL OF REPENTED SIN.

Did not Paul give Luke this information concerning himself? and cause it to be recorded in the Acts of the Apostles?

It was well for Paul to remember his sin before conversion.

It will be well for us to remember ours.

1. To create and renew feelings of humility.
2. To inflame love and zeal.
3. To deepen our love to the doctrines of sovereign grace.
4. To make us hopeful and zealous for others.

Let dying Stephen be cheered by the hope of young Saul's salvation.

Let wicked young Saul repent of his wrong to Stephen.

Observanda

A Spanish painter, in a picture of Stephen conducted to the place of execution, has represented Saul as walking by the martyr's side with melancholy calmness. He consents to his death from a sincere, though mistaken, conviction of duty; and the expression of his countenance is strongly contrasted with the rage of the baffled Jewish doctors and the ferocity of the crowd who flock to the scene of bloodshed. Literally considered, such a representation is scarcely consistent either with Saul's conduct immediately afterwards, or with his own expressions concerning himself at the later periods of his life. But the picture, though historically incorrect, is poetically true. The painter has worked according to the true idea of his art in throwing upon the persecutor's countenance the shadow of his coming repentance. We cannot dissociate the martyrdom of Stephen from the conversion of Paul. The spectacle of so much constancy, so much faith, so much love, could not be lost. It is hardly too much to say with Augustine, that "the church owes Paul to the prayer of Stephen." —*Conybeare and Howson*

Here first comes in view an individual destined to be the most extraordinary character in the church of God. Had a prophet stood near on this occasion and said, "Ah! Saul, you will by-and-by be stoned for the same profession, and die a martyr in the same cause;" he would have been filled with surprise and indignation, and have exclaimed, "What, is thy servant a dog, that he should do this thing?" —*William Jay*

As soon as Satan heard of the conversion of Saul, he ordered the devils into deep mourning. —*John Ryland, Senior*

Among the leaders of the great revival of the eighteenth century were Captain Scott and Captain Toriel Joss, the former a captain of dragoons, the latter a sea-captain. Both became famous preachers. Whitefield said of them, "God, who sitteth upon the flood, can bring a shark from the ocean, and a lion from the forest, to show forth his praise."

The following lines by *William Hone*, author of the "Every-day Book," were written to describe his own experience:

> The proudest heart that ever beat
>   Hath been subdued in me;
> The wildest will that ever rose
> To scorn thy cause, and aid thy foes,
>   Is quelled, my God, by thee.
>
> Thy will, and not my will, be done;
>   My heart be ever thine;
> Confessing thee, the mighty Word,
> My Savior Christ, my God, my Lord,
>   Thy cross shall be my sign.

Might they not have been written by the young man, "whose name was Saul"?

192

To you is the word of this salvation sent.
—*Acts 13:26*

 AUL and Barnabas first preached the gospel to the seed of Abraham.

These Jews contradicted and blasphemed, and therefore, in verse 46, the servants of the Lord boldly exclaimed, "We turn to the Gentiles." A blessed turning this for you and for me!

Herein is a warning to ourselves, lest we refuse the gospel, and find it taken from us, and sent to others.

At this moment, to our hearers we earnestly say, "To you is the word of this salvation sent."

Let us then consider:

I. WHAT IS THE WORD OF THIS SALVATION?

1. It is the testimony that Jesus is the promised Savior (verse 23).
2. The word which promises forgiveness to all who exhibit repentance of sin, and faith in the Lord Jesus (verses 38–39).
3. In a word, it is the proclamation of perfect salvation, through the risen Savior (verses 32–33).

It is comparable to a *word* for conciseness and simplicity.

It is a word, as being spoken by God, and as being his present utterance even at this moment.

It is a word; for it reveals Him who is truly "the Word."

It is a word *of salvation*; for it declares, describes, presents, and presses home salvation.

It is a word *sent*, for the Gospel dispensation is a mission of mercy from God, the Gospel is a message, Jesus is the Messiah, and the Holy Ghost himself is *sent* to work salvation among men.

II. IN WHAT MANNER IS THE GOSPEL SENT TO YOU?

1. In the general commission, which ordains that it be preached to every creature.
2. In the fact that the gospel is preached in our land, the Bible is in every house, and the word is proclaimed in our streets.
3. In the providence which has brought you this day to hear the word. Very specially may you be sent to the preacher, the preacher sent to you, and the special message be sent through the preacher to you.
4. In the peculiar adaptation of it to your case, character, and necessity. A medicine which suits your disease is evidently meant for you.

5. In the power which has attended it, while you have been hearing it, though you may have resisted that power.

It would be a sad thing if we had to single out even one, and say, "This word is *not* sent to you;" but we are under no such painful necessity.

III. IN WHAT POSITION DOES IT PLACE YOU?

In a position:

1. Of singular favor. Prophets and kings died without hearing what you hear (Matt. 13:16).
2. Of notable indebtedness to martyrs and men of God, in past ages, and in these days; for these have lived and died to bring you the gospel.
3. Of great hopefulness; for we trust you will accept it and live.
4. Of serious responsibility; for if you neglect it, how will you escape (Heb. 2:3)?

It puts it out of your power to remain unaffected by the gospel It must either save you, or increase your condemnation.

IV. IN WHAT MANNER WILL YOU TREAT THIS WORD?

1. Will you decidedly and honestly refuse it? This would be a terrible determination; but the very idea of so doing might startle you into a better mind.
2. Will you basely and foolishly delay your reply? This is a very dangerous course, and many perish in it.
3. Will you play the hypocrite, and pretend to receive it, while in your heart you reject it?
4. Will you act the part of the temporary convert?
5. Will you not rather accept the word of salvation with delight?

Suppose the gospel should be taken from you by your removal to a place where it is not preached, or by the death of the minister whom you so greatly esteem. It would be just. It may happen. It has happened to others Refuse the heavenly message no longer, lest your day of grace should end in an eternity of woe.

Personalities

A minister having to preach in the city jail, was accompanied by a young man of fine mind and cultivated manners, but who was not a Christian. As the minister looked at the audience, he preached to them Jesus with so much earnestness as deeply to impress his companion. On their return home, the young man said, "The men to whom you preached today must have been moved by the utterance of such truth. Such preaching cannot fail to influence." "My dear young friend," answered the minister, "were *you* influenced? Were you impelled by the words you heard today to choose God as your portion?" "You were not preaching to me, but to your convicts," was the quick reply. "You mistake. I was preaching to you as much as to them. You need the same Savior as they. For all there is but one way of salvation. Just as much for you as for these poor prisoners was the message of this afternoon. Will you heed it?" The word so faithfully spoken was blessed of God.

Jesus said, "Preach the gospel to every creature." I can imagine Peter was asking him: "What, Lord! Shall we offer salvation to the men who crucified you?" And I can imagine Jesus answering him: "Yes, Peter, I want you to preach my gospel to everybody, beginning at Jerusalem. Proclaim salvation to the men who crucified me. Peter, I'd like you to find that man who put the crown of thorns on my head. Tell him, if he'll take salvation as a gift he shall have a crown of glory from me, and there shan't be a thorn in it. Look up that Roman soldier who thrust that spear into my side, to my very heart, and tell him that there's a nearer way to my heart than that. My heart is full of love for his soul. Proclaim salvation to him." —*D. L. Moody*

To whom is it that the God of salvation sent "the word of salvation"? He sent it to all sinners that hear it. It is a word that suits the case of sinners; and therefore is it sent to them. If it be inquired, for what *purpose* is it sent to sinners?. . . It is sent as a word of *pardon* to the condemned sinner. Hence may every condemned sinner take hold of it, saying, This word is sent to me. It is sent as a word of *peace* to the rebellious sinner. It is sent as a word of *life* to the dead. It is a word of *liberty* to the captives, of *healing* for the diseased, of *cleansing* to the polluted. It is a word of *direction* to the bewildered, and of *refreshment* to the weary. It is sent as a *comforting* word to the disconsolate; and as a *drawing word* and a *strengthening* word to the soul destitute of strength. It is sent, in short, as a *word of salvation*, and *all sorts* of salvation and redemption to the lost soul, saying, "Christ came to seek and to save that which was lost." —*Condensed from Ralph Erskine*

193

And many that believed came, and confessed, and showed their deeds. Many of them also which used curious arts brought their books together and burned them before all men: and they counted the price of them, and found it fifty thousand pieces of silver. So mightily grew the word of God and prevailed.

—*Acts 19:18–20*

 HIS last verse is a despatch from the seat of war announcing a glorious victory for the royal arms.

Past triumphs of the gospel may be used as encouragements.

We, too, shall see the Word of God grow and prevail, for:

- The gospel is the same as ever.
- The human race is unchanged at heart.
- The sins to be overcome are the same.
- The Holy Spirit is just as mighty to convince and renew.

The trophies of victory may be expected to be the same.

Men, magic, books, and the love of money shall all be subdued.

Let us turn aside to see:

I. THE WORD OF GOD PLANTED.

Planted it was, or it could not have grown.

The work proceeded in the following fashion:

1. Certain disciples were further enlightened, aroused, and led to seek a higher degree of grace. This was an admirable beginning, and revivals thus commenced are usually lasting.
2. These became obedient to an ordinance which had been overlooked (verse 5), and also received the Holy Ghost, of whom they had heard nothing: two great helps to revival.
3. A bold ministry proclaimed and defended the truth.
4. Opposition was aroused. This is always a needful sign. God is not at work long without the devil working also.
5. Deceitful counterfeiting commenced, and was speedily ended in the most remarkable manner.
6. Paul preached, pleaded, made the gospel to sound forth, and on departing could say, "I am pure from the blood of all men."

Read this and the following chapter, and see how three years were well spent in planting the church at Ephesus.

II. THE WORD OF GOD GROWING.

"So mightily grew the word of God." The measure of it was seen:

1. In a church formed with many suitable elders.
2. In a neighborhood fully aware of the presence of the gospel among them. It touched them practically, so much so, that important trades were affected.
3. In a people converted, and openly confessing their conversion.
4. In a general respect paid to the faith. Even those who did not obey it, yet yielded it homage and owned its power.

Here we see Paul's work and God's work. Paul labored diligently in planting, and God made it to grow, yet it was all of God.

Is the word of God growing among us? If not, why not?

- It is a living seed, and should grow.
- It is a living seed, and will grow unless we hinder it.

III. THE WORD OF GOD PREVAILING.

Growth arouses opposition; but where the word grows with inward vitality it prevails over outward opposition.

The particular proof of prevalence here given is the burning of magical books.

1. Paul does not appear to have dwelt continually upon the evil habit of using magical arts; but gospel light showed the guilt of witchcraft, and providence cast contempt on it.
2. The sin being exposed, it was confessed by those who had been guilty of it, and by those who had commenced its study.
3. Being confessed, it was renounced altogether, and, though there was no command to that effect, yet in a voluntary zeal of indignation the books were burned. This was right because:
   - If sold, they would do harm.
   - They were so detestable that they deserved burning.
   - Their public burning lighted up a testimony.
4. Their destruction involved expense, which was willingly incurred, and that expense gave weight to the testimony.

No other proof of power in our ministry will equal that which is seen in its practical effect upon our hearers' lives.

Will you who attend our preaching see to it that you purge yourselves from all filthiness of the flesh and of the spirit?

Sparks

It's a blessed time in a soul, it's a blessed time in a family, it's a blessed time in a congregation, it's a blessed time in a country—when the word of God grows mightily and prevails.... It's a blessed time when open sinners are seen leaving their sins and seeking the Savior; when men are seen giving up their unholy gains; when tavern-keepers take down their signs and burn them—when they give up their licenses; and it's a blessed time when card-players throw away their cards and take the Bible instead. It's a blessed time when the lovers of gaudy dress take their gaudy dresses and destroy them. —*Robert Murray McCheyne*

The gospel, like a plant of great vigor, will grow almost among stones. Thus have I seen it to grow among hypocrites, formalists, and worldlings; and I have seen it laying hold of one, and another, and indeed of many, however untoward the surrounding soil "So mightily grew the word of God and prevailed."

When the leaven of the gospel begins to work, there will be no need of a train of arguments to prove how inexpedient, how utterly unworthy it is for a Christian to turn aside after the vain amusements and trifling books used by the world: "Ephraim shall say, What have I to do any more with idols?" What have I to do with black arts, or dealing with a lie? Those who first trusted in Christ were willing to forsake all and follow him. The grace of the gospel produces a new taste—it alters everything about us—our friends, our pursuits, our books, etc. —*Richard Cecil*

Agesilaus, when he saw the usurer's bonds and bills blazing in the fire, said, "I never saw a better or a brighter fire in all my life!" and it were heartily to be wished that all scandalous, blasphemous, and seditious books and pamphlets were on the fire, too. —*John Spencer*

Yes, God blessed the self-denial, and gave them compensation and a compensation, too, remarkably appropriate. They who burned books, obtained books. They burned books for Christ, and they received books from him. Have you never heard of Paul's Epistle to the Ephesians? Do you recollect no such letter as one from the Savior "to the Angel of the church at Ephesus"? —*T. R. Stevenson*

The Earl of Rochester, of whom it has been said that he was "a great wit, a great scholar, a great poet, a great sinner, and a great penitent," left a strict charge to the person in whose custody his papers were, to burn all his profane and lewd writings, as being only fit to promote vice and immorality, by which he had so highly offended God, and shamed and blasphemed the holy religion into which he had been baptized.

194

"Saul, Saul, why persecutest thou me? It is hard for thee to kick against the pricks."

—Acts 26:14

JESUS even out of heaven speaks in parables, according to his wont. To Paul he briefly utters the parable of the rebellious ox.

Note the tenderness of the appeal: it is not, "Thou art harming me by thy persecutions," but, "Thou art wounding thyself." He saith not, "it is hard for *me*," but "hard for *thee*."

May the Lord thus speak in pity to those who are now resisting his grace, and thus save them from wounding themselves.

Listen attentively to the simple comparison, and observe:

I. **THE OX.** A fallen man deserves no higher type.

1. You are acting like a brute beast, in ignorance and passion. You are unspiritual, thoughtless, unreasonable.
2. Yet God values you more than a man does an ox.
3. Therefore he feeds you, and does not slay you.
4. You are useless without guidance, and yet you are unwilling to submit to your Master's hand.

5. If you were but obedient you might be useful, and might find content in your service.

6. You have no escape from the choice of either to obey or to die, and it is useless to be stubborn.

II. THE OX-GOAD. You have driven the Lord to treat you as the husbandman treats a stubborn ox.

1. The Lord has tried you with gentle means, a word, a pull of the rein, etc.: by parental love, by tender admonitions of friends and teachers, and by the gentle promptings of his Spirit.

2. Now he uses the more severe means:
   - Of solemn threatening by his law.
   - Of terrors of conscience and dread of judgment.
   - Of loss of relatives, children, friends.
   - Of sickness, and varied afflictions.
   - Of approaching death, with a dark future beyond it.

3. You are feeling some of these pricks, and cannot deny that they are sharp. Take heed lest worse things come upon you.

III. THE KICKS AGAINST THE GOAD. These are given in various ways by those who are resolved to continue in sin.

1. There are early childish rebellions against restraint.
2. There are sneers at the gospel, at ministers, at holy things.
3. There are willful sins against conscience and light.
4. There are revilings and persecutions against God's people.
5. There are questionings, infidelities, and blasphemies.

IV. THE HARDNESS OF ALL THIS TO THE OX. It hurts itself against the goad, and suffers far more than the driver designs.

1. In the present. You are unhappy: you are full of unrest and alarm, you are increasing your chastisement, and fretting your heart.

2. In the best possible future. You will feel bitter regrets, have desperate habits to overcome, and much evil to undo. All this if you do at last repent and obey.

3. In the more probable future. You are preparing for yourself increased hardness of heart, despair, and destruction.

Oh, that you would know that no possible good can come of kicking against God, who grieves over your infatuations!

Yield to the discipline of your God.

He pities you now, and begs you to consider your ways.

It is Jesus who speaks; be not so brutish as to refuse him that speaks from heaven.

You may yet, like Saul of Tarsus, become grandly useful, and plow many a field for the Lord Jesus.

Striking Thoughts

Did not Lord Byron feel the sharpness of the goad when he exclaimed, concerning the gospel, "The worst of it is, I believe it"?

You have heard of the swordfish. It is a very curious creature, with a long and bony beak, or sword, projecting in front of its head. It is also very fierce, attacking other fishes that come in its way, and tries to pierce them with its sword. The fish has sometimes been known to dart at a ship in full sail, with such violence as to pierce the solid timbers. But what has happened? The silly fish has been killed outright by the force of its own blow. The ship sails on just as before, and the angry sword-fish falls a victim to its own rage. But how shall we describe the folly of those who, like Saul of Tarsus, oppose the cause of Christ? They cannot succeed: like the sword-fish, they only work their own destruction. —*Illustrative Teaching*

Dr. John Hall, in one of his sermons, compared the attacks of infidelity upon Christianity to a serpent gnawing at a file. As he kept on gnawing, he was greatly encouraged by the sight of the growing pile of chips; till feeling pain, and seeing blood, he found that he had been wearing his own teeth away against the file, but the file was unharmed.

> Oh cursed, cursed Sin! Traitor to God,
> And ruiner of man! Mother of Woe,
> And Death, and Hell!
> —*Pollok*

Cowper describes Voltaire as "An infidel in health, but what when sick? Oh, then a text would touch him at the quick."

Men complain of their circumstances and cry, "*This* is hard—hard as for the bird of plumage to beat against the wires of its cage." Nay, harder far than that. It is hard for loss of time, for loss of temper, for loss of strength, for loss of trusting, loving obedience. And because no good can come of it, no success can be gained in the vain, Utopian, and worse than foolish struggle. Let every man struggle to improve *himself*; and he will not fail to improve his lot also. But let him never "kick" against his earthly lot; for so, if hurt at all, he hurts himself the more. He "kicks against the pricks." —*Pulpit Commentary*

The Spirit of God can make use of any agency to bring sinners to repentance and faith in the Redeemer. Commenting once upon the words, "The ox knoweth his owner, and the ass his master's crib; but Israel doth not know, my people doth not consider," the speaker sought to impress upon his people how strangely guilty the human heart is, despising the goodness of God, and forgetting his very existence. Three or four days after, a farmer, who had been present, was giving provender to his cattle, when one of his oxen, evidently grateful for his care, fell to licking his bare arm. Instantly, with this simple incident, the Holy Spirit flashed conviction on the farmer's mind. He burst into tears, and exclaimed, "Yes, it is all true. How wonderful is God's word! This poor dumb brute is really more grateful to me than I am to God, and yet I am in debt to him for everything. What a sinner I am!" The lesson had found its way to his heart, and wrought there effectually to lead him to Christ.

195

And the barbarous people showed us no little kindness, for they kindled a fire, and received us every one, because of the present rain, and because of the cold.

—*Acts 28:2*

 ERE was an early Shipwrecked Mariners' Society. Among rough people there is much of genuine kindness.

Let not people of a gentler mold, greater education, and larger possessions come behind them in deeds of kindness.

Their kindness was thoroughly practical. We have too much of "Be ye warmed" and too little kindling of fires.

There may be spiritual as well as physical cold, and for this last the kindling of a fire is needed.

This is our present subject.

I. THAT WE ARE VERY APT TO BE COLD.

1. The world is a cold country for gracious men.
2. By reason of our inbred sin, we are cold subjects, and far too apt to be lukewarm, or frozen.
3. Cold seasons also come, when all around lies bound in frost. Ministers, churches, saints, are too often cold as ice.
4. Cold corners are here and there, where the sun seldom shines. Some good men live in such cold harbors.
5. Chilling influences are now abroad. Modern thought, worldliness, depression in trade, depreciation of prayer, etc.

If we yield to the power of cold, we become first uncomfortable, next inactive, and then ready to die.

II. THAT THERE ARE MEANS OF WARMTH.

1. The Word of God is as a fire. Heard or read, it tends to warm the heart.
2. Private, social, and family prayer. This is as coals of juniper.
3. Meditation and communion with Jesus. "While I was musing the fire burned" (Ps. 39:3). "Did not our heart burn within us, while he talked with us by the way?" (Luke 24:32).
4. Fellowship with other Christians (Mal. 3:16).
5. Doing good to others. Job prayed for his friends, and then his captivity was turned (Job 42:10).
6. Returning to first love and doing first works, would bring back old warmth (Rev. 2:4–5).

Let us get to these fires ourselves, lest we be frost-bitten and benumbed.

III. THAT WE SHOULD KINDLE FIRES FOR OTHERS.

We need the fire of revival, seeing so many are washed upon our shores in dying circumstances.

Concerning a true revival, let it be remembered that it both resembles the fire in the text, and differs from it.

1. It must be lighted under difficulties—"because of the present rain." The sticks are wet, the hearth is flooded, the atmosphere is damp. It is not easy to make a fire in such circumstances, and yet it must be done.
2. The fire we need cannot, however, be kindled by barbarians: the flame must come from above.
3. Once get the flame, the fire begins with littlest. Small sticks are good for kindling.
4. It is well to nourish the flame by going down on your knees, and breathing upon it by warm and hearty supplications.
5. It must be fed with fuel. Think of the great Paul picking up a bundle of sticks. Let each one bring his share.
6. This fire must be kindled for "every one." We must not be content till all the shivering ones are comforted.
7. The fire will be of great service, and yet it may warm into life more than one viper. Thank God, the fire which revived the creature into venomous life will also destroy it.

What can we each do towards this fire? Can we not each one either kindle or feed the fire? Bring a stick.

Let no one damp the flame.

Let us pray.

Kindling

How to maintain spiritual warmth. Philip Henry's advice to his daughter was, "If you would keep warm in this cold season (January, 1692), take these four directions: (1) Get into the sun. Under his blessed beams there are warmth and comfort. (2) Go near the fire. 'Is not my word like a fire?' How many cheering passages are there! (3) Keep in motion and action—stirring up the grace and gift of God that is in you. 4. Seek Christian communion. 'How can one be warm alone?'" —*Feathers for Arrows*

"Ane stick'll never burn! Put more wood on the fire, laddie; ane stick'll never burn!" my old Scotch grandfather used to say to his boys. Sometimes, when the fire in the heart burns low, and love to the Savior grows faint, it would grow warm and bright again, if it could only touch another stick. What we need, next to earnest prayer to God and communion with Christ, is communion with each other. "Where two or three are gathered together," the heart burns; love kindles to a fervent heat. Friends, let us frequent the society of those who are fellow-pilgrims with us to Canaan's happy land. "Ane stick'll never burn," as a great generous pile will be sure to. —*Anonymous*

I will tell you a story, which I have from very good hands, of two very eminent men, both for learning and piety, in the beginning of the last century, one of them a great prelate (indeed, a primate), and the other a Churchman of great note. These two eminent men often met together to consult upon the interests of learning and the affairs of the church; and when they had dispatched that business, they seldom parted from one another without such an encounter as this. "Come, good doctor," saith the bishop, "let us talk now a little of Jesus Christ;" or, on the other side, said the doctor, "Come, my lord, let me hear your Grace talk of the goodness of God with your wonted eloquence; let us warm one another's hearts with heaven, that we may better bear this cold world." Here is now an example of holy conference without a preface and yet without exception; a precedent easy to imitate wherever there is a like spirit of piety. A few such men would put profaneness out of countenance, and turn the tide of conversation. —*Goodman*

> See how great a flame aspires,
> Kindled by a spark of grace!
> Jesus' love the nations fires,
> Sets the kingdoms in a blaze:
> To bring fire on earth he came,
> Kindled in some hearts it is:
> Oh that all might catch the flame,
> All partake the glorious bliss!
> —*C. Wesley*

196

Or despisest thou the riches of his goodness and forbearance and longsuffering; not knowing that the goodness of God leadeth thee to repentance?

—*Romans 2:4*

 T is an instance of divine condescension that the Lord reasons with men and asks this question and others like it (Isa. 1:5; 55:2; Jer. 3:4; Ezek. 33:11).

God not only acts kindly to sinners, but when they misuse his kindness, he labors to set them right (Isa. 1:18; Hosea 11:8).

It is a sad thing that any who have seen God's judgments on others and have escaped themselves should draw from this special mercy a reason for adding sin to sin (Jer. 3: 8).

From the Lord's earnest question, let us learn wisdom.

I. LET US HONOR THE LORD'S GOODNESS AND FORBEARANCE.

A reverent sense of it will be a sure safeguard against despising it.

1. It is manifested to us in a threefold form:
   * Goodness which has borne with past sin (Ps. 78:38).
   * Forbearance which bears with us in the present (Ps. 103:10).
   * Long-suffering which, in the future as in the past and the present, is prepared to bear with the guilty (Luke 13:7–9).
2. It is manifested in great abundance: "riches of his goodness."
   * Riches of mercies bestowed, temporal and spiritual (Ps. 68:19).
   * Riches of kindness seen in gracious deliverance, measured by evils averted which might have befallen us, such as sickness, poverty, insanity, death, and hell (Ps. 86:13).
   * Riches of grace promised and provided for all needs.
3. It is manifested in its excellence by four considerations:
   * The person who shows it. It is "the goodness *of God*" who is omniscient to see sin, just to hate it, powerful to punish it, yet patient towards the sinner (Ps. 145:8).
   * The being who receives it. It is dealt out to man, a guilty, insignificant, base, provoking, ungrateful being (Gen. 6:6).
   * The conduct to which it is a reply. It is love's response to sin. Often God forbears, though sins are many, wanton, aggravated, daring, repeated (Mal. 3:6).
   * The boons which it brings. Life, daily bread, health, gospel, Holy Spirit, new birth, hope of heaven (Ps. 68:19).
4. It has been in a measure manifested to you. "Despisest *thou*?"

II. LET US CONSIDER HOW IT MAY BE DESPISED.

1. By allowing it to remain unnoticed, ungratefully passing it over.
2. By claiming it as our due and talking as if God were bound to bear with us.
3. By opposing its design and refusing to repent (Prov. 1:24–25).
4. By perverting it into a reason for hardness of heart, presumption, infidelity, and further sin (Zeph. 1:12; Eccles. 8:11).
5. By urging it as an apology for procrastination (2 Pet. 3:3–4).

III. LET US FEEL THE FORCE OF ITS LEADINGS.

The forbearance of God should lead us to repentance.

For we should argue thus:

1. He is not hard and unloving, or he would not have spared us.
2. His great patience deserves recognition at our hands. We are bound to respond to it in a generous spirit.
3. To go on to offend would be cruel to him and disgraceful to ourselves. Nothing can be baser than to make forbearance a reason for provocation.
4. It is evident from his forbearance that he will rejoice to accept us if we will turn to him. He spares that he may save.
5. He has dealt with each one personally, and by this means he is able to put it, as in the text, "God leadeth *thee* to repentance." He calls us individually to himself. Let each one personally remember his own experience of sparing mercies.
6. The means are so gentle; let us yield to them cheerfully. Those who might refuse to be driven should consent to be drawn.
   - O sinner, each gift of *goodness* draws thee to Jesus!
   - *Forbearance* would fain weep thee to Jesus!
   - *Long-suffering* waits and woos thee to Jesus!

Wilt thou not turn from sin and return unto thy God, or "despisest thou the riches of his goodness?"

Arguments

Here is a select variety of admirable words, where the critics tell us that the first word signifies the infinite goodness and generosity of the divine nature, whereby he is inclined to do good to his creatures, to pity and relieve. The second expresses his offers of mercy upon repentance, and the notices and warnings sinners have to amend. The third is his bearing the manners of bold sinners, waiting long for their reformation, and from year to year deferring to give the final stroke of vengeance. In what an apt opposition do *riches* of Divine *goodness*, and *treasures of wrath* to come, stand to one another! —*Anthony Blackwall.*

The forbearance and longsuffering of God towards sinners is truly aston-ishing. He was longer destroying Jericho than in creating the world. —*Benjamin Beddome*

According to the proverb of the Jews, "Michael flies but with one wing, and Gabriel with two," God is quick in sending angels of peace, and they fly apace; but the messengers of wrath come slowly. God is more hasty to glorify his servants than to condemn the wicked. —*Jeremy Taylor*

It is observable that the Roman magistrates, when they gave sentence upon any one to be scourged, a bundle of rods tied hard with many knots was laid before them. The reason was this: that whilst the beadle, or flagellifer, was untying the knots, which he was to do in a certain order and not in any other hasty or sudden way, the magistrate might see the deportment and carriage of the delinquent, whether he were sorry for his fault and showed any hope of amendment, that then he might recall his sentence or mitigate the punishment; otherwise he was to be corrected the more severely. Thus God in the punishment of sinners, how patient is he! how loath to strike! how slow to anger if there be but any hopes of recovery! How many knots doth he untie! How many rubs doth he make in his way to justice! He doth not try us by martial law, but pleads the case with us, "Why will ye die, O house of Israel?" And all this to see whether the poor sinner will throw himself down at his feet, whether he will come in and make his peace and be saved. —*Thomas Fuller*

To sin against law is daring, but to sin against love is dastardly. To rebel against justice is inexcusable, but to fight against mercy is abominable. He who can sting the hand which nourishes him is nothing less than a viper. When a dog bites his own master and bites him when he is feeding him and fondling him, no one will wonder if his owner becomes his executioner.

197

Jesus our Lord.
—*Romans 4:24*

 T is the part of faith to accept great contrasts, if laid down in the word, and to make them a part of her daily speech.

This name, Lord, is a great contrast to incarnation and humiliation.

In the manger, in poverty, shame, and death, Jesus was still Lord.

These strange conditions for "our Lord" to be found in are no difficulties to that faith which is the fruit of the Spirit.

For she sees in the death of Jesus a choice reason for his being our Lord (Phil. 2:7–11). "Wherefore God hath highly exalted him."

She delights in that lordship as the fruit of resurrection; but there could have been no resurrection without death.(Acts 2: 32–36).

She hears the voice of Jehovah behind all the opposition endured by Jesus proclaiming him Lord of all (Ps. 2:110).

It never happens that our faith in Jesus for salvation makes us less reverently behold in him the Lord of all. He is "Jesus" and also "our Lord." "Born a child and yet a King." "My Beloved," and yet "my Lord and my God."

Our simple trust in him, our familiar love to him, our bold approaches to him in prayer, our near and dear communion with him, and most of all, our marriage union with him, still leave him "our Lord."

I. HIS TENDER CONDESCENSIONS ENDEAR THE TITLE. "Jesus our Lord" is a very sweet name to a believer's heart.

1. We claim to render it to him specially as man, "who was delivered for our offenses, and was raised again for our justification" (verse 25). As Jesus of Nazareth, he is Lord.
2. We acknowledge him as Lord the more fully and unreservedly because he loved us and gave himself for us.
3. In all the privileges accorded to us in him, he is Lord:
   - In our salvation, we have "received Christ Jesus the Lord" (Col. 2: 6).
   - In entering the church, we find him the Head of the body, to whom all are subject (Eph. 5: 23).
   - In our lifework, he is Lord. "We live unto the Lord" (Rom. 14:8). We glorify God in his name (Eph. 5:20).
   - In resurrection, he is the firstborn from the dead (Col. 1:18).
   - At the Advent, his appearing will be the chief glory (Titus 2:13).
   - In eternal glory, he is worshipped forever (Rev. 5:12–13).
4. In our dearest fellowship at the table, he is "Jesus our Lord."
   It is the Lord's Table, the Lord's Supper, the cup of the Lord, the body and blood of the Lord; and our object is to show the Lord's death (1 Cor. 11:20, 26–27, 29).

II. OUR LOVING HEARTS READ THE TITLE WITH PECULIAR EMPHASIS.

1. We yield it to him only. Moses is a servant, but Jesus alone is Lord. "One is your Master " (Matt. 23:8, 10).
2. To him most willingly. Ours is delighted homage.
3. To him unreservedly. We wish our obedience to be perfect.
4. To him in all matters of lawmaking and truth-teaching. He is Master and Lord: his word decides practice and doctrine.

5. To him in all matters of administration in the church and in providence. "It is the Lord, let him do what seemeth him good" (1 Sam. 3:18).

6. To him trustfully, feeling that he will act a lord's part right well. No king can be so wise, good, great as he (Job 1:21).

7. To him for ever. He reigns in the church without successor. Now, as in the first days, we call him Master and Lord (Heb. 7:3).

III. WE FIND MUCH SWEETNESS IN THE WORD "OUR."

1. It makes us remember our personal interest in the Lord.
Each believer uses this title in the singular and calls him from his heart, "My Lord."
   - David wrote, "Jehovah said unto my Lord."
   - Elizabeth spoke of "the mother of my Lord."
   - Magdalene said, "They have taken away my Lord."
   - Thomas said, "My Lord and my God."
   - Paul wrote, "The knowledge of Christ Jesus my Lord."

2. It brings a host of brethren before our minds, for it is in union with them that we say "our Lord." And so it makes us remember each other (Eph. 3:14–15).

3. It fosters unity and creates a holy clanship as we all rally around our "one Lord." Saints of all ages are one in this.

4. His example as Lord fosters practical love. Remember the footwashing and his words on that occasion (John 13:14).

5. Our zeal to make him Lord forbids all self-exaltation. "Be not ye called Rabbi: for one is your Master, even Christ. Neither be ye called masters" (Matt. 23:8, 10).

6. His position as Lord reminds us of the confidence of the church in doing his work. "All power is given unto me in heaven and in earth. Go ye therefore, and teach," etc. (Matt. 28:18–19). "The Lord working with them" (Mark 16:20).

7. Our common joy in Jesus as our Lord becomes an evidence of grace and, thus, of union with each other (1 Cor. 12:3).

Let us worship Jesus as our Lord and God.

Let us imitate him, copying our Lord's humility and love.

Let us serve him, obeying his every command.

Gems

It ought to be the great care of every one of us to follow the Lord fully. We must in a course of obedience to God's will and service to his honor follow him universally, without dividing; uprightly, without dissembling; cheerfully, without disputing; and constantly, without declining: and this is following him fully.
—*Matthew Henry*

A disciple of Christ is one that gives up himself to be wholly at Christ's disposing; to learn what he teaches, to believe what he reveals, to do what he commands, to avoid what he forbids, to suffer what is inflicted by him or for him, in expectation of that reward which he hath promised. Such a one is a disciple of Christ, and he, and none else, is a Christian. —*David Clarkson*

It was thought a wondrous act of condescension when King George III visited the tent of the dying gypsy woman in Windsor forest and entered into religious conversation with her. What shall we think of him, who, though he was the King of glory, came down to us, and took our sins and sorrows upon himself, that he might bring us into fellowship with himself for ever?

A little child, hearing others speak of the Lord Jesus, asked, "Father, was it *our* Jesus?" In the same sweet simplicity of faith, let us speak of "Jesus *our* Lord."

Some years ago, an aged minister, who had long and lovingly known Christ, was on his deathbed. Memory had gone. In relation to those he loved best, it was a perfect blank. But someone whispered in his ear, "Brother, do you know Jesus Christ?" With a voice of rapture, he exclaimed,

> "Jesus, my Lord! I know his name;
> His name is all my trust;
> Nor will he put my hope to shame,
> Nor let my soul be lost."

198

Likewise reckon ye also yourselves to be dead indeed unto sin, but alive unto God through Jesus Christ our Lord. Let not sin therefore reign in your mortal body, that ye should obey it in the lusts thereof.

—*Romans 6:11–12*

How intimately the believer's duties are interwoven with his privileges! Because he is alive unto God, he is to renounce sin, since that corrupt thing belongs to his estate of death.

How intimately both his duties and his privileges are bound up with Christ Jesus his Lord!

How thoughtful ought we to be upon these matters, *reckoning* what is right and fit and carrying out that reckoning to its practical issues.

We have in our text:

I. A GREAT FACT TO BE RECKONED UPON. "Likewise reckon ye also yourselves to be dead indeed unto sin, but alive unto God through Jesus Christ our Lord."

1. We are dead with Christ to sin by having borne the punishment in him. In Christ we have endured the death penalty and are regarded as dead by the law (verses 6 and 7).
2. We are risen with him into a justified condition and have reached a new life (verse 8).
3. We can no more come under sin again than he can (verse 9).
4. We are therefore forever dead to its guilt and reigning power: "Sin shall not have dominion over you" (verses. 12–14).

This reckoning is based on truth, or we should not be exhorted to it.

To reckon yourself to be dead to sin so that you boast that you do not sin at all would be a reckoning based on falsehood and would be exceedingly mischievous. "There is no man that sinneth not" (1 Kings 8:46; 1 John 1:8). None are so provoking to God as sinners who boast their own fancied perfection.

The reckoning that we do not sin must either go upon the Antinomian theory that sin in the believer is no sin, which is a shocking notion.

Or else our conscience must tell us that we do sin in many ways: in omission or commission, in transgression or shortcoming, in temper or in spirit (James 3:2; Eccles. 7:20; Rom. 3:23).

To reckon yourself dead to sin in the scriptural sense is full of benefit both to heart and life. Be a ready reckoner in this fashion.

II. A GREAT LESSON TO BE PUT IN PRACTICE. "Let not sin therefore reign in your mortal body, that ye should obey it in the lusts thereof."

1. Sin has great power. It is in you and will strive to reign.
   - It remains as an outlaw, hiding away in your nature.
   - It remains as a plotter, planning your overthrow.
   - It remains as an enemy, warring against the law of your mind.
   - It remains as a tyrant, worrying and oppressing the true life.
2. Its field of battle is the body.
   - Its wants—hunger, thirst, cold, etc.—may become occasions of sin by leading to murmuring, envy, covetousness, robbery.
   - Its appetites may crave excessive indulgence and, unless continually curbed, will easily lead to evil.
   - Its pains and infirmities, through engendering impatience and other faults, may produce sin.
   - Its pleasures, also, can readily become incitements to sin.
   - Its influence upon the mind and spirit may drag our noble nature down to the groveling materialism of earth.

3. The body is *mortal*, and we shall be completely delivered from sin when set free from our present material frame, if indeed grace reigns within. Till then, we shall find sin lurking in one member or another of "this vile body."

4. Meanwhile, we must not let it reign.

   - If it reigned over us, it would be our god. It would prove us to be under death and not alive unto God.
   - It would cause us unbounded pain and injury if it ruled only for a moment.

Sin is within us, aiming at dominion. This knowledge, together with the fact that we are nevertheless alive unto God, should:

- Help our peace, for we perceive that men may be truly the Lord's, even though sin struggles within them.
- Aid our caution, for our divine life is well worth preserving and needs to be guarded with constant care.
- Draw us to use the means of grace, since in these the Lord meets with us and refreshes our new life.

Let us come to the Table of Communion, and to all other ordinances, as alive unto God. In that manner, let us feed on Christ.

Instructive Words

In the fourth century, when the Christian faith was preached in its power in Egypt, a young brother sought out the great Macarius. "Father," said he, "what is the meaning of being dead and buried with Christ?"

"My son," answered Macarius, "you remember our dear brother who died and was buried a short time since? Go now to his grave, and tell him all the unkind things that you ever heard of him and that we are glad he is dead and thankful to be rid of him, for he was such a worry to us and caused so much discomfort in the church. Go, my son, and say that, and hear what he will answer."

The young man was surprised and doubted whether he really understood; but Macarius only said, "Do as I bid you, my son, and come and tell me what our departed brother says."

The young man did as he was commanded and returned.

"Well, and what did our brother say?" asked Macarius.

"Say, father!" he exclaimed. "How could he say anything? He is dead."

"Go now again, my son, and repeat every kind and flattering thing you have ever heard of him. Tell him how much we miss him, how great a saint he was, what noble work he did, how the whole church depended upon him, and come again and tell me what he says."

The young man began to see the lesson Macarius would teach him. He went again to the grave and addressed many flattering things to the dead man, and then returned to Macarius.

"He answers *nothing*, father. He is dead and buried."

"You know now, my son," said the old father, "what it is to be dead with Christ. Praise and blame equally are nothing to him who is really dead and buried with Christ." —*Anonymous*

Though the lowest believer be above the power of sin, yet the highest believer is not above the presence of sin. Sin never ruins but where it reigns. It is not *destroying* where it is *disturbing*. The more evil it receives from us, the less evil it does to us. —*William Secker*

Sin may rebel, but it shall never reign in a saint. It fareth with sin in the regenerate as with those beasts that Daniel speaks of "that had their dominion taken away, yet their lives were prolonged for a season and a time." —*Thomas Brooks*

Men must not suffer a single sin to survive. If Saul had destroyed all the Amalekites, no Amalekite would have lived to destroy him. —*David Roland*

199

And if children, then heirs; heirs of God, and joint-heirs with Christ; if so be that we suffer with him, that we may be also glorified together.

—*Romans 8:17*

HIS chapter is like the Garden of Eden, which had in it all manner of delights. If one were shut up to preach only from the eighth of Romans, he would have a subject which might last a lifetime. Every line of the chapter serves for a text. It is an inexhaustible mine. Paul sets before us a golden ladder, and from every step he climbs to something yet higher: from sonship, he rises to heirship and from heirship to joint-heirship with the Lord Jesus.

I. THE GROUND OF HEIRSHIP. "If children, then heirs."

1. It does not follow from ordinary creation. It is not written "if creatures, then heirs."
2. Neither is it found in natural descent. It is not written "if children of Abraham, then heirs" (Rom. 9:7–13).
3. Nor can it come by meritorious service. It is not written "if servants, then heirs" (Gal. 4:30).
4. Nor by ceremonial observances. It is not written "if circumcised or baptized, then heirs" (Rom. 4:9–12).

Our being regenerated or born again unto God by his Holy Spirit is our one ground of heirship.

Let us inquire:

• Have we been born again (John 3:3)?

- Have we the spirit of adoption (Gal. 4:5)?
- Are we fashioned in the likeness of God (Col. 3:10)?
- Have we believed on Jesus (John 1:12)?

II. THE UNIVERSALITY OF THE HEIRSHIP. "Children, then heirs."

1. The principle of priority as to time cannot enter into this question. The elder and the younger in the divine family are equally heirs.
2. The love of God is the same to them all.
3. They are all blessed under the same promise (Heb. 6:17).
4. They are all equally related to that great Firstborn Son through whom their heirship comes to them. He is the Firstborn among many brethren.
5. The inheritance is large enough for them all.

They are not all prophets, preachers, apostles, or even well-instructed and eminent saints. They are not all rich and influential, they are not all strong and useful, but they are all heirs.

Let us, then, all live as such and rejoice in our portion.

III. THE INHERITANCE WHICH IS THE SUBJECT OF HEIRSHIP. "Heirs of God."

Our inheritance is divinely great. We are:

Heirs of all things. "He that overcometh shall inherit all things" (Rev. 21:7). "All things are yours" (1 Cor. 3:21).

- Heirs of salvation (Heb. 1:14).
- Heirs of eternal life (Titus 3:7).
- Heirs of promise (Heb. 6:17).
- Heirs of the grace of life (1 Pet. 3:7).
- Heirs of righteousness (Heb. 11:7).
- Heirs of the kingdom (James 2:5).

Whereas we are said to be "heirs of God," it must mean that we are:

1. Heirs of all that God possesses.
2. Heirs of all that God is: of his love, for God is love. Hence, heirs of all possible good, for God is good.
3. Heirs of God himself. What an infinite portion!
4. Heirs of all that Jesus has and is as God and man.

IV. THE PARTNERSHIP OF THE CLAIMANTS TO HEIRSHIP. "And joint heirs with Christ."

1. This is the test of our heirship. We are not heirs except with Christ, through Christ, and in Christ.
2. This sweetens it all. Fellowship with Jesus is our best portion.
3. This shows the greatness of the inheritance. Worthy of Jesus. Such an inheritance as the Father gives to the well-beloved.

4. This ensures it to us, for Jesus will not lose it. His title deed and ours are one and indivisible.

5. This reveals and endears his love. That he should become a partner with us in all things is love unbounded.

- His taking us into union with himself secures our inheritance.
- His prayer for us attains it.
- His going into heaven before us prepares it.
- His coming again will bring us the full enjoyment of it.

6. This joint heirship binds us faster to Jesus, since we are nothing and have nothing apart from him.

Let us joyfully accept present suffering with Christ, for it is part of the heritage.

Let us believe in the glorification which is sure to follow in due time, and let us anticipate it with immediate rejoicing.

Notes

How God treats men. "He pardons them and receives them into his house, he makes them all children, and all his children are his heirs, and all his heirs are princes, and all his princes are *crowned*." —*John Pulsford*

As a dead man cannot inherit an estate, no more can a dead soul inherit the kingdom of God. —*Salter*

It is not easy to imagine a more cautious, lawyer-like record than the following entry in a MS. book written by the celebrated Lord Eldon: "I was born, *I believe*, on the 4th June, 1751." We may suppose that this hesitating statement refers to the date, and not to the fact, of his birth. Many, however, are just as uncertain about their spiritual birth. It is a grand thing to be able to say, "We know that we have passed from death unto life," even though we may not be able to put a date to it.

As justification is union and communion with Christ in his righteousness; and sanctification is union and communion with Christ in his holiness or his holy character and nature, so, by parity of reasoning, adoption must be held to be union and communion with Christ in his sonship, surely the highest and best union and communion of the three. —*Dr. Candlish*

Inheritance—What is it? The pay of a soldier is not inheritance, neither are the fees of a lawyer, nor of a physician, nor the gains of trade, nor the wages of labor. The rewards of toil or skill, these are earned by the hands that receive them. What is inherited, on the other hand, may be the property of a new-born babe; and so the coronet, won long ago by the stout arm of valor and first blazoned on a battered shield, now stands above the cradle of a wailing infant. —*Dr. Guthrie*

The question lies in that first word "*if*." Can you cast out all uncertainty from that matter by proving your sonship? "*Then*"—ah! then, no doubt remains as to your heirship. No man need question that heaven will be his if he is the Lord's. The inheritance is to be glorified together with Christ. What more could a child desire than to inherit as much as his eldest brother? If we are as favored as Jesus, what more can we be?

200

But they have not all obeyed the gospel. For Esaias saith, Lord, who hath believed our report?

—Romans 10:16

AN is the same disobedient creature under all dispensations. We bemoan his rejection of the gospel, and so did Isaiah, who spoke in the name of the whole company of the prophets.

It is one of the greatest proofs of the depravity of man's heart that he will no more obey the gospel than the law, but disobeys his God, whether he speaks to him in love or in law.

Men will sooner be lost than trust their God.

When any receive the gospel, it is a work of grace: "the arm of the Lord is revealed." But when they refuse it, it is their own sin: "they have not obeyed the gospel."

I. THE GOSPEL COMES TO MEN WITH THE FORCE OF A COMMAND.

It is not optional to men to accept or refuse it at pleasure. "God now commandeth all men every where to repent" (Acts 17:30). He also commands them to repent and believe the gospel (Mark 1: 15).

To refuse to believe is to incur great sin (John 16:8).

There is a death penalty attached to disobedience (Mark 16:16).

It is so put:

1. To secure the honor of God. It is not the offer of an equal to an equal, but of the great God to a condemned sinner.
2. To embolden the proclaimer of it. The minister now speaks boldly with his Master's authority.
3. To remind man of his obligations. Repentance and faith are natural duties from which the gospel does not exonerate a man, although it blesses him by bestowing them upon him.
4. To encourage the humble seeker. He must be at full liberty to believe in Jesus, since he is commanded to do so and threatened if he does not do so.
5. To suggest to men the urgent duty of seeing to their souls' welfare. Suicide, whether of the body or of the soul, is always a great crime. To neglect the great salvation is a grave offense.

The gospel is set forth as a feast, to which men are bound to come under penalty of the King's displeasure (Matt. 22:1–7).

The prodigal was right in returning to his father; and if he was right in doing so, so would each one of us be in doing the same.

II. WHAT, THEN, ARE THE CLAIMS OF THE GOSPEL TO OBEDIENCE?

1. The authority of the sender. Whatever God commands, man is under bonds to do.
2. The motive of the sender. Love shines in the gospel command, and no man should slight infinite love. To refuse to obey the gospel of salvation is an insult to divine love.
3. The great gift of the sender: He has given us his only begotten Son. To refuse Jesus is a high affront to measureless love.
4. The reasonableness of the demand of the sender. Should not men believe their God and trust their Savior?
5. The earnestness of the sender. His whole heart is in the gospel. Note the high position which the scheme of salvation occupies in the esteem of God. Shall we not obey an appeal put before with such energy of compassion?

Ask your own consciences whether you do right to refuse or neglect the gospel of the grace of God.

Ask those who are now saved what they think of their long unbelief.

Do not incur a world of regrets in after years by long delays.

Do not jeopardize your souls by refusing the gospel.

III. WHAT IS THE OBEDIENCE REQUIRED BY THE GOSPEL?

Not mere hearing, crediting, liking, professing, or proclaiming; but a hearty obedience to its command. It claims:

1. Faith in the Lord Jesus Christ.
2. Renunciation of self-righteousness and confession of guilt.
3. Repentance and practical quittance of sin.
4. Discipleship under the Lord Jesus. This means obedience both to his teaching and to his example.
5. Public confession of his name in his own way, namely, by baptism.
   If you refuse to obey the gospel:
   • Your hearts will harden to a deeper unbelief.
   • Others will obtain the blessing which you refuse; and this will deepen your own condemnation (Rom. 10:19).
   • You will die in your sins with your blood on your own heads.

Enforcements

A powerful argument to prove the enmity of man's heart against God is the unsuccessfulness of the gospel, which can be resolvable into nothing else but such an enmity. The design of the gospel is to bring us into a union with the Son of God and to believe on him whom the Father hath sent. Christ seeks to gather in souls to God, but they will not be gathered. This is matter of fearful consideration, that when God is calling after men by his own Son, there be so few that will come to him. How few there are that say, "Give me Christ, or I am lost!

None can reconcile me to God, but Christ!" You are daily besought in Christ's stead to be reconciled, but in vain! What does this signify but obstinate, invincible enmity? —*John Howe*

"All God's biddings are enablings," says an old writer.

Obedience is faith incarnate.

To disobey the gospel is far worse than to break the law. For disobedience to the law, there is a remedy in the gospel, but for disobedience to the gospel no remedy can be found. "There remaineth no more sacrifice for sins."

It is reported of the old kings of Peru that they were wont to use a tassel or fringe made of red wool, which they wore upon their heads. When they sent any governor to rule as viceroy in any part of their country, they delivered unto him one of the threads of their tassel, and, for one of those simple threads, he was as much obeyed as if he had been the king himself—yea, it hath so happened that the king hath sent a governor only with this thread to slay men and women of a whole province without any further commission; for of such power and authority was the king's tassel with them, that they willingly submitted thereunto, even at the sight of one thread of it. Now, it is to be hoped that if one thread shall be so forcible to draw heathen obedience, there will be no need of cart-ropes to haul on that which is Christian. Exemplary was that obedience of the Romans which was said to have come abroad to all men. And certainly gospel obedience is a grace of much worth and of great force upon the whole man; for when it is once wrought in the heart, it worketh a conformity to all God's will. Be it for life or death, one word from God will command the whole soul as soon as obedience hath found admittance into the heart." —*Spencer's Things New and Old*

201

Rejoice with them that do rejoice.
—*Romans 12:15*

 T is supposed that some are rejoicing, and this is a happy supposition. You are invited to sympathize with them, and this is a happy duty.

Sympathy is a duty of our common humanity, but far more of our regenerated manhood. Those who are one in the higher life should show their holy unity by true fellow feeling.

Joyful sympathy is doubly due when the joy is spiritual and eternal.

I invite you to this joy because of those who have lately been brought to Jesus and are now to be added to the church. The occasion is joyous. Let the joy spread all around.

I. REJOICE WITH THE CONVERTS.

1. Some delivered from lives of grievous sin. All saved from that which would have ruined them eternally, but certain of them from faults which injure men in society.
2. Some of them rescued from agonizing fear and deep despair. Could you have seen them under conviction, you would indeed rejoice to behold them free and happy.
3. Some of them have been brought into great peace and joy. The blissful experience of their first love should charm us into sympathetic delight.
4. Some of them are aged. These are called at the eleventh hour. Rejoice that they are saved from imminent peril.
5. Some of them are young with years of happy service before them.
6. Each case is special. In some we think of what they would have been and in others of what they will be.

There is great gladness in these newborn ones, and shall we be indifferent? Let us welcome them with hearty joy.

II. REJOICE WITH THEIR FRIENDS.

1. Some have prayed long for them, and now their prayers are heard.
2. Some have been very anxious, have seen much to mourn over in the past, and feared much of evil in the future.
3. Some are relatives with a peculiar interest in these saved ones, parents, children, brothers, etc.
4. Some are expecting, and in certain cases already receiving, much comfort from these newly saved ones. They have already brightened family circles and made heavy hearts glad.

Holy parents have no greater joy than to see their children walking in the truth. Do we not share their joy?

III. REJOICE WITH THOSE WHO BROUGHT THEM TO JESUS.

The spiritual parents of these converts are glad.

- The pastor, evangelist, missionary, author.
- The parent, elder sister, or other loving relation.
- The teacher in the Sunday school or Bible class.
- The friend who wrote or spoke to them of Jesus.

What a joy belongs to those who by personal effort win souls!

Endeavor to win the same joy for yourself, and meanwhile be glad that others have it.

IV. REJOICE WITH THE HOLY SPIRIT.

1. He sees his strivings successful.
2. He sees his instructions accepted.

3. He sees his quickening power operating in new life.

4. He sees the renewed mind yielding to his divine guidance.

5. He sees the heart comforted by his grace.

Let us rejoice in the love of the Spirit.

V. REJOICE WITH THE ANGELS.

- They have noted the repentance of the returning sinner.
- They will henceforth joyfully guard the footsteps of the pilgrim.
- They expect his lifelong perseverance or their joy would be premature. He is and will be forever their fellow servant.
- They look one day to bear him home to glory.

The evil angels make us groan. Should not the joy of good angels make us sing in harmony with their delight?

VI. REJOICE WITH THE LORD JESUS.

1. His joy is proportioned to the ruin from which he has saved his redeemed ones.

2. His joy is proportioned to the cost of their redemption.

3. His joy is proportioned to the love which he bears to them.

4. His joy is proportioned to their future happiness and to the glory which their salvation will bring to him.

Do you find it hard to rejoice with these newly baptized believers? Let me urge you to do so, for:

- You have your own sorrows, and this communion of joy will prevent brooding too much over them.
- You will renew the love of your espousals by communion with these young ones.
- It will comfort you for your own erring ones if you rejoice with the *friends* of converts.
- It will forbid envy if you rejoice with *workers* who are successful.
- It will elevate your spirit if you endeavor to rejoice with the Holy Spirit and the angels.
- It will fit you to partake in a like success if you rejoice with Jesus, the sinner's friend.

Sympathetics

About three hundred years after the time of the apostles, Caius Marius Victonus, an old pagan, was converted from his impiety and brought over to the Christian faith. When the people of God heard this, there was a wonderful rejoicing and shouting and leaping for gladness, and psalms were sung in every church, while the people joyously said one to another, "Caius Marius Victorius is become a Christian! Caius Marius Victorius is become a Christian!"

Mr. Haslam, telling the story of his conversion, says: "I do not remember all I said, but I felt a wonderful light and joy coming into my soul. Whether it was something in my words, or my manner, or my look, I know not; but all of a sudden a local preacher, who happened to be in the congregation, stood up, and putting up his arms, shouted out in Cornish manner, "The parson is converted! The parson is converted! Hallelujah!" And in another, his voice was lost in the shouts and praises of three or four hundred of the congregation. Instead of rebuking this extraordinary 'brawling,' as I should have done in a former time, I joined in the outburst of praise and to make it more orderly, I gave out the Doxology, 'Praise God from whom all blessings flow,' which the people sung with heart and voice, over and over again."

An ungodly youth accompanied his parents to hear a certain minister. The subject of the discourse was the heavenly state. On returning home, the young man expressed his admiration of the preacher's talents. "But," said he turning to his mother, "I was surprised that you and my father were in tears." "Ah, my son!" replied the anxious mother, "I did weep, not because I feared my own personal interest in the subject or that of your father; but I wept for fear that you, my beloved child, would be forever banished from the blessedness of heaven." "I supposed," said the father, turning to his wife, "that those were your reflections, the same concern for our dear son made me weep also." These tender remarks found their way to the young man's heart and led him to repentance. —*Arvine*

202

For whatsoever things were written aforetime were written for our learning, that we through patience and comfort of the scriptures might have hope.

—*Romans 15:4*

 HIS is the text from which old Hugh Latimer preached continually in his latter days. Certainly, it gave him plenty of sea room.

The apostle declares that the Old Testament Scriptures are meant to teach New Testament believers.

Things written aforetime were written for our time.

The Old Testament is not outworn; the apostles learned from it.

Nor has its authority ceased; it still teaches with certainty.

Nor has its divine power departed, for it works the graces of the Spirit in those who receive it: patience, comfort, hope.

In this verse, the Holy Ghost sets his seal upon the Old Testament and forever enters his protest against all undervaluing of that sacred volume.

The Holy Scriptures produce and ripen the noblest graces.

Let us carefully consider:

I. THE PATIENCE OF THE SCRIPTURES.

1. Such as they inculcate:
   - Patience under every appointment of the divine will.
   - Patience under human persecution and satanic opposition.
   - Patience under brotherly burdens (Gal. 6:2).
   - Patience in waiting for divine promises to be fulfilled.
2. Such as they exhibit in examples:
   - Job under many afflictions triumphantly patient.
   - Abraham, Isaac, and Jacob patiently waiting as sojourners with God, embracing the covenant promise in a strange land.
   - Joseph patiently forgiving the unkindness of his brethren and bearing the false accusation of his master.
   - David in many trials and under many reproaches, patiently waiting for the crown and refusing to injure his persecutor.
   - Our Savior patient under all the many forms of trial.
3. Such as they produce by their influence.
   - By calling us to the holiness which involves trial.
   - By revealing the design of God in our tribulations, and so sustaining the soul in steadfast resolve.
   - By declaring to us promises as to the future which make us cheerfully endure present griefs.

II. THE COMFORT OF THE SCRIPTURES.

1. Such as they inculcate.
   - They bid us rise above fear (Ps. 46:1-3).
   - They urge us to think little of all transient things.
   - They command us to find our joy in God.
   - They stimulate us to rejoice under tribulations because they make us like the prophets of old.
2. Such as they exhibit:
   - Enoch walking with God.
   - Abraham finding God his shield and exceeding great reward.
   - David strengthening himself in God.
   - Hezekiah spreading his letter before the Lord.
   - Many other cases are recorded, and these stimulate our courage.
3. Such as they produce:
   - The Holy Spirit as the Comforter uses them to that end.

- Their own character adapts them to that end.
- They comfort us by their gentleness, certainty, fullness, graciousness, adaptation, personality.
- Our joyous experience is the best testimony to the consoling power of the Holy Scriptures.

III. THE HOPE OF THE SCRIPTURES.
- Scripture is intended to work in us a good hope.
- A people with a hope will purify themselves and will in many other ways rise to a high and noble character.

By the hope of the Scriptures we understand:

1. Such a hope as they hold forth:
   - The hope of salvation (1 Thess. 5:8).
   - "The blessed hope, and the appearing of our Lord" (Titus 2:13).
   - The hope of the resurrection of the dead (Acts 23:6).
   - The hope of glory (Col. 1:27).

This is a good hope, a lively hope, the hope set before us in the gospel.

2. Such a hope as they exhibit in the lives of saints. A whole martyrology will be found in Hebrews eleven.

3. Such a hope as they produce:
   - We see what God has done for his people and therefore hope.
   - We believe the promises through the word and therefore hope.
   - We enjoy present blessing and therefore hope.
   - Let us hold constant fellowship with the God of patience and consolation, who is also the God of hope. And let us rise from stage to stage of joy as the order of the words suggests.

Comforts

How much important matter do we find condensed in this single verse! What a light and glory does it throw on the Word of God! It has been well noted that we have here *its authority*, as it is a written word; *its antiquity*, as it was written aforetime; *its utility*, as it is written for our learning. We may also infer from what immediately follows, *its Divine origin*; for, if by means of the Holy Scriptures, and the accompanying lively power of the Holy Spirit (Isa. 59:21), God imparts to our soul patience, and comfort, and hope, it is because he is himself, as the apostle here expressly teaches, *the God of patience and comfort*, and *the God of hope* (verse 13). He is the fountain of these gifts and graces, which by the channel of his inspired Word, flow down into our hearts and lives, to strengthen them for his service. Nor must we fail to notice the gracious method of their communication, their regular development within us, as we find this to be the order of their course: (1) *patience*; (2) *comfort*; (3) *hope*. From a calm sense of inward peace and comfort, we are led by the same Spirit to feel a blessed and, it may be, a joyous hope. But, in order to this, there must always be in us the groundwork of *patience* in our suffering or doing the will of God. —*James Ford*

Oliver Cromwell once read aloud Phil. 4:11–13, and then remarked, "There, in the day when my poor child died, this Scripture did go nigh to save my life."

When George Peabody was staying at Sir Charles Reed's house, he saw the youngest child bringing to his father a large Bible for family prayers. Mr. Peabody said, "Ah! my boy, you carry the Bible now; but the time is coming when you will find that *the Bible must carry you.*"

"Speak to me now in Scripture language alone," said a dying Christian. "I can trust the words of God; but when they are the words of man, it costs me an effort to think whether I may trust them." —*G. S. Bowes*

As an instance of the patience, comfort, and hope which come from the gospel, note the following from *Dr. Payson*: "Christians might avoid much trouble if they would believe that God is able to make them happy without anything else. God has been depriving me of one blessing after another; but as every one was removed, he has come in and filled up its place. Now when I am a cripple and not able to move, I am happier than ever I was in my life before or ever expected to be. If I had believed this twenty years ago, I might have been spared much anxiety."

203

Know ye not that...ye are not your own, for ye are bought with a price: therefore glorify God in your body and in your spirit, which are God's.

—*1 Corinthians 6:19–20*

ITH what ardor does the apostle pursue sin to destroy it!

He is not so prudish as to let sin alone, but cries out in plainest language, "Flee fornication." The shame is not in the rebuke, but in the sin which calls for it.

He chases this foul wickedness with arguments (see verse 18).

He drags it into the light of the Spirit of God, "What? Know ye not that your body is the temple of the Holy Ghost?" (verse 19).

He slays it at the cross: "Ye are bought with a price."

Let us consider this last argument that we may find therein death for our sins.

I. A BLESSED FACT. "Ye are bought with a price."

"Ye are bought." This is that idea of redemption which modern heretics dare to style "mercantile." The mercantile redemption is the scriptural one, for the expression, "bought with a price" is a double declaration of that idea.

Redemption is a greater source of obligation than creation or preservation. Hence, it is a wellspring of holiness.

"With a price." This indicates the greatness of the cost. The Father gave the Son. The Son gave himself: his happiness, his glory, his repose, his body, his soul, his life.

Measure the price by the bloody sweat, the desertion, the betrayal, the scourging, the cross, the heartbreak.

Our body and spirit are both bought with the body and spirit of Jesus

1. This is either a fact or not. "Ye are bought," or ye are unredeemed. Terrible alternative.
2. If a fact, it is *the* fact of your life, a wonder of wonders.
3. It will remain to you eternally the grandest of all facts. If true at all, it will never cease to be true, and it will never be outdone in importance by any other event.
4. It should therefore operate powerfully upon us both now and ever.

II. A PLAIN CONSEQUENCE. "Ye are not your own."

NEGATIVE. It is clear that if bought, ye are *not* your own.

1. This involves privilege.
   - You are not your own provider; sheep are fed by their shepherd.
   - You are not your own guide; ships are steered by their pilot.
   - You are not your own father; children loved by parents.
2. This also involves responsibility.
   - We are not our own to injure, neither body nor soul.
   - Not our own to waste in idleness, amusement, or speculation.
   - Not our own to exercise caprice and follow our own prejudices, depraved affections, wayward wills, or irregular appetites.
   - Not our own to lend our service to another master.
   - Not our own to serve self. Self is a dethroned tyrant. Jesus is a blessed husband, and we are his.

POSITIVE. "Your body and your spirit, which are God's."

- We are altogether God's. Body and spirit include the whole man.
- We are always God's. The price once paid, we are forever his.

We rejoice that we know we are God's, for thus:

- We have a beloved owner.
- We pursue an honored service.
- We fill a blessed position. We are in Christ's keeping.

III. A PRACTICAL CONCLUSION. "Glorify God in your body, and in your spirit, which are God's."

Glorify God *in your body*:

By cleanliness, chastity, temperance, industry, cheerfulness, self-denial, patience, etc.

Glorify God:

- In a suffering body by patience unto death.
- In a working body by holy diligence.
- In a worshipping body by bowing in prayer.
- In a well-governed body by self-denial.
- In an obedient body by doing the Lord's will with delight.

Glorify God *in your spirit*:

By holiness, faith, zeal, love, heavenliness, cheerfulness, fervor, humility, expectancy.

Remember, O redeemed one, that:

1. You will be closely watched by Christ's enemies.
2. You will be expected to be more gracious than others and rightly so, since you claim to be Christ's own.
3. If you are not holy, the sacred name of your Redeemer, your Proprietor, and your Indweller will be compromised.
4. But if you live a redeemed life, your God will be honored.

Let the world see what Redemption can do.

Let the world see what sort of men "God's own" are.

Pieces of Money

Why should so vast a price be required? Is man worth the cost? A man may be bought in parts of the world for the value of an ox. It was not man simply, but man in a certain relation that had to be redeemed. See one who has been all his days a drunken, idle, worthless fellow? We appropriate to him the epithet "worthless," worth nothing. But if he commits a crime for which he is sentenced to be hanged or to be imprisoned for life, try to buy him now. Redeem him and make him your servant. Let the richest man in Cambridge offer every shilling he possesses for that worthless man, and his offer would be wholly vain. Why? Because now there is not only the man to be considered, but the law. It takes a great price to redeem one man from the curse of the law of England; but Christ came to redeem all men from the curse of the Divine law. —*William Robinson*

Does not justice demand the dedication of yourself to your Lord? God has not only procured a title for you, but a title to you, and unless you devote yourself to his service, you rob him of his right. What a man has bought, he deems his own, especially when the purchase has been costly. And has not God bought you with a price of infinite value? And would you rob him of a servant from his family; of a vessel from his sanctuary? To take what belongs to a man is robbery, but to take what belongs to God is sacrilege. —*William Jay*

The Lord Jesus is everything in redemption, for he is both the Buyer and the price.

A silly child when he plays at selling would like to take the price and keep the article too; but everybody knows that this cannot be. If you keep the goods, you cannot have the price, and if you accept the price, the goods are no longer yours. You may have either the one or the other, but not both. So you may be your own, if you wish; but then the redemption price is not yours. If you accept the ransom, then the thing redeemed is no longer yours, but belongs to him who bought it. If I am redeemed, I am Christ's. If I am resolved to be my own, I must renounce my Redeemer and die unransomed.

204

And when he had given thanks, he brake it, and said, Take, eat: this is my body, which is broken for you: this do in remembrance of me.
—*1 Corinthians 11:24*

EN have made evil use of this most blessed ordinance. Yet they have no excuse from any obscurity of Scripture. Nothing is said of a sacrifice or an altar, but everything is plain. The Supper, as we find it in Holy Scripture, is a service of remembrance, testimony, and communion, and nothing more.

No pompous ceremony is arranged for. Not even a posture is prescribed, but merely the providing of bread and the juice of the vine: taking, breaking, eating, drinking, and no more.

The spiritual action is specially prescribed. The remembrance of our Lord must be there, or we fail to keep the feast.

I. OTHER MEMORIES WILL COME, BUT MUST NOT CROWD OUT THE ONE MEMORY.

The following remembrances may be natural, allowable, and profitable, but they must be kept in a secondary place:

1. Of ourselves when we were strangers and foreigners.
2. Of our former onlooking and wishing to be at the table.
3. Of our first time of coming and the grace received since then.
4. Of the dear departed who once were with us at the table.
5. Of beloved ones who cannot be with us at this time because they are kept at home by sickness.
6. Of many present with us and what grace has done in their cases. We may think of their needs and of their holy lives.
7. Of the apostates who have proved their falseness, like Judas.

However these memories may press upon us, we must mainly remember *him* for whose honor the feast is ordained.

II. THE ORDINANCE IS HELPFUL TO THAT ONE SACRED MEMORY.

1. Set forth, the signs display the person of our Lord as really man, substantial flesh and blood.
2. Placed on the table, their presence betokens our Lord's dear familiarity with us and our nearness to him.
3. Broken and poured forth, they show his sufferings.
4. Separated, bread apart from wine, the flesh divided from the blood, they declare his death for us.
5. Eating, we symbolize the life-sustaining power of Jesus and our reception of him into our innermost selves.
6. Remaining when the Supper is ended, the fragments suggest that there is yet more bread and wine for other feasts; and, even so, our Lord is all-sufficient for all time.

Every particle of the ordinance points at Jesus, and we must therein behold the Lamb of God.

III. THAT SACRED MEMORY IS IN ITSELF MOST NEEDFUL FOR US.

It is needful to remember our crucified Lord, for:
1. It is the continual sustenance of faith.
2. It is the stimulus of love.
3. It is the fountain of hope.
4. It is a recall from the world, from self, from controversy, from labor, from our fellows—to our Lord.
5. It is the *reveille*, the up-and-away. It is the prelude of the marriage supper and makes us long for "the bridal feast above."

Above all things, it behoves us to keep the name of our Lord engraved on our hearts.

IV. THIS SYMBOLIC FESTIVAL IS HIGHLY BENEFICIAL IN REFRESHING OUR MEMORIES AND IN OTHER WAYS.

1. We are yet in the body, and materialism is a most real and potent force. We need a set sign and form to incarnate the spiritual and make it vivid to the mind.

   Moreover, as the Lord actually took upon him our flesh and blood and as he means to save even the material part of us, he gives us this link with materialism, lest we spirit things away as well as spiritualize them.
2. Jesus, who knew our forgetfulness, appointed this festival of love; and we may be sure he will bless it to the end designed.
3. Experience has often proved its eminent value.

4. While reviving the memories of the saints, it has also been sealed by the Holy Spirit, for he has very frequently used it to arouse and convince the spectators of our solemn feast.
- To observe the Supper is binding on all believers.
- It is binding to the extent of "oft."
- Only as it assists *remembrance* can it be useful. Seek grace lovingly to remember your Lord.

Memorials

It is common enough in human history to meet with periodical celebrations, anniversaries of the day of their birth or of their death, held in honor of those who have greatly distinguished themselves by their virtues, their genius, or their high services to their country or to mankind. But where except here do we read of any one in his own lifetime originating and appointing the method by which he was to be remembered, himself presiding at the first celebration of the rite and laying an injunction upon all his followers regularly to meet for its observance? Who among all those who have been the greatest ornaments of our race, the greatest benefactors of humanity, would ever have risked his reputation, his prospect of being remembered by the ages that were to come, by exhibiting such an eager and premature desire to preserve and perpetuate the remembrance of his name, his character, his deeds? They have left it to others after them to devise the means for doing so, neither vain enough, nor bold enough, nor foolish enough to be themselves the framers of those means. Who, then, is he who ventures to do what none else ever did? Who is this, who, ere he dies, by his own act and deed sets up the memorial institution by which his death is to be shown forth? Surely he must be one who knows and feels that he has claims to be remembered such as none other ever had—claims of such a kind that, in pressing them in such a way upon the notice of his followers, he has no fear whatever of what he does being attributed to any other, any lesser motive than the purest, deepest, most unselfish love! Does not Jesus Christ, in the very act of instituting in his own lifetime this memorial rite, step at once above the level of ordinary humanity, and assert for himself a position toward mankind utterly and absolutely unique? —*Dr. Hanna*

Miss Edgeworth, in one of her tales, relates an anecdote of a Spanish artist, who was employed to depict the "Last Supper." It was his object to throw all the sublimity of his art into the figure and countenance of the Master; but he put on the table in the foreground some chased cups, the workmanship of which was exceedingly beautiful, and when his friends came to see the picture on the easel, every one said, "What beautiful cups they are!" "Ah!" said he, "I have made a mistake. These cups divert the eyes of the spectator from the Master, to whom I wished to direct the attention of the observer." He took his brush and rubbed them from the canvas, that the strength and vigor of the chief object might be seen as it should. —*G. S. Bowls*

He that remembers not Christ's death, so as to endeavor to be like him, forgets the end of his redemption and dishonors the cross on which his satisfaction was wrought. —*Anthony Horneck*

205

But let a man examine himself, and so let him eat of that bread, and drink of that cup.

—*1 Corinthians 11:28*

 HE Lord's Supper is not for all men, but only for those who are able spiritually to discern the Lord's body.

It is not meant for the conversion of sinners, but for the edification of disciples.

Hence, the need of examination, lest we intrude ourselves where we have no right to be.

I. THE OBJECT OF THE EXAMINATION.

1. That the communicant may eat and drink. "Examine, and so let him eat." He is not to examine in order to justify his stopping away.
2. That he may know that the responsibility rests with himself. The examination is not by priest or minister; he examines *himself.*
3. That he may communicate solemnly and not come to the table carelessly as a matter of course. He is to make heartsearching inquiry and so approach the table with self-humiliation.
4. That he may come to the table intelligently, knowing to what he comes, and why, and wherefore.
5. That he may do so with appreciative confidence and joy. After examination, he will know his right to come and feel at ease.

Many good results would follow if this examination were universally practiced. "A man" in this text means "any man" and "every man."

The examination should be as frequent as the eating of the bread. No man has reached a point at which he is beyond the need of further self-searching.

II. THE MATTER OF THE EXAMINATION.

Points of examination may be suggested by the following thoughts:
1. It is a feast.
   • Have I life? The dead sit not at banquets.
   • Have I appetite? Else how can I eat?

- Have I a friendship toward the Lord who is the Host?
- Have I put on the wedding garment?

2. Jesus bids us show forth his death.
   - Have I faith in his death?
   - Do I live by his death?
3. Jesus bids us do this by eating bread.
   - Is this eating a symbol of a fact, or is it a mere mockery?
   - Is Jesus really and truly the food of my soul?
4. Jesus bids each believer do this in union with others.
   - Am I truly one of his people, and one with them?
   - Am I dwelling in love with them all?
5. This cup is the New Covenant in Christ's blood.
   - Am I in covenant with God in Christ Jesus?
   - Do I rest in that covenant for all my hopes?
6. Jesus calls his people to remember him in this supper.
   - Can I remember Christ, or am I attempting a vain thing?
   - Do I know him? How else can I remember him?
   - Are my past dealings with him such as I wish to remember?
   - Is he so loved by me that I wish to bear him in my memory?

Our profession, experience, conduct, hopes, and designs should all pass the test of this self-examination.

III. THE DUTY AFTER EXAMINATION.

1. To eat of the bread

   Not to neglect communion, or postpone it, or go away trembling from the table; but to partake reverently.

2. To drink of the cup

   This is specially commanded. Hence, we cannot go to popish mass where there is no cup.

3. To eat and drink so as to discern the Lord's body, having the mind awake to see Jesus symbolized in this ordinance.

4. To give thanks unto the Lord for so great a privilege. Twice did our Lord give thanks during the Supper, and at the close he sang. It is not a funeral, but a festival.

Ye who have come to this table heedlessly, repent of your wicked intrusion, and keep away till ye can come aright.

Ye who have never come at all, remember, if you are not fit for the communion below, you are not fit for heaven above.

All of you, bethink yourselves of Jesus, and having examined yourselves to your humbling, behold him to your consolation.

Observations

The three questions which Philip Henry advised people to put to themselves in self-examination before the sacrament were, What am I? What have I done? and, What do I want? —*John Whitecross*

It is every man's duty solemnly and seriously to examine himself about his interest in Christ, his habitual grace, his actual right and fitness for the Lord's Supper before his approach to it. It is not said as to the first time of our partaking, but as to every time, "*so* let him eat." Now, the second and third time, as well as before, we are so to eat. Great preparations are necessary for great duties. The particle so bars men from coming without this previous work of examination. Let a man come only in such a manner; if he neglects this self-examination, let him not venture upon this great mystery. Thus, "I will wash my hands in innocency: so will I compass thine altar, O Lord" (Ps. 26:6), alluding to the ancient custom of testifying the purity of their souls by the cleansing of their hands or to the washings used before sacrifices. If we take the gloss of Ambrose, it will read, "I will with a purity of heart embrace the Messiah, signified both by the altar and sacrifice. "*So* will I compass thy altar." Without such an inward purification, I dare not presume upon an approach unto it. —*Stephen Charnock*

The duty required for preventing the sin and danger of unworthy communicating is the great and necessary duty of self-examination. It is a metaphor taken from goldsmiths, who try the truth of their gold by the touchstone, the purity of their gold by the fire, and the weight of it by the scale. We have here: I. The person examining: "Let a man examine." II. The person examined; it is "himself"; he is to call himself to the bar of conscience and to put questions to himself. (1) Concerning his state, whether he has a right to come or not. (2) His sins and shortcomings. (3) His wants and necessities. (4) His ends and designs; whether it be to obey the charge of his dying Savior, to show forth his death, renew and seal his covenant with God, get nearness and communion with him, nourishment to his soul, and supply to his wants. And (5) concerning his graces and qualifications, particularly as to knowledge, faith, repentance, fear, love, thankfulness, holy desires, and new obedience. —*John Willison*

206

Some are fallen asleep.
—*1 Corinthians 15:6*

 ES, the companions of Jesus died one by one. Consider the great value of such men and of all good men to the church and the loss caused by their removal.

Yet, no word of lamentation is used. It is not said that they have perished or passed into the land of shades, but that "they are fallen asleep."

The spirit is with Jesus in glory; the body rests till his appearing.

"Fallen asleep" suggests a very different idea from that which distressed the minds of the heathen when they thought of death.

I. THE FIGURE HERE USED.

1. An act of the most natural kind: "fallen asleep."
   - It is the fit ending of a weary day.
   - It is not painful, but the end of pain.
   - It is so desirable that, if denied, we should pray for it.
   - It is most sweet when the place of our sleep is Jesus.
2. A state of which rest is the main ingredient.
3. A position of safety from a thousand dangers such as beset the pilgrim, the worker, the warrior.
4. A condition by no means destructive.
   - Neither sleep nor death destroys existence nor even injures it.
   - Neither sleep nor death should be viewed as an evil.
5. A posture full of hope.
   - We shall awake from this sleep.
   - We shall awake without difficulty.
   - We shall arise greatly refreshed.

II. THE THOUGHTS AROUSED BY THAT FIGURE.

1. How did we treat those who are now asleep?
   - Did we value their living presence, work, and testimony?
   - Ought we not to be more kind to those who are yet alive?
2. How can we make up for the loss caused by their sleep?
   - Should we not fill their vacant places?
   - Should we not profit by their examples?
3. How fit that we also should be prepared to fall asleep!
   - Is our house in order?
   - Is our heart in order?
   - Is our Christian work in order?
4. How much better that the faithful should fall asleep than that the wicked should die in their sins!
5. How patiently should we bear up under the labors and sufferings of the day, since there remaineth a rest for the people of God!

III. THE HOPES CONFIRMED BY THAT FIGURE.

1. The sleepers are yet ours, even as those in the house who are asleep are numbered with the rest of the inhabitants.

- They have the same life in them which dwells in us.
- They are part of the same family. "We are seven."
- They make up one church. "One church above, beneath."

2. The sleepers will yet awake.
    - Their Father's voice will arouse them.
    - They shall be awake indeed, full of health and energy.
    - They shall have new clothes to dress in.
    - They shall not again fall asleep.

3. The sleepers and ourselves will enjoy sweet fellowship.
    - Sleep does not destroy the love of brothers and sisters now.
    - We shall arise as one unbroken family, saved in the Lord.

Let us not hopelessly sorrow over those asleep.

Let us not ourselves sleep till bedtime comes.

Let us not fear to sleep in such good company.

Night Thoughts

A pious Scotch minister being asked by a friend during his last illness whether he thought himself dying, answered: "Really, friend, I care not whether I am or not, for if I die, I shall be with God. If I live, he will be with me." —*Arvine*

God's finger touched him, and he slept. —*Tennyson*

S. T. Coleridge speaking of a dear friend's death, said, "It is recovery, and not death. Blessed are they that sleep in the Lord; his life is hidden in Christ. In his Redeemer's life, it is hidden, and in his glory will it be disclosed. Physiologists hold that it is during sleep chiefly that we grow. What may we not hope of such a sleep in such a bosom?"

There must be life in Christ before death can become sleep in him. "Louis, the beloved, sleeps in the Lord," said the priest who announced the death of Louis the Fifteenth. "If," was Thomas Carlyle's stern comment, "if such a mass of laziness and lust sleeps in the Lord, who, think you, sleeps elsewhere?"

207

Blessed be God, even the Father of our Lord Jesus Christ, the Father of mercies, and the God of all comfort; Who comforteth us in all our tribulation, that we may be able to comfort them which are in any trouble, by the comfort wherewith we ourselves are comforted of God.

—2 Corinthians 1:3–4

HE apostle began with invoking the blessing of God (verse 1).

He then went on to bless God.

He was much tried, but he was in a grateful and cheerful humor, for he wrote of most comfortable things.

Here we have:

I. THE COMFORTABLE OCCUPATION. Blessing God. "Blessed be God."

If a man under affliction blesses the Lord:

1. It argues that his heart is not vanquished
   - So as to gratify Satan by murmuring, or
   - So as to kill his own soul with despair.
2. It prophesies that God will send to him speedy deliverances to call forth new praises. It is natural to lend more to a man when the interest on what he has is duly paid.

   Never did man bless God but sooner or later God blessed him.
3. It profits the believer above measure.
   - It takes the mind off from present trouble.
   - It lifts the heart to heavenly thoughts and considerations.
   - It gives a taste of heaven, for heaven largely consists in adoring and blessing God.
   - It destroys distress by bringing God upon the scene.
4. It is the Lord's due in whatsoever state we may be.

II. THE COMFORTABLE TITLES.

1. A name of affinity, "The Father of our Lord Jesus Christ."
2. A name of gratitude, "The Father of mercies."
3. A name of hope, "The God of all comfort."
4. A name of discrimination, "Who comforteth *us*." The Lord has a special care for those who trust in him.

III. THE COMFORTABLE FACT. "The God of all comfort who comforteth us in all our tribulation."

1. God personally condescends to comfort the saints.
2. God habitually does this. He has always been near to comfort us in all past time, never once leaving us alone.
3. God effectually does this. He has always been able to comfort us in all tribulation. No trial has baffled his skill.
4. God everlastingly does this. He will comfort us to the end, for he is "the God of all comfort," and he cannot change.

Should we not be always happy since God always comforts us?

IV. **THE COMFORTABLE DESIGN.** "That we may be able to comfort."

1. To make us comforters of others. The Lord aims at this: the Holy Ghost, the Comforter, trains us up to be comforters. There is great need for this holy service in this sin-smitten world.
2. To make us comforters on a large scale. "To comfort them which are in any trouble." We are to be conversant with all kinds of grief and ready to sympathize with all sufferers.
3. To make us experts in consolation, "able to comfort," because of our own experience of divine comfort.
4. To make us willing and sympathetic so that we may through personal experience instinctively care for the state of others.

Let us now unite in special thanksgiving to the God of all comfort.

Let us drink in comfort from the word of the Lord and be ourselves happy in Christ Jesus.

Let us be on the watch to minister consolation to all tried ones.

Comfortable Words

Music is sweetest near or over rivers where the echo thereof is best rebounded by the water. Praise for pensiveness, thanks for tears, and blessing God over the floods of affliction make the most melodious music in the ear of heaven.
—*Thomas Fuller*

> Many an Alleluia
>   That rings through the Father's home,
> Sobbed out its first rehearsal
>   In the shades of a darkened room.

When we try to comfort one another, let it be God's comfort that we give.
—*T. T. Lynch*

We have no more religion than what we have in times of trial. —*Andrew Fuller*

Away over in India a poor native woman, like Naomi, "was left of her two sons." She did not, perhaps, know enough to think about God at all in her grief, but she would take no comfort. To everything that could be said, she had one answer: "I had but two, and they are both gone."

Day after day she pined and fretted, going listlessly about, her life "empty" of all but a blank despair. One morning, as she wandered here and there among the people of the mission, one of them again remonstrated; but the poor thing gave her old reply: "I had but two, and they are both gone." "Look," said the worker, turning and pointing towards a group near by where a white lady of the mission stood directing some dusky natives. "Do you see *her*?" The woman looked and saw a sweet, pale face; patient, gentle, glad, as clear as a sky washed blue with storms, but wearing that unmistakable look which tells that storms have been. "Yes," she said, "I see her." "Well," said the other, "she has lost her sons, too!"

The poor native mother gazed for a minute spell-bound; then she sprang towards her. "Oh, lady!" she cried, "did you have two sons and are they both gone?"

And now the white mother on her part turned and looked. "Yes," she said, "I had two."

"And are they both gone?"

"Both."

"But they were all I had," cried the other, "and they are both gone!"

"And mine are both gone," said the white lady, clasping the hands of her poor sister in sorrow. "But Jesus took them; and they are with Jesus, and Jesus is with me. And by-and-by I shall have them again."

From that hour the native woman sat at her white sister's feet, followed her about, hung on her words, and from her would take comfort, "the comfort wherewith she herself was comforted of God." —*From "What Aileth Thee?"*

He would put off a meditated journey rather than leave a poor parishioner who required his services. From his knowledge of human nature, he was able, and in a remarkable manner, to throw himself into the circumstances of those who needed his help. No sympathy was like his. —*Chambers, on George Crabbe*

208

Who delivered us from so great a death, and doth deliver: in whom we trust that he will yet deliver us.

—*2 Corinthians 1:10*

 RAMMARIANS have here a lesson in the tenses, and Christians may profitably join in the exercise.

We may consider the past, present, and future, each one by itself.

We may also view them in their relation to each other.

Our text points out the delivering mercy of God as at all times working out the safety of his people. The case of Paul did not stand alone; hence he uses the plural, "who delivered us," "we trust."

We shall take the words out of the apostle's mouth and apply them to our own cases.

I. THE TEXT SUGGESTS THREE TRAINS OF THOUGHT.

1. Memory tells of deliverances in the past:

- From violent death. In Paul's case, "so great a death" may mean death by fierce mobs or by the emperor.
- From our death in sin: "So great a death" indeed.
- From fierce despair when under conviction.
- From total overthrow when tempted by Satan.
- From faintness under daily tribulation.
- From destruction by slander and the like.

The Lord has most graciously delivered us hitherto. Let us express our gratitude.

2. Observation calls attention to present deliverance.
   By the good hand of the Lord, we are at this time preserved:
   - From unseen dangers to life.
   - From the subtle assaults of Satan.
   - From the rampant errors of the times.
   - From inbred sin and natural corruption.
   - From the sentence of death within and from the greater danger of self-trust. See the preceding verse.

   Our present standing is wholly due to the grace of God, and, trusting in that grace, we may indulge a happy confidence.

3. Expectation looks out of the window upon the future.
   Faith rests alone in God, "in whom we trust," and through him, she looks for future deliverance:
   - From all future common trials.
   - From coming losses, afflictions, and sicknesses which may be coming upon us.
   - From the infirmities and wants of age. From the peculiar glooms of death.

   This expectation makes us march on with cheerfulness.

II. THE TEXT SUPPLIES THREE LINES OF ARGUMENT.

That the Lord will preserve us to the end is most sure. We can say of him, "In whom we trust that he will yet deliver us."

1. From the Lord's beginning to deliver, we argue that he will yet deliver, for:
   - There was no reason in us for his beginning to love us. If his love arises out of his own nature, it will continue.
   - He has obtained no fresh knowledge. He foreknew all our misbehaviors; hence, there is no reason for casting us off.
   - The reason which moved him at first is operating now, and none better can be required.

2. From the Lord's continuing to deliver, we argue that he will yet deliver, for:
   - His deliverances have been so many.
   - They have displayed such wisdom and power.
   - They have come to us when we have been so unworthy.

- They have continued in such an unbroken line that we feel sure he will never leave nor forsake us.
3. From the Lord himself, "in whom we trust," we argue that he will yet deliver, for:
   - He is as loving and strong now as aforetime.
   - He will be the same in the future.
   - His purpose never changes, and it is to his glory to complete what he has begun. Verily, "he will yet deliver us."

III. THE TEXT IS OPEN TO THREE INFERENCES.

1. We infer that we shall always be so in danger as to need to be delivered: wherefore, we are not high-minded, but fear.
2. We infer our constant need of God's own interposition. He alone has met our case in the past, and he only can meet it in the future; wherefore, we would ever abide near our Lord.
3. We infer that our whole life should be filled with the praise of God, who, for past, present, and future, is our Deliverer.

For the Times

First, God hath a time, as for all things, so for our deliverance. Secondly, God's time is the best time. He is the best discerner of opportunities. Thirdly, this shall be when he hath wrought his work upon our souls, specially when he hath made us to trust in him. As here, when Paul had learned to trust in God, then he delivered him. —*Richard Sibbes*

The Roman noblemen could give no greater proof of their confidence in their city and army than when they bought the land on which their Carthaginian enemies were encamped around the city. And we can give no greater proof of our confidence in God than by trusting him in the land which our enemies, darkness, sickness, and trouble, seem to possess, and acting as if God were their master and mightier than they all. This is but to act upon the truth.

There is an ante-war incident which illustrates the power for despair which lies in forgetfulness of God and the hope which leaps up when God is fully believed in. A dark cloud hung over the interests of the African race in our land. There seemed no way of deliverance. Frederick Douglas, at a crowded meeting, depicted the terrible condition. Everything was against his people. One political party had gone down on its knees to slavery; the other proposed not to abolish it anywhere, but only to restrict it. The Supreme Court had given judgment against black men as such. He drew a picture of his race writhing under the lash of the overseer and trampled upon by brutal and lascivious men. As he went on with his despairing words, a great horror of darkness seemed to settle down upon the audience. The orator even uttered the cry for blood. There was no other relief. And then he showed that there was no relief even in that. Everything, every influence, every event was gathering, not for good, but for evil, about the doomed race. It seemed as if they were fated to destruction. Just at the instant when the cloud was most heavy over the audience, there slowly rose, in the front seat, an old black woman. Her name, "Sojourner Truth." She had given it to herself. Far and wide, she was known as an African prophetess. Every eye was on her. The orator paused. Reaching out towards him her long bony finger as every eye followed her pointing, she cried out, *"Frederick, is God dead?"* It was a lightning flash upon that darkness. The cloud began to break, and faith and hope and patience returned with the idea of a personal and ever-living God. —*Sword and Trowel, 1887*

> Who murmurs that in these dark days
> His lot is cast?
> God's hand within the shadow lays
> The stones whereon his gates of praise
> Shall rise at last.
> —*J. G. Whittier*

209

For all the promises of God in him are yea, and in him Amen, unto the glory of God by us.

—*2 Corinthians 1:20*

AUL had altered his mind about visiting Corinth.

He had done this from the best of reasons.

The prejudices of certain Corinthians made them misconstrue his conduct and speak of him as one whose word was not to be relied on.

He asserted that he did not use lightness and that his mind was not of the "yea and nay" order, even upon so small a matter as a journey to Corinth at a certain date.

This led him to say that his preaching "was not yea and nay."

This further brought out the declaration that the promises of God are not "yea and nay."

Thus, a trivial circumstance and an ungenerous remark led to the utterance of a most precious truth. This has often been the case.

From these words, let us be led carefully to consider:

I. THE DIGNITY OF THE PROMISES. They are "the promises *of God*."

1. They were each one made by him according to the purpose of his own will.
2. They are links between his decrees and his acts, being the voice of the decree and the herald of the act.

3. They display the qualities of him who uttered them. They are true, immutable, powerful, eternal, etc.
4. They remain in union with God. After the lapse of ages, they are still *his* promises as much as when he first uttered them.
5. They are guaranteed by the character of God who spoke them.
6. They will glorify him as he works out their fulfillment.

II. THE RANGE OF THE PROMISES. "*All* the promises."

It will be instructive to note the breadth of the promises by observing that:
1. They are found both in the Old and New Testaments from Genesis to Revelation, running through centuries of time.
2. They are of both sorts—conditional and unconditional: promises to certain works and promises of an absolute order.
3. They are of all kinds of things—bodily and spiritual, personal and general, eternal and temporal.
4. They contain blessings to varied characters, such as:
   • The penitent (Lev. 26:40–42; Isa. 55:7; 57:15; Jer. 3:12–13).
   • The believing: (John 3:16, 18; 6:47; Acts 16:31; 1 Pet. 2:6).
   • The serving: (Ps. 37:3; 9:40; Prov. 3:9–10; Acts 10:35).
   • The praying: (Isa. 14:11; Lam. 3:25; Matt. 6:6; Ps. 145:18).
   • The obeying: (Exod. 19:5; Ps. 119:1–3; Isa. 1:19).
   • The suffering: (Matt. 5:10–12; Rom. 8:17; 1 Pet. 4:12–14).
5. They bring us the richest boons: pardon, justification, sanctification, instruction, preservation, etc.

What a marvelous wealth lies in promises, "all the promises"!

III. THE STABILITY OF THE PROMISES. "All the promises *in him are yea, and in him Amen.*"

A Greek word "yea" and a Hebrew word "amen" are used to mark certainty, both to Gentile and Jew.
1. They are established beyond all doubt as being assuredly the mind and purpose of the eternal God.
2. They are confirmed beyond all alteration. The Lord hath said, "Amen," and so must it be forever.
3. Their stability is in Christ Jesus beyond all hazard, for he is:
   • The witness of the promise of God
   • The surety of the covenant
   • The sum and substance of all the promises
   • The fulfillment of the promises by his actual incarnation, his atoning death, his living plea, his ascension power, etc.
   • The security and guarantee of the promises, since all power is in his hand to fulfill them.

IV. THE RESULT OF THE PROMISES. "The glory of God by us."

By us, his ministers and his believing people, the God of the promises is made glorious.

1. We glorify his condescending love in making the promise.
2. We glorify his power as we see him keeping the promise.
3. We glorify him by our faith, which honors his veracity, by expecting the boons which he has promised.
4. We glorify him in our experience which proves the promise true.

Let us confidently rest in his sure word.

Let us plead the special promise applicable to the hour now passing.

Gatherings

A speaker at the Fulton Street prayer meeting said, "I count all checks as cash when I am making up my money and striking a balance." So when we feel that we have not much of this world's goods, we can at least take hold of God's promises, for they are just so many drafts at sight upon divine mercy, and we may count them among our possessions. Then we shall feel rich, and the soul is rich who trusts God's word and takes his promises as something for present use.

In the streets of ancient Pompeii, there still remain the three stepping stones placed here and there, by which men crossed over the street when the water was high. The promises are such stepping stones on which "the wayfaring man" may place his footstep and be enabled the better to cross some stream of trouble or doubt or, perhaps, with more ease and safety to escape the mire of some Slough of Despond.

Promises are like the clothes we wear. If there is life in the body, they warm us, but not otherwise. When there is living faith, the promise will afford warm comfort, but on a dead, unbelieving heart it lies cold and ineffectual. It has no more effect than pouring a cordial down the throat of a corpse. — *William Gurnell*

If thou lean upon the promises of God themselves and not upon Jesus Christ in them, all will come to nothing. . . . Whence is it that so many souls bring a promise to the throne of grace and carry so little away from it? They lean upon the promises without leaning on Christ in the promise. — *Faithful Teate*

"By us" as *ministers*—publishing, explaining, applying them. A promise is often like a box of ointment, very precious, but the fragrance does not fill the room till the preacher breaks it. Or it is like the water that was near Hagar, which she saw not, till the angel of the Lord opens our eyes and shows us the well. "By us" as *believers* realizing the excellency and efficacy of them in our character and conduct. It is when these promises are reduced to experience—when they are seen cleansing us from all filthiness of flesh and spirit, making us partakers of the divine nature, leading us to walk worthy of the vocation wherewith we are called, filling us with kindness and benevolence, supporting us cheerfully under all our trials—it is then they glorify God "by us." — *William Jay*

210

Having therefore these promises, dearly beloved, let us cleanse ourselves from all filthiness of the flesh and spirit, perfecting holiness in
the fear of God.

—2 Corinthians 7:1

INDLING with strong emotion, constrained by the love of Christ,
and animated by the fellowship of all spiritual blessings, the apostle here strikes out an exhortation. He appeals to the noblest passions of the children of God, to their possession of divine lineage,
a present endowment, and their expectation of an exalted destiny. These he uses
as incentives to holiness of life.

To stir up in us this godly ambition, he sets before us the Christian in various lights:

I. AS POSSESSED OF MOST GLORIOUS PRIVILEGES. "Having these
promises." Not promises in reversion merely, but in actual possession, received,
embraced, enjoyed.

The promises referred to are mentioned in the previous chapter.
1. Divine indwelling: "I will dwell in them" (2 Cor. 6:16).
2. Divine manifestation: "I will walk in them."
3. Divine covenanting: "I will be their God, and they shall be my people."
4. Divine acceptance: "I will receive you" (6:17).
5. Divine adoption: "I . . . will be a Father unto you, and ye shall be my sons
   and daughters, saith the Lord Almighty" (6:18).
These promises are already fulfilled in our experience.

II. AS LABORING TO BE RID OF OBNOXIOUS EVILS. "Let us cleanse
ourselves." The matter has in it:
1. Personality: "Let us cleanse *ourselves.*"
2. Activity. We must continue vigorously to cleanse both body and mind.
3. Universality: "From all filthiness."
4. Thoroughness: "Of the flesh and spirit."
If God dwells in us, let us make the house clean for so pure a God.

Has the Lord entered into covenant with us that we should be his people?
Does not this involve a call upon us to live as becometh godliness?

Are we his children? Let us not grieve our Father, but imitate him as dear
children.

III. AS AIMING AT A MOST EXALTED POSITION. "Perfecting holiness."

1. We must set before us perfect holiness as a thing to be reached.
2. We must blame ourselves if we fall short of it.
3. We must continue in any degree of holiness which we have reached.
4. We must agonize after the perfecting of our character.

IV. AS PROMPTED BY THE MOST SACRED OF MOTIVES. "Perfecting holiness *in the fear of God.*"

1. The fear of God casts out the fear of man and thus saves us from one prolific cause of sin.
2. The fear of God casts out the love of sin, and with the root, the fruit is sure to go.
3. The fear of God works in and through love to him, and this is a great factor of holiness.
4. The fear of God is the root of faith, worship, obedience, and so it produces all manner of holy service.

See how promises supply arguments for precepts.

See how precepts naturally grow out of promises.

Outpourings

"*Cleanse ourselves.*" It is the Lord that is the sanctifier of his people; he purges away their dross and tin. He pours clean water, according to his promises, yet doth he call us to cleanse ourselves; having such promises, let us cleanse ourselves. He puts a new life into us and causes us to act, and excites us to excite it, and call it up to act in the progress of sanctification. Men are strangely inclined to a perverse construction of things Tell them that we are to act and work and give diligence; then they would fancy a doing in their own strength and be their own saviors. Again, tell them that God works all our works in us and for us, then they would take the ease of doing nothing. If they cannot have the praise of doing all, they will sit still with folded hands and use no diligence at all. But this is the corrupt logic of the flesh, its base sophistry. The apostle reasons just contrary, Philippians 2:13: "It is God that worketh in us both to will and to do." Therefore, would a carnal heart say, we need not work, or at least, may work very carelessly. But he infers, "Therefore, let us work out our salvation with fear and trembling," *i.e.*, in the more humble obedience to God and dependence on him, not obstructing the influences of his grace, and, by sloth and negligence, provoking him to withdraw or abate it. Certainly, many in whom there is truth of grace are kept low in the growth of it by their own slothfulness, sitting still, and not bestirring themselves and exercising the proper actions of that spiritual life by which it is entertained and advanced. —*Archbishop Leighton*

> Virtue, forever frail, as fair, below,
> Her tender nature suffers in the crowd,
> Nor touches on the world without a stain:
> The world's infectious; few bring back at eve,
> Immaculate, the manners of the morn—
> Something we thought is blotted; we resolved,
> Is shaken; we renounc'd, returns again.
> —*Edward Young*

"Let us *go on* to perfection" (Heb. 6:1) should rather be rendered, "Let us be *carried* on."... If we are unable to *go on*, we are surely able to be *carried* on to perfection. —*Charles Stanford*

The promises, as they have a quickening, so they have a purging power; and that upon sound reasoning. Doth God promise that he will be my Father and I shall be his son? and doth he promise me life everlasting? and doth that estate require purity? and no unclean thing shall come there? Certainly, these promises being apprehended by faith, as they have a quickening power to comfort, so they purge with holiness. We may not think to carry our filthiness to heaven. Doth the swearer think to carry his blasphemies thither? Filthy persons and liars are banished thence; there is "no unclean thing." He that hath these promises purgeth himself and "perfecteth holiness in the fear of God." "He that hath this hope purifieth himself, as he is pure" (1 John 3:3). —*Richard Sibbes*

A spiritual mind has something of the nature of the sensitive plant: a holy shrinking from the touch of evil. —*Richard Cecil*

211

> For godly sorrow worketh repentance to salvation not to be repented of: but the sorrow of the world worketh death.
> —*2 Corinthians 7:10*

IME was when inner experience was considered to be everything, and experimental preaching was the order of the day.

Now it is apt to be too much slighted.

Introspection was formerly pushed to the extreme of morbid self-searching; yet it ought not now to be utterly abandoned.

A correct diagnosis of disease is not everything, but yet it is valuable.

A sense of poverty cannot by itself enrich, but it may stimulate.

Sinners were unwisely influenced by certain ministries to look to their own feelings. Many began to seek comfort from their own misery.

Now it is "only believe." And rightly so; but we must discriminate. *There must be sorrow for sin working repentance.* Upon this point we must:

I. REMOVE CERTAIN ERRONEOUS IDEAS WITH REGARD TO REPENTANCE AND SORROW FOR SIN.

Among popular delusions, we must mention the suppositions:

1. That mere sorrow of mind in reference to sin is repentance.
2. That there can be repentance without sorrow for sin.
3. That we must reach a certain point of wretchedness and horror or else we are not truly penitent.
4. That repentance happens to us once and is then over.
5. That repentance is a most unhappy feeling.
6. That repentance must be mixed with unbelief and embittered by the fear that mercy will be unable to meet our wretched case.

II. DISTINGUISH BETWEEN THE TWO SORROWS MENTIONED IN THE TEXT.

1. The godly sorrow which worketh repentance to salvation is:
   - Sorrow for sin as committed against God.
   - Sorrow for sin arising out of an entire change of mind.
   - Sorrow for sin which joyfully accepts salvation by grace.
   - Sorrow for sin leading to future obedience.
   - Sorrow for sin which leads to perpetual perseverance in the ways of God. The ways of sin are forsaken because abhorred.

This kind of repentance is never repented of.

2. The sorrow of the world is:
   - Caused by shame at being found out
   - Is attended by hard thoughts of God
   - Leads to vexation and sullenness
   - Incites to hardening of heart
   - Lands the soul in despair.
   - Works death of the worst kind.

This needs to be repented of, for it is in itself sinful and terribly prolific of more sin.

III. INDULGE OURSELVES IN GODLY SORROW FOR SIN.

Come, let us be filled with a wholesome grief that we:

1. Have broken a law, pure and perfect.
2. Have disobeyed a gospel, divine and gracious.
3. Have grieved a God, good and glorious.
4. Have slighted Jesus, whose love is tender and boundless.

5. Have been ungrateful, though loved, elected, redeemed, forgiven, justified, and soon to be glorified.

6. Have been so foolish as to lose the joyous fellowship of the Spirit, the raptures of communion with Jesus.

Let us confess all this, lie low at Jesus' feet, wash his feet with tears, and love, yea, love ourselves away.

For Discrimination

A cognate text in Romans 2:2, 4, will help us here. These two allied but distinct intimations may be placed in parallel lines and treated like an equation, thus:

"The goodness of God leadeth thee to repentance."

"Godly sorrow worketh repentance."

We learn as the result of the comparison that the goodness of God leads to repentance by the way of godly sorrow. The series of cause-and-effect runs thus: goodness of God; godly sorrow; repentance.

Do not mistake; a fear of hell is not sorrow for sin. It may be nothing more than a regret that God is holy.

So hard is a heart long accustomed to evil that nothing can melt it but goodness, and no goodness but God's, and no goodness of his but the greatest. "Thanks be to God for his unspeakable gift." "Looking unto Jesus" is the grand specific for producing godly sorrow in a human heart. It was a hard heart that quivered under the beams of his loving eye on the threshold of Pilate's judgment hall. When Jesus looked on Peter, Peter went out and wept. Emmanuel's love has lost none of its melting power; the hardest hearts laid fairly open to it must ere long flow down. God's goodness, embodied in Christ crucified, becomes, under the ministry of the Spirit, the cause of godly sorrow in believing men. — *William Arnot*

> The mind that broods o'er guilty woes,
>   Is like the scorpion girt by fire;
> In circle narrowing as it glows,
> The flames around their captive close,
> Till inly searched by thousand throes,
>   And maddening in her ire,
> One sad and sole relief she knows,
> The sting she nourished for her foes,
> Whose venom never yet was vain,
> Gives but one pang and cures all pain,
> And darts into her desperate brain;
> So do the dark in soul expire,
> Or live like scorpion girt by fire.
> So writhes the mind Remorse has riven,
> Unfit for earth, undoomed for heaven,

Darkness above, despair beneath,
Around it flame, within it Death.
—*Byron*

Once a mother told her pastor that she was troubled about her daughter who was going to join the church. "She has not conviction enough," was the complaint , "and yet I have talked to her about her sins over and over again, setting them all in order before her till both of us were in tears. Oh, what can I do more?" Then he gave her in her own hands a Bible, and he read aloud to her slowly Isaiah 6:1-5. She saw, without any word of his, that the prophet became intelligent as the sight of God flashed upon him and grew penitent at the moment when the seraphim cried, "Holy." Then he turned to Job 42:5-6. She saw in silence that the patriarch repented, not when his exasperating friends pelted him with accusations, but when his eyes were opened to see God. She went away quietly to talk, with a wondering and awestruck heart, about the *holiness of Jehovah*. Thus, her child melted into contrition before the vision and wept.
—*C. S. Robinson*

Sin, repentance, and pardon are like to the three vernal months of the year, March, April, and May. Sin comes in like March, blustering, stormy, and full of bold violence. Repentance succeeds like April, showering, weeping, and full of tears. Pardon follows like May, springing, singing, full of joys and flowers. Our eyes must be full of *April*, with the sorrow of repentance, and then our hearts shall be full of *May*, with the true joy of forgiveness. —*Thomas Adams*

212

Immediately I conferred not with flesh and blood.
—*Galatians 1:16*

 HE conversion of Paul is a memorable proof of the truth of Christianity. A consideration of it has been the means of the conversion of many thoughtful persons.

His case is a noble instance of the gospel's power over men of mark, men of learning, men of zealous mind, and men of energetic character.

Paul, being converted, took an independent course.

Being taught of God:

- He did not consult those who were already believers, lest he should seem to have received his religion secondhand.
- He did not consult his relatives, who would have advised caution.
- He did not consult his own interests, which all lay in the opposite direction. These he counted loss for Christ.

- He did not consult his own safety, but risked life itself for Jesus. In this independent course, he was justified and should be imitated.

I. FAITH NEEDS NO WARRANT BUT THE WILL OF GOD.

1. Good men in all ages have acted upon this conviction.
    Noah, Abraham, Jacob, Moses, Samson, David, Elijah, Daniel, the three who were cast into the furnace, etc.
2. To ask more is virtually to renounce the Lord as our Commander and Guide and to lift man into his place.
3. To hesitate from self-interest is openly to defy the Lord.
4. To submit the claims of duty to the judgment of the flesh is diametrically opposed to the character and claims of the Lord Jesus, who gave himself to us and expects us to give ourselves to him without question or reserve.
5. To delay duty until we have held such consultation almost always ends in not doing the right thing at all. Too often it is sought after that an excuse may be found for avoiding an unpleasant duty.

II. THE PRINCIPLE HAS A WIDE RANGE OF APPLICATION.

1. To known duties:
    - In forsaking sin, we are not to consult society.
    - In upright dealing, we are not to consult the custom of trade.
    - In consecration to Christ, we are not to follow the lower standard so common among our fellow Christians.
    - In service, we are not to consult personal liking, ease, honor, prospect of advancement, or remuneration.
2. To needful sacrifices. We are not to shrink from:
    - Losses of situation through honesty or holiness.
    - Losses in trade through religion.
    - Losses of friendships and kindly feeling through faithfulness.
    - Losses of position and worldly honor through inability to lie, bribe, cringe, flatter, compromise, conceal, or change.
    We had better not confer with flesh and blood, for:
    - Good men may be self-indulgent, and so consult their own flesh.
    - Bad men may practically be consulted by our fearing that they will ridicule us and by our acting on that fear.
    - Our own flesh and blood may be consulted by unduly considering wife, husband, brother, child, friend, etc.
3. To special service. We are not to be held back from this by:
    - Considerations of personal weakness.
    - Considerations of want of visible means.
    - Considerations of how others will interpret our actions.

Consult not even your brethren here, for:
- Good men may not have your faith.
- They cannot judge your call.
- They cannot remove your responsibility.

4. To an open avowal of Christ. We must not be deterred from it by:
- The wishes of others, who think themselves involved in our act.
- The dread of contempt from those who deride godliness.
- The fear of not holding on and of thus disgracing religion.
- Reluctance to give up the world and a secret clinging to its ways. This is a very perilous vice. "Remember Lot's wife."

III. THE PRINCIPLE COMMENDS ITSELF TO OUR BEST JUDGMENT.

It is justified by:

1. The judgment which we exercise upon others. We blame them if they have no mind of their own. We applaud them if they are bravely faithful.
2. The judgment of an enlightened conscience.
3. The judgment of a dying bed.
4. The judgment of an eternal world.

Let us be in such communion with God that we need not confer with flesh and blood.

Let us not wait for second thoughts, but at once carry out convictions of duty and obey calls for help or impulses of love.

Confirmations

An Indian missionary says that the Hindus do not act on their own convictions, but according to their own phrase, "I do as ten men do." Let the maxim of the Christian be, "I do as my God would have me do."

"Sir," said the Duke of Wellington to an officer of engineers who urged the impossibility of executing the directions he had received, "I did not ask your opinion. I gave you my orders, and I expect them to be obeyed." Such should be the obedience of every follower of Jesus. The words which he has spoken are our law. We are not permitted to oppose thereto our judgments or fancies. Even if death were in the way, it is:

> Not ours to reason why—
> Ours but to dare and die,

and, at our Master's bidding, advance through flood or flame. —*"Feathers for Arrows"*

But this is a hard lesson to learn. I read some time ago of a German captain who found this out. He was drilling a company of volunteers. The parade ground was a field by the seaside. The men were going through their exercises very nicely, but the captain thought he would give them a lesson about obeying orders. They were marching up and down in the line of the water at some distance from it. He concluded to give them an order to march directly towards the water and see how far they would go. The men are marching along. "Halt, company," says the captain. In a moment, they halt. "Right face" is the next word, and instantly they wheel round. "*Forwart martch*" is then the order. At once, they begin to march directly towards the water; on they go, nearer and nearer to it. Soon they reach the edge of the water. Then there is a sudden halt. "Vat for you stop? I no say, Halt," cried the captain. "Why, captain, here is the water," said one of the men. "Vell, vot of it?" cried he, greatly excited, "vater is nothing, fire is nothing, everything is nothing. Ven I say, Forwart martch, then you must forwart martch." The captain was right; the first duty of a soldier is to learn to obey. —*Dr. Richard Newton*

What God calls a man to do, he will carry him through. I would undertake to govern half-a-dozen worlds if God called me to do it; but if he did not call me to do it, I would not undertake to govern half-a-dozen sheep. —*Dr. Payson*

213

But before faith came, we were kept under the law, shut up unto the faith which should afterwards be revealed.

—*Galatians 3:23*

ERE we have a condensed history of the world before the gospel was fully revealed by the coming of our Lord Jesus.

The history of each saved soul is a miniature likeness of the story of the ages. God acts upon the same principles both with the race and with individuals.

I. THE UNHAPPY PERIOD. "Before faith came."

1. We had no idea of faith by nature. It would never occur to the human mind that we could be saved by believing in Jesus.
2. When we heard of faith as the way of salvation, we did not understand it. We could not persuade ourselves that the words used by the preacher had their common and usual meaning.
3. We saw faith in others and wondered at its results; but we could not exercise it for ourselves.
4. We could not reach to faith, even when we began to see its necessity, admitted its efficacy, and desired to exercise it.

The reason of this inability was moral, not mental:
- We were proud and did not care to renounce self-righteousness.
- We could not grasp the notion of salvation by faith because it was contrary to the usual run of our opinions.
- We were bewildered because faith is a spiritual act, and we are not spiritual.

5. We were without the Spirit of God and therefore incapable.

We do not wish to go back to the state in which we were "before faith came," for it was one of darkness, misery, impotence, hopelessness, sinful rebellion, self-conceit, and condemnation.

II. THE CUSTODY WE WERE IN. "Kept under the law, shut up."

1. We were always within the sphere of law. In fact, there is no getting out of it. As all the world was only one prison for a man who offended Caesar, so is the whole universe no better than a prison for a sinner.
2. We were always kicking against the bounds of the law, sinning, and pining because we could not sin more.
3. We dared not overleap it altogether and defy its power. Thus, in the case of many of us, it checked us and held us captive with its irksome forbiddings and commandings.
4. We could not find rest. The law awakened conscience, and fear and shame attend such an awakening.
5. We could not discover a hope, for, indeed, there is none to discover while we abide under the law.
6. We could not even fall into the stupor of despair; for the law excited life, though it forbade hope.

   Among the considerations which held us in bondage were these:
   - The spirituality of the law, touching thoughts, motives, desires.
   - The need of perfect obedience, making one sin fatal to all hope of salvation by works.
   - The requirement that each act of obedience should be perfect.
   - The necessity that perfect obedience should be continual throughout the whole of life.

III. THE REVELATION WHICH SET US FREE. "The faith which should afterwards be revealed." The only thing which could bring us out of prison was faith. Faith came, and then we understood:

1. What was to be believed.
   - Salvation by another.
   - Salvation of a most blessed sort, gloriously sure, and complete.
   - Salvation by a most glorious person.
2. What it was to believe.

- We saw that it was "trust," implicit and sincere.
- We saw that it was ceasing from self and obeying Christ.

3. Why we believed:
   - We were shut up to this one way of salvation.
   - We were shut out of every other.
   - We were compelled to accept free grace or perish.

Our duty is to show men how the way of human merit is closed.

We must shut them up to simple faith only and show them that the way of faith is available.

To Arrest Attention

The Law and the Gospel are two keys. The law is the key that shutteth up all men under condemnation, and the gospel is the key which opens the door and lets them out. —*William Tyndale*

"Shut up unto the faith." To let you more effectually into the meaning of this expression, it may be right to state that in the preceding clause, "kept under the law," the term, *kept* is, in the original Greek, derived from a word which signifies a sentinel. The mode of conception is altogether military. The law is made to act the part of a sentry, guarding every avenue but one, and that one leads those who are compelled to take it to the faith of the gospel. They are shut up to this faith as their only alternative—like an enemy driven by the superior tactics of an opposing general to take up the only position in which they can maintain themselves or fly to the only town in which they can find a refuge or a security. This seems to have been a favorite style of argument with Paul, and the way in which he often carried on an intellectual warfare with the enemies of his Master's cause. It forms the basis of that masterly and decisive train of reasoning which we have in his epistle to the Romans. By the operation of skillful tactics, he (if we may be allowed the expression) maneuvered them and shut them up to the faith of the gospel. It gave prodigious effect to his argument when he reasoned with them, as he often does, upon their own principles, and turned them into instruments of conviction against themselves. With the Jews, he reasoned as a Jew. He made use of the Jewish law as a sentinel to shut them out of every other refuge and to shut them up to the refuge laid before them in the gospel. He led them to Christ by a schoolmaster whom they could not refuse; and the lesson of this schoolmaster, though a very decisive, was a very short one: "Cursed be he that continueth not in all the words of the law to do them." But in point of fact, they had not done them. To them, then, belonged the curse of the violated law. The awful severity of its sanctions was upon them. They found the faith and the free offer of the gospel to be the only avenue open to receive them. They were shut up unto this avenue; and the law, by concluding them all to be under sin, left them no other outlet but the free act of grace and of mercy laid before us in the New Testament. —*Dr. Chalmers*

The law was meant to prepare men for Christ by showing them that there is no other way of salvation except through him. It had two especial ends: the first was to bring the people who lived under it into a consciousness of the deadly dominion of sin, to shut them up, as it were, into a prison-house out of which only one door of escape should be visible, namely, the door of faith in Jesus. The second intention was to fence about and guard the chosen race to whom the law was given—to keep them as a peculiar people separate from all the world so that at the proper time the gospel of Christ might spring forth and go out from them as the joy and comfort of the whole human race. —*T. G. Rooke*

214

Ye did run well; who did hinder you that ye should not obey the truth?

—*Galatians 5:7*

 EVER censure indiscriminately. Admit and praise that which is good that you may the more effectually rebuke the evil. Paul did not hesitate to praise the Galatians and say, "Ye did run well."

It is a source of much pleasure to see saints running well. To do this, they must run in the right road, straight forward, perseveringly, at the top of their pace, with their eye on Christ, etc.

It is a great grief when such are hindered or put off the road.

The way is the truth, and the running is obedience. Men are hindered when they cease to obey the truth.

It may be helpful to try and find out who has hindered us in our race.

I. WE SHALL USE THE TEXT IN REFERENCE TO HINDERED BELIEVERS.

1. You are evidently hindered:
   - You are not so loving and zealous as you were.
   - You are quitting the old faith for new notions.
   - You are losing your first joy and peace.
   - You are not now leaving the world and self behind.
   - You are not now abiding all the day with your Lord.
2. Who has hindered you?
   - Did I do it? Pray, then, for your minister.
   - Did your fellow-members do it? You ought to have been proof against them. They could not have intended it. Pray for them.
   - Did the world do it? Why so much in it?

- Did the devil do it? Resist him.
- Did you not do it yourself? This is highly probable.
    Did you not overload yourself with worldly care?
    Did you not indulge carnal ease?
    Did you not by pride become self-satisfied?
    Did you not neglect prayer, Bible reading, the public means of grace, the Lord's Table, etc.?
    Mend your ways, and do not hinder your own soul.
- Did not false teachers do it, as in the case of the Galatians?
    If so, quit them at once, and listen only to the gospel of Christ.

3. You must look to it, and mend your pace.
- Your loss has been already great. You might by this time have been far on upon the road.
- Your natural tendency will be to slacken still more.
- Your danger is great of being overtaken by error and sin.
- Your death would come of ceasing to obey the truth.
- Your wisdom is to cry for help that you may run aright.

II. WE SHALL USE THE TEXT IN REFERENCE TO DELAYING SINNERS.

1. You have sometimes been set a-running.
- God has blessed his word to your arousing.
- God has not yet given you up; this is evident.
- God's way of salvation still lies open before you.

2. What has hindered you?
- Self-righteousness and trust in yourself?
- Carelessness, procrastination, and neglect?
- Love of self-indulgence or the secret practice of pleasurable sins?
- Frivolous, skeptical, or wicked companions?
- Unbelief and mistrust of God's mercy?

3. The worst evils will come of being hindered.
- Those who will not obey truth will become the dupes of lies.
- Truth not obeyed is disobeyed, and so sin is multiplied.
- Truth disregarded becomes an accuser, and its witness secures our condemnation.

God have mercy on *hinderers*. We must rebuke them.
God have mercy on the *hindered*. We would arouse them.

Spurs

Cecil says that some adopt the Indian maxim that it is better to walk than to run, and better to stand than to walk, and better to sit than to stand, and better to lie than to sit. Such is not the teaching of the gospel. It is a good thing to be walking in the ways of God, but it is better to be running—making real and visible progress, day by day advancing in experience and attainments. David likens the sun to a strong man rejoicing to run a race; not dreading it and shrinking back from it, but delighting in the opportunity of putting forth all his powers. Who so runs, runs well. —*The Christian*

The Christian race is by no means easy. We are sore let and hindered in running "the race that is set before us," because of: (1) Our sinful nature still remaining in the holiest saints. (2) Some easily besetting sin (Heb. 12:1). (3) The entanglements of the world, like heavy and close-fitting garments, impeding the racer's speed. (4) Our weakness and infirmity, soon tired and exhausted when the race is long or the road is rough. —*"In Prospect of Sunday," by G. S. Bowes*

Some are too busy. They run about too much to run well. Some run too fast at the outset; they run themselves out of breath. —*T. T. Lynch*

Henry Ward Beecher, in a sermon on this text, describes one of the hindrances to Christian progress thus: "We have fallen off immensely on the side of religious culture—earnest, prolonged, habitual, domestic, religious culture, conducted by the reading of God's Word and by prayer and its family influences. And this tendency is still further augmented by the increase of religious books, of tracts, of biographies and histories, of commentaries, which tend to envelop and hide the Word of God from our minds. In other words, these things which are called 'helps' have been increased to such a degree and have come to occupy so much of our attention, that when we have read our helps, we have no time left to read the things to be helped; and the Bible is covered down and lost under its 'helps.'"

It is possible that *fellow-professors* may hinder. We are often obliged to accommodate our pace to that of our fellow-travelers. If they are laggards, we are very likely to be so, too. We are apt to sleep as do others. We are stimulated or depressed, urged on or held back by those with whom we are associated in Christian fellowship. There is still greater reason to fear that in many cases *worldly friends and companions* are the hinderers. Indeed, they can be nothing else. None can help us in the race but those who are themselves running it; all others must hinder. Let a Christian form an intimate friendship with an ungodly person, and from that moment all progress is stayed. He must go back; for when his companion is going in the opposite direction, how can he walk with him except by turning his back upon the path which he has formerly trodden? —*P.*

A sailor remarks: "Sailing from Cuba, we thought we had gained sixty miles one day in our course; but at the next observation, we found we had lost more than thirty. It was an undercurrent. The ship had been going forward by the wind, but going back by the current." So a man's course in religion may often seem to be right and progressive, but the undercurrent of his besetting sins is driving him the very contrary way to what he thinks. —*Cheever*

215

Then is the offence of the cross ceased.
—*Galatians 5:11*

AUL intends here to declare that the offense of the cross never has ceased and never can cease. To suppose it to have ceased is folly.

The religion of Jesus is most peaceful, mild, and benevolent.

Yet, its history shows it to have been assailed with bitterest hate all along. It is clearly offensive to the unregenerate mind.

There is no reason to believe that it is one jot more palatable to the world than it used to be. The world and the gospel are both unchanged.

I. WHEREIN LIES THE OFFENSE OF THE CROSS?

1. Its doctrine of atonement offends man's pride.
2. Its simple teaching offends man's wisdom and artificial taste.
3. Its being a remedy for man's ruin offends his fancied power to save himself.
4. Its addressing all as sinners offends the dignity of Pharisees.
5. Its coming as a revelation offends "modern thought."
6. Its lofty holiness offends man's love of sin.

II. HOW IS THIS OFFENSE SHOWN?

1. Frequently by the actual persecution of believers.
2. More often by slandering believers and sneering at them as old-fashioned, foolish, weak-minded, morose, self-conceited, etc.
3. Often by omitting to preach the cross. Many nowadays preach a Christless, bloodless gospel.
4. Or by importing new meanings into orthodox terms.
5. Or by mixing the truth of Christ with errors.
6. Or by openly denying the deity of him who died on the cross and the substitutionary character of his sufferings.

Indeed, there are a thousand ways of showing that the cross offends us in one respect or another.

III. WHAT THEN?

1. Herein is folly, that men are offended:
   • With that which God ordains.
   • With that which must win the day.
   • With the only thing which can save them.
   • With that which is full of wisdom and beauty.

2. Herein is grace:

That we who once were offended by the cross, now find it to be:

The one hope of our hearts.

The great delight of our souls.

The joyful boast of our tongues.

3. Herein is heart-searching.

- Perhaps we are secretly offended at the cross.
- Perhaps we give no offense to haters of the cross. Many professed Christians never cause offense to the most godless.

Is this because they bear no testimony to the cross?

Is this because they are not crucified to the world?

Is this because there is no real trust in the cross and no true knowledge of Christ?

Let us not follow those preachers who are not friends to the cross.

Let us have no fellowship with those who have no fellowship with Christ.

Preachers who have caught the spirit of the age are of the world, and the world loves its own; but we must disown them.

Let us not be distressed by the offense of the cross, even when it comes upon us with bitterest scorn.

Let us look for it and accept it as a token that we are in the right.

Annotations

There is a want in the human mind which nothing but the Atonement can satisfy, though it may be a stumbling-block to the Jew and foolishness to the Greek. In the words of Henry Rogers, "It is adapted to human nature as a bitter medicine may be to a patient. Those who have taken it, tried its efficacy, and recovered spiritual health, gladly proclaim its value. But to those who have not and will not try it, it is an unpalatable potion still."

I open an ancient book written in opposition to Christianity by Arnobius, and I read: "Our gods are not displeased with you Christians for worshipping the Almighty God; but you maintain the deity of one who was put to death on the cross, you believe him to be yet alive, and you adore him with daily supplications." Men showed me at Rome in the Kircherian Museum a square foot of the plaster of a wall of a palace not many years ago uncovered on the Palatine hill. On the poor clay was traced a cross bearing a human figure with a brute's head. The figure was nailed to the cross, and before it a soldier was represented kneeling and extending his hands in the Greek posture of devotion. Underneath all was scratched in rude lettering in Greek, *"Alexamenos adores his God."* That representation of the central thought of Christianity was made in a jeering moment by some rude soldier in the days of Caracalla; but it blazes there now in Rome, the most majestic monument of its age in the world. —*Joseph Cook*

If any part of the truth which I am bound to communicate be concealed, this is sinful artifice. The Jesuits in China, in order to remove the offense of the cross, declared that it was a falsehood invented by the Jews that Christ was crucified; but they were expelled from the empire. This was designed, perhaps, to be held up as a warning to all missionaries that no good end is to be answered by artifice. —*Richard Cecil*

The cross is the strength of a minister. I, for one, would not be without it for the world. I should feel like a soldier without weapons, like an artist without his pencil, like a pilot without his compass, like a laborer without his tools. Let others, if they will, preach the law and morality. Let others hold forth the terrors of hell and the joys of heaven. Let others drench their congregations with teachings about the sacraments and the church. Give me the cross of Christ. This is the only lever which has ever turned the world upside down hitherto and made men forsake their sins. And if this will not do it, nothing will. A man may begin preaching with a perfect knowledge of Latin, Greek, and Hebrew; but he will do little or no good among his hearers unless he knows something of the cross. Never was there a minister who did much for the conversion of souls who did not dwell much on Christ crucified. Luther, Rutherford, Whitefield, M'Cheyne were all most eminent preachers of the cross. This is the preaching that the Holy Ghost delights to bless. He loves to honor those who honor the cross. —*J. C. Ryle*

> My thoughts once prompt round hurtful things to twine,
> What are they now, when two dread deaths are near?
> The one impends, the other shakes his spear.
> Painting and sculpture's aid in vain I crave:
> My one sole refuge is that love Divine,
> Which from the cross stretched forth its arms to save.
> —*Last lines written by Michaelangelo, when over eighty*

216

Bear ye one another's burdens, and so fulfil the law of Christ. . . . For every man shall bear his own burden.

—*Galatians 6:2, 5*

ALATIANS were apparently fond of the law and its burdens. At least, they appeared to be ready to load themselves with ceremonies, and so fulfill the law of Moses.

Paul would have them think of other burdens, by the bearing of which they would fulfill the law of Christ.

We are not under law, but under love.

But love is also law in the best sense. The law of Christ is love.

Love is the fulfilling of the law. "Bear ye one another's burdens, and so fulfil the law of Christ."

Lest this principle should be presumed upon, he mentions the principle of individual responsibility. "Every man shall bear his own burden."

I. COMMUNITY. "Bear ye one another's burdens."

1. Negatively:

It tacitly forbids certain modes of action.

- We are not to burden others. Some take a liberty to do so from this very text, as if it said, "Let others bear your burdens," which is just the reverse of what it urges.
- We are not to spy out others' burdens and report thereon.
- We are not to despise them for having such loads to bear.
- We are not to act as if all things existed for ourselves, and we were to bend all to our own purposes.
- We are not to go through the world oblivious of the sorrows of others. We may not shut our eyes to the woes of mankind.

2. Positively:

We are to share the burdens of others:

- By compassion, bear with their former sins (verse 1).
- By patience, bear with their infirmities and even their conceit (verse 2).
- By sympathy, bear their sorrows (verses 2–3).
- By assistance, bear their wants (verses 6, 10).
- By communion, in love and comfort, bear their struggles.
- By prayer and practical help, bear the burden of their labors and, thus, lighten it (verse 6).

3. Specially, we ought to consider:

- The erring brother. Referred to in verse 1 as "overtaken in a fault." We must tenderly restore him.
- The provoking brother, who thinks himself to be something (see verse 3). Bear with him; his mistake will bring him many a burden before he has done with it.
- The brother who is peculiarly trying is to be borne with to seventy times seven, even to the measure of the law of Christ.
- The greatly tried is to have our greatest sympathy.
- The minister of Christ should be released from temporal burdens, that he may give himself wholly to the burden of the Lord.

II. IMMUNITY. "For every man shall bear his own burden."

We shall not bear all the burdens of others.

We are not so bound to each other that we are partakers in willful transgression, negligence, or rebellion.

1. Each must bear his own sin if he persists in it.
2. Each must bear his own shame, which results from his sin.
3. Each must bear his own responsibility in his own sphere.
4. Each must bear his own judgment at the last.

III. PERSONALITY. "Every man . . . his own burden."

True godliness is a personal affair, and we cannot cast off our individuality. Therefore, let us ask for grace to look well to ourselves in the following matters:

1. Personal religion. The new birth, repentance, faith, love, holiness, fellowship with God, etc., are all personal.
2. Personal self-examination. We cannot leave the question of our soul's condition to the judgment of others.
3. Personal service. We have to do what no one else can do.
4. Personal responsibility. Obligations cannot be transferred.
5. Personal effort. Nothing can be a substitute for this.
6. Personal sorrow. "The heart knoweth its own bitterness."
7. Personal comfort. We need the Comforter for ourselves, and we must personally look up to the Lord for his operations.

All this belongs to the Christian, and we may judge ourselves by it.

So bear your own burden as not to forget others.

So live as not to come under the guilt of other men's sins'.

So help others as not to destroy their self-reliance.

Pithy Brevities

An old anecdote of the great Napoleon records that, while walking along a country road attended by some of his officers, he encountered a peasant heavily laden with faggots for fuel. The peasant was about to be jostled aside as a matter of course by his social superiors, when the Emperor, laying his hand on the arm of the foremost member of his escort, arrested the whole party, and gave the laboring man the use of the road, with the remark, "Messieurs, respect the burden."

Let him who expects one class in society to prosper to the highest degree while others are in distress try whether one side of his face can smile while the other is pinched. —*Thomas Fuller*

There is a proverb, but none of Solomon's, "Every man for himself, and God for us all." But where every man is for himself, the devil will have all. —*William Secker*

"Every man shall bear his own burden"; this is the law of necessity. "Bear ye one another's burdens"; this is the law of Christ. Let a man lighten his own load by sharing his neighbor's burden. —*T. T. Lynch*

There is a gateway at the entrance of a narrow passage in London over which is written, "No burdens allowed to pass through." "And yet we do pass constantly with ours," said one friend to another as they turned up this passage out of a more frequented and broader thoroughfare. They carried no visible burdens, but they were like many who, although they have no outward pack upon their shoulders, often stoop inwardly beneath the pressure of a heavy load upon the heart. The worst burdens are those which never meet the eye.

Bishop Burnet, in his charges to the clergy of his diocese, used to be extremely vehement in his declamations against pluralities. In his first visitation to Salisbury, he urged the authority of St. Bernard, who being consulted by one of his followers, whether he might accept of two benefices, replied, "And how will you be able to serve them both?" "I intend," answered the priest, "to officiate in one of them by a deputy." "Will your deputy suffer eternal punishment for you, too?" asked the saint. "Believe me, you may serve your cure by proxy, but you must suffer the penalty in person." This anecdote made such an impression on Mr. Kelsey, a pious and wealthy clergyman then present, that he immediately resigned the rectory of Bernerton, in Berkshire, worth two hundred a year, which he then held with another of great value. —*Whitecross*

With many, personal service in the cause of humanity is commuted for a money payment. But we are to be colliers in the campaign against evil and not merely to pay the war tax. —*"Ecce Homo"*

217

Be not deceived; God is not mocked: for whatsoever a man soweth, that shall he also reap.

—*Galatians 6:7*

 OTH Luther and Calvin confine these words to the support of the ministers of the word, and certainly therein they have weighty meaning. Churches that starve ministers will be starved themselves.

But we prefer to take the words as expressing a general principle.

I. GOD IS NOT TO BE TRIFLED WITH.

1. Either by the notion that there will be no rewards and punishments.
2. Or by the idea that a bare profession will suffice to save us.
3. Or by the fancy that we shall escape in the crowd.
4. Or by the superstitious supposition that certain rites will set all straight at last, whatever our lives may be.

5. Or by a reliance upon an orthodox creed, a supposed conversion, a presumptuous faith, and a little almsgiving.

II. THE LAWS OF HIS GOVERNMENT CANNOT BE SET ASIDE.

1. It is so in nature. Law is inexorable. Gravitation crushes the man who opposes it.
2. It is so in providence. Evil results surely follow social wrong.
3. Conscience tells us it must be so. Sin must be punished.
4. The word of God is very clear upon this point.
5. To alter laws would disarrange the universe and remove the foundation of the hopes of the righteous.

III. EVIL SOWING WILL BRING EVIL REAPING.

1. This is seen in the present result of certain sins.
   - Sins of lust bring disease into the bodily frame.
   - Sins of idolatry have led men to cruel and degrading practices.
   - Sins of temper have caused murders, wars, strifes, and misery.
   - Sins of appetite, especially drunkenness, cause want, misery, delirium, etc.
2. This is seen in the mind becoming more and more corrupt and less able to see the evil of sin or to resist temptation.
3. This is seen when the man becomes evidently obnoxious to God and man so as to need restraint and invite punishment.
4. This is seen when the sinner becomes himself disappointed in the result of his conduct. His malice eats his heart; his greed devours his soul; his infidelity destroys his comfort; his raging passions agitate his spirit.
5. This is seen when the impenitent is confirmed in evil and eternally punished with remorse. Hell will be the harvest of a man's own sin. Conscience is the worm which gnaws him.

IV. GOOD SOWING WILL BRING GOOD REAPING.

The rule holds good both ways. Let us, therefore, enquire as to this good sowing:

1. In what power is it to be done?
2. In what manner and spirit shall we set about it?
3. What are its seeds?
   - Towards God, we sow in the Spirit, faith and obedience.
   - Towards men, love, truth, justice, kindness, forbearance.
   - Towards self, control of appetite, purity, etc.
4. What is the reaping of the Spirit?
   Life everlasting dwelling within us and abiding there forever.

Let us sow good seed always.

Let us sow it plentifully that we may reap in proportion.
Let us begin to sow it at once.

Seeds

They that would mock God mock themselves much more. —*John Trapp*

It is not an open question at all whether I shall sow or not today. The only question to be decided is, Shall I sow good seed or bad? Every man always is sowing for his own harvest in eternity, either tares or wheat. According as a man soweth, so shall he also reap. He that sows the wind of vanity shall reap the whirlwind of wrath. Suppose a man should collect a quantity of small gravel and dye it carefully so that it should resemble wheat and sow it in his fields in spring, expecting that he would reap a crop of wheat like his neighbor's in harvest. The man is mad; he is a fool to think that by his silly trick he can evade the laws of nature and mock nature's God. Yet equally foolish is the conduct and far heavier the punishment of the man who sows wickedness now and expects to reap safety at last. Sin is not only profitless and disastrous; it is eminently a deceitful work. Men do not of set purpose cast themselves away; sin cheats a sinner out of his soul.

But sowing righteousness is never and nowhere lost labor. Every act done by God's grace and at his bidding is living and fruitful. It may appear to go out of sight, like seed beneath the furrow; but it will rise again. Sow on, Christians! Sight will not follow the seed far; but when sight fails, sow in faith, and you will reap in joy soon. —*William Arnot*

"Whatsoever a man soweth, that shall he also reap." No blight, nor mildew, nor scorching sun, nor rain deluge, can turn that harvest into failure.

Cast forth thy act, thy word into the ever-living, ever-working universe. It is a seed-grain that cannot die; unnoticed today, it will be found flourishing as a Banyan grove (perhaps, alas! as a Hemlock forest) after a thousand years. —*Thomas Carlyle*

So it is with all temptations and lusts. They are ever scattering seeds—as weeds do. What a power there is in seeds! How long-lived they are, as we see in the mummies of Egypt, where they may have lain for thousands of years in darkness, but now come forth to grow. What contrivances they have to continue and to propagate themselves. They have wings, and they fly for miles. They may float over wide oceans and rest themselves in foreign countries. They have hooks and attach themselves to objects. Often they are taken up by birds which transport them to distant places. As it is with the seeds of weeds, so it is with every evil propensity and habit. It propagates itself and spreads over the whole soul and goes down from generation to generation. —*Dr. James McCosh*

Doth any think he shall lose by his charity? No worldling, when he sows his seed, thinks he shall lose his seed; he hopes for increase at harvest. Darest thou trust the ground and not God? Sure, God is a better paymaster than the earth;

grace doth give a larger recompense than nature. Below, thou mayest receive forty grains for one, but in heaven (by the promise of Christ) a hundred-fold: a measure heapen, and shaken, and thrust together, and yet running over. "Blessed is he that considereth the poor"; there is the seeding. "The Lord shall deliver him in the time of trouble" (Ps. 12:1); there is the harvest. Is that all? No. Matthew 25:35: "Ye fed me when I was hungry, and gave me drink when thirsty"—comforted me in misery; there is the sowing. *Venite, beati.* "Come, ye blessed of my Feather, inherit the kingdom prepared for you"; there is the harvest. —*Thomas Adams*

218

But God forbid that I should glory, save in the cross of our Lord Jesus Christ, by whom the world is crucified unto me, and I unto the world.

—*Galatians 6:14*

 AUL vigorously rebuked those who went aside from the doctrine of the Cross (verses 12–13).

When we rebuke others, we must take care to go right ourselves; hence, he says, "God forbid that I should glory, save in the cross."

Our own resolute adherence to truth, when practically carried out, is a very powerful argument against opponents.

Paul rises to warmth when he thinks of the opponents of the cross. He no sooner touches the subject than he glows and burns.

Yet, he has his reasons and states them clearly and forcibly in the latter words of the text.

Here are three crucifixions:

I. CHRIST CRUCIFIED. "The cross of our Lord Jesus Christ."

He mentions the atoning death of Jesus in the plainest and most obnoxious terms. The cross was shameful as the gallows tree.

Yet with the clearest contrast as to the person enduring it, for to him he gives his full honors in the glorious title, "our Lord Jesus Christ."

He refers to the doctrine of free justification and full atonement by the death of Jesus upon the cross.

In this he gloried so as to glory in nothing else, for he viewed it:

1. As a display of the divine character. "God was in Christ" (2 Cor. 5:19).
2. As the manifestation of the love of the Savior (John 15:13).
3. As the putting away of sin by atonement (Heb. 9:26).

4. As the breathing of hope, peace, and joy to the desponding soul.

5. As the great means of touching hearts and changing lives.

6. As depriving death of terror, seeing Jesus died.

7. As ensuring heaven to all believers.

In any one of these points of view, the cross is a pillar of light, flaming with unutterable glory.

II. THE WORLD CRUCIFIED. "The world is crucified unto me."

As the result of seeing all things in the light of the Cross, he saw the world to be like a felon executed upon a cross.

1. Its character condemned (John 12:31).

2. Its judgment contemned. Who cares for the opinion of a gibbeted felon?

3. Its teachings despised. What authority can it have?

4. Its pleasures, honors, treasures, rejected.

5. Its pursuits, maxims, and spirit cast out.

6. Its threatenings and blandishments made nothing of.

7. Itself soon to pass away, its glory and its fashion fading.

III. THE BELIEVER CRUCIFIED. "And I unto the world."

To the world, Paul was no better than a man crucified.

If faithful, a Christian may expect to be treated as only fit to be put to a shameful death.

He will probably find:

1. Himself at first bullied, threatened, and ridiculed.

2. His name and honor held in small repute because of his association with the godly poor.

3. His actions and motives misrepresented.

4. Himself despised as a sort of madman or of doubtful intellect.

5. His teaching described as exploded, dying out, etc.

6. His ways and habits reckoned to be Puritanic and hypocritical.

7. Himself given up as irreclaimable and therefore dead to society.

Let us glory in the cross, because it gibbets the world's glory, and honor, and power!

Let us glory in the cross when men take from us all other glory.

Memoranda

It is a subject of rejoicing and glorying that we have *such* a Savior. The world looked upon him with contempt, and the cross was a stumbling-block to the Jew and folly to the Greek. But to the Christian, that cross is the subject of glorying. It is so because: (1) of the love of him who suffered there; (2) of the purity and holiness of his character, for the innocent died there for the guilty; (3) of the honor there put on the law of God by his dying to maintain it unsullied; (4)

of the reconciliation there made for sin, accomplishing what could be done by no other oblation and by no power of man; (5) of the pardon there procured for the guilty; (6) of the fact that through it we become dead to the world and are made alive unto God; (7) of the support and consolation which go from that cross to sustain us in trial; and (8) of the fact that it procured for us admission into heaven, a title to the world of glory. All is glory around the cross. It was a glorious Savior who died; it was glorious love that led him to die; it was a glorious object to redeem a world; and it is unspeakable glory to which he will raise lost and ruined sinners by his death. Oh, who would not glory in such a Savior! —*Albert Barnes*

If you have not yet found out that Christ crucified is the foundation of the whole volume, you have hitherto read your Bible to very little profit. Your religion is a heaven without a sun, an arch without a key stone, a compass without a needle, a clock without spring or weights, a lamp without oil. It will not comfort you; it will not deliver your soul from hell. —*J. C. Ryle*

Do not be satisfied with so many others only to know the cross in its power to atone. The glory of the cross is that it was not only to Jesus the path to life, but that each moment it can become to us the power that destroys sin and death and keeps us in the power of the eternal life. Learn from your Savior the holy art of using it for this. Faith in the power of the cross and its victory will day by day make dead the deeds of the body, the lusts of the flesh. This faith will teach you to count the cross, with its continual death to self, all your glory. Because you regard the cross not as one who is still on the way to crucifixion with the prospect of a painful death, but as one to whom the crucifixion is past, who already lives in Christ, and now only bears the cross as the blessed instrument through which the body of sin is done away (Rom. 6:6, RV). The banner under which complete victory over sin and the world is to be won is the cross. —*Andrew Murray*

When Ignatius, pastor of the church at Antioch, was condemned by the emperor Trajan to suffer death at Rome, he was apprehensive that the Christians there, out of their great affection for him, might endeavor to prevent his martyrdom; and therefore wrote a letter from Smyrna to the Roman Christians, which he sent on before him, wherein he earnestly besought them to take no measures for the continuance of his life, and amongst other things, said, "I long for death," adding as a reason why he was desirous of thus testifying his love to Christ, "My love is crucified."

Love makes the cross easy, amiable, admirable, delicious.

Brethren, the cross of Christ is your crown, the reproach of Christ your riches; the shame of Christ your glory. —*Joseph Alleine, written from "The Common Prison"*

219

That holy Spirit of promise, which is the earnest of our inheritance.
—Ephesians 1:13–14

EAVEN is ours by inheritance. It is not purchased by merit nor won by strength, but obtained by birthright.

Of this inheritance, we have a foretaste here below; and that foretaste is of the nature of a pledge or earnest, guaranteeing our coming to full possession.

An earnest is of the same nature as the ultimate blessing of which it is an earnest. A pledge is returned, but an earnest is retained as part of the thing promised.

Great enjoyment attends the possession of the earnest of our inheritance when rightly understood

I. THE HOLY SPIRIT IS HIMSELF THE EARNEST OF THE HEAVEN-LY INHERITANCE.

He is not only the pledge, but the foretaste of everlasting bliss.

1. His entrance into the soul brings with it that same life which enters heaven, namely, the eternal life.
2. His abiding in us consecrates us to the same purpose to which we shall be devoted throughout eternity, namely, the service of the Lord our God.
3. His work in us creates that same holiness which is essential to the enjoyment of heaven.
4. His influence over us brings us that same communion with God which we shall enjoy forever in heaven.
5. His being ours is as much as heaven being ours, if not more; for if we possess the God of heaven, we possess heaven and more.

The possession of the Spirit is the dawn of glory.

II. THE HOLY SPIRIT BRINGS TO US MANY THINGS WHICH ARE BLESSED FORETASTES OF THE HEAVENLY INHERITANCE.

1. Rest. This is a leading idea of heaven, and we have rest at this moment in Jesus Christ (Heb. 4:3).
2. Delight in service. We serve the Lord with gladness even now.
3. Joy over repenting sinners. This we can now attain.
4. Communion with saints. How sweet even in this imperfect state!
5. Enlarged knowledge of God and of all divine things. Here also we know in part the same things which are known above.
6. Victory over sin, Satan, and the world.

7. Security in Christ Jesus.

8. Nearness to our Beloved.

By these windows, we look into the things which God has prepared for them that love him. "He hath revealed them unto us by his Spirit."

III. THERE IS A VERY DARK CONTRAST TO THIS BRIGHT THEME.

There are "evident tokens of perdition," pledges of woe.

There are also earnests and foretastes of the eternal state of misery.

Ungodly men may pretty clearly guess what sin will bring them to when it has ripened. Let them learn from:

1. The fruit of some sins in this life: shame, rags, disease, etc.

2. Their fear of death, alarm at the thought of it.

3. Their frequent unrest and foreboding. "They flee when no man pursueth"; they are "tossed to and fro as the locust."

4. Disappointments in their companions, mutual quarrels and hates. What will it be to be shut up with such persons for ever?

5. Their distaste for good things, inability to pray, etc., all earnests of the impossibility of their joining saints and angels in heaven.

Oh, to be filled by the Spirit so as to find heaven begun below!

Striking Extracts

There is great resemblance betwixt an earnest and the indwelling of the Spirit with the graces which he works in us. (1)The earnest is part of the whole sum, which is on a certain account to be paid at the time appointed. So the Spirit we have and his grace are the beginning of that glorious being which we shall ultimately receive—the same for substance, though differing in degree. (2) An earnest is but little in comparison of the whole. Twenty shillings is earnest sufficient to make sure of a hundred pounds; thus, all the grace we have is but a small thing in comparison of the fullness we look for, even as the first-fruits were in comparison of the full harvest. (3)An earnest doth assure him that receiveth it of the honest meaning of him with whom he contracteth; so the Spirit and grace which we receive from God do assure us of his settled purpose of bringing us to eternal glory. —*Paul Bayne*

Christians! God is nearer to us than our nearest friend, nearer to us than Christ himself would be if we *only* felt the touch of his hand and the sweep of his vesture; for he takes up his abode *within* us. Plato seemed to have a glimpse of this glorious truth when he said, "God is more inward to us than we are to ourselves." What was to him a beautiful speculation is to us an inspiring reality; for we are the "temple of the Holy Ghost." —*Dr. Charles Stanford*

As soon as we have set out on our journey to go home, our home by foretastes comes to meet us. The peace of our home embraces us; the Spirit, like a dove, rests upon our hearts; the glory of our home allures us; and angel-servants from our home bear us company and help us on our road. Oh, what a sweet home ours must be that can send us such pledges of its sweetness while we are yet a great way off! —*John Pulsford*

"*The earnest.*" The Greek word is *arrhâbôn*. It is Hebrew (at least, Semitic) by derivation; the identical Hebrew word appearing in Genesis 38. By derivation it has to do with *exchange*, and so first means a *pledge*; but usage brought it to the kindred meaning of an *earnest*. It was used for the bridegroom's betrothal gifts to the bride, a case exactly in point here. In ecclesiastical Latin, it appears usually in the shortened form, *arra*. It survives in the French *arrhes*, the money paid to strike a bargain. *Arrhâbôn* occurs elsewhere in the New Testament: 2 Corinthians 1:22; 5:5. There, as here, it denotes the gifts of the Holy Spirit given to the saints, as the part payment of the coming "weight of glory," the inmost essence of which is the complete attainment (1 John 3:2) of that likeness to the Lord which the Spirit begins and develops here (2 Cor. 3:18). A kindred expression is "*the first fruits of the Spirit*" (Rom. 8:23). —"*Cambridge Bible for Schools and Families.*" *A work which we commend to all ministers.*

220

Of whom the whole family in heaven and earth is named.
—*Ephesians 3:15*

 ANY are the weights which drag us toward earth and the cords which bind us to it.

Among these last our families are not the least.

We need an upward impulse. Oh, that we may find it in the text!

There is a blessed connection between saints below and saints above.

Oh, to feel that we are one family!

I. LET US UNDERSTAND THE LANGUAGE OF THE TEXT.

1. The *keyword* is "*family.*"
   - A building sets forth the unity of the builder's design.
   - A flock, unity of the shepherd's possession.
   - The title of citizen implies unity of privilege.
   - The idea of an army displays unity of object and pursuit.

   Here we have something closer and more instructive still: "family"
   - The same Father, and thus unity of relationship.
   - The same life, and so unity of nature.
   - The same mutual love growing out of nature and relations.

- The same desires, interests, joys, and cares.
- The same home for abode, security, and enjoyment.
- The same inheritance to be soon possessed.

2. The *link word* is *"whole."* "Whole family in heaven and earth."
There is but one family, and it is a whole.
   On earth we find a portion of the family:
   - Sinning and repenting, not yet made perfect.
   - Suffering and despised, strangers and foreigners among men.
   - Dying and groaning, because yet in the body.

   In heaven, we find another part of the family:
   - Serving and rejoicing. Sinless and free from all infirmity.
   - Honoring God and honored by him.
   - Free from sighing and engrossed in singing.

The militant and the triumphant are one undivided family.

3. The *crowning word* is *"named."*
We are named after the Firstborn, even Jesus Christ.
   - Thus are we all acknowledged to be as truly sons as the Lord Jesus, for the same name is named on us.
   - Thus is he greatly honored among us. His name is glorified by each one who truly bears it.
   - Thus are we greatly honored in him by bearing so august a name.
   - Thus are we taught whom to imitate. We must justify the name.
   - Thus are we forcibly reminded of his great love to us, his great gift to us, his union with us, and his value of us.

II. LET US CATCH THE SPIRIT OF THE TEXT.

Let us now endeavor to feel and display a family feeling.

1. As members of one family, let us enjoy the things we have in common.
   We all have:
   - The same occupations. It is our meat and drink to serve the Lord, to bless the brotherhood, and to win souls.
   - The same delights: communion, assurance, and expectation.
   - The same love from the Father.
   - The same justification and acceptance with our God.
   - The same rights to the throne of grace, angelic ministration, divine provision, and spiritual illumination.
   - The same anticipations: growth in grace, perseverance to the end, and glory at the end.

2. As members of one family, let us be familiar with each other.

3. As members of one family, let us practically help each other.

4. As members of one family, let us lay aside all dividing names, aims, feelings, ambitions, and beliefs.

5. As members of one family, let us strive for the honor and kingdom of our Father who is in heaven.

Let us seek out the lost members of the family.

Let us cherish the forgotten members of the family.

Let us strive for the peace and unity of the family.

Choice Words

The Scripture knows but two places for the receipt of all believers, either heaven or earth. So when the apostle will tell us where all they were who were gathered under Christ as their Head and Redeemer, he arranges them in these orders, "things in heaven, and things in earth" (Eph. 1:10); the apostle forgot limbo there, and purgatory here. As the Scripture doth know but two sorts of saints, so but two places, heaven for the triumphant, earth for the militant. —*Paul Bayne*

"The *whole* family in heaven and earth," not the two families, nor the divided family, but the whole family in heaven and earth. It appears, at first sight, as if we were very effectually divided by the hand of *death*. Can it be that we are one family when some of us labor on, and others sleep beneath the greensward? There was a great truth in the sentence which Wordsworth put into the mouth of the little child, when she said, "O master, we are seven."

> "But they are dead: those two are dead,
> Their spirits are in heaven!"
> 'Twas throwing words away; for still
> The little maid would have her will,
> And said: "Nay, we are seven."

Should we not thus speak of the divine family? for death assuredly has no separating power in the household of God. —*C. H. S.*

"When I was a boy," says one, "I thought of heaven as a great shining city, with vast walls and domes and spires, and with nobody in it except white tenuous angels, who were strangers to me. By-and by my little brother died; and I thought of a great city with walls and domes and spires, and a flock of cold unknown angels, and one little fellow that I was acquainted with; he was the only one I knew in that time. Then another brother died, and there were two that I knew. Then my acquaintances began to die, and the flock continually grew. But it was not till I had sent one of my little children to his Grandparent— God—that I began to think I had got a little in myself. A second went, a third went, a fourth went; and by that time I had so many acquaintances in heaven that I did not see any more walls and domes and spires. I began to think of the residents of the celestial city. And now there have so many of my acquaintance gone there, that it sometimes seems to me that I know more in heaven than I do on earth." —*Handbook of Illustration*

Stein, a great German statesman and head of the Prussian government in 1807, wrote in 1812 to Count Munster, "I am sorry your excellency suspects a Prussian in me, and betrays a Hanoverian in yourself. I have but one Fatherland, and that is Germany; and as under the old constitution I belonged to Germany alone, and not to any part of Germany, so to Germany alone, and not to any part of it, I am devoted with my whole heart."

Thomas Brooks mentions a woman who lived near Lewes, in Sussex, who was ill, and therefore was visited by one of her neighbors, who to cheer her, told her that if she died she would go to heaven, and be with God, and Jesus Christ, and the saints and angels. To this the sick woman in all simplicity replied, "Ah, mistress, I have no relations there! Nay, not so much as a gossip, or acquaintance; and as I know nobody, I had a great deal sooner stop with you and the other neighbors, than go and live among strangers." It is to be feared that if a good many were to speak their thoughts they would say much the same.

221

That he would grant you, according to the riches of his glory, to be strengthened with might by his Spirit in the inner man; that Christ may dwell in your hearts by faith; that ye, being rooted and grounded in love, may be able to comprehend with all saints what is the breadth, and length, and depth, and height; and to know the love of Christ, which passeth knowledge, that ye might be filled with all the fulness of God.

—*Ephesians 3:16–19*

 HE ability to comprehend and measure described in our text was the subject of the apostle's prayer, and therefore we may be quite sure that it is a most desirable attainment.

Observe how he prays and how wisely he arranges his petitions.

He would have us measure the immeasurable, but he would first have us made fit to do so.

We shall make our chief point the fourfold measurement, but we shall note that which comes before and that which follows after.

I. THE PREVIOUS TRAINING REQUIRED FOR THIS MEASUREMENT.

1. He would have their spiritual faculties vigorous.
   - "Your inner man." Understanding, faith, hope, love—all need power from a divine source.

- "Strengthened." Made vigorous, active, healthy, capacious.
- "With might." No low degree of force will suffice.
- "By his Spirit." The power required is spiritual, holy, heavenly, divine, actually imparted by the Holy Ghost.

2. He would have the subject always before them: "that Christ may dwell in your hearts by faith."
   - "In your hearts." Love must learn to measure Christ's love. It is revealed to the heart rather than to the head.
   - "By faith." A carnal man measures by sight, a saint by faith.
   - "May dwell." He must be ever near that we may learn to measure him. Communion is the basis of this knowledge.

3. He would have them exercised in the art of measurement: "that ye, being rooted and grounded in love."
   - We must love him ourselves if we would measure Christ's love.
   - We must, by experience of his love, be confirmed in our own love to him, or we cannot measure his love.
   - We must also have a vital grip of Christ. We must be rooted as a tree, which takes many a hold upon the soil.
   - We must settle down on his love as our foundation on which we are grounded, as a building.
   - We must also show fixedness, certainty, and perseverance in our character, belief, and aim; for thus only shall we learn.

II. THE MENSURATION ITSELF.

This implies a sense of the reality of the matter.

It includes a coming near to the object of our study.

It indicates an intimate study and a careful survey.

It necessitates a view from all sides of the subject.

The order of the measurement is the usual order of our own growth in grace: breadth and length before depth and height.

1. *The breadth.* Immense.
   - Comprehending all nations: "Preach the gospel to every creature."
   - Covering hosts of iniquities: "all manner of sin."
   - Compassing all needs and cares.
   - Conferring boundless boons for this life and worlds to come.

It were well to sail across this river and survey its broad surface.

2. *The length.* Eternal.

We wonder that God should love us at all. Let us meditate upon:
   - Eternal love in the fountain: election and the covenant.
   - Ceaseless love in the flow: redemption, calling, perseverance.
   - Endless love in endurance: longsuffering, forgiveness, faithfulness, patience, immutability.

- Boundless love, in length exceeding our length of sin, suffering, backsliding, age, or temptation.

3. *The depth.* Incomprehensible.

- Stoop of divine love, condescending to consider us, to commune with us, to receive us in love, to bear with our faults, and to take us up from our low estate.
- Stoop of love personified in Christ.
    He stoops and becomes incarnate, endures our sorrows, bears our sins, and suffers our shame and death.
- Where is the measure for all this?

Our weakness, meanness, sinfulness, and despair make one factor of the measurement.

His glory, holiness, greatness, and deity make up the other.

4. *The height.* Infinite.

- As developed in present privilege, as one with Jesus.
- As to be revealed in future glory.
- As never to be fully comprehended throughout the ages.

III. THE PRACTICAL RESULT OF THIS MENSURATION. "That ye might be filled with all the fulness of God."

Here are words full of mystery, worthy to be pondered.

- Be *filled.* What great things man can hold!
- Filled *with God.* What exaltation!
- Filled *with the fullness* of God. What must this be?
- Filled *with all the fullness of God.* What more can be imagined?

This love and this fullness will lead to the imitation of Christ's love.

Our love to him will be broad, long, deep, high.

Insertions

In the gospel history, we find that Christ had a fourfold entertainment amongst the sons of men: some received him into house, not into heart as Simon the Pharisee who gave him no kiss nor water to his feet; some into heart, but not into house, as Nicodemus and others; some neither into heart nor house, as the graceless, swinish Gergesenes; some both into house and heart, as Lazarus, Mary, Martha. And thus let all good Christians do: endeavor that Christ may dwell in their hearts by faith, that their bodies may be fit temples of his Holy Spirit, that now in this life, whilst Christ stands at the door of their hearts, knocking for admission, they will lift up the latch of their souls, and let him in; for if ever they expect to enter into the gates of the city of God hereafter, they must open their hearts, the gates of their own city, to him here in this world. —*John Spencer*

Faith makes man's heart,
   That dark, low, ruin'd thing,
By its rare art,
   A palace for a king.
Higher than proud Babel's tower by many a story;
By faith Christ dwells in us, the hope of glory.
                        —*F. Tate*

The more we know, the more are we conscious of our ignorance of that which is unknown, or, as Dr. Chalmers used to put it in his class, borrowing an illustration from his favorite mathematics, "The wider the diameter of light, the greater is the circumference of darkness." The more a man knows, he comes at more points into contact with the unknown.

    'Tis hard to find God; but to comprehend
    Him as he is, is labor without end.
                        —*Robert Herrick*

A gentleman passing a church with Daniel Webster, asked him, "How can you reconcile the doctrine of the Trinity with reason?" The statesman replied by asking, "Do you understand the arithmetic of heaven?"

222

The head, even Christ: from whom the whole body fitly joined together and compacted by that which every joint supplieth, according to the effectual working in the measure of every part, maketh increase of the body unto the edifying of itself in love.
                        —*Ephesians 4:15–16*

 HE words are as "compacted" as the body itself.

We shall not attempt full or even accurate exposition of the original, but dwell on the figure of the English text, undoubtedly a scriptural one, and full of profitable instruction.

Four subjects are brought before us in the text:

I. OUR UNION TO CHRIST. "The head, even Christ."

1. Essential to life. Severed from him, we are dead.
2. Essential to growth. We grow up into him who is the Head.
3. Essential to perfection. What should we be without a Head?

4. Essential to every member. The strongest needs union to the head as much as the weakest.

II. OUR INDIVIDUALITY. "Every joint"; "every part."

Each one must mind his own office.

1. We must each one personally see to his own vital union with the body and chiefly with the Head.
2. We must be careful to find and keep our fit position in the body.
3. We must be careful of our personal health for the sake of the whole body, for one ailing member injures the whole.
4. We must be careful of our growth, for the sake of the whole body.

The most careful self-watch will not be a selfish measure, but a sanitary duty involved by our relationship to the rest.

III. OUR RELATIONSHIP TO EACH OTHER. "Joined together"; "that which every joint supplieth."

1. We should in desire and spirit be fitted to work with others. We are to have joints. How could there be a body without them?
2. We should supply the joint-oil of love when so doing; indeed, each one must yield his own peculiar influence to the rest.
3. We should aid the compactness of the whole by our own solidity and healthy firmness in our place.
4. We should perform our service for all. We should guard, guide, support, nourish, and comfort the rest of the members, as our function may be.

IV. OUR COMPACT UNITY AS A CHURCH. "The body edifying itself in love."

1. There is but one body of Christ, even as he is the one Head.
2. It is an actual, living union, not a mere professed unity, but a body quickened by "the effectual working" of God's Spirit in every part.
3. It is a growing corporation. It increases by mutual edification, not by being puffed up, but by being built up. It grows as the result of its own life, sustained by suitable food.
4. It is an immortal body. Because the Head lives, the body must live also.

Are we in the body of Christ?

Are we not concerned to see it made perfect?

Are we ministering the supply which the body may fairly expect from us as members?

To Fit In

There is great fitness in the figure of the head and the members. The head is: (1) The highest part of the body, the most exalted. (2) The most sensitive part, the seat of nerve and sensation, of pleasure and pain. (3) The most honorable part, the glory of man, the part of man's body that receives the blessing, wears the crown, and is anointed with the oil of joy and of consecration. (4) The most exposed part, especially assailed in battle, and liable to be injured, and where injury would be most dangerous. (5) The most expressive part, the seat of expression, whether in the smile of approval, the frown of displeasure, the tear of sympathy, the look of love. —*G. S. Bowes*

Everyone knows that it would be far better to lose our feet than our head. Adam had feet to stand with, but we have lost them by his disobedience: yet, glory be to God, we have found a Head, in whom we abide eternally secure, a Head which we shall never lose. — *"Feathers for Arrows"*

The moment I make of myself and Christ two, I am all wrong. But when I see that we are one, all is rest and peace. —*Luther*

What a happy condition the Church and members of Christ are in! (1) Interested in the same love as the Head. (2) Under the same decree of election with the Head. (3) Allied to the same relations, interested in the same riches, and assured by membership of the same life and immortality in the world to come: "Because I live, ye shall live also." —*Benjamin Keach*

Of all the symbols which set forth Christ's church, I prefer this. Bringing out, as well as any other, our relationship to Christ, and better than any other our relationship to each other, it teaches us lessons of love, and charity, and tender sympathy. When bill-hook or pruning-knife lops a branch from the tree, the stem bends; it seems for a while to drop some tears, but they are soon dried up; and the other boughs suffer no pain, show no sympathy—their leaves dancing merrily in the wind over the poor dead branch that lies withering below. But a tender sympathy pervades the body and its members. Touch my finger roughly, and the whole body feels it; wound this foot, and thrilling through my frame, the pang shoots upward to the head; let the heart, or even a tooth, ache, and all the system suffers disorder. With what care is a diseased member touched! What anxious efforts do we make to save a limb! With what slow reluctance does a patient, after long months or years of suffering, consent to the last remedy, the surgeon's knife! Many holy lessons of love, charity, and sympathy, our Lord teaches by this figure. —*Dr. Guthrie*

We must work in concert. Stress is laid on this in Scripture, as may be seen from such expressions as these: "if two of you shall agree," "fellow-helpers to the truth," "with one mind striving together for the faith of the gospel." It is as with the human hand. Take one of the fingers, the forefinger, for example; it can do many things by itself separately. I lay it on my pulse, to know how my heart beats; I turn over the leaf of a book with it; I use it to point a stranger the way; I place it on my lips to signify silence; I single out the individual to whom I would say, *"Thou art the man"*; I shake it in warning or remonstrance. But the hand can do, not five times as much as a single finger, not fifty times as much, not five hundred times as much, but five thousand times—and more. So with Christian churches; there must not merely be individual effort, but combined and united effort, on the New Testament principle, "As every man hath received the gift, even so let him minister." —*Dr. Culross*

223

But ye have not so learned Christ; if so be that ye have heard him, and have been taught by him, as the truth is in Jesus.

—Ephesians 4:20–21

THE distinction between the Christian and others: "but ye."

There must be this separation as long as the world is "the world."

The means of this distinction is our discipleship. We have learned Christ and learned him in a different way from that which satisfies many who profess to know him.

We have not so learned Christ as to be able to profess his name and yet practice lasciviousness.

We are converted into learners and are under the tutelage of the Holy Spirit. How we learn is a test question. Some have learned Christ and yet are not saved; others have not so learned him but are truly his disciples.

I. OUR LESSON. "Learned Christ."

This learning Christ is:
- Much more than learning doctrine, precept, or ceremony.
- Much more than knowing about Christ or learning from Christ.

It includes several forms of knowledge:

1. To know him as a personal Christ.
2. To know his nature and to treat him accordingly.
3. To know his offices and how to use them.
4. To know his finished work for God and for us.
5. To know his influence over men and to test it.
6. To know by learning Christ the way to live like him.

II. HOW WE HAVE *NOT* LEARNED IT.

1. So as to remain as we were before, unchanged and yet at peace.
2. So as to excuse sin because of his atonement.
3. So as to feel a freedom to sin because of pardon.

4. So as even to commit sin in Christ's name.

5. So as to reckon that we cannot conquer sin and so sit down under the dominion of some constitutional temptation.

6. So as to profess reverence for his name and character and then think little of the truth which he reveals.

III. HOW WE HAVE LEARNED IT.

We know the truth and know it in its best light:

1. As directly taught by his own self and by his own Spirit.

2. As distinctly embodied in his life and character.

3. As it relates to him and honors him.

4. Consequently, as it is in him. Truth is in Jesus, indeed and of a truth, for in him everything is real.

5. Consequently, as it works a total change in us and makes us like him in whom truth is embodied.

See, then, that we not only learn of Jesus, but we learn Jesus.

It is not enough to hear him and to be taught by him; we want to know himself.

Knowing him, we know the truth; for it is in him.

Thoughts

Instead of *"if so be that,"* many very competent scholars propose to render the original "inasmuch as" or "since ye have heard," etc., for the apostle is not referring to a supposed case, but stating a fact, as verse 20 proves. —*W. O'Neill*

He exhorts not to an outward reformation of their converse only, but to that truth and sincerity of sanctification, which the doctrine and power of grace in Christ teacheth and worketh in all true Christians: "If so be," saith he, "ye have learned the truth as it is in Jesus." Which doeth not, as other doctrines of philosophers, etc., teach you to put off the evils of your outward converse only, and to put on a new conversation over an old nature, as a sheepskin over a wolfish nature; he that doth no more falls short of that truth of grace which Christ requires; but it teacheth principally to put off the old man, as the cause of all the evils in the outward converse; and that is his meaning, when he saith, "As concerning the outward converse put off the old man," without which it is impossible to reform the converse. —*Thomas Goodwin*

An illustration of the foregoing remarks is found in Lord Chesterfield, who trained his only son, not to abandon vice, but to be a gentleman in the practice of it.

Some persons, instead of "putting off the old man," dress him up in a new shape. —*St. Bernard*

Unsanctified wisdom is the devil's greatest tool.

A handful of good life is worth a bushel of learning.

224

And have no fellowship with the unfruitful works of darkness, but rather reprove them.

—Ephesians 5:11

IRECTIONS on how to live while here below are very needful. We constantly come into contact with ungodly men; this is unavoidable. But here we are taught to avoid such communion with them as would make us partakers in their evil deeds.

Three truths are incidentally mentioned: evil works are sterile, they are works of darkness, and they deserve reproof.

We must have *no* fellowship with them, neither at any time, nor in any manner, nor in any degree.

I. WHAT IS FORBIDDEN? "Fellowship with works of darkness."

This fellowship may be produced in several ways:

1. By personally committing the sins so described or by joining with others in bringing them about.
2. By teaching wrong doing, either by plain word or by just inference.
3. By constraining, commanding, or tempting: by threat, request, persuasion, inducement, compulsion, bribery, or influence.
4. By provoking, through exciting anger, emulation, or discouragement.
5. By neglecting to rebuke: especially by parents and masters misusing their office and allowing known evils in the family.
6. By counseling and advising, or by guiding by example.
7. By consenting, agreeing, and cooperating. By smiling at an evil attempt, and, in the rend, partaking in the spoil. Those who join with churches in error come under this head.
8. By conniving at sin: tolerating, concealing, and making light of it.
9. By commending, countenancing, defending, and excusing the wrong already done and contending against those who would expose, denounce, and punish it.

II. WHAT IS COMMANDED? "Reprove them."

"Reprove" in the original is a word of large meaning.

1. Rebuke. Declare the wrong of it, and show your hatred thereof.
2. Convict. As the Holy Spirit reproves the world of sin, so aim at proving the world guilty by your holy life and bold witness.
3. Convert. This is to be your continual aim with those about you. You are so to reprove as to win men from ways of evil.

Oh, that we had more of honest and loving reproof of all evil!

III. WHY IT IS COMMANDED TO ME.

It is specially my duty to be clear of other men's sins:

1. As an imitator of God and a dear child (verse 1).
2. As one who is an inheritor of the kingdom of God (verses 5–6).
3. As one who has come out of darkness into marvelous light in the Lord (verse 8).
4. As one who bears fruit, even the fruit of the Spirit, which is in all goodness, righteousness, and truth (verse 9).
5. As one who would not be associated with that which is either shameful or foolish (verses. 12, 15).

If our fellowship is with God, we must quit the ways of darkness.

IV. WHAT MAY COME OF OBEDIENCE TO THE COMMAND.

Even if we could see no good result, yet our duty would be plain enough; but much benefit may result:

1. We shall be clear of complicity with deeds of darkness.
2. We shall be honored in the consciences of the ungodly.
3. We may thus win them to repentance and eternal life.
4. We shall glorify God by our separated walk and by the godly perseverance with which we adhere to it.
5. We may thus establish others in holy nonconformity to the world.

Let us use the text as a warning to worldly professors.

Let us take it as a directory in our conversation with the ungodly.

Examples

A member of his congregation was in the habit of going to the theater. Mr. Hill went to him and said, "This will never do—a member of my church in the habit of attending the theater!" Mr. So-and-so replied that it surely must be a mistake as he was not in the habit of going there, although it was true he did go now and then *for a treat*. "Oh!" said Rowland Hill, "then you are a worse hypocrite than ever, sir. Suppose any one spread the report that I ate carrion, and I answered, 'Well, there is no wrong in that; I don't eat carrion every day in the week, but I have a dish now and then *for a treat*.' Why, you would say, 'What a nasty, foul, and filthy appetite Rowland Hill has to have to go to carrion for a treat!' Religion is the Christian's truest treat, Christ is his enjoyment." —*Charlesworth's Life of Rowland Hill*

On one occasion, traveling in the Portsmouth mail, Andrew Fuller was much annoyed by the profane conversation of two young men who sat opposite. After a time, one of them, observing his gravity, accosted him with an air of impertinence, inquiring, in rude and indelicate language, whether on his arrival at Portsmouth he should not indulge himself in a manner evidently corresponding with their own intentions. Mr. Fuller, lowering his ample brows, and looking the inquirer full in the face, replied in measured tones: "Sir, I am a man that fears God." Scarcely a word was uttered during the remainder of the journey. —*Memoir of Andrew Fuller*

Matthew Wilks once rode by coach with a young nobleman and a female passenger. The nobleman entered upon an improper conversation with the coachman and the woman. At a favorable opportunity, Mr. Wilks attracted his attention, and said, "My lord, maintain your rank!" The reproof was felt and acted upon. Let the Christian ever maintain his rank.

A distinguished Christian lady was recently spending a few weeks in a hotel at Long Branch, and an attempt was made to induce her to attend a dance in order that the affair might have the prestige bestowed by her presence, as she stood high in society. She declined all the importunities of her friends, and finally an honorable senator tried to persuade her to attend, saying, "Miss B., this is quite a harmless affair, and we want to have the exceptional honor of your presence." "Senator," said the lady, "I cannot do it. I am a Christian. I never do anything in my summer vacation, or wherever I go, that will injure the influence I have over the girls of my Sunday-school class." The senator bowed, and said, "I honor you. If there were more Christians like you, more men like myself would become Christians." —*Dr. Pentecost*

Rebukes should always be dealt in love; never wash a man's face in vitriol. Some persons would burn a house down to get rid of a mouse. The smallest fault is denounced as a great crime, and a good brother is cut off from fellowship, and bad feeling is raised, when a gentle hint would have done the work much more effectually. —*C. H. S.*

225

Husbands, love your wives, even as Christ also loved the church, and gave himself for it.

—*Ephesians 5:25*

 HE love of Christ to his church is the pattern for husbands.

It should be a pure, fervent, constant, self-sacrificing love.

The conduct of Jesus was the best proof of his love: He "loved the church, and gave himself for it."

Our conduct should be the genuine outcome of our love.

I. HOW CHRIST LOVED HIS CHURCH.

He loved his own church with:

1. A love of choice and special regard.
2. A love of unselfishness. He loved not hers, but her.
3. A love of complacency. He calls her, "Hephzibah, my delight is in her."
4. A love of sympathy. Her interests are his interests.
5. A love of communion. He manifests himself to his chosen bride.
6. A love of unity. A loving, living, lasting union is established.
7. A love of immutable constancy. He loves unto the end.

II. HOW HE PROVED HIS LOVE. "Gave himself for it."

1. He gave himself to his church by leaving heaven and becoming incarnate that he might assume her nature.
2. He gave himself throughout his life on earth by spending all his strength to bless his beloved.
3. He gave himself in death, the ransom for his church.
4. He gave himself in his eternal life: rising, ascending, reigning, pleading—all for the church of his choice.
5. He gave himself in all that he now is as God and man, exalted to the throne, for the endless benefit of his beloved church.

III. HOW WE SHOULD THINK OF IT.

It is set before us as a love which should influence our hearts.
We should think of it:

1. In a way of gratitude, wondering more and more at such love.
2. In a way of obedience, as the wife obeys the husband.
3. In a way of reverence, looking up to love so great, so heavenly, so perfect, so divine.
4. In a way of holiness, rejoicing to be like our holy husband.
5. In a way of love, yielding our whole heart to him.
6. In a way of imitation, loving him and others for his sake.

Let us enter into the love of Jesus, enjoy it in our own hearts, then imitate it in our families.

Concerning Love

Rowland Hill often felt much grieved at the false reports which were circulated of many of his sayings, especially those respecting his publicly mentioning Mrs. Hill. His attentions to her till the close of life were of the most gentlemanly and affectionate kind. The high view he entertained of her may be seen from the following fact: A friend having informed Mr. Hill of the sudden death of a lady, the wife of a minister, remarked, "I am afraid our dear minister loved his wife too well, and the Lord in wisdom has removed her." "What, sir?" replied Mr.

Hill, with the deepest feeling, "can a man love a good wife too much? Impossible, sir, unless he can love her better than Christ loves the church: 'Husbands, love your wives, *even as* Christ also loved the church, and gave himself for it.'"

"Let all things be done in love," saith the apostle. If all thy actions towards others, then, much more all things that concern thy wife, should be done in love. Thy thoughts should be thoughts of love; thy looks should be looks of love; thy lips, like the honeycomb, should drop nothing but sweetness and love; thy instructions should be edged with love; thy reprehensions should be sweetened with love; thy carriage and whole conversation towards her should be but the fruit and demonstration of thy love. Oh, how did Christ, who is thy pattern, love his spouse! His birth, life, and death were but, as it were, a stage whereon the hottest love imaginable, from first to last, acted its part to the life. It was a known, unknown love. Tiberius Gracchus, the Roman, finding two snakes in his bed, and consulting with the soothsayers, was told that one of them must be killed; yet, if he killed the male, he himself would die shortly; if the female, his wife would die. His love to his wife, Cornelia, was so great, that he killed the male, saith Plutarch, and died quickly. —*George Swinnock*

The Spanish poet Calderon, in one of his dramas, describes a beautiful Roman girl, Daria by name, eventually a Christian convert and martyr, who declares, while yet a pagan, that she will never love until she finds some one who has died to prove his love for her. She hears of Christ, and her heart is won.

226

And your feet shod with the preparation of the gospel of peace.
—*Ephesians 6:15*

 HRISTIANS are meant to be steadfast, active, moving, progressing, ascending; hence, their feet are carefully provided for.

They are feeble in themselves and need protection. Their road also is rough, and hence they need the shoes which grace provides.

I. LET US EXAMINE THE SHOES.

1. They come from a blessed maker, one who is skillful in all arts and knows by experience what is wanted, since he has himself journeyed through life's roughest ways.
2. They are made of excellent material: "the preparation of the gospel of peace," well-seasoned, soft in wear, lasting long.

- Peace with God as to the past, the future, the present.
- Peace of full submission to the divine mind and will.
- Peace with the word and all its teachings.
- Peace with one's inner self, conscience, tears, desires.
- Peace with brethren in the church and the family.
- Peace with all mankind: "As much as lieth in you, live peaceably with all men" (Rom. 12:18).

3. They are such as none can make except the Lord, who both sends the gospel and prepares the peace.
4. They are such shoes as Jesus wore and all the saints.
5. They are such as will never wear out. They are old, yet ever new. We may wear them at all ages and in all places.

II. LET US TRY THEM ON.
Observe with delight:
1. Their perfect fitness. They are made to suit each one of us.
2. Their excellent foothold. We can tread with holy boldness upon our high places with these shoes.
3. Their marching powers for daily duty. No one grows weary or footsore when he is thus shod.
4. Their wonderful protection against trials by the way. "Thou shalt tread on the lion and adder" (Ps. 91:13).
5. Their pleasantness of wear, giving rest to the whole man.
6. Their adaptation for hard work, climbing, and ploughing.
7. Their endurance of fire and water (Isa. 43:2). By peace of mind, we learn to pass through every form of trial.
8. Their fighting qualities. They are really a part of "the whole armour of God." (See the chapter in which the text is found.)

III. LET US LOOK AT THE BAREFOOTED AROUND US.
- The sinner is unshod, yet he kicks against the pricks. How can he hope to fulfill the heavenly pilgrimage?
- The professor is slipshod or else he wears tight shoes. His fine slippers will soon be worn out. He loves not the gospel, knows not its peace, seeks not its preparation.

The gospel alone supplies a fit shoe for all feet.
To the gospel, let us fly at once. Come, poor shoeless beggar!

Fastenings
"Put shoes on his feet" were among the first words of welcome to the returning prodigal. To be shoeless was in Israel a mark of great disgrace, indicating a lost inheritance, a state of misery, and penury (Deut. 25:10).

The Chinese advertise shoes which enable the wearer to walk on the clouds. Compare Isaiah 40:31: "They that wait upon the Lord shall renew their strength. They shall *run*, and not be weary; they shall *walk*, and not faint." "*Run* with patience, looking unto Jesus" (Heb. 12:1–3).

"Your feet shod with the preparation of the gospel of peace" (Eph. 6:15). The passage has been paraphrased, "Shod with the firm footing of the solid knowledge of the gospel." The word "preparation" signifies *preparedness* or *readiness*. Compare 2 Timothy 4:2: "Instant in season, out of season"; also Romans 1:15 : "I am ready to preach the gospel." This preparedness is well-pleasing to God. "How *beautiful* are thy feet with shoes, O prince's daughter! (Song of Sol. 7:1; Isa. 52:7). —*Mrs. Gordon*

Christian in the palace Beautiful: "The next day they took him, and had him into the armory, where they showed him all manner of furniture which their Lord had provided for pilgrims, as sword, shield, helmet, breast-plate, all-prayer, and shoes that would not wear out. And there was here enough of this to harness out as many men for the service of their Lord as there be stars in the heaven for multitude." —*Bunyan*

None can make a shoe to the creature's foot, so that he shall go easy on a hard way, but Christ; he can do it to the creature's full content. And how doth he do it? Truly, no other way than by underlaying it, or, if you will, lining it with the peace of the gospel. What though the way be set with sharp stones? If this shoe go between the Christian's foot and them, they cannot much be felt.

It is the soldier's shoe that is meant, which, if right, is to be of the strongest make, being not so much intended for finery as for defense.

The gospel shoe will not come on thy foot so long as that foot is swelled with any sinful humor (I mean any unrighteous or unholy practice). This evil must be purged out by repentance, or thou canst not wear the shoe of peace.

The Jews were to eat their passover with their loins girded, their shoes on their feet, and their staff in their hand, and all in haste (Exod. 12:11). When God is feasting the Christian with present comforts, he must have this gospel shoe on; he must not sit down as if he were feasting at home, but stand and eat even as he takes a running meal in an inn on his way, willing to be gone as soon as ever he is a little refreshed for his journey.

The conceited professor, who hath a high opinion of himself, is a man shod and prepared, he thinks; but not with the right gospel shoe. He that cannot take the length of his foot, how can he of himself fit a shoe to it?

Is not thy shoe, Christian, yet on? Art thou not yet ready to march? If thou hast it, what hast thou to dread? Canst fear that any stone can hurt thy foot through so thick a sole? —*William Gurnall*

Paul was thus shod: Romans 8:38: "I am persuaded, nothing shall separate me from the love of God." "All things, I know, work together for the good of them that are beloved of God" (Rom. 8:28). And this furniture made him go such hard ways cheerfully, in which showers of afflictions did fall as thick as hailstones. This doth make God's children, though not in the letter, yet in some sort, tread upon the adder and the basilisk, yea, to defy vipers, and receive no hurt; whereas, if the feet be bared a little with the absence of this peace, anything causeth us sore smart. —*Paul Bayne*

227

Rejoice in the Lord alway: and again I say, Rejoice.

—*Philippians 4:4*

OY drives out discord. See how our text follows as a remedy upon a case of disagreement in the church (verses 1–2).

Joy helps against the trials of life. Hence, it is mentioned as a preparation for the rest of faith which is prescribed in verse 6.

I. THE GRACE COMMANDED "Rejoice"

1. It is delightful. Our soul's jubilee has come when joy enters.
2. It is demonstrative. It is more than peace; it sparkles, shines, sings. Why should it not? Joy is a bird. Let it fly in the open heavens, and let its music be heard of all men.
3. It is stimulating and urges its possessor to brave deeds.
4. It is influential for good. Sinners are attracted to Jesus by the joy of saints. More flies are caught with a spoonful of honey than with a barrel of vinegar.
5. It is contagious. Others are gladdened by our rejoicing.
6. It is commanded. It is not left optional, but made imperative.
   We are as much commanded to rejoice as to keep the Sabbath.
   * It is commanded because joy makes us like God.
   * It is commanded because it is for our profit.
   * It is commanded because it is good for others.

II. THE JOY DISCRIMINATED. "In the Lord."

1. As to sphere: "in the Lord." This is that sacred circle wherein a Christian's life should be always spent.
2. As to object: "in the Lord."
   We should rejoice in the Lord God, Father, Son, and Spirit.
   We should rejoice in the Lord Jesus, dead, risen, etc.:
   * Not in temporals, personal, political, or pecuniary.
   * Nor in special privileges, which involve greater responsibility.

- Nor even in religious successes. "In this rejoice not, that the devils are subject unto you through my word, but rather rejoice that your names are written in heaven" (Luke 10:20).
- Nor in self and its doings (Phil. 3:3).

III. THE TIME APPOINTED. "Always."
1. When you cannot rejoice in any other, rejoice in God.
2. When you can rejoice in other things, sanctify all with joy in God.
3. When you have not before rejoiced, begin at once.
4. When you have long rejoiced, do not cease for a moment.
5. When others are with you, lead them in this direction.
6. When you are alone, enjoy to the full this rejoicing.

IV. THE EMPHASIS LAID ON THE COMMAND. "Again I say, Rejoice."
Paul repeats his exhortation:
1. To show his love to them. He is intensely anxious that they should share his joy.
2. To suggest the difficulty of continual joy. He twice commands, because we are slow to obey.
3. To assert the possibility of it. After second thoughts, he feels that he may fitly repeat the exhortation.
4. To impress the importance of the duty. Whatever else you forget, remember this: Be sure to rejoice.
5. To allow of special personal testimony. "Again I say, Rejoice."
   Paul rejoiced. He was habitually a happy man.
   This epistle to the Philippians is peculiarly joyous.
   Let us look it through. The apostle is joyful throughout:
   - He sweetens prayer with joy (1:4).
   - He rejoices that Christ is preached (1:18).
   - He wished to live to gladden the church (1:25).
   - To see the members likeminded was his joy (2:2).
   - It was his joy that he should not run in vain (2:16).
   - His farewell to them was, "Rejoice in the Lord" (3:1).
   - He speaks of those who rejoice in Christ Jesus (3:3).
   - He calls his converts his joy and crown (4:1).
   - He expresses his joy in their kindness (4:4, 10, 18).

To all our friends, let us use this as a blessing: "Rejoice in the Lord."
This is only a choicer way of saying, Be happy; fare-you-well.

Fare ye well, and if forever,
Still forever fare ye well.

Joy Bells

It is not an indifferent thing to rejoice, or not to rejoice; but we are commanded to rejoice, to show that we break a commandment if we rejoice not. Oh, what a comfort is this, when the Comforter himself shall command us to rejoice! God was wont to say, *Repent*, and not *rejoice*, because men rejoice too much; but God here commandeth to *rejoice*, as though some men did not rejoice enough: therefore you must understand to whom he speaketh. In Psalm 149:5, it is said, "Let the saints be glad," not, let the wicked be glad. And in Isa. 40:1, he saith, "Comfort my people," not, comfort mine enemies, showing to whom this commandment of Paul is sent, "Rejoice evermore." —*Henry Smith*

The thing whereunto he exhorteth, as ye see, is to rejoice; a thing which the sensual man can quickly lay hold on, who loves to rejoice, and to cheer himself in the days of his flesh; which yet might now seem unreasonable to the Philippians, who lived in the midst of a naughty and crooked nation, by whom they were even hated for the truth's sake which they professed. Mark, therefore, wherein the apostle would they should rejoice, namely, in the Lord; and here the sensual man, that haply would catch hold when it is said, *Rejoice*, by-and-by when it is added, *in the Lord*, will let go his hold. But they that, by reason of the billows and waves of the troublesome sea of this world, cannot brook the speech when it is said, *Rejoice*, are to lay sure holdfast upon it when it is added, *Rejoice in the Lord*; which holdfast once taken, that they might for ever keep it sure, in the third place it is added, *Rejoice in the Lord alway*, to note the constancy that should be in Christian joy. —*Henry Airay*

Another note to distinguish this joy in the Lord from all other joys is the fullness and exuberancy of it, for it is more joy than if corn and wine and oil increased. Else what needed the apostle, having said, "Rejoice in the Lord alway," to add, "and again I say, Rejoice"? What can be more than *always*, but still adding to the fullness of our joy, till our cup do overflow?

Upon working days, rejoice in the Lord who giveth thee strength to labor and feedeth thee with the labor of thy hands. On holidays, rejoice in the Lord who feasteth thee with the marrow and fatness of his house. In plenty, rejoice again and again, because the Lord giveth. In want, rejoice because the Lord taketh away, and as it pleaseth the Lord, so come things to pass. —*Edward Marbury*

The calendar of the sinner has only a few days in the year marked as festival days; but *every day* of the Christian's calendar is marked by the hand of God as a day of rejoicing. —*Anonymous*

'Tis impious in a good man to be sad. —*Edward Young*

Napoleon, when sent to Elba, adopted, in proud defiance of his fate, the motto, "*Ubicunquce felix*." It was not true in his case, but the Christian may be truly "happy everywhere" and always.

228

For by him were all things created, that are in heaven, and that are in earth, visible and invisible, whether they be thrones, or dominions, or principalities, or powers: all things were created by him, and for him.

—*Colossians 1:16*

 NY theme which exalts the Savior is precious to the saints.

This is one in which the preacher cannot hope to do more than to show how vastly his theme is above him.

All things were created by God and for him, yet by Jesus and for him, because he is truly God and one with the Father.

I. CONSIDER THE STATEMENT ITSELF.

1. Heaven itself was created by and for Christ Jesus.
   - There is such a place as well as such a state, and of that place Jesus is the center. Enoch and Elijah in their bodies are there, Jesus as man is there, and there all his people will be. God, as a pure Spirit, needed no such place, nor angels, for everywhere they would see God.
   - It was created for Jesus and for the people whom he will bring there to be one forever with himself.
   - It exists by Jesus and for Jesus.
     Everything in heaven prepared by Jesus. He is the designer of it.
     Everything in heaven reflects Jesus. He is the soul of it.
     Everything in heaven praises Jesus. He is the King of it.
2. The angels. All their ranks were made by him and for him:
   - To worship him and glorify him with their adoration.
   - To rejoice with him and in him, as they do when sinners repent.
   - To guard Christ's people in life and bring them to him in death.
   - To carry out his purposes of judgment, as with Pharaoh, etc.
   - To achieve his purposes of deliverance, as Peter from prison.
3. This world was made by him to be:
   - A place for him to live and die upon.
   - A stage for his people to live and act upon.
   - A province to be fully restored to his dominion.
   - A new world in the ages to come to bless other worlds, if such there be, and to display forever the glories of Jesus.
4. All the lower creatures are for Jesus. "And that are in earth."
   - They are needful to man and so to our Lord's system of grace.
   - They are illustrations of Christ's wisdom, power, and goodness.
   - They are to be treated kindly for his sake.

5. Men were created by and for Christ.
- That he might display a special phase of power and skill, in creating spiritual beings embodied in material forms.
- That he might become himself one of them.
- That he might himself be the head of a remarkable order of beings who know both good and evil, are children of God, are bound to God by ties of gratitude, and are one with his Son.
- That for these he might die to save them, and to make them his companions, friends, and worshippers forever.
- That human thrones, even when occupied by wicked men, might be made to subserve his purpose by restraint or by overruling.

II. REVIEW THE REFLECTIONS HENCE ARISING.
1. Jesus, then, is God. "By him were all things created."
2. Jesus is the clue of the universe, its center and explanation. All things are to be seen in the light of the cross, and all things reflect light on the cross. For him all things exist.
3. To live to Jesus, then, is to find out the true object of our being and to be in accord with all creation.
4. Not living to Jesus, we can have no blessing.
5. We can only live *for* him as we live *by* him, for so all things do.
6. It is clear that he must triumph. All is going well. If we look at history from his throne, all things are "for him." "He must reign." Let us comfort one another with these words.

What an honor to be the smallest page in the retinue of such a prince!

Words of Homage

When the Christian martyr Pionius was asked by his judges, "What God dost thou worship?" he replied, "I worship him who made the heavens, and who beautified them with stars, and who has enriched the earth with flowers and trees." "Dost thou mean," asked the magistrates, "him who was crucified (*illum dicis qui crucifixus est*)?" "Certainly," replied Pionius, "him whom the Father sent for the salvation of the world." As Pionius died, so died Blandina and the whole host of those who in the first three centuries, without knowing anything of the Nicene creed, held it implicitly, if not explicitly, and proclaimed it in flames and in dungeons, in famine and in nakedness, under the rack and under the sword. —*Joseph Cook*

In creation God shows us his hand, but in redemption God gives us his heart. —*Adolphe Monod*

What sublime views does this subject (the creation of angels) furnish us of the greatness of Christ! By him, says the apostle, were all those illustrious beings created, together with all their attributes, importance, and dignity. The character of every workman is seen, of course, in the nature of the work which he has made. If this be insignificant and worthless, it exhibits nothing but the insignificance and worthlessness of the maker. If curious and excellent, if sublime and wonderful, it unfolds strongly and certainly his greatness, wisdom, and glory. Of what faculties are angels the subjects! Of what intelligence, purity, power, loveliness, and elevation of mind! What, then, must be the perfections of him who contrived and formed angels, who with a word called them into being, who preserves, informs, directs, controls, and blesses them for ever! Great and excellent as they are, they are exhibited as "unclean in his sight" and as "charged with folly" before him. How amazing, then, must be the perfection of his character! How great, how wise, how good! —*Timothy Dwight*

Paul would prevent the shadow of a doubt crossing our minds about our Lord having a right to the divine honors of the Creator. "By him," he says, "all things were created"; and as if an angel, standing at his side when he penned these words, had stooped down to whisper in his ear that men, attempting to rob Jesus of his honor, would rise to throw doubt upon that truth and explain it away, to make the truth still more plain, he adds, "that are in heaven, and that are in earth." Not content with that, he uses yet more comprehensive terms; and to embrace all the regions of God's universe above the earth and beyond the starry bounds of heaven, he adds, "visible and invisible." Nor leaves his task till, sweeping the highest and the lowest things, men and worms, angels and insects, all into Christ's hands, he adds, "whether they be thrones, or dominions, or principalities, or powers." —*Dr. Guthrie*

It was well said of a heathen, *Si essem luscinia*: If I were a nightingale, I would sing as a nightingale; *si alauda*: If I were a lark, I would soar as a lark. Since I am a man, what should I do but know, love, and praise God without ceasing, and glorify my Creator? Things are unprofitable or misplaced when they do not seek or serve their end; therefore, for what use are we meet, if we are unmeet for our proper end? We are like the wood of the vine, good for nothing, not so much as to make a pin whereon to hang anything (Ezek. 15:2); good for nothing but to be cast into the fire unless it be fruitful. What are we good for if we be not serviceable to the ends for which we were created? —*Thomas Manton*

229

As ye have therefore received Christ Jesus the Lord, so walk ye in him.

—Colossians 2:6

HERE is great safety in going back to first principles.

To make sure of being in the right way, it is good to look back at the entrance gate. Well begun is half done.

The text is addressed, not to the ungodly, nor to strangers, but to those who "have received Christ Jesus the Lord." They have commenced well; let them go on as they have begun.

For the spiritual good and establishment of such in the faith, the apostle longs, and to this end he gives the exhortation.

I. NOTICE IN THE TEXT THE FACT STATED. Sincere believers have in very deed "*received* Christ Jesus the Lord."

This is the old gospel word. Here is no evolution from within, but a gift from without, heartily accepted by the soul.

This is free-grace language: "received," not earned or purchased.

It is not said that they received Christ's *words*, though that is true, for they prize every precept and doctrine, but they received Christ.

Carefully observe:

1. The personality of him whom they received, "Christ Jesus the Lord": his person, his godhead, his humanity, himself. They:
   - Received him into their knowledge.
   - Received him into their understanding.
   - Received him into their affections.
   - Received him into their trust.
   - Received him as their life at their new birth. When they received him, he gave them power to become the sons of God.
2. The threefold character in which they received him.
   The words of the text, "Christ Jesus the Lord," indicate this.
   They received him:
   - As Christ, anointed and commissioned of God.
   - As Jesus, the Savior, to redeem and sanctify them.
   - As the Lord, to reign and rule over them with undivided sway.
3. The looking away from self in this saving act of reception.
   It is not said, as ye have fought for Jesus and won him, or studied the truth and discovered Christ Jesus, but, as ye have "received" him. This strips us of everything like boasting, for all we do is receive.
4. The blessed certainty of the experience of those to whom Paul wrote, "As ye *have* received Christ Jesus the Lord." They had really received Jesus; they had found the blessing to be real: no doubt remained as to their possession of it.

II. NOTICE, NEXT, THE COUNSEL GIVEN. "So walk ye in him."

There are four things suggested by that word "walk."

1. Life. Vitally enjoy the Lord Jesus.
2. Continuance. Remain in Christ. Make him your constant place of daily movement and occupation.
3. Activity. Busy yourselves, but not with a new way of salvation. Work for Jesus, with him, and in obedience to him.
4. Progress. Advance, but ever let your most advanced thought remain in him.

III. NOTICE, LASTLY, THE MODEL WHICH IS PRESENTED TO US.

We are to walk in Christ Jesus the Lord "as we received him."

And how was that?

1. We received him gratefully. How we blessed his name for regarding our low estate!
2. We received him humbly. We had no claim to his grace, and we confessed this and were lowly.
3. We received him joyfully. Our first joy was bright as the dew of the morning. Have we lost it?
4. We received him effectually. We brought forth many spiritual fruits and abounded in life, faith, love, and every grace.
5. We received him unreservedly. We made no conditions with him, and we reserved nothing for the flesh.

Thus, we should continue to walk in him, evermore in our daily life excelling in all these points.

Alas, some have never received Jesus!

Our closing words must be addressed to such.

If you will not receive Jesus, you refuse mercy here and heaven hereafter. What! will you not receive so great a boon?

Explanatory

Inquirers are not infrequently counseled to give their hearts to Christ or to consecrate themselves to the Lord. We would not be overcritical with what is well meant; but really this is not the gospel. The good news of grace is that God hath given to us eternal life and redemption through his Son, and that in order to be saved, the sinner has nought to do but to accept it.

But having received the gift of God and having become partakers of his converting grace, then and therefore the divine obligation for service begins to press upon us. The Lord becomes an asker as soon as we have become recipients. "As ye have therefore received Christ Jesus the Lord, so walk ye in him." Let consecration crown conversion, let self-devotion to Christ answer to his self-devotion for you. —Dr. A. J. Gordon

If you would know how faith is to be exercised in thus abiding in Jesus, to be rooted more deeply and firmly in him, you have only to look back to the time when first you received him. You remember well what obstacles at that time there appeared to be in the way of your believing. There was first your vileness and guilt: it appeared impossible that the promise of pardon and love could be for such a sinner. Then there was the sense of weakness and death: you felt not the power for the surrender and the trust to which you were called. And then there was the future: you dared not undertake to be a disciple of Jesus while you felt so sure that you could not remain standing, but would speedily again be unfaithful and fall. These difficulties were as mountains in your way. And how were they removed? Simply by the word of God. That word, as it were, compelled you to believe that, notwithstanding guilt in the past, and weakness in the present, and unfaithfulness in the future, the promise was sure that Jesus would accept and save you. On that word, you ventured to come and were not deceived: you found that Jesus did indeed accept and save you.

Apply this, your experience in coming to Jesus, to the abiding in him. By faith you became partakers of the initial grace; by that same faith you can enjoy the continuous grace of abiding in him. —*Andrew Murray*

Since they had received the doctrine of Christ, they could not again part with it without convicting themselves either of imprudence in having mistaken a false doctrine for a true one or of instability, in quitting and altering a doctrine which they knew to be good and sufficient when they received it. If your belief be good, why do you change it? If it be otherwise, why did you entertain it? Though it be a heinous sin not to receive the Lord Jesus when he presents himself to us in his gospel, yet it is much more evil to cast him out after having received him; as it is a greater outrage to thrust a man from your house when you have admitted him, than to shut your doors against him at the first. —*Jean Daille*

230

Where there is neither Greek nor Jew, circumcision nor uncircumcision, Barbarian, Scythian, bond nor free: but Christ is all, and in all.
—*Colossians 3:11*

 HERE are two worlds, the old and the new.

These are peopled by two sorts of manhood: the old man, and the new man, concerning whom, see verses 9 and 10.

In the first are many things which are not in the second.

In the second are many things which are not in the first.

Our text tells us what there is not and what there is in the new man.

Let us begin by asking whether the hearer knows *where* he is; for the text turns on that word *"where."*

I. WHAT THERE IS NOT IN THE NEW.

When we come to be renewed after the image of him that created us, we find an obliteration of:

1. National distinctions: "Where there is neither Greek nor Jew."
   - Jesus is a man. In the broadest sense, he is neither Jew nor Gentile. We see in him no restrictive nationality. Our own peculiar nationality sinks before union with him.
   - Jesus is now our nationality, our charter, and our fatherland.
   - Jesus is our hero, legislator, ancestor, leader.
   - Jesus gives us laws, customs, history, genealogy, prestige, privilege, reliance, power, heritage, conquest.
   - Jesus furnishes us with a new patriotism, loyalty, and clanship, which we may safely indulge to the utmost.
2. Ceremonial distinctions: "There is neither circumcision nor uncircumcision." The typical separation is removed.
   - The separating rite is abolished, and the peculiar privilege of a nation born after the flesh is gone with it.
   - Those who were reckoned far off are brought near.
   - Both Jew and Gentile are united in one body by the cross.
3. Social distinctions: "There is neither bond nor free."
   We are enabled through divine grace to see that:
   - These distinctions are transient.
   - These distinctions are superficial.
   - These distinctions are of small value.
   - These distinctions are nonexistent in the spiritual realm.

What a blessed blending of all men in one body is brought about by our Lord Jesus! Let us all work in the direction of unity.

II. WHAT THERE IS IN THE NEW.

"Christ is all and in all," and that in many senses.

1. Christ is all our culture. In him we emulate and excel the "Greek."
2. Christ is all our revelation. We glory in him even as the "Jew" gloried in receiving the oracles of God.
3. Christ is all our ritual. We have no "circumcision," neither have we seven sacraments nor a heap of carnal ordinances; he is far more than these. All Scriptural ordinances are of him.
4. Christ is all our simplicity. We place no confidence in the bare Puritanism which may be called "uncircumcision."
5. Christ is all our natural traditions. He is more to us than the freshest ideas which cross the mind of the "Barbarian."
6. Christ is all our unconquerableness and liberty. The "Scythian" had not such boundless independence as we find in him.

7. Christ is all as our Master, if we be "bond." Happy servitude of which he is the Head!

8. Christ is our Magna Charta, yea, our liberty itself if we be "free."

In closing, we will use the words "Christ is all and in all" as our text for application to ourselves. It furnishes a test question for us.

Is Christ so great with us that he is our all?

Is Christ so broadly and fully with us that he is all in our all?

Is he, then, all in our trust, our hope, our assurance, our joy, our aim, our strength, our wisdom—in a word, "all in all"?

If so, are we living in all for him?

Are we doing all *for* him, because he is all to us?

Embroideries

What a rich inheritance have all those who are truly interested in Jesus Christ! *Christus meus et omnia.* They possess him that is all in all, and in possessing him, they possess all. "I have all things, my brother," saith Jacob to Esau (Gen. 33:11, margin). He that hath him that is all in all cannot want anything. "All things are yours," saith the apostle, "whether things present or things to come, and ye are Christ's" (1 Cor. 3:22–23). A true believer, let him be never so poor outwardly, is in truth the richest man in all the world; he hath all in all, and what can be added to all? —*Ralph Robinson*

Christ is not valued at all unless he be valued above all. —*Augustine*

> He is a path, if any be misled;
>   He is a robe, if any naked be;
> If any chance to hunger, he is bread;
>   If any be a bondman, he is free;
>   If any be but weak, how strong is he!
> To dead men life he is, to sick men health,
> To blind men sight, and to the needy wealth;
> A pleasure without loss, a treasure without stealth.
> —*Giles Fletcher*

All, then, let him be in all our desires and wishes. Who is that wise merchant that hath heart large enough to conceive and believe as to this? Let him go sell all his nothings, that he may compass this pearl, barter his bugles for this diamond. Verily, all the haberdash stuff the whole pack of the world hath, is not worthy to be valued with this jewel.

I cannot but reverence the memory of that reverend divine (Mr. Welsh) who, being in a deep muse after some discourse that had passed of Christ, and tears trickling abundantly from his eyes before he was aware, being urged for the cause thereof, he honestly confessed that he wept because he could not draw his dull heart to prize Christ aright. I fear this is a rare mind in Christians, for many think a very little to be quite enough for Jesus, and even too much for him! —*Samuel Ward*

"At length, one evening, while engaged in a prayer-meeting, the great deliverance came. I received the full witness of the Spirit that the blood of Jesus had cleansed me from all sin. I felt I was nothing, and Christ was all in all. Him I now cheerfully received in all his offices: my Prophet, to teach me; my Priest, to atone for me; my King, to reign over me. Oh, what boundless, boundless happiness there is in Christ, and all for such a poor sinner as I am! This happy change took place in my soul March 13th, 1772." —*William Carvosso*

Dannecker, the German sculptor, spent eight years in producing a face of Christ; and at last wrought out one in which the emotions of love and sorrow were so perfectly blended that beholders wept as they looked upon it. Subsequently, being solicited to employ his great talent on a statue of Venus, he replied, "After gazing so long into the face of Christ, think you that I can now turn my attention to a heathen goddess?" Here is the true secret of weanedness from worldly idols, "the expulsive power of a new affection."

> I have heard the voice of Jesus,
> Tell me not of aught beside;
> I have seen the face of Jesus,
> All my soul is satisfied.
> —*Dr. A. J. Gordon*

231

For this cause also thank we God without ceasing, because, when ye received the word of God which ye heard of us, ye received it not as the word of men, but as it is in truth, the word of God, which effectually worketh also in you that believe. For ye, brethren, became followers of the churches of God which in Judea are in Christ Jesus: for ye also have suffered like things of your own countrymen, even as they have of the Jews.

—*1 Thessalonians 2:13–14*

 AUL unbosoms his heart to the loving church at Thessalonica.

He knew what it was to be worried by the Corinthians and the Galatians, but he found rest when thinking of the Thessalonians.

The most tried ministers have some bright spots.

In setting forth his joyful memories of Thessalonica, Paul gives us a sight of three things:

I. MINISTERS GIVING THANKS. "We also thank God."

Ministers are not always groaning and weeping, though they often do so. They have their times of thanksgiving, as in Paul's case.

1. This followed upon sore travail (see verse 9). Only as we sow in tears do we reap in joy.
2. This was backed by holy living. Dwell upon each point in verses 10 and 11. Unholy ministers will have scant cause for joy.
3. It prevented all self-laudation. They thanked God, and this is the opposite of glorifying self.
4. It was of a social character. "*We* thank God": Paul, Silas, and Timothy. We hold a fraternal meeting of joy when God blesses us among our beloved people.
5. It was of an abiding character: "without ceasing." We can never cease praising the Lord for his goodness in saving souls.
6. It cheered them for further service. They wished, according to verse 17, to visit the friends again, and further benefit them.

What a mercy for us all when God's servants are glad about us!
Their joy is in our salvation.

II. HEARERS RECEIVING THE WORD. "Ye received the word of God."

Not all receive it. How badly do some treat the gospel!
Not all receive it as did the Thessalonians, for:

1. They received the word of God. They heard it calmly, attended to it candidly, considered it carefully.
2. They received the word of God with a hearty welcome. They accepted it by faith with personal confidence and joy.
3. They did not receive the word of man. It is well to keep the doors locked in that direction. We cannot receive everything. Let us reject merely human teaching and leave the more room in our minds for the Lord's word.
4. They did not receive the gospel as the word of men. Their faith was not based on the clever, eloquent, logical, dogmatical, or affectionate way in which it was preached.
5. They received it as God's revealed word and therefore received it:
   - With reverence of its divine character.
   - With assurance of its infallibility.
   - With obedience to its authority.
   - With experience of its sacred power.
6. They received it so that it effectually worked in them. It was practical, efficient, and manifestly operative upon their lives and characters.

III. CONVERTS EXHIBITING THE FAMILY LIKENESS.

1. They were like Judean Christians, the best of them, in faith, in experience, in afflictions.

2. Yet many of them as heathen began at a great disadvantage.
3. They had never seen the church of God in Judea and were no copyists; yet they came to be facsimiles of them.
4. This is a singular confirmation of the divine character of the work.
   • The same Lord works in all believers. In the main, the same experience occurs in all the saints, even though they may never have seen each other.
   • This similarity of all regenerated men furnishes a valuable set of experimental evidences of the divine origin of conversion.

Let us not be daunted by opposition, for at Thessalonica Paul was persecuted and yet triumphant.

Let us rejoice in the effects of the word everywhere.

Memoranda

There was a minister of the gospel once, a true preacher, a faithful, loving man, whose ministry was supposed to be exceedingly unsuccessful. After twenty years' labor, he was known to have brought only one soul to Christ. So said his congregation. Poor worker in the trench! His toil was not seen by men, but the eye of God rested upon it. To him, one day, came a deputation from his people, representing to him, respectfully enough, that, inasmuch as God had not seen fit to bless his labors among them, it were better for him to remove to another sphere. They said that he had only been instrumental in the conversion of one sinner. He might do more elsewhere. "What do you say?" said he. "Have I really brought one sinner to Christ?" "Yes," was the reply, "one, but only one." "Thank God," cried he, "for that! Thank God! I have brought one soul to Christ. Now for twenty years' more labor among you, God sparing me, perhaps I may be the honored instrument of bringing two." —*Calthrop*

"Whoever made this book," said a Chinese convert, "made me. It tells me the thoughts of my heart."

A celebrated Frenchman said, "I know the Word of God is the sword of the Spirit because it has pierced me through."

Loskiel's "Account of the Moravian Missions Among the North American Indians" has taught me two things. I have found in it a striking illustration of the uniformity with which the grace of God operates on men. *Crantz*, in his "Account of the Missions in Greenland" has shown the grace of God working on a man-fish—on a stupid, sottish, senseless creature, scarcely a remove from the fish on which he lived. *Loskiel* shows the same grace working on a man-devil—a fierce, bloody, revengeful warrior, dancing his infernal war-dance with the mind of a fury. Divine grace brings these men to the same point. It quickens, stimulates, and elevates the Greenlander; it raises him to a sort of new life; it seems almost to bestow on him new senses; it opens his eye and bends his ear, and rouses his heart; and what it adds, it sanctifies. The same grace tames the high spirit of the Indian—it reduces him to the meekness, docility, and simplicity of a child. The evidence arising to Christianity from these facts is perhaps seldom sufficient by itself to convince the gainsayer; but, to a man who already believes, it greatly strengthens the reason of his belief. I have seen, also, in these books, that the fish-boat, and the oil, and the tomahawk, and the cap of feathers excepted, a Christian minister has to deal with just the same sort of creatures as the Greenlander and the Indian among civilized nations. —*Richard Cecil*

The edition of those living epistles is the same the world over; the binding only may differ.

232

But ye, brethren, be not weary in well doing.
—*2 Thessalonians 3:13*

 EAD the two previous verses, and mark the apostle's censure of those who are busy-bodies, "working not at all."

A church should be like a hive of working bees.

There should be order, and there will be order where all are at work. The apostle condemns disorder in verse 11.

There should be quietness, and work promotes it (verse 12).

There should be honesty, and work fosters it.

The danger is, lest we first tire of work, and then fancy that we have done enough, are discharged from service by our superior importance, or by our subscribing to pay a substitute. While any strength remains, we may not cease from personal work for Jesus.

Moreover, some will come in who are not busy bees but busybodies. They do not work for their own bread, but are surprisingly eager to eat that of others. These soon cause disturbance and desolation, but they know nothing of "well doing."

The apostle endeavors to cure this disease, and therefore gives:

I. A SUMMARY OF CHRISTIAN LIFE. He calls it "well doing."

1. Religious work is well doing. Preaching, teaching, writing books and letters, temperance meetings, Bible classes, tract distributing, personal conversation, private prayer, praise.
2. Charitable work is "well doing." The poor, the widow and the fatherless, the ignorant, the sick, the fallen, and the desponding are to be look' after with tender care.
3. Common labor is "well doing."

This will be seen to be the point in the text, if we read the previous verses. Well-doing takes many forms: among the rest:

- Support of family by the husband.
- Management of house by the wife.
- Assistance in housework by daughters.
- Diligence in his trade by the young man.
- Study of his books by the child at school.
- Faithful service by domestics in the home.
- Honest toil by the day laborer.

4. Certain labor is "well doing" in all these senses, since it is common labor used for charitable and religious ends:

- Support of aged persons by those who work for them.
- Watching over infirm or sick relatives.
- Bringing up children in the fear of the Lord.
- Work done in connection with the church of God to enable others to preach the gospel in comfort.

Everything is "well doing" which is done from a sense of duty with dependence upon God and faith in his word, out of love to Christ, in good will to other workers, with prayer for direction, acceptance, and blessing.

Common actions become holy, and drudgery grows divine when the motive is pure and high.

We now think it will be wise to gather from the epistle:

II. A WARNING AS TO CAUSES OF WEARINESS IN WELL DOING.

1. Unworthy receivers of charity weary generous workers (verse 10).
2. Idle examples tempt the industrious to idleness (verse 11).
3. Busybodies and disorderly persons in the church hinder many from their diligent service (verses 11–12).
4. Troublers, such as "unreasonable and wicked men," dispirit those who would serve the Lord (verse 2).
5. Our own flesh is apt to crave ease and shun difficulties.

We can make too much of works, and it is equally easy to have too few of them. Let us watch against weariness.

Let us now conclude with:

III. AN ARGUMENT AGAINST WEARINESS IN WELL DOING. "But ye, brethren, be not weary in well doing."

1. Lose not what you have already wrought.
2. Consider what self-denial others practice for inferior things: soldiers, wrestlers, rowers in boat races, etc.
3. Remember that the eye of God is upon you, his hand with you, his smile on you, his command over you.

4. Reflect upon the grandeur of the service in itself as done unto the Lord and to his glorious cause.

5. Think upon the sublime lives of those who have preceded you in this heavenly service.

6. Fix your eye on Jesus and what he endured.

7. Behold the recompense of reward: the crown, the palm.

If others tire and faint, don't be weary.

If others meanly loaf upon their fellows, be it yours rather to give than to receive.

If others break the peace of the church, be it yours to maintain it by diligent service and so to enjoy the blessing of verse 16.

Whetstones

A true Christian must be a worker. Industry, or diligence in business, is a prime element in piety; and the industry God demands is the activity of our whole complex nature. Without this, a man may be a dreamer, but not a "doer"; and just so far as any faculty of our nature is left unemployed do we come short of a complete Christian character. I must be doing—I, my entire self, my hand, my foot, my eye, my tongue, my understanding, my affections—must be all, not only resolving, purposing, feeling, willing, but actively doing. "Let us be doing."

But more than this. I must be "well doing." The Greek word expresses beauty, and this enters into the apostolic thought. True piety is lovely. Just so far as it comes short in the beautiful, it becomes monstrous. But, as used by Paul, it goes far beyond this, and signifies all moral excellence. Activity is not enough; for activity the intensest may be evil. Lucifer is as active, as constant, and earnest as Gabriel. But the one is a fiend and the other a seraph. Any activity that is not good is a curse always and only. Better be dead, inert matter—a stone, a clod— than a stinging reptile or a destroying demon; and herein lies the great practical change in regeneration. It transforms the mere doer into a well-doer. It is not so much a change in the energy as in the direction. —*Charles Wadsworth, D.D.*

The Hebrews have a saying that God is more delighted in adverbs than in nouns: 'tis not so much the matter that's done, but the matter how 'tis done, that God minds. *Not how much, but how well!* 'Tis the well-doing that meets with a well-done. Let us therefore serve God, not nominally or verbally, but adverbially. —*Ralph Venning*

Think nothing done while aught remains to do. —*Samuel Rogers*

D'Israeli tells the following story of two members of the Port Royal Society. Arnauld wished Nicolle to assist him in a new work, when the latter replied, "We are now old. Is it not time to rest?" "Rest!" returned Arnauld, "have we not all eternity to rest in?" So *Gerald Massey* sings:

Let me work now, for all Eternity,
With its immortal leisure, waiteth me.

233

This is a faithful saying, and worthy of all acceptation, that Christ
Jesus came into the world to save sinners; of whom I am chief.
—*1 Timothy 1:15*

 AUL had described his ordination in verse 12.

He then went on to speak of the grace manifested in the call of
such a person to the ministry (verse 13), and of the further grace
by which he was sustained in that ministry.

Incidentally, he was led to mention the message of his ministry.

We may profitably use the text on this occasion.

I. HOW WE PREACH THE GOSPEL.

1. As a certainty. It is a "faithful saying." *We* do not doubt the truth of our
message, or how could we expect *you* to believe it? We believe and are
sure because:
   - It is a revelation of God.
   - It is attested by miracles.
   - It bears its witness within itself.
   - It has proved its power upon our hearts.
2. As an everyday truth. It is to us a "saying" or proverb.

The gospel affects us at home, in business, in sickness, in health, in life, in
youth and age, in death.

3. As having a common bearing, therefore, a "saying" to be heard by all
kinds of people, especially the most sinful.
   - All have sinned and need a Savior.
   - All who believe in Jesus have a Savior.
   - All believers show by their lives that Jesus has saved them.
4. As claiming your attention. "Worthy of all acceptation."
   - You must believe it to be true.
   - You must appropriate it to yourself.
   - You ought to do so, for it is worthy of your acceptance.

II. WHAT GOSPEL DO WE PREACH?

1. The gospel of a person: "Christ Jesus."
   - He is the Anointed of God: "Christ."
   - He is the Savior of men: "Jesus."
   - He is God and man in one person.
   - He died and yet he lives for ever.
2. The gospel of divine visitation. Jesus came into the world:
   - By his birth as a man.

- By his mingling with men.
- By his bearing our sorrows and our sins for us.

3. The gospel for sinners:
  - For such Jesus lived and labored.
  - For such he died and made atonement.
  - For such he has sent the gospel of pardon.
  - For such he pleads in heaven.

4. The gospel of a finished work.
  - He finished the work of salvation before he left the world.
  - That work continues complete to this day.
  - He is ready to apply it to all who come to him.

5. The gospel of effectual deliverance. "To save sinners."
  - Not to half save them.
  - Nor to make them salvable.
  - Nor help them to save themselves.
  - Nor to save them as righteous.
  - But to save them wholly and effectually from their sins.

III. WHY DO WE PREACH IT?

1. Because we have been saved by it.
2. Because we are now in sympathy with Jesus and wish to save sinners, even the chief of them.
3. Because we believe it will be a blessing to all of you who hear it. If you are saved by it, you will be happy, and so shall we.
4. Because we cannot help it, for an inward impulse compels us to tell of the miracle of mercy wrought upon us.

Will you not believe a saying so sure?

Will you not accept a truth so gladsome?

Will you not come to a Savior so suitable?

Sayings

A visitor to Rome says, "I was struck with the frequency with which the priests and other exhibitors of church curiosities use the phrase, 'It is said' (*on dit*) when describing relics and rarities. They do not vouch for their being what they are reputed to be." "It is said." Are they ashamed of their curiosities? Do they thus try to satisfy their consciences? They do not express their personal belief, but—*it is said*. Not thus do gospel preachers speak. "That which we have seen and heard declare we unto you."

There's a nice word in the text: it is the word "acceptation." It's all provided for you. It's very much like a supper. You'll find the table laid, and everything all ready. You're not expected to bring anything at all. I was once invited out to tea by a poor widow, and I took something in my pocket. But I'll never do it again.

It was two cakes; and, when I brought them out and laid them on the table, she picked them up and flung them out into the street and said, "I asked you to tea; I didn't ask you to provide tea for me." And so with Christ: he asks, he provides, and he wants nothing but ourselves; and if we take aught else, he'll reject it. We can only sup with him when we come as we are. Who will accept salvation? Who'll say,

> I take the blessing from above,
> And wonder at thy boundless love?
> —*John Wold Ackrill, in "The Sword and the Trowel"*

Mr. Moody said, "I remember preaching on the subject 'Christ as a Deliverer,' and walking away, I said to a Scotchman, 'I didn't finish the subject.' 'Ah, man! You didn't expect to finish, did ye? It'll take all eternity to finish telling what Christ has done for man.'"

Luther says, "Once upon a time, the devil said to me, 'Martin Luther, you are a great sinner, and you will be damned!' 'Stop! Stop!' said I. 'One thing at a time. I am a great sinner, it is true, though you have no right to tell me of it. I confess it. What next?' 'Therefore, you will be damned.' 'That is not good reasoning. It is true I am a great sinner, but it is written, "Jesus Christ came to save sinners." Therefore, *I shall be saved!* Now go your way.' So I cut the devil off with his own sword, and he went away mourning because he could not cast me down by calling me a sinner."

The Jews have a saying that the manna tasted to each one precisely like that which he liked best. The gospel is suited to every man, whatever his needs or desires may be.

One of William Carey's last visitors was the Rev. Alexander Duff who talked with him of his past life, then knelt down and prayed by his bedside. Leaving the room, Mr. Duff thought he heard himself recalled. He turned back, and the dying man addressed him in a whisper, "Mr. Duff, you have been talking about *Doctor* Carey, *Doctor* Carey. When I am gone, say nothing about Doctor Carey. Speak about Doctor Carey's *Savior*."

234

Howbeit for this cause I obtained mercy, that in me first Jesus Christ might shew forth all longsuffering, for a pattern to them which should hereafter believe on him to life everlasting.

—1 Timothy 1:16

HE notion is common that Paul's conversion was something uncommon and not at all to be expected in the usual order of things.

The text flatly contradicts such a supposition: the very reason for his salvation was that he might be a type of other conversions.

I. IN THE CONVERSION OF PAUL, THE LORD HAD AN EYE TO OTHERS.

The fact of his conversion and the mode of it:

1. Would tend to interest and convince other Pharisees and Jews.
2. Would be used by himself in his preaching as an argument to convert and encourage others.
3. Would encourage Paul as a preacher to hope for others.
4. Would become a powerful argument with him for seeking others.
5. Would, long after Paul's death, remain on record to be the means of bringing many to Jesus.

We are each one saved with an eye to others.

For whose sake are *you* saved?

Are you making the fullest use of your conversion to this end?

II. IN HIS ENTIRE LIFE, PAUL SPEAKS TO OTHERS.

He was foremost in sin and also in grace, and thus his life speaks to the extremes on each side.

1. In sin. His conversion proves that Jesus receives great sinners.
   - He was a blasphemer, a persecutor, and injurious.
   - He went as far as he could in hatred to Christ and his people.
   - Yet, the grace of God changed him and forgave him.
2. In grace. He proved the power of God to sanctify and preserve.
   - He was faithful in ministry, clear in knowledge, fervent in spirit, patient in suffering, diligent in service.
   - And all this notwithstanding what he once was.

The foremost in sin may be saved, and so none are shut out.

These should be and may be foremost in faith and love when saved.

III. IN HIS WHOLE CASE, HE PRESENTS A PICTURE OF OTHERS.

1. As to God's long-suffering to him. In his case:
   - Long-suffering was carried to its highest pitch.
   - Long-suffering was so great that *all* the patience of God seemed to be revealed in his one instance.
   - Long-suffering was concentrated. All the long-suffering that has ever been seen or ever will be seen in others met in him.
   - Long-suffering which displayed itself in many ways, so as:
     To let him live when persecuting saints.

To allow him the possibility of pardon.

To call him effectually by grace.

To give him fullness of personal blessing.

To put him into the ministry and send him to the Gentiles.

To keep and support him even unto the end.

2. As to the mode of his conversion.

He was saved remarkably, but others will be seen to be saved in like manner if we look below the surface of things:

- Saved without previous preparation on his own part.
- Saved at once out of darkness and death.
- Saved by divine power alone.
- Saved by faith wrought in him by God's own Spirit.
- Saved distinctly and beyond all doubt.

Are we not also saved in precisely the same way?

It is possible for us to realize in ourselves a full parallel with Paul:

- There is a sad resemblance in our sin.
- There is a similarity in the divine longsuffering towards us.
- There is a likeness in some degree in the revelation, for the Lord Jesus asks us from heaven, "Why persecutest thou me?"
- Shall there not be a similarity also in the faith?
- Will we not ask, "Who art thou, Lord?" and "What wilt thou have me to do?"

Proof Impressions

The word "pattern" in the original is expressive: a pattern from which endless copies may be taken. You have heard of stereotype printing. When the types are set up, they are cast—made a fixed thing, so that from one plate you can strike off hundreds of thousands of pages in succession without the trouble of setting up the types again. Paul says, "That I might be a plate never worn out—never destroyed, from which proof impressions may be taken to the very end of time." What a splendid thought that the apostle Paul, having portrayed himself as the chief of sinners, then portrays himself as having received forgiveness for a grand and specific end, that he might be a standing plate from which impressions might be taken forever, that no man might despair who had read his biography! —*Dr. Cumming*

An infidel, during his sickness, became convinced of his wretched condition, and by the assistance of a Sabbath-school teacher was led to the Savior and found salvation in his blood. After the change which had passed in his heart, he often spoke of the Savior's love and the heaven into which he hoped soon to enter. Finding his life drawing rapidly to a close, he urged the teacher to proceed in his glorious work of doing good; then, opening his bedroom window, which overlooked a bustling and crowded thoroughfare, as he gazed upon the human forms beneath, summoning his last remaining strength, he cried at the top of his voice, "There is mercy for all! None need despair, since I, a poor infidel, have obtained mercy." This, his last work, accomplished, exhausted by the effort, he fell back on his bed and instantly died. —*Haughton, in Bate's Cyclopaedia*

John Newton, speaking of the sudden death of Robinson, of Cambridge, in the house of Dr. Priestly, said: "I think Dr. Priestly is out of the reach of human conviction; but the Lord can convince him. And who can tell but this unexpected stroke may make some salutary impression upon his mind? I can set no limits to the mercy or the power of our Lord, and therefore I continue to pray for him. I am persuaded he is not farther from the truth now than I was once." In the same spirit, Newton wrote the lines:

> Come, my fellow sinners, try,
> Jesus' heart is full of love;
> Oh that you, as well as I,
> May his wondrous mercy prove!
> He has sent me to declare,
> All is ready, all is free;
> Why should any soul despair,
> When he saved a wretch like me?

Every conversion of a great sinner is a new copy of God's love; it is a repeated proclamation of the transcendency of his grace. This was his design in Paul's conversion. He sets up this apostle as a white flag to invite rebels to treat with him and return to their loyalty. As every great judgment upon a grand sinner is as the hanging a man in chains to deter others from the like practice, so every conversion is not only an act of God's mercy to the convert, but an invitation to the spectators. —*Stephen Charnock*

235

For the which cause I also suffer these things: nevertheless I am not ashamed: for I know whom I have believed, and am persuaded that he is able to keep that which I have committed unto him against that day.

—*2 Timothy 1:12*

AUL, much buffeted and persecuted, is sustained by faith and by a sense of personal security in Christ Jesus.

The meaning which may be in the text: The gospel deposited with Paul the Lord Jesus was able to keep until the judgment. This is well worthy of being explained. The gospel is safe in the care of Jesus.

Paul felt great comfort as the result of committing his soul to Jesus.
Let us consider:

I. WHAT HE HAD DONE.

Feeling the value of his soul, knowing its danger, conscious of his own weakness, believing in the grace and power of the Lord Jesus, he had placed his soul in his hands.

1. His soul's case was there for Jesus to heal him as a *Physician*.
2. His soul's calls were there to be supplied by Jesus as a *Shepherd*.
3. His soul's course was there to be directed by Jesus as a *Pilot*.
4. His soul's cause was there to be pleaded by Jesus as an *Advocate*.
5. His soul's care was there to be guarded by Jesus as a *Protector*.

He had committed his soul to Jesus by an act of faith, which act he persevered in continually.

II. WHAT HE KNEW. "I know whom I have believed."

He speaks not of believing *in* him, but of believing him: a personal faith in a personal Savior. This trusted one he knew.

1. He knew the Lord Jesus by his personal meeting with him on the road to Damascus and at other times.
2. By what he had read and heard concerning him and made his own by meditation thereon.
3. By communion with him. This way is open to all the saints.
4. By experience, through which he had tried and proved his love and faithfulness. He had received a practical education, by which he was made to know his Lord by entering into the fellowship of his sufferings and death.

Have we this personal acquaintance with the Lord?

If so, we shall gladly commit our all to him.

III. WHAT HE WAS SURE OF. "That he is able to keep."

His assurance was reasonable and deliberate; hence he says, "I am persuaded."

Our apostle was persuaded of:

1. The ability of Jesus to keep all souls committed to him.
   • He is divine and therefore omnipotent to save.
   • His work is finished, so that he meets all the demands of the law.
   • His wisdom is perfect, so that he will ward off all dangers.
   • His plea is constant and ever prevails to preserve his own.
2. The ability of Jesus to keep Paul's own soul.
3. The ability of Jesus to keep his soul under the heavy trials which were then pressing upon him. "I suffer . . . I am not ashamed, for I am persuaded that he is able to keep."

4. The ability of Jesus to keep his soul even to the close of all things: "against that day."

Of this Paul was persuaded. Be this our persuasion.

Many would persuade us to the contrary; but we *know*, and are not therefore to be persuaded into a doubt upon the matter.

IV. WHAT, THEREFORE, HE WAS.

1. Very cheerful. He had all the tone and air of a thoroughly happy man.
2. Very confident. Though a prisoner, he says, "I am not ashamed." Neither of his condition, nor of the cause of Christ, nor of the cross, was he ashamed.
3. Very thankful. He gladly praised the Lord in whom he trusted. The text is a confession of faith or a form of adoration.

Let us seek more knowledge of our Lord as the Keeper of our souls.

Let us be of that brave persuasion which trusts and is not afraid.

Instances and Illustrations

When *Dr. James W. Alexander* was dying, his wife sought to comfort him with precious words, as she quoted them to him: "I know in whom I have believed." Dr. Alexander at once corrected her by saying, "Not *in* whom I have believed," but, "I know *whom* I have believed." He would not even suffer a little preposition to be between his soul and his Savior.

"I have lost that weary bondage of doubt, and almost despair, which chained me for so many years. I have the same sins and temptations as before, and I do not strive against them more than before, and it is often just as hard work. But whereas I could not before see why I *should* be saved, I cannot now see why I should *not* be saved if Christ died for sinners. On that word, I take my stand and rest there." —*F. R. Havergal*

Justyn Martyr was asked ironically by the Roman prefect if he believed that after his decapitation he would ascend to heaven. He replied: "I am so sure of the grace which Jesus Christ hath obtained for me that not a shadow of doubt can enter my mind."

Donald Cargill, on the scaffold, July 27th, 1681, as he handed his well-used Bible to one of his friends that stood near, gave this testimony: "I bless the Lord that these thirty years and more I have been at peace with God and was never shaken loose of it. And now I am as sure of my interest in Christ and peace with God as all within this Bible and the Spirit of God can make me. And I am no more terrified at death or afraid of hell because of sin than if I had never had sin. For all my sins are freely pardoned and washed thoroughly away through the precious blood and intercession of Jesus Christ."

Faith, Hope, and Love were questioned what they thought
Of future glory, which religion taught:
Now Faith believed it firmly to be true,
And Hope expected so to find it, too:
Love answered, smiling, with a conscious glow,
"Believe? Expect? I know it to be so!"

—John Byrom

A child that hath any precious thing given him cannot better secure it than by putting it into his father's hands to keep. So neither can we better provide for our souls' safety than by committing them to God. *—John Trapp*

236

The Lord grant unto him that he may find mercy of the Lord in that day.

—2 Timothy 1:18

THE best method of showing our gratitude to some men for their kindness would be to pray for them. Even the best of men will be the better for our prayers.

Paul had already prayed for the household of Onesiphorus, and now he concludes by a specially hearty prayer for the good man himself. The repetition of the word "Lord" makes the prayer peculiarly solemn.

Onesiphorus had remembered Paul in his day of peril, and Paul begs the Lord to give him a gracious return in the day of judgment.

Yet the utmost he can ask even for so excellent a man is *mercy*. Even the merciful need mercy; and it is their benediction from the Lord himself that "they shall obtain mercy."

Let us consider this prayer under three heads:

I. "THAT DAY."

"That day": It is not specifically described, because well-known and much thought of among Christians. Do we sufficiently think of that day? If so, we shall feel our great need to find mercy of the Lord when it comes.

- Its date is not given. It would but gratify curiosity.
- Its length is not specified. Will it be a common day? It will be long enough for the deliberate judgment of all men.
- Its coming will be solemnly proclaimed. We shall know it. Ushered in with pomp of angels and sound of trumpet, none will be ignorant of it.

- Its glory: the revelation of Jesus from heaven upon the throne of judgment. This will make it most memorable.
- Its event: the assembly of quick and dead and the last assize.
- Its character: excitement of joy or terror. It will be the day of days, for which all other days were made.
- Its personal interest to each one of us will be paramount.
- Its revealings of secrets of thought, word, deed for good or for evil will be most astounding.
- Its decisions will be strictly just, indisputable, unchangeable.
- It will be the last day, and henceforth the state of men will be fixed for joy or woe.

How much we shall need mercy in the judgment! Every thought connected with it makes us feel this. Let us pray about it.

II. THE MERCY.

All will need it. Assuredly we shall need it ourselves.

To arouse us, let us think of those who will find no mercy of the Lord in that day:

- Those who had no mercy on others.
- Those who lived and died impenitent.
- Those who neglected salvation. How shall they escape?
- Those who said they needed no mercy: the self-righteous.
- Those who sought no mercy: procrastinators and the indifferent.
- Those who scoffed at Christ and refused the gospel.
- Those who sold their Lord, and apostatized from him.
- Those who made a false and hypocritical profession.

III. TODAY.

Our address at this moment is to those for whom we would specially breathe the prayer of the text.

The prospect of judgment for preacher and hearers leads us at once to pray for you and at the same time to urge you to seek the Lord while he may be found.

We would not have you despair as to the future but hope to find mercy in the present that you may find it in "that day."

- Remember that now is the accepted time, for:
- You are not yet standing at the judgment bar.
- You are yet where prayer is heard.
- You are where faith will save all who exercise it towards Christ.
- You are where the Spirit strives.
- You are where sin may be forgiven at once and forever.
- You are where grace reigns, even though sin abounds.

Today is the day of grace; tomorrow may be a day of another sort, for you at least and possibly for all mankind. The Judge is at the door.

Seek mercy immediately, that mercy may be yours forever.

Trumpet Notes

I would rather have the gift of a brother's faithful prayers than of his plentiful substance. And I feel that when I have given to a brother my faithful prayers, I have given him my best and greatest gift. —*Edward Irving*

There is a machine in the Bank of England which receives sovereigns as a mill receives grain for the purpose of determining wholesale whether they are of full weight. As they pass through, the machinery, by unerring laws, throws all that are light to one side and all that are of full weight to another. That process is a silent but solemn parable for me. Founded as it is upon the laws of nature, it affords the most vivid similitude of the certainty which characterizes the judgment of the great day. There are no mistakes or partialities to which the light may trust; the only hope lies in being of standard weight before they go in. —*William Arnot*

An infidel was introduced by a gentleman to a minister with a remark, "He never attends public worship." "Ah!" said the minister, "I hope you are mistaken." "By no means," said the stranger. "I always spend Sunday in settling my accounts." "Then, alas!" was the calm, but solemn reply, "you will find, sir, that the day of judgment will be spent in the same manner." —*G. S. Bowes*

When *Thomas Hooker* was dying, one said to him, "Brother, you are going to receive the reward of your labors." He humbly replied, "Brother, I am going to receive *mercy.*"

By that tremendous phrase, "*eternal* judgment," consider your ways, and be wise! If its true meaning could lighten upon you at this moment, what consternation would strike upon each spirit! Every man, though serene as death before, would spring to his feet and cry, "Tell me, tell me this moment, what I must do!" —*Charles Stanford, D.D.*

It is a pathetic tale to tell, and I do not vouch for its absolute truth, that once a famous composer wrote a great anthem to be sung at a festival. He sought to picture the scenes of the final judgment and introduced a strain of music representing the solemn lamentations of the lost. But no singer was found willing to take such a part. So the wailings and woes were omitted; and when the passage was reached, the leader simply beat the time in silence till the awful chasm was passed, and the musicians took up gloriously the strains of celestial unison lying on the other side of it: "the shout of them that triumph and the song of them who feast." —*Dr. C. S. Robinson*

237

Wherein I suffer trouble, as an evil-doer, even unto bonds; but the word of God is not bound.

—*2 Timothy 2:9*

 HE resurrection of Christ was Paul's sheet-anchor. Enlarge upon verse 8, wherein he mentions it as the essence of the gospel.

He himself is suffering and bound, but he is not without comfort. His great joy is that the word of God is not bound.

I. IN WHAT SENSES THIS IS TRUE.

"The Word of God is not bound":

1. So that it cannot be made known.
   - The ministers who preach it may be imprisoned, but not the word.
   - The book which contains it may be burned, but the truth abides.
   - The doctrine may become almost extinct as to open testimony, and yet it will revive.
2. So that it cannot reach the heart.

   It will not be hindered of its divine purpose:
   - Through the obduracy of the sinner, for grace is omnipotent.
   - Through absence of the means. The Holy Spirit can reach the conscience without the hearing or reading of the word.
   - Through actual derision of it. Even the scoffer and skeptic can yet be convinced and converted.
3. So that it cannot comfort the soul.
   - Conviction of sin will not hinder consolation when faith is given.
   - Constitutional despondency will give way before the light of the word.
   - Confirmed despair shall be overcome, even as Samson snapped the cords wherewith he had been bound.
4. So that it cannot be fulfilled.
   - Providence will carry out the promise to the individual.
   - Providence will perform the threat to the rebellious.
   - Providence will achieve the prophecies of the millennial future.
5. So that it cannot prevail over error.

   Infidelity, ritualism, popery, fanaticism shall not bind the gospel so as to retain their mischievous power over men. The gospel must and will accomplish the purposes of God.

II. FOR WHAT REASONS THIS IS TRUE.

The word of God cannot be bound since:

1. It is the voice of the Almighty.
2. It is attended by the energetic working of the Holy Ghost.
3. It is so needful to men. As men will have bread, and you cannot keep it from them, so must they have the truth. The gospel is in such demand that there must be free trade in it.
4. It is in itself a free and unbound thing, the very essence of liberty.
5. It creates such enthusiasm in the hearts wherein it dwells, that men must declare it abroad. It must be free.

III. WHAT OTHER FACTS ARE PARALLEL WITH THIS?

As the binding of Paul was not the binding of the word of God, so:

- The death of ministers is not the death of the gospel.
- The feebleness of workers is not its feebleness.
- The bondage of the preacher's mind is not its bondage.
- The coldness of men is not its coldness.
- The falsehood of hypocrites does not falsify it.
- The spiritual ruin of sinners is not the defeat of the gospel.
- The rejection of it by unbelievers is not its overthrow.

Rejoice, that the word of the Lord has free course.

Arouse yourselves to work with it and by it.

Accept its free power, and be yourself free at once.

Illustrations

"But the Word of God is not bound." It runs and is glorified (2 Thess. 3:1), being free and not fettered. "I preach, though a prisoner," saith Paul; so did Bradford and other martyrs. "Within a few days of Queen Mary's reign, almost all the prisons in England were become right Christian schools and churches," saith Mr. Fox, "so that there was no greater comfort for Christian hearts than to come to the prisons to behold their virtuous conversation and to hear their prayers, preachings, etc." The Earl of Derby's accusation in the Parliament House against Mr. Bradford was that he did more hurt (so he called good evil) by letters and conferences in prison than ever he did when he was abroad by preaching. —*John Trapp*

In a portrait of Tyndale still preserved in this country, beside the heroic man is a device: a burning book is tied to a stake, while a number of similar books are seen flying out of the fire. The meaning is an historic fact. Tonstal, the Bishop of London, had bought up some scores of Tyndale's Testaments and burned them. The money paid for them enabled Tyndale to bring out a new and more correct edition.

Towards the close of the last century, before the days of the great Bible societies, there was for a season a woeful want of Bibles in America, caused partly by the prevalence of French infidelity and partly by the general religious apathy which followed the Revolutionary War. In that period, a man went into a book-store in Philadelphia and asked to buy a Bible. "I have none," said the bookseller. "There is not a copy for sale in the city; and I can tell you further," said he (for he was of the French way of thinking), "in fifty years there will not be a Bible in the world." The rough answer of the customer was, "There will be plenty of Bibles in the world a thousand years after you are dead and gone to hell." —*The Christian Age*

When the daughter of the Mayor of Baune had lost her canary bird, her wise parent gave strict orders that all the gates of the town should be shut that the creature might not escape. The bird was soon over the hills and far away, despite the locking of the gates. When a truth is once known, no human power can prevent its spreading. Attempts to hinder its progress will be as ineffectual as the mayor's proclamation. As a bird of the air, truth flies abroad on swift wings. As a ray of light, it enters palaces and cottages. As the unfettered wind, it laughs at laws and prohibitions. Walls cannot confine it nor iron bars imprison it. It is free, and maketh free. Let every freeman be upon its side, and being so, let him never allow a doubt of its ultimate success to darken his soul. —*C. H. S.*

The monument in Westminster Abbey to the memory of the two Wesleys bears the sentence, "God buries his workmen, but carries on his work."

Truth is more incompressible than water. If compressed in one way, it will exude through the compressing mass, the more visible through the attempts to compress it. —*Dr. Pusey*

238

That they may adorn the doctrine of God our Saviour in all things.
—*Titus 2:10*

 HE apostle greatly values the doctrine of the gospel, or he would not care so much to have it adorned.

The apostle highly esteems the practical part of religion; hence he regards it as the beauty and ornament of the gospel.

What a wide range of practical instruction we find in this short letter! With what holy ingenuity is this interwoven with the doctrine! We are bidden to obey the precept that we may adorn the doctrine. We have in our text:

I. A NAME OF ADORNMENT FOR THE GOSPEL. "The doctrine of God our Saviour."

1. It sets forth its greatness: "doctrine of God."
   • Our fall, ruin, sin, and punishment were great.

- Our salvation and redemption are great.
- Our safety, happiness, and hopes are great.

2. It sets forth its certainty. It is "of God."
- It comes by revelation of God.
- It is guaranteed by the fidelity of God.
- It is as immutable as God himself.

3. It sets forth its relation to Christ Jesus: "of God our Saviour."
- He is the author of it.
- He is the substance of it.
- He is the proclaimer of it.
- He is the object of it. The gospel glorifies Jesus.

4. It sets forth its authority.
- The whole system of revealed truth is of God.
- The Savior himself is God, and hence he must be accepted.
- The gospel itself is divine. God's mind is embodied in the doctrine of the Lord Jesus and to reject it is to reject God.

Let us believe, honor, defend, and propagate this "doctrine of God our Saviour." What else is so worthy of our love and zeal?

II. A METHOD OF ADORNMENT FOR THE GOSPEL.

This is a remarkable verse. Observe:

1. The persons who are to adorn the gospel.
- In Paul's day, bond servants or slaves.
- In our day, poor servants of the humblest order.

Strange that these should be set to such a task!

Yet, the women slaves adorned their mistresses, and both men and women of the poorest class were quite ready to adorn themselves.

From none does the gospel receive more honor than from the poor.

2. The way in which these persons could specially adorn the gospel:
- By obedience to their masters (verse 9).
- By endeavors to please them: "please them well."
- By restraining their tongues: "not answering again."
- By scrupulous honesty: "not purloining" (verse 10).
- By trustworthy character: "showing all good fidelity."

All this would make their masters admire the religion of Jesus.

3. The way of adornment of the doctrine in general.
Negatively, it is found:
- Not in the decoration of the building, the priest, the choir, or the worshippers.
- Nor in the attraction of peculiar garb and speech.
- Nor in the finery of philosophical thought.
- Nor in the tawdriness of rhetorical speech.

Positively, it lies in another direction.
- We must adorn it by our godly lives.
- Adornment, if really so, is *suitable to beauty*. Holiness, mercifulness, cheerfulness are congruous with the gospel.
- Adornment is often a *tribute to beauty*. Such is a godly conversation; it honors the gospel.
- Adornment is *an advertisement of beauty*. Holiness calls attention to the natural beauty of the gospel.
- Adornment is *an enhancement of beauty*. Godliness gives emphasis to the excellence of doctrine.

Let us all endeavor to adorn the gospel, by:
- Strict integrity in business.
- Constant courtesy of behavior.
- Unselfish love to all around us.
- Quick forgiveness of injuries.
- Abundant patience under trials.
- Holy calm and self-possession at all times.

Gems

Yes, and mark you, this is to be done not as the prerogative of a few grandly gifted spirits and on some occasion which may lift them proudly up to the gaze of the universe. As found in the text, it was of the power of the poor Cretan slaves the apostle was writing, of their power, too, not in some tremendous trial, as of torture or martyrdom, to which the cruelty of their masters sometimes subjected their faith, but of their power to do it "in all things": in the daily, lowly, degrading service of a menial; in the small things as well as the great; in the squalid stall and fold as well as in the splendor of the palace; absolutely, in "all things" to adorn the glorious gospel of God. O blessed bondsmen of Crete, going forth under the lash and the chain, yet with hearts of faith under their burdens and smiles of love amid their tears, doing work for God impossible to an angel! —*Charles Wadsworth, D.D.*

We have all heard the story of the girl who said she had been converted, for she now "swept under the mats." Koba, an Indian warrior, recently gave evidence of his conversion by saying, "I pray every day, and hoe onions." An Indian could not give a much better evidence of his sincerity than that. Manual labor is not the chief joy or pride of an Indian warrior.

Fox says, "When people came to have experience of Friends' honesty and faithfulness and found that their yea was yea and their nay was nay; and that they kept to a word in their dealings, and that they could not cozen and cheat them; but that if they sent a child to their shops for anything, they were as well used as if they had come themselves, the lives and conversations of Friends did preach. All the inquiry was, Where was a draper, or shopkeeper, or tailor, or shoemaker, or any other tradesman that was a Quaker?"

A Brahmin wrote to a missionary, "We are finding you out. You are not as good as your Book. If your people were only as good as your Book, you would conquer India for Christ in five years."

Light conceits and flowers of rhetoric wrong the Word more than they can please the hearers. The weeds among the corn make it look gay, but it were all the better they were not amongst it. —*Leighton*

> All may of thee partake:
>   Nothing can be so mean,
> Which with this tincture (for thy sake)
>   Will not grow bright and clean.
>
> A servant with this clause
>   Makes drudgery divine:
> Who sweeps a room, as for thy laws,
>   Makes that and th' action fine.
>   —*George Herbert*

239

For the word of God is quick, and powerful, and sharper than any twoedged sword, piercing even to the dividing asunder of soul and spirit, and of the joints and marrow, and is a discerner of the thoughts and intents of the heart.

—*Hebrews 4:12*

 HE word of God is a name for Christ as well as for the Scriptures. The Scriptures are meant in this place, but the Lord Jesus is never dissevered therefrom: indeed, he is the substance of the written word.

Scripture is what it is because the Lord Jesus embodies himself in it.

Let us consider from this text:

I. THE QUALITIES OF THE WORD.

1. It is divine. It is the word of God.
2. It is living. "The word of God is quick."
   - In contrast to our words, which pass away, God's word lives on.
   - It has life in itself. It is "the living and incorruptible seed."
   - It creates life where it comes.
   - It can never be destroyed and exterminated.

3. It is effectual: "quick, and powerful."
  - It carries conviction and conversion.
  - It works comfort and confirmation.
  - It has power to raise us to great heights of holiness and happiness.
4. It is cutting: "Sharper than any two-edged sword."
  - It cuts all over. It is all edge. It is sharpness itself.
  - It wounds more or less all who touch it.
  - It kills self-righteousness, sin, unbelief.
5. It is piercing: "even to the dividing asunder."
  - It forces its way into the hard heart.
  - It penetrates the smallest opening, like the arrow which entered between the joints of the harness.
6. It is discriminating: "to the dividing asunder of soul and spirit."
  - It separates things much alike: natural and spiritual religion.
  - It divides the outer from the inner: external and internal religion, "joints and marrow."
  - It does this by its own penetrating and discerning qualities.
7. It is revealing: "a discerner of the thoughts and intents of the heart."
  - It cleaves the man as the butcher cleaves a carcase and opens up the secret faculties and tendencies of the soul.
  - Laying bare thoughts, intents, and inner workings.
  - Criticizing them and putting a right estimate on them.
  - Tracing their windings and showing their dubious character.
  - Approving that which is good and condemning the evil.

All this we have seen in the preaching of the word of God.

Have you not felt it to be so?

II. THE LESSONS WHICH WE SHOULD LEARN THEREFROM.

- That we do greatly reverence the word, as truly spoken of God.
- That we come to it for quickening for our own souls.
- That we come to it for power when fighting the battles of truth.
- That we come to it for cutting force to kill our own sins and to help us in destroying the evils of the day.
- That we come to it for piercing force when men's consciences and hearts are hard to reach.
- That we use it to the most obstinate to arouse their consciences and convict them of sin.
- That we discriminate by its means between truth and falsehood.
- That we let it criticize us, our opinions, projects, acts, and all about us.

Let us keep to this sword of the Lord, for none other is living and powerful as this is.

Let us grasp its hilt with firmer grip than ever.

Sharpeners

All the great conquests which Christ and his saints achieve in this world are got with this sword. When Christ comes forth against his enemies, this sword is girded on his thigh (Ps. 14:3): "Gird thy sword upon thy thigh, O most mighty"; and his victory over them is ascribed to it (verse 4), "And in thy majesty ride prosperously because of truth," that is, the word of truth.

We read of Apollos (Acts 18:28), that he "mightily convinced the Jews." He did, as it were, knock them down with the weight of his reasoning. And out of what armory fetched he the sword with which he so prevailed? See the same verse, "Showing by the Scriptures that Jesus was Christ." He, therefore, is said to be "mighty in the Scriptures" (verse 24).

Bless God for the efficacy of the word upon thy soul. Did ever its point prick thy heart, its edge fetch blood of thy lusts? Bless God for it. You would do as much to a surgeon for lancing a sore, and severing a putrified part from thy body, though he put thee to exquisite torture in the doing of it. And I hope thou thinkest God hath done thee a greater kindness. . . . There is not another sword like this in all the world that can cure with cutting; not another arm could use this sword, to have done thus with it besides the Spirit of God. None could do such feats with Scanderberg's as himself.

The word of God is too sacred a thing and preaching too solemn a work to be toyed and played with, as is the usage of some who make a sermon but matter of wit and fine oratory. If we mean to do good, we must come unto men's hearts, not in word only, but with power. Satan moves not for a thousand squibs and wit-cracks of rhetoric. Draw, therefore, this sword out of your scabbard, and strike with its naked edge; this you will find the only way to pierce your people's consciences and fetch blood of their sins. —*William Gurnall*

When the heathen saw the converts reading the book which had produced the change, they enquired if they talked to it. "No," they answered, "it talks to us, for it is the Word of God." "What then!" replied the strangers. "Does it speak?" "Yes," rejoined the Christians, "it speaks to the heart." —*Life of Moffat*

Miss Whateley says, "To rouse the torpid and unexercised mind of a Moslem woman is wonderful, for they are sunk in ignorance and degradation. But while I was reading to one of them a few weeks ago, she exclaimed, 'Why, it is just as if I were out in the dark, and you held a lamp to me that I might see my way.'"

The *Rev. James Wall*, of Rome, relates the following instances of conversion through the reading of the Scriptures: One of the converts, when first presented with a New Testament, said, "Very well; it is the very size for me to make my cigarettes," and so he began to smoke it away. He smoked away all the Evangelists, till he was at the tenth chapter of John, when it struck him that he must read a bit of it, for if he didn't, there would soon be no more left to read. The first word struck home, and the man read himself into Christ.

A secret society of political conspirators, who sought to achieve their purposes by assassination, were in the habit of placing a Bible (as a blind) on the table of the room where they met for deliberation. One night, when there happened to be little business to transact, and they were all rather sleepy, a member of the society opened the Bible and saw a verse that went right to his heart. He soon returned to the book and read more of it, and now he was a very earnest follower of the Lord Jesus. —*Missionary Herald*

240

Let us therefore come boldly unto the throne of grace, that we may obtain mercy, and find grace to help in time of need.

—*Hebrews 4:16*

 RAYER occupies a most important place in the life of the Christian. His vigor, happiness, growth, and usefulness depend thereon. In Scripture, the utmost encouragements are held out to prayer. This verse is one of the sweetest of invitations to prayer.

I. HERE IS OUR GREAT RESORT DESCRIBED. "The throne of grace."

Once it was called "the mercy *seat*," but now "the throne."

In drawing near to God in prayer, we come:

1. To God as a King, with reverence, confidence, and submission.
2. To one who gives as a King; therefore we ask largely and expectantly. He has riches of grace and power.
3. To one who sits upon a throne "of grace" on purpose to dispense grace. It is his design, his object in displaying himself as King.
4. To one who in hearing prayer is enthroned and glorified. Grace is at its utmost when believers pray; it is grace on the throne.
5. To one who even in hearing prayer acts as a sovereign, but whose sovereignty is all of grace.

To the throne of the great God, poor sinners are invited to come. Oh, the privilege of having audience with the King of Grace!

II. HERE IS A LOVING EXHORTATION. "Let us come."

It is the voice of one who goes with us. It is an invitation:

1. From Paul, a man like ourselves, but an experienced believer who had much tried the power of prayer.
2. From the whole church speaking in him.

3. From the Holy Spirit, for the apostle spoke by inspiration. The Spirit, making intercession in us, says, "Let us come."

Let us not be indifferent to this sympathetic call. At once let us draw near to God.

III. HERE IS A QUALIFYING ADVERB. "Let us come boldly."

Not proudly, presumptuously, nor with the tone of demand, for it is the throne, yet "boldly," for it is the throne of *grace*.

By this adverb, "boldly," is meant:
1. We may come constantly, at all times.
2. We may come unreservedly, with all sorts of petitions.
3. We may come freely, with simple words.
4. We may come hopefully, with full confidence of being heard.
5. We may come fervently, with importunity of pleading.

IV. HERE IS A REASON GIVEN FOR BOLDNESS. "Let us *therefore* come."

1. "That we may obtain mercy, and find grace;" not that we may utter good words; but may actually obtain blessings.
   - We may come when we need great mercy, because of our sin.
   - We may come when we have little grace.
   - We may come when we are in great need of more grace.
2. There are many other reasons for coming at once, and boldly.
   - Our character may urge us. We are invited to come for "mercy," and therefore undeserving sinners may come.
   - The character of God encourages us to be bold.
   - Our relation to him as children gives us great freedom.
   - The Holy Spirit's guidance draws us near the throne.
   - The promises invite us by their greatness, freeness, sureness, etc.
   - Christ is already given to us, and therefore God will deny us nothing.
   - Our former successes at the throne give us solid confidence.
3. The great reason of all for bold approach is in Jesus.
   - He once was slain, and the mercy-seat is sprinkled with his blood.
   - He is risen and has justified us by his righteousness.
   - He has ascended and taken possession of all covenant blessings on our behalf. Let us ask for that which is our own.
   - He is sympathetic, tender, and careful for us; we *must* be heard.

Let us come to the throne, when we are sinful, to find mercy.
Let us come to the throne, when we are weak, to find help.
Let us come to the throne, when we are tempted, to find grace.

Expositions

When God enacts laws, he is on a throne of legislation: when he administers these laws he is on a throne of government: when he tries his creatures by these laws, he is on a throne of judgment, but when he receives petitions, and dispenses favors, he is on a *throne of grace.*

The idea of a throne inspires awe, bordering upon terror. It repels rather than invites. Few of us could approach it without trembling. But what is the throne of the greatest earthly monarch that ever swayed a scepter? The God we address is the King of kings. In his eye an Alexander is a worm; yea, all nations before him are less than nothing and vanity. How can we approach his infinite majesty? Blessed be his name, he is on a throne of grace; and we are allowed, and even commanded, to come to it *boldly.* —*William Jay*

It is styled a throne of grace, because God's gracious and free favor doth there accompany his glorious majesty. Majesty and mercy do there meet together. This was, under the law, typified by the ark. At each end thereof was an angel, to set forth God's glorious majesty. The cover of it is styled a "mercy-seat" (Exod. 25:17–18). —*William Gouge*

A holy boldness, a chastened familiarity, is the true spirit of right prayer. It was said of Luther that, when he prayed, it was with as much reverence as if he were praying to an infinite God, and with as much familiarity as if he were speaking to his nearest friend. —*G. S. Bowes*

This word *boldly* signifies liberty without restraint. You may be free, for you are welcome. You may use freedom of speech. The word is so used, (Acts 2:29; 4:13). You have liberty to speak your minds freely; to speak all your heart, your ails, and wants, and fears, and grievances. As others may not fetter you in speaking to God by prescribing what words you should use; so you need not restrain yourselves, but freely speak all that your condition requires. —*David Clarkson*

A petitioner once approached Augustus with so much fear and trembling that the emperor cried, "What, man! do you think you are giving a sop to an elephant?" He did not care to be thought a hard and cruel ruler. When men pray with a slavish bondage upon them, with cold, set phrases, and a crouching solemnity, the free Spirit of the Lord may well rebuke them. Art thou coming to a tyrant? Holy boldness, or at least a childlike hope, is most becoming in a Christian.

Obtaining mercy comes first; then finding grace to help in time of need. You cannot reverse God's order. You will not find grace to help in time of need till you have sought and found mercy to save. You have no right to reckon on God's help and protection and guidance, and all the other splendid privileges which he promises to "the children of God by faith in Jesus Christ," until you have this first blessing, the mercy of God in Christ Jesus; for it is "in" Jesus Christ that all the promises of God are yea and Amen. —*F. R. Havergal*

241

Who can have compassion on the ignorant, and on them that are out of the way.

—Hebrews 5:2

EN who are ignorant should not be met with scorn, nor fault-finding, nor neglect, for they need compassion.

We should lay ourselves out to bear with such for their good.

A disciple who has been taught all that he knows by a gracious Savior should have compassion on "the ignorant."

A wanderer who has been restored should have compassion on "them that are out of the way."

A priest should have compassion on the people with whom he is one flesh and blood, and assuredly our Lord, who is our great High Priest, has abundant compassion upon the ignorant.

Let us think of his great pity towards them.

I. WHAT IS THIS IGNORANCE?

It is moral and spiritual, and deals with eternal things.

1. It is fearfully common among all ranks.
2. It leaves them strangers to themselves.
   - They know not their own ignorance.
   - They are unaware of the heart's depravity.
   - They are unconscious of the heinousness of their actual sin.
   - They dream not of their present and eternal danger.
   - They have not discovered their inability for all that is good.
3. It leaves them unacquainted with the way of salvation. They choose other ways.
   - They have a mixed and injurious notion of the one way.
   - They often question and cavil at this one and only way.
4. It leaves them without the knowledge of Jesus.
   They know not his person, his offices, his work, his character his ability, his readiness to save them.
5. It leaves them strangers to the Holy Spirit.
   - They perceive not his inward strivings.
   - They are ignorant of regeneration.
   - They cannot comprehend the truth which he teaches.
   - They cannot receive his sanctification.
6. It is most ruinous in its consequences.
   - It keeps men out of Christ.
   - It does not excuse them when it is willful, as it usually is.

II. WHAT IS THERE IN THIS IGNORANCE WHICH IS LIABLE TO PROVOKE US, AND THEREFORE DEMANDS COMPASSION?

1. Its folly. Wisdom is worried with the absurdities of ignorance.
2. Its pride. Anger is excited by the vanity of self-conceit.
3. Its prejudice. It will not hear nor learn; and this is vexatious.
4. Its obstinacy. It refuses reason; and this is very exasperating.
5. Its opposition. It contends against plain truth, and this is trying.
6. Its density. It cannot be enlightened: it is profoundly foolish.
7. Its unbelief. Witnesses to divine truth are denied credence.
8. Its willfulness. It chooses not to know. It is hard teaching such.
9. Its relapses. It returns to folly, forgets and refuses wisdom, and this is a sore affliction to true love.

III. HOW OUR LORD'S COMPASSION TOWARDS THE IGNORANT IS SHOWN. "He can have compassion on the ignorant." This he clearly shows:

1. By offering to teach them.
2. By actually receiving them as disciples.
3. By instructing them little by little, most condescendingly.
4. By teaching them the same things over again, patiently.
5. By never despising them notwithstanding their dullness.
6. By never casting them off through weariness of their stupidity.

To such a compassionate Lord let us come, ignorant as we are.

For such a compassionate Lord let us labor among the most ignorant, and never cease to pity them.

Notes

It is a sad thing for the blind man who has to read the raised type when the tips of his fingers harden, for then he cannot read the thoughts of men which stand out upon the page; but it is far worse to lose sensibility of soul, for then you cannot peruse the book of human nature, but must remain untaught in the sacred literature of the heart. You have heard of the "iron duke," but an iron Christian would be a very terrible person: a heart of flesh is the gift of divine grace, and one of its sure results is the power to be very pitiful, tender, and full of compassion. —*C. H. S.*

Ignorance is the devil's college. —*Christmas Evans*

What the Papists cry up as the mother of devotion, we cry down as the father of superstition. —*William Secker*

That there should one man die ignorant who had capacity for knowledge, this I call a tragedy. Were it to happen more than twenty times in the minute, as by some computations it does, what a line of tragedies!

The miserable fraction of science which our united mankind, in a wide universe of nescience, has acquired, why is not this, with all diligence, imparted to all? —*Thomas Carlyle*

Utter ignorance is a most effectual fortification to a bad state of the mind. Prejudice may perhaps be removed; unbelief may be reasoned with; even demoniacs have been compelled to bear witness to the truth; but the stupidity of confirmed ignorance not only defeats the ultimate efficacy of the means for making men wiser and better, but stands in preliminary defiance to the very act of their application. It reminds us of an account, in one of the relations of the French Egyptian Campaigns, of the attempt to reduce a garrison posted in a bulky fort of mud. Had the defenses been of timber, the besiegers might have set fire to and burnt them; had they been of stone, they might have shaken and ultimately breached them by the battery of their cannon, or they might have undermined and blown them up. But the huge mound of mud had nothing susceptible of fire or any other force; the missiles from the artillery were discharged but to be buried in the dull mass; and all the means of demolition were baffled. —*John Foster*

In *"Eyesight, Good and Bad,"* by Dr. R. B. Carter, the writer says, "Nothing is more common than for defective sight to be punished at obstinacy or stupidity. For my own part, I have long learned to look upon obstinate and stupid children as mainly artificial productions, and shall not readily forget the pleasure with which I heard from the master of the great elementary school at Edinburgh, where twelve hundred children attend daily, that his fundamental principle of management was that there were no naughty boys and no boobies."

I used to reproach myself for *religious stupidity* when I was not well; but I see now that God is my kind Father, not my hard taskmaster expecting me to be full of life and zeal when physically exhausted. It takes long to learn such lessons. One has to penetrate deeply into the heart of Christ to begin to know its tenderness and sympathy and forbearance.

> The love of Jesus—what it is
> Only His *sufferers* know.
> —*Elizabeth Prentiss*

242

Though he were a Son, yet learned he obedience by the things which he suffered.

—Hebrews 5:8

 T is always consoling to us to behold the footsteps of our Lord. When we see him tried, we cheerfully submit to the like trial. When we perceive that in his case an exception to the rule of chastening might have been expected, and yet none was made, we are encouraged to bear our sufferings patiently.

When we see the great Elder Brother put to more rather than less of trial, we are fully drawn to obey the will of God by submission.

I. SONSHIP DOES NOT EXEMPT FROM SUFFERING.

1. Not even Jesus, as a Son, escaped suffering.
   - He was *the* Son, peculiarly, and above all others.
   - He was the honored and beloved first-born.
   - He was the faithful and sinless Son.
   - He was soon to be the glorified Son in an eminent sense.
2. No honor put upon sons of God will exempt them from suffering.
3. No holiness of character, nor completeness of obedience, can exempt the children of God from the school of suffering.
4. No prayer of God's sons, however earnest, will remove every thorn in the flesh from them.
5. No love in God's child, however fervent, will prevent his being tried.

The love and wisdom of God ensure the discipline of the house for all the heirs of heaven without a single exception.

II. SUFFERING DOES NOT MAR SONSHIP.

The case of our Lord is set forth as a model for all the sons of God.

1. His poverty did not disprove his Sonship (Luke 2:12).
2. His temptations did not shake his Sonship (Matt. 4:3).
3. His endurance of slander did not jeopardize it (John 10:36).
4. His fear and sorrow did not put it in dispute (Matt. 26:39).
5. His desertion by men did not invalidate it (John 16:32).
6. His being forsaken of God did not alter it (Luke 23:46).
7. His death cast no doubt thereon (Mark 15:39). He rose again and, thus, proved his Father's pleasure in him (John 20:17).

Never was there a truer, or lovelier, or more beloved Son than the sufferers. "A man of sorrows, and acquainted with grief."

III. OBEDIENCE HAS TO BE LEARNED EVEN BY SONS.

Even he in whom there was no natural depravity, but perfect, inherent purity, had to learn obedience.

1. It must be learned experimentally.
   - What is to be done and suffered can only be learned in the actual exercise of obedience.
   - How it is done must be discovered by practice.
   - The actual doing of it is only possible in trial.
2. It must be learned by suffering.
   - Not by words from the most instructive of teachers.
   - Nor by observation of the lives of others.

- Nor even by perpetual activity on our own part. This might make us fussy rather than obedient; we must suffer.
3. It must be learned for use in earth and in heaven.
   - On earth by sympathy with others.
   - In heaven by perfect praise to God growing out of experience.

IV. SUFFERING HAS A PECULIAR POWER TO TEACH TRUE SONS.

It is a better tutor than all else, because:

1. It touches the man's self: his bone, his flesh, his heart.
2. It tests his graces, and sweeps away those shams which are not proofs of obedience, but presences of self-will.
3. It goes to the root, and tests the truth of our new nature. It shows whether repentance, faith, prayer, etc., are mere importations, or home-grown fruits.
4. It tests our endurance, and makes us see how far we are established in the obedience which we think we possess. Can we say, "Though he slay me, yet will I trust in him"?

The anxious question: Am I a son?

The aspiring desire: Let me learn obedience.

The accepted discipline: I submit to suffer.

Blossomings of the Rod

Corrections are pledges of our adoption and badges of our sonship. One Son God hath without sin, but none without sorrow. As God corrects none but his own, so all that are his shall be sure to have it, and they shall take it for a favor, too (1 Cor. 11:32).—John Trapp

I bear my willing witness that I owe more to the fire, and the hammer, and the file, than to anything else in my Lord's workshop. I sometimes question whether I have ever learned anything except through the rod. When my school-room is darkened, I see most. —*C. H. S.*

> If aught can teach us aught, Affliction's looks,
>   Making us look unto ourselves so near,
> Teach us to know ourselves beyond all books,
>   Or all the learned schools that ever were.
> This mistress lately plucked me by the ear,
>   And many a golden lesson hath me taught;
> Hath made my senses quick, and reason clear,
>   Reformed my will, and rectified my thought.
>   —*Sir John Davies*

"I never," said Luther, "knew the meaning of God's word, until I came into affliction. I have always found it one of my best schoolmasters." On another occasion, referring to some spiritual temptation on the morning of the preceding day, he said to a friend (Justin Jonas), "Doctor, I must mark the day; I was yesterday at school." In one of his works, he most accurately calls affliction "the theology of Christians": "Theologium Christianorum." "I have learned more divinity," said Dr. Rivet, confessing to God of his last days of affliction , "in these ten days that thou art come to visit me, than I did in fifty years before. Thou teachest me after a better manner than all those doctors, in reading whom I spent so much time."—*Charles Bridges*

A minister was recovering from a dangerous illness, when one of his friends addressed him thus, "Sir, though God seems to be bringing you up from the gates of death, yet it will be a long time before you will sufficiently retrieve your strength, and regain vigor enough of mind to preach as usual." The good man answered: "You are mistaken, my friend; for this six weeks' illness has taught me more divinity than all my past studies and all my ten years' ministry put together." —*New Cyclopedia of Anecdote*

> Not to be unhappy is unhappiness,
> And misery not to have known misery;
> For the best way unto discretion is
> The way that leads us by adversity;
> And men are better showed what is amiss
> By the expert finger of calamity
> Than they can be with all that fortune brings,
> Who never shows them the true face of things.
>
> —*Samuel Daniel*

243

He taketh away the first, that he may establish the second.
—*Hebrews 10:9*

 THE way of God is to go from good to better.
This excites growing wonder and gratitude.
This makes men desire, and pray, and believe, and expect.
This aids man in his capacity to receive the best things.
The first good thing is removed, that the second may the more fitly come.
Upon this last fact we will meditate, noticing:

I. THE GRAND INSTANCE. First came the Jewish sacrifices, and then came Jesus to do the will of God.

1. The removal of instructive and consoling ordinances.

While they lasted they were of great value, and they were removed because, when Jesus came:

- They were needless as types.
- They would have proved burdensome as services.
- They might have been dangerous as temptations to formalism.
- They would have taken off the mind from the substance which they had formerly shadowed forth.

2. The establishment of the real, perfect, everlasting atonement.

This is a blessed advance, for:

- No one who sees Jesus regrets Aaron.
- No one who knows the simplicity of the gospel wishes to be brought under the perplexities of the ceremonial law.
- No one who feels the liberty of Zion desires to return to the bondage of Sinai.

Beware of setting up any other ordinances; for this would be to build again what God has cast down; if not to do even worse.

Beware of imagining that the second can fail as the first did. The one was "taken away"; but the other is *established* by God himself.

II. INSTANCES IN HISTORY. These are many. Here are a few:

1. The earthly paradise has been taken away by sin; but the Lord has given us salvation in Christ, and heaven.
2. The first man has failed; behold the Second Adam.
3. The first covenant is broken, and the second gloriously takes its place.
4. The first temple, with its transient glories, has melted away; but the second and spiritual house rises beneath the eye and hand of the Great Architect.

III. INSTANCES IN EXPERIENCE.

1. Our first righteousness is taken away by conviction of sin, but the righteousness of Christ is established.
2. Our first peace has been blown down as a tottering fence, but we shelter in the Rock of Ages.
3. Our first strength has proved worse than weakness, but the Lord is our strength and our song; he also has become our salvation.
4. Our first guidance led us into darkness; now we give up self, superstition, and philosophy, and trust in the Spirit of our God.
5. Our first joy died out like thorns which crackle under a pot; but now we joy in God.

IV. INSTANCES TO BE EXPECTED.

1. Our body decaying shall be renewed in the image of our risen Lord.
2. Our earth passing away, and its elements being dissolved, there shall be new heavens and a new earth.

3. Our family removed one by one, we shall be charmed by the grand reunion in the Father's house above.

4. Our all being taken away, we find more than all in God.

5. Our life ebbing out, the eternal life comes rolling up in a full tide of glory.

Let us not grieve at the taking away of the first.

Let us expect the establishment of the second.

Meliora

The Law is a Gospel pre-figured, and the Gospel a Law consummated. —*Bishop Hall*

The sin-destroyer being come, we are no longer under the sin-revealer. —*Martin Boos*

> No need of prophets to inquire:
> The Sun is risen—the stars retire:
> The Comforter is come, and sheds
> His holy unction on our heads.
> —*Josiah Conder*

When Alexander went upon a hopeful expedition, he gave away his gold; and when he was asked what he kept for himself, he answered, "Spem majorum et meliorum"—the hope of greater and better things. . . . A Christian's motto always is, or always should be, *Spero meliora*—I hope for better things. —*Thomas Brooks, in "The Best Things Reserved Till Last"*

On a cold, windy March day, a gentleman stopped at an apple-stand, whose proprietor was a rough-looking Italian. He alluded to the severe weather, when, with a cheerful smile and tone, the Italian replied: "Yes, pritty cold; but by-and-by—tink of dat!" In other words, the time of warm skies, flowers, and songs was near, and was to be thought of. The humble vendor little thought of the impression made by his few words. "By-and-by—think of that!"

The Jewish rabbins report (how truly is uncertain) that when Joseph, in the times of plenty, had gathered much corn in Egypt, he threw the chaff into the River Nile, that so, flowing to the neighboring cities and nations more remote, they might know what abundance was laid up, not for themselves alone, but for others also. So God, in his abundant goodness, to make us know what glory there is in heaven, hath thrown some husks to us here in this world, that so, tasting the sweetness thereof, we might aspire to his bounty that is above, and draw out this happy conclusion to the great comfort of our precious souls—that if a little earthly glory do so much amaze us, what will the heavenly do? If there be such glory in God's footstool, what is there in his throne? If he give us so much in the land of our pilgrimage, what will he not give us in our own country? If he bestoweth so much on his enemies, what will he not give to his friends? —*John Spencer*

There are certain words which, occurring frequently, are like a bunch of keys, and enable us to unlock the treasures in this epistle. Such a key is *"better"*; and we find the Lord Jesus described as being better than angels (1:4; illustrated in John 5:4–6), better than Moses (3), Joshua (4), and Aaron (7); his blood speaking better things than that of Abel (12:24); himself the Surety of a better testament, established upon better promises (7:22; 8:6). The old covenant based upon man's *promise* (Exod. 19:8; 24:7–8) was broken in forty days; but the *performance* by the Son of God was the foundation of the better covenant. "The two tables of the testimony were in the *hand* of Moses" (Exod. 32:15; Gal. 3:19), but God's law is within the *heart* of our Surety (Ps. 40:8; compare Deut. 10:1–2). That word was spoken by angels (Heb. 2:2; Acts 7:53); but this by him who is "so much *better* than angels." —*E. A. H. (Mrs. Gordon)*

244

And make straight paths for your feet, lest that which is lame be turned out of the way; but let it rather be healed.

—*Hebrews 12:13*

E sometimes meet with those who are fleet of foot and joyous of spirit. Would to God that all were so! But as they are not, the lame must be considered.

The road should be cleared for tottering steps.

Our desire is that the whole band may reach the journey's end in safety.

I. IN ALL FLOCKS THERE ARE LAME SHEEP.
1. Some are so from their very nature and birth.
   - Ready to despond and doubt.
   - Ready to disbelieve and fall into error.
   - Ready to yield to temptation, and so to prove unstable.
   - Unready and feeble in all practical duties.
2. Some have been ill-fed. This brings on a foot-rot and lameness.
   - Many are taught false doctrine.
   - Many more receive indefinite, hazy doctrine.
   - Many others hear light, insubstantial, chaffy doctrine.
3. Some have been worried, and so driven to lameness.
   - By Satan, with his insinuations and temptations.
   - By persecutors, with their slander, taunting, ridicule, etc.
   - By proud professors, unkindly pious, severely critical, etc.
   - By a morbid conscience, seeing evil where there is none.

4. Some have grown weary through the roughness of the road.
- Exceeding much ignorance has enfeebled them.
- Exceeding much worldly trouble has depressed them.
- Exceeding much inward conflict has grieved them.
- Exceeding much controversy has worried them.
5 Some have gradually become weak.
- Backsliding by neglect of the means of grace.
- Backsliding through the evil influence of others.
- Backsliding through pride of heart and self-satisfaction.
- Backsliding through general coldness of heart.
6. Some have had a terrible fall.
- This has broken their bones so as to prevent progress.
- This has snapped the sinew of their usefulness.
- This has crippled them as to holy joy.

II. THE REST OF THE FLOCK MUST SEEK THEIR HEALING.

1. By seeking their company, and not leaving them to perish by the way through neglect, contempt, and despair.
2. By endeavoring to comfort them and to restore them. This can be done by the more experienced among us; and those who are unfit for such difficult work can try the next plan, which is so plainly mentioned in our text.
3. By making straight paths for our own feet.
- By unquestionable holiness of life.
- By plain gospel teaching in our own simple way.
- By manifest joy in the Lord.
- By avoiding all crooked customs which might perplex them.
- By thus showing them that Jesus is to us "the way, the truth, and the life." No path can be more straight than that of simple faith in Jesus.

III. THE SHEPHERD OF THE FLOCK CARES FOR SUCH.

1. Their fears: they conclude that he will leave them.
2. The reason: to do so would be by far the easier plan for him.
3. Their dread: if he did so, they must inevitably perish.
4. Their comfort: he has provided all the means of healing the lame.
5. Their hope: he is very gentle and tender, and wills not that any one of them should wander and perish.
6. Their confidence: healing will win him much honor and grateful affection; wherefore we conclude that he will keep them.

Let us be careful to cause no offense or injury to the weakest.

Let us endeavor to restore such as are out of the way, and comfort those who are sorely afflicted.

Sheep-Lore

Sheep are liable to many diseases, many of them are weak and feeble; these a good shepherd taketh pity of, and endeavors to heal and strengthen. So the saints of God are subject to manifold weaknesses, temptations, and afflictions, which moved the Almighty to great compassion, and sorely to rebuke the shepherds of Israel for their cruelty and great remissness towards his flock: "The diseased have ye not strengthened, neither have ye healed that which was sick," etc. And therefore he saith he would himself take the work into his own hands; "I will bind up that which was broken, and will strengthen that which was sick," etc. —*Benjamin Keach*

Many preachers in our days are like Heraclitus, who was called *"the dark doctor."* They affect sublime notions, obscure expressions, uncouth phrases, making plain truths difficult, and easy truths hard. "They darken counsel with words without knowledge" (Job 38:2). Studied expressions and high notions in a sermon, are like Asahel's carcass in the way, that did only stop men and make them gaze, but did no ways profit them or better them. It is better to present Truth in her native plainness than to hang her ears with counterfeit pearls. —*Thomas Brooks*

Now Mr. Feeble-mind, when they were going out at the door, made as if he intended to linger; the which, when Mr. Great-heart espied, he said, "Come, Mr. Feeble-mind, pray do you go along with us; I will be your conductor, and you shall fare as the rest."

Feeble-mind: "Alas! I want a suitable companion: you are all lusty and strong; but I, as you see, am weak: I choose, therefore, rather to come behind, lest, by reason of my many infirmities, I should be both a burden to myself and to you. I am, as I said, a man of a weak and feeble mind, and shall be offended and made weak at that which others can bear. I shall like no laughing: I shall like no gay attire: I shall like no unprofitable questions. Nay, I am so weak a man as to be offended with that which others have a liberty to do. I do not know all the truth: I am a very ignorant Christian man. Sometimes, if I hear any rejoice in the Lord, it troubles me because I cannot do so, too. It is with me as it is with a weak man among the strong, or as with a sick man among the healthy, or as 'a lamp despised,' so that I know not what to do. 'He that is ready to slip with his feet is as a lamp despised in the thought of him that is at ease' (Job 12:5)."

"But, brother," said Mr. Great-heart, "I have it in commission to 'comfort the feeble-minded,' and 'to support the weak.' You must needs go along with us: we will wait for you; we will lend you our help; we will deny ourselves of some things, both opinionate and practical, for your sake; we will not enter into 'doubtful disputations' before you; we will be 'made all things' to you, rather than you shall be left behind." —*John Bunyan*

It should be between a strong saint and a weak as it is between two lute strings that are tuned one to another; no sooner one is struck but the other trembles; no sooner should a weak saint be struck, but the strong should tremble." Remember them that are in bonds, as bound with them" (Heb. 13:3). —*Thomas Brooks*

245

See that ye refuse not him that speaketh. For if they escaped not who refused him that spake on earth, much more shall we not escape, if we turn away from him that speaketh from heaven.

—Hebrews 12:25

 ᴇsus still speaks to us in the gospel. What a privilege to hear such a voice, with such a message! What cruel sin to refuse Jesus a hearing! Here is a most urgent exhortation to yield him reverent attention.

I. THERE IS NEED OF THIS EXHORTATION FROM MANY CONSIDERATIONS.

1. The excellence of the word. It claims obedient attention.
2. The readiness of Satan to prevent our receiving the divine word.
3. Our own indisposition to receive the holy, heavenly message.
4. We have rejected too long already. It is to be feared that we may continue to do so, but our right course is to hearken at once.
5. The word comes in love to our souls; let us therefore heed it, and render love for love.

II. THERE ARE MANY WAYS OF REFUSING HIM THAT SPEAKETH.

1. Not hearing. Absence from public worship, neglect of Bible reading. "Turn away from him."
2. Hearing listlessly, as if half asleep, and unconcerned.
3. Refusing to believe. Intellectually believing, but not with the heart.
4. Raising quibbles. Hunting up difficulties, favoring unbelief.
5. Being offended. Angry with the gospel, indignant at plain speech, opposing honest personal rebuke.
6. Perverting his words. Twisting and wresting Scripture.
7. Bidding him depart. Steeling the conscience, trifling with conviction, resorting to frivolous company for relief.
8. Reviling him. Denying his Deity, hating his gospel, and his holy way.
9. Persecuting him. Turning upon his people as a whole, or assailing them as individuals.

III. THERE ARE MANY CAUSES OF THIS REFUSING.

1. Stolid indifference, which causes a contempt of all good things.
2. Self-righteousness, which makes self an idol, and therefore rejects the living Savior.
3. Self-reliant wisdom, which is too proud to hear the voice of God.

4. Hatred of holiness, which prefers the willful to the obedient, the lustful to the pure, the selfish to the divine.

5. Fear of the world, which listens to threats, or bribes, or flatteries, and dares not act aright.

6. Procrastination, which cries "tomorrow," but means "never."

7. Despair and unbelief, which declare the gospel to be powerless to save, and unavailable as a consolation.

IV. REFUSING TO HEAR CHRIST, THE HIGHEST AUTHORITY IS DESPISED.

"Him that speaketh from heaven."

1. He is of heavenly nature, and reveals to us what he has known of God and heaven.

2. He came from heaven, armed with heavenly authority.

3. He speaks from heaven at this moment by his eternal Spirit in Holy Scripture, the ordinances and the preaching of the gospel.

4. He will speak from heaven at the judgment.

He is himself God, and therefore all that he saith hath divinity within it.

V. THE DOOM TO BE FEARED IF WE REFUSE CHRIST.

Those to whom Moses spake on earth, who refused him, escaped not.

1. Let us think of their doom, and learn that equally sure destruction will happen to all who refuse Christ.
   - Pharaoh and the Egyptians.
   - The murmurers dying in the wilderness.
   - Korah, Dathan, and Abiram.

2. Let us see how some have perished in the church.
   - Judas, Ananias and Sapphira, etc.

3. Let us see how others perish who remain in the world, and refuse to quit it for the fold of Christ.
   - They shall not escape by Annihilation, nor by Purgatory, nor by Universal Restitutions.
   - They shall not escape by infidelity, hardness of heart, cunning. or hypocrisy. They have refused the only way of escape, and therefore they must perish for ever.

Instead of refusing, listen, learn, obey.

Instead of the curse, you shall gain a blessing.

Warning Words

Our blessed Lord is represented as "now speaking from heaven" to Christians generally; and even if we were, contrary to all just reason, to confine the reference to the persons to whom the Epistle was immediately written, he is said to speak to multitudes who never saw or heard him in the days of his flesh. This could be only by the agency of inspired men, whose commission to teach and command "in the name of Christ" was proved by miracles. Those miracles they attributed to him, as is plain from many passages in the Acts and the Epistles. Thus Christ stands in the very position of power, authority, and action, continually ascribed to Jehovah in the Old Testament, *speaking by his prophets.* "This," observes Michaelis, "is saying of Christ the greatest thing that can be said." —*Dr. J. Pye Smith*

We seem to have done with the Word as it has passed through our ears; but the Word, be it remembered, will never have done with us, till it has judged us at the last day. —*Judge Hale*

A nobleman, skilled in music, who had often observed the Hon. Rev. Mr. Cadogan's inattention to his performance, said to him one day, "Come, I am determined to make you feel the force of music; pay particular attention to this piece." It was accordingly played. "Well, what do you say now?" "Why, just what I said before." "What! can you hear this and not be charmed? Well, I am quite surprised at your insensibility. Where are your ears?" "Bear with me, my lord," replied Mr. Cadogan, "since I, too, have had my surprise. I have often, from the pulpit, set before you the most striking and affecting truths; I have sounded notes that might have raised the dead; I have said, 'Surely he will feel now,' but you never seemed to be charmed with my music, though infinitely more interesting than yours. I, too, have been ready to say, with astonishment, 'Where are his ears?'"

One of the modern thinkers had been upholding the doctrine of universal salvation at a certain house with much zeal. A child who had listened to his pestilent talk was heard to say to his companion, "We can now steal, and lie, and do wicked things, for there is no hell when we die." If such preachers gain much power in this country we shall not need to raise the question of a hell hereafter, for we shall have one here. —*C. H. S.*

246

He hath said, I will never leave thee, nor forsake thee.
—*Hebrews 13:5*

 ERE is a divine word, directly from God's own mouth: "For himself hath said." (See Revised Version.)

Here is a promise which has been frequently made: "He hath said." This promise occurs again and again.

Here are some of the fat things full of marrow. The sentence is as full of meaning as it is free from verbiage.

Here is the essence of meat, the quintessence of medicine.

May the Holy Spirit show us the treasure hid in this matchless sentence!

I. VIEW THE WORDS AS A QUOTATION.

The Holy Spirit led Paul to quote from the Scriptures, though he could have spoken fresh words.

Thus, he put honor on the Old Testament.

Thus, he taught that words spoken to ancient saints belong to us.

Our apostle quotes the sense, not the exact words, and thus he teaches us that the spirit of a text is the main thing.

We find the words which Paul has quoted.

- In Genesis 28:15, "I will not leave thee, until I have done that which I have spoken to thee of." Spoken to Jacob when quitting home, and thus to young saints setting out in life.
- In Deuteronomy 31:8, "He will be with thee, he will not fail thee, neither forsake thee." To Joshua, and so to those who have lost a leader, and are about to take the lead themselves, and to enter upon great wars and fightings, in which courage will be tried.
- In 1 Chronicles 28:20, "He will not fail thee, nor forsake thee, until thou hast finished all the work." To Solomon, and thus to those who have a weighty charge upon them, requiring much wisdom. We build a spiritual temple.
- In Isaiah 41:10, "Fear thou not; for I am with thee." To Israel, and so to the Lord's tried and afflicted people.

II. VIEW THEM AS A HOUSEHOLD WORD FROM GOD.

1. They are peculiarly a saying of God: "He hath said." This has been said, not so much by inspiration as by God himself.
2. They are remarkably forcible from having five negatives in them in the Greek.
3. They relate to God himself and his people. "I"... "thee."
4. They ensure his presence and his help. He would not be with us, and be inactive.
5. They guarantee the greatest good. God with us means all good.
6. They avert a dreadful evil which we deserve and might justly fear; namely, to be deserted of God.
7. They are such as he only could utter and make true. Nobody else can be with us effectually in agony, in death, in judgment.
8. They provide for all troubles, losses, desertions, weaknesses, difficulties, places, seasons, dangers, etc., in time and eternity.

9. They are substantiated by the divine love, immutability, and faithfulness.
10. They are further confirmed by our observation of the divine proceeding to others and to ourselves.

III. VIEW THEM AS A MOTIVE FOR CONTENTMENT. "Let your conversation be without covetousness, and be content with such things as ye have."

These most gracious words:
- Lead us to live above visible things when we have stores in hand.
- Lead us to present satisfaction however low our stores may be.
- Lead us to see provision for all future emergencies.
- Lead us into a security more satisfactory, sure, ennobling, and divine, than all the wealth of the Indies could bestow.
- Lead us to reckon discontent a kind of blasphemy of God.

Since God is always with us, what can we want besides?

IV. VIEW THEM AS A REASON FOR COURAGE. "So that we may boldly say, The Lord is my helper, and I will not fear what man shall do unto me."

1. Our Helper is greater than our foes. "Jehovah is my helper."
2. Our foes are entirely in his hand. "I will not fear what man shall do."
3. If permitted to afflict us, God will sustain us under their malice.

What a blessed deliverance from fretting and from fearing have we in these few words!

Let us not be slow to follow the line of things which the Spirit evidently points out to us.

Notes on "Nots"

Lord, the apostle dissuadeth the Hebrews from covetousness with this argument, because God said, "I will not leave thee, nor forsake thee." Yet I find not that God ever gave this promise to all the Jews; but he spake it only to Joshua, when first made commander against the Canaanites, yet this (without violence to the analogy of faith) the apostle applieth to all good men in general. Is it so, that we are heirs apparent to all promises made to thy servants in Scripture? Are the charters of grace granted to them good to me also? Then will I say with Jacob, "I have enough." But because I cannot entitle myself to thy promises to them except I imitate their piety to thee, grant I may take as much care in following the one as comfort in the other. —*Thomas Fuller*

Our friend, Dr. William Graham of Bonn, has lately departed this life, and we are told that on his death bed one said to him, "He hath said, 'I will never leave thee, nor forsake thee,'" to which the good man replied, with his dying breath, "Not a doubt of it! Not a doubt of it!" —*C. H. S., in the Sword and the Trowel, 1884*

It is right to be contented with what we have, never with what we are. —*Mackintosh*

I have read, says *Brooks*, of a company of poor Christians who were banished into some remote part; one standing by, seeing them pass along, said that it was a very sad condition these poor people were in, to be thus hurried from the society of men, and made companions with the beasts of the field. "True," said another, "it were a sad condition indeed if they were carried to a place where they should not find their God. But let them be of good cheer, God goes along with them, and will exhibit the comforts of his presence whithersoever they go."

A heathen sage said to one of his friends, "Do not complain of thy misfortunes, as long as Caesar is thy friend!" What shall we say to those whom the Prince of the kings of the earth calls his sons and his brethren? "I will never leave thee, nor forsake thee" Ought not these words to cast all fear and care for ever to the ground? He who possesses him, to whom all things belong, possesseth all things. —*F. W. Krummacher*

> The soul that on Jesus has leaned for repose
> I will not, I will not desert to his foes;
> That soul though all hell should endeavor to shake,
> I'll never, no never, no never forsake.
>
> —*George Keith*

247

Blessed is the man that endureth temptation: for when he is tried, he shall receive the crown of life, which the Lord hath promised to them that love him.

—*James 1:12*

o be *blessed* is to be happy, favored, prosperous, etc.

But it has a secret, sacred emphasis all its own; for the favor and prosperity are such as only God himself can bestow.

Who would not desire to be blessed of God?

Most men mistake the whereabouts of blessedness.

It is not bound up with wealth, rank, power, talent, admiration, friendship, health, pleasure, or even with a combination of all these.

It is often found where least expected: amid trials, temptations, etc.

I. THE BLESSED IN THIS LIFE.

1. Blessedness is not in our text connected with ease, freedom from trial, or absence of temptation.

    Untested treasures may be worthless; not so those which have endured the fire. No man may reckon himself blessed if he has to fear that a trial would wither all his excellence.

2. Blessedness belongs to those who endure tests.
    - These have faith, or it would not be tried; faith is blessed.
    - These have life which bears trials, the spiritual life is blessed.
    - These possess uprightness, purity, truth, patience; all these are blessed things.

3. Blessedness belongs to those who endure trials out of love to God. The text speaks of "them that love him."
    - He that has love to God finds joy in that love.
    - He also finds blessedness in suffering for that love.

4. Blessedness belongs to those who are proved true by trial.
    - After the test comes approval. "When he hath been approved" is the rendering of the Revised Version.
    - After the test comes assurance of our being right. Certainty is a most precious commodity.

5. Blessedness comes out of patient experience.
    - Blessedness of thankfulness for being sustained.
    - Blessedness of holy dependence under conscious weakness.
    - Blessedness of peace and submission under God's hand.
    - Blessedness of fearlessness as to result of further trial.
    - Blessedness of familiarity with God enjoyed in the affliction.
    - Blessedness of growth in grace through the trial.

He who, being tested, is supported in the ordeal, and comes out of the trial approved, is the blessed man.

II. THE BLESSED IN THE LIFE TO COME.

Those who have endured trial inherit the peculiar blessedness:

1. Of being crowned. How crowned if never in the wars?
    - Crowned because victorious over enemies.
    - Crowned because appreciated by their God.
    - Crowned because honored of their fellows.
    - Crowned because they have kept the conditions of the award.

2. Of attaining the glory and "crown of life" by enduring trial, thus only can life be developed till its flower and crown appear.
    - By trial brought to purest health of mind.
    - By trial trained to utmost vigor of grace.

- By trial developed in every part of their nature.
- By trial made capable of the highest glory in eternity.

3. Of possessing a living crown of endless joy. "Crown of life" or living crown: amaranthine, unfading.
   - If such fierce trials do not kill them, nothing will.
   - If they have spiritual bliss, it can never die.
   - If they have heavenly life, it will always be at its crowning point.

4. Of receiving this life-crown from God.
   - His own promise reveals and displays it.
   - His peculiar regard to those who love him doubly ensures it.
   - His own hand shall give it.

Let us encounter trial cheerfully.

Let us wait for the time of approval patiently.

Let us expect the crown of life most joyfully and gather courage from the assurance of it.

Extracts

"Blessed"; that is, already blessed. They are not miserable as the world judgeth them. It is a Christian paradox, wherein there is an allusion to what is said (Job 5:17). "Behold, happy is the man whom God correcteth;" it is a wonder, and therefore he calleth the world to see it. *Behold!* So the apostle, in an opposition to the judgment of the world, saith, *Blessed.*

Afflictions do not make the people of God miserable. There's a great deal of difference between a Christian and a man of the world: his best estate is vanity (Ps. 39:5), and a Christian's worst is happiness. He that loveth God is like a die; cast him high or low, he is still upon a square: he may be sometimes afflicted, but he is always happy. —*Thomas Manton*

Times of affliction often prove times of great temptations, and therefore afflictions are called temptations. —*Thomas Brooks*

The most durable and precious metal in the ancient arts was the Corinthian bronze, which was said to have first been caused by the fusing of all the precious metals when Corinth was burned. The most precious products of experience are got in the fire of trial. —*John Legge*

An old sailor was asked for what purpose shoals and rocks were created, and the reply was, "That sailors may avoid them." A Christian philosopher, using that axiom, upon being asked for what purpose trials and temptations are sent, answered, "That we may overcome and use them." The true dignity of life is not found in escaping difficulties, but in mastering them for Christ's sake and in Christ's strength. —*Dean Stanley*

Many were the sorts of crowns which were in use amongst the Roman victors: (1) *Corona civica,* a crown made of oaken boughs, which was given by the

Romans to him that saved the life of any citizen in battle against his enemies. (2) *Obsidionalis*, which was of grass, given to him that delivered a town or city from siege. (3) *Muralis*, which was of gold, given to him that first scaled the wall of any town or castle. (4) *Castralis*, which was likewise of gold, given to him that first entered the camp of the enemy. (5) *Navalis*, and that also of gold, given to him that first boarded the ship of an enemy. (6) *Ovalis* (and that of myrtle), which was given to those captains that subdued any town or city, or that won any field easily, without blood. (7) *Triumphalis*, which was of laurel, given to the chief general or consul who, after some signal victory, came home triumphing. These, with many others, as imperial, regal, and princely crowns (rather garlands or coronets than crowns), are not to be compared to the crown of glory which God hath prepared for those that love him. Who is able to express the glory of it; or to what glorious thing shall it be likened? If I had the tongue of men and angels, I should be unable to decipher it as it worthily deserveth. It is not only a crown of glory, but hath divers other titles of pre-eminency given unto it, of which all shall be true partakers that are godly; a crown of righteousness, by the imputation of Christ's righteousness; a crown of life, because those that have it shall be made capable of life eternal; a crown of stars, because they that receive it shall shine as stars for ever and ever. —*John Spencer*

> The same who crowns the conqueror, will be
> A coadjutor in the agony.
> —*Robert Herrick*

248

But he giveth more grace.
—*James 4:6*

 RACTICAL as is the Epistle of James, the apostle does not neglect to extol the grace of God, as unevangelical preachers do in these times. We err if we commend the fruits regardless of the root from which they spring. Every virtue should be traced to grace.

We must clearly point out the fountain of inward grace as well as the stream of manifest service which flows from it.

The principle of grace produces the practice of goodness, and none can create or preserve that principle but the God of all grace.

If we fail anywhere, it will be our wisdom to get more grace.

See the bounty of God: ever giving, and ever ready to give more!

I. OBSERVE THE TEXT IN ITS CONNECTION.

1. It presents a contrast. "But he giveth more grace."

   Two potent motives are confronted. "The spirit that dwelleth in us lusteth to envy"; on God's part this is met by "but he giveth more grace."

2. It suggests a note of admiration.
   - What a wonder that when sin aboundeth, grace still more abounds!
   - When we discover more of our weakness, God gives more grace.

3. It hints at a direction for spiritual conflict.
   - We learn where to obtain the weapons of our warfare; we must look to him who gives grace.
   - We learn the nature of those weapons: they are not legal, nor fanciful, nor ascetical, but gracious: "he giveth more grace."
   - We learn that lusting after evil must be met by the fulfillment of spiritual desires and obtaining more grace.

4. It encourages us in continuing the conflict.
   - As long as there is one passion in the believing soul that dares to rise, God will give grace to struggle with it.
   - The more painfully we mourn the power of sin, the more certainly will grace increase if we believe in Jesus for salvation.

5. It plainly indicates a victory.

   "He giveth more grace" is a plain promise that:
   - God will not give us up, but that he will more and more augment the force of grace, so that sin must and shall ultimately yield to its sanctifying dominion.

Glory be to God, who, having given grace, still goes on to give more and more grace till we enter into glory! There is no stint or limit to the Lord's increasing gifts of grace.

II. OBSERVE THE GENERAL TRUTH OF THE TEXT.

God is ever on the giving hand. The text speaks of it as the Lord's way and habit: "He giveth more grace."

1. He giveth new supplies of grace.
2. He giveth larger supplies of grace.
3. He giveth higher orders of grace.
4. He giveth more largely as the old nature works more powerfully.

This should be:

1. A truth of daily use for ourselves.
2. A promise daily pleaded for others.
3. A stimulus in the contemplation of higher or sterner duties, and an encouragement to enter on wider fields.
4. A solace under forebodings of deeper trouble in common life.
5. An assurance in prospect of the severe tests of sickness and death.

Seeing it is the nature of God to give more and more grace, let us have growing confidence in him.

III. BRING IT HOME BY SPECIAL APPROPRIATION.

1. My spiritual poverty, then, is my own fault, for the Lord giveth more grace to all who believe for it.
2. My spiritual growth will be to his glory, for I can only grow because he gives more grace. Oh, to grow constantly!
3. What a good God I have to go to! Let me rejoice in the present and hope for the future. Since the further I go the more grace shall I know, let me proceed with dauntless courage.

Brethren, let us trust the liberality of God, try it by prayer, prove it by faith, bear witness to it with zeal, and praise it with grateful joy.

Encouragements

When Lord North, during the American war, sent to the Rev. Mr. Fletcher, of Madeley (who had written on that unfortunate war, in a manner that had pleased the minister), to know what he wanted, he sent
him word, that he wanted but one thing, which it was not in his lordship's power to give him, and that was *more grace.* —*John Whitecross*

When a man gives a flower, it is a perfect gift; but the gift of grace is rather the gift of a flower *seed.*

When Matthew Henry was a child he received much impression from a sermon on the parable of the "mustard-seed." On returning home, he said to his child sister, "I think I have received a grain of grace." It was the seed of the Commentary "cast upon the waters." —*Charles Stanford*

I have grace every day! every hour! When the rebel is brought, nine times a day, twenty times a day, for the space of forty years, by his prince's grace, from under the ax, how fair and sweet are the multiplied pardons and reprievals of grace to him! In my case here are multitudes of multiplied redemptions! Here is plenteous redemption! I defile every hour, Christ washeth; I fall, grace raiseth me; I come this day, this morning, under the rebuke of justice, but grace pardoneth me; and so it is all along, till grace puts me into heaven. —*Samuel Rutherford*

Were you to rest satisfied with any present attainments to which you have reached, it would be an abuse of encouragement. It would be an evidence that you know nothing of the power of divine grace in reality, for:

> Whoever says, I want *no more,*
> Confesses he has *none.*

Those who have seen their Lord, will always pray, "I beseech thee, show me thy glory." Those that have once tasted that the Lord is gracious, will always cry, "Evermore give us this bread to eat." —*William Jay*

A little grace will bring us to heaven hereafter, but great grace will bring heaven to us now. —*An old Divine*

Oh, what a sad thing it is when Christians are what they always were! You should have more grace; your word should be, ego non sum ego—I am not the same I, or, *nunc oblita mihi*—now my old courses are forgotten; or, as the apostle, 1 Peter 4:3, "The time past may suffice to have walked in the lusts of the flesh." —*Thomas Manton*

> Have you on the Lord believed?
> Still there's more to follow;
> Of his grace have you received?
> Still there's more to follow;
> Oh, the grace the Father shows!
> Still there's more to follow I
> Freely he his grace bestows;
> Still there's more to follow!

249

Receiving the end of your faith, even the salvation of your souls.
—*1 Peter 1:9*

 HE greater benefits of salvation are usually classed among things to come, but indeed a large portion of them may be received here and now.

I. WHAT OF SALVATION IS RECEIVED HERE?

1. The whole of it by the grip of faith, and the grace of hope.
2. The absolute and final pardon of sin is ours at this moment.
3. Deliverance from slavish bondage, and from a sense of awful distance from God is a present relief.

   Peace, reconciliation, contentment fellowship with God, and delight in God, we enjoy at this hour.
4. Rescue from the condemning power of sin is now complete.
5. Release from its dominion is ours. It can no longer command us at its will, nor lull us to sleep by its soothing strains.
6. Conquest over evil is given to us in great measure at once.
   - Sins are conquerable. No one should imagine that he must necessarily sin because of his constitution or surroundings.

- Holy living is possible. Some have reached a high degree of it. Why not others?

7. Joy may become permanent in the midst of sorrow.

The immediate heritage of believers is exceedingly great.

Salvation is ours at this day, and with it "all things."

II. HOW IS IT RECEIVED?

1. Entirely from Jesus, as a gift of divine grace.
2. By faith, not by sight or feeling. We believe to see, and this is good. To require to see in order to believe is vicious.
3. By fervent love to God. This excites to revenge against sin and so gives present purification. This also nerves us for consecrated living and, thus, produces holiness.
4. By joy in the Lord. This causes us to receive peace unspeakable, not to be exaggerated, nor even uttered. Too great, too deep to be understood, even by those who enjoy it.

Much of heaven may be enjoyed before we reach it.

III. HAVE YOU RECEIVED IT, AND HOW MUCH?

1. You have heard of salvation, but hearing will not do.
2. You profess to know it? But mere profession will not do.
3. Have you received pardon? Are you sure of it?
4. Have you been made holy? Are you daily cleansed in your walk?
5. Have you obtained rest by faith and hope and love?

Make these inquiries as in God's sight.

If the result is unsatisfactory, begin at once to seek the Lord.

Look for the appearing of the Lord as the time for receiving in a fuller sense "the end of your faith."

Breviates

An evangelist said in my hearing: "He that believeth *hath* everlasting life. H-A-T-H—that spells 'got it.'" It is an odd way of spelling, but it is sound divinity. —*C. H. S.*

This is the certainty of their hope, that it is as if they had already received it. If the promise of God and the merit of Christ hold good, then they who believe in him, and love him, are made sure of salvation. The promises of God in Christ "are not yea and nay; but they are in him yea, and in him amen." Sooner may the rivers run backward, and the course of the heavens change, and the frame of nature be dissolved, than any one soul that is united to Jesus Christ by faith and love can be severed from him, and so fall short of the salvation hoped for in him, and this is the matter of their rejoicing. —*Archbishop Leighton*

To fall into sin is a serious thing, even though the guilt of it be forgiven. A boy who had often been disobedient was made by his father to drive a nail into a post for each offense. When he was well-behaved for a day he was allowed to draw out one of the nails. He fought against his temper bravely, and at last all the nails were gone from the post, and his father praised him. "Alas, father," said the lad, "the nails are all gone, but the holes are left!" Even after forgiveness it will require a miracle of grace to recover us from the ill effects of sin.

In St. Peter's, at Rome, I saw monuments to James III., Charles III., and Henry IX., kings of England. These potentates were quite unknown to me. They had evidently a name to reign, but reign they did not: they never received the end of their faith. Are not many professed Christians in the same condition? —*C. H. S.*

250

If the righteous scarcely be saved, where shall the ungodly and the sinner appear?

—*1 Peter 4:18*

"SCARCELY saved" points out the difficulty of salvation.

Some think it easy to begin by believing, but the prophet cries, "Who hath believed?" and Jesus asks, "When the Son of man cometh, shall he find faith on the earth?"

Some may also think it easy to persevere to the end, but the godly are hard put to it to keep their faces Zionward.

It is no light thing to be saved; omnipotent grace is needed.

It is no trifling thing to be lost, but it can be done by neglect.

I. THE FACT. *"The righteous scarcely are saved."*

1. From the connection we conclude that the righteous are saved with difficulty because of the strictness of divine rule. "The time is come that judgment must begin at the house of God."
   - There is equity and fitness in this specialty of examination.
   - These tests are many, varied, repeated, applied by God himself.
   - Good corn endures the sickle, the flail, the fan, the sieve, the mill, the oven.
   - The great test of all is the omniscient judgment of the jealous God. What grace will be needed to pass that ordeal!
2. From the experience of saints we come to the same conclusion. They find many saving acts to be hard, as for instance:
   - To lay hold on Christ simply and as sinners.

- To overcome the flesh from day to day.
- To resist the world with its blandishments, threats, and customs.
- To vanquish Satan and his horrible temptations.
- To perform needful duties in a humble and holy spirit.
- To reach to gracious attainments and to continue in them.
- To pass the tribunal of their own awakened and purified conscience, and to receive a verdict of acquittal there.

3. From the testimony of those who are safely landed.

"These are they which came out of great tribulation."

II. THE INFERENCE FROM THE FACT. *"Where shall the ungodly and the sinner appear?"*

1. If even the true coin is so severely tested, what will become of "reprobate silver"?
2. If saints scarcely reach heaven, what of the ungodly?
   - What can they do who have no God?
   - What can they do who have no Savior?
   - What can they do who are without the Spirit of God?
   - What without prayer, the Word, the promise of God, etc.?
   - What without diligence? When the tradesman, though careful, is losing all his capital, what of the spendthrift?
   - What without truth? When the fire consumes houses strongly built, what must become of wood, hay, stubble?
3. If saints are so sorely chastened, what will justice mete out to the openly defiant sinner?

III. ANOTHER INFERENCE. *Where will the mere professor appear?*

If the truly godly have a hard fight for it:

- The formalist will find ceremonies a poor solace.
- The false professor will be ruined by his hypocrisy.
- The presumptuous will find his daring pride a poor help.
- He who trusted to mere orthodoxy of creed will come to a fall.
- Height of office will do no more than increase responsibility.

IV. ANOTHER INFERENCE. *Then the tempted soul may be saved.*

It seems that even those who are truly saints are saved with difficulty; then we may be saved, though we have a hard struggle for it.

- Uprising corruption makes us stagger.
- A persecuting world tries us sorely.
- Fierce temptations from without cause us perplexity.
- Loss of inward joys brings us to a stand.
- Failure in holy efforts tests our faith.

But in all this we have fellowship with the righteous of all ages. They are saved, and so shall we be.

V. ANOTHER INFERENCE. *How sweet will heaven be!*
There the difficulties will be ended for ever.
There the former trials will contribute to the eternal bliss.

Enforcements

When the apostle uses the phrase, *"If the righteous scarcely be saved,"* he does not, assuredly, mean that there is any doubt about the absolute and infinite sufficiency of the ground of their salvation, or that there is any uncertainty in the result, or that there is any stintedness or imperfection in the final enjoyment, or that, when believers come to stand before the judgment seat at last, it will go hard with them, so that they may barely come off with acquittal, the poised balance vibrating in long uncertainty, and barely turning on the favorable side, the justifying righteousness of their Lord forming no more than a counterpoise, and hardly that, to their demerits. He means none of these things. *His language refers to the difficulty of bringing them through* to their final salvation; to the necessity of employing the rod and furnace; the process, in many instances severe, of correction and purification; of bringing them "to the wealthy place through the fire and the water;" of their "entering the kingdom through much tribulation"; of their being "chastened of the Lord, that they might not be condemned with the world." If "fiery trial" be required, and his hatred of sin and his love to his children will not allow him to withhold it, to purge out the remaining alloy of their holiness, what must his enemies have to look for from his abhorrence of evil, in whom sin is not the mere alloy of a better material, *but all is sin together? —Dr. Wardlaw*

There is much ado to get Lot out of Sodom, to get Israel out of Egypt. It is no easy matter to get a man out of the state of corruption. —*Richard Sibbes*

Of this I am assured, that no less devotion than that which carried the martyrs through the flames, will carry us unpolluted through this present world. —*Mrs. Palmer*

Do you grieve and murmur that you must be saved with difficulty? Ungrateful creatures! you had deserved certain damnation. The vengeance of God might have appeared armed for your destruction; and he might long ago have sworn in his wrath that you should never enter into his rest. And will you complain of the Lord's leadings because he does not always strew your path with roses? —*Dr. Doddridge*

"Where shall the ungodly and the sinner appear?" Surely nowhere. Not before saints and angels, for holiness is their trade. Not before God, for he is of "more pure eyes than to behold them." Not before Christ, for he shall come in flaming fire rendering vengeance. Not in heaven, for it is an undefiled inheritance. —*John Trapp*

Where shall he appear, when to the end that he might not appear, he would be glad to be smothered under the weight of the hills and mountains, if they could shelter him from appearing? —*Archbishop Leighton*

251

The elders which are among you I exhort, who am also an elder, and a witness of the sufferings of Christ, and also a partaker of the glory that shall be revealed.

—*1 Peter 5:1*

HE apostle's care. He was anxious that the elders should tend the flock of God, and make themselves examples to it.

The apostle's gentleness. "I exhort," not command, etc.

The apostle's humility: "also an elder." He does not insist upon his apostleship, though this was much the greater office.

The apostle's wisdom: "also an elder." In this capacity he would have most weight with them in his exhortation.

Besides this, he mentioned two other characters, and calls himself "a witness of the sufferings of Christ, and a partaker of the glory that shall be revealed."

I. A WITNESS OF THE SUFFERINGS OF CHRIST.

So far as possible, let us be witnesses with Peter.

1. An eye-witness of those sufferings. Apostles must have seen Jesus.

He had seen the passion and death of our Lord.

In this we cannot participate, nor need we desire to do so.

2. A faith-witness of those sufferings.
   - He had personally believed on Jesus at the first.
   - He had further believed through after-communion with him.
3. A testifying witness of those sufferings.
   - He bore witness to their bitterness when borne by Jesus.
   - He bore witness to their importance as an atonement.
   - He bore witness to their completeness as a satisfaction.
   - He bore witness to their effect in perfect salvation.
4. A partaking witness of those sufferings.
   - In defense of truth he suffered from opposers.
   - In winning others he suffered in the anguish of his heart.
   - In serving his Lord he suffered exile, persecution, death.

What he witnessed in all these ways became a motive and a stimulus for his whole life.

II. A PARTAKER OF THE GLORY TO BE REVEALED.

It is important to partake in all that we preach, or else we preach without vividness and assurance.

1. Peter had enjoyed a literal foretaste of the glory on the holy mount. We, too, have our earnests of eternal joy.
2. Peter had not yet *seen* the glory which shall be revealed, and yet he had partaken of it in a spiritual sense; our participation must also be spiritual. Peter had been a spiritual partaker in the following ways:
   • By faith in the certainty of the glory.
   • By anticipation of the joy of the glory.
   • By sympathy with our Lord, who has entered into glory.
3. Peter had felt the result of faith in that glory:
   • In the comfort which it yielded him.
   • In the heavenliness which it wrought in him.
   • In the courage with which it endowed him.

These two things, his witnessing and his partaking, made our apostle intense in his zeal for the glory of God. Because he had seen and tasted of the good word, he preached it with living power and vivid speech. All preachers need to be witnesses and partakers.

These made him urgent with others to "feed the flock of God." Such a man could not endure triflers.

These are the essentials for all eminently useful and acceptable service. The Lord will only bless witnesses and partakers.

Hints

I remember a story which runs thus: To a saint who was praying the evil spirit showed himself radiant with royal robes, and crowned with a jewelled diadem, and said, "I am Christ; I am descending on the earth; and I desire first to manifest myself to thee." The saint kept silence, and looked on the apparition; and then said, "I will not believe that Christ is come to me save in that state and form in which he suffered: he must wear the marks of the wounds and the cross." The false apparition vanished. The application is this: Christ comes not in pride of intellect or reputation for ability. These are the glittering robes in which Satan is now arraying himself. Many false spirits are abroad, more are issuing from the pit: the credentials which they display are the precious gifts of mind, beauty, richness, depth, originality. Christian, with the saint, look hard at them in silence, and ask them for the print of the nails. —*Dr. J. S. Howson*

'Tis a very sad thing when preachers are like printers, who compose and print off many things, which they neither understand, nor love, nor experience; all they aim at is money for printing, which is their trade. It is also sad when ministers are like gentlemen ushers, who bring ladies to their pews, but go not in themselves; bring others to heaven, and themselves stay without. —*Ralph Venning*

252

The Lord knoweth how to deliver the godly out of temptations, and to reserve the unjust unto the day of judgment to be punished.

—*2 Peter 2:9*

 " HE Lord knoweth." Our faith in the superior knowledge of God is a great source of comfort to us:
- In reference to perplexing doctrines.
- In reference to puzzling prophecies.
- In reference to amazing promises.
- In reference to distressing providences.
- In reference to grievous temptations.
- In our entrance upon an unknown world in the last solemn article in death.

The government of this world and the next is in the hands of the all-knowing One, who cannot be mistaken, nor taken at unawares.

I. THE LORD'S KNOWLEDGE IN REFERENCE TO CHARACTER.

1. He knows the godly:
- Under trial, when they are not known to others.
- Under temptation, when scarcely known to themselves.
2. He knows the unjust:
- Though they may make loud professions of piety.
- Though they may be honored for their great possessions.

No error either as to partiality or severity is made by God.

II. THE LORD'S KNOWLEDGE IN REFERENCE TO THE GODLY.

A people knowing, fearing, trusting, loving God.

He knows how to let them suffer, and yet to deliver them in the most complete and glorious manner.

1. His knowledge answers better than theirs would do.
2. His knowledge of their case is perfect. Before, in, and after temptation he knows their sorrows.
3. He knows in every case how to deliver them.
4. In every case there must therefore be a way of escape.
5. He knows the most profitable way of deliverance for themselves.
6. He knows the way which will be most glorifying to himself.
7. His knowledge should cause them to trust in him with holy confidence, and never to sin in order to escape.

III. THE LORD'S KNOWLEDGE IN REFERENCE TO THE UNJUST.

They are unjust in all senses, for they are:

- Not legally just, by keeping the law;
- Nor evangelically just, through faith in Jesus;
- Nor practically just, in their daily lives.

The Lord knows best:

1. How to deal with them from day to day.
2. How to reserve them under restraints. He makes it possible to reprieve them, and yet to maintain law and order.
3. How to punish them with unrest and fears even now.
4. How and when to strike them down when their iniquities are full.
5. How to deal with them in judgment, and throughout the future state. The mysteries of eternal doom are safe in his hand.

Two fine illustrations of the Lord's dealings with the righteous and the wicked may be found in Acts 12, in connection with Peter's life.

Peter in prison was unexpectedly set free.

Herod on the throne was eaten of worms.

Brevia

On the headstone of a little grave containing a little child who was washed ashore during the gales, without any clue to birth, name, or parentage, was placed the epitaph: "God knows." —*Leisure Hour*

"The Lord knoweth how." It is set down indefinitely. No man, no apostle, no angel, can know all the means of God's delivering his; it is enough that he himself knows. This gives a check to all saucy inquirers that will not believe help from the Lord, unless he tells them how. . . . Deliverance we look for; how or when the Lord will deliver thee or me, that is in his own bosom, and in the breast of his Privy Counselor, Jesus Christ. —*Thomas Adams*

In the *Life and Letters of G. Ticknor*, a remark is made to the effect that when in Brussels, and conversing with some of the *elite* of society there, he could not avoid constantly remembering that two of the high-minded intellectual persons with whom he was sitting were under sentence of death, if found within the grasp of Austria. We cannot forget that many around us are now "under condemnation" and are "reserved until the day of judgment."

253

It doth not yet appear what we shall be: but we know that when he shall appear, we shall be like him, for we shall see him as he is.

—*1 John 3:2*

HE present condition of the believer, notwithstanding its imperfection, is a state of much joy and honor. Looked at in the light of faith it is sublime, for "now are we the sons of God."

We are near to God's heart as his children.

We nestle under the wings of God for protection.

We abide in his pavilion for communion.

We are fed in his pasture for provision.

For all this, our earthly existence is not a life which we would desire to be perpetual. It is as a traveler's pilgrimage, a sailor's voyage, a soldier's warfare; and we look forward to its end with joyful expectation.

We will let the text divide itself verbally.

I. "IT DOTH NOT YET APPEAR WHAT WE SHALL BE."

At present we are veiled, and we travel through the world *incognito*.

1. Our Master was not made manifest here below.
   - His glory was veiled in flesh.
   - His Deity was concealed in infirmity.
   - His power was hidden under sorrow and weakness.
   - His riches were buried under poverty and shame.

The world knew him not, for he was made flesh.

2. We are not fit to appear in full figure as yet.
   - The son is treated as a servant while under age.
   - The heir is kept a pensioner till his majority.
   - The prince serves as a soldier before he reaches the throne.

We must needs have an evening before our morning, a schooling before our college, a tuning before the music is ready.

3. This is not the world to appear in.
   - There are none to appreciate us, and it would be as though kings showed their royalty at a wake, or wise men discoursed philosophy before fools.
   - A warring and waiting condition like the present would not be a fit opportunity for unveiling.

4. This is not the time in which to appear in our glory.

   The winter prepares flowers, but it does not call them forth.
   - The ebb-tide reveals the secrets of the sea, but many of our rivers no gallant ship can then sail.
   - To everything there is a season, and this is not the time of glory.

II. "BUT WE KNOW THAT WHEN HE SHALL APPEAR."

1. We speak of our Lord's manifestation without doubt. "We know."
2. Our faith is so assured that it becomes knowledge.
   - He will be manifest upon this earth in person.
   - He will be manifest in perfect happiness.

- He will be manifest in highest glory.
- He will appear surely, and so we speak of it as a date for our own manifesting: "when he shall appear."

Oh the hope, the glory, the bliss, the fullness of delight which cluster around this great appearing!

III. "WE SHALL BE LIKE HIM."

We shall then be as manifested, and as clearly seen, as he will be.

The time of our open presentation at court will have come.

1. Having a body like his body.

Sinless, incorruptible, painless, spiritual, clothed with beauty and power, and yet most real and true.

2. Having a soul like his soul.

Perfect, holy, instructed, developed, strengthened, active, delivered from temptation, conflict, and suffering.

3. Having such dignities and glories as he wears.

Kings, priests, conquerors, judges, sons of God.

We must be made in a measure like him now, or else we shall not be found so at his appearing.

IV. "WE SHALL SEE HIM AS HE IS."

1. This glorious sight will perfect our likeness.
2. This will be the result of our being like him.
3. This will be evidence of our being like him, since none but the pure in heart can see God.
   - The sight will be ravishing.
   - The sight will be transforming and transfiguring.
   - The sight will be abiding, and a source of bliss for ever.

Behold what glories come out of our being the sons of God!

Let us not rest till by faith in Jesus we receive power to become sons of God, and then let us go on to enjoy the privileges of sonship.

Lights

God showed *power* in making us creatures, but *love* in making us sons. Plato gave God thanks that he had made him a man, and not a beast; but what cause have they to adore God's love, who hath made them children! The apostle puts an *ecce* to it, *Behold!* —*Thomas Watson*

And here, reader, wonder not if I be at a loss, and if my apprehensions receive but little of that which is in my expressions. If to the beloved disciple that durst speak and inquire into Christ's secrets, and was filled with his revelations, and saw the New Jerusalem in her glory, and had seen Christ, Moses, and Elias in part of theirs, if it did not appear to him what we shall be, but only in general, that when Christ appears, we shall be like him, no wonder if I know little. —*Richard Baxter, in "The Saint's Everlasting Rest"*

Such divine, God-given glimpses into the future reveal to us more than all our thinking. What intense truth, what divine meaning there is in God's creative word: "Let us make man in our image, after our likeness!" To show forth the likeness of the Invisible, to be partaker of the divine nature, to share with God his rule of the universe, is man's destiny. His place is indeed one of unspeakable glory. Standing between two eternities, the eternal purpose in which we were predestined to be conformed to the image of the first-born Son, and the eternal realization of that purpose when we shall be like him in his glory. We hear the voice from every side: O ye image-bearers of God! on the way to share the glory of God and of Christ, live a Godlike, live a Christlike life! —*Andrew Murray*

A converted blind man once said, "Jesus Christ will be the first person I shall ever see, for my eyes will be opened in heaven."

> Then shall we see Thee as Thou art,
> For ever fixed in no unfruitful gaze,
> But such as lifts the new-created heart,
> Age after age, in worthier love and praise.
> —*John Keble*

"You are going to be with Jesus, and to see him as he is," said a friend to Rowland Hill on his deathbed. "Yes," replied Mr. Hill with emphasis, "and I shall be *like* him; *that* is the crowning point."

To see him as he is, and in himself, is reserved till we shall have better eyes: these eyes we have are carnal and corruptible, and cannot see God till they have put on incorruption. —*Sir Richard Baker*

> One view of Jesus as he is
> Will strike all sin for ever dead.
> —*W. Cowper*

254

And every man that hath this hope in him purifieth himself, even as he is pure.

—*1 John 3:3*

THE Christian is a man whose main possessions lie in reversion. Most men have a hope, but his is a peculiar one; and its effect is special, for it causes him to purify himself.

I. THE BELIEVER'S HOPE. "Everyone that hath this hope in him."

1. It is the hope of being like Jesus.
   Perfect, Glorious, Conqueror over sin, death and hell.
2. It is based upon divine love. See verse 1.
3. It arises out of sonship. "Called the sons of God."
4. It rests upon our union to Jesus. "When he shall appear."
5. It is distinctly hope in *Him*. "We shall be like him," etc.
6. It is the hope of his second Advent.

II. THE OPERATION OF THAT HOPE. "Purifieth."

It does not puff up, like the conceit of Pharisees.

It does not lead to loose living, like the presumption of Antinomians.

It shows us what course is grateful, is congruous to grace, is according to the new nature, and is preparatory to the perfect future.

1. The believer purifies himself from:
   - His grosser sins. From evil company, etc.
   - His secret sins, neglects, imaginings, desires, murmurings, etc.
   - His besetting sins of heart, temper, body, relationship, etc.
   - His relative sins in the family, the shop, the church, etc.
   - His sins arising out of his nationality, education, profession, etc.
   - His sins of word, thought, action, and omission.
2. He does this in a perfectly natural way.
   - By getting a clear notion of what purity really is. By keeping a tender conscience, and bewailing his faults.
   - By having an eye to God and his continual presence.
   - By making others his beacons or examples.
   - By hearing rebukes for himself, and laying them to heart.
   - By asking the Lord to search him, and practicing self-examination.
   - By distinctly and vigorously fighting with every known sin.
3. He sets before him Jesus as his model. "He purifieth himself, even as HE is pure."
   - Hence he does not cultivate one grace only.
   - Hence he is never afraid of being too precise.
   - Hence he is simple, natural, and unconstrained.
   - Hence he is evermore aspiring after more and more holiness.

III. THE TEST OF THAT HOPE. "He purifieth himself."

Actively, personally, prayerfully, intensely, continually, he aims at the purification of himself, looking to God for aid.

- Some defile themselves willfully.
- Some take things as they are.
- Some believe that they need no purifying.

- Some talk about purity, but never strive after it.
- Some glory in that which is a mere counterfeit of it.

The genuine Hoper does not belong to any of these classes: he really and successfully purifies himself.

What must it be to be without a good hope?

How can there be hope where there is no faith?

Grace adopts us; adoption gives us hope; hope purifies us, till we are like the Firstborn.

Animating Words

(1) *The Workman.* "Every one that hath this hope in him," every one that looks to be like the Lord Jesus in the Kingdom of Glory is the man that must set about this task. (2) *The work* is a work to be wrought by himself. He is a part of the Lord's husbandry, and he must take pains as it were to plow his own ground, to weed his own corn, he must purify himself; this is his present and personal work. (3) the *pattern* by which he must be directed is the Lord Jesus: his purity. Take him for a pattern and instance; look unto him that is the author and finisher of our faith; as you have seen him do, so do you; as he is pure, so labor you to express in your lives the virtue of him who hath redeemed you. —*Richard Sibbes*

Then thou comportest with thy hopes of salvation when thou laborest to be as holy in thy conversation as thou art high in thy expectation This the apostle urgeth from the evident fitness of the thing (2 Pet. 3:11) "What manner of persons ought ye to be in all holy conversation and godliness, looking for and hastening unto the coming of the day of God?" Certainly, it becomes such to be holy, even to admiration, who look for such a blessed day; we hope then to be like the angels in glory, and therefore should, if possible, live now like angels in holiness. Every believing soul is Christ's spouse. The day of conversion is the day of espousals, wherein she is betrothed by faith to Christ, and, as such, lives in hopes for the marriage-day, when he shall come and fetch her home to his father's house, as Isaac did Rebekah to his mother's tent, there to dwell with him, and live in his sweet embraces of love, world without end. Now, would the bride have the bridegroom find her in sluttery and vile raiment? No, surely: "Can a bride forget her attire (Jer. 2:32)? Was it ever known that a bride forgot to have her wedding clothes made against the marriage-day, or to put them on when she looks for her bridegroom's coming? Holiness is the raiment of needlework in which, Christian, thou art to be brought to thy King and husband (Ps. 45:14). Wherefore is the wedding-day put off so long, but because this garment is so long a-making? When this is once wrought, and thou art ready dressed, then that joyful day comes. Remember how the Holy Spirit wordeth it in the Book of Revelation, "The marriage of the Lamb is come, and his wife hath made herself ready" (Rev. 19:7). —*William Gurnall*

A good hope, through grace, animates and gives life to action, and purifies as it goes; like the Highland stream that dashes from the rock, and purifies itself as it pursues its course to the ocean. —*G. Salter*

The Christian needs Christ in his redemption as the object of Faith, for salvation; Christ himself the object of Love, for devotion and service; and Christ in his coming glory, the object of Hope, for separation from the world. —*W. Haslam*

The biographer of Hewitson says of him: "He not only believed in the speedy appearing, but loved it, waited for it, watched for it. So mighty a motive power did it become, that he ever used to speak of it afterwards as *bringing with it a kind of second conversion.*" —*A. J. Gordon, D.D.*

255

We know that we have passed from death unto life, because we love the brethren.

—*1 John 3:14*

 HE spiritual things which we speak of are matters of knowledge. John, in almost every verse of this epistle, uses the words "we know." The philosophical distinction between believing and knowing is mere theory. "We know and have believed."

I. WE KNOW THAT WE WERE DEAD.
1. We were without feeling when law and gospel were addressing us.
2. Without hunger and thirst after righteousness.
3. Without power of movement towards God in repentance.
4 Without the breath of prayer or pulse of desire.
5. With signs of corruption; some of them most offensive.

II. WE KNOW THAT WE HAVE UNDERGONE A SINGULAR CHANGE.
1. The reverse of the natural change from life to death.
2. No more easy to describe than the death change would be.
3. This change varies in each case as to its outward phenomena, but it is essentially the same in all.
4. As a general rule its course is as follows:
   - It commences with painful sensations.
   - It leads to a sad discovery of our natural weakness.
   - It is made manifest by personal faith in Jesus.
   - It operates on the man by repentance and purification.

- It is continued by perseverance in sanctification.
- It is completed in joy, infinite, eternal.

5. The period of this change is an era to be looked back upon in time and through eternity with grateful praise.

III. WE KNOW THAT WE LIVE.

1. We know that we are not under condemnation.
2. We know that faith has given us new senses, grasping a new world, enjoying a realm of spiritual things.
3. We know that we have new hopes, fears, desires, delights, etc.
4. We know that we have been introduced into new surroundings and a new spiritual society: God, saints, angels, etc.
5. We know that we have new needs; such as heavenly breath, food, instruction, correction, etc.
6. We know that this life guarantees eternal bliss.

IV. WE KNOW THAT WE LIVE, BECAUSE WE LOVE. "We love the brethren."

1. We love them for Christ's sake.
2. We love them for the truth's sake.
3. We love them for their own sake.
4. We love them when the world hates them.
5. We love their company, their example, their exhortations.
6. We love them despite the drawbacks of infirmity, inferiority, etc.

Let us prove our love by our generosity.

Thus shall we supply ourselves with growing evidences of grace.

Love-Lines

Just as in his gospel he rescues the word *logos* from antichristian uses, so in this Epistle he rescues the word *"know,"* and aims at making his "little children" Gnostics in the divine sense. Knowledge is excellent, but the path to it is not through intellectual speculation, however keen and subtle, but through faith in Jesus Christ and subjection to him, according to those most Johannine words in the Gospel of Matthew: "Neither knoweth any man the Father save the Son, and he to whomsoever the Son will reveal him." —*Dr. Culross*

The Christian apologist never further misses the mark than when he refuses the testimony of the Agnostic to himself. When the Agnostic tells me he is blind and deaf, dumb, torpid, and dead to the spiritual world, I must believe him. Jesus tells me that. Paul tells me that. Science tells me that. He knows nothing of this outermost circle; and we are compelled to trust his sincerity as readily when he deplores it as if, being a man without an ear, he professed to know nothing of a musical world, or being without taste, of a world of art. The nescience of the Agnostic philosophy is the proof from experience that to be carnally minded is death. —*Professor Henry Drummond*

The world always loves to believe that it is impossible to know that we are converted. If you ask them, they will say, "I am not sure; I cannot tell," but the whole Bible declares we may receive, and know that we have received, the forgiveness of sins. —*R. M. McCheyne*

In the writings of Paul, "Faith in the Lord Jesus, and love to all the saints," constitute a well-understood and oft-recurring sequence. It is a straitening about that upper spring of faith that makes the streams of love fail in their channels. —*W. Arnot*

> No outward mark have we to know
>   Who thine, O Christ, may be,
> Until a Christian love doth show
>   Who appertains to thee:
> For knowledge may be reached unto,
>   And formal justice gained,
> But till each other love we doe,
>   Both faith and workes are feigned.
>   —*George Wither, 1588–1667*

Yes, brethren in Christ have all one common Father, one common likeness, one object of faith, love, and adoration, one blessed hope, one present employment, alike in trials, alike in prayer. They lean upon the same hand, appear daily before the same mercy-seat, feed at the same table. How much all these things link them together, not in profession only, but in heart! Hence this is a decisive test: "We know that we have passed from death unto life, because we love the brethren." —*D. Katterns*

In the early days of Christianity, when it triumphed over the old heathenism of the Roman world, it founded a new society bound together by this holy mutual love. The catacombs of Rome bear remarkable testimony to this gracious brotherhood. There were laid the bodies of members of the highest Roman aristocracy, some even of the family of the Caesars, side by side with the remains of obscure slaves and laborers. And in the case of the earliest graves the inscriptions are without a single allusion to the position in society of him who was buried there: they did not trouble themselves whether he had been a consul or a slave, a tribune of the legion or a common soldier, a patrician or an artisan. It sufficed that they knew him to have been a believer in Christ, a man who feared God. They cared not to perpetuate in death the vain distinctions of the world; they had mastered the glorious teaching of the Lord, "One is your master, even Christ, and all ye are brethren." —*E. De Pressense*

256

For if our heart condemn us, God is greater than our heart, and knoweth all things. Beloved, if our heart condemn us not, then have we confidence toward God.

—*1 John 3:20–21*

 HE fault of many is that they will not lay spiritual things to heart at all, but treat them in a superficial manner. This is foolish, sinful, deadly. We ought to put our case upon serious trial in the court of our own conscience.

Certain of a better class are satisfied with the verdict of their hearts and do not remember the higher courts; and therefore either become presumptuous, or are needlessly distressed. We are about to consider the judgments of this lower court. Here we may have:

I. A CORRECT VERDICT AGAINST OURSELVES.

Let us sum up the process.

1. The court sits under the King's arms, to judge by royal authority. The charge against the prisoner is read. Conscience accuses, and it quotes the law as applicable to the points alleged.
2. Memory gives evidence. As to the fact of sin in years past and of sin more lately committed. *Items* mentioned. Sabbath sins. Transgressions of each one of the ten commandments. Rejection of the gospel. Omissions in a thousand ways. Failure in motive, spirit, temper, etc.
3. Knowledge gives evidence that the present state of mind and heart and will is not according to the Word.
4. Self-love and pride urge good intents and pious acts in stay of proceedings. Hear the defense! But alas! it is not worth hearing. The defense is but one of "the refuges of lies."
5. The heart, judging by the law, condemns. Henceforth the man lives as in a condemned cell under fear of death and hell.

If even our partial, half-enlightened heart condemns, we may well tremble at the thought of appearing before the Lord God.

The higher court is more strictly just, better informed, more authoritative, and more able to punish. God knows all. Forgotten sin, sins of ignorance, sins half seen are all before the Lord.

What a terrible case is this! Condemned in the lower court, and sure to be condemned in the higher!

II. AN INCORRECT VERDICT AGAINST OURSELVES.

The case as before. The sentence apparently most clear.

But when revised by the higher court it is reversed, for good reasons.

1. The debt has been discharged by the man's glorious Surety.
2. The man is not the same man; though he sinned he has died to sin, and he now lives as one born from above.
3. The evidences in his favor, such as the atonement and the new birth, were forgotten, undervalued, or misjudged in the lower court; hence he was condemned. Sentence of condemnation does not stand when these matters are duly noted.
4. The evidence looked for by a sickly conscience was what it could not find, for it did not exist, namely, natural goodness, perfection, unbroken joy, etc. The judge was ignorant, and legally inclined. The verdict was therefore a mistaken one. An appeal clears the case: "God is greater than our heart, and knoweth all things."

III. A CORRECT VERDICT OF ACQUITTAL.

Our heart sometimes justly "condemns us not."

The argument for non-condemnation is good: the following are the chief items of evidence in proof of our being gracious:

1. We are sincere in our profession of love to God.
2. We are filled with love to the brethren.
3. We are resting upon Christ, and on him alone.
4. We are longing after holiness.

The result of this happy verdict of the heart is that we have:

- Confidence towards God that we are really his.
- Confidence as to our reconciliation with God by Jesus Christ.
- Confidence that he will not harm us, but will bless us.
- Confidence in prayer that he will accept and answer.
- Confidence as to future judgment that we shall receive the gracious reward at the last great day.

IV. AN INCORRECT VERDICT OF ACQUITTAL.

1. A deceived heart may refuse to condemn, but God will judge us all the same. He will not allow self-conceit to stand.
2. A false heart may acquit, but this gives no confidence Godward.
3. A deceitful heart pretends to acquit while in its center it condemns.

If we shrink now, what shall we do in judgment?

What a waking, to find ourselves condemned at the last!

Quotations

When Sir Walter Raleigh had laid his head upon the block, says an eloquent divine, he was asked by the executioner whether it lay aright. Whereupon, with the calmness of a hero and the faith of a Christian, he returned an answer, the power of which we all shall feel when our head is tossing and turning on death's uneasy pillow: "It matters little, my friend, how the head lies, providing the heart be right." —*Steele*

As Luther says: "Though conscience weigh us down and tell us God is angry, yet God is greater than our heart. The conscience is but one drop; the reconciled God is an ocean of consolation." —*Critical English Testament*

A seared conscience thinks better of itself, a wounded worse than it ought; the former may account all sin a sport, the latter all sport a sin; melancholy men, when sick, are ready to conceive any cold to be the cough of the lungs, and an ordinary pustule to be no less than a plaguesore. So wounded consciences conceive sins of infirmity to be sins of presumption, sins of ignorance to be sins of knowledge, apprehending their case to be far more dangerous than it is indeed. —*Thomas Fuller*

Conscience works after the manner so beautifully set forth in the ring that a great magician, according to an Eastern tale, presented to his prince. The gift was of inestimable value, not for the diamonds and rubies and pearls that gemmed it, but for a rare and mystic property in the metal. It sat easily enough on the finger in ordinary circumstances, but as soon as its wearer formed a bad thought, designed or committed a bad action, the ring became a monitor. Suddenly contracting, it pressed painfully on his finger, warning him of sin. Such a ring, thank God, is not the peculiar property of kings; the poorest of us, those that wear none other, may possess and wear this inestimable jewel; for the ring of the fable is just that conscience which is the voice of God within us, which is his law, engraved by the finger of God, not on Sinai's granite tables, but on the fleshy tablets of the heart, which, enthroned as a sovereign in every bosom, commends us when we do right, and condemns us when we do wrong. —*Dr. Guthrie*

The spirit of man, that candle of the Lord, often gives but a faint and glimmering light; but the Spirit of God snuffs it, that it may burn brighter. —*Benjamin Beddome*

257

For whatsoever is born of God overcometh the world; and this is the victory that overcometh the world, even our faith.

—*1 John 5:4*

 HAT is meant by this world?

The power of sin all around us: the influence which operates towards evil, and makes the commandments and purposes of God grievous to society. The Prince of this world has much to do with this evil power.

This world is our foe, and we must fight with it.

We must contend till we overcome the world, or it will overcome us.

I. THE CONQUEST ITSELF. *"Overcometh the world."*

We are not to be litigious, eager to contradict everybody.

We are not, however, to be cowardly, and anxious to flee the fight.

We mingle among men of the world, but it must be as warriors who are ever on the watch, and are aiming at victory. Therefore:

1. We break loose from the world's customs.
2. We maintain our freedom to obey a higher Master in all things.

    We are not enslaved by dread of poverty, greed of riches, official command, personal ambition, love of honor, fear of shame, or force of numbers.
3. We are raised above circumstances, and find our happiness in invisible things: thus we overcome the world.
4. We are above the world's authority. Its ancient customs or novel edicts are for its own children; we do not own it as a ruler, or as a judge.
5. We are above its example, influence, and spirit. We are crucified to the world, and the world is crucified to us.
6. We are above its religion. We gather our religion from God and his Word, not from human sources.

As one in whom this conquest was seen, read the story of Abraham. Think of him in connection with his quitting home, his lonely wanderings, his conduct towards Lot, Sodom and her king, Isaac, etc.

II. THE CONQUERING NATURE. *"Whatsoever is born of God."*

1. This nature alone will undertake the contest with the world.
2. This nature alone can continue it. All else wearies in the fray.
3. This nature is born to conquer. God is the Lord, and that which is born of him is royal and ruling.
    - It is not an amendment of the former creation.
    - It is not even a new creation without relationship to its Creator; but it is a birth from God, with eminence of descent, infusing similarity of nature, and conferring rights of heirship.
    - The Creator cannot be overcome, nor those born of him.
    - Jesus, the firstborn, never was defeated, nor will those conformed to him fail of ultimate triumph.
    - The Holy Spirit in us must be victorious, for how should he be vanquished? The idea would be blasphemous.

III. THE CONQUERING WEAPON. *"Even our faith."*

We are enabled to be conquerors through regarding:

1. The unseen reward which awaits us.
2. The unseen presence which surrounds us. God and a cloud of witnesses hold us in full survey.
3. The mystic union to Christ which grace has wrought in us. Resting in Jesus, we overcome the world.
4. The sanctifying communion which we enjoy with the unseen God.

In these ways faith operates towards overcoming sin.

IV. **THE SPECIALITY OF IT.** "This is *the* victory."
1. For salvation, finding the rest of faith.
2. For imitation, finding the wisdom of Jesus, the Son of God.
3. For consolation, seeing victory secured to us in Jesus.

Behold your conflict: born to battle.

Behold your triumph: bound to conquer.

War Cries

When a traveler was asked whether he did not admire the admirable structure of some stately building, *"No,"* said he, *"for I have been at Rome where better are to be seen every day."* O believer, if the world tempt thee with its rare sights and curious prospects, thou mayst well scorn them, having been by contemplation in heaven, and being able by faith to see infinitely better delights every hour of the day!" This is the victory that overcometh the world, even our faith." —*Feathers for Arrows*

The danger to which Christians are exposed from the influence of the visible course of things, or the world (as it is called in Scripture), is a principal subject of St. John's General Epistle. He seems to speak of the world as some False Prophet, promising what it cannot fulfill, and gaining credit by its confident tone. Viewing it as resisting Christianity, he calls it the "Spirit of Antichrist," the parent of a numerous progeny of evil, false spirits like itself, the teachers of all lying doctrines, by which the multitude of men are led captive. The antagonist of this great tempter is the Spirit of Truth, which is "greater than he that is in the world;" its victorious antagonist, because gifted with those piercing Eyes of Faith which are able to scan the world's shallowness, and to see through the mists of error into the glorious kingdom of God beyond them. "This is the victory that overcometh the world," says the text, "even our faith." —*J. H. Newman*

The believer not only overcomes the world in its deformities, but in its seeming excellences. Not in the way that Alexander and other conquerors overcame it, but in a much nobler way; for they, so far from overcoming the world, were slaves to the world. The man who puts ten thousand other men to death does not overcome the world. The true conqueror is he who can say with Paul, "Thanks be to God, who giveth us the victory through our Lord Jesus Christ," and, "Who shall separate us from the love of Christ? Shall tribulation? etc." "Nay, in all these things we are more than conquerors, through him that loved us." Such a one has recourse, by faith, to an infallible standard: the Word of God: indeed, there is no other. He detects the world, and will not be imposed upon by it. When he is tempted to take the world's good things as his portion, he rejects them; because he has something better in hand. Thus, faith in Christ overcometh the corrupt influence, the inordinate love, the slavish fear, the idolatry, the friendship, the false wisdom, and the maxims of the world: it overcometh not only the folly, but the very religion of the world, as far as it is a false religion. The Christian has hold of a superior influence, and engages superior strength. Doubtless, says he, I have great enemies to attack, but greater is he that is with me than he that is in the world. —*Richard Cecil*

It is asserted of this elegant creature (the Bird of Paradise) that it always flies against the wind; as, otherwise, its beautiful but delicate plumage would be ruffled and spoiled. Those only are Birds of Paradise, in a spiritual sense, who make good their way against the wind of worldliness; a wind always blowing in an opposite direction to that of heaven. —*J. D. Hull*

Believers, forget it not I you are the soldiers of *the Overcomer.* —*J. H. Evans*

258

Beloved, I wish above all things that thou mayest prosper and be in health, even as thy soul prospereth.

—*3 John 2*

THE gospel made a marvelous change in John. Once he could call fire from heaven on opposers; now, having received the Holy Ghost, he is full of love and kind desires.

The gospel makes the morose cheerful, the gay serious, the revengeful loving. Coming to such a one as John, it made him the mirror of love.

A man's private letters often let you into the secrets of his heart.

Instance Rutherford, Kirke White, Cowper, and John Newton.

In this letter, John gratefully wishes Gaius every blessing, and above all things better health.

Health is an invaluable mercy; it is never properly valued till lost.

But John puts soul-prosperity side by side with it.

Man has two parts; the one corporeal and earthy, the other immaterial and spiritual. How foolish is the man who thinks of his body and forgets his soul, neglects the tenant and repairs the house, prizes the earthen vessel and yet despises the treasure!

I. WE WILL EXAMINE THE WORDS OF THE TEXT.

1. "I wish"; more correctly, as in the margin, "I pray." Prayer is a wish sanctified. Turn your wishes into prayers.
2. "That thou mayest prosper." We may ask for prosperity for our friends, especially if, like Gaius, they serve God and his cause with their substance.
3. "And be in health." This is necessary to the enjoyment of prosperity. What would all else be without it?
4. "Even as thy soul prospereth." We are startled at this wish; the spiritual health of Gaius is made the standard of his outward prosperity! Dare we pray thus for many of our friends?

Dare we pray thus for ourselves? What would be the result if such a prayer were answered? Picture our bodies made like our souls.

Some would have fever, others paralysis, others ague, etc.

Let us bless God that the body is not the invariable index of the soul.

Few would care to have their spiritual condition expressed in their external condition.

II. WE WILL MENTION THE SYMPTOMS OF ILL-HEALTH.

1. A low temperature.
   - Lukewarmness is an ill sign. In business, such a man will make but little way; in religion, none at all.
   - This is terrible in the case of a minister.
   - This is dangerous in the case of a hearer.
2. A contracted heart.
   - While some are latitudinarian, others are intolerant, and cut off all who do not utter their Shibboleth.
   - If we do not love the brethren, there is something wrong with us.
3. A failing appetite as to spiritual food.
4. A difficulty in breathing.
   When prayer is an irksome duty, everything is wrong with us.
5. A general lethargy: unwillingness for holy service, want of heart, etc.
6. An ungovernable craving for unhealthy things. Some poor creatures will eat dirt, ashes, etc. Some professors are ill in a like way, for they seek groveling amusements and pursuits.

III. WE WILL SUGGEST MEANS OF RECOVERY.

We will not here dwell upon the means God uses, though he is the great Physician; but we will think of the regimen we must use for ourselves.

1. Seek good food. Hear a gospel preacher. Study the Word.
2. Breathe freely. Do not restrain prayer.
3. Exercise yourself unto godliness. Labor for God.
4. Return to your native air; breathe the atmosphere of Calvary.

5. Live by the sea. Dwell near to God's all-sufficiency.

6. If these things fail, here is an old prescription: *"Carnis et Sanguinis Christi."* This taken several times a day, in a draught of the tears of repentance, is a sure cure.

God help you to practice the rules of the heavenly Physician!

IV. WE WILL CONCLUDE WITH AN EXHORTATION.

Brother Christian, is it a small matter to be weak and feeble? Thou needest all thy vigor. Go to Calvary, and recruit thyself.

Sinner, thou art dead, but life and health are in Christ!

Nota Medica

An ancient Roman wished that he had a window in his breast that all might see his heart, but a sage suggested that in such a case he would have urgent need of shutters, and would keep them closed. We could not afford to wear the signs of our spiritual condition where all could see. We should then need all our blood for blushing. —*C. H. S.*

Sin is called in Scripture by the names of diseases. It is called the plague of the heart: I Kings 8:38. There are as many diseases of the soul as there are of the body. Drunkenness is a spiritual dropsy; security is a spiritual lethargy; envy is a spiritual canker; lust is a spiritual fever (Hosea 7:4). Apostasy or backsliding is the spiritual falling sickness; hardness of heart is the spiritual stone; searedness of conscience is a spiritual apoplexy; unsettledness of judgment is a spiritual palsy; pride a spiritual tumor; vainglory a spiritual itch. There is not any sickness of the body but there is some distemper of the soul that might be paralleled with it, and bear the name of it. —*Ralph Robinson*

The fact of the Scriptures furnishing nutriment and upbuilding to the soul is the most real experience of which we have knowledge. None of us, "by taking thought, can add one cubit unto his stature." But how many, by taking in God's great thoughts, feeding on them, and inwardly digesting them, have added vastly to their spiritual stature! —*A. J. Gordon, D.D.*

If a portrait were taken of a person in strong, vigorous health, and another was taken of the same man after a severe illness, or when he had been almost starved to death, or weakened by confinement, we should scarcely recognize them as the likeness of the same man, the dear old friend we loved! Still greater would be the change could we draw the *spiritual* portrait of many a once hearty, vigorous saint of God, whose soul has been starved for want of the proper spiritual nourishment, or by feeding upon "ashes" instead of bread. —*G. S. Bowes*

Oh, that our friends were well in soul! We are not sufficiently concerned about this best of health! When they are well in soul we are grieved to see them ailing in body; and yet this is often the case. The soul is healed, and the body is still suffering! Well, it is by far the smaller evil of the two! If I must be sick, Lord, let the mischief light on my coarser nature, and not on my higher and diviner part!—*C. H. S.*

259

Now unto him that is able to keep you from falling, and to present you faultless before the presence of his glory with exceeding joy. To the only wise God our Savior, be glory and majesty, dominion and power, both now and ever. Amen.

—Jude 24–25

 E will joyfully praise the Lord with Jude's doxology.

It is well to be called full often to adoring praise, and the specific statement of the reason for praise is helpful to fervor of gratitude.

Our great danger is falling and faultiness.

Our great safety is divine ability and faithfulness, by which we are kept from stumbling so as to dishonor our Lord.

I. LET US ADORE HIM WHO CAN KEEP US FROM FALLING.

1. We need keeping from falling, in the sense of preservation from:
   - Error of doctrine; which is rife enough in this age.
   - Error of spirit: such as want of love, or want of discernment, or unbelief, or credulity, or fanaticism, or conceit.
   - Outward sin. Alas, how low may the best fall!
   - Neglect of duty: ignorance, idleness, want of thought.
   - Backsliding. Into this state we may insensibly descend.
2. None but the Lord can keep us from falling.
   - We cannot keep ourselves without him.
   - No place guarantees security; the church, the closet, the communion table—all are invaded by temptation.
   - No rules and regulations will secure us from stumbling. Stereotyped habits may only conceal deadly sins.
   - No experience can eradicate evil, or protect us from it.
3. The Lord can do it. He is "able to keep," and he is "the only wise God, our Savior." His wisdom is part of his ability.
   - By teaching us so that we fall not into sins by ignorance.
   - By warning us; this may be done by our noting the falls of others, or by inward monitions, or by the Word.
   - By providence, affliction, etc., which remove occasions of sinning.

- By a bitter sense of sin, which makes us dread it as a burnt child dreads the fire.
- By his Holy Spirit, renewing in us desires after holiness.

4. The Lord will do it. According to the Revised Version he is "the only God our Savior." He will assuredly save.

From final falls, and even from stumblings (R V), his divine power can and will keep us.

II. LET US ADORE HIM WHO WILL PRESENT US IN HIS COURTS FAULTLESS.

1. None can stand in those courts who are covered with fault.
2. None can deliver us from former guilt, or keep us from daily faultiness in the future, but the Savior himself.
3. He can do it as our Savior. He is divinely wise to sanctify.
4. He will do it. We should not be exhorted to praise him for an ability which he would not use.
5. He will do it "with exceeding joy," both to himself and to us.

III. LET US ADORE HIM WITH HIGHEST ASCRIPTIONS OF PRAISE.

1. Presenting our praise through Jesus, who is himself our Lord.
2. Wishing him glory, majesty, dominion and power.
3. Ascribing these to him as to the past, for he is "before all time."
4. Ascribing them to him "now."
5. Ascribing them to him "forever."
6. Adding to this adoration, and to the adoration of all his saints, our own fervent "Amen." Heartily consenting to all his praise.

Come let us praise our Guardian *now*, in memory of past upholdings.

Let us praise him in foretaste of what he will do for us.

Let us praise him with "exceeding joy."

A Statement and an Instance

We cannot stand a moment longer than God upholdeth us; we are as a staff in the hand of a man; take away the hand, and the staff falleth to the ground; or rather, as a little infant in the nurse's hand (Hos. 11:3); if we are left to our own feet, we shall soon fall. Created grace will never hold out against so many difficulties. One of the fathers bringeth in the flesh, saying, *Ego deficiam*, I shall fail; the world, *Ego decipiam*, I will deceive them; the devil, *Ego eripiam*, I will sweep them away. But God saith, *Ego custodiam*, I will keep them, I will never fail them, nor forsake them. There lieth our safety. —*Thomas Manton*

Philip Dickerson, an aged Baptist minister, who died October 22nd, 1882, just before his death said, "Seventy years ago the Lord took me into his service without a character. He gave me a good character, and by his grace I have kept it."

260

Behold, he cometh with clouds; and every eye shall see him, and they also which pierced him; and all kindreds of the earth shall wail because of him. Even so, Amen.

—Revelation 1:7

HE doxology which precedes our text is most glorious.

It runs well in the Revised Version: "To him that loved us and loosed us."

Keeping to our Authorized Version, we can get the alliteration by reading "loved us and laved us."

To him who has made us kings, is himself a King, and is coming into his kingdom; to him be glory.

Our adoration is increased by our expectation. "He cometh."

Our solemnity in praise is deepened by the hope that our expectation will be speedily realized. The coming is in the present tense.

John, who once heard the voice, "Behold the Lamb of God!" now utters the voice, "Behold, he cometh!"

I. OUR LORD JESUS COMES.

1. This fact is worthy of a note of admiration: "Behold!"
2. It should be vividly realized till we cry, "Behold, he cometh!"
3. It should be zealously proclaimed. We should use the herald's cry, "Behold!"
4. It is to be unquestioningly asserted as true. Assuredly he cometh.
   - It has been long foretold. Enoch. Jude 14.
   - He has himself warned us of it. "Behold, I come quickly!"
   - He has made the sacred supper a token of it. "Till he come."
   - What is to hinder his coming? Are there not many reasons for it?
5. It is to be viewed with immediate interest.
   - "Behold!" for this is the grandest of all events.
   - "He cometh," the event is at the door.
   - "He," who is your Lord and Bridegroom, comes.
   - He is coming even now, for he is preparing all things for his advent, and thus may be said to be on the road.
6. It is to be attended with a peculiar sign: "with clouds."
The clouds are the distinctive tokens of his Second Advent.
   - The tokens of the divine presence. "The dust of his feet."
   - The pillar of cloud was such in the wilderness.
   - The emblems of his majesty.
   - The ensigns of his power.

- The warnings of his judgment. Charged with darkness and tempest are these gathered clouds.

II. OUR LORD'S COMING WILL BE SEEN OF ALL.

1. It will be a literal appearance. Not merely every mind shall think of him, but "Every eye shall see him."
2. It will be beheld by all sorts and kinds of living men.
3. It will be seen by those long dead.
4. It will be seen by his actual murderers, and others like them.
5. It will be manifest to those who desire not to see the Lord.
6. It will be a sight in which *you* will have a share.

Since you must see him, why not at once look to him and live?

III. HIS COMING WILL CAUSE SORROW. "All kindreds of the earth shall wail because of him."

1. The sorrow will be very general. "All kindreds of the earth."
2. The sorrow will be very bitter. "Wail."
3. The sorrow proves that men will not be universally converted.
4. The sorrow also shows that men will not expect from Christ's coming a great deliverance.
   - They will not look to escape from punishment.
   - They will not look for Annihilation.
   - They will not look for Restoration.
   - If they did so, his coming would not cause them to wail.
5. The sorrow will in a measure arise out of his glory, seeing they rejected and resisted him. That glory will be against them.
6. The sorrow will be justified by the dread result. Their fears of punishment will be well grounded. Their horror at the sight of the great Judge will be no idle fright.

To his Lord's coming the believer gives his unfeigned assent, whatever the consequences.

Can you say, "Even so, Amen"?

Advent Thoughts

Even so, Lord Jesus, come quickly! In the meanwhile, it is not heaven that can keep thee from me; it is not earth that can keep me from thee; raise thou up my soul to a life of faith with thee; let me even enjoy thy conversation, whilst I expect thy return. —*Bishop Hall*

"*Every eye shall see him.*" Every eye, the eye of every living man, whoever he is. None will be able to prevent it. The voice of the trumpet, the brightness of the flame, shall direct all eyes to Him, shall fix all eyes upon him. Be it ever so busy an eye, or ever so vain an eye, whatever employment, whatever amusement it had the moment before, wilt then no longer be able to employ it, or to amuse it. The eye will be lifted up to Christ, and will no more look down upon money, upon books, upon land, upon houses, upon gardens. Alas! these things will then all pass away in a moment; and not the eyes of the living alone, but also all the eyes that have ever beheld the sun, though but for a moment; the eyes of all the sleeping dead will be awakened and opened. The eyes of saints and sinners of former generations. The eyes of Job, according to those rapturous words of his, which had so deep and so sublime a sense, "I know that my Redeemer liveth, and that he shall stand in the last day on the earth; in my flesh I shall see God, whom my eyes shall behold, and not another." The eyes of Balaam, of which he seems to have had an awful foreknowledge when he said, "I shall see him, but not now; I shall behold him, but not nigh." Your eyes and mine. O awful thought! Blessed Jesus! May we not see thee as through tears; may we not then tremble at the sight! —*Dr. Doddridge*

"And the Lord turned, and looked upon Peter . . . And Peter went out and wept bitterly." So shall it be, but in a different sense, with sinners at the day of judgment. The eye of Jesus as their judge shall be fixed upon them, and the look shall awake their sleeping memories, and reveal their burdens of sin and shame—countless and cursed crimes, denials worse than Peter's, since life-long and unrepented of, scoffings at love that wooed them, and despisings of mercy that called them—all these shall pierce their hearts as they behold the look of Jesus. And they shall go out and flee from the presence of the Lord—go out never to return, flee even into the outer darkness, if so be they may hide them from that terrible gaze. And they shall weep bitterly—weep as they never wept before, burning, scalding tears, such as earth's sorrow never drew—weep never to be comforted, tears never to be wiped away. Their eyes shall be fountains of tears, not penitential and healing, but bitter and remorseful—tears of blood—tears that shall rend the heart in twain, and deluge the soul in fathomless woe. —*Anonymous*

261

And the temple of God was opened in heaven, and there was seen in his temple the ark of his testament; and there were lightnings, and voices, and thunderings, and an earthquake, and great hail.

—*Revelation 11:19*

I T may not be easy to work out the connection of the text; but taken by itself it is eminently instructive.

Much that is of God we fail to see; to us the temple of God in heaven is still in a measure closed.

There is need that it be opened to us by the Holy Spirit.

Jesus has rent the veil, and so laid open, not only the holy place, but the Holy of holies; and yet by reason of our blindness it still needs laying open, so that its treasures may be seen.

There are minds that even now see the secret of the Lord. We all shall do so above; and we may do so in a measure while below.

Among the chief objects which are to be seen in the heavenly temple is the ark of the covenant of God. This means that the covenant is always in the mind of God, and that his most holy and most secret purposes have a reference to that covenant.

It is "covenant," not testament (see the Revised Version, which is the better translation in this place).

I. THE COVENANT IS ALWAYS NEAR TO GOD. "There was seen in his temple the ark of his covenant."

Whatever happens, the covenant stands secure.

Whether we see it or not, the covenant is in its place, near to God.

The covenant of grace is for ever the same, for:

1. The God who made it changes not.
2. The Christ who is its Surety and Substance changes not.
3. The love which suggested it changes not.
4. The principles on which it is settled change not.
5. The promises contained in it change not; and, best of all,
6. The force and binding power of the covenant change not.

It is, It must be, for ever where God at first placed it.

II. THE COVENANT IS SEEN OF SAINTS. "There was seen in his temple."

We see in part, and blessed are we when we see the covenant.

We see it when:

1. By faith we believe in Jesus as our Covenant-head.
2. By instruction we understand the system and plan of grace.
3. By confidence we depend upon the Lord's faithfulness, and the promises which he has made in the covenant.
4. By prayer we plead the covenant.
5. By experience we come to perceive covenant-love running as a silver thread through all the dispensations of providence.
6. By a wonderful retrospect we look back when we arrive in heaven, and see all the dealings of our faithful covenant God.

III. THE COVENANT CONTAINS MUCH THAT IS WORTH SEEING.

The ark of the covenant may serve us as a symbol.

In it typically, and in the covenant actually, we see:

1. God dwelling among men: as the ark in the tabernacle, in the center of the camp.
2. God reconciled, and communing with men upon the mercy-seat.
3. The law fulfilled in Christ: the two tables in the ark.
4. The kingdom established and flourishing in him: Aaron's rod.
5. The provision made for the wilderness: for in the ark was laid up the golden pot which had manna.
6. The universe united in carrying out covenant purposes, as typified by the cherubim on the mercy-seat.

IV. THE COVENANT HAS SOLEMN SURROUNDINGS. "There were lightnings, and voices, and thunderings," etc.

It is attended by:
1. The sanctions of divine power: confirming.
2. The supports of eternal might: accomplishing.
3. The movements of spiritual energy: applying its grace.
4. The terrors of eternal law: overthrowing its adversaries.

Study the covenant of grace.

Fly to Jesus, who is the Surety of it.

Remarks of Sound Divines

The great glory of the covenant is the certainty of the covenant; and this is the top of God's glory, and of a Christian's comfort, that all the mercies that are in the covenant of grace are "the sure mercies of David," and that all the grace that is in the covenant is sure grace, and that all the glory that is in the covenant is sure glory, and that all the external, internal, and eternal blessings of the covenant are sure blessings. —*Thomas Brooks*

The covenant stands unchangeable. Mutable creatures break their leagues and covenants, and when they are not accommodated to their interests, snap them asunder, like Samson's cords. But an unchangeable God keeps his: "The mountains shall depart, and the hills be removed; but my kindness shall not depart from thee, nor shall the covenant of my peace be removed" (Isa. 54:10). —*Stephen Charnock*

The ark was a special type of Christ, and it is a very fit one; for in a chest or coffer men put their jewels, plate, coin, treasure, and whatsoever is precious, and whereof they make high account. Such a coffer men use to have in the house, where they dwell continually, in the chamber where they lie, even by their bedside; because his treasure is in his coffer, his heart is there also. Thus, in Christ "are hid all the treasures of wisdom and knowledge" (Col. 2:3). He is "full of grace and truth" (John 1:14). "It pleased the Father that in him should all fullness dwell" (Col. 1:19). Hereupon Christ is "the Son of God's love" (Col. 1:13); "his elect in whom his soul delighteth" (Isa. 42:1); and he is "ever at the right hand of God" (Heb. 10:12). —*William Gouge*

A friend calling on the Rev. Ebenezer Erskine, during his last illness, said to him, "Sir, you have given us many good advises; pray, what are you now doing with your own soul?" "I am doing with it," said he, "what I did forty years ago; I am resting on that word, *I am the Lord thy God,*" and on this I mean to die. "To another he said, "The covenant is my charter, and if it had not been for that blessed word, *I am the Lord thy God,*" my hope and strength had perished from the Lord." —*Whitecross*

The rainbow of the covenant glitters above, lightnings of wrath issue from below. This is the fire that breaks forth from the sanctuary to consume those who profane its laws. It is the wrath of the Lamb that bursts from the altar upon those who trample under foot his blood. It is the savor of death unto death to those who have rejected the gospel as a savor of life unto life. It is the reply of Christ to those who command him upon their own authority to come down from his lofty elevation, and commit himself into their hands. "If I be a man of God, let fire come down from heaven and consume you." Humiliation brings Christ himself from heaven to earth; imperiousness brings down consuming fire. From the same temple, in which some behold the ark of the covenant, lightnings, voices, thunderings, earthquake and great hail descend upon those who have profaned its courts with their abominations. —*George Rogers*

262

And the fourth angel poured out his vial upon the sun; and power was given unto him to scorch men with fire. And men were scorched with great heat, and blasphemed the name of God, which hath power over these plagues; and they repented not to give him glory.
—*Revelation 16:8–9*

HAT forces God has at his disposal, since all *angels* serve him! These bring forth the vials of his wrath.

What power these beings have over nature, for on the sun the angel empties his bowl, and men are scorched with fire!

No men are beyond the power of the judgments of God. He can reach them by any medium. He can make ill effects flow from our best blessings: in this case burning heat poured from the sun.

The judgments of God do not of themselves produce true repentance; for these men "repented not to give him glory."

I. THEY MAY PRODUCE *A* REPENTANCE.

1. A carnal repentance caused by fear of punishment. Cain.

2. A transient repentance which subsides with the judgment. Pharaoh.

3. A superficial repentance which retains the sin. Herod.

4. A despairing repentance which ends in death. Judas.

There is nothing about any of these which gives glory to God.

II. THEY DO NOT PRODUCE *THE* REPENTANCE WHICH GIVES GOD GLORY.

True repentance glorifies God:

1. By acknowledging his omniscience, and the wisdom of his warnings, when we confess the fact and folly of sin.

2. By admitting the righteousness of his law, and the evil of sin.

3. By confessing the justice of the Lord's threatenings, and bowing before his throne in reverent submission.

4. By owning that it lies with the sovereign mercy of God further to punish us, or graciously to forgive us.

5. By accepting the grace of God as presented in the Lord Jesus.

6. By seeking sanctification so as to live in holy gratitude, in accordance with favor received.

In the case before us in the chapter, the men under the plague went from bad to worse, from impenitence to blasphemy; but where there is godly sorrow, sin is forsaken.

III. THEY INVOLVE MEN IN GREATER SIN WHEN THEY DO NOT SOFTEN.

1. Their sin becomes more a sin of knowledge.

2. Their sin becomes more a sin of defiance.

3. Their sin becomes a sin of falsehood before God. Vows broken, resolutions forgotten: all this is lying unto the Holy Ghost.

4. Their sin becomes a sin of hate towards God. They even sacrifice themselves to spite their God.

5. Their sin becomes more and more deliberate, costly, and stubborn.

6. Their sin is thus proven to be ingrained in their nature.

IV. THEY ARE TO BE LOOKED UPON WITH DISCRETION.

Hasty generalization will lead us into great errors in reference to divine judgments.

1. Used by the grace of God, they tend to arouse, impress, subdue, humble, and lead to repentance.

2. They may not be regarded as of themselves beneficial.

   • Satan is not bettered by his misery.

   • The lost in hell grow more obdurate through their pains.

   • Many wicked men are the worse for their poverty.

- Many sick are not really penitent, but are hypocritical.

3. When we are not under judgment and terror, we should repent.
  - Because of God's long-suffering and goodness.
  - Because we are not now distracted by pain.
  - Because now we can think of the sin apart from the judgment, and are more likely to be honest in repentance.
  - Because we shall find it sweeter and nobler to be drawn than to be like "dumb driven cattle."

Be it our one aim "to give HIM glory."

Begin with this object in repentance, continue in it by faith, rise nearer to it in hope, abide in it by zeal and love.

From Great Authors

Trees may blossom fairly in the spring, on which no fruit is to be found in the harvest; and some have sharp soul exercises which are nothing but foretastes of hell. —*Boston*

Richard Sibbes says, "We see, by many that have recovered again, that have promised great matters in their sickness, that it is hypocritical repentance, for they have been worse after than they were before." *Dr. Grosart* adds, by way of illustration, the testimony of a prison chaplain, to the effect that of *"reprieved"* criminals who, in the shadow of the gallows, had manifested every token of apparent penitence and *heart*-change, the number whose subsequent career gave evidence of reality is as 1-to-500, perhaps as awful a fact as recent criminal statistics reveal.

I believe it will be found that the repentance of most men is not so much sorrow for sin as sin, or real hatred of it, as sullen sorrow that they are not allowed to sin. —*Adam's Private Thoughts*

There is no repentance in hell. They are scorched with heat, and blaspheme God's name, but repent not to give him glory. They curse him for their pains and sores, but repent not of their deeds. True repentance ariseth from faith and hope; but there can be no faith of releasement where is certain knowledge of eternal punishment: knowledge and sense exclude faith. There can be no hope of termination where be chains of desperation. There shall be a desperate sorrow for pain, no penitent sorrow for sin. None are now saved but by the blood of the Lamb; but when the world is ended, that fountain is dried up. The worm of conscience shall gnaw them with this remorse, bringing to their minds the cause of their present calamities: how often they have been invited to heaven, how easily they might have escaped hell. They shall weep for the loss of the one and gain of the other, not for the cause of either, which were repentance. . . . They suffer, and they blaspheme. —*Thomas Adams*

How awful to read, "men blasphemed God because of the plague of the hail"! How true it is that affliction makes good men better, and bad men worse! Wrath converts no man. It is grace that saves. The chastisement that does not soften hardens. Judgments lead men to blaspheme; and the greater the plague, the more they blaspheme. What a solemn, but truthful, representation of the consequence of oft-neglected warnings! See the employment of man in the future state—in heaven, to praise; in hell, to blaspheme. —*George Rogers*

263

And he saith unto me, Write, Blessed are they which are called unto the marriage supper of the Lamb.

—*Revelation 19:9*

 MAZED by what he saw and heard, John might have failed to write but he was warned to do so on this occasion, because of:

- The value of the statements herein recorded.
- Their absolute certainty, as sure promises and true sayings of God.
- The necessity of keeping such facts in remembrance throughout all time for the comfort of all those who look for the Lord's appearing.

This fact, that men shall partake of the marriage supper of the Lamb, might seem too good to be true if it were not specially certified by order of the Lord, under the hand and seal of the Spirit of God.

In the historical order, the false harlot-church is to be judged (see previous chapter), and then the true bride of Christ is to be acknowledged and honored.

In meditating upon this august marriage festival, we shall note:

I. THE DESCRIPTION OF THE BRIDEGROOM.

The inspired apostle speaks of him as "the Lamb."

This is John's special name for his Lord. Perhaps he learned it from hearing the Baptist cry by the Jordan, "Behold the Lamb."

What we learn early abides with us late.

John uses this name continually in this Book of the Revelation.

The last book of the Bible still reveals Jesus in this character as the Lamb of God.

In this passage the marriage of the Lamb may even seem incongruous as a figure, but John looks at the sense, and not at the language.

He wishes us above all things to remember that as the sacrifice for sin our Lord appears in his glory, and that as a Lamb he will manifest himself in the consummation of all things when his church is perfected.

1. As the Lamb he is the one everlasting sacrifice for sin: he will not be other than this in his glory.

2. As the Lamb suffering for sin, he is especially glorious in the eyes of the angels and all other holy intelligences, and so in his joyous day he wears that character.

3. As the Lamb he most fully displayed his love to his church; and so he appears in this form on the day of his love's triumph.

4. As the Lamb he is best loved of our souls. Behold, how he loved us even to the death!

Ever as a victim for sin he rejoices to display himself to the universe.

II. THE MEANING OF THE MARRIAGE SUPPER.

In the evening of time, in the end of the gospel day, there shall be:

1. The completion and perfection of the church. "His bride hath made herself ready."

2. The rising of the church into the nearest and happiest communion with Christ in his glory. "The marriage of the Lamb is come." The espousals lead up to this.

3. The fulfillment of the long expectations of both.

4. The open publication of the great fact of mutual love and union.

5. The overflowing of mutual delight and joy. "Be glad and rejoice."

6. The grandest display of magnificent munificence in a banquet.

7. The commencement of an eternally unbroken rest. "He shall rest in his love." The church, like Ruth, shall find rest in the house of her husband.

III. THE PERSONS WHO ARE CALLED TO IT.

Not those who have the common call and reject it, but:

1. Those who are so called as to accept the invitation.

2. Those who now possess the faith which is the token of admission.

3. Those who love Bridegroom and bride.

4. Those who have on the wedding garment of sanctification.

5. Those who watch with lamps burning.

These are they which are called to the marriage supper.

IV. THE BLESSEDNESS WHICH IS ASCRIBED TO THEM.

1. They have a prospect which blesses them even now.

2. They have great honor in being called to such a future.

3. They will be blessed indeed when at that feast, for:

   • Those who are called will be admitted.

   • Those who are admitted will be married.

   • Those who are married to Jesus will be endlessly happy. How many a marriage leads to misery! but it is not so in this case.

Alas, some are not thus blessed! To be unblessed is to be accursed.

Marriage Music

As they that have invited a company of strangers to a feast do stay till the last be come, so there will not. be a glorious coming of Christ until all the elect be gathered into one body. And then shall be the coming of all comings, which is the glorious coming of Christ, to take us to himself. —*Richard Sibbes*

How blessed it will be to those "called" ones, to "sit down" at "the marriage supper of the Lamb!" Then will "the King sit indeed at his table," and "the spikenard will send forth the smell thereof."

He who once hung so sad upon the cross for every one will look around that bright company, and in every white robe, and in every lighted countenance, he will behold the fruit of his sufferings. He will "see of the travail of his soul, and will be satisfied." It will be the eternal union of God fulfilled in its deepest counsel: a people given to Christ from before all worlds; and that they are, that day, all chosen, all gathered, all washed, all saved, and not one of them is lost! —*James Vaughan*

We dare not say that our Lord will love us more than he loves us now, but he will indulge his love for us more; he will manifest it more, we shall see more of it, we shall understand it better; it will appear to us as though he loved us more. He will lay open his whole heart and soul to us, with all its feelings, and secrets, and purposes, and allow us to know them, as far at least as we can understand them, and it will conduce to our happiness to know them. The love of this hour will be the perfection of love. This marriage-feast will be the feast, the triumph, of love—the exalted Savior showing to the whole universe that he loves us to the utmost bound love can go, and we loving him with a fervor, a gratitude, an adoration, a delight, that are new even in heaven.

The provisions made by him for our enjoyment will astonish us. Conceive of a beggar taken for the first time to a splendid monarch's table, and this at a season of unusual splendor and rejoicing. How would he wonder at the magnificence he would see around him, and the profusion of things prepared for his gratification; some altogether new to him, and others in an abundance and an excellence he had never thought of! So will it be with us in heaven. We shall find it a feast and a monarch's feast. It will have delights for us, of which we have no conception; the pleasures we anticipate in it will be far higher and more abundant than our highest expectations have ever gone. We shall have a provision made for us, which will befit, not our rank and condition, but the rank and condition, the greatness, the magnificence, of a glorious God. —*Charles Bradley*

264

And he saith unto me, These are the true sayings of God.
—*Revelation 19:9*

HESE words relate to that which immediately precedes them.

- The judgment of the harlot church (verse 2).
- The glorious and universal reign of Christ (verse 6).
- The sure reward and glory of Christ with his saved ones in the glorious period at the last (verses 7–8).
- The existence, beauty, purity, simplicity, and glory of the church.
- The union of Christ and the church in love, joy, glory.
- The blessedness of all who have to do with this union.

The subjects thus referred to make up a summary of what the Lord has said upon future human history.

The words before us we shall use as expressing:

I. A RIGHT ESTIMATE OF HOLY SCRIPTURE.

1. These words which we find in the Old and New Testaments are true. Free from error, certain, enduring, infallible.
2. These are divine words. Infallibly inspired, so as to be, in very truth, "the sayings of God."
3. These words are thus true and divine in opposition to:
   - Words of man. These may or may not be true.
   - Pretended words of God. False prophets and men with addled intellects profess to speak in the name of God; but they lie.
4. These words are all of them truly divine. "These are the true sayings of God."
   - Neither too severe to be true, nor too terrible to be uttered by a God of love, as some dare to say.
   - Nor too good to be true, as tremblers fear.
   - Nor too old to be true, as novelty-hunters affirm.
   - Nor too simple to be truly divine, as the worldly-wise insinuate.
5. These words are a blessing to us for that reason.
   - What else can guide us if we have no sure revelation from God?
   - How can we understand the revelation if it is not all true? How could we discriminate between the truth and the error on subjects so much beyond us?

II. THE RESULT OF FORMING SUCH AN ESTIMATE.

If you believe that "these are the true sayings of God":

1. You will listen to them with attention, and judge what you hear from preachers by this infallible standard.
2. You will receive these words with assurance.
   - This will produce confidence of understanding.
   - This will produce rest of heart.
3. You will submit with reverence to these words, obey their precepts, believe their teachings, and value their prophecies.
4. You will expect fulfillment of divine promises under difficulties.
5. You will cling to revealed truth with pertinacity.
6. You will proclaim it with boldness.

III. OUR JUSTIFICATION FOR FORMING SUCH AN ESTIMATE.

In these days we may be accused of bibliolatry, and other new crimes, but we shall hold to our belief in inspiration, for:

1. The Scriptures are what they profess to be—the word of God.
2. There is a singular majesty and power in them, and we see this when the truth of God is preached.
3. There is a marvelous omniscience in Scripture, which is perceived by us when it unveils our inmost souls.
4. They have proven themselves true to us.
   - They warned us of the bitter fruit of sin, and we have tasted it.
   - They told us of the evil of the heart, and we have seen it.
   - They told us of the peace-giving power of the blood, and we have proved it by faith in Jesus.
   - They told us of the purifying energy of divine grace: we are already instances of it, and desire to be more so.
   - They assured us of the efficacy of prayer, and it is true.
   - They assured us of the upholding power of faith in God, and by faith we have been upheld in trial.
   - They assured us of the faithfulness of God to his people as shown in providence, and we have experienced it. All things have worked together for our good hitherto.
5. The witness of the Holy Spirit in our hearts confirms our faith in Holy Scripture. We believe and are saved from sin by believing. Those words must be truly divine which have wrought in us such gracious results.

What follows upon this? We believe all the Scripture.

We now accept as true sayings of God:

- The proclamation that our Lord is coming.
- The doctrine that the dead will be raised at his call.
- The fact that there will be a judgment of the quick and dead. The truth that saints will enjoy eternal life, and that sinners will go away into everlasting punishment.

Worth Quoting

Whence but from heaven could men unskilled in arts,
In several ages born, in several parts,
    Weave such agreeing truths? or how, or why
    Should all conspire to cheat us with a lie?
    Unasked their pains, ungrateful their advice,
    Starving their gain, and martyrdom their price.
                                  —*Dryden.*

Of most things it may be said, "Vanity of vanity, all is vanity;" but of the Bible it may be truly said, "Verity of verity, all is verity." —*Arrowsmith*

The True is the one asbestos which survives all fire, and comes out purified. —*Thomas Carlyle*

A young man had fallen into loose habits, and was living a wild, fast life. Late hours were frequent with him, and he would pay no regard to the remonstrances of a Christian father. At last it came to a point. The father told his son that he must either leave his home or conform to rules. He followed his old ways, went into lodgings, and was rather pleased to be free from the restraint he felt at home. After a while he picked up some young companions who professed infidel opinions, and soon, like them, he even scoffed at religion, and made light of all his parents had taught him. But the prayers of his father and mother followed him, and in a remarkable way were abundantly answered. One night the young fellow lay awake and began to think. "I tell people," said he to himself, "that there is no truth in the Bible, but there must be truth somewhere, and if not there, where is it? I wonder what the Bible says about truth."

In this way he was led to go to the Scriptures, and read every passage where truth is spoken of. The Bible became its own witness. It so took hold of him that he was persuaded that it was the very Word of the Living God. He was convinced of the evil of his past life, and was led to see Jesus as the Way, the Truth, and the Life. His whole future was the reverse of his former course. —*G. Everard*